Encyclopedia of Military Technology and Innovation

Encyclopedia of Military Technology and Innovation

Stephen Bull

GREENWOOD PRESS
Westport, Connecticut • London

Library of Congress Cataloging-in-Publication Data

Bull, Stephen.
 Encyclopedia of military technology and innovation / Stephen Bull.
  p. cm.
 Includes bibliographical references and index.
 ISBN 1–57356–557–1 (alk. paper)
 1. Military art and science—Dictionaries. 2. Military weapons—Dictionaries. I. Title.
 U24.B85 2004
 623'.03—dc22   2004040431

British Library Cataloguing in Publication Data is available.

Library of Congress Catalog Card Number: 2004040431
ISBN: 1–57356–557–1

First published in 2004

Greenwood Press, 88 Post Road West, Westport, CT 06881
An imprint of Greenwood Publishing Group, Inc.
www.greenwood.com

Printed in the United States of America

The paper used in this book complies with the
Permanent Paper Standard issued by the National
Information Standards Organization (Z39.48–1984).

10   9   8   7   6   5   4   3   2   1

Contents

List of Entries

List of Entries

List of Entries

List of Entries

List of Entries

List of Entries

Guide to Related Topics

Aircraft (powered, winged, and piloted types)

Aardvark, F-111

Airacobra (and Kingcobra)

Airacomet

Aircraft

Albatros

Avenger, TBF

B-29 Superfortress

B-47 Stratojet

B-52 Stratofortress

Bear, Tu-95

Beaufighter

Blackbird, SR-71A

Black Widow, P-61, F-61

Blenheim Bomber

Buffalo, F2A

C-47 Skytrain

C-97 Stratofreighter

Catalina

Cessna

Condor, Fw 200

Curtiss; Hawk, Warhawk, Kittyhawk

Dauntless, SBD

Defiant

Dewoitine, 520 etc.

Dive Bomber

Dornier; Do 17, 215, 217

Douhet, Guilio

Eagle, F-15

Fighting Falcon, F-16

Flying Fortress, B-17

Focke-Wulf Fw 190

Folgore, C.202, and Saetta, M.C. 200

Forger, Yak-38

Gladiator

Global Hawk

Goblin, XF-85

Gotha

Gripen ("Griffin")

Harrier, Sea Harrier

Havoc, Douglas A-20

Hawkeye, E-2

He 111 Bomber

He 219, Uhu

He 280

Hellcat, F6F

Helldiver

Hercules, C-130

Hien, Kawasaki Ki-61

Hornet, F-18

Hunter

Hurricane

Intruder, A-6

Invader, A-26

Joint Strike Fighter (F-35)

Ju-88

Kamikaze

Lancaster

Liberator, B-24

Lightning, English Electric

Lightning, Lockheed P-38

Me 109

LAW 80

Milan Missile

Panzerfaust (Klein, 60, 150, etc.)

Panzerschreck

PIAT

RPG-7

Armor (personal protection)

Armor

Buff Coat

Chemico Armor

Helmet

Sappenpanzer

Shield

Variable Armor

Artillery and Mortars

8-Inch Howitzer, M1; M115

18-Pounder Gun

25-Pounder Gun

75 mm Gun

88 mm Gun

105 mm Howitzer, M1, M3, M102

Artillery

Bofors, "Bofors Gun"

Böhler Gun

Bombard

Carronade

Flak

Hedgehog

Howitzer

Katyusha

"Knee" Mortar

Leather Gun

Mortar

Oerlikon Gun

PAK (PaK)

Paladin, M109

Paris Guns, Paris Kanonen, Wilhelmgeschutze

Phalanx, Close-In Weapon System

Recoilless Gun; Recoilless Rifle

Self-Propelled Gun; Self-Propelled Artillery

Supergun

V3

Balloons and Airships

Airship

Balloon

Zeppelin

Biological Warfare

Anthrax

Biological Warfare

NBC; NBC Suit

Bows and Catapult Weapons

Bow

Catapult; Ballista; Mangonel; Trebuchet

Crossbow

Chemical Warfare

Agent Orange

Chlorine

Gas

Gas Masks

Mustard Gas

NBC; NBC Suit

Phosgene

Sarin

Soman

Tabun

V-Agents

Communications, Observation, Detection, Navigation, Avionics, and Computation

America's Army

AWACS

Bombe

Camouflage

Chaff

Colossus

ENIAC

Enigma

Gee

Head-Up Display, HUD

Guide to Related Topics

Hydrophone

Hyposcope; Hyposcope Rifle

Image Intensifier

Infrared Systems

Laser

Personnel Detector, Chemical

Radar

Radio

Satellites

Sonar; Sonobuoy

Stealth

Strategic Defense Initiative

Telegraph

Telescope; Binoculars

Tiara

Edged, Bladed and Pole and Club Weapons

Axe; Poleaxe

Bayonet

Dagger; Knife

Flail; Flail Tank

F-S Fighting Knife

Halberd

Knobkerrie

Knuckle Knife

Mace

Machete

Spear

Sword

Trench Club

Explosives, Ammunition, Shells, Mines, Ignition Systems

Ammunition, Ammunition Box

Boobytrap

Bouncing Bomb

Brennan Torpedo

Cartridge

Case Shot; Canister Shot

Cluster Bomb; Cluster Munition

Copperhead, M712

Depth Charge, Depth Bomb

Dum Dum Bullet

Explosives

Flechette

Flintlock

Fragmentation Grenade, M11A1

Fritz-X

Fuel-Air Explosive Bomb

Fuse; Fuze

Grenade, Granadoe

Gunpowder

Hedgehog

HESH, High-Explosive Squash Head

Hobos

Hollow Charge

Kaiten "Human Torpedo"

Maiale Manned Torpedo

Match, Matchlock

Microwave Bomb

Mills Bomb

Mines; Land Mine

Minié Ball

Molotov Cocktail

Nipolit

Ohka Piloted Bomb

Petard

Percussion Cap; Percussion Ignition

Rifle Grenade

Sabot; APDS; FSADS

Sea Mines

Semtex

Shell

Shrapnel

Smart Bomb

Snot

Steil *Handgranate*

Thermobaric Bomb

Torpedo

Wheel lock

Firearms

Antimaterial Rifle

Arisaka Rifle

Assault Rifle, "Sturmgewehr"

AUG Steyr Rifle

Baker Rifle

Barrett M82A1, "Light Fifty"

Bolt Action

Borchardt Pistol

Box Lock

Breech Loading

Bren Gun

Brown Bess

Bullpup, Gun/Missile

Carbine

Chassepot

Chauchat Automatic Rifle

Degtyarev DP28; DPM

Double Action

Dragon, Dragoon

Dux Submachine Gun

FA MAS Rifle

FIST

G3 Rifle

Galil

Garand Rifle, M1

Gatling

General Purpose Machine Gun

Glisenti Handguns

Glock 17

Goryunov Machine Gun

Hotchkiss Machine Guns

Howdah; Howdah Pistol; Elephant

Ingram Submachine Gun, Models 6, 10, 11

Interrupter Gear

Johnson, M1941

Kalashnikov, AK-47, AKM, AIM, Tabuk, Type 56

Krag-Jorgensen Rifle

Lahti Pistol

Lewis Gun

Liberator ("OSS") Pistol

Luger Pistol

M1 Carbine

M3 "Grease Gun"

M14 Rifle

M16 Rifle

M60 Machine Gun

M79 Grenade Launcher

Machine Gun

Madsen Machine Gun

Mannlicher Rifle

Martini Henry Rifle

Mauser

Maxim

MG 08; MG 08/15

MG 34

MG 42

Minimi; Squad Automatic Weapon

Mosin-Nagant Rifle

MP 5 Submachine gun

MP 38, MP 40

Musket; Musket Rest

Nambu Pistol

Peabody Rifle

PPsh-1941G

Reising Submachine Gun

Revolver

Rifle, Rifling

Ross Rifle

SA 80 Rifle

Schmeisser

Schwarzlose

Semiautomatic

Sharps Carbine; Sharps Rifle

Shotgun

SIG-Sauer

Silencer

Skorpion Submachine Gun

Smith and Wesson

SMLE, Short Magazine Lee Enfield

Snider Rifle

Sniper Rifles

Spandau

Guide to Related Topics

Spencer Rifle

Springfield; Springfield Rifle

Sten Gun

Stoner 63 System

Submachine Gun, SMG

Thompson Submachine Gun

Type 92

Type 94 Pistol

Uzi

Vickers Gun

Walther; PP; PPK

Webley; Webley and Scott

Welrod Pistol

Flame and Incendiary devices

Flamethrower

Flaming Bayonet

Greek Fire

Napalm; Napalm B

Fortifications and Obstacles

Atlantic Wall

Barbed Wire

Caltrop; Caltrap; Calthrop; Tribulus

Fort; Fortification

Maginot Line

McNamara Line

Pillbox

Manufacturers and Inventors

Armstrong

Astra

Aviatik

Beretta

Birmingham Small Arms, "BSA"

Boeing

Bristol Aircraft; Bristol Fighter; "Brisfit"; Bristol Scout

British Aerospace Systems

Browning

Cessna

Christie

Colt

Congreve, Sir William

Curtiss

Dryse

Enfield

Fabrique Nationale

Fokker

Gatling

Grumman

Hall, John H.

Handley Page

Hawker, Hawker Siddeley

Junkers

Krupp

Maxim

McDonnell Douglas

Potez; Potez 630

Schmeisser

SIG-Sauer

Smith and Wesson

Sopwith

Webley; Webley and Scott

Winchester Repeating Arms

Miscellaneous

Airgun

Conger

Double-L Sweep

Douhet, Guilio

Ejection Seat

Flail; Flail Tank

Goliath

Interrupter Gear

Meatball

Mulberry Harbor

Oboe

Oropesa Sweep

Parachute

PLUTO

Railroads, Railways

Ramrod

Rations

Roborat

Saddle

Schnorkel; Schnorchel; Snorkel

Skis

Spur

Stirrup

Missiles and Missile Systems

Acrid (AA-6)

Alkali (AA-1) missile

Apex (AA-7) missile

Arrow TMD

AS.11 (AGM-22A)

AS.20 and AS.30

Aspide

ASROC

Bloodhound Missile

Blowpipe Missile

Bomarc

Bullpup, Missile

Cannonball, D-40

Chaparral (MIM-72A)

Congreve, Sir William

Crotale Missile

Cruise Missile

Dragon (M-47) missile

Exocet Missile

Falcon Missile

Frog Missile

Gainful (SA-6)

Gecko (SA-8) Missile

Guideline (SAM-2) Missile

Hale Rocket

Harpoon Missile

Hawk (MIM-23, etc.) Missile

Hellfire Missile

Honest John (MGR-1) Missile

Intercontinental Ballistic Missile (ICBM)

Katyusha

Milan Missile

Minuteman

Mistral

Moskito Missile Launcher

Multiple Launch Rocket System, M270

Nebelwerfer

Patriot Missile

Phoenix Missile

Polaris Missile

Poseidon Missile

Pulse Jet

Rapier Missile

Redeye Missile

Sagger Missile

Scud (SS-1) Missile

Seawolf Missile

Sidewinder Missile

Sparrow Missile

Stinger Missile

Swingfire

Terrier Missile

TOW Missile

Trident Missile

V1

V2

Nuclear Warfare

Force de Frappe

Hydrogen Bomb

NBC; NBC Suit

Nuclear, Thermonuclear, "Atomic" Weapons

Submarines

Albacore

Astute Class

Delta Class (I, II, III, and IV)

Echo Class

Foxtrot Class

Gato Class

George Washington Class

H Class

K Class

KD6 Class

Kilo Class

Kursk

L Class

Guide to Related Topics

Bradley, M2, M3

BRDM

Bren Carrier, Carden Lloyd, Universal Carrier, Cargo Carrier T16

Chariot

Commando Armored Car

Duck, DUKW

Ferret

Fox Armored Car

FV 430, 432, "Trojan" APC

Gama Goat

Gillois EWK

Goer

Greyhound M8, armored car

Haflinger Trucks

Half-Track

Hovercraft

Humvee (HMMWV)

Jeep

Kettenkrad

Landing Craft Retriever

Land Rover; Range Rover; "Pink Panther"

Light Strike Vehicle

M113, 113A APC

Marsh Screw

Mini-Moke

Mulo Meccanico

"Nellie," NLE Trenching Machine

Ontos

Overland Train

Panhard

PATA

Pony

RAT

Rome Plough

Saladin

Saracen, FV 603

Schwimmwagen

Sidewinder Articulated Cargo

SKOT

Snowcat

Stalwart

Tank Transporter

Teracruzer

Tricar Parachutable

Unimog

Vespa "ACMA" TAP

Warrior Armored Personnel Carrier

Wheelbarrow

Warships

Adelaide, HMAS

Admirable Class

Aircraft Carrier

Akagi

Alabama, CSS

Alaska Class

Algérie

Arethusa Class

Arizona, USS

Arleigh Burke Class

Atlanta Class

Atlantic Conveyor

Auk Class

Baltimore Class

Battleship

Belfast, HMS

Bismarck

Bogue Class

Bomb Vessel

Brigantine, Brig

Brooklyn Class

Campania, HMS

Captain Class

Carrack

Ceres Class

Cleveland Class

Cog

Constitution, USS

Corvette

Couronne

Cruiser

D-Class Cruisers

Descubierta Class

Guide to Related Topics

Preface

Few things have occasioned such human misery as military technology; it may reasonably be argued that all our lives would have been better, without, for example, the bayonet or Semtex. Yet this is but part of the story, for military technology has done much to shape all human history, and the human race and the arms race seem inextricably entwined. Catapults, swords, armor and arrows helped to define medieval Europe; sailing ships and gunpowder both reshaped European society and made European states masters of much of the world. The rifle in the hands of individuals was one factor that helped bring about American independence, leaving a constitutional legacy that is still debated today. The Civil War would have been totally different without the rifle, ironclad, field fortifications, and mortars.

World War I was first brought to a standstill by the technologies of artillery, machine guns, and barbed wire—then rekindled by tanks, aircraft, new shells, and new tactics. The early part of World War II was dominated by the existence of German tanks and dive bombers, the latter part by American and British aircraft, Russian tanks, code-breaking machinery, and finally the atomic bomb. "Mutually assured destruction" could not have brought the strange but lethal stability of the Cold War without the strategic bomber or the nuclear missile. Vietnam might have been a different war, or no war at all, without belief in military technology. More recently technology appears to have acquired the power to mollify the voters of the democracies in difficult situations. In the Gulf in 1991, "smart" bombs and cruise missiles were expended instead of coalition lives,

leaving superior armored forces at an advantage.

At the time of writing the same has so far been largely true of Afghanistan, where unmanned surveillance, daisy-cutter bombs, and a very small number of special forces units have taken the place of the "big battalions" and plane loads of body bags. Sadly this may be less true of Iraq. Whether the development of artificially intelligent systems and unmanned craft will continue apace remains to be seen. If it does, the world of movie science fiction, in which men do battle with machines, never actually seeing a human adversary, may not be so far away. Whether such engagements could ever solve anything remains an open question. Fighting machines do not yet perform satisfactorily many of the tasks that are the province of infantry on the ground; still less are they capable of winning "hearts and minds."

On a more hopeful note, the nightmare chemical and biological "weapons of mass destruction" have so far proved gratifyingly ineffective. Inept "anthrax by post" has killed fewer innocent bystanders than have misfits who rampage with conventional weapons. Gas has continued to be as difficult to target effectively as it was in 1915. So far, terrorist groups have also failed to master nuclear weaponry—but this is undoubtedly an area that demands continuous vigilance.

Even if we feel untouched by these great dramas of history, military technology has still had a major influence on all our lives. Early social organization was a product not only of tribe, survival, and genetics but the ability to provide warriors, weapons, horses, and other material for waging of war. In the nineteenth and twentieth centuries the many, rather than the few, were touched by conscription. Railways, roads, and communications had important strategic dimensions from the start. Early steamship, automotive, and aircraft advances were underpinned by government subsidies and by interests that were primarily strategic. The *autobahn* was as much a military as a civil routeway. Mass air travel would not have evolved as and when it did without bomber and troop-carrier technology. Industrial giants like Krupp, Boeing, and Rolls-Royce might not have existed without the march of military progress. On smaller scales, computers; canned, frozen, and dried food; certain medical techniques, and man-made fibers all owe something to military technologies.

Having filled complete libraries already, the scope and complexity of the story of military technology defies truly comprehensive treatment by any one book. However, it is hoped that this volume will prove useful in a number of ways. Nonspecialists may come across the "ballista" or the "longbow" in historical novels, museums, and drama and want to have them defined; they are likely to see documentaries on aircraft in which "Natter," "A-20," and "Fritz-X" are mentioned, and here their curiosity can be quickly satisfied. In military hardware, arcane names and strange acronyms abound, and it maybe that the layman can use this book to get a small but much-needed grasp on our often violent world.

It should be pointed out that some names have been used time and time again. In the U.S. military, names like Washington, Lexington, Dragon, and Langley have been used and re-used, and sometimes ship names have been duplicated on aircraft and land-based systems. Eagle, Buccaneer, Lightning, Hurricane, Manchester, and many others, have referred to different things at different times on either side of the Atlantic. In the United Kingdom, names like *Ark Royal* and *Invincible* go back centuries and will probably be reused well into the future. In Germany names like *Deutschland, Emden,* and *Scharnhorst* have totemic status and have been used several times on different types of

vessel. There have been many different rifles called Springfields, Mausers, and Enfields. Typhoon is both an aircraft name and a class of submarine. In the most extreme example *P38* has referred to a pistol, an aircraft, and a lightweight can opener. Where such duplication occurs, effort has been made to note the existence of a popular name—but the reader is advised to double check, where possible, using date or model numbers, to obtain the correct reference.

The more expert reader will probably gain most satisfaction from the bibliographic references. Many entries end with a note on additional reading, and the full titles of these works are provided in the listings at the end of the book. No such bibliography can be exhaustive, and new books are appearing all the time, but by being directed to a few titles in each subject area the reader can be led deeper into the chosen field. The bibliographic entries are biased toward readable printed material in the English language. Though some technical manuals have been included, no attempt has been made to tackle scientific papers, periodicals, or manuscripts. It should also be observed that Western terminology has been adopted throughout. Where a missile or aircraft has a NATO designation or a popular English-language name, it has been used.

Several hundred Web sites have been perused in the writing of this work. Most, however, have not been referenced. This is not only because web sites tend to contain more errors but because they are often transient and may have disappeared by the time the reader wants them. Many, perhaps a majority, are also commercial marketing tools, and their information is slanted toward the products they contain. Nevertheless the effectiveness of this volume may be multiplied with judicious use of the World Wide Web.

The observant reader will notice a definite partiality toward the United States, United Kingdom, Germany, and Russia in the pages that follow. This is partly by virtue of circumstance, but it is also the case that it is these countries that have dominated the military advances of the period since 1800. Minuteman, Dreadnought, V-2, and T-34 ought to be part of our common vocabulary, for they are examples of military technology that have genuinely changed the world in which we live today. Other countries—notably Italy, Japan, China, and France—get limited coverage, and it is sometimes surprising what contributions they have made over the centuries.

Nevertheless, with limited space and about 700 entries, there has been some subjectivity, and many difficult choices concerning what to put in and what to leave out. Sometimes the decision has come down to what the reader is likely to encounter in everyday life and want information about. Thus it is that "B-17 Flying Fortress" receives a lengthy report, while the "Beech Model 17," a stagger-wing communi-

cations aircraft, was excluded at an early stage. Moreover effort has been made to arrange the entries in a manner that the reader will find easy to cope with. So it is that if one happens to have forgotten that the "Flying Fortress" was the "B-17," it can be found by looking under either "Flying" or "B." Additionally there has been an attempt to cross-reference the entries internally by the use of bold type. By this method "Boeing" will take the reader to aircraft and "B-17," as well as to a score of other related products. Major companies likely to be household names, like Fokker or Boeing, have short entries of their own, while less familiar manufacturers may be mentioned with the tank, ship, or other hardware, if at all.

Encyclopedia of Military
Technology and Innovation

Numeric Entries

0/100. *See* **Handley Page**

2S25. *See* **Tank Destroyer**

.30-06. *See* **Springfield**

8-Inch Howitzer, M1; M115   ARTILLERY

Development of 8-inch **howitzers** by the United States began soon after World War I, a new M1 being introduced in 1942. More than a thousand had been produced by 1945, and the weapon had gained a reputation for hard-hitting accuracy. It fired a 200 lb **shell** to a range of over ten miles, twice a minute. After World War II it was redesignated as the M115 and saw extensive service in Vietnam.

18-Pounder Gun   ARTILLERY

The British 18-pounder "Q.F." (quick-firing) gun was an **artillery** piece introduced in 1904 in the wake of the Boer War. With a range of over 6,000 yards it was designed primarily to fire **shrapnel shells**, though during World War I it was called upon to be used in conjunction with high-**explosive ammunition**. Advanced at the time of its introduction, it was of limited utility by 1918.

Additional Reading: Trawin, *Early British Quick Firing Artillery*, 1997.

25-Pounder Gun   ARTILLERY

First mounted on the same carriage as the **18-pounder** and thus originally called the "18/25-pounder," the 25-pounder was a British **artillery** piece developed in the interwar period.

Usually towed into action behind a Quad tractor, it had a range of about 13,000 yards. It remained the main U.K. field gun until well after World War II.

Additional Reading: Hogg, *British and American Artillery*, 1978.

75 mm Gun   ARTILLERY

The 75 mm caliber gun, approximately three inches, has been used for numerous pieces of **artillery** over more than a century. It has been a particularly common size in Germany and the United States, but the most famous "75" of all was the French model 1897 field gun, development of which was pushed through by General Deloye. It was one of the first real "QF" field guns, had a range of 6,860 meters, and was towed into action by a team of six horses. For short periods it could fire a round every four seconds. Revolutionary in its time, it was soon copied, and even surpassed, by the German 77 mm and British **18-pounder**. A modified version of the French 75 mm was used by the U.S. Army.

88 mm Gun   ARTILLERY

More properly known by the German expression *8.8 cm*, the dreaded "88" was not just one type of **artillery** piece but a family of guns. Development of these started as early as 1915, leading to the introduction of the antiaircraft **Krupp** and Rheinmettal 8.8 cm K-Zugflak L/45 in the following year. In the interwar period further development resulted in the **Flak** 18 L/56, produced from 1933; it had a folding cruciform platform, all-round traverse, detachable wheel units for mobility, and a power-assisted rammer.

The weapon was powerful and quick firing, as it ejected the empty **cartridge** during recoil and cocked itself ready for the next round. The maximum range was about 10,000 meters. Barrels needed replacement after about 900 rounds, and in the mid-1930s a clever, if expensive, method of replacement was devised in which just the worn part could be changed. The models 18, 36 and 37 all served in World War II, with still more impressive types being produced in 1941 and 1943. The 8.8 cm Flak 41 was 6.55 meters long with an electric firing system, mobile turntable, and a service ceiling of 15,000 meters. The full crew was 12.

Yet the real strength of the 88 was not its technological sophistication but its tactical flexibility. For though some weapons were fitted with mounts that were specifically antitank, and others were fitted to tanks, as in the case of the **Tiger**, many guns could be used in either role. The guns could also fire a variety of **shell** types.

Using the armor-piercing 40/43, the 8.8 cm Pak 43 could shatter a stunning 241 mm of armor plate. So it was that the 88 was deployed to useful effect against Allied bombers, British tanks in North Africa, the Americans at Omaha, on the Russian front, and pretty well anywhere powerful artillery was needed.

Additional Reading: Ellis and Chamberlain, *The 88*, 1998; Hogg, *German Artillery of World War II*, 1997.

105 mm Howitzer, M1, M3, M102
ARTILLERY

For decades 105 mm has been a standard caliber for field **howitzers** in nations as diverse as the United States, Germany, and South Korea. The original M1 U.S. howitzer was standardized as early as 1928, with a lightweight M3 appearing in 1943. The M102 was first used in Vietnam. Its main advantages were lightness and flexibility, its maximum range of over 16,000 yards, and its ability to fire ten rounds per minute.

A

A4. *See* V2

A-6. *See* **Intruder**

A7V Tank   TANK

The A7V was the only **tank** produced by Germany in World War I. Its design was commenced in 1916 to answer the appearance of British tanks. The designation "A7V" was a contraction of the title of the committee of the War Ministry responsible for its production. It saw action in 1918, but few were produced.

Effectively a large steel box on a Holt tractor chassis, the A7V was neither fast, at 5 mph maximum, nor good at coping with obstacles. The full crew was an astonishing 18 men, with one 5.7 cm gun and up to seven **machine guns**. Given the relative lack of success of the A7V, the later German **panzers** are all the more remarkable.

Additional Reading: Hundleby and Strasheim, *The German A7V Tank*, 1990.

A-10. *See* **Thunderbolt**

A-20. *See* **Havoc, Douglas A-20**

AA Gun. *See* **Flak**

Aardvark, F-111   AIRCRAFT

Variously described as both a "harbinger of new technologies" and a "big ugly bird with loose wings," the F-111 multirole U.S. combat **aircraft** was one of the most interesting and controversial of modern times. It was born as response to "Specific Operational Requirement 183," an ambitious document that sought to replace many existing fighters and bombers with a single machine, thus achieving a high degree of cost-effective "commonality" between the army and navy. A General Dynamics design was selected, and a storm of protest followed. Nevertheless, the F-111 made its first flight, piloted by Dick Johnson, on 21 December 1964.

Much was new. The F-111 had revolutionary swing wings, was powered by twin turbofans, was intended to have a "rough landing" capability, and had a most extraordinary cockpit (indeed, so unusual was it that it took longer to finalize than the plane, with the result that the first Aardvarks had to fly with an interim arrangement). Within the cockpit "module," the two crewmen sat side by side, a configuration preferred by navy pilots for night and bad weather.

Rather than simply ejecting when the escape handles were pulled, a complex automatic sequence of events was initiated. First a "shielded mild detonating cord" caused a controlled explosion that operated guillotines severing control cables, antenna leads, and anything else in the way, while the crew harnesses were tightened. A third of a second later, a new flurry of pyrotechnics cut the module free of the fuselage and blasted it into a rocket nozzle–controlled trajectory. At the same time, a radio beacon was activated and **chaff** scattered, marking the point of ejection for rescuers. As the **parachutes** deployed, an air cushion "mattress" inflated under the module to cushion landing. Dropping into water was a practical option, as the unit was intended to be watertight, and the control columns acted as bilge pump handles in an emergency. Exit was possible at all speeds and altitudes, though the system worked best when the Aardvark was flying at reasonable height. A successful ejection was achieved from an F-111 at Mach 2 during a roll.

Though the F-111 had been intended for **aircraft carrier** use, expensive tests eventually determined that it was too heavy for the purpose, and "Seavark" development was halted in the late 1960s. (The **Tomcat** eventually filled this niche.) Moreover it was soon realized that the plane was much more of a bomber than a fighter, and in the low-level bombing the remarkable terrain-following **radar** was invaluable. The F-111A first saw action in Operation Combat Lancer in Vietnam in 1968, but three were lost in quick succession. Defective valve welds were discovered, and another plane lost its wings in flight. The result was media hysteria about the "suicide" aircraft. The F-111 was now grounded for seven months.

The Aardvark would come back from this trial better and wiser. There were numerous improvements, and its later performance was markedly better. In Vietnam it would demonstrate that it could outrun any **MiG**, and it soon developed something of a specialist combat repertoire; though it seldom used its Vulcan **Gatling**, it proved able to act as a Pathfinder for **F-4s**, and it excelled in "beacon bombing" guided by a ground observer. During the 1980s laser and **infrared** optronics were introduced, making possible the delivery of highly accurate precision-guided munitions. In 1986 Aardvarks were used in the bombing of Libya during Operation El Dorado Canyon. The plane's finest hour was the Gulf War of 1991 when 88 Aardvarks were used, with much improved avionics, to great effect.

Arguably the most powerful Aardvark was the nuclear-capable FB-111A, manufactured in 1969–1971. This variant was 75 feet long, had a 75-foot wingspan with the wings fully open, and weighed 47,481 empty. The maximum thrust from each engine, with afterburner, was 20,350 lb. It had four different radar systems, including the APQ-114 attack radar. Among

other safety systems, the dropping of nuclear weapons required that both crewmen depress their "pickle buttons," thereby giving joint consent for the action. In training crew would pull down flash curtains and practice supersonic dashes to escape shock waves. Another interesting variant was the Raven, or "Sparkvark," developed for jamming and reconnaissance.

Though discontinued with U.S. forces, Aardvarks were still flying with the Australians in 2003. A good number have also been preserved on both sides of the Atlantic. Of these Aarvark 68-0033, *Hat Trick*, is at the Pima County Museum Arizona; *My Lucky Blonde* is at Hill Air Force Base, Utah; and *The Chief* is at Duxford, Cambridgeshire, United Kingdom.

Additional Reading: Davies and Thornborough, *F-111*, 1997; Pace, *X-Fighters: USAF Experimental and Prototype Fighters, XP-59 to YF-23*, 1991.

A and AA Sweep. *See* **Sea Mine**

ABL. *See* **Strategic Defense Initiative**

Abrams M1 Battle Tank   TANK

Developed during the 1970s as a result of the XM1 program, the Abrams tank was intended as a replacement for the **M60**. Trials commenced in 1976, and the first full-production models were completed in 1980. By 2000 almost 10,000 Abrams had been made. Of these the improved M1A1 was the most numerous, with existing early-model M1s planned for conversion to M1A1 standard. Users outside the United States include Egypt, Kuwait, and Saudi Arabia.

The most distinctive feature of the Abrams is its large angular turret, protected by British-developed Chobham armor and reportedly resistant to all battlefield tank missiles and guns. In the M1A1 a special "heavy armor" package is extended to the hull, where high-density metals encased in steel are intended to provide extra protection against the latest kinetic-energy rounds. The M1A1 also boasts a Rheinmetall M256 120 mm smoothbore gun and three **machine guns**. Though relatively hot and noisy,

A U.S. Army M1A1 Abrams MBT or "Main Battle Tank" of the 64th Armored engages in mock battle at Fort Stewart, Georgia, March 1999. The Abrams has repeatedly shown its worth, not least in two Gulf Wars. Courtesy of the Department of Defense.

the Textron Lycoming AGT-1500 gas turbine provides 1,500 horsepower, giving a remarkable 41 mph road speed. For a heavy tank the M1A1 also has excellent acceleration, reaching 20 mph in six seconds. Deployed in numbers during the Gulf Wars, the Abrams met nothing that could stand in its way.

Technologically interesting is the fact that the gun can readily be fired on the move using a laser range finder and computer. Marine Corps M1A1s are fitted with a deep-water fording kit. A total of 77 new M1A2s were built in 2000. Following "Block I" improvements, it is expected that the latest M1A2 will feature better command and control and optical systems and improvements to the suspension. The latest tank research is that on the **Future Combat System**.

Additional Reading: Green, *M1 Abrams*, 1992; Zaloga, *M1 Abrams Battle Tank*, 1985; Zaloga and Green, *Tank Attack*, 1991.

AC-47. *See* C47 Skytrain

Acoustic Hammer. *See* Sea Mines

Acrid (AA-6)   MISSILE

A large Soviet air-to-air missile, in service c. 1980. Equipped with both **infrared** and semiactive radar homing devices, the Acrid was carried by MiG-25 **Foxbat** interceptor **aircraft**. It had a high-explosive warhead, a range of about 25 miles and a total length was 20 feet.

Additional Reading: *Jane's Weapons Systems*, various editions.

Adelaide, *HMAS*

Adelaide, **HMAS**   WARSHIP

The 5,500-ton *Birmingham*-class **cruiser** *Adelaide* was the largest warship to be built in Australia. Laid down at the Cockatoo Island dockyard in 1917, she took until 1922 to complete, delays being caused by the loss of parts supplied from Britain en route. She was therefore nicknamed "Her Majesty's Australian Ship Long Delayed." The *Adelaide* was 462 feet long, powered by ten Yarrow boilers, and had a top speed of just over 24 knots.

Just before and during World War II she underwent refitting and additions so that ultimately she could boast six 6-inch guns, copious antiaircraft guns, **depth-charge** throwers, and types 271, 285, and U.S. SC **radar**. She served as a convoy escort and patrol ship, sinking the German blockade runner *Ramses* in 1942. Finally used as a gunnery target, she was broken up in 1949.

Admirable **Class**   WARSHIP

The U.S. *Admirable* class of World War II comprised 130 completed vessels. These minesweepers were 180 feet long and displaced 650 tons. They were fitted for wire and double-L sweeping, and they had **sonar** and **depth charges**. Some also had hedgehog. Like the *Auk* class, many were named after birds—hence the *Jackdaw, Gull, Linnet*, and *Dunlin*. Some saw service with the Soviets, others with the Chinese Nationalists.

Additional Reading: Lenton, *American Gunboats and Minesweepers*, 1974.

Admiral Hipper. See **Prinz Eugen**

Aegis. *See* **Radar**

Aerobus   VEHICLE

Perhaps the ultimate in military stretched limousines, the Chrysler Checker A12W8C "Aerobus" was an 11-passenger transporter for road use, in U.S. service from 1963. Powered by a 190-horsepower V8 engine, it had power-assisted steering and braking. There were four doors on either side. The Aerobus was by no means unique, as a number of similar military stretches have since been produced.

Aerocycle. *See* **Flying Platform**

Agent Blue. *See* **Agent Orange**

Agent Orange   CHEMICAL WARFARE

Though foliage has been destroyed on a regular basis in warfare for centuries to improve fields of fire or deny crops or cover to the enemy, chemical defoliants are essentially a twentieth-century phenomenon. In the United States, important work was done during the 1950s when the Army Biological Warfare Laboratories devised chemical systems for clearing artillery ranges of vegetation that were too dangerous for personnel to clear manually.

The best known of the chemical defoliants is Agent Orange, so named because of the colored identification marks on its containers. Properly described as a "systemic herbicide," it was a mixture of the chemicals 2,4 D and 2,4,5 T, substances, which had been developed as weed killers in the 1940s. It was manufactured by Monsanto, Dow, and others. In Vietnam, Operation Ranch Hand, saw the use of about 11,000,000 gallons of Agent Orange from 1962 to 1970. The peak of activity was in 1967, when 1,700,000 acres were treated. The usual practice was to mix the chemical with kerosene or diesel and spray it from C-123 transport **aircraft**. It worked, to the extent that it destroyed large areas of crops and forest, but was criticized, initially because of the negative world publicity it generated, later because of health fears for U.S. personnel. In 1977 remaining stocks were destroyed at sea by the furnace ship *Vulcanus.*

Though the most important, Agent Orange was just one of 15 herbicides used in Vietnam. Agent Blue was less permanent in its effects, being a desiccant, or drying agent, which caused foliage to die back, often without killing the whole plant. Agents Purple, Green, and Pink also saw use up until about 1964; a new formulation of Orange, also known as "Super Orange" or "Orange II," was used in 1968 and

1969. Agents other than Orange types accounted for approximately 8,000,000 gallons used in Vietnam.

Though Agent Orange has passed, the idea of chemicals and bioweapons aimed at crops and foliage remains current, research being continued in the West and East. According to newspaper reports of 2002, Britain has developed the use of a living fungal organism, *Pleospora papaveracea*, and has tested it in conjunction with former Soviet republics. Its purpose is selectively to destroy opium poppies, while leaving it possible to grow other types of crop.

Air Gun   FIREARM

Air guns are projectile weapons that use air or gas for motive force; they have been known since the sixteenth century. Mechanisms may include compressed springs, bellows, air reservoirs, and carbon dioxide (CO_2) cylinders, dependent on type. The Austrian army introduced a repeating air rifle designed by Bartolomeo Girandoni in 1780. Since that time air guns have played a part in military training, most notably with the British SAS (Special Air Service), where they have been used as a realistic but nonlethal aid to jungle warfare practice. Compressed-air **mortars** have also been used. Though quiet, and often inexpensive, air weapons are now commonly perceived as insufficiently powerful or reliable for general military use.

Additional Reading: Smith, *Standard Encyclopaedia of Gas, Air, & Spring Guns of the World*, 1957.

Airacobra (and Kingcobra)   AIRCRAFT

The Bell P-39 Airacobra, a U.S. single-seater fighter **aircraft**, went into production in 1939. It was heavily armed, having a 37 mm nose cannon and six **machine guns**. It saw action with the British, Soviet, and other air forces, as well as U.S. formations. Approximately 9,558 were made. It was novel in that it was the first U.S. Army single-seat fighter with a tricycle undercarriage, a feature made desirable by its mid-engine position. Unfortunately, it suffered from poor climb rate and high-altitude performance, factors that were later put down to the deletion of the intended turbocharger from the final specification. It was therefore best used in a ground-attack role.

A larger and more powerful P-63 Kingcobra with a 1,325 horsepower Allison engine was produced from 1942. About 3,300 of these were made, serving mainly with the Soviets.

Additional Reading: Dorr & Scutts, *Bell P-39 Airacobra*, 2000.

Airacomet   AIRCRAFT

The Bell P-59 Airacomet was a twin turbojet–engined fighter developed in the United States during World War II. Using **jet** technology provided by Frank Whittle in the United Kingdom, it was the first aircraft to mount American-built gas turbines. Flown by a trials unit of 412th Fighter Group, it was found to have inadequate performance and was not volume produced.

Aircraft   AIRCRAFT

Though **balloons** and **airships** have a longer history, aircraft for military use only slightly postdate the first powered, manned, heavier-than-air flight by the Wright brothers in 1903. Government sponsorship of races and research hastened development, and soon many countries were forming military air services, mainly for observation purposes. Air communications were rudimentary at first, early experiments including message dropping, light signaling, and flares. The first military reconnaissance flight on active service was made in October 1911 during the Italo-Turkish War, and it was also an Italian aircraft that dropped the first bombs, on 1 November 1911.

The British Royal Flying Corps was founded in 1912, and some surprisingly large military air organizations came into existence at an early date. At the end of 1913 the Russians were reported as being in the process of forming a 350-strong air fleet, using predominantly **Nieuport** and Farman monoplanes. At the outbreak of war in 1914 the French army claimed to have 600 aeroplanes, mainly Breguet and Farman biplanes, Briot, Nieuport, Deperdussin, and Hanriot monoplanes. An *escadrille* or squadron of Nieuport "aircraft destroyers" was formed with machine gun–armed machines, capable of about 90 mph, boasting limited armored protection.

Yet most aircraft still lacked dedicated armament, and in the earliest days of combat aviation pilots and observers went aloft with pistols, **shotguns**, or even **grenades**. Aerial darts or **flechettes** for dropping on troops also made an early appearance. The first victim of air-to-air combat is believed to have been a German **Aviatik** shot down near Rheims by a Hotchkiss gun mounted in a French Voisin. The French plane was piloted by Sergeant Fantz, his gunner being Corporal Qunault. **Parachutes** were not recognized as part of aircraft equipment at this time.

One of the biggest handicaps to efficient combat was the lack of a satisfactory means to fire through the propeller. Early solutions included giving machine guns to a second crew member, whose arc of fire was to the sides or rear; mounting guns high on wings to fire over the screw; using "pusher planes" with rear engines; or armoring the propeller. A real breakthrough came in 1915, when practical **interrupter gear** was produced.

The quality of air observation was similarly improved in 1915 by the mounting of cameras on aircraft in such a way as to take vertical pictures and eliminate vibration. Aerial photography would rapidly become an important science providing much of the best military intelligence, though **camouflage** and dummy ground installations were also developed. Wireless sets were also taken aloft in 1915, and coded messages were soon being sent for the immediate correction of **artillery** fire.

Progress in First World War led to remarkable fighters like the **Fokker, Albatros, Sopwith, Spad**, and **Bristol** types, and to the first air aces. These would include German Manfred von Richtofen, with 80 victories; Frenchman Rene Fonck, with 75; Canadian Billy Bishop, with 72; and Eddie Rickenbacker of the United States, with 26. **Junkers** produced the first all-metal aircraft. There was also an increasing use of specialized types. Ground attack was soon

possible. The emergence of large bombers like the **Gotha** and **Handley Page** suggested that aircraft might have more than a purely tactical battlefield role and take significant part in future strategic campaigns. Long-distance forays, both by aircraft, and by German **zeppelins**, brought the first taste of bombing to civilian populations. Seaplanes and early **aircraft carriers** demonstrated that there were aerial dimensions to war at sea.

Despite interwar financial stringency, there were theorists who saw a future in which air power might be decisive. These did not always get their way. Italian Giulio Douhet postulated that trench stalemate might be avoided by the single-minded application of strategic bombing, which would shatter enemy morale and lead to a collapse of the war effort. In the United States, Brigadier General Billy Mitchell argued for the creation of an independent air force but was court-marshaled in 1925 following a series of attacks on military policy. In Germany, Walter Wever, chief of staff of the new Luftwaffe, declared that though fighters and antiaircraft guns were necessary, the "decisive weapon of air warfare is the bomber." His broad-based and coordinated approach to air power was summed up in *Die Luftkriegführung* (or the *Conduct of Air War*), which appeared in 1935, but he died the next year, leaving the Luftwaffe in arguably less capable hands. Britain had a narrow lead in jet technology, for though Germany had the **pulse jet**, Sir Frank Whittle was the first to run a true jet engine experimentally, in April 1937.

World War II would see exponential technological advance. In 1939 biplanes like the Gloster **Gladiator** were commonplace; by 1945 jet aircraft, **kamikaze** attacks, **radar** guidance, bombers capable of delivering **nuclear weapons, ejection seats**, pressurized cabins, **chaff**, and unmanned aircraft had all been invented. Among the numerous important craft of the war were the **Mustang, Spitfire, Hurricane, Zero, Me 109, Me 110, Focke-Wulf 190**, and **Hellcat** fighters; the **He 280, Me 262**, and Gloster **Meteor** jet craft; and bombers like the **He 111, Lancaster, Liberator, Wellington, B-17**, and **B-29**. Well-known dive bombers and ground-attack machines included the **Stuka,**

British RAF officer Frank Whittle (1907–96) pictured at his desk in World War II. Though Whittle invented the jet engine, jet propulsion would first be exploited in battle by the German Luftwaffe. The concept revolutionized air warfare. © Hulton/Getty Images.

Shturmovik, and **Dauntless**. The practicality of tank busting with rockets was demonstrated by craft like the **Typhoon**. Guided aerial munitions made their first appearance, and the insertion of large numbers of parachute and **glider** troops became reality.

Though there were many conventional craft like the **Skyraider** operating after 1945, new military jet and rocket planes now set records for speed and altitude. Among these the **X-1** made world news—but service aircraft like the **Hunter** also set records, and the remarkable **MiG-15** showed that jet technology was not the exclusive prerogative of the West. Now a household name, the original **B-52** was designed surprisingly soon after the war. Some advances were directly assisted by captured German technology; links can be seen not only to immediate postwar designs like the excellent **Sabre** and **B-49** but to **stealth** concepts.

Teamed with atomic weapons, long-range bombers were the key deterrent of the early Cold War, but the period also saw new twists on old ideas—for example, the Vulcan-type **Gatling** gun. Rapid, vertical, and near-vertical takeoff had early expressions in **ZELL**, the **helicopter**, and the wartime **Natter**, but it was not until the early 1960s that the **Harrier** perfected

vertical takeoff and landing in a practical and reliable combat aircraft. The **Phantom** was arguably the definitive plane of the time, but soon after the remarkable **F-111** was pushing the envelope yet again with "swing wings" and other new technologies.

Military aircraft were now not only hugely complex but hugely expensive. Consolidation was a major way of sharing costs and technologies. In the United States, mergers and acquisitions brought together huge players like **Boeing** and **McDonnell Douglas**. The United Kingdom's last true solo fighter production was the **Lightning**, after which European cooperation would become more common. Nevertheless some countries, such as Sweden with its Saab aircraft, would maintain independent traditions. The development of new missiles, like **Sidewinder**, Maverick, and **Hellfire**, increased the combat capacity of aircraft beyond recognition. Though the Soviet bloc would produce a surprising number of good aircraft, among them the **MiG**-21 and MiG-23, and the **Sukhoi Su-27**, the dominance of the West, and the United States in particular, would become steadily more apparent. Carrier-based formations with new planes like the **F-14** would ensure control of the sea, while the **F-15** would become a pace setter over land. **AWACS** revoultionized early-warning systems.

In recent times the air technology race has by no means slowed. New materials, carbon fibers, fiber optics, and the silicon chip are just a few of the things that have made new revolutions possible. First computer modeling, then computer-aided design, and finally virtual reality have made possible plans and experiments before a single component is constructed. Fly-by-wire, engines with nozzles that turn, new sensors, new software, new control systems, and the latest **head-up** and helmet-mounted displays are just some of the areas in which new aircraft compete. **Smart bombs** give relatively small numbers of aircraft considerable tactical and strategic power. Just some of the leaders in the modern fighter field are the **F-16, F-22, Eurofighter Typhoon**, and the **Joint Strike Fighter**. Just as remarkable, but very different, is the extraordinary **Osprey**.

Additional Reading: Sweetman, *Advanced Fighter Technology*, 1997; Angelucci, *World Encyclopaedia of Military Aircraft*, 1985; Clarke, *British Aircraft Armament*, 1993, 1994; Francillon (ed), *World Military Aviation*, 1997; Huenecke, *Modern Combat Aircraft Design*, 1987; Collinson, *Introduction to Avionics*, 1986; Taylor, *Combat Aircraft of the World*, 1969.

Aircraft Carrier   WARSHIP

Long-range vision has always been significant at sea—hence the early development of spotting tops, crow's nests, and other observation platforms. The idea of ships that carry **aircraft** therefore caught on very rapidly at the beginning of the twentieth century. As early as 1903 towed kites and **balloons** were in experimental use, and takeoff from the sea itself was achieved by Henri Fabre in 1910. The same year, U.S. aviator Eugene Ely made the first takeoff from a ship, using a **Curtiss** Pusher plane from a platform on the light cruiser *Birmingham*.

Early ship launches relied on downward-sloping ramps to give rapid acceleration, but landing was generally impossible, though Ely did succeed in alighting on a specially constructed platform in 1911. An apparently more practical method was pioneered by Glenn Curtiss when his seaplane was hoisted on board the USS *Pennsylvania* in 1911. **Catapults** for launching aircraft were invented in 1911 and 1912, first using a wire and counterweight, then a compressed-air system. They were in use on a ship by 1915.

In 1913 the Royal Navy sent the cruiser *Hermes* on an exercise with aircraft on board. The British continued to be early pioneers of the carrier, using converted vessels like the *Campania* and *Furious*, often with **Sopwith**-type aircraft. During World War I turret-mounted and retrofitted forecastle launch platforms were in use. In trolley-assisted takeoffs the aircraft was moved along on a wheeled carriage to gain speed. This allowed float planes to become airborne more rapidly and made their paths more predictable. In systems where the trolley was arrested, it could be reused.

Aircraft-carrying ships played a particular role in anti-**zeppelin** defense.

Though the Washington Naval Treaty limited tonnages, the interwar period saw considerable advances; the first U.S. carrier, the *Langley*, was commissioned in 1922. Though it was realized that flat "through decks" offered considerable advantage in both takeoff and landing, there was much debate over design. The need for funnels and navigation superstructures was particularly problematic. In the early plans for both the HMS *Eagle* and the USS *Lexington*, superstructures were positioned on both sides of the flight deck. In the Japanese *Kaga* a trunking system took smoke to the rear. The Japanese also built merchantmen designed for easy conversion to carriers, this "shadow carrier" fleet helping circumvent the treaties. Eventually, however, an "island" layout became commonplace in which the funnel, command, and navigation equipments were grouped and offset to one side. Planes were slowed on landing with arresting gear, engaging a hook trailing the aircraft.

Carriers were critical during World War II, often dictating naval strategy. In many actions, including Pearl Harbor and Midway, carrier **torpedo** bombers and **dive bombers** played crucial parts. Carriers also took on several distinct roles. Fleet carriers were major strike weapons, while escort carriers defended convoys and other potential targets. Many had antisubmarine duties. Some served principally as transports, often moving land-based planes from one area to another. Important vessels of the period included the U.S. *Yorktown, Bogue, Essex*, and *Independence* classes; the Japanese *Akagi, Taiho*, and *Shokaku*; and the British *Ark Royal* and *Illustrious*. Significant carrier-based planes included the **Helldiver, Dauntless, Hellcat, Swordfish, Val**, and **Zero**. There were more carriers in service in 1945 than at any other time before or since.

After the war, the United States emerged as the main proponent of carrier warfare, with particular emphasis on antisubmarine and nuclear-strike capability. The new technologies and increasing size of aircraft led to extensive conversions of existing carriers, as in the *Midway* class. It also led to startling new designs like the abortive **United States**, and to the building of bigger vessels, like the nuclear-powered **Enterprise** and the **Forrestal** class. In the majority of new carriers a distinctive angled deck and steam catapults were included. With the advent of **helicopter** and vertical takeoff, it was, however, also possible to build smaller special-purpose carriers, including the **Iwo Jima** and **Tarawa** classes, and the British **Invincible** class.

The Soviets were never enamored of large carriers; nevertheless their fleet included the *Moskva* class and the famous **Kiev** class, built 1970–1982. The largest Russian carrier today is the **Kuznetzov**. France kept a major carrier capability with the building of the *Clemenceau* and *Charles de Gaulle*. Press reports of 2004 state that Britain is intending to replace **Invincible, Ark Royal**, and *Illustrious* with two 65,000-ton vessels carrying up to 48 aircraft each. These are scheduled to enter service in 2012 and 2015.

The first of the U.S. *Nimitz* class was commissioned in 1975. Recent additions to this class are the USS **John C. Stennis** and **Harry S. Truman**, 97,000-ton carriers. Vessels of this size form the nuclei of significant task forces, or "carrier groups," allowing major actions even where no land base is available. It is thought that the *Ronald Reagan* will be the last carrier of the *Nimitz* type; thereafter a CVNX series, currently under development will likely enter service, over the next two decades. The cost of a single carrier is expected to be 6.6 billion dollars. Important carrier-based planes of the last quarter-century have included the **Harrier, Hornet, F-4B**, and **F-14A**.

Additional Reading: Chesneau, *Aircraft Carriers*, 1992; Beaver, *British Aircraft Carriers*, 1984; Jordan, *Soviet Warships 1945 to the Present*, 1991; Hone, *American and British Aircraft Carrier Development 1919–1941*, 1999.

Airgeep. *See* Flying Platform

Airship   BALLOON

During the nineteenth century, the idea of the "dirigible"—a navigable **balloon** or airship— gained currency. As early as 1852 a steam-powered balloon managed a short flight, but as yet the power-to-weight ratio was insufficient to make such a device practical. In France experiments with electric motors achieved some success, with the first powered lighter-than-air flight being that of the *La France* on 9 August 1884, but weight of batteries proved a serious handicap. Brazilian-born inventor Alberto Santos-Dumont built and flew various craft between 1898 and 1907. Yet it was with the internal combustion engine that the powered airship became viable, the **Zeppelin** *LZ 1* taking to the skies in July 1900.

Though the German machines were deservedly the best-known military airships, they were by no means unique. Count Almerigo da Schio's Italian airship appeared in 1905. In Britain, balloon maker Stanley Spencer produced an experimental model in 1902; the *Willows No. 2*, built by E. T. Willows of Cardiff, flew the Channel in 1910. Eventually a later Willows type would be the model for the "Sea Scout" design. The British Army Balloon Factory was making airships by 1907, and the Vickers company, working with the Admiralty, produced the Mayfly in 1909. The French Astra-Torres and German Parseval designs influenced British thinking. During World War I British C, or Coastal, type craft were used for maritime patrol and submarine detection.

The French Naval Air Service and army also flew limited numbers of machines of Astra-Torres, Zodiac, and Clement-Bayard types. Italian airships, which had been active against the Turks before 1914, made 197 raids during World War I, Italian craft being of the P and M types. Airship construction continued well into the interwar period, and civil airships have undergone something of a revival in recent years.

Additional Reading: Hartcup, *Achievement of the Airship*, 1974; Collier, *The Airship*, 1974; Mowthorpe, *Battlebags: British Airships of the First World War*, 1998; Treadwell and Wood, *Airships of the First World War*, 1999.

AK-47, AKM. *See* Kalashnikov

Akagi WARSHIP

The Japanese **aircraft carrier** *Akagi* was a 30,000-ton vessel commissioned in 1927. The keel had originally been laid for a battle cruiser but was later converted. The distinctive outline of the *Akagi* was a product of this ancestry, combining a double-level hangar layout and a downward-curving funnel intended to keep smoke away from the flight decks. A major refit improved capacity to 91 aircraft. Though surprisingly useful for her age, she was sunk in 1942.

Akula Class SUBMARINE

The *Akula* class Russian type 971 attack **submarines** are nuclear powered vessels of a double hulled construction with a distinctive high aft fin. The seven *Akula* I types were commissioned between 1986 and 1992, with a further three of an improved *Akula* II design built later. Slightly longer than the originals at 110 meters long they displace 12,770 tons. The main armament of the *Akula* is up to 12 Granat **cruise** type submarine launched missiles. There are also eight **torpedo** launch tubes. In addition to the main turbine there are two auxiliary diesels—the top submerged speed being 33 knots. Recent reports suggest that the Indian Navy intends to lease two *Akula* class vessels from Russia in 2004.

Additional Reading: Hutchinson, *Submarines*; www. naval-technology.com; *Jane's Warships*.

Alabama, CSS WARSHIP

Completed on the Mersey in the United Kingdom in 1862, the controversial CSS *Alabama* was the most successful Confederate commerce raider, accounting for 65 vessels. Sometimes defined as an "auxiliary bark," she was 220 feet long, was fitted with both steam and sail, and mounted eight guns. The $5,000,000 losses caused by the *Alabama* were blamed on the theoretically neutral Britain. The wreck of the *Alabama* was located in 1984.

Additional Reading: Bowcock, *CSS* Alabama, 2002; Hollet, *Alabama Affair*, 1993.

Alaska Class WARSHIP

The U.S. *Alaska*-class heavy **cruisers,** *Alaska* and *Guam*, completed in 1944, were **battleships** in all but name. Designed to counter Japanese heavy cruisers and the German commerce raiders, the *Alaska* class ships were 808 feet in length with a displacement of 30,000 tons. Their nine 12-inch guns comfortably outclassed the weaponry of ships like the ***Scharnhorst***; their armor had a maximum thickness of 9.5 inches and was slightly inclined. Both ships fought in the Pacific in the later stages of World War II. A third vessel, the *Hawaii*, was never completed.

Additional Reading: Garzke & Dulin, *Battleships: United States Battleships, 1935–1992*, 1995.

Albacore SUBMARINE

The 204-foot U.S. **submarine** *Albacore* (AGSS 569), launched at Portsmouth Navy Yard in August 1953, was a technological landmark that served as a test bed for many new ideas. Her tear-drop shape, then revolutionary, was the result of wind tunnel tests. Made of low-carbon steel, she incorporated experimental control surfaces and measures to decrease noise. From 1955 she underwent many modifications, including the use of Aquaplas, a sound-dampening elastic material, and the fitting of active and passive **sonar** systems. In 1962 a refit saw the installation of a larger engine, concentric contra-rotating propellers, and new silver-zinc batteries. Further modification in 1968 increased her top speed still further so that eventually she was claimed capable of 26 knots on the surface and 30 submerged. Her pioneering work has influenced the design of many modern submarines. Decommissioned in 1972, she was later displayed at the Portsmouth Maritime Museum, New Hampshire.

Additional Reading: Paine, *Ships of the World*, 1997; Hutchinson, *Submarines: War beneath the Waves*, 2001.

Albatros AIRCRAFT

Albatros fighters were among the best German **aircraft** of the First World War. Following the

C series the successful D series commenced in 1916 with the Albatros D. I. This single-seat biplane featured an aerodynamic elliptical fuselage, was fitted with a powerful Benz Bz III or Mercedes D.III engine, and was armed with synchronized **machine guns**. In the D.II model the top wing was lowered; the climb rate improved to 1,000 meters in five minutes.

The D.V, which appeared in the spring of 1917, was built in large numbers. It was powered by a 180-horsepower engine, had a ceiling of 18,700 feet, and could climb to 1,000 meters in four minutes. A little over seven meters in length, it weighed just 687 kg empty.

Alberich. *See* **Stealth**

Algérie   WARSHIP

Laid down in 1931, the 10,000-ton French **cruiser** *Algérie* has been acknowledged as one of the best cruisers built within the constraints of the Washington Treaty, and something of a departure from existing designs. A flush deck enhanced strength, while a single funnel saved space. Her main armament was eight 8-inch guns, backed by 12 of 100 mm. Before World War II her range finders and antiaircraft armament were improved. Following service on the Allied side in the Mediterranean and Atlantic, she was included in the Vichy fleet, but like most of the *Suffren* and *La Galissonniere* classes, was scuttled by her crew at Toulon in 1942.

Al-Hussein. *See* **Scud**

Alkali (AA-1) Missile   MISSILE

A Soviet air-to-air missile with semiactive radar homing, in service c. 1970. Carried by the MiG-19 and other interceptor **aircraft**, the Alkali was six feet in length and weighed about 200 lb. Its range was about five miles.

Alouette   HELICOPTER

The French Aerospatiale Alouette (or "lark") multirole **helicopter**, which first flew in 1955, has been described as "the most successful" European model. It has been produced in many different variants in several different countries. The Mark II, produced in the early 1970s, was a five-seater type; the "HAL Lama" was a high-altitude weight lifter; and the Mark III was a seven-seater. More than 60 countries have operated the Alouette, these being as diverse as India (whose army refers to the Alouette as the Cheetah, or Chetak), Zimbabwe, Sweden, Chile, Denmark, and Germany.

AM-39. *See* **Exocet**

America's Army   COMMUNICATIONS

"America's Army" is the title of a computer game unveiled at Los Angeles Electronic Expo 2002. During play enemies are stalked and killed; missions accomplished with the least loss of life are most highly rewarded. Developed by the Defense Department entirely at public expense, the game is to be given away free to any who want it. America's Army is primarily a recruiting tool, marketed with the explicit intention of finding computer-literate individuals who will be happy in a high-technology environment.

Ammunition, Ammunition Box
                                              EXPLOSIVES

The word "ammunition" originated as a corruption of the older word "munition"; until comparatively recently "ammunition" could be used to indicate any type of military store—hence references to "ammunition **boots**" and also to **rations**, such as "ammunition bread." Trains of **artillery** and "ammunition trains" could therefore include all manner of supplies. Over the last two centuries, however, the term has become applied in a much more specific sense to mean items used in the charging of guns—as, for example, **gunpowder, shells, cartridges,** and **explosives**. Improvements in the packing and storage of ammunition have made considerable, but often unsung, contributions to the advance of military technology.

By the Middle Ages, for example, the manufacture, storage, and transport of **arrows** had become a highly organized process. Leather spacers with circular holes were made to con-

tain set numbers and to protect delicate fletch-
ings. By 1600 it was realized that that
gunpowder left stored for long periods tended
to degrade, separate out, or absorb moisture.
Therefore not only was it kept in barrels, but
records were kept so that stocks could be rotated; any that exceeded a certain date would
be sent back to the supplier for exchange or
remanufacture. During the nineteenth century,
wooden storage boxes and paper and card
wrappings for ammunition became the norm,
with symbols and color-coded markings for different types of munition. In many instances
sheet-lead linings provided protection from
damp. The advent of fixed or one-piece cartridges made easy-to-reuse metal ammunition
boxes practical, though disposable plastics and
cardboards have become more common since
World War II.

Additional Reading: Hoyem, *The History and Development of Small Arms Ammunition*, 1981; Hawkins, *Treatise on Ammunition*, 1887; Allsop and
Toomey, *Small Arms*, 1999.

AMR. *See* **Antimaterial Rifle**

AMX-13   TANK

Designed by Atelier de Construction d'Issy-les-
Moulineaux, the AMX-13 is a French three-
man light **tank** first manufactured in 1952. The
usual main armament is a 90 mm gun. It has a
hull of all-steel welded construction giving armored protection of up to 40 mm, and its top
speed is 37 mph. The most novel features are
the turret and gun mounting, as the turret is
made in two parts with the gun rigidly fixed in
the upper part, which elevates as a complete
unit. The gun itself is fitted with an automatic
loader. The AMX-13 remained in production
for well over 30 years, during which time 7,700
were made, including engineer, recovery,
missile-launching, and other variants. It has
been widely used in South America and Southeast Asia as well as Europe.

AMX-30, 32   TANK

The French AMX-30 main battle **tank** was
manufactured from 1966, soon replacing the

M-47 in French service. With cast and welded
construction it has a maximum armor of 79 mm
and an Hispano-Suiza 12-cylinder multifuel engine giving a maximum speed of 40 mph. The
normal main armament is a 105 mm gun, in
addition to which a 20 mm and one or more
machine guns may be fitted. The coaxial gun
is unusual in that it may be elevated independently, allowing fire against **helicopters**.

There have been many variants over the
years, one of the more recent being the AMX-
30S, intended for desert operations. In this
model a new fire control system with **laser**
range finder was fitted, as were sand shields and
a modified transmission. The AMX-32, a prototype of which was completed as early as
1979, is a much uprated variation that was originally intended for the export market. This had
increased armor protection, provision for a 120
mm gun, and a TV camera mounted with the
main armament. It was steered with wheel
rather than the stick controls usual in tanks. It
has been substantially superseded by the **Leclerc**.

Andros Robot. *See* **Wheelbarrow**

Anthrax   BIOLOGICAL WARFARE

The naturally occuring "Bacillus anthracis" was
discovered by German bacteriologist Robert
Koch (1843–1910) in 1876. It is the cause of
what was commonly known as wool sorter's
disease, or anthrax. The rod-shaped microor-
ganism lives on sheep and cattle, and it can
infect man through the skin or lungs—the former not usually being fatal, while the latter is
almost always so. Particulate size is therefore
important.

Under General Shiro Ishii, the Japanese
made progress in adapting anthrax as a weapon
before World War II, testing it on the Chinese.
Anthrax was seen as a potential wonder
weapon, since the disease was not epidemic in
man yet on a weight-for-weight basis it was
many times more effective than any chemical
agent yet known.

Further work at Porton in the United Kingdom led to tests at Penclawdd on the Gower

coast, and at the now-infamous Gruinard Island, Scotland, which would remain polluted for half a century. In the United States, the Chemical Warfare Service established production facilities at Camp Detrick. Soviet military scientists followed suit. Methods developed for the use of anthrax included cluster-bomb dispersal for attacking human targets and putting anthrax into cattle cakes to destroy livestock. Fortunately, a recent terrorist use of anthrax in powder form has proved relatively ineffective, though very disruptive.

Additional Reading: Parker, *The Killing Factory: The Top Secret World of Germ and Chemical Warfare,* 1996.

Antimaterial Rifle FIREARM

An "anti-material rifle" is a **rifle**-type weapon of relatively large caliber designed to attack such vulnerable targets as vehicles and communication centers. It is essentially a modern version of the **antitank rifles** of old. The **Barrett** is sometimes put in this category, but the most obvious example is the Austrian Steyr 15 mm AMR. This high-velocity weapon has a muzzle brake and hydropneumatic sleeve to dampen the recoil and is claimed to have an effective range of about 2 km. Fired from a bipod, it can be broken down into two loads for transport by the crew.

Additional Reading: Hogg and Weeks, *Military Small Arms of the Twentieth Century,* 1977, 1994.

Antitank Rifle FIREARM

To all intents and purposes a very large and especially powerful rifle, the antitank **rifle** came into existence in 1918 with the appearance of the 13 mm **Mauser** T-Gewehr. While **tank** armor remained thin, the idea remained popular; the heyday of the antitank rifle lasted until about 1940.

Significant antitank rifles included the Polish Karabin Przecipancerny wz 35 Ur, which was relatively light and incorporated a four-round magazine, and the German PzB 38. The Japanese Type 97 was remarkable in that it was a 20 mm automatic weighing 52.5 kg. Named af-

ter Captain Boys, the British .55-inch Boys antitank rifle, introduced in 1937, was capable of penetrating about 21 mm of armor at 300 yards. It was obsolete by 1941. Nevertheless it was retained in small numbers for some interesting experiments. These included the breaking of unexploded bombs at a distance and super-long-range **sniping** in an antiterrorist role. It may therefore be claimed as a predecessor to the **antimaterial** rifle.

Apache, AH-64 HELICOPTER

The Apache AH-64 is one of the most significant **helicopters** of recent times. The U.S. Army Advanced Attack Helicopter program of 1972 was intended to create a machine capable of taking on enemy armor and absorb hits from **machine guns** and light **flak**. Following submissions from several manufacturers, the field was reduced to two competing designs in 1973, these being the Bell model 409 (YAH-63) and the Hughes 77 (YAH-64). The Hughes helicopter was announced the winner in 1976, and in the 1982 Defense bill $537.5 million was allocated for the production of the first 11 machines. Hughes built a new plant at Mesa, Arizona, and the first production vehicle, PV01, rolled out on 30 September 1983.

Apart from its ability to fire the latest **Hellfire** missiles, the Apache incorporated a number of then-novel technological features. Each blade of the rotor had five bars of high-strength stainless steel lined with glass fiber and a trailing edge of composite honeycomb structure, making it possible to fly even when any one spar had been shot through. The load paths were so arranged that the transmission could be removed while the rotor was kept in place. The transmission itself was designed to operate for an hour even after a total loss of oil. Dual control systems meant that the failure of the primary system did not automatically lead to a crash.

The avionics were installed as modular units, designed so that maintenance staff could replace them in seconds even in cold weather when wearing mittens. "Nap of the earth" flying was made possible by a battery of sensors including the AAQ-11 PNVS, or "Pilot's Night Vision Sensor," serving the rear of the two pilot seats. A "TADS," or Target Acquisition Designation Sight, was linked to the fire control computer allowing engagement in poor light and weather with 30 mm chain gun, rockets, or missiles. Data of 1986 showed that the AH-64A, with its twin General Electric T700-GE-701 turboshaft engines, was capable of a maximum speed of 184 mph and a climb of 2,460 feet per minute. The service ceiling was 21,000 feet, or 10,800 on one engine. It weighed 10,760 lb empty.

Since then the Apache has been built under the **McDonnell Douglas** name, and there have been many improvements. These include the fitting of **GPS**, extended fuel tanks, and **laser** warning receivers. The late 1990s saw the appearance of the Longbow Apache AH-64D, incorporating seeker-equipped "fire and forget" Hellfire anti**tank** guided missiles. Perhaps most importantly, the Longbow **radar** was mast mounted, allowing the helicopter to adopt a lower and less vulnerable in-flight profile.

Additional Reading: Gunston, *AH-64 Apache*, 1986; Moeng, *Military Aircraft*, 1994.

APDS. *See* **Sabot**

Apex (AA-7) Missile   MISSILE

Soviet air-to-air missile in service c. 1980. Carried by the MiG-23 Flogger and similar **aircraft**, the Apex had alternative infrared and semiactive radar-homing guidance systems. Powered by a solid-fuel rocket motor, it weighed 705 lb and had a range of about 17 miles.

Aquaplas. *See* **Albacore**

AR-5; AR-10; AR-15. *See* **M16**

Archer. *See* **Tank Destroyer; Bow**

Arethusa **Class**   WARSHIP

The British *Arethusa* class of four *cruisers* was laid down in the early 1930s and completed by November 1937. Delays and modifications during construction meant variations in detail: *Aurora*, for example, had no aircraft, and *Arethusa* and *Galatea* were slightly lighter than *Penelope* and *Aurora*. All had six 6-inch guns, but secondary armament also varied. All fought in World War II, with *Galatea* torpedoed and sunk by *U-557* in 1941, and *Penelope* sunk by *U-410* during Anzio operations in 1944. *Aurora* was sold to Nationalist China in 1948 and later defected to the communists, being known thereafter by at least four different Chinese names.

Arisaka Rifle   FIREARM

Designed by Colonel Nariake Arisaka in the 1890s, the Japanese Arisaka **rifle** was a **bolt-action** model of the **Mauser** type. Originally in 6.5 mm, the Arisaka became the Japanese standard model, but later types were in 7.7 mm. Variations included **carbines**, paratrooper models, and an extraordinary **sniper** type fitted with a monopod; all were used in World War II.

Additional Reading: Markham, *Japanese Infantry Weapons of World War II*, 1976.

Arizona, **USS**   WARSHIP

The U.S. **battleship Arizona** (BB 39) was a vessel of the *Pennsylvania* class laid down in 1914 and completed in 1916. Displacing 31,400 tons, her main armament was 12 14-inch guns. Following service in the Atlantic she underwent a major modernization at Norfolk Navy Yard, from 1929 to 1931. Further works were carried out in 1939 and 1941. At Pearl Harbor on 7 December she was hit by eight bombs and a **torpedo**, and her magazines exploded. She was dedicated as a memorial in 1962 and remains so to this day.

Additional Reading: Stillwell, *Battleship Arizona*, 1991; Terzibaschitsch, *Battleships of the US Navy in World War II*, 1977.

Arjun Main Battle Tank   TANK

The Indian Arjun, four-man, main battle **tank** was a highly ambitious project originally intended for completion in 1990. This was not actually achieved until a decade later. Problems included the lack of availability of a suitable Indian-made diesel power plant, with the result that German **Leopard** engines were fitted as a stopgap.

Nevertheless, about 100 Ajun tanks were known to be in service by 2000, and its statistics are impressive enough. Top speed is claimed as 45 mph, and the main armament is a **rifled** 120 mm gun. The tank's length is 33 feet, its armor a composite type, and the all-up weight 129,000 lb.

Ark Royal, HMS   WARSHIP

Since the medieval period there have been a number of vessels named *Ark Royal* in Britain's navies. Most recently the name has been applied to four **aircraft carriers**. The one purchased in 1914 was begun as a cargo ship but was converted to service seaplanes, or trolley-launch aircraft. With the commission of a new purpose-built carrier to be known as *Ark Royal*, the original was renamed *Pegasus*. The second carrier *Ark Royal* was the first large British carrier to be designed from scratch. Laid down in 1935, she was commissioned in 1938 and was sunk by a **U-boat** in 1941.

The third carrier *Ark Royal* was of the *Eagle* class and was much larger, at 37,000 tons. Though laid down at the Cammell Laird yard as early as 1943, she was not commissioned until 1955. Capable of taking 80 aircraft, her angled flight deck had two lifts and two catapults. Later in her service life she would undergo various modifications, enabling her to operate Buccaneer aircraft and new **radar**. Several thousand tons were added to her displacement. *Ark Royal* (III) was scrapped in 1980. The present *Ark Royal*, launched in 1981, is of the *Invincible* class and was dispatched to the Persian Gulf early in 2003.

Additional Reading: Johnstone-Bryden, *Ark Royal IV*, 1999; McCart, *Three Ark Royals*, 1999; Jameson, *Ark Royal 1939–1941*, 1957; Beaver, *Ark Royal*, 1979; Apps, *Four Ark Royals*, 1976; Poolman, *Ark Royal*, 1956.

Arleigh Burke **Class**   WARSHIP

The *Arleigh Burke* guided missile **destroyers** are an important part of the modern U.S. Navy. Types I and II of the class were constructed from 1988, with a total of 28 vessels completed by 1999. These were remarkable as being the first U.S. warships to have a "collective protection system" against nuclear-biological-chemical (**NBC**) threat, incorporating such features as double air-lock hatches. They use elements of **stealth** technology in the design of their hull shapes and incorporate measures designed to reduce **infrared** signature. *Cole* (DDG 67) was damaged by terrorist attack at Aden in October 2000.

A further eight vessels of the improved *Arleigh Burke* "IIa" type have also been commissioned, the first of these being the *Oscar Austin* (DDG 79) in August 2000. With a displacement of 9,200 tons and a crew of 344 the *Arleigh Burke* IIa has a main armament of **Tomahawk** and **Harpoon** as well as various surface-to-air missiles. The type also carries a 5-inch gun, **torpedoes**, and two **helicopters**.

Additional Reading: Saunders (ed), *Jane's Fighting Ships 2001–2002*, 2001.

Armor   ARMOR

The word "armor" has been applied to many different sorts of protection, and though once commonly understood to mean a defense for the human body it is now often applied to "armored vehicles," such as **tanks**. In prehistory the earliest armors were of natural materials like tree bark, horn, leather, and bone. Multi-layered linen was in use by the Egyptians by about 3000 B.C., and textiles then became important for protection. The use of padded jackets in particular has continued into modern times. The **helmet** remains in use today.

Metal armor came into use in the Bronze Age, and by about 1500 B.C. armor supported by straps over the shoulders came into use. Plate defenses for the breast followed and were popular for senior officers in Greece and Rome. The breastplate was often called a "cuirass," in reference to the fact that they had once often been made of leather. Metal scales were also applied to textiles at an early date and were seen in ancient China. Such composite protection continued to be important right through the classical and medieval eras, in forms known latterly as brigandines, jacks, or "coats of plate."

Mail, popularly called "chain mail" but more properly "ring mail," is believed to have been a Celtic development about the fifth century B.C. This defense of interlocking rings was a technological breakthrough, since it was a little lighter than solid plates and gave greater flexibility of movement. In the form of a coat, known as a hauberk or byrnie, mail was the primary defense of early medieval warriors and the Normans. Mail saw limited use—for example, in face defenses—as late as the First World War.

While scale, mail, and textile defenses remained popular over much of the globe, the "plate" armor associated with knightly Europe began to evolve during the thirteenth century. Gutter shaped greaves and vambraces for the arms were later developed into a full "cap à pied" or "head to foot" suit, better described as a "harness." By the mid-fifteenth century armor had reached a high point in sophistication and complexity, with particularly fine pieces produced in northern Italy and southern Germany —hence the expressions "Milanese" and "Gothic." Plates were angled and fluted to deflect **swords** and **arrows**, and made in different thickness to protect different parts of the body. The rich used special harnesses for war, the joust, and foot combat. The most technically advanced suits were modular; parts could be interchanged for different purposes.

These suits and their individual parts acquired a complex terminology. "Sabatons," for example, is the name applied to foot defenses— which, like modern shoes, changed in style over the centuries. Besagaws were discs to protect the armpits, and the bevor covered the neck and lower face, while the codpiece, ever more elaborate, protected the groin. Even horse armor had its own lexicography, with the chamfron to

protect the head and a peytral for the breast being parts of the full "bard" for an animal.

With first the long**bow**, and later the growing importance of firearms, armor became more decorative and less practical. While some **bows** and arrows in the hands of skilled archers would pierce some types of armor, muskets proved able to penetrate all but the heaviest. It was now impractical to cover the soldier's entire body and still expect him to fight. Nevertheless, prestige armor makers, such as those at Innsbruck, Augsburg, and Greenwich, continued to manufacture for royalty and nobility.

By 1600 battlefield armor of the horseman had been reduced to "half armor," or a simple back, breast, and helmet. The **pike**man was reduced to a corselet consisting of a breast and back, with tassets for the thighs and a helmet. **Musket**-armed troops seldom had as much as a helmet. Though some cavalry retained helmets and breastplates, and engineers might have siege armor, for most practical purposes armor was in abeyance in the Western world from 1700 to 1914.

During World War I positional warfare, which seldom required trench garrisons to move far and often exposed only a man's head and shoulders to **shrapnel**, brought about conditions in which armor was suddenly viable. The **Chemico**, Dayfield shield, Portobank, and Star were just a few of the commercial body armors put into production. General Angust-Louis Adrian set about the provision of shoulder defenses for French troops, and the Germans later made the *Sappenpanzer*. Italy produced a number of armors, including the Ansaldo type, which doubled as a **shield** when rested on the ground. The United States experimented with a sentinel's armor, light body armor cushioned internally with sponge rubber, laminated plates, and the Zeglin bulletproof "silken matting." A relatively small but significant percentage of troops on the western and southern european fronts were therefore armored by 1918.

In contrast, World War II would see very few combatants in body armor. Nevertheless, there was research and new types were devised, some of the most significant being for aviators. In the U.S. Air Force an M1 vest armored front and back was worn by bomber crews, often with the M3 or M4 apron. Yet the great modern resurgence of personal armor was made possible by the advent of new materials. As early as May 1943, the Dow company succeeded in making a strong material of glass fiber filaments bonded with an ethyl cellulose resin under pressure. Known as Doron, after General G. F. Doriot, this was used in combination with nylon, steel, and other materials in **flak** jackets as early as the battle of Okinawa in 1945, and again in the Korean War (as the "Vest, Armored, M-1951").

Though Doron and ballistic nylon were used in quantity in Vietnam in garments such as the **M69 vest**, other materials now proved promising. Hard ceramics, such as aluminum oxide, silicon carbide, and boron carbide, were found able to resist missiles when backed with softer materials, such as plastics and textiles. New body armors were developed for air crew, and by 1969 **"variable body armor"** was being issued to U.S. ground troops. In a number of protections ceramic plates were made to be slipped into pockets on vests made of flexible ballistic materials.

In recent years Kevlar has made the biggest contribution in the field of personal armor. First developed by the Du Pont company in 1965 as a substitute for rubber in industry, it was strong and light—an ideal combination for armor. By the 1970s it had been turned to both police and military use, and from 1980 it was also used in helmets. Kevlar body armor is currently in use with many nations.

Additional Reading: Dunstan, *Flak Jackets*, 1984; Stone, *A Glossary of the Construction, Decoration and Use of Arms and Armor*, 1934; Scott, *European Arms and Armour*; Robinson, *Armour of Imperial Rome*, 1975; Spring, *African Arms and Armour*, 1993; Pfaffenbichler, *Armourers*, 1992; Grancsay, *Arms and Armour*, 1964; Holmes, *Arms and Armour in Tudor and Stuart London*, 1957; Blair, *European Armour*, 1958; Edge and Paddock, *Arms & Armour of the Mediaeval Knight*; Long, *Modern Ballistic Armor*, 1986; *Jane's Infantry Weapons*, various editions.

Armored Car   VEHICLE

Development of the armored car began in 1896. The first U.S. experiment was in 1898. Though general acceptance was slow, some soon recognized the armored car as a useful reconnaissance vehicle and weapons platform. Early models included the Austrian Daimler of 1904, the German Erhardt of 1906, and the French Hotchkiss of 1909. One of the best was the Rolls Royce of 1914; it was based on a Silver Ghost chassis, weighed 3.5 tons, and mounted a **machine gun** in a revolving turret. Even so, very few armored cars were in the hands of the troops at the outbreak of war. Some British cavalry units actually purchased a few armored cars privately, while Belgian officers modified touring cars. A Royal Naval Armoured Car Division was formed in late 1914, and by 1915 it had squadrons serving in France.

Unfortunately, trenches and poor cross-country performance would prevent the armored car from reaching its full potential on the western front until the resumption of open warfare in 1918. More was achieved in South West Africa, where a Rolls Royce squadron was sent in 1915, and in East Africa, where Lanchesters and Leyland lorries were deployed. Perhaps most famously, British armored cars were also operated in North Africa and Palestine. In Palestine armored cars were operated by Colonel T. E. Lawrence against the Arabs.

By now the armored car was accepted as a major weapon. Faster than **tanks** on roads and good ground, they were cheaper to produce and often used technologies recognized in the civil sphere. With the gradual decline of cavalry armored cars carried out many of the tasks formerly performed by horsemen. During World War II some, mounted with large guns, were used in the role of **tank destroyers**. Others were devoted specifically to communications tasks. The best known U.S. type of the period was the **Greyhound** M8. Since 1945 armored cars have continued to be important, and in

A British Rolls-Royce armored car outside the Royal Ulster Constabulary police station on York Street, Belfast, following riots after an Orange Order parade, 1935. Previous "wars on terrorism" have had their own technology. © Hulton/Getty Images.

some instances, such as the **Saracen**, the traditional functions of the armored car have been combined with that of the personnel carrier. There have been dozens of models since World War II, including **Panhards**, the **Commando**, and **Ferret**.

Additional Reading: Hunnicutt, *Armored Car: A History of American Wheeled Combat Vehicles*, 2002; Terry, *Fighting Vehicles*, 1991.

Armstrong INVENTOR

William G. Armstrong (1810–1900) was a British hydraulic engineer who turned his mind to military matters with a design for a submarine **mine** in 1854. Commissioned to produce a field gun, he manufactured his first **rifled, breech-loading artillery** piece of forged iron in 1855.

After two years experimentation he perfected a weapon. The barrel, rifled with a large number of shallow grooves, was made by winding iron around a mandril, was welded solid, and then machined out to the correct dimension. The piece had a screw breech closure, and the projectile was lead covered so as to engage closely with the rifling. The result was an advanced and highly accurate gun.

Armstrong guns of various sizes were produced for the British forces and for export, but competition was fierce, and Whitworth muzzle-loaders and old smoothbores remained in service as well. In the 1860s Armstrong worked on heavier guns with wedge-type breeches. During the late 1870s and 1880s Armstrong experimented with slow-burning gunpowders for long-barreled guns, and he produced a new breech-loading cannon with wire-wound cylinders. Armstrong guns have been hailed as a significant advance in ships' armament, allowing firing "over the horizon" for the first time. Armstrong's Elswick Engineering works merged with **Vickers** in 1927 to form Vickers Armstrong.

Additional Reading: Rogers, *A History of Artillery*, 1975.

Arrow. *See* **Bow**

Arrow TMD   MISSILE

The Arrow Theater Missile Defense system is a joint U.S.-Israeli project utilizing technological developments of the U.S. **Strategic Defense Initiative** for the interception of ballistic missiles using missile batteries. The three-phase program commenced in 1988, and Arrow I achieved its first successful test intercept in 1994. Arrow II achieved its first intercept of a **Scud**-type target in 1996. The first operational Arrow antimissile batteries were deployed in Israel in 2000. Other countries, including the United Kingdom, Turkey, Japan, and India, have expressed interest.

It is claimed that the Arrow II command system can detect hostile missiles as much as 500 km away and deal with as many as 14 simultaneous intercepts. Its own missiles are said to be able to intercept a projectile traveling at up to nine times the speed of sound at altitudes from ten to 40 km.

Artillery   ARTILLERY

Like the word "**ammunition**," "artillery" originally denoted military stores in a general sense. It is sometimes asserted that artillery meant any weapon with a "tiller," or stock. So it is that the "artillator" John Cornewaille supplied the king of England with **crossbows** as well as guns in 1361. The word was broadly used in Chaucer's writings in the 1380s, and it has also been applied to **catapults** and siege engines. With the advance of technology the term began to take on more specific meaning. By the sixteenth century the word was used to describe all forms of firearm large or small: so it was

that the Honourable Artillery Company, first incorporated in England in 1537, primarily used handheld guns. What we might now think of as artillery was then called "great guns," or "great ordnance." A 1617 dictionary definition of artillery was "engines or instruments of war."

Terminology had moved on again by 1700, and the Royal Regiment of Artillery, formed in 1716, dealt with large guns from the outset. We now commonly assume that artillery means guns that are too big to be moved or operated by one person, and within the definition we may include **mortars, self-propelled guns**, and certain missiles. Artillery equipments commonly include some form of stand or carriage.

Gunpowder artillery was used in Europe c. 1300, the first documentary evidence being an illustration in a manuscript by Walter de Milemete of 1326. This shows a vase-shaped piece with an arrowhead projecting at the muzzle laid on a trestle or stand. A soldier is lighting the gun with a match. Thereafter artillery became steadily more useful in sieges, where castles and towns presented large static targets. There was also early, if limited, battlefield use. Most early guns appear to have been of wrought iron, fabricated with hoops and staves. Larger **bombards** were important in the fifteenth century. The addition of trunnions, or small spigots either side of the barrel at about the center of gravity, allowed guns to be elevated more easily and to be fitted with wheeled carriages.

The advent of casting, with bronze artillery now made by gun "founders" in a similar way to bells, was a significant advance of the later fifteenth century. The use of **cartridges** to load the **gunpowder** made artillery far more practical for the battlefield. The use of cheaper iron from the sixteenth century onward was also a technological breakthrough, though bronze and iron guns would coexist for many years. Gunnery instruments such as the "gunner's rule," shot gauge, and quadrant began to appear, and calculation was now applied to aim.

Standardization of gun types, with the categorization of pieces by the weight of shot, was a significant process that appears to have begun in the late sixteenth century and was largely complete in the West a century later. Old and

The 12pdr "Napoleon" gun—just one of many artillery pieces used in the American Civil War. Courtesy of the Library of Congress.

ill-defined categories like the "falcon," "saker," and "basilisk" slowly gave way to the three-pounder and six-pounder. This was important because it improved compatibility in terms of supply and training, and made possible range tables by which the fire of all guns of a certain class could be predicted. The study of what we would now call ballistics began, and not for the first time military technology became a significant contributor to science.

Artillery was now a dominating feature of war. In the late fifteenth and sixteenth centuries it ended the militarily usefulness of castles, and helped bring in low, thick-walled **forts** with bastions. The development of mortars and **grenades** complemented the guns. At sea it was the ships with the most heavy guns that tended to win naval battles. In the seventeenth century light "frame" guns and **"leather" guns** pointed to new mobility. On land, by the eighteenth century better organization and supply was increasing effectiveness on the battlefield. The French lit upon a system of five standard calibers in 1732, with the heaviest gun in the French artillery "train" a 24-pounder, the lightest a four-pounder. Reform under General General Gribeauval, and the introduction of the "system Gribeauval" three decades later, would define the field guns as 4, 8 and 12-pounders, supported by the **howitzer**, while the 16 and 24-pounders made up the siege artillery.

During the early nineteenth century the greatest progress was made with ammunition and ignition systems. The friction tube, used from the 1820s, produced quicker and more reliable ignition. It consisted of a roughened wire within a tube of saltpeter and antimony, with a small charge. A sharp pull on the wire created friction and set off the device. Spherical "common" **shells** and **shrapnel** were supplemented by elongated projectiles. The midcentury saw the advent of the RML, or **rifled** muzzle-loading gun, which increased both range and accuracy.

After that, much work was done to perfect reliable **breech-loading** systems. These would ultimately lead to quicker fire, practical reloading in turreted **battleships**, and less danger to gunners. Numerous solutions were tried to the problem of "obturation," or preventing gas escape. Radically different methods were pioneered by **Armstrong** in the United Kingdom, de Beaulieu in France, and Broadwell in the United States. Ultimately, however, the system that had most immediate impact was that of **Krupp**, whose sliding wedge incorporated Broadwell rings and was used to great advantage in Prussia's wars of the later nineteenth century. From the 1880s the "plastic obturator" of the French colonel C. R. de Bange came to prominence. Combined with the de Beaulieu "interrupted screw" breech, the basics of modern breech-loading systems were now in place.

Further revolutionary changes appeared before the end of the century. Perhaps the most significant were three: the fixed charge shell, hydraulic buffers that absorbed recoil, and the latest breech mechanisms, which could be thrown open to eject the used **cartridge** case with a single movement. Together these made possible the advent of quick-firing, or "QF," artillery. The gun that set the pace was the French **75 mm**.

During the early years of the twentieth century, and particularly during World War I, artillery development continued apace. The British **18-pounder** and German 77 mm brought the Q.F. idea to new perfection, but now there were more radical ideas. Predicted fire using maps and tables first supplemented, then largely replaced, shooting over open sights. Flash spotting and sound ranging helped to locate for counterbattery fire enemy batteries that might not otherwise have been engaged.

More heavy guns and newer categories of them helped gradually to negate the advantage of trenches, while ever more complex fire plans were introduced. Creeping barrages walked ahead of the infantry, and box barrages isolated the enemy from support. New **shells** and **gas** made the artillery more flexible. Railway mountings offered mobility to some of the most unwieldy pieces, including British 14-inch guns. The 14-inch railway gun "Boche-buster," in the presence of King George V, fired a first-shot direct hit on Douai railway station at a range of 18 miles. New **flak** guns were also developed, and the first tracked **self-propelled guns** appeared. Arguably, however, the most impressive pieces of the period were the **Paris guns**.

During World War II there were further improvements, with interesting advances in ammunition, **radar** direction, and antitank (**PaK**) artillery. Field artillery was now generally fitted with modern pneumatic tires and was often towed by motor vehicles. Significant pieces like the **88 mm** dominated the battlefield, and guns like the **25-pounder** and **105 mm** were the general workhorses. Taper-bored artillery was used on a limited scale. These pieces fired tungsten-cored jacketed shells through tapered barrels, which reduced the dimension of the shot during firing. The resultant increase in pressure made the shell fly much faster, more accurately, and with much better penetration.

In **recoilless guns**, an opening, or Venturi, at the rear allowed controlled gas escape, reducing or eliminating entirely the recoil effect. Such weapons could be much lighter than conventional types. RAP, or rocket-assisted projectiles, were used to increase the range of artillery. Yet the most exciting developments of the middle twentieth century were in fields beyond traditional guns with "tubes" (barrels)—that is, the appearance of new missiles and rocket projectors like the **Nebelwerfer**.

Nevertheless artillery and missile systems have coexisted since 1945 and maintain distinct niches in the order of battle. Noteworthy artillery pieces of the past half-century include the U.S. M102 105 mm howitzer, the Soviet 122 mm D-30, and the 155 mm F-70.

Additional Reading: Gravett, *Medieval Siege Warfare*, 1990; Dastrup, *The Field Artillery: History and Sourcebook*, 1994; Marsden, *Greek and Roman Artillery*; Teesdale, *Gunfounding in the Weald in the Sixteenth Century*, 1991; Hall, *Weapons and Warfare in Rennaissance Europe*, 1997; Hughes, *Firepower*, 1974; Caruana, *The History of English Sea Ordnance*, 1994; Hogg, *British and American Artillery of World War II*, 1978; Kennard, *Gunfounding and Gunfounders*, 1986; Foss, *Artillery of the World*,

AS.11 (AGM-22A)

1976; ffoulkes, *Gun Founders of England*, London, 1969; *Journal of the Ordnance Society*, Continuing.

AS.11 (AGM-22A)   MISSILE

The French Aerospatiale AS.11 air-to-surface wire-guided tactical missile was widely produced from 1960. Weighing 66 lb, it cruised at 360 mph to a range of about two miles and was available in a variety of subtypes, including high-explosive and antiarmor. Used by many countries, including the United States, it was often fired from **helicopters**. The AS-12 and AS-15 were developed later; larger but slower but with much-increased ranges, they were intended to tackle ships, submarines, and other bigger targets.

AS.20 and AS.30   MISSILE

The French AS.20 and AS.30 air-to-surface missiles were developed in 1960, and were widely used, particularly by European air forces. The supersonic radio-guided AS.20 featured a two-stage solid-fuel propulsion system. At 12 feet 7 inches in length, the AS.30 has been described as a scaled-up version with a five-mile range. The AS.30L was a subsequent model that featured laser homing, first tested in 1977.

ASAT. *See* Satellites

Asdic. *See* Sonar

Aspide   MISSILE

The first flight of the Italian Aspide air-to-air and surface-to-air missile was in 1974. Featuring semiactive **radar** homing, it was designed to be effective at both high and low altitude, and against multiple targets. Capable of being mounted in many different interceptor **aircraft**, the Aspide could also be used from ships having an Albatros missile control system. It was 12 feet long, weighed 485 lb, and had a range of 62 miles at Mach 4.

Additional Reading: Taylor, *Missiles of the World*, 1980.

ASROC   MISSILE

The 15-foot-long ASROC anti**submarine** rocket began development in 1956 and was in service with the U.S. and other navies from 1961. The system relied on sonar and a shipboard computer to work out the submarine's course and speed, so that the missile could be fired over the right spot. Here ASROC dropped a homing torpedo or small **depth charge** into the water. The depth charge could be conventional or nuclear.

Assault Gun. *See* Self-Propelled Gun

Assault Rifle, "Sturmgewehr"   FIREARM

Commonly defined as a **rifled** automatic, or repeating, long arm capable of being used by one man during the attack, the modern assault rifle came into existence during World War II. Nevertheless, the search to find such a weapon had a history going back to the end of the nineteenth century.

Following **Maxim's** experiments, other designers sought to come up with practical semiautomatic and automatic rifles, and as early as 1885 Mannlicher invented a recoil operated rifle with a mechanism that unlocked and that incorporated an accelerator to assist the movement of the breechblock. By 1891 he had a species of practical automatic rifle. **Browning** made a **semiautomatic shotgun** by 1897, and **Mauser** likewise produced an automatic rifle in 1898. In 1908 the Mexican general Mondragon unveiled a workable military automatic rifle, operated by the gas produced by the **cartridge**. The **Lewis** gun, later regarded as a light machine gun, appeared soon afterward. **Submachine guns**, such as the **MP 18** and **Thompson**, appeared at the end of, and just after, World War I, while the U.S. Pedersen device of 1917, enabled a **Springfield** rifle to be converted to semiautomatic fire.

The problem was that a rifle that fired automatically was too much for one man to carry and fire on the move, while on the other hand submachine guns, which generally used **pistol** cartridges, were usually very short-range. By the 1930s German manufacturers had come up with a solution: an "intermediate" cartridge, neither so powerful that it made automatic fire difficult nor so limited that it lacked the force and accuracy for normal battle ranges. A Vollmer automatic carbine was tested from 1935, and a Walther 7 mm machine carbine appeared in 1937. Nevertheless, it was the Polte 7.92 mm Kurz Patrone—literally, "short cartridge"—that showed most promise.

A contract to find the right weapon to fire the Kurz Patrone was placed in 1938, but the specification was demanding. The new gun was to be no heavier than an ordinary rifle, simple, resistant to dirt and cold, give effective semiautomatic and burst fire to 400 meters, and be able to take a **grenade** launcher. It took until 1941 for the firms of Haenel and Walther to find a practical answer; tests were conducted in 1942, with limited production of the Mkb42 the same year. By 1943 the new gun, now known as the MP 43, was adopted as a standard, and there were plans that it would replace **bolt-action** rifles in the infantry. Minor changes, and Hitler's personal endorsement, brought the new name "Sturmgewehr 44" in 1944.

It would not be too much to suggest that the "StG 44" brought about a revolution in military small arms, the effects of which are still with us in the twenty-first century. Simply, even crudely, made and easy to understand, the gun could lay down destructive bursts of accurate fire to most combat ranges and be quickly reloaded using 30-round box magazines. It could do nearly anything any other rifle could do at 600 meters. In only two respects could the Sturmgewehr be bettered by Allied rifles like the **Garand** and **Lee Enfield**: one was how close the firer could get his face to the ground when firing lying down, the other was long-range **sniping**. Attempts were made to use the MP43 and StG 44 with telescopic sights, but the results were disappointing. Though there were production problems, almost half a million Sturmgewehr had been made by the end of World War II. In a rare but celebrated variant, a curved barrel was fitted allowing the firer to remain under cover or shoot out of a **tank**, clearing areas not swept by the normal armament.

Though production ceased in April 1945 the influence of the weapon continued, setting the tone for moderate-length, box-magazine, pistol-grip, intermediate-cartridge, automatic assault rifles. Greater firepower for less weight now seemed attainable. Though very different weapons, distinct similarities can be seen with the **Kalashnikov AK-47**, Spanish CETME, and Swiss StG 57. Though there would be exceptions that retained more powerful cartridges, the movement to short rounds, and ultimately 5.56 mm assault weapons, was inexorable. Modern arms in this category include the French **FA-MAS**, Austrian **AUG**, British **SA 80**, U.S. **M16**, Israeli **Galil**, and the Finnish Valmet M71S; there are many others as well.

Additional Reading: Musgrave and Nelson, *World's Assault Rifles*, (undated); Senich, *German Assault Rifle*; Ezell, *Small Arms of the World*, various editions; HMSO, *Patents for Inventions Class 119; Jane's Infantry Weapons*, various editions; Hogg and Weeks, *Military Small Arms of the Twentieth Century*, 1977, 1994.

Astra   MANUFACTURER

The Spanish arms manufacturing firm Astra was established by Pedro Unceta and Juan Esperenza at Eibar in 1908; it moved to Guernica in 1913. The company has been known by various names, including Esperenza y Unceta and Astra-Union. **Semiautomatic** pistols were supplied to France, Germany, and Italy, the model 1921 becoming the official sidearm of the Spanish army. The company's Compogiro range, based on ideas by Count Giro, was distinctive for the large recoil spring around the barrel. Astra also made revolvers from 1958.

Additional Reading: Walter, *Dictionary of Guns and Gunmakers*, 2001.

Astrolite. *See* Mine

***Astute* Class**   SUBMARINE

Due to enter service in 2005, being built at Barrow-in-Furness the *Astute* class is Britain's latest generation of nuclear-powered **submarines**. Just over 318 feet long, they will have

Atlanta *Class*

a complement of 98 and be armed with submarine-launched **cruise** missiles, **Harpoon** missiles, and Starfish **torpedoes**.

Atlanta Class   WARSHIP

The U.S. *Atlanta* class of 11 **cruisers** was commenced in 1940, and the *Atlanta* herself was completed in December 1941. Seven more were finished during the war. The last three of the group, *Juneau* (II), *Spokane*, and *Fresno*, were completed in 1946. These 6,800-ton ships were armed with 16 5-inch guns, and were 541 feet in length. In a somewhat unusual layout, there were eight twin turrets, five aft and three forward. The hull form was similar to that of the **Brooklyn** class, but the armor, which was a maximum of just under four inches thick, formed an integral element for the first time.

All of the ships completed prior to the cessation of hostilities saw active service, with *Atlanta* and *Juneau* (I) both being lost in the Pacific on 13 November 1942. The end of the *Atlanta* was particularly tragic; having engaged the Japanese off Savo Island and sustained damage, she was mistakenly attacked by the *New Orleans*–class cruiser *San Francisco*. Terminally damaged, the *Atlanta* was scuttled off Guadalcanal. *Juneau* (I) was repeatedly torpedoed, with the loss of all but ten of her crew.

Additional Reading: Friedman, *US Cruisers*, 1985.

Atlantic Conveyor   WARSHIP

The *Atlantic Conveyor* was a civilian cargo carrying ship taken up by the Royal Navy during the Falklands War of 1982. Accompanying the task force to the South Atlantic, it was hit and sunk by an **Exocet** missile. With it went the entire British reserve of **Chinook** helicopters. This repeated a cardinal error in the stowage of military stores that had been identified as early as the Crimean War, in the midnineteenth century—that is, of putting all of one type of important munitions in the same vessel. Fortunately, the Marines and paratroops proved able to march tens of miles at a time to their objectives. It has been claimed that the presence of a large vessel like *Atlantic Conveyor* distracted the Argentines from their most important target, the task force **aircraft carriers**.

Atlantic Wall   FORTIFICATION

The Atlantic Wall was a line of German coastal **fortifications** stretching from Norway to the Spanish border, erected from 1940 to 1944. Though by no means continuous, they were formidable in places, especially on the French Pas de Calais. The biggest guns mounted were those of the Lindemann Battery, where 40.6 cm SK c/34 pieces had a range of 42,800 meters, but thousands of guns of many different calibers were included, many from warships. Many of the bunkers and casemates were built according to standardized designs. According to the statistics of the Organization Todt, almost 11,000,000 cubic meters of concrete went into the Atlantic Wall. The busiest construction month was April 1943, when 769,000 cubic meters were poured.

Additional Reading: Partridge, *Hitler's Atlantic Wall*, 1976; Schmeelke, *Fortress Europe: The Atlantic Wall Guns*, 1993; Saunders, *Hitler's Atlantic Wall*, 2001.

Atoll. *See* Sidewinder

Atomic Bomb. *See* Nuclear Weapons

AUG Steyr Rifle   FIREARM

At the time of its first production in 1978 the Austrian AUG, or Army Universal Gun, was one of the most innovative **rifles** anywhere. Its **bullpup** design, clean lines, futuristic look, and relative simplicity soon made it a winner in various parts of the world. It was made as part of a system of arms including a **submachine gun** and **carbine**. Weighing just 3.6 kg in the rifle version, it had an optical sight in the carrying handle and could be fitted with plastic box magazines of up to 42 rounds capacity.

Additional Reading: *Jane's Infantry Weapons*, various editions; Walter, *Dictionary*, 2001.

Auk **Class**   WARSHIP

The U.S. *Auk*-class minesweeper was built at great speed during World War II, with the *Auk* herself being launched in August 1941, a few months before the United States became involved. The design of the class was influenced by the *Osprey* and *Raven*, two prototypes authorized in 1938. As completed the *Auk*s were 221 feet long, displaced 890 tons, had a complement of 105, and were capable of 18 knots. Armament varied but included antiaircraft guns up to 3-inch. They performed good service but had steel hulls that limited their usefulness against magnetic **sea mines**. Many of the early *Auk*s were named after birds—hence the *Nuthatch, Pheasant, Skylark*, etc.

Additional Reading: Lenton, *American Gunboats and Minesweepers*, 1974.

Avenger A30. *See* **Tank Destroyer**

Avenger, TBF   AIRCRAFT

The U.S. **Grumman** Avenger TBF **torpedo** bomber **aircraft** was designed in 1940 as a replacement for the Douglas Devastator. It first flew in 1941 and was rushed into action against the Japanese at Midway in 1942. Despite initial heavy losses, the Avenger would go on to be one of the most important U.S. Navy planes of World War II. It was produced by the Eastern Division of General Motors as well as Grumman.

The Avenger was a three-seat, single-engine design, weighing 10,700 lb empty. In the late-war TBM-3 the power plant was a 1,750-horsepower Wright Cyclone engine giving a top speed of 267 mph. In addition to two forward-firing .5-inch machine guns, there was a .30-caliber and a .5 mounted in a power-operated turret at the rear of the main cockpit. The bomb bay could take 2,000 lb of weapons, and rockets and a **radar** pod could be mounted externally. Some planes were used in **mine**laying. After the war, the radar capabilities of certain Avengers were enhanced so that they could be used in **submarine** location.

Aviatik   MANUFACTURER

The Aviatik company had branches in both Germany and Austria during World War I. The latter produced the most numerous model of Austro-Hungarian fighter, the D.I., or Berg Scout, designed by Julius von Berg. This biplane with a 26-foot wingspan was surprisingly efficient but had two peculiarities. The first was an early propensity to wing failure—which caused leading Austian pilots to avoid flying it. The second was that certain models featured a side-mounted radiator, giving good forward visibility but a tendency to overheat.

Avrocar   AIRCRAFT

Looking, and behaving, very much like a small flying saucer, the experimental Avrocar was made by the Avro Canada plant at Malton. Initially known as "Project Y," it consisted of an 18-foot-diameter ring built on a triangular metal frame. In the center was a multibladed turbo rotor for lift. In the ring were two cockpits with bubble canopies. The project lasted from 1955 to 1961, when it was abandoned due to the basic instability of the craft.

Additional Reading: Rogers, *VTOL Military Research Aircraft*, 1989.

AWACS   COMMUNICATION

Standing for "Airborne Warning and Control System," AWACS **radar** was first flown experimentally in 1971. It has been used by the U.S. Air Force on modified **Boeing** aircraft since 1977. From the first, these E-3 Sentry planes carrying this early-warning radar were readily identifiable by the large mushroomlike radome on top. By the mid-1980s a total of 45 AWACS systems had been delivered by Westinghouse to the USAF and NATO customers. More recent models have been widely deployed, notably to Bosnia and Iraq. A Russian variation on the AWACS theme is the A-50 Mainstay.

Axe; Poleaxe   CLUB WEAPON

The first axes date back to the handheld worked flints of the Paleolithic period; they were used as multipurpose tools. Wooden hafts, added perhaps 40,000 years ago, made them far more practical as weapons, and it is natural that during the Bronze Age axes should have been cast of metal for the first time. The iron battleaxe later became a feared weapon in the hands of the Vikings, Danes, and Normans. In the later Middle Ages specialized versions of the axe, such as the long-shafted poleaxe, appeared.

Certain types of axe, such as the Native American tomahawk and the naval boarding axe, remained in use until comparatively recently. Interestingly, though early tomahawks were stone, many nineteenth-century examples were fitted with metal heads, sometimes imported from Europe.

Additional Reading: Stone, *A Glossary of the Construction, Decoration and Use of Arms and Armor,* 1934.

B

B-2 Stealth Bomber. *See* **Spirit**

B-9. *See* **Boeing**

B-17. *See* **Flying Fortress**

B-24. *See* **Liberator**

B-29 Superfortress AIRCRAFT

An initial idea for the B-29 Superfortress bomber **aircraft** was put forward by **Boeing** to the U.S. Army as early as 1940, in response to a request for designs for a VH, or "very heavy," LR (long-range) bomber. Its maiden flight, in prototype form, was in September 1942. As finally delivered in the autumn of 1943 the Superfortress was a modern and highly innovative design. Special features included a pressurized crew compartment, the ability to fly up to 32,000 feet, four remote-control gun turrets, and a maximum speed of 358 mph with four 2,200 horsepower Wright turbocharged radial engines. With a wingspan of 141 feet and a weight of 70,000 lb empty, the B-29 was one of the most massive planes of the period. It was also heavily armed, with a total of ten machine guns, a 20 mm cannon, and a 20,000 lb bomb load.

Production of the B-29 has been hailed as Americas largest aircraft manufacturing project of World War II, with thousands of subcontractors supplying the main contractors—Boeing, Bell, and Martin. Total output was about 3,000, with the majority made at Boeing's Wichita plant. The Superfortress was deployed to the Pacific, where best use could be made of its 3,250-mile range. On the night of 9 March 1945 a single B-29 raid from Guam on Tokyo is believed to have rendered a million people homeless and killed about 80,000. On 6 August the B-29 *Enola Gay* of the 393rd Bombardment Squadron carried out the first operational dropping of an **atomic bomb**, on Hiroshima; three days later *Bock's Car* of the same unit hit Nagasaki, bringing World War II to a close. See also **C-97**.

Additional Reading: Freeman and Anderton, *B-17 Fortress and B-29 Superfortress at War*, 1996.

B-47 Stratojet AIRCRAFT

The idea of multiengined jet bomber **aircraft** had occurred to the Allied powers as early as 1942. It was actually achieved by the end of the war—for example, by the Germans on a small scale with the **Me 262**. The breakthrough for **Boeing** came when aerodynamicist George Schairer was able to compare German data on swept-wing craft with home-grown wind tunnel results. From this came the experimental XB-47, which made use of a "jet assisted takeoff," or JATO, system of small rockets. Fast landing speeds were addressed with a tail **parachute** to increase drag.

The B-47 first flew in December 1947, becoming the first U.S. multiengined swept-wing bomber. Over 2,000 were produced by 1956, the majority by Boeing, with smaller numbers at **Douglas** and **Lockheed**. The craft became a mainstay of the Strategic Air Command. With six GE J-35 engines and a top speed of 587 mph, the B-47 had a range of 4,000 miles. Bomb loads were up to 22,000 lb.

A B-29 Superfortress Chase plane (in the background), accompanies an experimental XNB-36H bomber aircraft through the skies over Fort Worth, Texas. Courtesy of the Department of Defense.

Additional Reading: Natola, *Boeing B-47 Stratojet*, 2002.

B-52 Stratofortress   AIRCRAFT

The very first XB-52 experimental long-range design selected by the U.S. Army Air Forces in 1946 was a conventional if massive straight-winged, six-engined, propeller-driven **aircraft**. Yet it was quickly realized that such a machine would be out of date before it was operational, because the days of propellers were numbered. **Boeing** lore has it that the chief of bomber development therefore instructed Chief Engineer Ed Wells to make drastic revision. He did so, very swiftly, and came up with a swept-wing eight-engined jet bomber, influenced no doubt by the work already done on the **B-47**. The war in Korea helped turn drawing-board design and prototype into the familiar super-long-range bomber that has now seen almost fifty years of service in various guises.

The first B-52A flew on 5 August 1954, though it was the heavier 52B, with larger engines, that went into full-scale production. The B-52H of 1961 remains in use. A total of 744 B-52s have been made by Seattle and Wichita plants. The bomber has seen use all over the world, most obviously in Vietnam, but it proved useful in the Gulf and Afghanistan as recently as 2003. What is perhaps most remarkable about the aircraft is its range and endurance. As early as 1962 a B-52 flew the 12,500 miles from Spain to Japan nonstop; the operational range is claimed as over 10,000 miles. About 7,500 miles can be covered operationally on one air refueling. The B-52H has a wingspan of 185 feet and a crew of five. The gross weight is 488,000 lb. The eight TF-33 turbofans give a top speed of 650 mph. Armament may include various bomb loads, a typical arrangement being 51 500-lb bombs, 24 on external pylons and 27 in the bomb bay. Other options include Hound Dog missiles, a 20 mm **radar**-directed cannon, and up to 20 missiles of SRAM or ALCM types.

As might be expected, the B-52 has undergone considerable adaptations over its service life. These are most important in the areas of engine improvement, electronic systems, and low-altitude capability. Recently Boeing put forward a proposal to replace the existing engines with four RB-211-535 engines.

Additional Reading: Boyne, *Boeing B-52*, 1994; Sgarlato, *Aircraft of the USAF*, 1978.

BAe. *See* **British Aerospace Systems**

Baka Bomb. *See* **Ohka**

Baker Rifle   FIREARM

Following tests in 1800 the **flintlock** short **rifle** designed by Ezekiel Baker of Whitechapel, London, was adopted by the British army for use with regiments of riflemen. Resembling the German Jäger rifle, it weighed 9 lb and had a 30-inch barrel. The barrel was rifled with seven grooves making a quarter of a turn. It could be fitted with a sword **bayonet**. Initially manufactured in **musket** bore, the size of the ball was later reduced to .625-inch carbine size. This smaller ball with a greased cloth patch made for easier loading. The Baker helped demonstrate the value of the military rifle; it served with distinction in the Napoleonic Wars and remained in use until 1838.

Balista, Ballista. *See* **Catapult**

Balloon   BALLOON

Balloons rise when they are lighter than air; the earliest examples capable of lifting people and animals were filled with hot air, which is of lower density than the surrounding atmosphere. The first manned flight, in a Montgolfier balloon, was made in 1783; a year later a balloon

was used for military observation at the battle of Fleurus. The French soon created a corps of balloonists, and in later years balloons filled with coal gas, hydrogen, and helium were produced. These would have the advantage of greater reliability, but hydrogen proved particularly dangerous.

Balloon observers were used by Federal forces in the American Civil War, and the Confederates are recorded as having a balloon made from the silk dresses of the patriotic ladies of Richmond. In 1870 during the siege of Paris, 65 balloons were used by the French to communicate with the outside world; it is believed that they transported as many as 3,000,000 letters. Balloons were used in the Boer War from 1899 and continued to be used for observation up to and including the Great War but by then **aircraft** and **airships** were becoming more important.

Captive balloons, known as "barrage" balloons, were also quite widely used, particularly in the early stages of World War II. Commonly raised and lowered by means of large winches, these cigar-shaped balloons served as countermeasures to enemy aircraft, which were endangered by their cables. Though relatively few planes fell victim, barrage balloons were a means of denying airspace.

Additional Reading: Evans, *War of the Aeronauts*, 2002; Mead, *The Eye in the Air*, 1983; Owen, *Lighter Than Air*, 1999.

Baltimore Class   WARSHIP

The *Baltimore* class of U.S. heavy **cruisers** was laid down from 1941 to 1945. Though several hulls were canceled at the end of World War II, 17 were completed, and a number saw war service. The *Quincy* was notable in that she supported the troops ashore at Utah beach, at Normandy. *Baltimore, Canberra, Boston, Pittsburgh*, and *St. Paul* fought in the Pacific. Important lessons had been learned from the previous *Wichita* and **Cleveland** classes with the result that stability and machinery layouts were improved in the *Baltimore* class.

The basic specification was a displacement

of 14,500 tons, length 673 feet, and a main armament of nine 8-inch guns. Top speed was 33 knots. The success of the design is perhaps demonstrated by the fact that the majority of the *Baltimore* class survived into the 1970s, with some serving in the Korean War and several being converted to guided missile cruisers. A few lasted until finally paid off in 1980.

Additional Reading: Whitley, *Cruisers of World War II*, 1985.

Bandvagn. *See* **Snowcat**

Bangalore Torpedo

The Bangalore Torpedo is an **explosive** device used for the clearance of obstructions. Commonly mounted on a pole, plank, or in a tube it may be pushed into place for subsequent detonation. It is particularly associated with World War I when it was used for the clearance of **barbed wire**.

BAR. *See* **Browning**

Barbed Wire   OBSTACLE

Wire with points or spikes added was used in the United States as early as the 1860s. What we understand as modern barbed wire was patented in 1874 by Joseph Glidden (1813–1906) of Dekalb, Illinois. Thereafter it was widely used, at first for agricultural purposes. Many other variants were registered in the next few years, including Crandall's "Zig Zag" (1879), and Harbaugh's "Torn Ribbon" (1881). From early "ribbon" wires, modern razor wires have evolved.

It was during the trench warfare of World War I that the use of barbed wire became of crucial military significance. Wiring became an art. "High" and "low wire" entanglements made their appearance, along with spider wire and portable knife rests to form temporary obstructions. Dannert wire formed concertinas that could be extended to produce barriers. Wire was secured with wood or metal pickets, which could be hammered or screwed into the ground. By the 1960s the Lane Myers Company was

the leading supplier of barbed wire to the U.S. Army.

Additional Reading: McCallum, *The Wire That Fenced the West*; War Office (UK), *Dannert Concertina Wire Obstacles*, 1939.

Bard. *See* **Armor**

Barham. *See* **Queen Elizabeth**

Barrage Balloon. *See* **Balloon**

Barrett M82A1, "Light Fifty"   FIREARM

The U.S. Barrett .50 **semiautomatic rifle** is designed for long range **sniping** or **antimaterial** use. It has a bipod but is compatible with **M60** and other mountings. Weighing 32.4 lb, it is not as light as might be expected, but it has an 11-round magazine and a muzzle brake to reduce the recoil.

Bastion. *See* **Fort**

Battle Cruiser. *See* **Battleship**

Battleship   WARSHIP

The word "battleship" was first used during the eighteenth century as a contraction of the phrase "**line of battle** ship." It thus originally referred to sail-propelled warships—or "ships of the line"—that fought in lines, to bring their "broadsides," or side-facing gun decks, to bear on the enemy. Since then "battleship" has commonly been used to mean a warship of the largest and most heavily armored class, or "capital" ship. The modern battleship, which dominated naval warfare from about 1905 to the latter part of World War II, began to emerge in the mid-nineteenth century with the evolution of steam propulsion, the rotating gun turret, and armor. "Cruiser battleships," or "battle cruisers," which appeared in the early twentieth century, constituted a type of battle ship designed primarily for speed.

A practical steam craft was devised as early as 1802. Within a few years steamships were employed towing military sailing vessels from

The USS *Missouri* at anchor c. 1906. Battleships were arguably the key military technology of the late nineteenth and early twentieth centuries, a reign brought to a sudden end by air power during World War II. Courtesy of the Library of Congress.

harbor; soon the idea of dual steam and sail propulsion was adopted for actual warships. The first steam-powered military vessel was the USS *Demologos*, originally named *Fulton the First*, laid down in 1814. Displacing 2475 tons, this ship had twin hulls with a paddle wheel between, as well as lateen sails and jibs. It was armed with 20 32-pounder guns and capable of seven knots. The last fleet action conducted entirely under sail was at Navarino in 1827; thereafter dual sail and steam propulsion was adopted on an ever-increasing scale. In Britain, 32 ships of the line originally powered by, or converted to, steam had been built by 1858. A significant example of the period was the triple-decker, 5,829-ton *Duke of Wellington*, which had been laid down as a sail vessel at Pembroke Dock in 1849 but converted to steam power in 1852.

The first seagoing armored "ironclad" fighting ship was the French *Gloire*, launched in 1859. Together with the *Couronne*, the British *Warrior*, and the U.S. coastal-going *Monitor*, the *Gloire* sparked a revolution in naval warfare in which, within twenty years wood, sail power,

and gundecks would all become obsolete. The year 1860 saw the commencement of the *Provence*-class battleships, the largest single group of French battleships ever built. In 1863 Britain produced the *Research*, which had its guns concentrated in an armored casemate amidships. Other vessels of this innovative period were the HMS *Devastation* and the large ocean going U.S. monitor *Dictator*. Rotating turrets or "cupolas" designed by the Swedish engineer John Ericsson, used on the early monitors, were now generally adopted by the U.S. Navy, and in 1866 Britain completed the *Prince Albert*, the first turreted battleship, designed by Captain Cowper Coles. The 3,880-ton *Prince Albert* featured four 111-ton turrets, which were hand cranked; the ship had a maximum speed of 11 knots. Coles himself was drowned when his second turreted ship, HMS *Captain*, sank in bad weather in 1870.

Denmark was the first Scandinavian country to boast a significant ironclad fleet. The Glasgow-built, 1,320-ton *Rolf Krake*, for example, served against Prussia, seeing action against shore batteries in 1864. Russia soon adopted ironclads; there were also advances in Austria, Germany, and Italy. The Italians converted wooden warships like the *Re d'Italia* and *Re di Portogallo*; they also ordered broadside ironclads, including the *Regina Maria Pia*, from France. Later the Italians built their own ironclads. The first of these were the *Palestro* and the *Principe Amedeo*. The battle of Lissa in 1866 between Austrian and Italian warships proved inconclusive, due in part to the inability of current naval armament to cope with armor, and helped make popular the "ramming bow" incorporated in many ships. Austrian vessels included the *Kaiser*, which fought at Lissa as a wooden battleship before conversion to an ironclad central-battery ship in 1869. Austria's first purpose-built ironclad was the *Salamander*.

With the formation of the Second Empire in 1871, Germany began to take an interest in seagoing capital ships. The 7,596-ton *Friedrich der Grosse* was an ironclad of a class of three vessels; its turrets were amidships, located behind bulwarks that could be lowered in battle. Despite the invention of the turret, many battleships were still built with their armament in central batteries. The central-battery ship *Friedrich Carl* was claimed as Germany's first battleship. The largest of the type was the 9,700-ton French vessel *Courbet*, laid down in the wake of the war with Prussia.

Innovation continued with the introduction of the **torpedo** and the appearance of the armored deck, first seen on HMS *Shannon* in 1877. Armament grew ever larger and more sophisticated, with battleships mounting muzzle loaders up to 16 inches in caliber prior to the introduction of **breechloaders**, which were general c. 1880. Barbette ships with big guns in mountings that were often open enjoyed a relatively brief popularity. The British pace setter of the time was HMS *Collingwood*, a 9,500-ton vessel capable of 17 knots; it had a waterline belt of armor up to 18 inches thick. It mounted four 12-inch and six 6-inch guns and had transverse water chambers to control rolling. Among the most massive armament of this era was that of the Italian battleship *Lepanto*, completed in 1887. It carried four 17-inch and eight 16-inch guns, and featured an armored redoubt amidships. At 15,900 tons and capable of 18 knots, the *Lepanto* was big and fast, but it was soon out of date due to the advance of **artillery** technology. Germany produced the novel *Brandenburg* class in 1892, with six main guns—two forward, two aft, and two amidships.

Better armor, using nickel steel, and enclosed armored turrets for the main armament, mounted for and aft, pointed the way ahead. Smaller ships, such as **destroyers**, were now introduced specifically for the purpose of guarding capital vessels. Searchlights and quick-firing guns were also mounted with an eye to close defense. In an age of empires, the battleship had become a symbol of power and pride, able to extend national influence to the wider world. It soon became the object of an international arms race. A huge expansion of Britain's Royal Navy following the Naval Defence Act of 1889 included the construction of seven ships in the ***Royal Sovereign*** class and 29 other battleships by 1904. Against this France produced only a string of basically one-off vessels, what critics called a "fleet of samples," until its program of 1900. Germany produced the new ***Deutschland*** class as a followup to her *Kaiser Friedrich III* and *Wittelsbach* classes.

Yet it was the appearance of ***Dreadnought*** in 1906 that helped bring about a revolution in battleship design. Fast vessels with a single category of long-range main armament became the new orthodoxy. In the U.S. ***Michigan*** class and the German ***Nassau*** class, big guns in twin turrets were the order of the day. Speed for outrunning the enemy was an additional priority in British Admiral Jackie Fisher's ***Invincible*** and ***Indefatigable*** classes prior to the outbreak of World War I; 15-inch guns were mounted in the latest ***Queen Elizabeth*** class. In the United States the ***Wyoming*** class was followed by the *Texas* and *New York*, completed in 1914. In the event, and with the major exception of Jutland in 1916, battleship actions were not common in World War I; numerically the greatest losses were to **submarine** and **sea mine**.

After the war construction would be curtailed by the Washington Treaty of 1921, which set agreed proportions of strength and total tonnages for capital ships. Nevertheless, technology continued to develop, with improvements to boilers, oil firing, and range finding. Important vessels of the interwar period would include the British *Nelson* and *King George V* types, and the US *North Carolina* class. Yet it is the German fast modern battle cruisers, such as *Bismarck* and *Scharnhorst*, that have captured the popular imagination. German commerce-raiding missions early in the Second World War led to the end of *Admiral Graf Spee*, the old British battle cruiser *Hood*, and ultimately the *Bismarck* herself.

In the Pacific the loss of or damage to *Maryland*, *West Virginia*, *Oklahoma, California*, and *Arizona* on "battleship row" at Pearl Harbor in December 1941, followed rapidly by the sinking of the British *Prince of Wales* and *Repulse*, demonstrated that battleships were no longer inviolate. The newer technologies of the **aircraft carrier, dive bomber, radar** and **submarine** were all making capital ships less useful. Though battleships continued to have a role as part of a battle group, and in shore bombardment, the sea war against the Japanese would be shaped by aircraft. Ultimately Japan lost most of her capital ships—six of them to air strikes, three to gunnery, and one each to submarine and accidental explosion. The casualties included the mighty *Yamato, Musashi,* and *Shinano*.

Post–World War II, only the United States would maintain a large battleship force, and just four, including *New Jersey*, would be in use by the 1960s. These would see limited action in Korea, Vietnam, and the Persian Gulf, primarily as shore-bombardment platforms, using missiles as well as guns. They were still in reserve in the late 1990s.

Additional Reading: Breyer, *Battleships and Battlecruisers*; Gardiner (ed), *The Eclipse of the Big Gun Warship, 1906–1945*, 1992; Whitley, *Battleships of World War II*, 1998; Simkins, *Battleship*, 1979; Silverstone, *Directory of the World's Capital Ships*, 1984; Willmot, *Pearl Harbor*, 2001; Wilson, *Battleships in Action*, 1995; Padfield, *Battleship*, 2000; Hodges, *The Big Gun: Battleship Main Armament 1860–1945*, 1981.

Bayonet   BLADED WEAPON

A blade or spike attached to a firearm for close combat, invented during the seventeenth century, and named after the town of Bayonne in France, bayonets were documented in military use at Ypres in 1647. The bayonet was of crucial battlefield importance c. 1700–1900, when it was used by formed bodies of infantry, often in squares, to resist cavalry. Though now often regarded as a general-purpose knife or tool, it continues to be issued.

The first bayonets consisted of a blade attached to a wooden handle, which was inserted into the muzzle of the **musket**. These "plug" bayonets did not allow the weapon to be fired once in place. The solution for this problem is often credited to a French marshal of about 1688 who introduced the "ring" or "socket" bayonet, which did not interfere with the use of the gun to which it was attached. Socket bayonets became increasingly common after 1700 and were used by most armies for the next century or more. One of the earliest patents was registered by Frenchman Deschamps for a retractable bayonet in 1718. These, and various folding or sprung bayonets that were permanently attached to firearms, especially **blunderbusses**, saw some use in the eighteenth century. Remarkably similar blades would reappear on certain Soviet bloc and Chinese firearms two centuries later. One of the earliest references to "sword"-type bayonets is Isaac de la Chalmette's patent of 1721 describing "swords which serve for bayonets." **Pistol** bayonets appeared in limited use at about the same time. Formalized exercises, like those of Wolrab, published in 1730, helped to coordinate the actions of troops in battle, making the bayonet more effective.

The nineteenth century would see a great diversification of bayonet types, with long "sword" bayonets in use on short **rifles**, saw-back blades for use by pioneers, cutlass-style hilts for navy units, and down-swept "yataghan" models. Some of the most extraordinary bayonets were used by the Confederate army in the Civil War. These included Captain Charles Broom's **shotgun** bayonet, Bowie bladed bayonets, and "sabre" bayonets. Other oddities included U.S. army Colonel Edmund Rice's "trowel" bayonet of 1868; the spade bayonet, patented by Myron Coloney of Missouri in 1878; and Scotsman Alexander Hogg's wire-cutting bayonet attachment of 1900.

Despite causing minimal casualties during World War I, bayonets continued to be carried by most combatants, and their use remained an essential skill. Though most major nations were using sword or knife-style bayonets, the French and Russians now favored a thin **stiletto**-type blade designed for maximum penetration. Given the frequency of raids and cramped trench conditions, many soldiers used modified bayonet blades for trench **knives**. Saw-backed bayonet blades, still in limited use with the Germans, were rapidly withdrawn when accusations were made of their use in atrocities. Perhaps the oddest type of World War I was the U.S. "**flaming bayonet.**"

World War II saw the British introduction of the spike bayonet, a cheap, crude, short, metal prong that was useful only as a thrusting weapon, calculated to be just long enough to kill even the most thickly clad enemy. The U.S. Army, which had been equipped with sword bayonets since 1905, moved toward shorter knife bayonets from 1944 with the appearance of the Bayonet Knife M4. The Australians experimented with a **machete** blade. Perhaps surprisingly, bayonets were also used in conjunction with many **submachine guns**.

Post 1945, bayonets remained an integral part of the weapon system. Though the Soviet **Kalashnikov** was not originally designed to take a bayonet one was soon added, and the U.S. **M16** has been used with the short Bayonet Knives AR 15 and M7. Recent developments have seen the reemergence of ring types; multipurpose bayonet tools, with additional functions such as wire cutting; increas-

ing use of plastics; and new forging and casting methods.

Additional Reading: Carter and Walter, *The Bayonet*, 1974; Watts and White, *The Bayonet Book*, 1975.

Bazooka ARTILLERY

The name "bazooka," now taken to mean any tube-type shoulder-launched missile system, was originally applied to the U.S. World War II 2.36-inch antitank rocket launcher. The word itself is borrowed from a slide wind instrument made popular by Bob Burns. Despite the comedic overtones, the bazooka was an important, even revolutionary, military technology that offered the possibility of putting infantry on equal terms with tanks. Though no one part of the bazooka was entirely new, the combination of **hollow-charge** warhead, rocket, and tube was remarkable.

As early as 1918, U.S. scientists had considered the possibility of firing rockets from tubes, and the theme was followed up in the 1930s when Captain Skinner of the U.S. Army and Lieutenant Uhl of the U.S. Navy began to cooperate on a rocket project. In 1940 the idea was put forward of matching a rocket motor to an M10 **grenade** and a light steel tube. The first bazookas were tested at Aberdeen Proving Ground in May 1942. They were immediately ordered for the army, the launchers being manufactured by General Electric and the projectiles by E. G. Budd. Various statistics have been cited, but it appears that the range of the basic M1 model was about 400 yards, with an armor penetration of a little over 80 mm—not great by modern standards but sufficient to inconvenience any **panzer** and tear Japanese tanks and other vehicles to shreds. Moreover, performance was increased in later types.

Perhaps the bazooka's greatest compliment was that it was rapidly copied by the Germans. The 3.5-inch rocket launcher, or "super bazooka," with its folding tube and enhanced capabilities, was rushed into production at the time of the Korean War.

Additional Reading: Gander, *Bazooka*; Weeks, *Men against Tanks*, 1975.

Beacon. *See* **Telegraph and Radio**

Beano. *See* **Grenade**

Bear, Tu-95   AIRCRAFT

The Soviet Bear swept-wing, four-engined, nuclear bomber aircraft, a Tupolev design, was introduced in 1956. With a 167-foot wing span and a 4,000-mile combat radius, the Bear was impressive, though the introduction of stand-off missiles soon necessitated improvements and new models. A new strategic bomber variant, the Tu-95-MS-6, was produced as late as 1983 for use with Kent-type **cruise** missiles. Bears remain in use with Russia, the Ukraine, and Kazakhstan.

Beaufighter   AIRCRAFT

The British Bristol Beaufighter was a twin-engined, long-range fighter aircraft that first flew in 1939. Based on the existing Beaufort **torpedo** bomber, the Beaufighter was heavily armed, with four 20 mm nose cannon and later six **machine guns** in the wings. Weighing 14,600 lb empty, the Beaufighter had a maximum speed of 333 mph and a ceiling of 26,500 feet.

Beaverette   VEHICLE

Based on the chassis of a Standard or Humber Super Snipe car, the Beaverette, or "Beaver-bug," was a British armored car rushed into production after the evacuation from Dunkirk in 1940. Instigated by Lord Beaverbrook, after whom they were named, Beaverettes had 45 horsepower engines and mounted a **Bren** gun or **antitank rifle**. Late models had a small turret.

Beehive. *See* **Flechette**

Beep. *See* **Jeep**

Beethoven. *See* **Ju 88**

Belfast, HMS   WARSHIP

The British **cruiser** Belfast, sister ship to the *Edinburgh*, was of the "Improved *Southampton*" type, designed to answer the appearance of the Japanese *Mogami* class. Commenced at the Belfast yard of Harland and Wolff in 1936, she was commissioned in 1939. At 13,385 tons she was then the largest cruiser in the Royal Navy. Her main armament was 12 6-inch guns. She saw much service in World War II, being damaged by a **sea mine** in 1939, taking part in the sinking of the *Scharnhorst* in 1942, and supporting the D-Day invasion in 1944. As part of the Imperial War Museum, she has been moored as a museum ship in the Thames since 1971. She is claimed to be Europe's last surviving World War II big-gun armored warship.

Additional Reading: Watton, *Belfast*; Imperial War Museum, *Review* (vol. 1); Raven and Roberts, *British Cruisers of World War II*, 1980.

Belgrano. *See* **General Belgrano**

Bell P-39. *See* **Airacobra**

Bell 47. *See* **Sioux**

Benet-Merci. *See* **Hotchkiss**

Bensen B-10. *See* **Flying Platform**

Bensen X-25   UNCONVENTIONAL
                        AIRCRAFT

The unusual Bensen Aircraft X-25 was devised in 1967 and 1968 as a "Discretionary Descent Vehicle," or, in plain English, a method of escape from stricken **aircraft**. In the first version it was essentially a small powered autogyro, in the second an unpowered gyro glider, which descended under control like a sycamore leaf, with the pilot seated underneath. This interesting idea was overtaken by advances in aircraft and ejection seats, and the experimental craft went to the U.S. Air Force Museum.

Additional Reading: Miller, *X-Planes*, 1988.

Beretta   MANUFACTURER

Established as long ago as the seventeenth century the Italian Beretta company came to world prominence as a maker of military **pistols** in the early twentieth century. During World War I the Beretta Model 1915 was selected for the Italian forces. One of the company's best designs was the handy 1934 model used in World War II; it combined features of earlier guns with the 9 mm **Browning** cartridge.

More recently the company has been noteworthy as the originator of the 9 mm, M9, or model 92 FS. This was selected in 1985 as successor to the **Colt** model 1911 for U.S. forces. Whilst undoubtedly a good weapon, the adoption of a foreign pistol caused a major outcry, since the United States itself had such a long history of handgun design and production.

Additional Reading: Hogg, *Infantry Weapons of World War II*, 1977; Department of the Navy, *Operator's Manual, Pistol Semiautomatic, 9mm, M9*; Walter, *Dictionary of Guns and Gunmakers*, 2001.

Bergmann. *See* **Submachine Gun**

Bicycle   VEHICLE

One of the first documented uses of the bicycle as a military vehicle was in Italy, when they were used for communications during exercises in 1875. Other European countries soon followed suit. British **Rifle** Volunteers are recorded using "ordinaries," or "penny farthings," in 1885, and cycle sections were in existence before the end of the decade. These were claimed to be able to move up to 50 miles in a single march. Four-wheeled tandem bicycles with their rims fitted to the **railway** lines saw use in the Boer War. Whole battalions of cyclists were raised in World War I, with most countries having such troops.

In the World War II cyclists were of particular importance to the Germans, who often lacked sufficient vehicles and used them for the transport of *Panzerfaust* teams in the latter part of the war. The Japanese used them along narrow tracks and found them easier than motor vehicles in river crossings. The British had a

BSA folding bicycle. Bicycles were widely used in Vietnam.

"Big Bertha." *See* **Krupp**

Binary Chemical Munitions. *See* **Gas**

Binocular. *See* **Telescope**

Biological Warfare   BIOLOGICAL
                               WARFARE

Though not described as such, biological warfare was known to the ancients, who poisoned wells with dead animals and threw carcasses over city walls with catapults to spread disease and terror. Such practices were quite common during medieval sieges. Plague and disease naturally followed war, when populations were weakened by hunger or infected by marauding armies. Well into the nineteenth century the casualties of such epidemics, military and civilian, were commonly greater than those of battle.

The scientific application of biology belongs essentially to the twentieth century, when specific microorganisms, bacteria, and fungi were identified and isolated for use. One of the first modern applications came in 1918, with the German idea of spreading glanders, a highly infectious disease of horses and men, among the Allies. In the 1920s experiments began in the Soviet Union, leading Poland to propose successfully that bacterial warfare should be included in the 1925 Geneva Protocol. Nevertheless, research advanced in the 1930s, with Japan and the Soviets establishing an early lead. Britain set up what was at first called an "Emergency Bacteriological Service" in 1938.

The current science of genetic modification makes it possible for man to engineer "new" diseases, though viruses such as influenza do in any case evolve and change in the natural world. Dispersal methods for biological agents now include bombs, aerosol sprays, contamination of water supplies, and the use of vectors, such as insects. Some biological weapons, such as **anthrax** and swine fever, may be applied indirectly, destroying livestock to undermine an enemy. Antiplant agents can be employed in a similar way to destroy crops.

Nevertheless, the major problem of ancient biological warfare is shared by its modern protagonists—such weapons cannot distinguish between friend and foe, and may attack either. It is also the case that biological weapons seldom cause instant casualties and must thus be regarded as delayed-action, or strategic, rather than tactical. Inoculations now make it possible to protect against many diseases, though "cocktails" of **chemicals** and inoculations given against chemical and biological weapons may themselves cause problems. This has been one explanation put forward for the so-called Gulf War syndrome.

Numerous biological agents have been identified, stored, and manufactured, and the following are just some of the more obvious. The rickettsiae rodlike micro organisms cause typhus and similar diseases. Rocky Mountain fever and scrub typhus are particularly virulent, sometimes causing in excess of 50 percent mortality in populations. Cholera similarly causes high mortality and has traditionally been resistant to drug therapies. Diptheria, caused by the *Corynebacterium diptheriae*, is also deadly if left untreated and can be epidemic. *Pasteurella pestis* is a particularly deadly bacterium causing various forms of plague, with untreated pnuemonic plague causing upward of 90 percent mortality in untreated cases.

The *Shigella dysenteriae* bacterium causes dysentery, which, though not usually fatal, is debilitating and highly contagious. The Brucella group of organisms is again not generally fatal but may cause various fevers and infections and is not commonly prevented by immunization. Among the myriad possible viruses for use in war, foot and mouth, rinderpest, hog cholera, fowl plague, encephalitis, smallpox, and yellow fever have all seen experimental use, and many have obvious application in the destruction of livestock. Some types of fungi can also be surprisingly effective under the right conditions.

Additional Reading: Gander, *Jane's NBC Protection Equipment*, 1988; Margiotta (ed), *Brassey's Encyclopedia of Land Forces and Warfare*, 1996; Parker, *The Killing Factory: The Top Secret World of Germ and Chemical Warfare*, 1996; Hersh, *Chemical and Biological Warfare*, 1970; Barnaby, *Plague Makers*, 1999.

Birmingham Small Arms, "BSA"
MANUFACTURER

Established following a meeting of the Birmingham small-arms trade in June 1861, BSA became one of Britain's leading gun makers. Its first government contract was an 1866 order for the conversion of **Enfield rifles** to **Snider** breechloaders. Thereafter significant contracts were completed for various countries, and it was soon claimed that this Small Heath company was the largest private arms concern in Europe. Though a shortage of work in 1878 almost proved terminal, BSA now diversified into other work, including bicycles.

During World War I the company was a major manufacturer of **SMLE** rifles, **Lewis guns**, motorcycles, and other munitions. In World War II it had an even greater range of products, including **Browning machine guns, Sten guns; shells**, primers; **armored cars, Boys antitank rifles, rockets**; and even a folding bicycle for airborne troops. Despite air raids, BSA produced 5,000,000,000 guns, munitions, and components between 1939 and 1945. BSA purchased Triumph in 1951, but fierce competition led to closures and mergers. However, even in 2002 the name continues as part of BSA Regal group and may still be found on motorcycles and **air guns**.

Additional Reading: Ward, *The Other Battle, Being a History of the Birmingham Small Arms Company Limited*, 1946; Walter, *Dictionary*, 2001.

Bismarck
WARSHIP

Named after the "iron chancellor" of imperial Germany, *Bismarck* was arguably the best known **battleship** of World War II. She and the *Tirpitz* were the first true battleships to be built by Germany after the Treaty of Versailles. Laid down at the Blöhm and Voss yard at Hamburg in 1936, Bismarck was launched in 1939 and commissioned in 1940. At 800 feet in length she displaced 41,700 tons and was powered by 12 Wagner superheated boilers, giving a laden speed of 30 knots and a range of 8,410 nautical miles. Her main armament was eight 38 cm guns, but she also mounted 12 15 cm, 16 10.5 cm, and 16 37 cm guns. She also carried six Arado aircraft, and her armor had a maximum thickness of 12.5 inches.

In Operation Rheinübung, under Admiral Gunther Lutjens, the *Bismarck* and the cruiser ***Prinz Eugen*** sailed out of the Baltic in May 1941, intending to attack enemy commerce. They were discovered and confronted in the Denmark Strait, where they were engaged by a British squadron including the battlecruiser *Hood* and battleship ***Prince of Wales***, and the **cruisers** *Norfolk* and *Suffolk*. With her excellent stereoscopic range finders and good gunnery the *Bismarck* quickly sank the *Hood*. Yet Bismarck received damage from the *Prince of Wales* and from air strikes, and so made haste for St. Nazaire. She could not escape her now-numerous adversaries. On 27 May the coup de grace was administered by the British battleships ***Rodney*** and *King George V*, and the cruisers *Norfolk* and *Dorsetshire*. *Bismarck* went down with her captain Ernst Lindemann and all but 115 of her 2,092-man crew.

Additional Reading: Kemp, *Bismarck and Hood*, 1991; Bercuson and Herwig, *Bismarck*, 2002; Müllenheim-Rechberg, *Battleship Bismarck*, 1990; Ballard, *Discovery of the Bismarck*, 1990; Koop and Schmolke, *Battleships of the Bismarck Class*, 1998; Beaver, *German Capital Ships*, 1980.

Blackbird, SR-71A   AIRCRAFT

The U.S. two-seater Lockheed Blackbird strategic reconnaisance **aircraft** was conceived as a successor to the **U-2**. The Central Intelligence Agency (CIA) asked for an craft that could not be shot down, and the Blackbird, which first flew in 1966, was the result. At just over 107 feet in length and of elongated, futuristic appearance, the Blackbird relied on extreme speed for its survivability, its Pratt and Whitney turbo ramjets providing 32,000 lb of thrust and a top speed of 2,309 mph in the SR-71A. Neverthe-

less, the Blackbird could also be armed with air-to-air missiles. An interesting feature of the SR-71A is that it actually changes size and shape very slightly in flight, so great are the forces exerted upon it by speed and altitude.

Additional Reading: Simonsen, *US Spy Planes*, 1985; Sgarlato, *Aircraft of the USAF*, 1978; Pace, *X-Fighters: USAF Experimental and Prototype Fighters, XP-59 to YF-23*, 1991.

Black Hawk, UH-60A, UH-60L
HELICOPTER

First flown in 1974, the Black Hawk **helicopter**, manufactured by the **Sikorsky** division of United Technologies, was selected in 1976 as a "Utility Tactical Support" for the U.S. Army. Designed to carry a squad of 11 men and three crew, the original army model weighed 10,624 lb empty. It was powered by two General Electric turboshaft engines driving a composite rotor made of titanium, glass fiber, and nomex honeycomb. Interesting technological features included **radar** warning, and **chaff** dispensers. Its maximum speed was 184 mph, and the cargo lift capability 8,000 lb. Army armament for the UH-60A was two **M60** machine guns.

The UH-60L, produced from 1989, is claimed to have a 24 percent power increase over its predecessor, allowing a 9,000 lb external payload. The service ceiling is 19,150 feet. Four removable pylons are fitted for 16 **Hellfire** missiles, and a variety of guns and rockets can be carried. The helicopter has the distinction of being one of the few modern weapons to be in the title of a major Hollywood film—Ridley Scott's *Black Hawk Down*.

Black Powder. *See* Gunpowder

Black Widow, P-61, F-61   AIRCRAFT

The Northrop P-61 Black Widow has the distinction of being the first purpose-designed U.S. night fighter **aircraft**. It was designed in answer to a specification for a heavily armed twin-engined machine capable of carrying **radar**. Flown in prototype in 1942, with production starting in 1943, it first saw combat in July

1944. The Black Widow was a twin-boom craft, had a wing span of 66 feet, was capable of 369 mph, and was armed with four 20 mm cannon. The first few produced also had four .5-inch machine guns in an upper remote-controlled mounting, but this was deleted when it was discovered to cause buffeting. Major Black Widow variants were the P-61A, B, and C.

Though there were early problems with the Massachusetts Institute of Technology's airborne interception radar, the Black Widow proved effective. It continued to serve until 1950, under the designation F-61.

Blenheim Bomber   AIRCRAFT

The British twin-engine Bristol Blenheim **aircraft** first flew in 1935 and served as both a bomber and a fighter in World War II. In the fighter role the three-seater featured a gun pack fitting beneath the fuselage. At the time of its introduction its design and its speed of 285 mph were impressive, though by 1940 it was outclassed. In the IF model its armament was six **machine guns**—four in the gun pack, one in the wing, and one in the turret. The later fitting of **radar** made the Blenheim practical as a night fighter.

Bloodhound Missile   MISSILE

The British Bloodhound missile system was first developed by the **Bristol** and Ferranti companies beginning in 1949. It was a large guided antiaircraft weapon, entering service in 1958. The Mark 2 version, which was active from 1964, was 27 feet 9 inches in length, relied on semiactive homing, and had a range in excess of 50 miles. Typically a missile section comprised four missiles and their launchers, a target-illuminating radar, and a launch-control post. The Bloodhound remained in use into the 1980s.

Blooper; Bloop Gun. *See* M79

Blowpipe Missile   MISSILE

The British Blowpipe shoulder-launched anti-aircraft missile was developed by Short Broth-ers of Belfast and entered service in 1966. Its essentials were a canister, containing the round, and an aiming unit. The firer pointed and shot, then used a small joystick and radio link to guide the round to its target. The improved Javelin version, in use from the 1980s, featured an improved rocket motor, a range of over two miles, and a better guidance system. In this SA-CLOS, or "semiautomatic command line of sight," system, all the firer had to do was keep the target in the center of the sight, guidance being transmitted to the missile automatically.

Additional Reading: Beaver and Gander, *Modern British Military Missiles*, 1986.

Blunderbuss. *See* Shotgun

BM-13. *See* Katyusha

BMP   VEHICLE

The BMP is a fully tracked infantry combat vehicle, which the Western powers identified in the Soviet inventory in 1967 and therefore initially christened the M-1967. At the time it was one of the most advanced in the world, being fully amphibious, with a magnesium welded hull and a turret with a 73 mm smoothbore gun fed from an automatic loader. On the gun barrel was a launcher rail for a **Sagger** guided missile. An **NBC** protection system and night-vision equipment were fitted, and a total of ten firing ports allowed the occupants to fire out. Carrying up to eight, the all-up weight was 25,000 lb.

Bobbin. *See* Funnies

Boeing   MANUFACTURER

Now the biggest **aircraft** producer in the world, Boeing was founded by William E. Boeing (1881–1956). Yale-educated Boeing made money in the timber industry prior to commencing his first aircraft in 1915. This was the "B&W," a floatplane constructed in conjunction with Navy engineer G. C. Westervelt; Boeing test-flew it himself in 1916. Thereafter Boeing incorporated the business as the Pacific Aero

Products Company, a name soon changed to the Boeing Airplane Company. Having hired a talented team including Claire Egtvedt, Phil Johnson, and Tsu Wong, the company now designed and built the Model C seaplane, which was bought in small numbers as a U.S. Navy trainer.

The end of hostilities in 1918 brought lean times, and survival entailed rapid diversification into civil aircraft and furniture. Yet Boeing continued to satisfy military orders, notably for Thomas-Morse MB-3A fighters for the Army Air Service. Under the company presidency of Edgar Gott, from 1922 to 1925 Boeing also made NB trainers for the U.S. Navy and export, and the Model 15, or PW-9, fighter, which first flew in 1923. The latter was significant in that it featured bracing made of arc-welded tubing. The plane helped establish a company reputation as a fighter manufacturer and led ultimately to the P-12/F4B series.

Stearman Aircraft was purchased in 1929, and by the 1930s Boeing was a significant player in the industry. William Boeing now also owned both parts manufacturers and airlines as well as his main concerns. The position was consolidated by the Monomail, an all-metal cargo-carrying monoplane, which, via the experimental XP-9, led to the building of the **P-26 "Peashooter"** fighter and also the B-9 bomber. The B-9 was advanced for 1931, with sleek all-metal construction and a 2,400 lb bomb load. Nevertheless, antitrust legislation in 1934 forced a division of Boeing assets, and Boeing himself resigned from the company. Under the presidency of Clairmont L. Egtvedt, Boeing now developed the experimental XB-15 and Model 299 bombers in conjunction with the U.S. Army. This would ultimately lead to the appearance both of the ubiquitous **B-17 (the Flying Fortress)** and the commercial Stratoliner.

World War II saw massive expansion of Boeing facilities, most notably in Wichita and Seattle. By March 1944 the company was making 362 planes per month. In addition to the B-17 and **B-29**, Boeing was involved in the construction of many craft, including the DB-7 or **Douglas A-20**, Waco **gliders, C-97** transports, Kaydet trainers, and flying boats. As might be expected, the end of the war brought

contraction, but it also led to the discovery of German experiments and to the beginnings of mass air travel. Important Boeing developments of the immediate postwar period would include the experimental XB-47, America's first multiengined swept-wing jet bomber, and the KC-97 tanker. The XB-47, produced with the aid of then-novel high-speed wind tunnel technology, saw service as the **B-47** Stratojet. Yet it would be the long-range **B-52**, first flown by test pilot Tex Johnston in 1952, that most captured public imagination; it remains in service after half a century in various models.

Though Boeing abandoned the fighter market, the later 1940s and 1950s were a key period for the firm's involvement in missile development. Analog computers were used to guide some of these weapons, and the Boeing Ground to Air Pilotless Aircraft, originally conceived as a supersonic antidote to German V weapons, helped lead the way to the **Bomarc** missile of 1957. Ultimately Boeing would also win the major contract for the **Minuteman ICBM** program. More recently Boeing has produced both the Short Range Attack Missile, or SRAM, and the Air Launched **Cruise** Missile, or ALCM.

The link between such military developments, the Dyna-Soar project for a reusable space vehicle, Apollo, and the space shuttle is readily apparent, Boeing being a key player in all. Likewise commercial airliner production has also enjoyed synergy with various federal and military projects. As early as 1962, Boeing 707s were converted for presidential use under the call sign "Air Force One." From 1976, 707 airframes were put to use as platforms for the E-3A Airborne Warning and Control System, **AWACS**. The 747 was later adapted for use in the E-4 Advanced Airborne Command Post, and the 767 has fulfilled similar roles since 1991. Jet technology has also been applied to the water, hence involvement in jet foils and the patrol hydrofoil. From the 1960s military **helicopters** have also been a key part of the portfolio, particularly as Boeing had acquired other companies, such as Vertol, which were skilled in this area. Thus it is that the **Chinook** and Sea Knight form part of the Boeing story. More recent helicopter developments, such as the V-22 **Osprey** tiltrotor and RAH-66 **Comanche**, have made use of more advanced technology.

The 1990s would also see Boeing work on the **B-2 stealth bomber**, the **Joint Strike Fighter**, and such futuristic projects as Dark Star. In 1996 Boeing acquired the Rockwell International aerospace and defense business. The seal was set on Boeing ascendancy, following Federal Trade Commission approval, when in August 1997 Boeing and **McDonnell Douglas** merged in a $13 billion deal, creating a company of 220,000 employees. The three main divisions created after the merger were Information, Space and Defense, Commercial Airplane, and a Shared Services Group for such things as computing and telecommunications.

In the new conglomerate Phil Condit remained chairman of the board, while Harry C. Stonecipher, former McDonnell Douglas president, became chief operating officer. As one newspaper report claimed, "Although the companies characterised it as a merger, the terms clearly show Boeing is buying McDonnell." Though this may have been true, Stonecipher was also correct when he observed that independence was being surrendered to create what he called "the first and only preeminent aerospace company in the history of aviation." Though Boeing has since sold some of its helicopter interests, the company remains a giant in the defense field. In addition to space and **GPS** (Global Positioning System), significant recent projects have included the **F-22 Raptor fighter**; the **F/A-18 Super Hornet**, the Airborne Laser, the AH-64 **Apache** Longbow, and the **Harpoon** missile.

Press reports of summer 2002 refer to the development of a family of unmanned submarines and an X45A pilotless combat jet. In early 2003 rumors of a merger involving the **BAE** were also reported.

Additional Reading: Taylor, *Boeing*, 1982. www.Boeing.com.

Bofors, "Bofors Gun"   ARTILLERY

The Bofors armaments company of Sweden has long been known as a manufacturer of **artillery**. Its best-known product was a 40 mm antiaircraft gun with automatic loading that enabled rapid fire against fast-moving targets. During World War II basically the same model was in use by both Allied and Axis forces, mounted on ships, emplaced, or towed on a trailer. More recently Bofors has diversified. One of its later weapons was the RBS-70 Ray Rider light air-to-air missile, which was steered by means of a **laser**.

Bogue Class   WARSHIP

The USS *Bogue* (CVE 9) was the first vessel of the *Bogue*-class **aircraft carrier** series. Build by Seattle-Tacoma in 1942, the 8,500-ton *Bogue* was based on a merchant vessel hull, helping to make up the shortage of carriers. It was 465 feet in length and capable of taking 28 aircraft. Defended by two 5-inch and ten 20 mm guns, it had a crew of 890. Bogue herself served mainly on Atlantic antisubmarine duties, being finally scrapped in Japan in 1960. Others in the class included *Card* (CVE 11), which saw active service in the Vietnam War, and *Croatan* (CVE 25), the varied deployments of which included a period in 1964 as an experimental platform for NASA.

Böhler Gun   ARTILLERY

First produced by the Böhler Brothers company of Kapfenberg, Austria, in the early 1930s, Böhler guns were innovative light **artillery** pieces, some of which were particularly adapted to antitank work. Capable of being towed by a single horse, they were small and easy to conceal. During World War II, 47 mm Böhler types were used especially by Italy.

Bolt Action   FIREARM

In bolt-action firearms, the breech is closed by means of a metal bolt that is manipulated like a door bolt. This was a significant advance over earlier systems, being a strong and positive method of locking and capable of containing the great pressures of discharge. Its application to firearms is generally credited to Johann **Dryse** and was general in military **rifles** by the late nineteenth century. The straight-pull bolt, requiring one motion rather than the "up and back" of the ordinary bolt, was introduced by **Mannlicher** in 1884. It was later applied to such rifles as the Swiss Schmidt-Rubin of 1889 and the **Ross**.

Additional Reading: Walter, *Dictionary*, 2001.

Bomarc   MISSILE

Named after **Boeing** and the Michigan Aeronautical Research Center, the Bomarc long-range air-defense system was developed from 1949 and deployed operationally in the 1960s. The 13-meter long guided missile with stubby wings was vertically launched; it was powered by two ramjets and a solid-fuel booster. It was intended to be flown against enemy bombers and could carry a nuclear warhead.

Bombard   ARTILLERY

Though the word "bombard" is now a verb, generally taken to mean "to attack with **artillery**" or to batter, during the fifteenth century a bombard was also a specific type of large bored cannon. Important surviving examples include Mons Meg at Edinburgh castle, Scotland; Dulle Griet, at Ghent, Belgium; the Basel bombard, now at the Historisches Museum Basel; and the Paris bombard, now at the French Musée de l'Armes, Paris. The Blacker Bombard was a much later device, being a form of spigot **mortar** used in World War II.

Additional Reading: Smith and Brown, *Bombards: Mons Meg and Her Sisters*, 1989.

Bomb Disposal Robot. *See* Wheelbarrow

Bombe   COMMUNICATIONS

A bombe is a code-breaking machine. The first use of the name appeared about 1930, when the Polish mathematician Marian Rejewski produced such a device during his work on the German **Enigma**. It has been suggested that the word is derived either from the ticking that the original made or that it is named after the ice cream "bombe."

Bomb Vessel   WARSHIP

The mounting of a **mortar** in a special vessel is generally credited to Bernard Renan d'Elicagary, though sketches by Prince Rupert of the Rhine also contain similar ideas. Whatever the inspiration, mortars were mounted in wide and stable Dutch galliots by 1682. Bomb vessels soon became widespread, being popular in the English and French navies. Many had names suitable to their function—hence the *Granado*, built at Rotherhithe in 1693, and the *Firedrake* and the *Mortar*, built at Blackwall in 1741. Bomb vessels continued into the nineteenth century, seeing action in the Crimean and American Civil War. The last known, a French ship, was decommissioned in 1907.

Additional Reading: Goodwin, *The Bomb Vessel Granado*, 1989.

Boobytrap   EXPLOSIVE DEVICE

The boobytrap is commonly defined in the modern military sense as "a harmless looking object which on being touched sets off an explosion." Nevertheless, the idea is an old one, with accounts of explosions triggered by hapless victims going back to at least the seventeenth century. Neither does the boobytrap have to contain an **explosive**. In Vietnam, for example, U.S. forces encountered ancient methods as simple as pits, snares, and sharp stakes. Some of the most effective are rigged to the ordinary movements of buildings, detonating when a door is opened or a toilet seat is lifted.

One of the best-known mass uses of boobytraps occurred during the German retreat to the Hindenburg Line in 1917. In World War II the Russians were noted using explosive devices as diverse as **cartridge boxes**, balls, and cognac bottles. The Japanese made a pipe that exploded in the victim's mouth. Both Britain and the United States manufactured switches, pull **fuses**, and other materials for use in boobytraps. More recently, such devices as televisions, computers, and light switches have offered useful covers for electrically initiated explosions.

Additional Reading: Department of the Army, *Field Manual 5-31* and *Technical Manual 31-200-1*.

Borchardt Pistol   FIREARM

Born in Magdeburg Germany, Hugo Borchardt (1844–1921) emigrated to the United States before the Civil War. He was employed by Pioneer Breech Loading Arms of Trenton, and later by Singer Sewing Machines, **Colt**, and **Sharps**. Though he worked on various weapons, he is best known for his **semiautomatic** pistol, patented in 1893. This used a toggle-lock system. In this arrangement a two-piece arm rose and flexed as the barrel recoiled, allowing the breech to unlock and ejecting the empty cartridge case. The basics of the toggle joint had been known to engineers for some time and had been used by **Maxim** in his machine gun, but its application to a handgun was novel.

Though an intriguing design, capable of impressively rapid and accurate fire, the Borchardt had serious drawbacks as a military arm. It was large, ungainly, and difficult to holster, with a nearly vertical grip. Sales were poor, and it is mainly for the subsequent success of the **Luger** that the Borchardt is remembered.

Additional Reading: Ezell, *Handguns of the World*, 1981; Walter, *The Luger Story*, 1995.

Boulton Paul Defiant. *See* Defiant

Bouncing Betty. *See* Mines

Bouncing Bomb   EXPLOSIVE DEVICE

Invented by Barnes Wallis specifically to attack the German Ruhr dams, the bouncing bomb was an **explosive**-filled metal cylinder weighing over 1,000 lb. The secret of the bomb was the application of two main principles: the propensity of projectiles to skip off the surface of water when delivered at low angle, and backspin that would prevent overshoot and cause the bomb to hug a dam wall. The bomb was set off by water pressure when it finally sank.

Modified aircraft were required for delivery. To this end **Lancaster** G production "specials" without bomb-bay doors were fitted with py-
lons under the fuselage. Using power from the planes' hydraulic systems, the bombs were spun by means of a belt drive to 500 revolutions per minute before release. Exact height was achieved by means of searchlights set so as to converge on the ground at a preset level, and primitive triangular bombsights were improvised to judge the precise distance to the target. On the night of 16 May 1943, 19 Lancasters of 617 Squadron, under Wing Commander Guy Gibson, attacked the dams in three waves. Despite the loss of eight aircraft, the attack was pressed home from heights as low as 60 feet. The Mohne and Eder dams were breached, causing flooding and loss of power and communications over a widespread area.

Additional Reading: Cooper, *The Dambusters Squadron*, 1993; Bennett, *617 Squadron*, 1986.

Bow   BOW

The bow is one of man's oldest weapons, known since the Mesolithic period, about 12,000 years ago. It was well nigh universal until the seventeenth century, being used by groups as disparate as the auxiliaries of ancient Rome, Native Americans, the Pygmy tribes of Africa, and the bodyguards of the Royal Company of Archers in Scotland. **Crossbows** were also widespread. In its basic form the bow consists of a flexible stave, ends of which are joined by a cord under tension. Drawing the cord bends the stave, briefly storing energy that is released to drive the arrow forward.

Bows may be simple, or "self" (that is, of one piece of material, normally wood or metal), or composite (in which different layers or sections impart greater flexibility). Two important types among the many composites are the *yumi* and the Turkish bow. The *yumi*, or Japanese longbow, was made of strips of bamboo at various stages of seasoning, creating different degrees of suppleness and strength. The Turkish bow, which was often highly ornamented, was short and "reflex"—that is, having a strong curvature in the opposite direction to the string.

In Europe the most important form of the military bow was the longbow—perhaps the most significant of all weapons during the fourteenth and fifteenth centuries. Traditionally of yew with a yard-long arrow fletched with goose feather, it played havoc with cavalry and could penetrate some **armor** at close range. Even at 200 yards it was capable of harassing the enemy. It could be shot several times a minute, putting more than one arrow in the air at any given moment. Its chief users were the English and Welsh peasantry, who inflicted catastrophic defeats on French knights at Crécy and Agincourt. Few authentic longbows survive; most of those that do emanate from the wreck of the *Mary Rose*.

Though bows were eclipsed by firearms in the late sixteenth century, periodic attempts have been made to revive them as weapons of war. Bows have also seen Third World and special-forces military use comparatively recently. Various ancillary archery equipment is encountered. The bracer is designed to protect the archer's arm; rings may be used for the thumb; spacers and quivers are used to hold sheaves of arrows. The archer's chest (container) is an "Ascham," named after Roger Ascham, tutor to Queen Elizabeth I.

Additional Reading: Hardy, *Longbow*, 1986; Heath (ed), *Bow versus Gun*; Grancsay (ed), *The Art of Archerie*, 1968; Spring, *African Arms and Armour*, 1993; Stone, *A Glossary of the Construction, Decoration and Use of Arms and Armor*, 1934; Tarassuk and Blair, *The Complete Encyclopaedia of Arms and Weapons*, 1979; Webb, *Archaeology of Archery*, 1991.

Bowser   VEHICLE

Bowsers are fuel tanker trucks, and they now regarded as indispensable to the operations of armies and air forces. There have been many types since World War I. The British AEC Mammoth Major of the late 1960s, for example, was an eight-wheeler, diesel-powered, 5000-gallon type with a limited off-road capability. From the 1950s Japan used a Hino refueler, while the U.S. Air Force in Europe used the Dutch DAF aircraft fueler from 1953. More innovative was the 1959 U.S. LeTourneau-Westinghouse 5000-gallon logistical tanker, which incorporated an independently

tilting front tractor unit and vast tires for rough-terrain mobility.

Box Lock   FIREARM

A type of firearm where the lock or ignition mechanism is enclosed in the center of the weapon, usually with the cock or arm on top. It had the advantage of making the weapon more compact and reducing the chances of moving parts catching on obstructions. **Flintlock** box lock pistols first became popular in the middle of the eighteenth century.

Additional Reading: Blair, *Pollard's History of Firearms*, 1983.

Boxer. *See* **Cartridge**

Boys Rifle. *See* **Antitank Rifle**

Bradley, M2, M3   VEHICLE

Manufactured by UDLP, the U.S. Bradley M2 and M3 are, respectively, the armored fighting vehicles of the infantry and cavalry. They are turreted, fully tracked, amphibious, and powered by VTA-903T engines, having a top speed of 41 mph. The main weapon is a 25 mm Bushmaster chain gun, but **TOW** missiles and machine guns are also carried. Produced since 1981, Bradleys now number about 7,000. An A3 upgrade commenced in 1998; it included improved thermal imaging systems, **laser** range finder, and digital information displays. In the infantry version the capacity is three crew plus six fully equipped troops.

BRDM   VEHICLE

The Soviet BRDM was an innovative small, armored, amphibious, four-wheel-drive scout car that entered service in the 1960s. Fitted with twin 70 horsepower engines, it weighed 15,500 lb and was capable of 70 mph on land and 6 mph in water using hydrojet propulsion. It was armed with two **machine guns** in the turret. The Hungarian FUG, also supplied to other communist countries, was similar, though it lacked the turret.

Breech Loading FIREARMS

Guns that load at the rear, or breech, end are of much greater antiquity than is commonly supposed, having been in regular use in the fifteenth century. Often **artillery** pieces were made with barrels with openings at either end; a chamber containing the charge was wedged into position at the back. Though breech loading was possibly swifter if a number of such charges were available, there were many early problems with achieving a good seal between the breech piece and barrel. Since that time breech loading has been in and out of fashion several times.

Pistols with "turn off" barrels that were removed from the weapon and loaded at the rear were reasonably common in the latter seventeenth and early eighteenth centuries. Breech-loading **rifled** weapons were specifically noted in England in 1747; some produced by Captain Patrick Ferguson saw limited military use in the American War of Independence. A "tip up" breech system for **muskets** was used by Henry Nock in the 1780s. **Hall** breechloaders were in use in the United States c. 1819, and the Prussian army issued **Dreyse** breechloaders from 1848. **Revolvers** were often loaded at the back of the cylinder, as was the case in many **Smith and Wesson** arms.

By 1860 breechloaders finally became cheap and reliable enough to become general-issue military arms in many countries, the **Sharps** carbine and **Snider** rifle being just two of this period. Within a few years all major powers were using breechloaders. Generally speaking, breech-loading weapons were now more accurate, reliable, and quicker than muzzle loaders. They also offered the advantage that the firer could lie down when loading. Significant breech-loading systems later included those of **Peabody; Martini; Lee**; and **Mauser**. Virtually all military arms were breech loading from 1870.

Bren Carrier, Carden Loyd, Universal Carrier, Cargo Carrier T16 VEHICLE

The idea of tracked carriers goes back to World War I, when converted British **tanks** were used

for supplies. In the 1920s British Dragon ("drag-gun") tracked carriers were used to tow **artillery** and carry gun crews. In 1925 a Major Martel put forward the idea of a "tankette," or small infantry carrier, which he built at his own expense in his garage. Though few of this design were completed, the Carden Loyd company was inspired to produce a 1.8-ton one-man carrier, and a two-man version was accepted for service as a **machine-gun** carrier in 1928. From 1934 Vickers-Armstrong began the development of a machine that could be used as tractor or machine-gun carrier. The company produced the "Carrier, Machine Gun, No 2 Mk 1" in 1937, and this was also manufactured by Thorneycroft, Morris, and others. In 1938 it was modified for the **Bren gun**, and so the Bren carrier was born. This served in World War II and was also made in Australia and New Zealand. Weapons mounted included **mortars** and the Boys **anti-tank rifle**.

Owing to the large number of models, it was decided to standardize, and the Universal carrier appeared in 1940. Many were made, Canada alone producing 33,987 before turning to the manufacture of her own more powerful Windsor carrier in 1943. Though there were many slightly differing specifications, the typical Universal carrier weighed about four tons, had up to 10 mm of armor, and was powered by a 65 or 85 horsepower engine giving a top speed of about 30 mph. A larger T16 cargo carrier was made in the United States. Among the many modifications produced were Wasp **flamethrower** carriers and the alterations made by the Germans to captured carriers. The last of the fully tracked, open-topped, carrier breed were the postwar Oxford and Cambridge Carriers, some of which were still in use as late as 1964.

Additional Reading: Chamberlain and Ellis, *Making Tracks: The British Carrier Story 1914–1972*, 1973; White, *British Tanks and Fighting Vehicles 1914–1945*, 1970.

Bren Gun FIREARM

The British Bren gun was one of the most successful light **machine guns** of the Second

World War, being highly accurate, robust, and reliable. Though formally introduced as early as 1938, the LMG, as it commonly became known in later years, was still in limited use in the 1990s.

The Bren took as its inspiration the innovative Czech ZB 26 and ZB 30 machine guns, which were tested in Britain in the early 1930s. Redesign adapted the basic idea for the .303 **cartridge**, shortened the barrel, and altered other detailing. Its ancestry was apparent from its name, the "Bren" being a composite of Bruno in Czechoslovakia and **Enfield**. The Bren had a curved 30-round box magazine and was commonly used as a squad-support weapon, though it could be mounted on a tripod and was sometimes supplied with large drum magazines for antiaircraft use. Its versatility was improved by the fact that ordinary rifle ammunition could be used to charge its magazines on the battlefield. The gun weighed just over 22 lb and had a cyclic rate of about 500 rounds per minute.

Additional Reading: Dugelby, *Bren Gun Saga*, 1986.

Brennan Torpedo   EXPLOSIVE DEVICE

Designed by Irish-Australian Louis Brennan between 1874 and 1877, the Brennan **torpedo** was one of the few designs to challenge seriously the near monopoly achived by Robert Whitehead in this field. Key to the ingenious Brennan system were two drums of wire attached to the shore, where winding engines pulled on the wire, providing the power to rotate a pair of propellors, thus driving the missile forward. The torpedo could be steered by varying the speed of one or other of the propellors. The shore operator was aided by a small mast atop the torpedo by means of which he could track its position. Many Brennan torpedoes were installed in British coastal defenses, but they were obsolete soon after the turn of the century.

Brewster. *See* Buffalo

Brigantine, Brig   WARSHIPS

The earliest brigantines were small vessels that could be sailed or rowed and were thus very maneuverable and useful for reconnaissance and espionage. Later the word "brig" was applied as a short version of the name, but brigs then began to develop different characteristics. They later came to be defined as small square-rigged ships, but with a gaff and boom on the main mast.

One well known example of an American warship defined as a brig was the *Oneida*, constructed on Lake Ontario for a reported $20,505. She carried 14 cannon firing through ports and a 32-pounder on a pivot mounting. The *Oneida* fought throughout the War of 1812. "Brig" is now used as slang for naval or military prison.

Bristol Aircraft; Bristol Fighter; "Brisfit"; Bristol Scout   MANUFACTURER

Founded in 1910 by Sir George White at Filton, Bristol, in the United Kingdom, the Bristol company was one of Britain's best known military **aircraft** manufacturers. Important products during World War I included the 1914 Scout biplane and the M1C monoplane of 1916. Yet easily the best was the Bristol Fighter F2B, nicknamed the "Brisfit." Designed by Frank Barnwell and in action by 1917, this two-seater had good all-round visibility, was fast and maneuverable, and could take punishment. Top speed was a then-healthy 123 mph.

After 1918 Bristol produced the Bulldog Fighter, and in World War II the **Blenheim**, Beaufort, **Beaufighter**, Buckingham, and Brigand. Bristol became part of the British Aircraft Corporation in 1963.

British Aerospace Systems   MANUFACTURER

Also known as "BAE" or "BAe," British Aerospace came into existence in 1977 as a "nationalized corporation" with the merger of the British Aircraft Corporation, **Hawker** Siddeley, and Scottish Aviation. The company was privatized in 1981; acquisitions in the 1980s included Royal Ordnance, the Rover Group, and Arlington Securities. Despite near collapse in 1992, targeted disposals and huge weapons contracts with Saudi Arabia helped secure the future. New European collaborations were forged with Dassault, Saab, Siemens, and others.

In 1999 the BAE and GEC defense businesses were merged, and in 2000 electronics concerns were purchased from **Lockheed Martin**, helping to make the company a major player in the United States. BAE was now a major supplier of land sea and air defense systems, with the capacity to build nuclear **submarines, radar** systems, **artillery** and guided weapons. Important work included contributions to both the **Joint Strike Fighter** and the **Eurofighter aircraft**. In 2002 under Executive Chairman Sir Richard Evans, BAE was Britain's biggest manufacturer, with annual sales of £13.2 billion and an order book of £43.8 billion. BAE is now the sixth-largest supplier to the Pentagon, with 28 percent of its sales in the United States.

Broadsword. *See* Sword and Type 22

Brooklyn Class   WARSHIP

The U.S. *Brooklyn* class of nine 10,000-ton **cruisers** was laid down in the mid-1930s and complete by 1939. This design was influenced by the London Naval Treaty of 1930 and by the appearance of the Japanese *Mogami* class. It therefore mounted 6-inch rather than 8-inch guns, having a total of 15 pieces, mounted in five triple turrets. The main belt of armor was almost six inches thick. Later modifications included copious antiaircraft weaponry.

The *Brooklyn* saw extensive war service in the Atlantic and Mediterranean, supporting the landings at Salerno and Anzio. Later sold to Chile, she was renamed *O'Higgins*. *Philadelphia* served all over the globe during World War II, being sold to Brazil in 1951. *Savannah* was badly damaged by a radio-controlled bomb in the Mediterranean but later served as a training ship and was not sold for scrap until 1966. *Nashville* saw extensive Pacific service, including their Aleutians, Guadalcanal, and New

Georgia before being damaged and requiring refit; she was soon back in action. Hit by a **kamikaze aircraft** on 13 December 1944, she was back to the fray by April 1945. Later sold to Chile, she survived until 1985. *Phoenix* fought in the Pacific but ultimately became better known as Argentina's *General Belgrano*.

The *Boise* was severely damaged at Cape Esperance in October 1942. Following repair she fought in both the European and Pacific theaters, being sold to Argentina in 1951. *Honolulu* suffered minor damage at Pearl Harbor and then fought in the Pacific, being one of the units responsible for the sinking of the **destroyer** *Niisuki*. The *Helena* was sunk in this same action. The ninth of the class, the *St. Louis*, fought extensively in the Pacific, being damaged in the Solomon Islands in 1944. She survived to fight at Saipan, the Philippine Sea, and Leyte Gulf, where she too was hit by a kamikaze. Sold to Brazil in 1951, she foundered on her way to scrapping in 1980.

Additional Reading: Friedman, *US Cruisers*, 1985; Terzibaschitsch, *Cruisers of the US Navy 1922–1962*, 1988.

Brown Bess   FIREARM

The term "Brown Bess" is popularly applied to **flintlock** military shoulder arms, especially British ones, of roughly the period 1715–1815. It is sometimes asserted that the "brown" part of the name refers either to stocks being brown or to "browned" barrels acquiring that color through antirust treatment. Though the "Brown Bess" is a handy concept, it should be noted that there were in fact many identifiable and slightly differing patterns in use during this period. These included the Land, Militia and India patterns. Similar weapons were used by many nations.

Additional Reading: Bailey, *British Military Longarms*, 1986.

Browning   MANUFACTURER

Prolific American inventor John Moses Browning (1855–1926) was the son of Mormon gunsmith Jonathan Browning, of Ogden, near Salt Lake City. The young Browning worked in his

A GI firing a pedestal mounted .30 caliber Browning machine gun, during training at Fort Knox, Kentucky, in June 1942. Courtesy of the Library of Congress.

father's shop as a child, making his first rifle at 14. An early breakthrough came with Browning's association with T. G. Bennet, general manager of **Winchester**. The company purchased a number of Browning designs, including that for the 1886-model lever-action rifle. A lever-action **shotgun** appeared a year later. About 1889, Browning's interest turned to automatic weapons, producing a **machine gun** in 1891 and the first of his famous **semiautomatic pistol** designs in 1895. A patent was taken out in 1897, and **Colt** received U.S. production rights. The same year Browning also signed agreements with **Fabrique Nationale**, or "FN," of Belgium.

The 1897 Browning .32 "blowback" pistol was a landmark in design and became a model for many small **pistols** that followed. It featured a recoil spring in a tunnel above the barrel; this transmitted pressure to the breechblock via a guide rod and provided the force to recock the striker. About 750,000 of a larger 1900-model pistol were manufactured for the military mar-

ket; thereafter Browning's reputation was made. Over the next few years he produced designs for many pistols that became military standards. Important among these were the 1905 model and the famous 1911 model, produced by Colt and others, which was adopted by many nations, including the United States, and remained in service for much of the twentieth century.

Of equal importance was the improved 9 mm semiautomatic pistol designed in the 1920s, which would later become known as the Browning High Power, or model 1935, "Grand Puissance." Though Browning laid the foundations, the project was brought to fruition by Dieudonn J. Saive. As completed it had a 13-shot, double-row box magazine and an external hammer. It also offered several mechanical simplifications, in the form of the slide and breechblock. An extremely practical military arm, the model 1935 was simple and powerful enough, but not so powerful as to be unmanageable by inexperienced shots. The large-capacity magazine proved useful and would set an example for pistols produced after World War II. The model 1935 was widely used in Europe and by Canada. It has also inspired Polish, Russian, and French designs.

Browning machine guns achieved similar prominence. He devised a reliable new recoil-operated, water-cooled weapon as early as 1910. In it the recoil of the barrel carried the bolt backward. After a short recoil, a vertically sliding lock withdrew, unlocking the bolt. A curved steel claw lever flipped the bolt back against a return spring, which operated the belt feed. Although this reliable gun failed to raise interest immediately, it was hurriedly adopted on U.S. entry into World War I, becoming the Browning model 1917, .30 caliber.

Eventually the Browning .30 caliber would serve not only as a water-cooled ground weapon but be converted for air cooling and become a standard in **aircraft** and **tanks**, seeing widespread service in many countries throughout the twentieth century. The .50-caliber Browning Heavy Machine Gun was originally conceived as an antitank weapon, but armor quickly outpaced its performance. Nevertheless the .50 gained importance as a support weapon, vehicle weapon, and aircraft/antiaircraft gun. The Browning Automatic Rifle, or BAR, was also an important design with a long working life, which stretched from World War I through World War II and Korea. Adopted by the U.S. Army in 1918, the BAR mechanism was based on a tipping bolt and gas piston. The total weight was 22 lb, including a 20-round detachable box magazine. Though billed as an "automatic rifle," it was used very much as a squad automatic weapon, in which role it found immediate favor. In Korea forty years later it was still viewed as "indispensable."

J. M. Browning registered approximately 130 firearms patents during his lifetime, and it is arguable that among inventors of military small arms he had the greatest single impact of any in modern times.

Additional Reading: Browning and Gentry, *John M. Browning: American Gunmaker*, 1964; Anon. *The Browning Heavy Machine Gun Made Easy*, (undated); Ezell, *Handguns of the World*, 1981; Patent Office, *Patents*; Walter, *Dictionary*, 2001; War Department, *Browning Machinegun Caliber .30*, 1940.

BSA. *See* **Birmingham Small Arms**

BT-7   TANK

The Soviet BT-7 light **tank**, which entered service in 1935, was the latest type in the prolific BT series. Based on a **Christie** design, the three-man BT-7 was capable of a healthy 46 mph on road using its wheels, or 33 mph on tracks. Its armor was much less impressive, at 22 mm maximum. The gun was a 45 mm. The tank was sometimes known to its crews as the "Betka," or beetle. Though innovative, its poor tactical use and relatively poor protection made it easy prey for the German **panzers** in 1941. Nevertheless, experimental work with sloped armor on a BT chassis helped with the development of the **T-34**.

Additional Reading: Bean and Fowler, *Russian Tanks of World War II*, 2002.

Buffalo, F2A   AIRCRAFT

The Brewster F2A Buffalo single-seat **aircraft** was the first monoplane fighter to equip a squadron of the U.S. Navy. Flying from 1937, the stubby Buffalo was thought promising but has since been described as "overweight, unstable and of poor maneuverability."

Buff Coat   ARMOR

The buff leather coat came into use in the sixteenth century as a protection against **swords** and other edged weapons. Lighter and more flexible than **armor**, it could be worn by itself or with a breast plate. Generally thick and stitched together in panels, it could be with or without sleeves and in different styles, but was generally worn longer as time progressed. It was common on the battlefields of the seventeenth century; Gustavus Adolphus, king of Sweden, was killed wearing one that survives to this day.

Additional Reading: Blackmore, *Arms & Armour of the English Civil Wars*, 1990; Bull, *An Historical Guide to Arms and Armor*, 1991.

Bullpup, Gun/Missile   FIREARM/MISSILE

When applied to small arms such as **rifles** and **machine guns** the description "bullpup" refers to weapons in which the trigger assembly is positioned forward of the magazine, often allowing a shorter overall length. Such is the case in the British **SA 80** and certain **Steyr** rifles.

The name was also applied to a U.S. Navy air-to-surface tactical missile that became operational in 1959. This radio-guided Bullpup A was based around a 250 lb bomb and was powered by a solid-fuel motor to a range of about seven miles. The Bullpup AGM-12E, made for the U.S. Air Force, was fitted with an antipersonnel warhead for use in Vietnam. The larger Bullpup B was built around the 1,000 lb bomb, had a range of ten miles, and could be either conventional or nuclear.

Burney. *See* **Recoilless Gun**

Busy Lizzie. *See* **V3**

Butterfly Bomb. *See* **Cluster bomb**

BYMS. *See* **Motor Minesweeper**

C

C4. *See* **Explosives**

C-47 Skytrain   AIRCRAFT

The Douglas C-47 Skytrain, also known as the Dakota, was one of the least glamorous but undoubtedly most important **aircraft** of World War II. The secrets of the Skytrain's success were numbers, versatility, and reliability. Descended from the commercial DC-1 prototype, which first flew in 1933, and the DC-3, which was in commercial use from 1936, it was purchased by the U.S. Army from 1940. Built at Long Beach and Tulsa, this all-metal light alloy plane was powered by twin Wasp engines and served in a variety of military transport and **glider**-tug roles. It was capable of 229 mph and had a load-carrying capacity of 6,000 lb. About 11,000 were made. Versions were also produced in Russia, and later Japan. Among its important contributions were delivering 60,000 Allied glider, paratroop, and other personnel to Normandy in a three-day period in June 1944, and the supplying of jungle operations by air drop.

In Vietnam C-47s were converted to AC-47 gunships for ground attack during 1965 and 1966. In this role they carried three **Gatling type** "minigun" pods. The C-47 was still in use as late as the 1980s.

Additional Reading: Bickers, *Airlift*, 1998.

C-97 Stratofreighter   AIRCRAFT

The C-97 was a military cargo or troop-carrying **aircraft** based on the B-29 bomber, with a double-lobed fuselage for high capacity. Flying in experimental form by 1944 it soon proved capable of shifting large quantities of supplies. The production version, active from 1949, featured outboard wing fuel tanks for increased range. It was also produced as a KC-97 tanker variant; 888 craft were produced between 1947 and 1958.

C-130. *See* **Hercules**

Cactus. *See* **Crotale**

Caltrop; Caltrap; Calthrop; Tribulus
                                               OBSTACLE

The caltrop is a defensive device that was in existence before Christ and has been used intermittently ever since. It consists of four limbs or spikes so arranged that a sharp point is always facing upward. Strewn in numbers, it can form a serious obstacle to infantry or cavalry. In the Roman variation the tribulus was reduced to a single spike attached to a piece of wood. Machine-finished steel caltraps were used in the World War I, and large versions were used as beach defenses in World War II. Similar devices are still used, especially to damage the tires of vehicles.

Camel. *See* **Sopwith**

Camouflage   DETECTION

The disguise and concealment of men and war material to avoid the attention of the enemy is one of the oldest military sciences. It has been suggested, for example, that the wearing of animal skins in prehistory was an early use of camouflage. Covered traps were certainly used against men as well as animals, and there is specific reference in Shakespeare to the use of foliage to cover the movement of troops. Nevertheless, use of camouflage in ancient, medieval, and early modern warfare was sporadic, since the weapons and tactics often required large bodies of troops to maneuver close to the enemy. In such circumstances the value of camouflage was limited.

With the advent of **rifles** and widespread skirmishing, personal concealment became a more practical proposition. During the eighteenth century green and grey uniforms were adopted by skirmish troops, particularly in America, Prussia, and Britain. Khaki and grey uniform made further advances in nineteenth-century colonial wars, aided by the discovery of cheap and fast chemical dye processes. Most major powers had adopted "service" uniforms of these colors by the outbreak of World War I.

Camouflage came of age from 1914. Scenic artists applied their skills to screens, netting, dummy trees, and sandbags. Green canvas splattered with different-colored paints created some of the first "disruptive patterns." In the French instance the repertoire included simulated dead bodies of horses and men, designed to conceal observation and **snipers.** Dummy heads and figures were used to attract snipers or to fool the enemy into thinking that an attack was coming. Face blacking was adopted by raiders. In the U.S. case complete battalions of camouflage troops would be formed.

Blotched patterns used by the Germans led eventually to the famous "lozenge" pattern camouflage of 1918 in which geometric patches of rust brown, ochre, and green were divided by finger-wide strips of black paint. Snow camouflage suits were in existence as early as 1917. At sea, "dazzle" paint was applied to ships in bold geometric patterns. This was not intended to conceal the vessel but to confuse the enemy as to its size, orientation, distance, and type.

From then, camouflage and concealment has been a regular part of military training the world over. Helmet nets and printed camouflage fabrics were widely used in World War II, and the increasing use of long-range **aircraft** led to civilian installations, such as factories,

being camouflaged. The lighting of fires, flooding of fields, and painting of roofs were just three of the major methods used to disorient air crews. An interesting U.S. experiment of the period was "Yahoody the Impossible," which involved brightly illuminating aircraft so they did not appear black against a bright sky. Black camouflage was applied to night fighters and bombers, and scientific research was applied to the nature of black—and which types of black were most compatible with night.

From World War II the advent of **infrared, radar,** heat, and other types of sensor have led to a battle to conceal what is already invisible to the naked eye. Modern camouflage netting may not only be fireproof but have chlorophyll-mimicking properties and textures designed specifically to match the environment. Camouflage patterns for clothing and materials may be varied to match the terrain and the season, "urban" camouflages of greys and blacks being applied to vehicles as well as uniform.

Additional Reading: Hartcup, *Camouflage*, 1979; Sowinski & Walkowiak, *United States Navy Camouflage of the World War II*, 1976; Hodges, *Royal Navy Camouflage*, 1973; Stanley, *To Fool a Glass Eye: Camouflage versus Photoreconnaissance in World War II*, 1998.

Campania, HMS WARSHIP

Launched as an 18,000-ton liner in 1892, the British *Campania* was the largest merchantman converted to **aircraft carrier** service during the First World War, for which purpose she was commissioned in 1915. Fitted with a launching ramp and capable of carrying six aircraft, she also had a plane specially made for her use. This "Fairey Campania," a patrol seaplane launched from a trolley system, first flew in 1917. The *Campania* was lost following collision in November 1918.

Cannon. *See* **Artillery**

Cannonball, D-40 MISSILE

Developed in 1952, the Cannonball was an experimental U.S. Army guided missile project.

As the name suggests, the missile was spherical. It flew at a relatively leisurely 280 mph and was guided by a joystick, depositing upward of 50 lb of **explosive** on the target. The ball was powered by a main jet and stabilized by smaller jets.

Additional Reading: Weeks, *Men against Tanks*, 1975.

Captain Class   WARSHIP

The 78 Captain class **frigates** commissioned into the Royal Navy in 1943 and 1944 were in fact U.S.-built ships previously categorized as *Evarts* and *Buckley*-class **destroyer** escorts. Some had actually been launched and given names in the U.S. Navy prior to transfer. Hence it was, for example, that the USS *Wintle* became HMS *Capel*, while USS *Bull* became HMS *Bentinck*.

With various propulsion systems, the Captains were capable of between 20 and 24 knots; they were armed primarily for anti submarine work. They were equipped with Type 144 **Asdic, depth charges, hedgehog**, and 3-inch guns. While they entered service relatively late in the Second World War, they were successful in their task, sinking 36 **U-boats**.

Additional Reading: Collingwood, *The Captain Class Frigates*, 1998.

Captor. *See* Torpedo

Carbine   FIREARM

Now commonly understood to mean a light shoulder arm shorter than a normal rifle, the meaning of the word "carbine" has shifted subtly over the last three centuries. Like the **dragon**, the carbine was initially the weapon of mounted troops, being easier to handle on horseback than longer weapons. The term was thus applied to weapons like the U.S. **Sharps** carbine. By the twentieth century the carbine was more widespread, the name being applied to the German **K98k** and to **semiautomatics** such as the **M1**. In British usage the term "machine carbine" was also applied to **submachine guns** such as the Sten.

Cargo Carrier T16. *See* Bren Carrier

Cargo Projectile. *See* Cluster Bomb

Carl Gustav M2. *See* Recoilless Guns

Carrack   WARSHIP

First mentioned in English in the midfourteenth century, the carrack was a large wooden vessel, thought to be the result of a fusion of northern and southern European sailing technologies. It was deep hulled and frequently three masted. When used as warships, as in the case of the *Mary Rose*, carracks could have considerable complements of guns and crew. The fighting power consisted of both archers and small arms on the decks, as well as **artillery** fired through ports on the sides.

Additional Reading: Gardiner (ed), *Cogs, Caravels and Galleons*, 1994; Hutchinson, *Mediaeval Ships and Shipping*, 1994.

Carro Veloce CV33 Tankette   TANK

The Italian Carro Veloce CV33 was a two-man small **tank**, or "tankette." Its design was originally based on that of the Carden-Loyd carrier (See **Bren carrier**). Produced from 1933 it mounted two **machine guns**, had a top speed of 26 mph, and carried armor of 15 mm. A slightly improved CV35 appeared in 1935. Total production, including command, **flamethrower**, bridging, and other variants, was about 2,500. Though its flimsy protection was rudely exposed as early as the Spanish Civil War, it went on to fight in North Africa and even in Russia in World War II; Allied tanks made short work of them.

Additional Reading: Riccio, *Italian Tanks and Fighting Vehicles of World War II*, 1975.

Carronade   ARTILLERY

Introduced in the 1770s, the carronade was a relatively short, large-bored piece of **artillery** usually mounted on ships. However authorities, have pointed out that the idea of what was effectively a "naval **howitzer**" was not new, since short, wide-bored ship's guns had been in use for over a hundred years at that date. The name came from that of the Carron company of Falkirk, Scotland, but use of the weapon was widespread. The Dutch navy, for example, not only carried carronades but developed a "**rifled** carronade" in the 1860s. One nickname connected with carronades is "the Smasher."

Cartridge AMMUNITION

The cartridge, or case containing the charge for a gun, has been in existence for much longer than is commonly assumed, being in regular use with **artillery** by the middle sixteenth century. The earliest examples were of cloth or paper, hence the term "cartridge paper." Cartridge-making materials featured among ships' stores, and in 1578 William Bourne was able to remark that the use of cartridges was by far the best way to load a gun. Initially cartridges were not manufactured and filled centrally but made up by ships' crews or garrison gunners. By period of the English Civil Wars, 1642–1651, individual charges of **gunpowder** for small arms were frequently wrapped in paper, and artillery cartridges were beginning to be supplied complete.

Artillery cartridges of the period were fed whole into the piece, followed by the ball, rammed tight enough to prevent air gaps. A reamer was pushed through the touch hole to pierce the cartridge. As John Vernon's "Young Horseman" of 1644 noted, cartridges for muskets were bitten or ripped open before the powder was tipped in, followed by the ball and paper, which, when rammed, served as wadding. Though there were minor modifications in terms of the cartridge wrapping for certain arms, this continued to be the essential picture from the later seventeenth century to the early nineteenth.

Rapid advances were made from 1812, when Swiss national Samuel J. Pauly (1766–1820) patented a cartridge that incorporated a metal base within which was a cavity for detonating powder and a striker. Though not immediately adopted by the military, it was the starting point for many new ideas. Frenchman Clement Pottet

took the theme a stage farther in 1829 with a design for a metal cartridge with either a depression in the base for a fulminate **explosive** initiator or a nipple for a **percussion** cap. In the 1830s Casimir Lefaucheux (1802–1852) experimented with a "pin fire" cartridge system in which a percussion cap inside the cartridge case was hit by a pin, which was struck by the hammer of the gun. This was actually used in the French 1858 Navy **revolver** and during the American Civil War. A cartridge with priming in the rim of the base was patented in 1846, thus beginning the development of what came to be known as "rim fire" cartridges, now commonly associated with **Smith and Wesson**.

The development of reliable metal cartridges with "center fire," or primers in the middle of the base, in the period 1855–1870 helped make possible the appearance of modern magazine **rifles** and **machine guns**. Important in the development of the modern cartridge were Englishman Charles Lancaster (1820–1878), who produced a drawn metal cartridge in 1854, and American G. W. Morse (1812–1888) who obtained a series of patents between 1856 and 1858. The French Schneider cartridge with a paper upper and a brass head, perfected in 1858, became the basis of the shotgun **shell**.

Ultimately the brass center-fire cartridge was perfected in two slightly different forms by Colonel E. M. Boxer and Colonel H. Berdan, who finalized their designs on each side of the Atlantic by 1866. In the Boxer cartridge there is a cap in the base, which is crushed against a plate called the "anvil." In the Berdan version there is a dome in the base. On a larger scale, brass one-piece "fixed" cartridges were adopted for field guns during the last decade of the nineteenth century. Though bagged charges would remain in use for the largest pieces, including many naval guns, the large cartridge or "shell case" would make "quick-firers" possible and make **ammunition** handling in battle far easier.

Though there have been many further developments, these have been mainly in the field of bullets, **shells**, and propellants rather than the body of the cartridge. However, trials in recent years have shown a particular interest in caseless rounds and various plastic cartridges. While the latter have proved useful under certain circumstances, truly caseless rounds have proved problematic for military use due to fouling and the difficulty of producing an explosive tough enough to work in gun mechanisms yet work cleanly and predictably. One other concept that recurs from time to time is that of "telescoped ammunition," in which the bullet rests within the propellant rather than sitting in the end of the cartridge case.

Additional Reading: Smith (ed), *British Naval Armaments*, 1989; Blair (ed) *Pollard's History of Firearms*, 1983; Brown, *The Big Bang*, 1998; Temple, *WWI Armaments and the .303 British Cartridge*, 1995; Hoyem, *The History and Development of Small Arms Ammunition*, 1981; Allsop and Toomey, *Small Arms*, 1999; Hawkins, *Treatise on Ammunition*, 1887; War Office (UK), *Small Arms Ammunition*, 1944; Sellier and Kneubuehl, *Wound Ballistics*, 1994.

Case Shot; Canister Shot   AMMUNITION

Case or canister shot, at some periods divided into "heavy" and "light," was a container of many smaller projectiles fired from an artillery piece. The container broke open as it cleared the barrel, showering the enemy like a huge **shotgun**. Devastating at close range, case shot was seldom useful at more than about 400 yards. The main reason for this was the rapid dispersion—according to one calculation, about 32 feet per hundred yards of range. Case shot is known to have been in use by the seventeenth century.

Grape shot, sometimes confused with case shot, was somewhat different. Grape shot were enclosed in canvas, or wired together, perhaps on a wooden base. Usually the individual shot were larger than in a case shot, 2 lb balls being used, for example, in a 24 lb grape round. Grape shot were commonly used sea rather than on land.

Additional Reading: Hughes, *Firepower*, 1974; Blackmore, *Ordnance*, 1976.

Catalina   AIRCRAFT

The U.S. twin-engined Consolidated PBY Catalina **aircraft** first flew in 1935. It became arguably the most ubiquitous Allied flying boat of World War II. Variants were built in Canada and the Soviet Union; a total of about 4,000 were produced. Though slow, it had a very useful 2,500-mile range, and it was interesting in that it landed on its hull, the wing tips having stabilizing floats that folded away in flight, thus reducing drag. Wheeled landing gear, fitted from 1939, allowed the Catalina to operate as an amphibian from land and sea.

Additional Reading: Creed, *PBY: The Catalina Flying Boat*, 1986; Donald, *American Warplanes of World War II*, 1995.

Catapult; Ballista; Mangonel; Trebuchet   CATAPULT

Catapults, or projectile-throwing engines, were known to the ancients. Very destructive but cumbersome to move, they were a staple of siege warfare. Arguably the earliest was the *gastraphetes*, or belly bow, an oversized **crossbow** of ancient Greece. This line of development would be continued on a larger scale with ground mounted *ampurius* or scorpions, and the later ballista—which were also bows, tensioned by a variety of mechanical means. In the mangonel, a beam was drawn back and locked while loaded with a missile. It was then released, allowing the power of a torsioned skein of ropes or hair to flip it to the vertical, releasing the projectile.

In a distinctively different family of machines, leverage was used to telling effect. The counterweight trebuchet, in use by the twelfth century, had a long arm pivoted between uprights. The longer end of the beam was held down, and a sling at its tip was loaded with the projectile. The shorter end, weighted with a container of stone or earth, was allowed to descend suddenly, whipping the projectile into the air. Modern experiment has determined that given sufficient time this could be done with sufficient range and accuracy to demolish sections of castle wall. Catapults did not end with the introduction of **gunpowder**, as **artillery** and mechanical engines coexisted for over two centuries.

Catapult weapons had a remarkable period of revival during the First World War when they were used to throw bombs and **grenades** into enemy trenches. The French "grasshopper" of 1914 was a light version of the old crossbow-type machines, capable of flinging a bomb about 100 meters. The Y-shaped wooden Leech catapult, manufactured by Gamages for the British army, used a sling of rubber springs to store its motive power. The West Spring Gun of 1915 was the most elaborate of the trench catapults to see widespread deployment; it had a "battery" of metal springs to jerk its long throwing arm. Others, which reached only the experimental stage, included complex centrifugal throwers powered by engines. Trench **mortars** replaced most of this bizarre equipment by early 1916. Since then catapults have resurfaced only briefly as weapons of guerrilla and clandestine warfare—a handheld model, for example, having featured among the weaponry of the U.S. Office of Strategic Services in World War II.

Additional Reading: Nicolle, *Medieval Siege Engines*, 2002; Kern, *Ancient Siege Warfare*, 1999; Gravett, *Medieval Siege Warfare*, 1990; Bradbury, *The Medieval Siege*, 1992; Connelly, *Greece and Rome at War*, 1981; Marsden, *Greek and Roman Artillery*; Saunders, *Weapons of the Trench War*, 1999.

Caterpillar, D7. *See* **Rome Plough**

Centurion Tank   TANK

The British Centurion **tank** was developed at the end of World War II and was in service by 1949. Though retired from frontline duty in Britain after the appearance of the **Chieftain**, it continued to serve with other nations, notably Israel. During its life it has been progressively rearmed, its original 17-pounder gun being replaced by first a 20-pounder, then a 105 mm.

With maximum armor of 152 mm and a top speed of 22 mph the Centurion has proved a successful and durable design.

***Ceres* Class**   WARSHIP

The five British *Ceres*-class **cruisers** were an improved subgroup of the C class. They were laid down in 1916 and completed between June 1917 and February 1918. They were 4,300-ton ships, mounting five 6-inch guns, with armor up to three inches thick. Three were lost in World War II: *Curlew* in the 1940 Norwegian campaign; *Coventry*, damaged while covering the Tobruk raid of 1942 and then scuttled; and *Curacoa*, accidentally rammed and sunk by the *Queen Mary*.

Cessna   MANUFACTURER

U.S. aviation pioneer Clyde Cessna built his first **aircraft** in 1911, and the Cessna Aircraft Company was founded in 1927. Though the firm is better known for commercial planes, a number of Cessna designs have seen military applications over the years. The twin-engined T-50 of 1939 and its variants, for example, saw uses as trainer, ferry, and light transport.

Chaff   DETECTION

Originally code-named "window," chaff was invented during World War II to confuse **radar**. Consisting of thin strips of aluminum, it was dropped from **aircraft**, giving false radar echoes. The size and shape of the pieces could be varied to give specific effects against radars of specific frequencies. Its use has continued to the present day, one of the major manufacturers being Chemring. It is now projected as well as dropped. Chaff systems used by U.S. forces in recent decades have included bulk dispensers, projectors that shoot out both flares and chaff, and machines that make preprogrammed drops or random ejections in automatic response to the detection of enemy radar. In some instances the chaff is automatically cut to different lengths onboard aircraft in flight.

Chaffee, M24 Light Tank   TANK

With the U.S. **Stuart** light tank out of date and outgunned, efforts were made to find a replacement. The Ordnance Department, working with Cadillac, produced a pilot that mounted a light 75 mm gun developed from an aircraft cannon. The armor was only 25 mm, but it was well sloped, and the modest 18-ton weight was rewarded with good maneuverability and a 35 mph maximum speed. The Chaffee first saw action during the battle of the Bulge and was also used in Korea, as well as by other countries.

Additional Reading: Forty, *United States Tanks of World War II*, 1983.

Chain Mail; Ring Mail. *See* Armor

Challenger Tank, 1 and 2   TANK

The Challenger main battle **tank** is currently the main equipment of British armored regiments. The Challenger 1 entered service in 1984, and despite early poor publicity it went on to serve with distinction in the Gulf War of 1991. A particularly neat trick achieved with its 120 mm was shooting right through Iraqi tanks at targets hidden behind them. Good night sights allowed Challengers to lurk out of view picking off targets safe from retaliation.

Such success led to the acceptance of the Challenger 2, developed by Vickers Defence. This has second-generation Chobham armor and a V12 diesel engine giving a 35 mph road speed. The L30 chrome-plated 120 mm gun is capable of firing dense depleted-uranium projectiles and is controlled and stabilized electrically. A **McDonnell Douglas** chain gun and a **machine gun** complete the armament.

Chaparral (MIM-72A)   MISSILE

The development of the Chaparral surface-to-air close-defense weapons system began in 1965. It uses four **Sidewinder** missiles mounted on a launcher, which can be fired by one man once the system has been set up. After 1978 Chaparral was used with **radar** guidance.

Char (French for "tank") *See* Tank

Char B1 Heavy Tank   TANK

The French Char B heavy **tank** was the result of development during the 1920s when General Jean Baptiste Estienne solicited designs for a vehicle capable of carrying a 75 mm hull-mounted gun. The original Char B, as completed about 1930, weighed 24.6 tons and was fitted with four **machine guns** in addition to the 75 mm. In the more familiar Char B1 "*bis,*" which entered service in 1936, a 47 mm gun was mounted in the turret, while the machine guns were reduced to two.

Though slow, at a maximum speed of 17 mph, the Char B had 60 mm armor that was capable of stopping most antitank guns of 1940. It was fitted with both electric and compressed-air starting, and had a novel gyroscopic direction indicator. Its relative ineffectiveness against the German blitzkrieg is therefore usually explained by the way in which it was used and by the fact that its small, one-man turret left the commander trying simultaneously to load and fire a gun while directing the tank. Nevertheless the Germans found captured Char Bs useful enough for training, fitting them with **flamethrowers** and **howitzers**, and other specialized gear.

Chariot   VEHICLE

Essentially an animal-pulled cart developed for battle, the chariot is of considerable antiquity, early existing examples having been discovered amongst the grave goods of the Egyptian pharaohs. Chariots were widespread, being popular in Persia, India, and Rome, as well as with the Celtic tribes of Western Europe. According to Diodorous, Roman war chariots were commonly pulled by two horses and were crewed by a driver and a soldier. Celtic chariots were relatively long and narrow, with the warrior positioned behind the driver.

Chariot (Naval). *See* Maiale

Chassepot   FIREARM

Antonie A. Chassepot (1833–1905), an employee of the St. Thomas d'Aquin artillery works, was the inventor of the famous **breech-**

loading rifle adopted by France in 1866. It was similar to the **Dreyse** but in some ways superior. One particular advantage was the form of the **cartridge**, which had the primer at the base, allowing for a shorter firing pin. A good seal was provided by a rubber disc, though this needed frequent changing. The Gras rifle of 1874, designed by Captain Basile Gras (1836–1904), had an improved barrel and breech mechanism to fire the latest **cartridges** but was essentially an update of the Chassepot.

Additional Reading: Walter, *Dictionary*, 2001.

Chauchat Automatic Rifle   FIREARM

Variously referred to as a machine **rifle**, automatic rifle, or light **machine gun**, the French Chauchat is an example of a very good idea that went horribly wrong. A number of weapons were developed by Captain Louis Chauchat and armorer Charles Sutter at the Atelier de Construction de Puteaux from 1903 onward. By 1913 they had what appeared to be a practical and simple machine weapon, and a few of these early Chauchat-Sutter Fusils Mitrailleur were used in **aircraft**. Given the shortage of machine guns and the fact that the Chauchat was light and appeared to offer the possibility of automatic "walking fire" going forward with the troops, it was decided to produce a 1915-model CSRG in large numbers.

This should have been a major coup, especially since the latest Chauchat was fabricated from very cheap and modern stampings and tubings. The result, however, was a nightmare that was not ergonomic, was prone to mechanical failure, and frequently smacked its user in the face with its recoil during firing. The version converted to fire U.S. .30–06 ammunition was even less effective.

Additional Reading: Bruce, *Machine Guns of World War I*, 1997.

Chemical Weapons. *See* Gas

Chemico Armor   ARMOR

The British Chemico body shield was one of many **armors** used in World War I. First man-

ufactured by the County Chemical Company of Birmingham about 1916, it was a heavily padded waist coat weighing about 6 lb. Its many layers included cotton, linen, and silk. It was able to stop low-velocity fragments and even some pistol bullets.

Additional Reading: Dean, *Helmets and Body Armor*.

Chetak. *See* Alouette

Chieftain Tank   TANK

Claimed to be the best armored **tank** of its generation, the British Chieftain entered service in 1967. About 900 were made at Leeds and Elswick. With the driver in a semireclined position and a flat cast turret, height was reduced to nine feet six inches. The gun was a powerful **rifled** 120 mm. Enhanced armor, code-named "Stillbrew," was fitted in 1986. Variants included a bridge layer and recovery vehicle. Perhaps the weakest part of the system was the engine, though after initial problems a respectable 30 mph road speed was achieved. Chieftains were later replaced by the **Challenger**.

Additional Reading: Norman, *Chieftain and Leopard*, 1971; Hilmes, *Main Battle Tanks: Developments in Design since 1945*, 1987; Dunstan, *The Chieftain Tank*, 1989; Foss, *Jane's Main Battle Tanks*, 1983.

Chi-Ha, Type 97   TANK

The Type 97 Chi-Ha medium tank was a Mitsubishi-designed machine that entered Japanese service in 1938. It was originally armed with a short-barreled 57 mm gun, but this was later changed to a longer, higher-velocity, 47 mm in the two-man turret. Powered by a 12-cylinder diesel engine at the rear, the Chi-Ha had a maximum speed of 24 mph and a maximum armor of 25 mm.

Chinook (CH-47); Sea Knight (CH-46)   HELICOPTER

The tandem-rotor Chinook **helicopter** has been in widespread use as a military load carrier for

40 years. Its earliest ancestor was the banana-shaped, two-rotor machine produced by Frank Piasecki's P-V Engineering Forum as early as 1945. P-V was renamed Vertol in 1956, and **Boeing** purchased the company in 1960. The first Chinook, the YHC-1B, appeared in 1961. The Chinook saw combat use in Vietnam; remarkably, one machine is reputed to have carried as many as 147 refugees in a single lift. Used by many nations, the basic design also serves as the base for several variants. Closely related to the Chinook is the Sea Knight, which was also under development by Vertol at the time of its takeover. Having won a design competition for an assault helicopter for the Marine Corps, it first flew in 1962. Over 600 were manufactured between 1964 and 1990. The Sea Knight has a top speed of 165 mph and can carry 17 troops in addition to three crew.

Chlorine   CHEMICAL WARFARE

Chlorine was the first **gas** used in quantity as a chemical weapon—by the Germans in April 1915. Acting primarily on the respiratory system, it choked and ultimately "drowned" its victims if a lethal dose was inhaled. Its deployment was no doubt facilitated by the fact that it was already known to industry and could be transported in liquid form in cylinders readily adaptable for use in war. It was widely used in gas attacks, creating distinctive greenish yellow clouds. Known to the Allies by the designation "Red Star," it could also be combined with **phosgene**.

Additional Reading: Hartcup, *The War of Invention: Scientific Developments, 1914–1918*, 1988; Haber, *The Poisonous Cloud*, 1986.

Christie   MANUFACTURER

U.S. engineer J. Walter Christie started his automotive career with a company for motorizing fire engines, and later motorized gun carriages and ultimately **self-propelled artillery**. He turned to **tank** design, producing his first innovative design in 1919. Though ultimately unsuccessful, it included such novel features as

sprung tracks and a barbette mounting for the gun.

In 1928 he produced what would later become known in U.S. service as the T3 tank. This innovative vehicle incorporated many new technological ideas and in a number of respects anticipated what would later become regarded standard tank features. Perhaps most remarkable was the suspension and the removable tracks, which allowed the tank to be run on large rubber-tired wheels on the road. The **Liberty tank** engine, originally designed for a much heavier vehicle, propelled the medium T3 at previously unobtainable speeds.

Though Christie produced few tanks, and these did not prove reliable, his ideas were widely influential. Britain and Poland expressed an immediate interest, but it is arguably in the USSR that the greatest impact was felt. Here the Christie tank became the BT-1, impacting not only on the design of a generation of Soviet light tanks but ultimately on that of the **T-34**.

Churchill Tank   TANK

Designed in the wake of the British army's retreat from Dunkirk, the Churchill **tank** first appeared in 1941. Though early models featured a 3-in **howitzer** in the hull, the turret gun was a relatively inadequate 2-pounder, and the engine was unsatisfactory, giving only 16 mph. Perhaps the best part was the armor, over 102 mm on early models, rising to a maximum of 152 mm on the Marks VII and VIII. Late models also had better turret armament, including a 75 mm or 6-pounder. Special types included bridging, flamethrowing "Crocodiles," and bunker-busting engineer models.

Additional Reading: Anon, *Churchill Tank: Vehicle History and Specification*, 1983.

CIRD. *See* **Flail**

Claymore. *See* **Sword, and Mine**

Cleveland Class   WARSHIP

The *Cleveland* class of light cruisers was numerically one of the most important in the U.S.

Navy in World War II. The series commenced with the *Cleveland* (CL 55), laid down at New York Shipbuilding in 1940; the final vessel was the *Dayton*, completed in January 1945. Despite cancelations and the completion of some of the hulls as much-needed light **aircraft carriers**, 27 *Cleveland*-class ships would sail. The basic design was 610 feet long, about 12,000 tons, and had a main armament of 12 6-inch guns. Interesting features included a triple bottom against mines and heavy antiaircraft armament. Nevertheless, the *Clevelands* were not the most stable vessels.

The *Cleveland* herself served in the Pacific, Mediterranean, and South China Sea during World War II, being finally sold off in 1960. Some of the class, notably *Pasedena, Springfield, Topeka, Providence, Amsterdam, Portsmouth, Wilkes-Barre*, and *Atlanta* (CL 104), survived into the 1970s. *Galveston* was interesting in that she was completed but not commissioned during the war, being later reworked, like certain others of the *Cleveland* class, as a guided missile cruiser. *Oklahoma City* served with the Naval Air Warfare Center Weapons Division until comparatively recently and was still afloat in the 1990s. *Little Rock* was towed to Buffalo, New York, in 1977 to become a museum ship.

Additional Reading: Friedman, *US Cruisers*, 1985.

CLGP. *See* Copperhead

Club. *See* Mace; Trench Club

Cluster Bomb; Cluster Munition
AMMUNITION

Cluster munitions contain many small bombs or bomblets and may be designed for use against personnel, armor, or other targets. They can be air dropped or fired using **artillery, mortars**, or rockets. The idea is by no means new, having seen experimental application in the nineteenth century. In one of the first practical uses, British Livens projectors of World War I were used with a special round that contained **Mills bombs**. By World War II many applica-

tions had been found for the general principle, as, for example in large German bomb cases that split open to shower enemy positions with smaller "butterly bombs."

In the United States, research after World War II led to the production of "cargo projectiles." By the 1960s these were in general service for use against personnel and armor; they survive as Dual-Purpose Improved Conventional Munitions (DPICMs). Some of the most advanced cargo munitions, such as the Israeli M85, contain an integral self-destruct mechanism that sets them off if not exploded on impact. This has the dual advantage of maximizing their effect while reducing the chances of accidental injuries after conflicts have ceased.

Air-dropped cluster bombs are of considerable diversity and may scatter delayed-action devices or **mines**, as well as bomblets. Particularly widespread has been the U.S. ISC Technologies Rockeye cluster bomb, which first entered service in the 1970s and has been used with many different aircraft, including the French **Mirage** and British Jaguar, as well as U.S. types. The 500 lb Rockeye II Mark 20 was capable of very low-level delivery and contained 100 lb of explosive in 247 dual-purpose bomblets. Its impact pattern would be altered by the speed and altitude of delivery, though a typical low-level dispersal spread the munitions over 2,700 square meters of ground.

Cog
WARSHIP

The cog was a general-purpose medieval wooden vessel with a large square sail; early examples are tentatively dated to seventh-century Germany. By 1200 they were common and the major sailing ship of northern Europe. In later examples a stern rudder replaced the original steering oar. Raised structures, or "castles," were also added fore and aft, providing fighting platforms. Though the expression "stern castle" has virtually died out, "forecastle," or fo'c'sle, survives as a description of the fore part of a ship under the main deck. Cogs were generally superseded by the larger **carrack**.

Colossus

Additional Reading: Gardiner (ed), *Cogs, Caravels and Galleons*, 1994; Hutchinson, *Mediaeval Ships and Shipping*, 1994.

Colossus   COMPUTATION

Collosus, the world's first programmable computer, was built at the General Post Office Research Centre at Dollis Hill, London, in 1943. It thus predated **ENIAC** by more than a year. Designed by Bletchley Park mathematician Max Newman, drawing on ideas from Alan Turing's so called "Universal Machine," it was produced to crack the German military's Lorenz cipher. As assembled by engineer Tommy Flowers, Colossus consisted of 1,500 electronic valves. It was considerably faster than the electromechanical relay switches of the **bombes** so far constructed for use against Enigma.

Additional Reading: Singh, *The Code Book*, 1999.

Colt   MANUFACTURER

Samuel Colt (1814–1862), of Hartford, Connecticut, was the son of a merchant. He had served as a seaman, but it was in his home town that he prevailed upon gunsmith Anson Chase to produce his prototype **revolver**. Though Colt both perfected and popularized the revolver, to the extent that his name is sometimes regarded as synonymous with that type of handgun, he did not invent it; revolving hand firearms had been in existence since the sixteenth century. Nevertheless Colt was a great showman and entrepreneur who made a significant technological step forward.

In 1835 he traveled to London obtaining patents for both a long arm and a revolver with folding trigger. French and U.S. patents followed. Arguably Colt's most important contribution was the idea of what he called a "lifter and ratchet" mechanism, turning the cylinder, which locked in the correct position behind the barrel. The Patent Arms Manufacturing Company of Patterson, New Jersey, was formed in 1836 and produced both the Paterson five-shot **percussion** revolvers and long arms to Colt's specifications. Yet business was slow, and the company failed in 1841.

The idea survived, however, and by 1847 Eli Whitney's factory was producing Walker Colt pistols, which had resulted from collaboration between Colt and Captain Samuel Walker of the Texas Rangers. Significantly, Whitney had been a pioneer of the manufacture of arms with interchangeable parts, which improved on practicality and decreased cost. Colt set up his own factory in Pearl Street, Hartford, in 1848, the same year he obtained a government order for **Dragoon** pistols.

The Pocket and Navy revolvers soon followed, and in 1851 Colt exhibited at the British Great Exhibition. A London works was set up in 1852, and two years later Charles Dickens marveled that not only could the Pimlico factory produce 600 weapons a week but that the workers were provided with heating, lighting, and bathing facilities. The English works soon closed, but Colt established a new manufactury on the Connecticut River near Hartford in 1855 that would be famous the world over. An early product was the Root-type revolver, a weapon with a solid frame, or top strap, connecting the barrel to the rear portion of the gun, devised by Colt employee E. K. Root. Though Colt died early in the Civil War, demand occasioned by the conflict would ensure the company's future.

Among the many revolvers produced by Colt over the next century were the famous .45 Peacemaker, the New Line, the Marine Corps .38 and .45, the New Service, the Official Police, and Police Positive. Yet the secret of continued success would be movement with the times and technology, and a widely sold **machine gun** was produced in 1895. Colt was abreast of **semi automatic** pistol development with its model of 1905, and its model 1911, also based on the **Browning** system, was a winner. The model 1911, originally produced in .45 caliber to use Colt Auto Pistol or ACP cartridges, was adopted as standard by the U.S. military and has been described as "a man stopper without parallel." There would be foreign models, including those of Norway and Argentina and versions in other calibers. The company would diversify further still during the later twentieth century, most notably as producer of the **M16 rifle**.

The Paterson Colt revolver. Samuel Colt's factory in the Old Gun Mill at Paterson New Jersey was opened in 1836 and closed in 1843. The Texas Paterson was a five shot .34 caliber arm with a concealed trigger. Courtesy of the Library of Congress.

Additional Reading: Ulrich, *A Century of Achievement 1836–1936*, 1936; Rosa, *Colt Revolvers*, 1988; Ezell, *Handguns of the World*, 1981; Moore, *Colt Single Action Army Revolvers*, 1999; Walter, *Dictionary of Guns and Gunmakers*, 2001.

Comanche, RAH-66　　　HELICOPTER

Developed during the 1990s, the **Boeing Sikorsky** (United Technologies) Comanche helicopter is billed by the manufacturer as the U.S. Army's "centerpiece for full spectrum dominance and total force protection" in the twenty-first century. While this is undoubtedly an overstatement of the potential of any weapon, the Comanche uses some interesting technology. Its **stealth**-influenced design avoids right angles,

has a folding undercarriage, and incorporates the tail rotor within the fuselage. The five-bladed composite rotor is of a bearingless type. A chin turret houses a 20 mm cannon, and load-bay doors double as missile pylons. The advanced avionics include flat screens, a moving map, and a wide-field-of-view **helmet**-mounted system.

Commando Armored Car　　　VEHICLE

Developed by Cadillac Gage in 1961, the U.S. Commando was a four-wheeled amphibious **armored car** powered by a Chrysler 361, 210 horsepower engine giving a top speed of 65 mph. There were several variants, including a personnel carrier, escort, and police vehicle.

Twin **machine guns** were mounted in turreted models. Supplied to the U.S. Army and Air Force in the mid-1960s, they saw extensive use in Vietnam.

Condor, Fw 200   AIRCRAFT

The German Focke-Wulf Condor was developed from 1936 primarily as a passenger **aircraft** and did indeed serve as a staff transport. Yet from 1940 the Fw-200C-3 found fame as a long-range maritime reconnaisance aircraft, being the ideal partner for **U-boats**. The Condor, with its 108-foot wingspan, was massive by standards of the day and capable of carrying 4,620 lb of bombs, but its main strength was its 2,210-mile range.

Additional Reading: Taylor, *Combat Aircraft of the World*, 1969.

Conger   MISCELLANEOUS

Made by the Chubb Company of Wolverhampton, in the United Kingdom, Conger was a **mine**-clearance device produced in 1944. It consisted of a 5-inch rocket projector and a long length of hose. The rocket was fired over the minefield dragging the hose behind it, and then the hose was pumped full of **explosive** using compressed air. When the explosive was detonated a path was cleared through the mine field.

Congreve, Sir William   INVENTOR

British artillery officer Sir William Congreve (1772–1828) invented a new gun for **frigates** but is best remembered for his pioneering work with rockets. These were first used as incendiaries but were later modified with explosive heads and deployed on the battlefield in rocket batteries. Moved by horses and fired from frames, Congreve rockets could achieve greater mobility than many artillery pieces. They saw action in small numbers at Leipzig in 1813 and in America. Though wildly inaccurate, Congreve rockets had a range of about 1,500 yards, great shock value, and were significant as inspiration for later rocket systems.

Constitution, USS   WARSHIP

The *Constitution*, launched in October 1797, is easily the oldest vessel on the U.S. Navy list. This warship, commonly described as a "heavy **frigate**" of 32 24-pounder guns and 20 32-pounder **carronades**, saw action in the War of 1812, gaining the nickname "Old Ironsides." Extensively restored from 1927 to 1930, it was further overhauled in 1992 to 1996. It actually took to sea again as part of its own bicentennial celebration in 1997.

Copperhead, M712   SHELL

As early as World War II the feasibility of guiding **artillery** rounds was considered, but the stresses of **shell** acceleration were found insurmountable. It was not until 1975 that the U.S. Martin Marietta Company was awarded a contract for the development of Cannon Launched Guided Projectiles, or CLGPs. The eventual result was Copperhead, a projectile with small flip-out wings and control fins, fired from 155 mm **howitzers**, and a HEAT (high-explosive antitank) warhead. With the target illuminated by the observer using a **laser**, Copperhead glides toward the target. Though used successfully in the Persian Gulf, Copperhead is no longer in production. A similar Russian device, the Krasnopol, carries a high-explosive head.

Corvette   WARSHIP

The name "corvette" is derived from that of a Spanish merchant vessel; nevertheless it was applied to small sailing warships during the eighteenth and nineteenth centuries. The American *General Pike*, for example, was a three-masted corvette 145 feet long armed with 28 24-pounder guns, launched in 1813.

By the twentieth century "corvette" was commonly used for fast naval escorts in the 500-to-700-ton range. The type remained popular with certain nations—hence, for example, the British *Flower*-class corvettes used in World War II. More recently, the 900-ton Soviet Grisha-class coastal antisubmarine vessel was rated as a corvette.

Additional Reading: Gardiner, *Line of Battle*, 1994.

Couronne   WARSHIPS

The name *Couronne* has been used for a number of French warships over the centuries. The most technologically significant was that laid down at Lorient in 1858 and now commonly regarded as the first iron-hulled **battleship**. Designed by Audenet, she was certainly a better ship than the more widely known *Gloire*. The 6,428-ton *Couronne* was of a sandwich construction, in which the four-inch-thick outer armor was backed with four inches of teak, then an iron lattice, then a further 11 inches of teak on top of the three-quarter-inch iron skin. Completed in 1862 she proved both seaworthy and durable. Undergoing several changes of armament during her life, she became a gunnery training ship in 1885 and was not finally broken up until 1934.

Crab. *See* Flail

Croatan (CVE 25). *See* Bogue

Crocodile. *See* Churchill Tank

Cromwell Tank   TANK

The British Cromwell **tank** first appeared in 1943. Despite a slow and often fraught development, it would prove a fast and popular machine. Nevertheless its armament, which varied from a 6-pounder to a 75 mm gun or 95 mm **howitzer**, was never on a par with that of the enemy.

Additional Reading: *Cromwell Tank*, 1983.

Crossbow   BOW

Known to have existed in China as long ago as the Han dynasty, about the time of Christ, the crossbow consisted of a **bow** mounted on a shaft, or "tiller." As with other bows, crossbows could be of composite materials. When the bow was drawn the string could be held back by a revolving nut or stop connected to a trigger, allowing the user to take aim. Crossbow projectiles are often referred to as bolts or quarrels, though some crossbows could shoot stones or lead balls.

While the longbow was superior in terms of speed and economy, the crossbow was accurate even in the hands of relatively untrained users and could offer mechanical advantages. These were most pronounced when a device was used to span the bow, which multiplied the muscular effort of the user. The Romans used a form of ratchet, while in the Middle Ages screws, belt hooks, pulleys, and windlasses were all known. The cranequin, which worked on a rack-and-pinion principle, was introduced in the fourteenth century.

Despite a papal ban, crossbows remained in military use until the sixteenth century. Since then there have been various small-scale experiments and special forces applications. At least two crossbow-type weapons were tried by the U.S. Office of Strategic Services in World War II. "Little Joe" was made of heat-treated aluminum, could be shot one-handed, weighed just over two pounds, and had a pistol-style grip and trigger. It was almost silent and claimed an accurate lethal range of 30 yards. The larger William Tell was a shoulder arm, with what was described as a "rubber propelling unit" to provide the power. It was intended to deal with sentries and guard dogs.

Additional Reading: Alm, *European Crossbows*, 1994; Payne-Gallwey, *The Crossbow*, 1990; Wilson, *Crossbows*, 1976; Melton, *OSS Special Weapons and Equipment*, 1991; Hall, *Weapons and Warfare in Rennaissance Europe*, 1997.

Crotale Missile   MISSILE

Also known as "Cactus," this close-range surface-to-air missile was developed by the French Matra company from 1964 to 1968. The primary customer for the weapon was South Africa. With a top speed of Mach 2.3, it could be used as close as 500 yards from the target, or as far as five miles. Its methods of target tracking included **infrared** locking, optical, and television. A battery consisted of four vehicles, three carrying a total of 12 of the nine-foot, five-inch-long missiles, the other a target acquisition radar. A more recent improved version is the Shahine.

Cruise Missile   MISSILE

First conceived in 1972, cruise missiles are subsonic weapons that fly like a conventional **aircraft** over much of their course. Where modern cruise missiles score substantially over their ancestors, like the **V1**, is in terms of launch methods, guidance systems, accuracy, and potential to carry a **nuclear** warhead. Cruise missiles are deemed particularly effective because they are difficult to detect, having a small cross-section and flying at low altitudes. Moreover, their turbofan engines emit relatively little heat, and their desirable characteristics can be enhanced by firing in batches. It was the nuclear capability that caused considerable protest on their deployment to Western Europe in the early 1980s.

There have been several distinct models in U.S. service, at least one of which is now obsolete. The two types now in use are the air-launched AGM-86 and the Tomahawk BGM-109 ship or submarine-launch weapon. The AGM-86 is 6.29 meters long, weighs 3,150 lb, and has a range of about 1,500 miles flying at 550 mph. The sea-based version is fractionally smaller and lighter with a range of 700 miles. A simpler Chinese version has a much shorter range still. The cost of a single U.S. missile is about $1.6 million.

When a cruise missile is launched, it receives an initial thrust from a detachable booster. Once it is airborne the stubby wings deploy, and the electronic systems are engaged; the Global Positional System (**GPS**) helps determine its situation. The missile now uses TERCOM, "terrain contour matching," to read the ground, comparing it against a three-dimensional route map provided by the U.S. National Imaging and Mapping Authority. Over the target, DSMAC, or "digital scene matching area correlation," confirms the point of impact, and the missile delivers 1,000 lb of **explosive**. An interesting variation reported in some sources is the ability to deploy a "lights out" warhead, which throws out spools of conductive fibers. These are useful for shorting out electric grids and power plant.

A figure of about 85 percent accuracy is claimed to within a few meters. The cruise mis-

The launch of a Tomahawk Cruise missile from the nuclear powered submarine USS *La Jolla* on the Pacific Missile Test Center range, April 1983. Courtesy of the Department of Defense.

sile is a fearsome weapon but not infallible, since it needs up-to-date, accurate, and specific data on which to be fired. The next generation is expected to be able to circle its target, sending back data. In the event of finding the primary target destroyed or abandoned the missile could then be reprogrammed to a new location.

Additional Reading: *Jane's Naval Weapons Systems, Various editions*; Webber et al., *Crisis over Cruise*, 1983.

Cruiser   WARSHIP

The cruiser is widely considered as the successor to the **frigate** of the age of sail, acting as a scout and protector to merchant shipping. The modern cruiser came into existence in the 1880s, with the British Admiralty taking the lead in developing "cruising ships" of steel, driven by screw propellers. It later produced several classes of what were called "protected cruisers." Though usually smaller than a true **battleship**, the cruiser is difficult to define in terms of size, since vessels as small as 2,600 tons have been regarded as cruisers, while at the other end of the scale pocket battleships, such as the German *panzerschiffe* ***Graf Spee, Scharnhorst***, and ***Gneisenau***, and the U.S.

Alaska have also been called "heavy cruisers" or "battle cruisers."

Amongst the first true cruisers were a series of ships produced by the firm of Elswick on the Tyne, supplied to countries as diverse as the United States, Japan, China, and Austria. France produced the well-protected 20-knot *Forbin* class in the mid-1880s. The German light cruiser *Gazelle* appeared in 1900, with a uniform battery of 10.5 cm guns, and ten similar ships were constructed by 1904. One of Germany's biggest cruisers was the 15,500-ton *Blücher* of 1909, often regarded as a "battle cruiser." Other major vessels included the *Roon, Yorck, Magdeburg*, and *Karlsruhe*. The *Breslau* and the battle cruiser *Goeben* were later used by Turkey. In addition to protected cruisers, Germany would ultimately construct 35 light cruisers by the time of the First World War.

Britain also continued building apace, producing about 90 ships of various cruiser classes by 1914. By the outbreak of World War I the United Kingdom would have by far the largest cruiser force. Among these the Town class, commenced in 1911, was particularly significant. Next in order of numbers was Germany, followed at some remove by France and Japan. New classes of cruiser commenced by the United Kingdom during the war included the *Caledon, Ceres, Carlisle,* **D**, and *Hawkins*. In the event, though cruiser-versus-cruiser actions did occur in World War I, the greatest losses would be to submarines and mines.

After 1918 there was an increasing use of oil firing, which the United Kingdom had used in the *Boaudicea* as early as 1909. There was also work with increasing boiler pressure, particularly in the United States and Germany. Despite international naval treaties that set strict limitations on battleships, cruisers were built in numbers around the world. The United States, which had built very few cruisers hitherto, now constructed a large force of her own, with the **Omaha** class being completed, and the beginning of the *Pensacola, Northampton, Portland,* **New Orleans, Brooklyn**, and *Wichita* classes between 1926 and 1936. This mirrored Japan, which had completed the *Nagara, Sendai, Yu-*

bari, and *Furutaka* classes by this time and was now working on the *Myoko,* **Takao, Mogami** and *Tone* classes.

In terms of scale, there was a marked diversification between light and heavy cruisers—which in practice tended to mount 6 and 8-inch guns, respectively. By the mid-1930s increasing concern over the potency of **aircraft** led to the fitting of greater antiaircraft armaments. In some classes, as, for example the Japanese *Takao*, it was intended that the main armament should be able to operate at high firing angles. In the British **Dido** class, antiaircraft work became the main role. In the United States the King Board resulted in a major drive to improve anti aircraft equipments, which were hastily added to most classes.

In World War II, Allied cruisers gained the hard-won upper hand, through technological advances such as **radar**, intelligence gleaned through **Enigma** and through industrial effort on the part of the United States, which had mastered the Japanese navy by 1944. Nevertheless Britain and the United States lost a total of 37 cruisers during 1939–1945, against 57 such enemy vessels. It was telling that the majority of these were sunk by **submarines** and aircraft.

After World War II, cruiser forces were drastically scaled down, with **aircraft carriers** seen as more important, particularly in the West. Many U.S. cruisers were put into reserve or sold to other countries. Nevertheless, the Soviet Union continued to build and plan, but not complete, 30 light cruisers under Admiral Sergei Gorshkov, the ten-year plan being commenced in 1946, with the **Sverdlov** completed in 1952. Guided missile cruisers specifically continued to have a place in the world's navies. The last cruiser to be sunk in action was the **General Belgrano**, in 1982.

Additional Reading: Whitley, *German Cruisers of World War II*, 1985; O'Brien, *Technology and Naval Combat*; Raven and Roberts, *British Cruisers of World War II*, 1980; Lacroix and Wells, *Japanese Cruisers of the Pacific War*, 1997; Rimington, *Fighting Fleets*, 1944.

CS. *See* **Gas**

Cuirass

Cuirass. *See* **Armor**

Curtiss; Hawk, Warhawk, Kittyhawk
MANUFACTURER/AIRCRAFT

The Curtiss Aeroplane and Motor Company established a relationship with the U.S. Army as early as 1914 with the supply of the JN, or Jenny, series. In the interwar period Curtiss-Wright, as the corporation had by then become, began to develop new monoplane fighter **aircraft**. In the 1935 Model 75, or Hawk, the company demonstrated a single-seat machine with such modern features as a retractable undercarriage and enclosed cockpit. Later versions included the refinement of wheels that swiveled to lie flush under the wing. A few were ordered, including some overseas purchases, the U.S. examples with Pratt and Whitney engines being known as the P-36.

A much more streamlined and elegant-looking P-40 Warhawk was developed from 1938 with a new powerplant. Over 13,700 Curtiss P-40s would be built in several slightly varying configurations for French, British, and Russian as well as U.S. service. Improved versions, of 1941 to 1944, included the Tomahawk and Kittyhawk. It is noteworthy that like the Bell **Airacobra**, the P-40 proved a relatively poor high-altitude performer and was best used in ground attack. Other of the many Curtiss machines of the period were the O-52 Owl observation plane, the Seamew, the Seahawk, the Seagull, the C-46 commando troop carrier, and the **Helldiver**.

Additional Reading: Johnsen, *P-40*, 1998; Dorr, *US Fighters of World War II*, 1991; Vader, *Pacific Hawk*, 1970.

CV33 Tankette. *See* **Carro Veloce CV33**

D

D3A. *See* **Val**

D-40. *See* **Cannonball**

D-Class Cruisers WARSHIP

The D class of British **cruisers** was laid down from 1916 to 1918 as a counter to new and more powerful German vessels. The basic design was an improvement on the existing C class, being a 5,000-ton ship with a main armament of six 6-inch guns, mounted in single-gun turrets, with a maximum armor of three inches. Eight ships were completed, with others canceled at the end of World War I. All had names beginning with D.

Danae and *Dragon* saw brief war service at the end of World War I, with others serving against revolutionary Russia in 1919. All eight were active in World War II: *Danae, Despatch,* and *Dragon* (as part of the Polish navy) all covered the Normandy landings, with *Durban* being sunk as a **Mulberry** breakwater. *Dragon* was damaged, then used as a breakwater. After several actions *Dunedin* was sunk by the *U-124.* The five ships that survived were scrapped in the late 1940s.

Dagger; Knife EDGED WEAPON

The short-bladed knife, or dagger, is an extremely old weapon, stone daggers having been identified from the neolithic period. It has been suggested that the dagger originated from detached **spear** heads, but given the antiquity of the stone hand **axe** and the early use of handheld thrusting weapons of bone and antler, this is likely to have been only one line of devel-

opment. During the Bronze Age, cast-metal daggers began to appear, and from thence a distinction may be made between longer **swords** and shorter daggers. By 1500 B.C. the Myceneans were making elaborately decorated bronze daggers of remarkable sophistication. Bronze, and later iron, daggers became part of the military equipment of many peoples. The *machaira* of the Greeks; the *sax,* or *scramasax,* of the Saxons; and the *kukri* of the Gurkhas were just three of the most significant.

With the development of **armor,** specialized daggers with strong, narrow points were developed. In Europe a particularly effective and long-lived design was the rondel dagger, with protective discs at either end of the grip. In the Middle Ages the dagger was used both by peasant conscripts and by the knightly classes, though in the latter case it was in a secondary role to the sword. During the sixteenth century a distinctive style of sword and dagger fighting emerged, with the dagger usually held in the left hand—hence the appearance of the so-called left-hand dagger. Some parrying daggers now acquired notched blades, allowing the enemy sword blade to be caught or even broken. Slender thrusting stilettos are also particularly associated with this period. The "gunner's stiletto" actually featured graduated marks on the blade so that it could be used as an impromptu measuring device.

By 1700 the usefulness of the dagger in European warfare was declining; firearms and the **bayonet** now predominated. In other parts, however, daggers continued to be significant. Just some of the many used by different ethnic groups around the world were the thrusting Indian *katar*, the Persian *kinjal*, the Khyber knife of the Afghans, and the traditional *kris* of the Malays. In Scotland the dirk remained a practical fighting weapon during the early eighteenth century, though it had become primarily ceremonial by the nineteenth. Distinctive types of knife and dagger were also used by Europeans in America, and of these the broad-bladed Bowie developed in the 1820s is best known. The Spanish *navaja*, with its folding blade, was popular in California.

The dagger underwent a dramatic revival during World War I, when trench knives were used for raiding. Important types included the German *Nahkampfmesser*, or close combat knife; the French "nail"; the thrust dagger, with its transverse grip; and the **knuckle dagger**. In World War II the fighting knife emerged as particular weapon of special forces, with the **F-S knife** the most influential pattern. Military survival knives also developed as a distinct class; some, issued to aircrew, were designed specifically for the cutting of **parachute** rigging lines. Ceremonial daggers were retained by certain nations, most notably Germany, which had a distinctive type for virtually every military and political organization.

Today there are numerous specialist knives in military use. These include the **machete**, diver's knives, survival knives, and combat patterns. Technological advances have been mainly in terms of the materials used, which may improve rust resistance, float, be nonreflective, or undetectable by X-ray, depending on the task to hand. Some types conceal additional tools within the handle, an idea explored by the Germans in World War II.

Additional Reading: Coe et al., *Swords and Hilt Weapons*, 1993; Hughes and Jenkins, *Primer of Military Knives*; Hughes, *German Military Fighting Knives*; Weland, *A Collectors Guide to Swords Daggers and Cutlasses*, 1991; Wallace, *Scottish Swords and Dirks*, 1970; Dufty, *European Swords and Daggers in the Tower of London*, 1974; Albaugh, *Confederate Edged Weapons*, 1960; Stone, *A Glossary of the Construction, Decoration and Use of Arms and Armor*, 1934; Stephens, *Fighting*

Knives, 1980; Stephens, *Edged Weapons of the Third Reich*, 1972.

Dakota. *See* C-47 Skytrain

Dauntless, SBD   AIRCRAFT

The Douglas SBD Dauntless is widely regarded as the most successful U.S. **dive-bomber aircraft** of World War II; it made a major contribution to the war in the Pacific. The Dauntless was inspired by the Northrop BT-1 of 1938 but incorporated many improvements. It was a two-seater, single-engine design, with dual controls, had a low cantilever wing configuration, and was of all-metal construction, excepting the control surfaces. Diving was facilitated by hyrdraulically activated air brakes, and an arresting hook was fitted for **aircraft carrier** operations. Its fuel tanks were self-sealing, being fitted with rubber liners. The Dauntless had a low stall speed of 78 mph and light responses, making it easy to fly. It was soon nicknamed the "Slow But Deadly." The plane was also cheap, reputedly costing only $85,000 to develop.

The SBD-1 Dauntless entered service with the Marine Corps in late 1940, with the improved models SBD-2, 3, 4, 5, and 6 following successively, for Navy and USMC use, as the war progressed. The U.S. Army also had an A-24 version, serving from 1941, which was similar to the SBD-3, and A-24A and B models, which approximated to the SBD-4 and 5. The SBD-3, delivery of which commenced in March 1941, had a wingspan of 41 feet 6 inches, weighed 6,345 lb empty, and was powered by a Wright 1000 horsepower engine giving a top speed of 245 mph level. The maximum bomb load was 1,200 lb, and four **machine guns** were fitted—two fixed .50-caliber and two .30-caliber operated by the gunner from the rear cockpit. The most common model, however, was the SBD-5, produced at the Tulsa plant; it began to arrive in May 1943. This featured a slightly more powerful engine and a better rate of climb. Total production of all Dauntless types was 5,936, of which about

30 survived in various states of preservation at the end of the century.

Additional Reading: Smith, *Douglas SBD Dauntless*, 1997; Tillman, *The Dauntless Dive Bomber of World War II*, 1976; Tillman and Lawson, *U.S. Navy Dive and Torpedo Bombers*, 2001.

Davis Gun. *See* **Recoilless Gun**

DCDI. *See* **Depth Charge**

DD. *See* **Duplex Drive**

Defiant   AIRCRAFT

The two-seater British Boulton Paul Defiant, which first flew in 1937, was one of the more unusual fighter **aircraft** of World War II. It had no fixed armament but mounted four .303 inch **machine guns** in a power-operated turret. When first used in action in May 1940 it had considerable surprise value, but when the enemy realized that it had no forward wing guns, many fell prey to head-on attack. The Boulton Paul Defiant was later fitted with **radar** and served as a night fighter.

Additional Reading: Brew, *Turret Fighters*, 2002; Clarke, *British Aircraft Armament*, 1993, 1994.

Defoliants. *See* **Agent Orange**

Degtyarev DP28; DPM   FIREARM

Designed by V. A. Degtyarev in the 1920s, the DP28 was an ungainly-looking light **machine gun** with a large flat, top-mounted, 49-round ammunition pan. The mechanism was gas operated, with a Kjellman-Friberg locking system. It was produced at the Tula arsenal from the 1930s. Despite appearances the Degtyarev was a robust design that had a minimum of moving parts and was easy to manufacture. A modified DPM model appeared in 1944, and the gun continued to be used long after World War II.

Additional Reading: *Jane's Infantry Weapons*; Barker and Walter, *Russian Infantry Weapons of World War II*, 1971; Walter, *Dictionary*, 2001.

Delta Class (I, II, III, and IV)
                                            SUBMARINE

Based on the old **Yankee** type, the Soviet Delta nuclear-powered **submarines** were first laid down in 1969. Eventually there would be four subtypes, progressively enlarged and improved to take new generations of ballistic missile. The Delta IV, construction of which commenced in 1981 and continued until 1992, is still current at time of writing, and the quietest of the group. Delta IVs are 544.5 feet in length with a surface displacement of 10,800 tons and a crew of 135. With a top speed of 24 knots they can dive to 1,000 feet. Armament includes Skiff ballistic missiles with 100-kiloton nuclear warheads, type 40 **torpedoes**, and the Starfish antisubmarine weapon.

Additional Reading: *Jane's Warships*; Jordan, *Soviet Submarines*, 1989.

Demologos. *See* **Battleship**

Depth Charge, Depth Bomb   EXPLOSIVE
                                            DEVICE

The depth charge is an **explosive** device, commonly large and cylindrical, used by ships and aircraft to attack **submarines**. As developed by the British for use against **U-boats** in 1915, they resembled oil drums and were rolled off the side or stern of the ship. They were set off by means of a hydrostatic valve, which enabled them to be detonated at preset depths. It was by no means necessary that the depth charge should hit the submarine, since pressure waves could crack hulls. From 1918 large low-velocity launchers were used to throw the charge well clear of the ship.

In World War II depth-charge technology was further improved, and a variety of weapons were employed. These included monster depth charges up to 3,000 lb in weight and smaller devices with greater ranges, such as **Hedgehog** and Squid. Submarines, on the other hand, now began to carry DCDI, or depth charge direction indicators, or **hydrophones** attached to lamp

Descubierta *Class*

systems to tell from which direction antisubmarine attacks were made.

Modern depth charges are sophisticated devices that can be fired from computer-controlled launch systems, often to ranges of 2,000 yards. The most destructive have nuclear payloads and have commensurately large killing zones. By 1990 the standard U.S. Navy nuclear depth bomb was the Mark 101, a 1200 lb weapon known as "Lulu," capable of being dropped from helicopters or fixed-wing aircraft.

Additional Reading: Friedman, *World Naval Weapons Systems*, 1991; Kemp, *Convoy Protection*, 1993.

Descubierta Class   WARSHIP

The 1970s Spanish *Descubierta* class of **frigates** were a modified version of the Portuguese *Joao Coutinho* class. Displacing 1,233 tons, they were well armed, and distinguished by an unusual split, or Y-shaped, funnel intended to keep fumes clear of the **radar** equipment. In the 1980s standard armament included **Harpoon** and **Sea Sparrow** missiles, **torpedoes** and **Bofors** guns.

De Soto County. See Landing Ship Tank

Destroyer; Destroyer Escort   WARSHIP

The destroyer is now generally understood to be a relatively small, fast, multipurpose warship with varied armament. Recent U.S. types include the *Spruance* and *Arleigh Burke* classes. Other significant models of the last half-century have included the Soviet Kashin, the Canadian *Iroquois*, the British County class, the Chinese *Luta*, the German *Hamburg* class, and the French *Suffren*.

Nevertheless, the destroyer as a type has a convoluted history, dependent on evolving technology. The advent of **torpedo boats** in the 1870s posed a significant problem, since it seemed possible that inexpensive "small craft" navies might now be able to neutralize some of the mightiest **battleship** fleets in the world. Therefore, by the 1880s some small vessels, very much like torpedo boats themselves, were

being made expressly to intercept and destroy them with their guns. The name *Destroyer* was actually given to at least one U.S. vessel of this period. Larger torpedo gunboats, or TGBs, were also produced.

In the 1890s Britain introduced the new concept of a ship, about 200 feet in length with superior seakeeping qualities, which was intended to hunt down torpedo boats. These would have relatively light armament, and a shallow draft that might allow torpedoes to pass harmlessly underneath. Thus was born the torpedo boat destroyer, or TBD, a name later shortened to "destroyer." It may thus be claimed that the ancestors of the modern destroyer were the six vessels, capable of 26 knots, that were ordered in the Royal Navy building program of 1892–1893. Even so, there were parallels in other countries like the "division boats" being built by Germany, and it was not long before the type was widespread. A particular premium was put on speed, but with time destroyers tended to be built larger. In the United States, new-style destroyers were under construction by 1900.

By 1914 destroyers were a significant part of the naval scene; their versatility had made them indispensable, with Germany alone boasting 133 destroyers at the outbreak of war. Many destroyers now doubled for antisubmarine, **raiding**, and sea **minelaying** duties. U.S. destroyers of the period included the *Alwyn*, *Sampson*, and *Wickes* classes. The myriad British types included the S class for patrol work, the V&W class, M class, and the *Shakespeare* class with the 4.7-inch gun. Though some hundreds were decommissioned after World War I and over 50 German destroyers were scuttled at Scapa Flow, destroyer development continued in the interwar period. Japan's buildup included the powerful *Fubuki* class, while Britain countered with the **Tribals**.

During World War II the U.S. building program was particularly impressive. The famous *Fletcher* class, built in greater numbers than any other, was faster and larger than what had gone before, though later improved upon with the *Allen M. Sumner* type. The *Evarts* and *Buckley* destroyer escort types were shared with the United Kingdom, becoming **Captain** class **frigates** in the British order of battle. In the latter part of the war several American destroyers were being finished every month, with eight of the *John C. Butler* class commissioned in June 1944 alone. Eventually the United States would produce 563 destroyer escorts.

Additional Reading: Polmar, *Ships and Aircraft of the U.S. Fleet*, 1981; Cocker, *Destroyers of the Royal Navy 1893–1981*, 1981; Whitley, *German Destroyers of World War II*, 1991; Preston, *V&W Class Destroyers, 1917–1945*, 1971; Whitley, *Destroyers of World War II*, 1988; Lyon, *The First Destroyers*, 2001.

Deutschland   WARSHIP

Meaning "Germany," the name *Deutschland* has been used for several German warships. Four of these are particularly significant. The *Deutschland* of the *Kaiser* class, built in Britain in 1874, was the last German capital ship to be built abroad. Originally constructed on a central-battery design, this 9,000-ton vessel featured a sailing rig as well as steam power and had eight 10-inch guns.

The *Deutschland* class of **battleships** constructed from 1903 to 1908 were a much more powerful proposition at 14,000 tons, with four 11-inch and 14 6.7-inch guns, and capable of 18 knots. They also featured small-tube boilers, which were to become standard for German naval vessels. Nevertheless, these battleships were outclassed by the Royal Navy's **dreadnoughts**, a factor that helped prompt Grand Admiral Alfred von **Tirpitz** into fresh building programs. The *Deutschland* that fought in World War II was originally known simply as Panzerschiffe A and was later renamed *Lützow*.

Deutschland was also the name of the first West German warship to exceed the tonnage limits imposed after World War II. Entering service in 1963, this *Deutschland* was a 3,000-ton light **cruiser**, with particular minelaying and training roles. With an armament of four 100 mm guns she was capable of 22 knots.

Additional Reading: Taylor, *German Warships of World War I*, 1969; Whitley, *German Capital Ships of World War II*, 1989.

Devastation, HMS   WARSHIP

The **battleship** HMS *Devastation*, built at the Plymouth dockyard in 1871, has been described as "the first true capital ship without a single sail." She was also remarkable in that her main armament of four 12-inch guns, mounted atop the hull, were the largest muzzleloaders. Displacing 9,188 tons, she had a maximum armor of 12 inches and a top speed of 12 knots. Retired in 1902, she was finally broken up in 1908.

Dewoitine, 520, etc.   AIRCRAFT

Emile Dewoitine's first fighter **aircraft** was produced at Toulouse in 1921. Its claim to technological significance was that it boasted a high proportion of light metal at a time when fabric was common. Despite this advance the Dewoitine company had an uncertain existence, going into liquidation in 1928, later producing craft in Switzerland. Following a number of high-wing monoplanes the company finally found its forte in the 500 series. By far the best of these was the D.520, which bore a superficial resemblance to the **Spitfire** and could manage 332 mph. Unfortunately, few were available when France fell in 1940, and those produced thereafter went to Vichy and Germany's allies.

Additional Reading: Taylor, *Combat Aircraft of the World*, 1969.

Dido **Class**   WARSHIP

The *Dido*, and modified *Dido*, classes of cruiser were numerically the most significant in the Royal Navy during World War II, totaling 16 vessels. The prime reason for their construction between 1937 and 1944 was the realization that the fleets lacked adequate antiaircraft protection. They therefore mounted eight or ten 5.25-inch guns as the main armament, these guns were capable of engaging at high or low angles. Other antiaircraft guns were also carried, and more, plus **radar** was added at later stages. A few of the many in the class worthy of note are: *Royalist*, which was converted to an escort **aircraft carrier**; *Argonaut*, which served all over the world, including the Far East, the Russian Arctic, and Normandy, surviving double torpedo strikes that blew off both bow and stern; and *Black Prince*, which saw extensive action in the Arctic, off Utah Beach, and in the Far East before being lent to New Zealand in 1946. *Bonaventure, Naiad, Hermione, Charybdis*, and *Spartan* were all lost in action in World War II. The last of the *Dido* class was scrapped in 1968.

Additional Reading: Raven and Roberts, *British Cruisers of World War II*, 1980.

Diphosgene. *See* **Phosgene**

"Dirty" Bomb. *See* **Nuclear Weapons**

Dive Bomber   AIRCRAFT

Diving attacks by **aircraft** were widely discussed as early as 1914. Practical pioneering work with "vertical bombing" was done by the British during the latter part of World War I. During 1918 tests under controlled conditions were carried out at the RAF armament experimental station using SE5a and **Sopwith** Camel aircraft. Many nations took up the idea in the interwar period, and in the mid 1920s it was the U.S. Navy that took the lead, important sponsors being Rear Admiral William A. Moffett and Captain J. M. Reeves.

What constitutes "dive bombing" has been open to various definitions concerning altitude and angle of dive, but in its most common form it consisted of flying fairly high toward a target, pitching over into a steep dive, and releasing bombs from perhaps 2,000 feet. The steep approach and low release significantly aided accuracy while unnerving troops on the ground. Even so, the practice was initially controversial, with some experts arguing that it was suicidal. The Swedes experimented with **Hawker** Hart S7 biplanes, but it was the Americans, Germans, and Japanese who became the greatest exponents of the technique during World War

II. Important dive bombers of that period include the **Stuka** and Junkers **Ju 88**.

Additional Reading: Tillman & Lawson, *U.S. Navy Dive and Torpedo Bombers of World War II*, 2001.

Dog Lock. *See* **Flintlock**

Doodle-Bug. *See* **V1**

Dornier; Do 17, 215, 217   AIRCRAFT

The development of German Dornier **aircraft** commenced in some secrecy as early as the late 1920s, with work in Switzerland as well as Germany. Types produced included both float planes and civil craft as well as the more famous bombers. The famous Do 17 "Flying Pencil" appeared in prototype in 1934 and was in service by 1937. A promising twin-engine bomber capable of carrying 2,200 lb of bombs, it was well nicknamed, having an extraordinarily sleek and slender fuselage. At the time of its introduction the 220 mph top speed was more than adequate, and this was later upped to 263 mph. Though it had some early success in the Spanish Civil War and World War II, it was rapidly overhauled by newer fighters like the **Spitfire**. The production of newer types like the Do 215 and 217 increased speed to over 300 mph—but in the West at least, this was a losing battle.

Additional Reading: Donald, *German Aircraft of World War II*, 1996.

Double Action   FIREARM

The term "double action" is commonly applied to firearms in which a pull on the trigger suffices both to cock and discharge the firing mechanism. This reduces the number of motions required, leading to greater speed. In many double-action **revolvers** it was also possible to use the weapon as though it were "single action"—cocking the hammer by hand, and then pulling the trigger. This was slower but had the advantage of greater accuracy. Double action **semiautomatics** such as the **Walther** PP and **SIG-Sauer** have the benefit that they may safely be carried loaded for swifter use.

Double-L Sweep   MINE (DEFENSE)

The double-L sweep was a device invented in late 1939 to counter German magnetic **sea mines**. It consisted of 750 feet of cables floated by rubber balls, towed behind a vessel (often a **motor minesweeper**). It was powered by two generators that passed 3,000 amps through the cables. This created a magnetic field, by means of which the mines were detonated. Magnetic sweeps were also extemporized by towing 300-ton magnets on skids behind tugs. Double-L was the standard basic sweep against magnetic mines for all Allied navies from 1940.

Additional Reading: Melvin, *Minesweeper*, 1992; Elliott, *Allied Minesweeping*, 1979.

Douglas Aircraft. *See* McDonnell Douglas

Douhet, Guilio   AIRCRAFT (THEORIST)

Italian soldier and aviation theorist Giulio Douhet (1869–1930) was court-martialed for critizing his country's military air policy in World War I but was soon reinstated, and by 1921 he held the rank of general. His book *Il Dominio dell'Aria* postulated that there could be no defense against **aircraft**. He expected that wars could be won by bombers devastating civilian targets. To his work may be traced the idea that "the bomber always gets through."

DP 1928. *See* Degtyarev DP28

DPICM. *See* Cluster Bomb

Dr I. *See* Fokker

Drache Fa 266, Fa 223   AIRCRAFT

The German Focke Achgelis F 61 first flew in 1936 and was one of the first practical *helicopters*. It overcame the problems of torque and control by having two rotors mounted at either end of transverse booms, and a tail at the end of the fuselage. The Fa 266, which appeared four years later, was essentially a larger version, and the Fa 223 Drache (or "dragon") incorporated further improvements. The Drache was powered by a 1,000 horsepower BMW engine, was 40 feet in length, and was capable of 109 mph. A single **machine gun** was mounted in the nose. The Drache could carry six troops and was equipped to take an externally slung load. Though mass production was intended, due to Allied bombing relatively few saw service.

Dragon, Dragoon   FIREARM

A dragon was a short shoulder firearm of large bore, a description of which was given by Gervase Markham in 1625. It was therefore similar to a "musketoon." It is generally considered that the weapon gave its name to "dragoons," or soldiers on horseback armed with firearms, in the sixteenth century. An alternative explanation offered by Sir James Turner in 1683 was that horsemen with **matchlock** weapons "riding with burning matches (especially in the night time) resembled "fiery dragons." In any case it was accepted that dragoons of the sixteenth and seventeenth centuries were essentially mounted infantry who would dismount to fight, rather than true cavalry. They were often mounted on smaller or inferior horses.

Definitions changed with time however, since dragoons of the mid-seventeenth and eighteenth centuries were often armed with full-length **muskets**, and short firearms carried by mounted troops became known as **carbines**. The distinction between the dragoon and the cavalryman was further blurred when many countries, including the French, raised units of dragoons that were intended to act much as ordinary cavalry. Other nations later subdivided dragoons into "light," "heavy," and "guard." It has been suggested that the widespread use of dragoons was in part due to the fact that they were originally less expensive troops than cavalry. The name "Dragoon" has since been applied to various military hardware, including, for example, Israeli four-wheel drives.

Dragon (M-47) Missile   MISSILE

The Dragon M-47 is a shoulder-launched medium antitank and assault missile, development of which commenced in the 1960s. The main manufacturer was **McDonnell Douglas**. In ser-

HMS *Dreadnought* being launched by the King at Portsmouth, 1906. The *Dreadnought* was the most powerful ship of its day, giving its name to a whole new type of battleship. © Hulton/Getty Images.

vice with U.S. and other forces from 1974 the Dragon comprises a launch tube and tracker unit. The system is wire guided so that as long as the operator keeps the sight on the target the missile will continue to fly toward it. The 27 lb missile is two feet five inches in length, with a range of about half a mile. Towards the back of the cylindrical body are mounted 30 pairs of small solid-propellant rocket motors that steer the missile. (The name "Dragon" was also applied to a British carrier; see **Bren Carrier**.)

Dragunov. *See* **Sniper Rifles**

Dreadnought, HMS   WARSHIP

Though the name has come to signify almost any heavily armed and armored **battleship**, the HMS *Dreadnought* was a specific British vessel launched in 1906, the ninth Royal Navy ship to bear the name (the first such having been commissioned in 1573). The early-twentieth-century *Dreadnought* set the pace in military naval design and arguably stoked the naval race that preceded World War I.

Though First Sea Lord Admiral Sir John A. "Jacky" Fisher claimed to have had the idea for *Dreadnought* as early as 1900, its actual construction was stimulated by world events. In 1903 Italian Vittorio Cuniberti called for 17,000-ton fighting vessels with 12-inch guns; and in 1904 the U.S. Navy approached Congress for funds to build similar ships. Japan laid down two 20,000-ton ships armed with 10 and 12-inch guns in 1905. Against this background Fisher created a Committee on Designs in late 1904, intending that it should come up with a vessel fitting what he saw as the two "governing conditions" of naval warfare, "guns and speed."

In the final design *Dreadnought* featured five turrets, each with two 12-inch guns. The turrets were so positioned that eight guns could be brought to bear either side, and six ahead or astern. With its ten 12-inch guns the *Dreadnought* carried approximately double the armament of most previous capital ships. Trials in 1907 saw her guns hurl 21,250 lb of shells from her guns in eight minutes, or 75 percent more than any other British battleship. The 23,000 horsepower steam-turbine engines gave her 21 knots, with increased efficiency and reduced vibration, though she carried 5,000 tons of armor. Her weight was 17,900 tons.

Significantly *Dreadnought* was seen to make the contemporary *Deutschland* class obsolete, leading to drastic changes in the German shipbuilding program. Critics pointed out that the "Cult of the Monster Ship" put too much at risk in individual vessels, and also meant that most of Britain's own fleet, and many of her docks, were now outdated. Conversely, Fisher claimed that Dreadnought-type ships were much more effective, being vastly more powerful for moderate increases in weight and expense. *Dreadnought* was scrapped in 1923.

Additional Reading: Massie, *Dreadnought: Britain Germany and the Coming of the Great War*, 1992; Hough, *Dreadnought*, 1964.

Dryse   INVENTOR

Johann Nikolaus von Dryse (1787–1867) of Sömmerda, Prussia, is significant in the history of military firearms for two innovations that were eventually brought together in the model 1841 *Zündnadelgewehr*, or "needle gun." The first of these was the use of a long pin within the breech mechanism of **a rifle** that when pushed smartly forward by a spring would pierce a **cartridge**. Within the cartridge was contained an **explosive** cap of fulminate of mercury, which would detonate when struck, thus setting off the main charge of the cartridge firing the shot. This basic idea was put forward as early as 1827.

A few years later Dryse combined this with a bolt-action **breech loading** mechanism. The **bolt action** itself may not have been a new invention, but the combination of firing needle or "firing pin," cartridge, and bolt action was a critical step, and a major influence on military firearms thereafter. Dreyse lived to see his invention triumph over the Austrians in the war of 1866.

Additional Reading: Walter, *The German Rifle*, 1979.

Duck, DUKW   MOTOR VEHICLE

The U.S. General Motors "Duck," or DUKW, was a wheeled marine amphibious truck first produced in 1941. It saw extensive use in World War II, proving especially useful in river crossings and the Pacific theater of war. Ducks remained in service with many nations after 1945. A much bigger "Superduck," with an increased load-carrying capacity, was produced in 1953, and a "Drake" in 1956. The official designation of such equipments was later changed to the less evocative "Landing Vehicle, Wheeled."

Duguay-Trouin   WARSHIP

The *Duguay-Trouin* class of French **cruisers** was laid down in the early 1920s. The class comprised three vessels—the *Duguay-Trouin, Lamotte-Piquet*, and *Primaguet*—which were completed by 1927, their design being broadly based on the U.S. *Omaha* class. They were relatively thin-skinned ships, displacing 7,249 tons, with a main armament of eight 155 mm guns. They served well (on both sides) in World War II.

Duke Class. *See* Type 23

Dum Dum Bullet   AMMUNITION

Dum Dum was the location of a small-arms factory in India where the superintendent, Captain N. S. Bertie Clay, designed a soft-nosed bullet for use in "savage warfare." The bullet deformed and expanded easily on impact, causing worse wounds. Since the 1890s the term "dumdum" has been used generally to refer to expanding, hollow-point, and even **explosive** bullets.

Though use of such **ammunition** was later forbidden by the Hague Convention and Britain abandoned the original bullet in 1902, there have been frequent controversies regarding dumdums. During World War I, for example, several nations were accused of using blunt-nosed rounds, bullets inverted in their **cartridges**, and mutilated bullets in order to cause worse injury. The Austrians manufactured and employ a genuine exploding rifle bullet; the Russians threatened to execute any soldier captured in possession of them.

Additional Reading: *Imperial War Museum, Review* (vol 5); Sellier and Kneubuehl, *Wound Ballistics*, 1994.

Duplex Drive   TANK

Developed by Hungarian-born engineer Nicholas Straussler, duplex-drive systems take power from the motor of a vehicle to drive a propeller. During World War II, "DD" was applied to tanks such as the Valentine and **Sherman** to produce "swimming tanks," which were also provided with collapsible canvas skirts to give buoyancy. Predictably, the troops nicknamed the DDs "Donald Ducks." Though many of the Shermans so used on D-Day were lost, the idea was an important one, and variations on the theme survive to this day.

Dux Submachine Gun   FIREARM

Based on a Finnish design, the West German Dux **submachine gun** was first produced in the early 1950s. It was used by the army and border guards but was effectively rendered obsolete by the **MP5**. The later 1959 model was 62 cm long with the stock folded and took 32 or 40 round box magazines. It weighed 3.6 kg.

Dynatrac. *See* Rat

E

E-2. *See* **Hawkeye**

E-3. *See* **AWACS**

***Eagle,* HMS;** *Eagle* **Class**   WARSHIP

The British **aircraft carrier** *Eagle* had a checkered career, being laid down in 1913 as a **battleship** for the Chilean navy. By 1918 it was decided that Britain needed the hull for a carrier, but the war was over before completion. At one stage it was proposed that she would be built with a funnel on either side and a 68-foot gap between the islands. She was finally commissioned in 1924 with a conventional one-sided island arrangement. Built, quite literally, like a battleship, she was tough but slow and capable of accommodating only 24 aircraft despite a 22,000-ton displacement. She was sunk by a **U-boat** in 1942. A new HMS *Eagle* of the *Eagle* class, sister ship to *Ark Royal* was completed in 1951.

Additional Reading: Chesneau, *Aircraft Carriers,* 1992.

Eagle, F-15   AIRCRAFT

The U.S. **McDonnell Douglas** F-15 Eagle is arguably one of the most successful fighter aircraft of modern times. It was an indirect result of the search to find a successor to the F-4 **Phantom** that began as early as 1965, with an RFP, or request for proposals, to which eight companies responded. Though McDonnell did not initially receive a contract, it continued to work up the concept and gained a contract-definition phase agreement in 1968. The de-

manding requirements now included an ability to fly to Europe without refueling, twin self-start engines, low wing loading, a top speed of Mach 2.5, and a minimum "fatigue life of 4,000 hours." A particular premium was put on structural integrity and high survivability in combat. It was intended that all this should be achieved with proven low-risk technology.

By the end of 1969 the McDonnell contender had emerged as the winning design, and the F-15 first flew on 27 July 1972. For weight saving and simplicity the airframe was fixed-wing, with a 45-degree sweep, which achieved the best compromise for both high and low-speed handling. The massive power required to achieve five-gravity turns, reach the required speed, and drive the relatively large airframe was provided by two Pratt and Whitney F100-PW-100 turbofans. Lightweight titanium fabrication and advanced cooling techniques allowed a permitted turbine temperature of 2,500 degrees with a compression ratio of 23:1.

A number of technologically significant features appeared in the cockpit, in which the pilot sat high up for good all-round visibility. The **head-up** display had a cathode-ray tube with automatic brightness control and a cine, later video-filming, capability. There was also a HOTAS system, or "hands on throttle and stick" control technique, contributed by designer Gene Adam. The pilot could operate much of the equipment through buttons on the throttle quadrant and control column. This obviated the need for groping around the cockpit for small switches at inopportune moments and so helped pilots to focus. While older men took time to

U.S. F-15 Eagles from 1st Fighter Wing patrol the no fly zone over southern Iraq, 2002. Courtesy of the Department of Defense.

acclimatize, the first generation of computer gamers were natural to the system. The pulse-Doppler **radar** was capable of tracking small high-speed targets and looking up and down to treetop level. Information from the radar was fed into the central computer; targets acquired and the information on them was projected on the head-up display. "Identification Friend or Foe" and electronic countermeasures were included.

Over the years there have been five major variants of the F-15—the models A, B, C, D, and E. The F-15E Strike Eagle first flew in 1980. Data published in 2001 suggests that it has a maximum speed of Mach 2.5 at 40,000 feet, a combat radius of 790 miles, a range of 2,762 miles, a maximum loaded weight of 81,000 lb, and an internal fuel load of 2,727 gallons. The two-seater Strike Eagle can carry a vast range of weaponry. Its bomb load may include guided "smart" bombs or precision-guided munitions, low-drag general-purpose (or LDGP) bombs, Mk 84 "dumb" bombs, and **cluster bombs**. Missiles can include AIM-7M, AIM-9M, AIM-120A, and Maverick. A 20 mm Vulcan-type rotary cannon, or **Gatling**-type gun, is usually fitted at the wing root. Maximum weapons load is 24,500 lb.

Though the F-15 had its origins as a Phantom successor it did not take over the navy role, which was ultimately filled by the F-14 **Tomcat**. However, the Eagle was soon paramount as a land-based multirole fighter, with the majority of the 1,500 units produced going to air force squadrons based in the United States, Europe, and Middle East, and later to the Air National Guard. They were also supplied to Israel, Japan, and Saudi Arabia. An F-15I Thunderer model has also been supplied to Israel since 1998. Though a good number of Eagles have been lost to accidents over the years, the combat record is unsurpassed, for none have been lost in action. On the other side of the coin, Israeli F-15s shot down several Syrian fighters during 1977 and 1982, and in the Gulf War there were 36 confirmed victories. In 1999 a further four hostile aircraft were shot down in the Balkans. Eagle pilots have also experienced multiple bird strikes, severe wing damage, turbine failures, and other mishaps yet lived to tell the tale.

Additional Reading: Davies and Thornborough, *F-15*; Pace, *X-Fighters: USAF Experimental and Prototype Fighters, XP-59 to YF-23*, 1991; Sgarlato, *Aircraft of the USAF*, 1978; Whitford, *Design for Air Combat*, 1987.

Echo Class   SUBMARINE

The Echo class of Soviet nuclear **submarine** was commenced in 1958 with the Echo I. The Echo boats were somewhat similar to the better-known November and Hotel classes but were the first true **cruise-missile** vessels built by the Soviets. In the 1970s the existing Echo I types were converted to **torpedo**-only vessels, while Echo II was introduced for use with the SS-N-3 and SS-N-12 missiles. By 1980 there were 29 Echo II class submarines. Though useful vessels they were relatively noisy and easy to detect; they were discontinued during the 1980s.

Additional Reading: Jordan, *Soviet Submarines*, 1989.

EFA. *See* Typhoon "Eurofighter"

Ejection Seat   MISCELLANEOUS

As speeds of military **aircraft** increased, crews experienced greater difficulties in escaping from stricken craft. The idea of expelling crewmen automatically was investigated during World War II, as in the **He 219** and **He 280**. Yet the concept was neither made general nor fully perfected. A more reliable solution to the problem was developed by the British Martin Baker company just after the war. In the first modern ejection system, the pilot pulled down a curtain to protect his face, and a gas cylinder provided the thrust to throw him and his seat clear of the plane at about 80 feet per second. A **parachute** then had to be activated manually. The process of parachute deployment was automated from 1953 with a clockwork mechanism.

In the United States, rocket-sled tests using human volunteers demonstrated that pilots could stand sudden decelerations from speeds of up to 1,800 mph; this pioneering work helped to design of the next generation of seats. By the 1960s, rocket-powered "zero-zero" systems were in use that could be activated even when a plane was stationary at ground level. Though rocket seats saved many lives, injuries including broken bones and spinal compression remained common. Responses to this problem have included various devices to pull the aviator back into his seat and restrain his limbs. Small boosters have also been incorporated to alter the direction in which the seat flies or to send crew members at different angles to avoid collision.

Though modern seats apply similar principles, they vary in detail. The K-36 Russian model, in use during the 1990s, includes a plastic shield for the pilot, and stabilizing arms. The US **F-16** uses the ACES, or Advanced Concept Ejection Seat. A new Mark 16 seat has been developed by Martin Baker, incorporating its own individual computer and sequencing system for use with the Joint Strike Fighter. The latest methods enable a pilot to be out of his aircraft and descending by parachute in just over a second from the moment he pulls the release handle. Most seats include an oxygen system for high-altitude ejection, a barostatic gauge to initiate parachute deployment, and a survival pack for use on the ground. Variations on the ejection-seat theme include complete capsules that separate from an aircraft, as in the **F-111**, and **helicopter** systems in which the rotor blades come off and are thrown clear before the pilot exits upward.

Elefant. *See* Tank Destroyer "Ferdinand"

Elektroboot. *See* U-boat

Elephant. *See* Howdah

Emden   WARSHIP

In the early twentieth century the famous name *Emden* was used by three German cruisers in the space of a decade. The 3,650-ton, three-funnel, light cruiser *Emden* disguised herself as a British vessel in 1914, surprising and sinking the Russian light cruiser *Jemtchug* at Penang. She also sank the French **torpedo** boat *Mousquet* and later fired on a customs patrol boat; realising the latter was unarmed, the *Emden* sent it an apology. Her Indian Ocean trail of havoc was finally brought to a conclusion by HMAS *Sydney*, which sank her at the Cocos Islands on 9 November 1914. A second *Emden* was built not long afterward.

The third German cruiser *Emden*, intended as a replacement for the *Ariadne*, and was laid down at Wilhelmshaven in 1921. She was built under very difficult circumstances, within the restrictions of the Versailles Treaty, and with marginal funding. Nevertheless, she incorporated such modern features as electric welding, and though originally provided with mixed oil and coal-fired boilers was later converted completely to oil. Her original armament was eight 15 cm guns. The *Emden* served as a training ship, one of her interwar captains being the future chief of the **U-boat** arm and the Third Reich's final leader, Karl Dönitz. Her active service included the Norwegian campaign of 1940 and action against the Russians in the Baltic. Bombed and put out of commission, her crew were put ashore to fight on land, while the ship was blown up on 3 May 1945.

Additional Reading: Taylor, *German Warships of World War I*, 1969; Whitley, *German Cruisers of World War II*, 1985.

EMP. *See* Nuclear Weapons

Enfield   MANUFACTURER

The British Royal Small Arms factory was established at Enfield Lock, Middlesex, in 1804. Much of its early work was in assembly of components supplied from elsewhere, but with the introduction of the 1853 Pattern Enfield **rifled musket** its work expanded to encompass the whole production cycle. Thereafter many British military firearms would include Enfield in the title, including several **revolvers**, and the SMLE, or **Short Magazine Lee Enfield**, used in both world wars. The site was run down in the 1980s after the takeover by Royal Ordnance and sold; production of the latest **SA80** rifle was started in Nottingham. The important Pattern Room collection of historic military small arms was also moved to Nottingham, but at the time of writing is again moving, this time to Leeds.

Additional Reading: Walter, *Dictionary*, 2001.

ENIAC   COMPUTATION

Developed by John Mauchly and J. Presper Eckert in 1945 at the University of Pennsylvania, the Electronic Numerical Integrator and Computer (ENIAC) was a machine for automating the production of fire tables. Though not the first computer, a title taken by **Colossus**, Eniac had a lasting legacy. It was used in computations for the development of **nuclear weapons** and was later found to have widespread applications.

Additional Reading: Goldstine, *The Computer from Pascal to von Neumann*, 1972.

Enigma   COMMUNICATIONS

The Enigma encoding machine, conceived by Arthur Scherbius (d. 1929), was first used by business but was adopted as the main encription device of German forces between the wars. The heart of the electrically powered machine was a series of wheels, or rotors—initially two but later anything up to twelve in number. These turned as the keys of the keyboard were depressed, allowing a vast number of potential connections for the encoding of messages, which could be deciphered by an operator using a similar machine with the same initial settings. Security was massively increased by a "plugboard," by means of which pairs of letters could be transposed to create many trillions of possible keys to the code. Though undoubtedly the most famous of the rotor machines, Enigma was not unique; others were patented by Alexander Koch in the Netherlands, Arvid Damm in Sweden, and Edward Heburn in the United States.

Neither was Enigma impenetrable. As early as the 1930s a Polish team led by mathematician Marian Rejewski succeeded in decoding messages encrypted on the three rotor machines. At the British Government Code and Cipher School at Bletchley Park during the early part of the Second World War, Alan Turing produced a new **bombe**, Christened "Agnus Dei," which proved capable of decoding Enigma messages within an hour. A complete Enigma machine was captured by the Royal Navy aboard the *U-110* in 1941. The Lorenz S40 machine, similar to but much more complex than Enigma, was eventually defeated by **Colossus**. In the Pacific, the U.S. Signal Intelligence Service would achieve similar success against "Purple," the Japanese version of Enigma. Taken together, the efforts of the Allied "Ultra" system codebreakers thoroughly penetrated enemy communications, making a significant contribution to the defeat of the Axis, though this was not revealed until 1974 with the publication of FW Winterbotham's *The Ultra Secret*.

Additional Reading: Sebag-Montefiore, *Enigma*, 2000; Singh, *The Code Book*, 1999; Smith, *Station*

X: The Codebreakers of Bletchley Park, 1998; Hinsley and Stripp, *Code Breakers*, 1994.

Enterprise, USS   WARSHIP

The remarkable USS *Enterprise* (CVAN 65), commissioned in November 1961, was a 76,000-ton vessel that was essentially America's prototype for all its nuclear-powered **aircraft carriers** since that date. With the capacity to carry 99 **aircraft** and a complement of over 5,000 she was a massive ship for the 1960s. Her 1,040-foot-long flight deck had an area of four and a half acres. She was also massively expensive, and it has been suggested that it was to save money that no fixed defensive battery was initially mounted. Later, **Sea Sparrow, Phalanx,** and other systems were added.

Additional Reading: Chesneau, *Aircraft Carriers,* 1992.

Eprouvette. *See* **Gunpowder**

Essex **Class**   WARSHIP

Commenced in 1941 the *Essex* class of U.S. **aircraft carriers** eventually numbered 24 vessels. At 820 feet long and 28,000 tons each, capable of carrying 91 aircraft, they were large for the period, making a substantial contribution to the war effort. They also had a good defensive armament, which included 12 5-inch, 32 40 mm, and 46 20 mm guns. None were lost in action. *Essex* (CV 9) was the first to be laid down, at Newport News in April 1941, being commissioned on 31 December 1942. The last, Philippine Sea (CV 47), was started in August 1944 but not finished until May 1946. Technologically interesting features included a deck-edge elevator that could be folded to allow these large ships to pass through the Panama Canal, and boilers and machinery spaces disposed in a staggered manner to improve survivability. At least some of the class remained in service until the 1980s, and many modifications were made over the decades. *Hancock* (CV 19) for example, was the first U.S. carrier to be fitted with steam catapults, in 1954.

Boxer (CV 21) served in both Korea and Vietnam, and along with *Princeton* (CV 37), Yorktown (CV 10), and *Valley Forge* (CV 45) was redesignated as an amphibious assault ship. *Hornet* (CV 12) still exists.

Eurofighter "EFA." *See* **Typhoon**

Exeter, **HMS**   WARSHIP

The 8,500-ton British cruiser *Exeter* was laid down at Devonport Dockyard in 1928 and completed in 1931. She was 575 feet long, with six 8-inch guns and a complement of 628, and had eight boilers and Parsons geared turbines. She fought the *Graf Spee* at the battle of the River Plate in 1939 and was badly damaged. In 1942 she was damaged in action at the battle of the Jarva Sea before finally being cornered and sunk by the Japanese.

Exocet Missile   MISSILE

The French Aerospatiale Exocet tactical missile was made front-page news by the Argentinians in 1982, when it was used with success against British forces in the Falklands. Its victims were the *Sheffield* and *Atlantic Conveyor*. In production as a ship-to-ship weapon from the 1970s, the Exocet was soon adapted for air-to-sea use as the MM38 and AM-39, being launched from **helicopters** and from the Super Etendard (in 1977). In the air versions a one-second delay is incorporated so that the missile will drop clear of the **aircraft** prior to firing. With a total launch weight of 1,433 lb and a length of 15 feet four inches, the Exocet is a substantial "fire and forget" missile with active homing by radar, and a range of up to 43 miles. In the Falklands the Argentinians also adapted it for land firing when their navy and air force were defeated.

Additional Reading: Beaver and Gander, *Modern British Military Missiles,* 1986.

Explosives   EXPLOSIVE

Propellants and explosives are chemical compounds or mixtures that rapidly produce large volumes of hot gases when properly initiated. The amount of energy liberated depends on the thermochemical properties of the material. The explosive reaction itself may be internal or a reaction between discrete oxidizers. Generally speaking, propellants, which are used in **ammunition** and missiles to move the projectile, are consumed more slowly than explosives, which are used for things like warheads and **shell** and **grenade** fillings.

It should be noted that detonation and burning are different—explosions involve high-pressure shock waves and do not depend on rates of heat transfer as in burning. It is also the case that the same compound may behave differently under various circumstances. Something that usually burns, for example, may explode when vaporized or confined in a certain way. Granular TNT burns when spread thinly but detonates when heaped. Since stability, ease of manufacture and transport, and price are all factors, military explosives tend to rely on a relatively small number of well proven ingredients. Pyrotechnic compounds also produce reduction reactions, with flame, smoke, or colors but relatively little gas. These compounds often consist of finely powdered metals and can be used for flares, signals, heating mixtures, and tracers. Thus it is that smoke munitions frequently contain high proportions of zinc, while flares often contain magnesium.

Though incendiaries, such as **Greek fire**, were known to the ancient world, and some incendiaries do explode under certain circumstances, it was not until the discovery of **gunpowder** in the thirteenth century that the development of explosives really commenced. This made possible both the gun and **artillery**. In the nineteenth century the nitration of various compounds led to rapid technological advances, including smokeless powders and more powerful explosives. Explosions may be triggered in a variety of ways, but in most cases heat is the ultimate cause of activation. Friction, lighting, flints, **fuses**, and striking all have long histories as initiators, as may be seen in early technologies like the **matchlock, wheel lock**, and **flintlock**. More sensitive explosives may be used to set off the less sensitive—hence the use

of detonators, gaines, and **percussion** caps. A simple distinction between "low" and "high" explosives is often drawn, in that it is generally possible to initiate the former by lighting whereas the latter require a shock wave to detonate.

Recently explosives have been improved with the application of a number of experimental techniques. These include high-speed photography, electronic instrumentation, and computers. Theoretical modeling may include use of the Ruby software and Kamlet equations. Explosives are tested against a wide range of criteria, though the military and scientific communities tend to judge their suitability under seven major headings: performance, sensitivity, thermal characteristics, physical properties, producibility, vulnerability, and environmental and safety concerns. The military place a particular premium on maximum energy, long shelf life and ability to withstand handling stresses, and adaptability to a wide range of environmental conditions. Despite apparent vulnerability, **fuel-air explosives** have also proved efficient since the 1960s.

Explosives are often categorized as "primary" or "secondary." The former are the most sensitive and are often used as initiators to larger charges of the latter. In the military, mercury fulminate, lead, and silver azide have been particularly significant. Lead azide has been widely used in U.S. military detonators, as it is stable, stores well, has good flow characteristics, and is compatible with most explosives.

The secondary explosives may be divided into the aliphatic nitrate esters, the nitroaromatics, and the nitramines. Of the first, a few have assumed particular military significance. Nitroglycerin is used in dynamites but by itself is very sensitive to shock or friction; pentaerythritol tetranitrate can be used for detonating cord. Much more important is nitrocellulose, which has proved invaluable in gun and rocket propellants. The cellulose in its fibrous composition is taken from wood, pulp, or cotton fiber. It can be unstable and is therefore often shipped wet. The size of its grains or strands is also important and can have a significant impact on its explosive or propellant properties.

Among the nitroaromatics, TNT or trinitrotoluene is probably the best known, being good for stability and storage. It may be steam melted and cast. Other explosives in the nitroaromatic group include picric acid (the first modern explosive to be used as a burster in shells) and ammonium picrate (the great stability of which made it suitable for projectiles intended to penetrate armor before exploding). The nitramines assumed much greater significance during the twentieth century and are important in high-performance rocket propellants and high-energy explosives. Important in this category are RDX, HMX, and Tetryl. C4 is one of the best known military plastic explosives, easily pressed into shape or stretched. It is 91 percent RDX, or "Research Department Explosive" mixed with polyisobutylene plasticizer. In the last couple of decades the search for even more powerful explosives has concentrated on four particular molecules known as PYX, ONC, TNAZ, and DINGU. Particularly important "brand name" explosives of the twentieth century include **Nipolit** and **Semtex**.

Additional Reading: Kroschwitz, *Encyclopedia of Chemical Technology*, 1993; Brown, *The Big Bang*, 1998.

F

F2A. *See* **Buffalo**

F2B. *See* **Bristol**

F-4. *See* **Phantom**

F4F. *See* **Wildcat**

F-5. *See* **Tiger F-5**

F6F. *See* **Hellcat**

F-14. *See* **Tomcat**

F-15. *See* **Eagle**

F-16. *See* **Fighting Falcon**

F-18. *See* **Hornet, F-18**

F-22. *See* **Raptor**

F-35. *See* **Joint Strike Fighter**

F-61. *See* **Black Widow**

F-86. *See* **Sabre**

F-104. *See* **Starfighter**

F-105. *See* **Thunderchief**

F-111. *See* **Aardvark**

F-117A. *See* **Stealth**

Fabrique Nationale   MANUFACTURER

The Belgian arms manufacturer FN was established in 1889 following a Belgian government decision to build a version of the 1888 model **Mauser rifle**. This brought together several companies that had previously been in competition, allowing sufficient scale of production and relatively easy interchangeability of parts. A new factory was built and the latest machinery purchased from Ludwig Loewe of Berlin. Although FN has produced other things, including bicycles and other vehicles, arms have been its most important line. Important FN weapons included the **Browning** model 1900, 1903, and 1910 pistols; the model 1935 Browning High-Power pistol; various **grenades** and **machine guns**; **shotguns**; and the FN or Self Loading Rifle (SLR) used by NATO. The company has also licensed many other manufacturers to make its products.

Additional Reading: Stevens, *The FAL Rifle*, 1993; Walter, *Dictionary*, 2001.

Fagot. *See* **MiG-15**

Fairbairn-Sykes. *See* **F-S Knife**

Falchion. *See* **Sword**

Falcon Missile   MISSILE

The Falcon air-to-air missile was developed by the U.S. Hughes Aircraft Company from 1947, and it was in production from 1954. Consisting of a body six feet seven inches long, and weighing 134 lb, the Falcon had a range of six miles at Mach 4. Originally reliant on semiactive **radar** homing, later versions incorporated infrared homing, optical target detection devices, and eventually a solid-state radar that would allow detonation in proximity, without the missile hitting the target. Sweden was a major user of Falcon, building it under license as the RB-27 and RB-28.

FA MAS Rifle   FIREARM

Entering French service at the end of the 1970s the 5.56 mm FA MAS rifle made by St. Etienne was a modernistic-looking **bullpup** design. Light at just under 3.5 kg it incorporated plastic furniture, a spring buffer in the butt, and sights protected within the top carrying handle. With an effective range of about 300 meters it could also fire rifle grenades. The standard magazine was a 25-round box.

Additional Reading: *Jane's Infantry Weapons.*

Fargo Class   WARSHIP

The U.S. *Fargo* class of **cruisers** was laid down from 1943 to 1945 and was intended to comprise 16 vessels. In the event, however, only three were actually launched, the remainder being canceled as the end of World War II came in sight. None saw war service, with the *Newark* being used for shock tests in 1948. *Huntington* remained in the reserve until 1961 and the *Fargo* herself until 1970. Similar to the *Cleveland* class, the *Fargo* type was an improvement in that it had a lower center of gravity and a single funnel. It was also stronger, since it was more divided internally.

Additional Reading: Whitley, *Cruisers*; Terzibaschitsch, *Cruisers of the US Navy 1922–1962*, 1988.

Ferret   VEHICLE

The Ferret **armored** car was the first postwar British wheeled armored vehicle. Entering service in 1951, it remained in use for approximately 30 years. Powered by a Rolls-Royce six-cylinder, 130 horsepower engine, it was small and maneuverable, with a crew of two.

The Mark 1 had no turret, but other marks featured a small turret mounting a **machine gun**.

Fighting Falcon, F-16   AIRCRAFT

Claimed to be one of the best current combat **aircraft**, the General Dynamics F-16 was originally conceived as a relatively simple, lightweight, U.S. fighter optimized for air combat. The prototype YF-16 flew in 1974 and the F-16A in 1976. Since then the craft has come a long way, with the addition of more advanced technology through a staged improvement plan. This includes upgraded **radar** for small-target detection, new cockpit control and display systems, and instrument automatic landing.

Nevertheless, the greatest strength of the F-16 remains its remarkable performance. It is able to withstand nine-gravity force when fully laden, has a maximum speed of 1,320 mph, and can climb 50,000 feet in a minute. The pilot enjoys particularly good visibility through the bubble-type canopy. Moreover, maneuverability is exceptional. The plane is "fly-by-wire," so there are no cables and linkages; there is a side stick controller, which is more convenient for use in high G-force conditions. F-16 C and D models were used in the Gulf in 1991, and they were also deployed to the Balkans in the mid-1990s. The F-16 has also been license-built in Europe, primarily to provide a replacement for the **Starfighter**.

Additional Reading: Senior, *F-16 Fighting Falcon*, 2002; Herzog, *Defense Reform and Technology: Tactical Aircraft*, 1994; Pace, *X-Fighters: USAF Experimental and Prototype Fighters, XP-59 to YF-23*, 1991; Whitford, *Design for Air Combat*, 1987.

Firebee. *See* UAV

FIST   FIREARM

News of the British billion-pound "Future Integrated Soldier Technology," or FIST, project was released in 2002. The idea is to produce an integrated system in which a gun, capable of firing **grenades** or bullets, will be linked to a helmet that has facilities for communication and identification, as well as a **head-up** display.

It is intended that the soldier will thus be able to use the **Global Positioning System** to find his place on the battlefield, viewed through the helmet visor, which also incorporates night-vision and thermal-imaging aids. Contenders for the contract at time of writing included **BAE** systems, Marconi, the U.S. Raytheon, and the French Thales companies. The major problem identified is to make FIST simple, reliable, and intuitive to use.

Firelock. *See* **Flintlock**

Fishbed. *See* **MiG-21**

Flail; Flail Tank   MISCELLANEOUS

Flails with wooden handles and flexible heads were used in ancient and medieval warfare. Originally identical to those used in agriculture—for threshing corn for example—specifically military types were developed later.

During World War II the flail idea was revived as a method of exploding enemy **mines**. Powered revolving drums were fitted to arms forward of a **tank**, and from these hung chains that pounded the ground, so clearing the mines. Best known of the flail tanks was the **Sherman** "Crab" conversion. An alternative to flails was the use of rollers—for example, the CIRD, or Canadian Indestructible Roller Device.

Additional Reading: Stone, *A Glossary of the Construction, Decoration and Use of Arms and Armor*, 1934.

Flak   ARTILLERY

The German acronym *Flak—Flugzeug Abwehr Kanon*, meaning literally "aircraft defense gun"—has been taken into common usage for antiaircraft **artillery**. **Krupp** and Erhardt had exhibited dedicated "AA" guns as early as 1909, but development was limited until World War I. Later flak guns included the 2 cm Rheinmetall 1930 design, the 3 cm Jaboschreck, or "fighter-bomber-terror," the four-barreled Flakvierling, and various models of **88 mm**. Flak guns are frequently emplaced but have also been mounted on railway trains, tanks

chassis, and other vehicles. Early improvements to flak included new **shell fuses**, dedicated sights, and "predictors," which helped guns aim ahead of aircraft, which would fly into the explosions. **Radar** guided guns became progressively more common from World War II.

In modern U.S. usage a distinction is often drawn between "AA" and "AAA" systems—the former are missile based, while the latter, "antiaircraft artillery," is gun based. Well known European manufacturers of such guns have included **Bofors** and **Oerlikon**.

Additional Reading: Hogg, *Anti Aircraft Artillery*, 2002.

Flamethrower   FLAME DEVICE

The projection of fire was familiar to the ancients, **Greek fire** being the best known incendiary. Fire **arrows** and flaming pitch were of significance in medieval sieges. A recognizably modern flamethrower was patented by German inventor Richard Fiedler in 1910. This consisted of a double cylinder containing fuel and compressed gas, which could deliver squirts via a flexible hose. A similar model was adopted by the Germans in 1912. This "backpack" type was later referred to as the klein, or "small," to distinguish it from the much larger ground-mounted models also developed in World War I.

Flamethrower technology at that point became widespread, and by World War II many nations adopted backpack models. These were commonly capable of ranges from 20 to 30 yards and might manage about a dozen short squirts before their fuel was exhausted. Flamethrowers were now also used from armored vehicles as well as fixed positions. Intermediate models were mounted on small trolleys.

Tactically they are most useful in defense or in attacks on fixed positions and bunkers. In the attacking role they are able to offer a considerable moral advantage; apart from burning they can exhaust the oxygen of an enemy in a confined space. They were thus of considerable use to the United States in the Pacific War against Japan. Flamethrowers in use after World War II have included the triple-cylinder

A U.S. flame-throwing tank of 6th Marine Division lays down a barrage of fire on Japanese positions on Okinawa, May 1945. © Hulton/Getty Images.

LPO-50, a standard model of the Warsaw Pact; the U.S. M9E1-7, capable of 50 meters using thickened fuel; and the Italian T-148. Flamethrowers have also been widely fitted to **tanks**, and in the U.S. case, to patrol boats.

Additional Reading: *Jane's Infantry Weapons*; Saunders, *Weapons of the Trench War*, 1999; Patent Office, *Patents*.

Flaming Bayonet   FLAME DEVICE

The U.S. experimental "flaming **bayonet**" of 1917 was one of the most unusual weapons ever made. Weighing just under a pound, it was fitted to the muzzle of a 1903 **Springfield** or Model 1917 **rifle**. When the soldier was engaged in bayonet fighting he was supposed to pull a trigger to release a gout of flame five to 15 feet in length, incinerating his opponent.

Flanker. *See* **Sukhoi Su-27**

Flechette   AMMUNITION

A flechette is a thin fin-stablized projectile looking not unlike a small arrow. Possible precursors are the "darts" used by the ancients, and the small hand-thrown arrows used in certain Eastern martial arts. In the modern western context they reappeared as aerial darts dropped from aircraft during World War I. Though they have been used as individual projectiles for **rifles**, their most successful exployment has been as a cluster from **artillery** rounds. A good example is the "beehive" used in Vietnam.

Fletcher **Class**   WARSHIP

Arguably the most famous U.S. **destroyer** type, the *Fletcher* class commenced construction in 1941. For destroyers of that period they were large, at 376 feet and 2,325 tons. A strong flush-decked design, the *Fletcher*s were armed with five 5-inch guns and **torpedoes**, and had

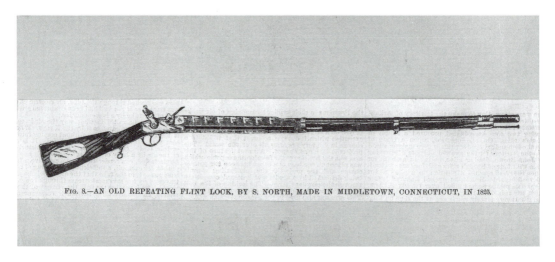

FIG. 8.—AN OLD REPEATING FLINT LOCK, BY S. NORTH, MADE IN MIDDLETOWN, CONNECTICUT, IN 1825.

An experimental repeating flintlock by S. North, made at Middletown, Connecticut in 1825. Before the advent of self contained cartridges there was limited success with repeating firearms. © Culver Pictures.

a crew of 273. Top speed was a very respectable 38 knots.

They were mainly used in the Pacific, and 18 of the class were lost in action. The *Colhoun, Luce, Little, Morrison, Longshaw, William D. Porter*, and *Callaghan* were all sunk by **kamikazes** during the Okinawa operations. Late in the war many *Fletcher*s received the so called "kamikaze" refit, which gave them quadruple batteries of 40 mm guns with blind fire control, and twin 20 mms. Over 150 *Fletcher*s were still in existence after 1945; they were both used in Korean War and passed on to other countries. Later users included South Korea, Germany, Argentina, Taiwan, Columbia, Turkey, Brazil, Mexico, Greece, and Spain. The *Fletcher* (DD 445) herself was stricken from U.S. Navy lists in August 1967, but a number of the class were still afloat toward the end of the twentieth century.

Additional Reading: Whitley, *Destroyers of World War II*, 1988.

Flettner Fl 282 Kolibri. *See* Kolibri

Flintlock   IGNITION SYSTEM

The flintlock mechanism sets off a firearm by means of sparks generated by a flint (or pyrites) striking against steel. Flintlock mechanisms

have been applied to **artillery** and tinder boxes as well as **pistols** and long arms. Gaining in importance during the seventeenth century, flintlock **muskets** became the main military arm during the eighteenth. Requiring no constant source of heat and easier to handle than the **matchlock**, the flintlock was also generally cheaper and less complex than the **wheel lock**. The flintlock may be divided into several subtypes that developed over time in different places.

The invention of a firearm ignited by a sparking flint is believed to date to the middle of the sixteenth century. A gun of 1556 with such a mechanism is in the Swedish Royal Armoury, though knowledge of the technology appears to have been reasonably widespread by that time. Such early pieces are often described as "snaphance" or "snap lock," terms derived from the Dutch as the cock, or flint-holding part of the mechanism, was held to resemble a pecking chicken, or *haan*. In these snap locks the cock is linked to a V-shaped spring, and the steel against which it strikes is pivoted vertically over a pan. Pulling a trigger releases a sear, or catch, allowing the flint to snap against the steel and sparks to fall into the pan, igniting the priming powder. The priming powder, communicating with the main charge in the barrel by means of a small hole, sets off the weapon.

Though basic snaphance guns continued to be produced for a century, particularly in Scandinavia and Russia; improvements were made continually. A sliding pan cover was incorporated into more advanced weapons in the late sixteenth century, and various forms of safety catch also began to appear. In "dog" locks a small pivoted hook was so placed as to engage the cock when drawn back. In the miquelet or patilla lock, used through much of the Mediterranean, full-cock and half-cock positions are possible. What is now generally defined as the true flintlock, with steel and pan cover in one piece and a cock with both full and half positions, probably evolved in France about 1610, with a documented example occurring c. 1620. The name "flintlock" does not itself seem to have been applied until rather later, though the term "fire lock" was used in English to refer to striking flint weapons for much of the century.

By the English Civil War of 1642–1651, fire locks had a well developed military niche, being thought especially useful for skirmishers, **snipers**, artillery guards, and sentinels. In any of these tasks a matchlock with its trailing smoldering match was seen as a liability, causing accidents among the **gunpowder**, being obvious to the enemy, and using up large amounts of match cord. It became customary to arm a company of each regiment, or special regiments, with flint-ignition weapons. In the Scottish army of 1648 there was such a unit, known as "Frazer's Firelocks." In France, long guns fitted with flint ignition were known as *fusils* as early as about 1630, and this term spread quite widely in the later seventeenth century. Regiments of fusiliers were formed as early as 1671. In the English-speaking world "fusil" came to mean a small or lightweight flintlock long arm; the Royal Regiment of Fusiliers was formed in 1685, armed with what was also described as a "Snaphance Musket . . . three foot eight inches long."

Nevertheless, flintlocks and matchlocks coexisted for a considerable period, and outside Europe early ignition systems would survive into the nineteenth century. On the European battlefield, the flintlock obtained primacy in the early eighteenth century, and it is also from this century that carefully defined and dated general "patterns" of military arm can first be readily identified.

Additional Reading: Blair (ed), *Pollard's History of Firearms*, 1983.

Flogger. *See* MiG-23

Flying Fortress, B-17   AIRCRAFT

The **Boeing** B-17 Flying Fortress U.S. bomber is one of the best known military **aircraft** of all time. The commencement of its development is usually taken to be the specification issued by the Army Air Corps in July 1934, which sought a machine to replace the Martin B-10. The new plane had to be capable of carrying a 2,000 lb bomb load and of cruising at speeds of 200 to 250 mph to a distance of 2,000 miles. Manufacturers were to build prototypes at their own expense. The Boeing board, headed by president Clairmont L. Egvedt, decided to put up $275,000 for the project, though ultimately the Boeing entry would cost $432,034.

The result was the Model 299, a sleek four-engined aluminum aircraft capable of carrying no less than 4,800 lb of bombs as far and as fast as the requirement. Moreover, it could mount five defensive **machine guns**. The prototype was first flown at Boeing Field, Seattle, on 28 July 1935 by test pilot Leslie Tower. In August 1935 the 299 flew to Wright Field at Dayton, Ohio, for competition with Martin and **Douglas** planes. Though the Boeing aircraft was quickly judged an excellent competitor, the test plane crashed, killing Tower and Major P. Hill. Understandably, no large order was forthcoming. Undaunted the manufacturers produced the 299B, or Y1B-17, in 1936. This suffered a bad landing, and congressional investigation followed.

Despite these adversities the Y1B-17 went into service trials in the summer of 1937 and soon gained a reputation for solid construction and safety. It would be 1939 however before further funding was forthcoming to expand the program and produce small numbers of the B-17B. The first model actually to see combat was the B-17C, supplied to Britain in the spring of 1941 and flown over Germany from July. Reports from combat experience were fed back to the United States, resulting in modifications to the later B-17E. Soon after U.S. entry into World War II, B-17s were in action over the Pacific.

The B-17F, produced from early 1942, was the first type to be made in very large numbers, Boeing, Douglas, and Lockheed manufacturing 3,400. The 75-foot-long B-17F was powered by four Wright Cyclone R-1820-97 engines, producing a maximum speed of 299 mph. It had a crew of ten, and ten .50-inch machine guns. With the maximum 6,000 lb load of bombs its range was 1,300 miles. Study into long-range Pacific operations would lead to the adoption of "Tokyo tanks" in the wings for extra fuel. Improvements over the E model included a new ball turret, a frameless plexiglass nose for better visibility, a dual braking system, and an AFCE (or "automatic flight control equipment") that gave the bombardier lateral control of the aircraft during the bomb run.

The most common Flying Fortress of all was the B-17G, a total of 8,680 of which were made from 1943 onward. This was very similar to the B-17F, but improvements included a small chin turret for forward defense, a redesigned tail turret, and staggered positions for the waist gunners. The B-17G could carry up to 13 machine guns, eight of them in four turrets. The maximum bomb load was now 9,600 lb. Despite remarkable armament, B-17s were still shot down by enemy fighters; in total more than a third were lost in combat. Indeed, it has been argued that the better the defense and bomb load of the B-17 became, the more vulnerable the aircraft. Nevertheless the 13,000 Flying Fortresses made a major contribution to the Allied bombing campaign, bearing a major share of the action, along with the **Lancaster** and **Liberator**.

Most B-17s were individually named by their crews. Among many outstanding machines were *Memphis Belle*, subject of a 1943 documentary and later feature film; *Nine-o-Nine* and *Milk Wagon*, veterans of 140 and 120 missions, respectively; and *Day's Pay* purchased for the U.S. Army Air Forces at a cost

of $300,000 by the employees of Hanford Engineering. *Bertie Lee* was nursed back from Brunswick by Lieutenant Edward S. Michael, one of 16 cases where USAAF B-17 crew members won the Medal of Honor.

Though the B-17 ceased to be used as a U.S. bomber soon after the war; other countries, including Taiwan and Israel, operated it for some time. The CIA also used the B-17 and with it developed the Fulton "Skyhook," the purpose of which was to snatch a person off the ground without landing. At the time of writing, 11 flying examples of the aircraft are known to exist, with possibly 40 others in various states of preservation. Confusingly, two surviving craft bear the name *Memphis Belle*, while a third is the *Miss Liberty Belle*.

Additional Reading: Bowman, *Boeing B-17 Flying Fortress*, 1998; Dorr, *US Bombers of World War Two*, 1989; Freeman, *The B-17 Flying Fortress Story*, 1998; Freeman and Anderton, *B-17 Fortress, B-29 Superfortress*, 1996.

Flying Pencil. *See* **Dornier**

Flying Platform   UNCONVENTIONAL AIRCRAFT

As early as 1946, Charles H. Zimmerman commenced research into small vertical takeoff military craft. Soon this line of thinking had given rise to the notion of the "flying platform," intended for battlefield use; a series of U.S. experimental designs were flown during the decade 1955 to 1965. Specific models included the de Lackner DH-5 Aerocycle, the Hiller VZ-1 Pawnee, and the Bensen B-10 Propcopter. This last flew in 1959; powered by two 72 horsepower engines, it had two propellers four feet in diameter and weighed 650 lb. More substantial were the **Curtiss**-Wright VZ-7 "flying truck," which had four propellers, and the Piasecki VZ-8P, also known as an "Airgeep."

Additional Reading: Rogers, *VTOL Military Research Aircraft*, 1989.

FN, FN Rifle. *See* **Fabrique Nationale**

Focke-Wulf Fw 190   AIRCRAFT

The outstanding German Fw 190 single-seat fighter **aircraft** was produced by the Focke-Wulf design team under the auspices of Kurt Tank. The prototype first flew in 1939, though it would not see actual combat until 1941. Its mean, big-engined appearance was by no means deceptive, since the **Junkers** Jumo motor gave well over 400 mph on later models. It was also maneuvrable and a good gun and bomb platform. In 1942 the Fw 190s were particularly active, providing air cover for *Scharnhorst* and her comrades as she headed for northern German ports. In the latter part of the war, the Fw 190 became a general workhorse; among its many duties were bomber interception, training, and ground attack. In this last role it made good use of its 20 mm cannon. The maximum bomb load on the 190G was a surprising 3,086 lb. Total production of all models was 20,051. The Fw 190 was supposed to be replaced by the Ta 152 model, which was similar in general appearance but was faster yet, with a top speed of 439 mph and a ceiling of 37,000 feet. Few were produced.

Focke-Wulf Fw 200. *See* Condor

Fokker   MANUFACTURER

The "flying Dutchman"—designer, pilot, and businessman—Anthon H. G. Fokker (1890–1939) was born in Java but moved to the Netherlands as a child. He studied in Germany and had early interests in automobiles and tires. His first aircraft was the Spin, variants of which were made between 1910 and 1913. He formed Fokker Aviatik company in 1912. He began to supply the German army air service and received Austrian orders after the outbreak of war in 1914.

Significant advances were made in 1915, when he produced a viable propeller-synchronized machine gun, or **interrupter gear**, and introduced the M series of monoplanes—later to be known as the E, or Eindecker, planes in service. Despite early, and sometimes fatal, problems, these innovative aircraft soon proved themselves, as reconnaissance platforms, later

as fighters. The E III, in action by September 1916, was powered by a 100 horsepower Oberursel engine and was armed with two synchronized **machine guns**. Yet rapid development of enemy aircraft demanded a response, and Fokker also began to build biplanes, the D I appearing in August 1916, and the D II, III, and IV soon after: he also manufactured C series trainers. A V, or test, model monoplane, nicknamed "the flea," which featured cantilever wings without connecting struts, was not greeted with enthusiasm, being perhaps ahead of its time.

Arguably Fokker's best known First World War aircraft was the triplane, or *Dreidecker*, Dr. I, immortalized by the "Red Baron," Manfred von Richtofen of the "Flying Circus." Chief designer on the project was Reinhold Platz. The plane weighed just 587 kg loaded and had an operational ceiling of 19,500 feet. Although capable of no more than 114 mph, the Dr Is "climbed like monkeys and manoeuvred like the devil," as von Richtofen put it. Between mid-1917 and May 1918 about 320 were built, and before being shot down Richtofen obtained 19 victories in this model.

In January 1918 Fokker won a contract to supply the D VII fighter. With a six-cylinder 185 horsepower BMW engine, the D VIIF was a biplane with twin machine guns; it was capable of 124 mph and had a good operational ceiling and rate of climb. Lack of capacity at Fokker's Schwerin works would see many D VIIs built under license by rival **Albatros**. Yet there were jealous rumors that good though Fokker products were, his contracts were obtained with the endorsement of aces whom Fokker wined, and supplied with female company, at the Hotel Bristol in Berlin. Nevertheless, he received ample official recognition, including both classes of the Iron Cross.

After World War I Fokker established a plant in the Netherlands, using many materials spirited out of German factories from under the noses of the Inter-Allied Control Commission. Aircraft civil and military were supplied to many powers. The Soviets took a consignment of D VII fighters, as did the Netherlands, Lithuania, and Switzerland. D XIII machines, then the fastest fighters in the world, supposedly bound for Argentina, landed up in the hands of the theoretically nonexistent Luftwaffe, which was training in the Soviet Union. The United States had PW5 types, and later D XIs as well as various test models; Fokker himself set up residence in the United States in 1925. New C and F series planes including light bombers and fighter bombers were developed, and the B series flying boats were constructed from 1922 to 1930.

The General Motors Corporation acquired a 40 percent holding in Fokker in 1929, but the partnership was stormy and Fokker retired from the position of director of engineering in 1931. Another serious blow was the appearance of the all-metal Douglas DC-1 in 1933, which spelled the end of Fokker supremacy. Nevertheless, many concerns had now purchased licenses to build Fokker products, and the name continued to be associated with planes as diverse as the Trimotor, PJ-1 flying boat, and TV bomber.

Though Anton Fokker died in 1939, Fokker aircraft would see service on both sides during World War II. The Dutch and Finns had many models, while the T VIII-W torpedo-bomber seaplane was used by the British and the Germans. The Danish army had C Is with BMW engines. Following liberation, a revived Fokker worked on jet models such as the S 14 trainer, license-built F8s and **Hunters**, and many joint U.S. ventures. Despite filing for bankruptcy in 1996, Fokker survived as a Stork subsidiary.

Additional Reading: Dierikx, *Fokker a Transatlantic Biography*, 1997; Hegener, *Fokker the Man and the Aircraft*, 1961; Leaman, *Fokker Aircraft of World War I*, 2001.

Folgore, C.202, and Saetta, M.C. 200
AIRCRAFT

The single-engined Saetta, or Lightning, Macchi M.C. 200, was one of Italy's major fighter **aircraft** at the outbreak of World War II. It made its first flight in 1937, and a total of 1151 were built. The much more impressive Folgore, or Thunderbolt, C.202 fighter, which was derived from the M.C. 200, entered service in 1941. In North Africa the new machine put up

a surprisingly good fight against aircraft like the **Curtiss P-40** and **Hurricane**. Key to its performance was the German-designed Daimler-Benz 601 engine, built under license by Alfa Romeo, which gave a top speed of 370 mph. The Folgore armament was two .5-inch **machine guns**.

Force de Frappe   NUCLEAR WARFARE

"Force de Frappe" comprises the independent French **nuclear** forces. These were first made public in 1955; France later built up a considerable nuclear power, including intermediate-range ballistic missiles, **aircraft**-dropped bombs, and submarine-launched **SLBM**s.

Forger, Yak-38   AIRCRAFT

The Soviet Yak-38 fighter **aircraft** flew in the early 1970s and was first deployed for naval use in 1976. Designed for vertical takeoff and landing, it is 52 feet long and has mid-mounted wings with a 25-foot span. Of comparable weight to the **Harrier**, it is carries a smaller payload. It has been used on **aircraft carriers**, including the *Kiev*.

Additional Reading: Rogers, *VTOL Military Research Aircraft*, 1989.

Forrestal Class   WARSHIP

James Vincent Forrestal (1892–1949) was under secretary, and then secretary, of the U.S. Navy during World War II. His name was perpetuated in a new class of **aircraft carrier** approved by Congress after the outbreak of the Korean War in 1950. Though originally conceived as straight and flush-deck carriers without islands, the design was quickly changed to incorporate an angled flight deck and small offset island. Significantly, this would be the first time that the flight deck became an integral member of the hull structure in U.S. carriers. The first vessel to be commissioned was *Forrestal* (CVA 59) in 1955; within four years it had been followed by *Saratoga, Ranger*, and *Independence*. The *Forrestal* class displaced 61,000 tons and could take 90 aircraft.

Advancing technology, however, soon put

the original four *Forrestal*s out of date, with the result that a further four ships—*Kitty Hawk, Constellation, America,* and the *John F. Kennedy* (CVA 67)—commissioned between 1961 and 1968, are often regarded as "improved *Forrestals.*" These featured, amongst other things, a deletion of conventional gun armament and the addition of **Terrier** launchers (Sea Sparrow on the *JFK*), an enlarged flight deck, and redistributed lifts. The *Forrestal*s saw action during the Vietnam War, the *Forrestal* itself being badly damaged by a fire. The *JFK* showed significant differences to the others including a remodelled landing deck and a funnel which angled outwords.

Additional Reading: Friedman, *US Aircraft Carriers,* 1983.

Fort; Fortification   FORTIFICATION

Fortification is one of the oldest military sciences. Defensive town walls feature in the Old Testament, and siege warfare was well established in ancient Greece. Western European Iron Age hill forts with banks and ditches have been dated to the eighth century B.C., with the elaborate example at Maiden Castle, Dorset, United Kingdom, as large as 1,000 meters in length. Roman camps and forts formed the nodes of road systems, which often dictated settlement and communication patterns.

Though the Great Wall of China is undoubtedly the most impressive linear defense, there have been many of considerable scale throughout history. Offa's Dyke and the Roman Hadrian's wall in the United Kingdom are excellent ancient examples, while in twentieth-century Europe the **Maginot Line**, West Wall, and **Atlantic Wall** were just three of the best known. Though "forts" are commonly thought of as earthworks or wooden structures, and "castles" are of masonry, this distinction was not applied historically. The first Norman castles, for example, were of wood on mounds or earthen "mottes," while many forts have incorporated stone facings or concrete.

The medieval castle showed considerable technological advance between 1100 and 1450. Simple rectangular Norman keeps gave way to increasingly sophisticated structures with shell or concentric designs and towers linked by curtain walls. One or more "baileys" ensured that attackers could not gain immediate access to the heart of the fortress. Square corners gave way to round towers, less vulnerable to **mining** and **catapults**. Both wet and dry moats were used to keep miners and siege engines at bay, while **arrow** slits, "murder holes," and finally gunports enabled castle garrisons to shoot at their besiegers.

The impact of **gunpowder artillery** upon fortification is difficult to overstress. The shot-resistant angled bastion appeared in embryonic form in a number of wedge-shaped towers built in the latter part of the fifteenth century. Fully formed bastions appeared in the 1490s, as exemplified by the fort of Civita Castellana, remodeled by Antonio da Sangallo the Elder from 1494. Thereafter modern fortifications appeared over much of northern Italy, spreading into France and Switzerland. Early in the following century, deep-set, drumlike, hybrid castle-fortresses were built by Henry VIII for the defense of the English coast. The borderlands of France were reinforced with such works as those at Metz and Toul.

By the end of the sixteenth century, complex pentagonal forts dominated Flanders and the Netherlands, to the extent that their durability largely determined the outcome Dutch wars of liberation against Spain. The dominance of forts was confirmed in the late sixteenth and early seventeenth centuries, when the French engineer Sebastien Vauban was the preeminent designer of fortifications. Star-shaped forts and bastioned traces now defended many European cities, and similar ideas would be spread to the Americas. **Mortars** and **howitzers** were of increasing importance.

Though nineteenth-century warfare was characterized by maneuver, there were many new fortresses, as well as campaigns where forts were crucial. The siege of Sevastopol in the Crimea lasted almost a year; while Vicksburg and Petersburg were of crucial importance in the American Civil War. In Europe, stone casemates, earthworks, and batteries with "bomb proof" shelters created new barriers. These included new works on the border of France, and Lord "Palmerston's follies," which protected the British coast in the 1860s. Though the forts of Paris were thirty years old by 1870, they sustained a Prussian siege of four months.

By the latter part of the nineteenth century new forts were being built with surprisingly modern characteristics. Earth banks with lines of trenches were being protected by obstacle zones and supplied by **railway**. In the ideal plan of the French general Brialmont, armor-plated batteries, cupolas, and rifled mortars were key features. The complementary significance of "field works"—small-scale defenses constructed in the field—was demonstrated in South Africa and the Russo-Japanese War of 1904–1905. Though it was trenches and **barbed wire** that dominated World War I, especially from 1915 to 1917, forts were far from valueless, as was demonstrated at Verdun. Technological improvements of the period included new **pillboxes** and the widespread use of reinforced concrete.

Since 1918 fortification has been in and out of fashion. The failure of the **Maginot Line**, the Siegfried Line, and the eventual reduction of Japanese works in the Pacific seemed to suggest that the time of forts was at an end. With certain exceptions, including Sweden, coastal defenses were widely discontinued. Nevertheless, fortified "fire bases" were an important part of the war in Vietnam. Moreover the advent of **nuclear weapons** and the Cold War led to the widespread building of shelters. These were designed to protect governmental and civilian installations as well as strictly military targets. In Switzerland, the building of shelters for new houses was made mandatory.

Additional Reading: Duffy, *Siege Warfare*, 1979; Clarke, *Fortification*, (undated); Fortress Study Group, *Fort: Journal of the Fortress Study Group*, (continuing); Bidwell, *Roman Forts in Britain*, 1997.

Fox Armored Car   VEHICLE

The British Fox **armored car** appeared in prototype in 1969. Developed from the Ferret and rather longer, at 13 feet 4 inches, it was powered by a Jaguar 195 horsepower engine.

Weight was reduced by the extensive use of aluminum.

Foxtrot Class   SUBMARINE

Produced from 1958 to 1984, the Soviet Foxtrot class **submarines** served not only the Soviet Union but India, Libya, and Cuba. Powered by diesel and electric engines, the Foxtrots had a maximum speed of 18 knots. The displacement was 2,475 tons and the crew 75 men. Ten **torpedo** tubes were arranged six in the bow and four in the stern. One of the 62 vessels that served with the Soviet Navy (Nato code *U-475*) is now moored as a visitor attraction in Folkestone Harbor, United Kingdom.

Additional Reading: Jordan, *Soviet Submarines*, 1989.

FR 12. *See* La Galissonniere

Fragmentation Grenade, M11A1
EXPLOSIVE DEVICE

Based on a French design, the standard fragmentation **grenade** was adopted by the U.S. Army in 1917. Minor improvements would produce the M11A1, which was used throughout World War II and beyond. With a cast-iron body and a four-and-a-half-second fuse, it weighed just over 1 lb. Using a grenade projector adaptor, it could be fitted with a fin assembly and fired from a **rifle**.

Freedom Fighter. *See* Tiger, F-5

Friction Tube. *See* Artillery

Frigate   WARSHIP

The name "frigate," first rendered "figat," or even "frygatte," is known to have been in use as early as the 1580s. As a midsized warship, the frigate was historically regarded as the largest not to warrant inclusion in the **line of battle**. Traditionally frigates featured raised quarterdecks and forecastles. An English commission of 1618 recommended that the wooden sailing frigate should be nimble and three times as long as wide. The term "frigate" was therefore particularly associated with speed and relative lightness of construction, and frigates tended to be used as multipurpose scouts and raiders. The English navy later rated such vessels as fifth and sixth rates.

Typical early frigates included the Dutch 34-gun *Delft* of 1667, the 42-gun French *Amazone* of 1707, and the British 20 and 40-gun ships produced on the 1719 establishment. Thereafter, with increasing rivalry between France and England, frigates tended to increase in power, with the French 40-gun single-decker setting the pace for the mideighteenth century. The British answer would be the *Southampton, Pallas,* and *Brilliant* classes mounting 32 to 36 guns. Later still the **Constitution** was described as a "heavy frigate."

During World War II "frigate" was applied to a new type of naval escort that has been defined as a "large **corvette**." The frigate has continued to be important for many duties, including antisubmarine warfare. Significant types have included the British **Leander** and **Type 22** classes, the French F2000, Australian River class, and the U.S. *Garcia* and **Oliver Hazard Perry** classes. In Russia some types of **destroyer** are called *fregats*, though the main Russian type recognized in the West as a frigate is the **Krivak**. Many other countries make extensive use of frigates. India, for example, has two major types: the Russian-built *Talwar* and the *Godavari*, built at Mazagon Dock, Bombay.

Additional Reading: Chapelle, *The History of the American Sailing Navy*, 1949; Gardiner, *Line of Battle*; Cocker, *Frigates Sloops and Patrol Vessels of the Royal Navy*, 1985; *Jane's Fighting Ships*; Henderson, *Frigates*, 1970.

Fritz-X   EXPLOSIVE DEVICE

The Fritz-X, also known as the FX 1400 or SD 1400, was a German World War II glide bomb, radio controlled by the aircraft that released it. Development began in 1939, and the weapon was in service by mid-1943. The bomb contained 1400 kg of explosive and was fitted with four wings. The tail contained radio equipment and gyroscopes; the bomb aimer guided the

missile by tracking its built-in flare to the target. A wire-guided version was developed later.

Additional Reading: Hogg, *German Secret Weapons of the Second World War*, 1999.

Frog Missile   MISSILE

The Soviet Frog missiles of the 1950s were relatively simple but large and destructive unguided surface-to-surface weapons suitable for bombardment. With a range of 30 miles, a length of 33 feet 6 inches, and a weight of 4,4000 lb, they could be moved by means of a tracked vehicle with the launch rail on top. The warhead could be nuclear or conventional. Many improved versions were produced, some with greater range or using wheeled launchers, during the remainder of the twentieth century.

FSADS. *See* Sabot

F-S Fighting Knife   EDGED WEAPON

Invented by W. E. Fairbairn and E. A. Sykes of the Shanghai Police in 1940 and manufactured by Wilkinson in the United Kingdom from January 1941, the "F-S" is important as the precursor of many modern military fighting knives. Its very sharp, slender, 7.5-inch blade has been widely imitated. Similar U.S. types included the Marine Corps Stiletto and the OSS knife.

Additional Reading: Stephens, *Fighting Knives*, 1980; Buerlein, *Allied Military Fighting Knives*, 2001.

FT-17. *See* Renault FT-17 Light Tank

Fubuki Class   WARSHIP

In their day the 388-foot-long Japanese *Fubuki* "Special Type" **destroyers** were some of the best in the world. The class was commenced with the laying down of the *Fubuki* in June 1926, and eventually 20 such ships were constructed. Displacing 1,750 tons, they possessed powerful armament that included six 5-inch guns, **torpedo** tubes, and **sea mines**. Their top speed was 37 knots. Some early structural problems were later rectified by moving weight lower within the vessel and reducing the torpedo load. Though they performed well in World War II the *Fubuki*s were virtually annihilated. Only the *Ushio* survived the conflict.

Fuel-Air Explosive Bomb   EXPLOSIVE DEVICE

Developed by U.S. Navy scientists in 1966, fuel-air **explosives** work by mixing a fuel with the surrounding air prior to detonation. Usually such bombs were air dropped and slowed by drogue **parachutes**. The bomb cannister ruptured on impact, creating a concentrated mist that was then ignited. Blast pressures of 300 lb per square inch resulted. In Vietnam, where such weapons were first used, they proved particularly adept at exploding minefields or blasting clear areas of jungle. The latest variation on the theme is the **thermobaric bomb**.

FUG. *See* BRDM

"Funnies"   TANK

"Funny" has been used as a popular term for special-purpose armored vehicles such as engineer tanks, **duplex drives**, and **flails**. Another important sort of funny was the "Bobbin," which laid trackway from a spool, allowing other vehicles and personnel to cross difficult terrain. The name was first applied in the United Kingdom, in World War II, to Major General P. C. S. Hobart's 79th Armored Division. In this formation were concentrated the special machines required for breaching the **Atlantic Wall** on D-Day.

Furious, HMS   WARSHIP

HMS *Furious*, one of Britain's earliest and most innovative **aircraft carriers**, was first laid down as a cruiser in 1915, undergoing various changes to specification before commissioning in 1917. She originally carried four **Sopwith** Pups and four Seaplanes; she had at first few dedicated facilities but was extensively modified in November 1917. She was then fitted with a 300-foot landing deck at the bow. Other novelties included primitive arresting wires and electric elevators serving the hangars.

After World War I *Furious* was repeatedly refitted to bring her up to date. The very extensive work included a differently shaped landing deck, new elevators capable of dealing with 8,000 lb at a time, and deck island added in 1939. Gunnery **radar** was one of the final improvements. She fought with distinction in both world wars and survived to be scrapped in 1948.

Fuse; Fuze   IGNITION SYSTEM

Fuzes may be used to initiate **explosive** devices such as **shells**, bombs and **mines**. A distinction is sometimes made between a "fuse," which is a train of combustible material, and a "fuze," which initiates the charge at a given moment. Some of the earliest were wooden tubes filled with compressed gun powder, used in **grenades**. These were known in the fifteenth century. Later, time fuzes had divisions on the outside to indicate the length of burning. Some of the first attempts to produce percussion, or "explode on impact" fusing, relied on gravity or shock to drive a heat source into gunpowder.

Fuze technology advanced with the industrial revolution, metal parts such as springs and strikers, clock components, and fulminates, making greater complexity possible. Bickford's fuse, patented in 1831, introduced a more reliable time element, having powder wound within a twine covering, varnished and protected externally. By the middle of the nineteenth century percussion fuzes had been joined by concussion fuzes, which were initiated by the shock of the discharge of the artillery piece that fired them. Colonel Breithaupt is credited with the invention of the metal time fuze with a rotating cap. Detonanting cord, or "cordeau," using liquid TNT in its manufacture, was invented in France before World War I.

Fuze technology accelerated from 1914 as the combatants sought means to answer many new technical problems, such as shells that would burst at ground level to clear barbed wire and trenches, and means to combat aircraft at height. New types of fuzing were also developed for such new weapons as the aircraft-dropped bomb and the rifle grenade. Various models were now armed by the spinning of small vanes or propellers as projectiles flew through the air, others by abrupt changes in velocity; some were fired by electricity. Pins, shear wires, uncoiling tapes, weights, and small drop-out bolts were all used as mechanical safety mechanisms.

Further advances during World War II would see experimentation with "continuously adjustable" fuses—set when they were actually in the gun, using the latest data. These would be overtaken by the appearance of "proximity" fuzes, activated when passing near their target. The U.S. T97, for example, contained a radio unit in the head. Proximity fuzes were pioneered by Forman, Butement, and Pollard in the United Kingdom and Tuve in the United States. The first battle success went to the USS *Helena* in 1943, when a Japanese aircraft became the first casualty to an electronic fuze. An idea of the scope presented by modern fuzes is given by the fact that during 1939 to 1945 the German army used roughly a hundred different models for artillery alone.

Current U.S. Army literature refers to several distinct categories of fuze type. Time fuzes may be subdivided into electrical, mechanical, and MTSQ (mechanical time and superquick). Explode-on-impact types are listed as either point-detonating or point-initiating/base-detonating. Proximity fuzes also known as "influence types" are listed and may be designated VT, or variable timed.

Additional Reading: Hogg, *British and American Artillery of World War II*, 1978; Brown, *The Big Bang*, 1998; Margiotta, *Brassey's Encyclopedia of Land Forces and Warfare*, 1996.

Fusil. *See* **Flintlock**

Future Combat System   TANK

"Future Combat System" is the working program title given to the latest generation of U.S. **tanks**, under development in 2002. They are expected to be of much lower silhouette than the existing **Abrams** and use **stealth** technology to help hide them from the enemy. The crews will view the world using large all-round screens inside the tank. Weight is to be kept under 40 tons for airlift into combat.

FV 430, 432, "Trojan" APC   VEHICLE

Developed at the UK Fighting Vehicles Research and Development Establishment in the late 1950s, the FV 430 series was a family of fully tracked armored personnel carriers inspired by the U.S. **M113** and M59. The commonest of the type was the FV 432, originally dubbed Trojan. Easy to drive, the 432 weighed 33,300 lb, was 16 feet 9 inches long, and was powered by a two-stroke Rolls-Royce engine giving a top speed of 35 mph. It carried a section of ten plus a commander and driver.

Among the many variants were included a recovery vehicle, minelayer, **Swingfire** launcher, signal vehicle, command vehicle, and **mortar**-locating **radar** platform. Some versions incorporated a small turret, and many were mounted with a **machine gun**. The 432 was the standard personnel carrier of British forces until the appearance of **Warrior**.

Additional Reading: Chamberlain & Ellis, *Making Tracks: The British Carrier Story 1914–1972*, 1973.

FZG 76. *See* **V1**

G

G3 Rifle   FIREARM

Adopted by the West German Bundeswehr in 1959, the 7.62 mm **Heckler and Koch** G3 **rifle** was one of the most successful designs of recent times, being widely used in other countries. With plastic furniture in the later models and weighing just over 4 kg, it has a full automatic capability and is effective to about 400 meters. Normally 102 cm long, there is also a retractable-butt version that reduces the length to 80 cm. It has similarities to the **MP 5 submachine gun**.

Additional Reading: *Jane's Infantry Weapons.*

G88, G98. *See* Mauser

Gainful (SA-6)   MISSILE

The Soviet Gainful surface-to-air missile, first displayed to the public in 1967, soon became a standard in the communist arsenal. Mounted in threes atop a tracked launcher vehicle, each semiactive radar homing missile weighed 1,212 lb and had a range of 37 miles to a ceiling of around 11 miles.

Galil   FIREARM

Developed by Yaccov Lior and Israel Galil, the Galil **assault rifle** was produced in the late 1960s and adopted by Israeli forces in 1972. Intended as a general-purpose arm to fill the roles of both **submachine gun** and **rifle**, it could also be used to project **grenades**. There are shortened models, a **sniper** derivative, and types with and without a bipod. The Galil bipod is interesting in that it doubles as a wirecutter.

Based on the **Kalashnikov** system, with a trigger similar to that of the **Garand**, the Galil is gas operated. It is fed from box magazines, some of which are plastic and contain up to 50 rounds.

Additional Reading: *Jane's Infantry Weapons*; Walter, *Kalashnikov*, 1999; Ezell, *Small Arms of the World*, various editions.

Galleon   WARSHIP

Probably derived from the early sixteenth-century Spanish *galeones*, the galleon dominated naval warfare from about 1540. Though the earliest included oars, like the older **galley**, the fully developed galleon was a fully rigged seagoing sailing vessel. The classic Spanish galleon of the late sixteenth century was used for both war and trade, had a high sterncastle, square stern, lower forecastle, and a beak below the bowsprit. Though commonly under 1,000 tons, the largest examples, like the French *Couronne* of 1636, were almost double this displacement. The Venetians, Dutch, and Portuguese were particular exponents of the galleon, in varying forms. Vessels such as the *Wasa, Mayflower*, and *Santiago* may generally be described as galleons.

Additional Reading: Gardiner (ed), *Cogs, Caravels and Galleons*, 1994.

Galley   WARSHIP

The dominant vessel of ancient naval warfare was the oared galley. Though oars were the main form of propulsion, many galleys also carried a sail. As early as the eighth century B.C., galleys with 50 oars, benches for the rowers, and a ram at the prow are described in Homer's *Odyssey*. Later, much greater numbers of oarsmen were employed; the amounts of timber required for the biggest galleys has been blamed for the deforestation of central Greece. Ships with two banks of oars are described as biremes, while triple-bank ships were triremes. Initially it was possible to man galleys without resort to force, though in later years galley slaves were used. Some galleys were equipped with **catapults**.

The galley survived as a military technology much longer than is commonly realized, being regularly seen in naval warfare, particularly in the Mediterranean, until late in the sixteenth century. They were employed not only by Phoenician, Greek, Carthaginian, and Roman navies but also by comparatively modern states, such as Venice and Spain.

Gama Goat   VEHICLE

The novel Gama Goat U.S. military vehicle was designed by Robert L. Gamaunt of Fawnskin, California, and was built in prototype by the Ling Temco Vought Corporation of Dallas in 1961. After grueling testing it was accepted in 1966, and it was later used in several variants produced by the Condec Corporation. Powered by a Chevrolet Corvair 80 horsepower engine or a GM Detroit 103 horsepower diesel, it was perhaps the most agile military vehicle of its day. The secret of the design was that it comprised two articulated units that could roll independently of each other and be uncoupled if required. The rear compartment of the cargo unit could accomodate eight troops.

Garand Rifle, M1   FIREARM

John Cantius Garand (1888–1974) was born in Quebec, Canada, but moved to Connecticut as a boy. Employed in a textile mill, he soon showed a flair for all things mechanical. By the First World War Garand was involved in weapons design, and from 1919 he worked at the **Springfield** Armory. His early essays in armaments included a light machine gun, but he is best known for the "U.S. Rifle, Caliber .30

M1," which was officially adopted in 1936 and is now more commonly known as the Garand rifle.

The prime importance of the Garand was that it was the first semiautomatic rifle to be generally adopted by any major power, giving the ordinary American soldier a firepower advantage over much of the opposition through World War II. Key to the Garand was a gas-operated system with a sliding and rotating bolt allied to an eight-round, clip-loaded magazine. After the eighth shot the clip was ejected with a distinctive "ping." The rifle was robust and reliable, with more than adequate power and accuracy for the job in hand.

From 1941 to 1945 just over four million Garands were produced by **Springfield** and **Winchester**. Garand was given the Civilian Medal of Honor for his efforts in 1944. With the Korean War, production was again stepped up, with International Harvester and Harrington and Richardson also making the rifle. In this conflict the Garand continued to receive praise for its suitability and ability to operate in harsh conditions, most notably from S.L.A. Marshall in his *Infantry Operations and Weapons Usage in Korea* (1953). The Garand was widely used in other countries and influenced the design of other weapons.

Additional Reading: Canfield, *A Collector's Guide to the M1 Garand and the M1 Carbine*, 1989; Pyle, *The Gas Trap Garand*, 1999.

Gardner Gun. *See* Machine Gun

Gas   CHEMICAL WARFARE

Though the use of smoke, incendiaries, and **Greek fire** in warfare dates back to biblical times, the first systematic use of chemical substances in a gaseous state belongs to the period of the First World War. The growth of the idea in the nineteenth century had led to a clause in the Hague Convention of 1899 in which the signatories agreed not to deploy "projectiles, the sole use of which is the diffusion of asphyxiating or harmful gases." Nevertheless, experiment had continued, and small-scale trials and uses of "lachrymators," or "tear" gases, had

STEEL MILLS.....

BRISTOL PYROMETERS HELP
STEEL MILLS TURN OUT BETTER
STEEL FOR GUNS.

PERFECT RIFLE BARRELS

FOR GARAND RIFLES ARE MADE
WITH THE HELP OF SUPERIOR
BRISTOL INSTRUMENTS.

Precision manufacture was vital to rifle accuracy. In this poster Bristol pyrometers claims its part in the manufacture of the U.S. Garand semiautomatic rifle, the GIs' mainstay of World War II. Courtesy of the National Archives.

followed, without significant effect. So it was that the first-large scale use of **chlorine gas**, by the Germans, who released it from cylinders at Ypres on 22 April 1915, came as a considerable shock and was widely regarded as an atrocity.

Thereafter many nations rushed to produce both gases and gas defenses, such as **gas masks**. As in other fields the combatants continually attempted to produce something more deadly than the weapon held by the enemy. The French soon formed a body called the Direction du Matériel Chimique de Guerre to supply

chemical warfare materials, while the British formed "special companies" for chemical warfare. Yet it was the Germans who first used **phosgene** in December 1915, and the blistering agent **mustard gas** in 1917. Though chlorine, phosgene, and various mustard type gases saw the most widespread deployment, many other substances were developed during the Great War. These included Jellite (a mixture of prussic acid, chloroform, and triacetyl cellulose), Vincennite (prussic acid, chloroform, stannic chloride, and arsenious chloride), sulphuretted hydrogen, chloropicrin, and various arsenical compounds.

Gas was horrible in its effects yet failed signally as a war-winning wonder weapon. As more lethal gases appeared, so did ever more effective protections. Surprise gave way to familiarity; gas became a weapon of harassment, forcing its victims to seek protection and making them become less efficient soldiers as a result. Rarely did it result in mass fatalities; often men were temporarily incapacitated, and some were permanently crippled, but usually chemical weapons proved less effective than shells or bullets.

Though the chemical compounds had widely varying effects, often requiring differing defensive precautions, it may be argued that the diverse delivery systems developed were of equal technological significance. Early discharges from cylinders, or "cloud attacks," suffered from the fact that they required very specific weather conditions and had to be released in one's own front line. Gas **shells** to be fired from **artillery** and **mortars** were therefore introduced. The gas shell had the great advantage that it could be fired with reasonable accuracy against distant targets, provided no warning of its arrival, and was less dangerous to friendly troops. On the debit side, gas shells carried relatively little active ingredient and were therefore required in large numbers to build up worthwhile concentrations of gas. The use of cylinders and shells therefore continued in parallel.

Delivery problems were much reduced with the introduction of "gas projectors," or large-bore, lightweight, mortars, which could be fired in batteries, giving most of the advantages of the gas shell combined with immediate large concentrations of gas. The first of these weapons was the Livens projector, developed by Captain Livens of the Royal Engineers in 1916. This consisted of a large metal tube with a sombrero-shaped base plate, usually sunk into the ground on a predetermined alignment; drums could be hurled about 350 yards. Originally intended as a long-range **flamethrower** the Livens was soon adapted for gas munitions;

it was made all the more deadly by remote electric firing.

Gas was used during the Allied intervention in Russia in 1919, and despite a Geneva Protocol in 1925 against its use, it was also used in Ethiopia by the Italians and in China by the Japanese. Though the blood agent Zyklon B was used during the genocide of the Holocaust and gas was accidentally released on at least one occasion during combat in World War II, there was no systematic battlefield deployment during 1939 to 1945. Even so, development of weapons continued apace, and a general capacity existed for the use of chemical munitions from large artillery pieces, mortars, and rocket projectors. Nerve agents such as **Tabun, Sarin**, and **Soman** made their appearance, renewing the debate over both the lethality and legality of chemical warfare.

After 1945 both the Eastern and Western powers built up large chemical weapons stockpiles. Actual use was rare, however, and was perhaps most widespread where chemicals were used as defoliants rather than man killers. Such was the case with the deployment of **Agent Orange** by the United States in Vietnam. While practical application was generally lacking, the advance of technology continued, and new chemical agents for military use were identified. An important advance was the development of binary chemical munitions, in which the ingredients of nerve gases were held apart during handling and storage, mixing and becoming lethal only after release from a delivery system. These delivery systems now included not only new types of bombs and shells but **aircraft** underwing reservoirs and rockets. The Iran-Iraq War, however, saw a resurgence in the use of chemical weapons including nerve and blistering agents, and at Halamjeh in 1988 Saddam Hussein used gas on his own people.

By the end of the twentieth century, chemical warfare weapons were generally divided into seven major categories. The first of these were the old choking agents, including phosgene or (CG), diphosgene, and chlorine, all of which attacked the respiratory tract, and were now seldom encountered as munitions. The nerve agents, including Tabun (GA), Sarin

(GB), Soman, and the so called V-Agents, worked by upsetting the balance in the nervous system by causing its continuous stimulation; they remained current, though they could be nullified by the rapid administration of autonomic blocking agents. The blood agents were defined as those absorbed into the body through breathing, thereafter preventing the transfer of oxygen from the blood; these included hydrogen cyanide (AC), cyanogen chloride (CK), and arsine (SA). The blister agents were the successors to the old Mustard gas and Lewisite; these now included distilled mustard (HD), nitrogen mustard (HN-1, HN-2, and HN-3), mustard-Lewisite (HL), phosgene oxime (CX), methyldichloroarsine (MD), and others.

Vomiting agents including diphenylchloroarsine (DA), Adamsite (DM), and diphenylcyanoarsine (DC) were designed primarily for riot control but could also cause serious illness or death in confined spaces. Tear agents, or lachrymators, such as chloroacetophenone (CN), CNC, CNS, CNB, and BBC, were similarly intended for riot situations but had substantially been replaced by CS—O-chlorobenzalmalonitrile, the ubiquitous CS gas—in general use. Incapacitating chemical agents, such as BZ, were intended to act by producing either temporary physical incapacity, such as paralysis or blindness, or temporary mental aberrations.

Additional Reading: Gander (ed), *Jane's NBC Protection Equipment*, 1988; Richter, *Chemical Soldiers*, 1992; Haber, *The Poisonous Cloud*, 1986; Croddy, *Chemical and Biological Warfare*, 2002; Burck and Flowerree, *International Handbook on Chemical Weapons Proliferation*, 1991; Conti, *Beyond Pepper Spray*, 2002; Palazzo, *Seeking Victory on the Western Front*, 2000.

Gas Masks CHEMICAL WARFARE

The first **gas** masks, produced in early 1915, were simple pads dipped in water or urine and held over the nose and mouth. These were soon joined by mine breathing apparatus and converted chloroform masks, often impregnated with neutralizing chemicals. A minor improvement was a pad held in place by tapes designed by the British lieutenant Barley that could be worn with goggles and was dipped in a neutralizing "hypo" solution. A French P2 model on similar lines was in service later in the year. Animal testing was used at an early stage, with rodents in jars sealed off by various fabrics impregnated with the different chemicals to be tried, being a prime research tool. By May 1915 Captain Cluny Macpherson, medical officer to the Newfoundland Regiment, had produced a radically new design of "gas helmet" or "smoke hood," in which a bag of impregnated flannel was pulled right over the head. In an improved "tube" model a mouthpiece for exhalation was incorporated. (Though of limited effectiveness, this design would be revived at the end of the twentieth century as a potential short-term protection for passengers escaping smoke-filled aircraft.)

Thereafter many new masks were manufactured, either for better sustained protection or to combat the new types of gas being introduced. A marked divergence now emerged between one-piece masks with a filter attached direct to the face, such as the German 1915 model and the French ARS, and the box respirators, such as the Harrison's Tower and the SBR, which became the C.E. Box Respirator in U.S. service. The "box" designs featured a tube from the face mask on the end of which was a container for the neutralizing substances, such as lime permanganate granules and charcoal. One-piece masks with attached filters had the advantage that they were compact and lacked any tube to snag; however, box respirators could deal with greater volumes of air, placed less weight on the face, and gave better overall protection. In the long term it also proved more practical to improve the boxes than to add ever more bulky filters to face masks.

Nevertheless the divergence between one-piece and box designs persisted, and World War II would see the U.S., British, Japanese, Polish, French, and Soviet militaries using box types, while the Germans and Hungarians had one-piece masks. The basic U.S. mask at the outbreak of war was the "Army Service," which had much in common with its 1918 predecessor. It was a heavy box-type carried in a canvas

Men of the First World War American Expeditionary Force ready for gas drill behind the front line trenches of Lorraine, Western Front, during the latter stages of the conflict. The "C.E."-type respirators are based on the tried and tested "Small Box" British model. © Culver Pictures.

carrier around the neck, had a brown rubber hose, and was fitted with a flutter-type exhaust valve. Yet as the war progressed without battlefield use of chemical weapons, a number of nations including the United States and United Kingdom introduced lightweight variant masks. "Anti-dim" kits with compounds to prevent misting of lenses of masks were now commonplace. Unlike in World War I, civilians were now also widely issued with masks, though generally of a simpler type than those given to soldiers, who were deemed to be at greater risk.

Gas masks have continued to be general-issue military technology ever since. A few are worthy of specific mention. The Soviet ShM was the standard protective helmet-type mask for much of the Warsaw Pact during the latter days of communism. It was a dual-purpose mask in which the filter (MO-2 or MO-4U type) could either be attached directly to the rubber head piece or onto the end of a hose, thus providing the benefits of both one-piece and box respirator designs. An additional anticarbon

monoxide filter could be fitted between the mask and main filter box. An interesting feature was that incoming air was directed across the eye pieces, thus automatically reducing misting. In a modified ShMS model there was provision for the fitting of optically corrective lenses to the mask. Though efficient, the ShM and its fabric carrier weighed about 2 kg.

The British Respirator **NBC** S10, produced by Avon Industrial Polymers, was developed as the result of a program commenced in 1982 and was accepted into service in 1985. With four different-sized molded face pieces, it incorporates a drinking aperture with a safety valve, and various communication devices. The filter can be side mounted on the mask, or the mask can be attached to remote filters. Tinted lenses can be provided against flash, and it weighs less than 1 kg. A version known as the US10 was developed for the American XM40 respirator selection program.

The multipurpose chemical-biological mask actually accepted as the U.S. XM40, replacing

Engraving showing an 1871 model Gatling gun, on the all metal Broadwell type carriage. © Culver Pictures.

the 1960s M17, has a somewhat convoluted history. Originally intended as a low-risk option to incorporate tried and tested features of existing equipments, it was the result of a protracted testing of competing masks between 1984 and 1987. Scott Aviation eventually won, though contractual problems dogged production and issue. At the bottom end of the scale in terms of sophistication must be the Italian Sekur-Pirelli NBC Facelet. This is a simple cloth bag, decribed as a precautionary measure, that may be slipped into the pocket; when fitted it covers only the nose and mouth, in the manner of the earliest masks. It incorporates three layers: an outer of water and oil repellant fabric, a fiberglass filter, and a foam inner layer impregnated with charcoal.

Additional Reading: Gander (ed), *Jane's NBC Protection Equipment*, 1988; Fisch, *Field Equipment of the Infantry 1914–1945*, 1989; *History of the Ministry of Munitions*; Conti, *Beyond Pepper Spray*, 2002.

Gatling Gun   FIREARM

As a young man, Dr. Richard J. Gatling (1818–1903), of North Carolina, was employed as a legal clerk and country storekeeper while inventing part-time. Early efforts included a form of screw propeller for ships, and a seed drill. While studying medicine, Gatling also found time to produce a machine for beating hemp fiber, a steam plow, and other devices. It was only with the outbreak of the Civil War that he turned to armaments.

The first Gatling gun was covered by Patent 36,836, granted on 4 November 1862. This was essentially a revolving cluster of six barrels arranged in a circle, worked by a hand crank, so arranged that turning the handle turned the barrels and cocked and released hammers to discharge bullets from small steel chambers. A hopper, or reservoir, replenished the barrels with fresh chambers by gravity feed. Even this first model, prone to gas leakage and excessive friction, was claimed to be capable of 200 rounds per minute. Modifications, the most important of which involved changing from chambers to metallic cartridges, gradually improved the practicality of the system. Small numbers were sold to the U.S. Army and Navy, but an 1865 improved model of the gun was not formally adopted until 1866.

Though sometimes referred to as a **"machine gun,"** the original Gatling was technically a mechanical "revolving battery" gun, as it required continuous externally applied motive power to keep firing. It is also the case that the Gatling was just the most successful of several weapons that operated on similar principles. As early as 1718 English inventor James Puckle had patented a tripod-mounted revolver-type weapon. A Belgian Fafschamps gun with 50 breechloading barrels was tested in 1857 to 1859 and appears to have inspired the Montigny Mitrailleuse. American Wilson Ager produced a "coffee mill" gun using preloaded steel tubes; it saw action as early as 1862. A cranked repeating gun designed by Ezra Ripley was patented in 1861.

Nevertheless, the Gatling proved to be an inspirational design. It was sold to Britain, Russia, and Turkey, and it saw successful action in numerous wars. By 1883 Gatling was experimenting with the use of steam to power his gun, and a significant breakthrough was achieved in 1890 when the harnessing of electricity to a Gatling produced an astonishing 1,500 rounds in a minute. By 1893 tests are said to have achieved as many as 3,000 rounds per minute, though the advent of truly automatic, self-contained, **Maxim** machine guns ensured that these did not see battlefield action.

Only in 1945 when high rates of fire were demanded for aircraft guns was the electric Gatling revived. Captain Melvin M. Johnson now extensively modified an existing Gatling to coax out of it 6,000 rounds per minute, with a noise that sounded "like a high speed outboard motor without a muffler." A year later General Electric's Project Vulcan was working on new models, and by 1952 a 20 mm Vulcan gun was produced; it went into production four years later as a U.S. Air Force and Army standard. The M61 Vulcan was installed on such aircraft as the **Starfighter, Thunderchief**, and Hustler, also seeing service in Europe and Japan. Three-barrel Vulcan guns were mounted in **helicopters**, and by the 1960s a "minigun" version of the Gatling idea was being mounted in a pod system for various craft. The basics of the Gatling system therefore remain in use to this day.

Additional Reading: Wahl and Toppel, *The Gatling Gun*, 1966; Calef, *Description and Service of Machine Guns*, 1886; Walter, *Dictionary*, 2001.

Gato **Class**   SUBMARINE

Constructed between 1940 and 1944, the U.S. *Gato* class **submarines** have rightly been described as the "Pacific warhorse." They were 312 feet long, with a top speed of 20 knots, and armed with ten torpedo tubes, six forward and four aft, plus deck guns. The main manufacturers were the Electric Boat Company of Connecticut; the Portsmouth and Mare Island Navy Yards; and Manitowoc Shipbuilding of Wisconsin. Between them, the 73 vessels of the class sank 1,700,000 tons of Japanese shipping, or roughly a third of the Japanese loss during the entire war. The three most successful submarines of the U.S. Navy in World War II, *Flasher, Rasher*, and *Barb*—which sank 300,000 tons between them—were all of the *Gato* class. Their commanders were not without fighting spirit; in one celebrated incident the *Wahoo* engaged an enemy vessel with petrol bombs after its guns jammed.

Despite these major triumphs the *Gato*s were not without problems; premature explosions and incidents in which **torpedoes** went in circles caused several accidents. Technological innovations experimentally applied to *Gato*s included the fitting of **radar**, electrically powered torpedoes, rockets, and other devices. Post–World War II, many were deployed as radar pickets, at least one saw service during Vietnam, and others were involved in the development of **Polaris**. The last was the *Rock*, decommissioned in 1969.

Additional Reading: Roscoe, *U.S. Submarine Operations in World War II*, 1949; Hutchinson, *Submarines, War beneath the Waves*, 2001.

Gazelle Helicopter   HELICOPTER

The Gazelle multirole five-seater **helicopter** was produced in the late 1960s as a joint venture between the French Aerospatiale company and Westland of the United Kingdom. Though more expensive than the **Alouette**, it is faster and can take a better weapons load. Specifications (c. 1990) gave a maximum cruise speed of 164 mph, empty weight of 2,000 lb, and possible armaments of pods of 36 mm rockets, **machine guns, TOW** missiles, or miniguns. Gazelles have been adopted specifically for an antitank role; in some models the exhaust gases go through a deflected jet pipe to reduce the **infrared** signature, while miniguns are mounted on the cabin roof, allowing the helicopter to keep largely concealed while firing.

Gecko (SA-8) Missile   MISSILE

The Soviet Gecko surface-to-air missile system was first seen publicly in 1975. Normally mounted on a quadruple launcher carried atop a six-wheeled vehicle, each missile is 10 feet 3 inches in length with a 100 lb high-explosive warhead. The range is about seven miles to a ceiling of 19,700 feet. The missiles were provided with infrared homing.

Gee   NAVIGATION

Gee was the most widespread Allied radionavigational aid of World War II. Trials began in 1941, and despite German jamming attempts was in regular use by 1942. It depended on a series of radio pulses sent out sequentially from three stations; it could create a fix by means of the minute delays between transitions and receptions. There were similarities with the **Oboe** system.

Additional Reading: Latham and Stobbs, *Radar*, 1996.

General Belgrano   WARSHIP

The ship later known as the *General Belgrano* was commissioned in October 1938 as the U.S. Navy's **Brooklyn**-class light cruiser *Phoenix*. Based at Pearl harbor during the Japanese attack of December 1941, she escaped damage and later served with distinction around Australia and Java, and at Leyte Gulf. She was purchased by Argentina in 1951, where she was at first known as the *17 de Octubre*, in commemoration of the date Peron came to power. After his fall she was renamed again as the *General Belgrano*. The vessel was sunk by the British **submarine** *Conqueror* on 2 May 1982; though her Captain, H. Bonzo, survived, 368 of her 1,138 man crew died.

Additional Reading: Rice and Gavshon, *The Sinking of the Belgrano*, 1984.

General O'Higgins   WARSHIP

The Chilean 7,796 ton **cruiser** *General O'Higgins* was laid down at Armstrong's in the United Kingdom in 1896. Designed by Sir Philip Watts, she featured a hull that was wood sheathed and coppered, and a main armament of four 8-inch guns backed by ten 6-inch guns, 13 3-inch guns, and torpedoes. Her first significant service was around Panama during the confrontation between the United States and Columbia in 1903; she remained with the Chilean navy until 1954.

Additional Reading: Brook, *Warships for Export 1867–1927*, 1999.

General Purpose Machine Gun FIREARM

More properly known as the FN Mitrailleuse á Gaz, or MAG, the GMPG was designed by M. E. Vervier in the early 1950s. It is a sturdy and reliable belt-fed **machine gun**, generally 7.62 mm in caliber. Air cooled and weighing 10.5 kg, it has an effective range of about 1,200 meters and a cyclic rate upward of 600 rounds per minute. As the name suggests it could be carried as a squad support, mounted on a tripod, or carried on vehicles. It has been very widely adopted, users having included the United Kingdom, Israel, Sweden, India, and many African countries.

Additional Reading: *Jane's Infantry Weapons*; MOD UK, *General Purpose Machine Gun*, 1966.

George Washington Class   SUBMARINE

Though a number of U.S. vessels have been called *George Washington*, including a *Nimitz*-class **aircraft carrier,** *George Washington* was also the name of the world's first strategic ballistic missile–carrying **submarine.** Five of this class were completed between 1959 and 1961. The *George Washington* (SSBN 598) began as a hull of the *Skipjack* class, but during the construction the decision was taken to increase her length massively and add a central section from which missiles could be launched. She was commissioned in December 1959, and on 28 June 1960 off Cape Canaveral she made the first submerged launch of a strategic missile.

Over the next year the *Patrick Henry, Theodore Roosevelt, Robert E. Lee,* and *Abraham Lincoln* were commissioned. Each vessel was 382 feet long with a complement of 112, was capable of over 25 knots, and could carry 16 **Polaris** missiles. In later life some of the *George Washington*s underwent conversion to nuclear attack–type submarines. All have now been scrapped, though parts of the *George Washington* herself are preserved at the Submarine Museum, New London, Connecticut.

Gigant. *See* **Me 321** and **323**

Gillois EWK   VEHICLE

Invented by a French officer named Gillois, the "Vehicle, Amphibious, Bridging and Ferrying" was produced in Germany and used by several NATO countries. Consisting of an elongated boat-shaped, four-wheel-drive truck with a ramp on top, it could be driven into water and floated by means of rubber bladders on the sides. The ramp could then be rotated to 90 degrees to act as a bridge, several units being used to span wide obstacles.

Gladiator   AIRCRAFT

Entering service in 1937, the Gloster Gladiator was the RAF's last biplane fighter, and something of an historical anachronism, given that aircraft like the **Hurricane** and **Me 109** were already in existence. Powered by a Bristol Mercury 840 horsepower engine, it had a top speed of 253 mph and was armed with four **machine guns.** Despite its antique design the Gladiator fought in World War II and also saw limited use in a Sea Gladiator variant.

Additional Reading: James, *Gloster Aircraft,* 1987.

Gliders   GLIDERS

Unpowered aircraft are undeniably less useful to the military than powered ones; nevertheless, they have historically found two niches. As they are relatively cheap, they have long had a role in training; before World War II, for example, they were vital to the embryonic Luftwaffe as a means of producing pilots when aircraft were limited. As a means of air landing they were also in vogue during and immediately after World War II. Usually towed by "tug" aircraft to the target area and then released, they were extremely risky but were able to carry stores, **jeeps,** and **light artillery,** and to put down small concentrated groups of infantry.

The German DFS 230 of 1932 is claimed as the first transport glider, and significant numbers of the Gotha 242 were also produced. British Hamilcar and Horsa gliders saw action on D-Day: the 88-foot-long Airspeed Horsa had a normal tow speed of about 130 mph and was could carry 25 troops. The most significant U.S. models of the period were the Waco types. The last military transport glider to be built in numbers was the Soviet Yak-14 of 1947. Gliders were faced with a simple countertechnology aimed at denying landing areas. Measures adopted by the Germans included ditches and obstacles nicknamed "Rommel's asparagus."

Glisenti Handguns   FIREARM

The Italian Glisenti steel concern was established by Francesco Glisenti in 1859. It produced its first **revolver** in 1872. Yet the company's best known military **pistols** were the **semiautomatics** designed by B. A. Revelli in the first decade of the twentieth century. Though an unusual design and soon superseded by **Beretta** types, Glisentis were actually tested by the United States.

Global Hawk · AIRCRAFT

The Northrop Grumman Global Hawk is a high-flying U.S. **UAV**, or unmanned aerial vehicle, with a 116-foot wingspan and bulbous nose. In use over Afghanistan since 2001, they may remain airborne for up to 36 hours, traveling to long ranges at up to 400 mph. Capable of imaging tens of thousands of square miles per sortie, each Global Hawk costs $47 million.

Glock 17 · FIREARM

The 9 mm Austrian-manufactured Glock 17 semiautomatic pistol is used by several forces. Mainly manufactured from a high-resistance polymer, it is easily stripped down, with a 17-round magazine and only 33 parts. Its mechanism uses elements of the tried and tested **Colt Browning** system, and there are two different internal safety devices.

Additional Reading: Boatman, *Living with Glocks*, 2002; Walter, *Dictionary*, 2001.

Gloire · WARSHIP

Launched in 1859 the French **battleship** *Gloire* was the worlds first "ironclad" armored warship. Designed by Dupuy de Lome, the 5,617-ton ship was 252 feet in length and was broadly based on the **line-of-battle** steamer *Napoleon*. With a wooden hull plated to the upper deck with four and a half inches of iron, backed by 26 inches of wood, the *Gloire* had 34 guns arranged in traditional batteries—17 down either side. Later, however, this layout was modified so that two guns were placed to fire forward and two aft. She had a range of about 4,000 miles at eight knots, with a maximum speed of 13 knots, and a crew of 570. Other vessels in her class included the ***Invincible*** and *Normandie*. The *Gloire* was broken up in the 1880s. Together with the *Couronne* it is arguable that the *Gloire* helped bring about a technological revolution in naval warfare. The name *Gloire* was also given to a cruiser of the ***La Galissonniere*** class in the 1930s.

Glonass. *See* Satellites

Gloster Gladiator. *See* Gladiator

Gneisenau · WARSHIP

Sister ship to the ***Scharnhorst***, the German *panzerschiff Gneisenau* was launched in 1936. She was a 230-meter vessel with a top speed of 31 knots and a main armament of nine 28 cm guns. Badly damaged by bombing at Kiel in 1942 she was sunk as a blockship at Gotenhafen in 1945.

Additional Reading: Whitley, *German Capital Ships of World War II*, 1989; Garzke and Dulin, *Battleships: Axis and Neutral Battleships in World War II*, 1985.

Goal Keeper. *See* Phalanx System

Goblin, XF-85 · AIRCRAFT

The U.S. experimental **McDonnell** Goblin XF-85 is claimed to be the smallest jet powered military aircraft ever built. It arose from the Parasite fighter program (Secret Project MX-472) commenced in 1945, the object of which was to find a combat plane sufficiently small to be carried in the bomb bay of the new Peacemaker B-36 long-range bomber. The idea was that the mother ship would carry its own fighter escort, releasing the minifighter when in danger of attack—and, if possible, retrieve it back on board. Nicknamed the "Bumble Bee" by those who worked on it, the single-seat Goblin was 14 feet 10.5 inches long, was armed with four .5-inch **machine guns**, and had a maximum speed of about 600 mph. By 1948 successful flights and in flight retrievals had been made using a "trapeze" device mounted on a B-29, but the project was canceled in April 1949.

Additional Reading: Pace, *X-Fighters: USAF Experimental and Prototype Fighters, XP-59 to YF-23*, 1991.

Goer · VEHICLE

The Goer series of vehicles were the result of a late-1950s U.S. Army program that investigated the applicability of technology and components used in earthmoving and other commercial activities to military purposes. Caterpillar, LeTourneau-Westinghouse, International, and other vehicles were involved; the results of the process included such models as eight-ton tanker and wrecker trucks, and ultimately the eight-ton cargo M520. Due to their articulated steering, Goer vehicles could be "duck-walked," swung from side to side over boggy ground. The viability of the idea was amply demonstrated in difficult terrain, as in Vietnam, and the concept of military "big wheelers" is now commonplace.

Goliath   TANK

The misleadingly named Goliath was in fact a World War II German miniature remote-controlled **tank**, just over five feet in length. It carried 200 lb of **explosive**. Steered by cable onto its target, it was then exploded. In an improved B-IV model a charge was dropped off and the vehicle saved for repeat use.

Additional Reading: U.S. War Department, *Handbook on German Military Forces*, 1945.

Goryunov Machine Gun   FIREARM

Designed by Pytor Maximovitch Goryunov during World War II, the Soviet Goryunov **machine gun** was a successful design commonly used in fixed positions, on vehicles, or on small wheeled carriages. Though firing from a belt and capable of sustained fire, it was air cooled. It was widely used and manufactured elsewhere as well, being eventually and gradually replaced by the PK series guns.

Gotha   AIRCRAFT

Produced by the Gothaer Waggonfabrik, Gothas were the main German twin-engine bomber **aircraft** of World War I. With their wingspans of 77 feet, they were approximately the same size as the less well known Friedrichshafen model. Appearing in 1916 the Gotha took over much of the long-range bombing previously executed by **zeppelins**. Their 1,000 lb load was carried in external racks, and, initially at least, they proved quite successful, as fighters

could not climb quickly enough to catch them. Amazingly, the fastest Gotha III model traveled at only 92 mph.

GPMG. *See* **General Purpose Machine Gun**

GPS. *See* **Satellites**

Graf Spee   WARSHIP

Laid down at Wilhelmshaven in 1932, the German warship *Admiral Graf Spee* was originally described as "Panzerschiff C." Capable of 28 knots, she had a main armament of six 28 cm guns: **radar** was added in 1938. Though stronger than any single adversary at the battle of the River Plate in 1939, she was overwhelmed by the faster British **cruisers**, suffering 20 hits from large shells. She was scuttled by her captain, Erich Langsdorff, at Montevideo on 17 December.

Additional Reading: Whitley, *German Capital Ships of World War II*, 1989.

Grail. *See* **Redeye**

Grape Shot. *See* **Case and Canister**

Gras. *See* **Chassepot**

"Grease Gun." *See* **M3 Grease Gun**

Greek Fire   INCENDIARY DEVICE

Greek fire was known to the ancients as a weapon, specifically useful in siege and naval warfare. It could be dropped, projected from **catapults**, and possibly even pumped. Later descriptions suggest that its constituents included such substances as pitch, petroleum, and sulphur. It is commonly regarded as an ancestor of the **flamethrower** and **napalm**.

Grenade, Granadoe EXPLOSIVE DEVICE

The word "grenade" is from the Spanish *granada*, meaning pomegranate; it was the resemblance of the early hand-thrown bomb, or small **shell**, to the fruit that gave it the name. Grenades have existed since the beginning of the sixteenth century, and though usually of metal have been made of glass and other materials. The "bomb" thrown from mortars was also often described as a grenade or "granadoe," and in German, for example, *granate* can still refer to such a projectile. In English, "grenade" is now usually taken to mean a hand-thrown bomb. Many grenades are explosive in nature, but there have also been **gas**, incendiary, pyrotechnic, and other sorts of grenade. **Rifle grenades** are projected from firearms.

During the 1600s the most common form of grenade was a hollow cast-metal sphere filled with **gunpowder**, with a tube-type wooden **fuse**. The thrower, or grenadier, lit the fuse and threw the bomb, which then exploded into fragments. Most armies contained some grenadiers by the later part of the century, and grenadier companies were common by the eighteenth century. Nevertheless, grenades were at their most useful in sieges and street fighting. Cuplike devices attached to the end of muskets for the projection of grenades or fireworks were also known by this time.

Archaeological examples of grenades recovered from the wreck of the *Invincible*, sunk in 1758, give a good idea of grenades of that period. These were iron, about three inches in diameter, and had wooden fuses protected with linen and canvas covers. An unused fuse was not drilled entirely through to the bottom, suggesting that these may have been filled first and the end of the fuse cut off when they were inserted.

There was relatively little technological improvement until the midnineteenth century, but in the American Civil War new types were invented. W. F. Ketchum's grenade of 1861 was elongated in form and had a **percussion** cap in a tube at the nose and fins at the rear. The grenade was thrown nose first; a plunger impacted with the target, set off the cap, and exploded the grenade. In W. W. Hane's spherical "Excelsior," patented in 1862, inner and outer metal spheres were used, between which were percussion nipples that made the bomb explode on impact. Though this design required no burning fuse, it was dangerous to handle. Fur-

ther advances were made in 1904 during the Russo-Japanese War, when troops also improvised grenades from **artillery** shell cases, bamboo tubes, and tins.

Even so, many nations were still using old-fashioned time-fused, "ball" grenades in 1914. In the French "bracelet" bomb, a friction tube and cord were fitted so that the fuse was lit as the grenade left the bomber's hand. The German 1913 Kugel grenade had a brass pull fuse and a spherical body divided into segments externally. In the dramatically different British No. 1, an elaborate brass head mounted on a stick featured such safety devices as a pin and turning cap, and a fragmentation collar. A long streamer ensured that it landed nose first, exploding on impact by means of a detonator.

The trench warfare of World War I would see a major renaissance of the grenade, with huge numbers of many new and different designs manufactured. When dire shortages occurred soldiers manufactured their own grenades using jam tins, pipes, wooden handles, gun cotton, and lengths of fuse. Among the most important types of the war were the German **Steil** or "stick" grenade, the U.S. **fragmentation grenade M11A1**, and the British **Mills** bomb. Yet these were just the best of dozens. Phosphorus grenades were made to produce smoke and burn injuries, and small "egg" bombs were made for long-range throws. Many nations experimented in the hope of finding the perfect explode-on-impact model.

Another massive crop of new grenades appeared in World War II; among these were some interesting innovations. The British No. 69 was made of plastic and exploded on impact, relying on blast for its effect. The British "No. 74" was a rather alarming "sticky bomb," with a head of glass, glue, and explosive designed to break and stick to a **tank**. In the U.S. M111A2 offensive hand grenade, for demolition and bunker clearance, the body of the bomb was made of fiberboard. The Office of Strategic Services produced the Beano—a grenade designed to be approximately the same size and weight as a baseball. This required a long throw, as it was armed in flight but exploded on impact; it was billed as suitable for attacks

A German army Gefreiter equipped with practice grenades and explosives, from a propaganda picture taken about 1940. © Hulton/Getty Images.

on standing aircraft or moving vehicles. The Soviets used a number of stick bombs, among them the RPGs 1940 and 1943, for use against tanks. Perhaps the most important invention was the German **Nipolit** grenade.

After 1945 the grenade continued to be a staple of infantry combat, with improvements in the areas of fragmentation, materials, reliability, and cost. Many of the latest grenades are small, on the basis that more may be carried and thrown farther, and that comparatively small charges of explosive are adequate to clear a room or bunker. Significant U.S. grenades have included the M67 and M61, both of which are time-fuse bombs with side levers. In the M61, fragmentation is improved by the presence of a coil under the outer shell, which breaks into small pieces when the grenade explodes. Both the M61 and M67 have an effective casualty radius of 15 meters. The M61, like the British L2, is based on the older U.S. M26 type.

In the Soviet Union, several grenades of World War II vintage, such as the F1 antipersonnel type, were continued, with versions remaining current in client states for many years. A new and smaller RGD-5 was also produced. The RPGs had been substantially replaced by the RKGs by the 1970s. These latter were quite effective for hand-thrown antitank bombs, with the RKG-3M, for example, having an armor penetration of about 165 mm. Like the RPGs the RKG-3M was equipped with a drogue, or fabric spoiler, which deployed from the rear ensuring correct nose impact.

A number of hand grenades are particularly notable among the many produced by other countries. The Austrian Type 69 came in offensive and defensive models, both of which were plastic bodied. In the latter, 3,500 tiny steel balls were contained in the plastic matrix, producing almost certain lethality at five meters. The Types 72 and 73 included various improvements. The Argentinean GME-FMK2-MO was just two inches in diameter, but its fragments were claimed to be capable of penetrating a steel **helmet** a meter away. The Spanish Posare came in both "minigrenade" and more normal formats, some of which could be made into "defensive" types by the addition of an external fragmentation coil.

Additional Reading: *Jane's Infantry Weapons*; Blazey (ed), *The Official Soviet Army Handgrenade Manual*, 1998; Lord, *Civil War Collector's Encyclopaedia*; Skennerton, *An Introduction to British Grenades*, 1988; Saunders, *Weapons of the Trench War*, 1999; Marshall, *British Grenades*, 1982; Department of the Army, *Field Manual 23–30*; Patent Office, *Patents for Inventions: Class 119, Small Arms*, 1993.

Greyhound M8, Armored Car   VEHICLE

The U.S. Greyhound, developed in late 1941 and early 1942, was standardized as the M8 light **armored car** in May 1942. Produced in large numbers, this six-wheeler was the main U.S. vehicle of the type. Usually armed with a 37 mm gun in the turret as well as machine guns, it was capable of a healthy 55 mph. In a modified M20 version it became a general purpose "armored utility car." It continued to be widely used after 1945—as, for example, with United Nations forces.

Gripen ("Griffin")   AIRCRAFT

The Swedish Saab Gripen is one of the world's most advanced fighter **aircraft** and a successor to the **Viggen**. First flown in 1988, the Gripen is powered by a Volvo/General Electric afterburning RM-12 turbojet engine. Its usual armament is a 27 mm cannon, plus Sky Flash or **Sidewinder** missiles. Weighing 14,600 empty, it is capable of 1,321 mph. Significant strengths are great maneuverability and relatively short takeoff.

A delta-wing craft with a fly-by-wire system, the Gripen makes extensive use of computer and communications technology. It features a wide-angle **head-up display**, and a tactical information data link system for real-time exchanges of data. Operational service commenced in 1997.

Grumman   MANUFACTURER

Founded at the time of the 1929 Wall Street crash by Leroy Randle Grumman (1895–1984), a former employee of Loening Brothers, the U.S. Grumman Aircraft Company eventually became one of the world's best-known military **aircraft** manufacturers. Early craft included flying boats and the Navy biplane FF-1, and F3F-3, but it was the monoplane **Wildcat** that made the real breakthrough. Thereafter Grumman produced the **Avenger** and **Hellcat**, which were so important in World War II. The Bearcat and Tigercat were developed at the end of the war.

After 1945 the company worked not only on amphibious aircraft but on missiles as well. The Panther carrier-borne jet fighter appeared in time for Korea; it was followed by the experimental XF10F-1 Jaguar and F11F Tiger. Yet Grumman had greater success in the field of antisubmarine warfare and reconnaisance, producing the AF-2 Guardian, which was in service by 1950, and the Tracker, Tracer, and Mohawk thereafter. Recent company stars have included the A-6 **Intruder**, F-14 **Tomcat**, and

E-2 **Hawkeye**. Grumman merged with Northrop in 1994 to produce Northrop Grumman.

Additional Reading: Treadwell, *The Ironworks: Grumman's Fighting Aeroplanes*, 1990.

Guardian Angel. *See* Parachute

Guideline (SAM-2) Missile   MISSILE

The Soviet Guideline (or SAM-2) surface-to-air missile was developed in the 1950s and was one of the most widely used Soviet types. Carried on a Zil 157 transporter and on ships, the SAM-2 was 35 feet in length, weighed 5,070 lb, and carried a 288 lb high-explosive warhead. With a radio guidance system, it could be detonated on command or by means of a proximity fuse. Its range was about 31 miles to a ceiling of over 11 miles.

Gun Motor Carriage. *See* Tank Destroyer

Gunpowder   EXPLOSIVE

Though fireworks may already have existed, the **explosive** gunpowder (or black powder) was discovered in Europe about the middle of the thirteenth century. Claims of invention have been put forward for English philosopher Roger Bacon (1214–1293), as for "Black Berthold," a mysterious south German monk, but the precise origin remains obscure. It was in use with **artillery** c. 1300.

Early gunpowder was laboriously hand produced and of relatively low power, consisting of roughly equal proportions of saltpeter, charcoal, and sulphur. The saltpeter, which was soon identified as the most active ingredient, was initially obtained by the boiling, evaporation, and refining of deposits found in dung heaps, graves, and old buildings. It is therefore unsurprising that gunpowder was sometimes considered a work of the devil. With time stronger powders with greater proportions of saltpeter were produced. By the sixteenth century gunpowders with four parts saltpeter to one each of charcoal and sulphur were being made. In 1635 English government gunpowder was officially specified at a proportion of six, to one,

to one. Powders could now be tested in *eprouvettes*, devices of varying design in which a small quantity would be exploded, lifting a lid or moving an indicator up a scale.

Another early advance was the realization that power and ignition was influenced by grain size. This led to the introduction of "corning," the sieving of damp powder to produce different-size granules for different types of gun. Corned powder also found favor because less of it was needed and it was easier to handle. Ease of use was further improved by the early use of **cartridges**. Fine powder that was not corned was referred to as "serpentine" powder and used mainly as a priming to set off the main charge in a gun.

By the end of the seventeenth century gunpowder mills had achieved a fairly standardized process and some use of machinery. Much of the production would be done with the powder wet to reduce accidents. The mill would first receive "stack," or pit-burnt charcoal, and refined or partly refined saltpeter and sulphur, often imported. The charcoal and sulphur would now be pulverized using "edgerunner" mills powered by animals. Next the ingredients were mixed using a mingling trough, and incorporated by mills, which were usually water powered. At this stage the resulting wet powder might be compacted or pressed to increase its specific gravity. The product would then be corned, using water-powered "shaking frames," and then glazed by tumbling in water-powered barrels. Powder drying was done spread out in trays, using the indirect heat radiated from a cast iron fireback or "gloom stove." It could then be finished and packed.

The advent of smokeless powders—which produced no, or very little, smoke—was a significant breakthrough, since this vastly improved battlefield visibility. Experimentation was under way by the 1860s, but generally the invention of smokeless powder is credited to French chemist Paul Vieille (1854–1934), who produced the so-called B powders in 1884. Smokeless powders are sometimes called "colloidal"—in reference to their structure, which allows the production of strands or flakes.

Gus

Additional Reading: Cocroft, *Dangerous Energy: The Archaeology of Gunpowder and Military Explosives Manufacture*, 2000; Tarassuk and Blair, *The Complete Encyclopaedia of Arms and Weapons*, 1979; Cockle, *A Bibliography of Military Books up to 1642*, 1978; Brown, *The Big Bang*, 1998.

Gus. *See* **Hovercraft**

H

H Class
EDGED WEAPON → SUBMARINE

The Royal Navy's H-class **submarines** were built during the period 1915 to 1920 in the United States and Canada as well as the United Kingdom, to three slightly varying specifications. Classed as a coastal-defense type, the H class was armed with four torpedo tubes and powered by a 480 horsepower engine. The *H32* was involved in the first **Asdic** experiments. H6 had a particularly bizarre career, being run aground, purchased by the Dutch, scuttled in World War II, refloated, and then serving the Germans as the *UD1*. Remaining H-class submarines were scrapped in 1945.

Haflinger Trucks
VEHICLE

Perhaps best described as the Austrian alternative to the **jeep**, the Haflinger series of four-wheel-drive light trucks and load carriers were developed by Steyr-Daimler-Puch chief designer Erich Ledwinka from the late 1950s. The name "Haflinger" was taken from a powerful breed of horse. Typical of these vehicles was the small wheeled 700 AP .4-ton truck, with a 643 cc two-cylinder engine, current from 1966.

Halberd
EDGED WEAPON

The halberd is an edged staff-mounted weapon in use from the early Middle Ages, and it has been suggested that the first were actually short **sword** blades attached to a wooden pole. Surviving examples, predominantly from the fifteenth and sixteenth centuries, are mainly of a much more axelike appearance, having commonly a blade on one side and spikes to the top

and back. By the late sixteenth century, with the growing importance of **pikes** and firearms, halberds were becoming more decorative, eventually a mark of rank.

Additional Reading: Bull, *An Historical Guide to Arms and Armor*, 1991.

Hale Grenade. *See* Rifle Grenade

Hale Rocket
MISSILES

William Hale (1797–1870), born in Colchester, England, was a prolific inventor but is best known as a rocket pioneer who improved on the efforts of **Congreve**. One of his key developments was the use of escape holes and shaped vanes that spun the missile in flight, resulting in greater stability. Manufactured in the United States, Hale rockets were deployed against Mexico in the war of 1846–1848. They were also used on a limited scale in the Crimean and Civil Wars.

Half-Track
VEHICLE

The idea of tractors and other vehicles combining wheels with **tank**-type tracks goes back to the First World War, Benz-Brauer working on such a project as early as 1917. Yet the large-scale development of half-tracked troop carriers is essentially an interwar phenomenon. An early leader in the field was France, which produced Citroen-Kegresse half-tracks (or *semi-chenilles*) during the 1920s; these were subsequently purchased and evaluated by other nations, including the United States and United Kingdom. In the United States the James Cunningham company of Rochester acquired a license, and General Motors and Marmon-Herrington produced prototypes, with an M2 model of 1937 being purchased in small numbers.

Yet it was Germany that would prove the most enthusiastic proponent of half-tracks prior to World War II, seeing in them a way both to provide cross-country movement of heavy equipment and to enable infantry to accompany tanks in **panzer** divisions. A Krauss Maffei MZ 10 four-wheel-drive tractor was made as early as 1927 that could be converted to half-track operation. In 1931 Daimler-Benz began a half-track project for Russia. In 1932 the German army asked Demag to develop an all-terrain tractor for pulling a one-ton load; a year later Hansa-Lloyd-Goliath (later Borgward) of Bremen requested to produce a tractor for three-ton loads.

While the Demag program eventually produced the small Sdkfz 250 series of radio vehicles, gun carriers and command vehicles, the latter scheme led to the Gepanzerter Mannschafts Transportwagen, or section armored personnel carrier Sdkfz 251 series. These were fitted with a protective superstructure designed by Bussing NAG. Mass production of the distinctive machines was commenced by the Hanomag in 1937, and though not all would be produced by this company, the name "Hanomag" has stuck as a popular name for German half-tracks of the period. Other manufacturers of whole vehicles, or major components, included Borgward, Auto Union, Skoda, Adler, and Wumag. Under the "Schnell Program" of 1939, attempts were made to standardize and to produce enough vehicles to equip panzer and motorized infantry units, though this was never fully achieved.

Many German half-tracks were eventually finished as tractors, rocket-launching platforms, antitank gun carriers, **flamethrower** vehicles, and the like. The mighty 18 ton SdKfz 9 was used as a prime mover for heavy artillery and armored recovery, and the SdKfz 4 and 5 were effectively rough-terrain trucks. Yet the majority of German half-tracks were infantry carriers. The basic SdKfz 251 was 19 feet long, weighed eight tons, and had a maximum armor of 14.5 mm. It was powered by a Maybach six-cylinder engine giving a top speed of 33 mph. It could cross water two feet deep and trenches six and a half feet wide; it made 3.5 miles to the gallon. The standard armament was two **machine guns**. Despite shortcomings it has been described as an example to other nations and "one of the most important armored fighting vehicles of its time."

Close on the heels of Germany was the United States, where the White company built on the M2 to produce a T7 prototype. The well-known M3 half-track soon followed. This was powered by a six-cylinder engine giving 153 horsepower. By 1944 the United States had produced over 41,000 half-tracks in about 70 different variants. These included a **howitzer** motor carriage, an M9 **artillery** towing tractor, M4 **mortar** carrier, and 75 mm and 105 mm gun vehicles. Yet the most impressive was probably the M16 antiaircraft half-track, which carried four .5-inch machine guns on a traversing Maxson mounting. This "meat chopper" could also be turned on ground targets to awesome effect.

Though production of half-tracks would continue in Czechoslovakia after 1945 and in some parts of the world they would stay in service until the 1980s, the era of the half-track was effectively at an end. Fully tracked carriers such as the **M113** and **FV432** and wheeled amphibians would now fulfill their role.

Additional Reading: Boniface and Jeudy, *US Army Vehicles of World War II*, 1991; Culver, *The SdKfz 251 Half Track*, 1983; Spielberger, *Schützenpanzerwagen SdKfz 251*, 1979; Vanderveen, *M3 Half Track*; Vanderveen, *Military Wheeled Vehicles*, 1972; Hunnicutt, *Half-Track*, 2001.

Halifax. *See* **Handley Page**

Hall, John H.   INVENTOR

Breechloading firearms inventor John Hancock Hall (1781–1841) was born in Falmouth, Maine, and was a member of the Portland Federal Volunteers. He took out his first firearms patent, together with William Thornton, in 1811, and his first sale of trial pieces to the U.S. government came two years later. A contract for 100 **rifles** was given in 1817. In Hall's system the breech and **flintlock** mechanism tipped up as one piece, but despite its modernity it was criticized for fouling, its catch, and gas leakage. Nevertheless a larger contract was forthcoming in 1819, and by 1825 the inventor was at the Harper's Ferry armory supervising the use of machines in their production. This was a small step forward, but important since it pointed the way to later mass production and widespread interchangeability of parts. In 1833 a Hall carbine became the first U.S. military arm to be converted to **percussion** ignition.

Additional Reading: Schmidt, *Hall's Military Breechloaders*, 1996.

Handley Page   MANUFACTURER

Founded by Frederick Handley Page in 1909, the Handley Page company commenced building the 0/100 aircraft in 1911. At the time this was the largest **aircraft** in Britain; it was later used as a heavy night bomber. Novel features included armor, bullet-proof glass, and folding wings. The company also made bombers during World War II, including the four-engine Halifax and Hampden, and the twin-engine Hereford and Heyford. Handley Page closed in 1970.

Additional Reading: Barnes, *Handley Page Aircraft since 1907*, 1976.

Hanomag. *See* Half-Track

Harpoon Missile   MISSILE

First developed at the end of the 1960s, the Harpoon is a versatile missile system with air-to-surface, surface-to-surface, and antishipping capabilities. Guided by active **radar** and computer, the Harpoon can be fired from a variety of launchers and has a range of 80 miles. Depending on type Harpoon missiles may be up to 15 feet in length and carry warheads of 500 lb. An important characteristic of the Harpoon is its wave or surface-skimming ability, made possible by a radar altimeter. The flight path is also programmed so that the missile will pitch upward toward the end of its trajectory, avoiding close-defense weapons and maximizing impact.

In submarine-launch systems the Harpoon leaves the vessel in a capsule. This rises to the surface, and the ends of the container are jettisoned as the missile ignites and exits. Made by **McDonnell Douglas** in the United States, Harpoon systems have been widely adopted elsewhere, including the British Royal Navy. The description "antiship **cruise missile**" has also been applied to Harpoon systems by the U.S. Navy.

Harrier, Sea Harrier   AIRCRAFT

The Harrier multirole **aircraft** is one of the most remarkable weapons of the modern era, and at the time of writing was still the only single-engine, vertical or short takeoff and landing (VSTOL) winged plane in western service. Its greatest strength is that it does not need an airfield, and various models have been at home operating from either **aircraft carriers** or woodland clearings. An aircraft that can stop in midair or fly straight up and down also causes surprises in aerial combat. Arguably the Harrier can be seen as the culmination of a long line of development, beginning with the German **Natter** in World War II, on through the U.S. Pogo and Salmon to the **Ryan X-13** Vertijet, and Vertifan. Yet the P.1127 project from which the Harrier ultimately sprang started with **Hawker** designer Ralph Cooper, who conceived an idea for a "high speed **helicopter**" in which an engine nozzle could be rotated to achieve lift.

By 1958 work had progressed to a high-wing monoplane craft with a BE-53 engine, four fuselage-mounted jets, and a "bicycle"-configuration undercarriage. A prototype achieved first tethered, and then free, hover during 1960. In May 1963 a trials machine made the first landing on the carrier HMS *Ark Royal*, and by the following year Britain, the United States, and Germany had formed a squadron of what were then known as Kestrels for evaluation. One unusual U.S. contribution to the program was an experimental instant artificial "launch

An AV-8B Harrier performs a vertical take off from the flight deck of USS *Bataan* in support of Operation Enduring Freedom. The remarkable Harrier, developed in the early 1960s, is still in service. In addition to British and U.S. forces it has also been used by Italy, Spain, and Thailand. Courtesy of the Department of Defense.

pad," made of a polyester slurry, which could be dropped by a helicopter and dried off into a heat-proof surface. Another remarkable idea, tried later, was the Skyhook—a crane mounted on a ship or **submarine** that could deposit the Harrier in midair and retrieve it afterward without the benefit of a flight deck.

The Harrier GR.1 finally entered British service in 1969. Now powered by a Rolls-Royce Pegasus 6 turbofan, it was capable of a maximum speed of 700 mph and a climb to 40,000 feet in two minutes 23 seconds. The AV-8A Harrier entered U.S. Marine Corps service in 1971, and Major Harry W. Blott of the Corps took the concept of "viffing," or "vectoring in forward flight," one stage farther. RAF pilots were already swiveling the engine nozzles of Harriers downward suddenly in flight, producing a dramatic vertical lift; Blott

threw his engine into full reverse at 500 mph, creating the apparently impossible phenomenon of a midair halt.

The first Sea Harrier FRS.1 (for "Fighter, Reconnaisance, and Strike") was delievered to the Royal Navy in 1979. Based on the land-model GR.3, the Sea Harrier was intended primarily as a fleet air defense aircraft and was accordingly fitted with Blue Fox **radar** and proofed against saltwater corrosion. Loads included both conventional missiles and nuclear weapons and depth charges. Other innovations included an improved-visibility "bubble" canopy, a Martin Baker Mk 10 **ejector seat**, and a Smiths Industries **head-up display** driven by a computer. The Sea Harrier would be operated by the new generation of commando carriers or through-deck cruisers, which were now replacing traditional aircraft carriers in the British fleet. Following a Southampton University study, a number of vessels were fitted with ski jumps, which allowed Harriers to take off at relatively slow speeds after a very short run, thus allowing them to get airborne with large payloads.

Proof of combat effectiveness came with the Falklands War of 1982, when the small Harrier force was successful against all manner of Argentine aircraft, destroying 32 of them, as well as performing ground-attack missions. Many foreign customers now appeared, and since then new generations of Harrier have been developed. In the United States the "big wing" **McDonnell** Harrier II, with NASA-based technology for reduced drag and increased lift, first entered service with the "Bumblebees" squadron in 1985. In the United Kingdom the land-based GR. 5 was superceded by the GR.7, and a new Sea Harrier, in the shape of the FA.2, made its first appearance in 1988. The FA.2 weighs 13,000 lb empty, has a ceiling of 51,000 feet and two 30 mm Aden cannon, and can carry **Sidewinder** and Sea Eagle missiles or bombs and **cluster bombs**. Harriers have seen active service in both the Balkans and Persian Gulf. A U.S. Harrier is one of the central exhibits at the new Imperial War Museum development at Manchester, England.

Additional Reading: Dibbs, *Harrier*, 1992; Evans, *BAe / McDonnell Douglas Harrier*, 1998; Spick, *BAe and McDD Harrier*, 1991; Rogers, *VTOL Military Research*, 1989; Mercer, *The Sharp End: Sea Harrier Front Line*, 1995; Treadwell, *Submarines with Wings*, 1985.

Harry S. Truman, USS   WARSHIP

Billed as the most powerful **aircraft carrier** in the world, the USS *Harry S. Truman* is a *Nimitz*-class vessel based in Norfolk, Virginia. Commissioned by President William Clinton on 25 July 1998, this behemoth of Carrier Group Nine is a 97,000-ton ship. It is powered by two nuclear reactors and propelled by four screws, each of which weighs 64,000 lb and is 21 feet across, to speeds about 30 knots. The flight deck is 1,096 feet long and 251 feet wide with an area of 4.5 acres. Its height is equal to a 20

stories. The 30-ton anchors were originally used by USS *Forrestal*. The crew numbers just under 6,000.

The *Harry S. Truman* has four catapults and four aircraft elevators to handle nine or ten squadrons totaling about 80 aircraft. The steam catapults propel planes from the deck, accelerating them at anything from 0–140 mph in 1.5 seconds; flaps rise from the deck to protect personnel from back blast. "**Meatball**" lights help guide the pilots. Recently seven different types of plane were carried; F-14A **Tomcats**; FA-18C **Hornets**; EA-6B **Prowlers**; S-3 **Vikings**; E-2C **Hawkeyes; Sea Hawk** helicopters; and C-2A Greyhounds. It is reputed that the ships munitions stores contain 4.5 million pounds of explosives and may include **nuclear weapons**.

The deck crew may number anything from 200 to 500 depending, on the missions in hand; its members wear color-coded clothing according to duties. The yellow team direct plane movements, while the blue are plane handlers, elevator operators, and tractor drivers. The purple team, the "grapes," deal with refueling. The green crew manages the catapults and maintenance, and the brown are the air wing plane captains and petty officers. Those dressed in white control safety and provide medical personnel. The red team are for ordnance and crash and salvage.

Havoc, Douglas A-20   AIRCRAFT

First designed as early as 1936 by the Douglas Aircraft Company, the A-20 was an attack **aircraft** that saw widespread use in World War II. Its twin-engine layout was novel at the time, being the first such in U.S. Army service. Another unusual feature was the interchangeable nose fuselage sections, for attack or bomber versions. Also known as the Douglas Boston, the plane was also used by the French, British, Russians, Dutch, and others, primarily in a three-seat light bomber role. Production ended in 1944, by which time 7,385 had been built.

Additional Reading: Mondey, *American Aircraft of World War II*, 1996; Donald, *American Warplanes of World War II*, 1995.

Hawk. *See* **Curtiss Hawk** and **Global Hawk**

Hawk (MIM-23, etc.) Missile   MISSILE

The Hawk, or "Homing All the Way Killer" missile, was a low-to-medium-altitude surface-to-air weapon first developed in the 1950s. In January 1960 a Hawk was launched to intercept an **Honest John** supersonic artillery rocket and thus became the first missile to bring down a ballistic missile. Guided by a semiactive **radar** homing system, Hawks were usually carried in threes on a launcher that could be towed or tracked. Hawk has been continuously developed and continues to be deployed: newer features include antijamming measures, a new motor, and a "frequency-agile" continuous-wave radar.

Hawker, Hawker Siddeley
                    MANUFACTURER

Harry G. Hawker (1889–1921) was born at South Brighton, Victoria, Australia, and worked with automobiles from the age of 12. Emigrating to England, he joined **Sopwith** in 1912 as a designer and test pilot, establishing several aviation records. With the demise of the original Sopwith Company, Hawker took over its Kingston premises. He was killed at the age of only 32 in an air accident at Hendon, but his name was perpetuated in the Hawker company, which has produced many military aircraft (such as the **Hurricane** and **Hunter**) since.

Eventually, through many amalgamations, the Hawker company became Hawker Siddeley, encompassing other such famous names as Blackburn and Roe. Military aircraft produced included the **Harrier**, Nimrod, and Buccaneer. In 1977 further mergers created **British Aerospace** (BAe).

Additional Reading: Mason, *Hawker Aircraft*; Endres, *British Aircraft Manufacturers since 1908*, 1995.

Hawkeye, E-2   AIRCRAFT

Developed during the early 1960s, the **Grumman** Hawkeye is a twin-engine U.S. airborne early warning **aircraft**. Its most distinctive feature is a 24-foot-diameter revolving **radar** disc, or radome. The main task of the Hawkeye is protection of carrier forces, and it is itself one of the largest planes to be carried on an **aircraft carrier**. Statistics current in the 1990s showed a maximum all-up weight of 59,880 lb, a wingspan of 80 feet 7 inches, and a top speed of 348 mph. The five-man crew included two pilots and operators for radar, air control, and a combat information center.

Additional Reading: Treadwell, *The Ironworks: Grumman's Fighting Aeroplanes*, 1990.

HE, High Explosive. *See* **Shell** and **Explosive**

He 111 Bomber   AIRCRAFT

Designed by Walter and Siegfried Gunther in 1934, the German Heinkel 111 twin-engine bomber was a sleek-looking **aircraft**. In its final form it had a distinctive glazed nose that gave excellent observation. During the Spanish Civil War its top speed of 250 mph and limited armament were more than adequate. In 1939 it seemed likely that the new-model He 111P would have similar success. Up to a point this was the case, but meeting **Spitfires** and **Hurricanes** during the battle of Britain the Heinkels were shot down in droves. The more daring fighter pilots learned that they could attack head-on with a significant advantage.

Nevertheless, numerous submodels of the He 111 were produced, and more weapons were added, including 20 mm cannon. In late models the crew was increased to as many as six. The He 111 continued to serve with the Spanish air force until the late 1960s. The He 111H-6 of the middle World War II period had a wingspan of 74 feet 2 inches and a maximum speed of 258 mph, carrying a bomb load of 4,400 lb over a combat range of up to 760 miles.

Additional Reading: Nowarra, *Heinkel He 111*, 1980; Dressel and Griehl, *The Luftwaffe Album*, 1999.

He 219, Uhu   AIRCRAFT

The German Heinkel He 219 project began as early as 1940, with plans for a twin-engine, high-speed, high-altitude **aircraft** for bombing and reconnaisance. The first flight came on 10 January 1943, by which time the primary purpose had been redefined as that of a night fighter equipped with **radar** for interception. Despite plans to build the Uhu (or Owl) in large numbers and the success of those that did see active service, relatively few were completed due to Allied bombing. Interesting technology trialed during the program included an **ejection seat**, a methanol-water injection system for the **Junkers** Jumo motors, and remote-control defensive armament. Specifications were changed frequently, but the 219A-7/R2 was armed with at least four 20 mm cannon and two other weapons, part of the weaponry being mounted so as to fire upward into the underbellies of Allied bombers. Maximum altitude was a respectable 32,000 feet.

He 280   AIRCRAFT

Claimed to be the world's first jet fighter, the German twin-engine Heinkel 280 existed as a test air frame as early as 1940. The first powered flight was made on 2 April 1941, a speed of 485 mph being achieved. Other advanced features in the design were cabin pressurization and a compressed-air **ejection seat**. Difficulties during a test on 13 January 1942 resulted in the pilot's making the first recorded emergency ejection from an aircraft. Though the prototype He 280 was well advanced by 1943, comparison to the Me 262 showed that its performance was likely to be inferior. Other than experimentation, work ceased, and the He 280 never flew in active service.

Head-Up Display, HUD   AVIONICS

In use since 1967, the head-up display is a method of showing information within the normal line of sight of pilots or drivers so that they do not have to take their attention from the outside world to study instrument panels. The HUD works by projecting words, numbers, and symbols, often appearing in focus out beyond the cockpit, thus minimizing the need for the user's eyes to adjust between data and targets. In the mid-1990s the idea was taken a stage farther with helmet-mounted displays; similar systems can now be mounted within a pair of goggles or glasses.

HEAT Rocket Launcher, M72, 66 mm
ANTITANK WEAPON

Used in Vietnam and also carried by many nations, including the United Kingdom, Israel, and Australia, the U.S. 66 mm HEAT, or "high-explosive antitank," weapon was a notable success. Consisting of a small rocket with folding fins and a **hollow-charge** warhead within a telescoping tube, it weighed just 2.4 kg total. The firer opened the tube and took aim through sights that popped up. Maximum range was 1,000 meters, though moving targets were best engaged at under 150 meters. The device was also known as LAW, or light antitank weapon.

Additional Reading: *Jane's Infantry Weapons.*

Heckler and Koch

Founded in 1949 at Oberndorf, Germany, The Heckler and Koch Company was initially a supplier of specialised machine tools. Later important military small arms such as the **MP5** and **G3** were produced. Following various mergers during the 1990s the business became part of **British Aerospace**.

Additional Reading: Walter, *Dictionary*, 2001.

Hedgehog   EXPLOSIVE DEVICE

The Hedgehog antisubmarine launcher began to be fitted to escort vessels in 1942 as one answer to the **U-boat** menace. Each launcher mounted 24 projectiles, each filled with 32 lb of Torpex **explosive**. Fired simultaneously, these fell about 200 yards in front of the escort in a pattern, detonating when they hit a solid object. The smaller Mousetrap version was a U.S. Navy device that fired either four or eight similar rockets.

In the larger Squid, three tubes fired 350 lb

charges a distance of 700 yards ahead of the vessel. These were set to explode at specific depths and would create pressure waves designed to fracture the submarine hull. The first victim of Squid was *U-333* on 31 July 1944. Similar weapons have continued in use in some navies to the present day.

Additional Reading: Friedman, *World Naval Weapons Systems*, 1991.

Heinkel 219. *See* **He 219**

Helicopter　　　　　　　　　　HELICOPTER

The principle of vertical flight has been known for centuries, and Leonardo da Vinci's drawings of the "helical air screw" are commonly regarded as a precursor of the helicopter. Rotary-wing toys were popular in the nineteenth century. Prior to the First World War, **Sikorsky** and others conducted experiments that suggested that manned flight by similar methods was possible. Two major obstacles needed to be overcome: the difficulty of control, and the lack of engines sufficiently powerful and reliable. During the 1920s a partial solution was Juan de la Cierva's autogyro, which used a rotor for lift and a conventional propeller for forward thrust. The autogyro itself would see limited military service, notably during World War II, when it was used in **radar** calibration.

In 1936 the remarkable German Focke Achgelis Fa 61 was produced. This solved the problems of control and stability by means of two rotors on outriggers. It was later developed into the Fa 266 and Fa 223 **Drache**. The smaller **Kolibri**, by Anton Flettner, flew in 1941. Though it ultimately took longer to develop, Sikorsky's favored answer to control problems, a than small tail rotor to prevent the fuselage from rotating, was ultimately the most successful. Now working in the United States, Sikorsky manufactured the remarkably modern-looking R-4 from 1942. It is interesting to note that in terms of role, military helicopters mirrored the advancement of early conventional aircraft, in that the first machines were primar-

ily for observation and communication, the ability to attack coming later.

Military helicopters became widespread during the immediate postwar period, with significant models including the Bell **Sioux** and **Huey**; the Sikorsky S-51, S-55, and S-56; the Hiller **Raven**; the Kaman **Huskie**; the Vertol H-21 "Flying Banana"; the Mil Mi series and Swidnik; the **Yak-24**; and the Bristol Sycamore. In Indochina and Korea, helicopters were seen with such armament as **machine guns** and rockets on a regular basis.

Thereafter the roles in which helicopters could be employed increased steadily with their improved power and technological sophistication. Beasts like the huge Soviet Harke and the U.S. Tarhe were sky cranes, lifting all but the heaviest armor. The S-61 and the **Chinook** became a general maids of all work for Western powers, carrying out everything from shuttle flights and special forces work to cargo carrying and rescue. Since then helicopters have more than maintained their niche, over the battlefield as taxis, observation platforms, and **tank** killers, and at sea, where their antisubmarine and reconnaisance abilities are invaluable. In the last quarter-century particularly significant machines have included the **Apache, Black Hawk, Comanche, Hind**, Wessex, Lynx, **Sea King**, and Sikorsky S-65.

The control system of a helicopter is totally unlike that of a conventional aircraft and requires very different skills on the part of the pilot. Cyclic control enables the rotor to be tilted: forward tilt results in forward flight, while banking turns and horizontal hover can also be achieved. The collective pitch lever connected to the swash plate alters the pitch of the rotor blades; these are shaped like wings in cross section and so enable climb and descent. The throttle increases and decreases engine speed, while foot pedals control the tail rotor. The use of the foot pedals and cyclic controls together produces left and right turns.

Additional Reading: Hunt, *Helicopter*, 1998; Fay, *The Helicopter*, 1987; Rogers, *VTOL Military Research*, 1989.

Hellcat, F6F   AIRCRAFT

Developed from the F4F **Wildcat**, the U.S. Grumman Hellcat was one of the most successful fighter **aircraft** of World War II. Piloted by Bob Hall, the first Hellcat flew in June 1942. Flying from U.S. Navy **aircraft carriers** Hellcats would eventually be credited with 4,947 enemy aircraft destroyed in air-to-air combat. Many of these were **Zeros**. Moreover, the Hellcat helped more U.S. pilots to become aces than any other aircraft, with 307 flyers being credited with five or more kills. On 6 April 1945 Navy pilot Lieutenant Bill Hardy became an ace, engaging and destroying five Japanese aircraft in just 70 minutes. Amazingly, this was bettered by Lieutenant Alex Vraciu, who destroyed six in a single engagement.

The Hellcat was an all-metal single-seater powered by the most powerful engine then available, the Pratt and Whitney R-2800-10. This made it capable of up to 380 mph, with a service ceiling of 37,300 feet. Using an external drop tank its range was up to 1,530 miles. For the time it was heavily armed, having six **Browning** .50 wing-mounted **machine guns** and in later models the ability to carry two 1,000 lb bombs. The Hellcat was equipped with hydraulically back-folding undercarriage, an arrester hook, and outer wing panels that folded for carrier stowage. Empty weight was 9,153 lb. It had a reputation of being easy to fly and service.

When production ceased in November 1945, 12,272 of all models had been manufactured. The Hellcat also served in small numbers with the British Fleet Air Arm, where it was initially known as the Gannet. In 1952 six U.S. Navy Hellcats were used as remote-controlled bombs against North Korean targets. As late as 1961 the plane was still in active military service with Argentina and Uruguay.

Additional Reading: Tillman, *Hellcat: The F6F in World War II*, 1979; Dorr, *US Fighters of World War II*, 1991; Brown, *Carrier Fighters*, 1975.

Hellcat M18. *See* Tank Destroyer

Helldiver   AIRCRAFT

The Curtiss SBC Helldiver was first developed as a two-seat biplane fighter for the U.S. Navy in 1932–1933. It was powered by a Wright Cyclone 9 engine and served as an **aircraft carrier**–based scout-bomber. It was hopelessly out of date and underarmed by 1939. Curtiss therefore carried out a complete redesign, coming up with monoplane two-seater with autopilot option, powered by a Cyclone 14. It had two wing-mounted cannon, two machine guns fired from the rear cockpit, and an improved 2,000 lb bomb carrying capacity. This SB2C Helldiver entered service in 1942. Seven thousand were built, including models with provision for rocket firing and **radar**.

Additional Reading: Tillman and Lawson, *U.S. Navy Dive and Torpedo Bombers of World War II*, 2001.

Hellfire Missile   MISSILE

The current U.S. Hellfire missile was originally designed for **helicopter** use against **tanks**, the name being derived from the description "heliborne-launched fire and forget." Development commenced in the 1970s, with deployment beginning a decade later. Its range has been published as 7,000 meters, and it has a **hollow-charge** warhead to maximize armor penetration. The first model used a **laser** seeker, but newer **infrared** systems enable its use in a wider variety of circumstances.

Additional Reading: *Jane's Weapons Systems*.

Helmet   ARMOR

Protective headgear, or helmets, have existed since prehistory, the earliest being of natural materials. One archaeological example is actually of boar's tusk. By the classical era, bronze **armored** headgear was highly developed, with Spartan hoplites of 500 B.C., for example, wearing full-face, crested Corinthian-style helmets. Roman soldiers and their allies wore a variety of leather, bronze, and iron types over a long period. Two of the best known were the Imperial Gallic, with cheek guards, and the relatively simple Montefortino. Roman cavalry and sporting helmets could be extremely elaborate, with full face masks, typified by the remarkable Ribchester helmet.

After the fall of Rome, the ordinary warrior's headgear tended to simpler designs, such as the Spangenhelm. Nevertheless there were still splendid helmets in the Dark Ages. Among these must be counted the helmet found among the grave goods at Sutton Hoo and the Coppergate helmet of York. Viking helmets show a familial similarity, with face guards, both of plate and mail.

The Middle Ages would see a dramatic development from the relatively simple rounded or conical designs of the Norman soldier and the Norse warrior to some of the most elaborate helmets ever produced. Great helms covered the whole head, bascinets and broad-brimmed kettle hats left the face clear. Pig-faced bascinets used a snout-shaped guard for the face. Sallets of the fifteenth century could be shallow, or deep and provided with slots for the eyes, or teamed with bevors to cover the lower face and neck. Except for the heavy cavalry and sappers, elaborate helmets began to decline in the sixteenth century, with the use of morions, pots, or cabassets. A seldom studied but important aspect was the continually developing helmet liner, which could make the difference between life and death.

The dramatic reemergence of the steel helmet, or "tin hat," was occasioned by the onset of trench warfare in World War I, where **shrapnel** and fragments were major killers. Though all parties were faced with similar problems, there were very different solutions around the world. The French Adrian helmet was of light multipart construction, quickly introduced but relatively weak. The German *Stahlhelm* gave better coverage and was initially teamed with a heavy brow plate for much better protection. The British type, designed by John L. Brodie, was similar to the kettle hat of old and gave good protection from falling objects but little to the sides or neck. This type was subsequently adopted by the United States and remained in service until World War II. Helmet covers

made a widespread appearance beginning in 1916.

Many of the types seen in 1918 would be used again in 1939 and 1941, sometimes in updated or lightened forms, as was the case with the famous 1935 model German steel helmet. The U.S. M1 was a radical and practical departure, having an inner fiber liner that could be worn separately. Specific protective helmets were also widely worn by tank drivers and some air crews.

After 1945, simple basins of steel remained in widespread use in most NATO countries and the Soviet bloc. New materials made a real impact from about 1980, with the introduction of new helmets of Kevlar and plastics. Just two of the best known would be the so called U.S. "Fritz," so nicknamed because of its Germanic appearance, and the British Mk 6. These were initially expensive but offered significant advantages in weight and lack of fragmentation when struck. It is interesting that the latest helmet research is now reexamining organic structures, and it is thought that the strong protective shapes created by nature will again be seen in protective headgear. The story of the helmet will thus be brought full circle.

Additional Reading: Reynosa, *M-1 Helmet*, 1996; Dean, *Helmets and Body Armor*; Blair, *European Armour*, 1958; Robinson, *Armour of Imperial Rome*, 1975; Haselgrove and Radovic, *Helmets of the First World War*, 2000; Tubbs, *Stahlhelm*, 2000; Baer, *The German Steel Helmet*, 1985; Paddock and Edge, *Medieval Knight*.

Hercules, C-130   AIRCRAFT

Cited as the West's "most widely used and versatile military transport," the C-130 **aircraft** has served in over 60 countries. The prototype first flew in 1954, and since then over 2,000 of many different variants have been produced. Within the pressurized cargo compartment a load of over 43,000 lb can be carried. This may equate to five **humvees**, or 64 fully equipped **parachute** troops, who exit over the large rear cargo ramp. In a specially stretched version, troop capacity rises to as many as 128 men. In the C-130F the power is provided by four Allison turboprops, giving a cruising speed of 370 mph.

The AC-130 series are gunship versions. The MC-130 types, the first of which served in Vietnam, are adapted for special forces and rescue. EC-130s may serve various communications and jamming roles, with the ABCC subtype being an Airborne Battlefield Command and Control Center. Though useful, the Hercules cannot be described as luxurious. Passengers are commonly provided with ear plugs while seated in their web slings and are treated to a view limited to the control mechanisms working above their heads.

Additional Reading: Bowman, *Lockheed Hercules C-130*, 1999; Bickers, *Airlift*, 1998; Donald and Lake, *U.S. Navy and Marine Corps Air Power Directory*, 1992.

Hermes, HMS   WARSHIP

The name *Hermes* has been applied to several British warships, the best known of which were a series of **aircraft carriers**. The first of these began life as a 5,600-ton protected **cruiser** launched in 1897, converted to carry a Short Folder and a Caudron amphibian in 1913. She was sunk by the *U-27* in 1914. The second aircraft-carrying HMS *Hermes* was a purpose-built carrier ordered in 1917, the first that the Royal Navy would operate. She was commissioned in 1923 and like the **USS *Langley*** was a pace setter of the day. A total of 548 feet long, the *Hermes* had a hangar 400 feet in length and was capable of carrying 20 aircraft. Her top speed was 25 knots. This *Hermes* was sunk by the Japanese in 1942.

Perhaps the most famous *Hermes* was laid down in 1944 at Vickers-Armstrong, Barrow, as one of the *Centaur* class. This *Hermes* was 650 feet in length with a capacity for 42 aircraft and a top speed of 29 knots. Not completed until well after World War II, she would incorporate an angled deck, fallout protection, Type 984 **radar**, and automatic boiler feed. Refitted several times, she had her flight deck widened for Sea Vixen and Buccaneer aircraft in 1966. In 1973 her designation was changed to amphibious assault ship, accommodating 750

troops; later **Harrier** aircraft and **Seacat** launchers were fitted. Flagship of the Falklands task force in 1982, she played a pivotal role in the campaign against Argentina.

Additional Reading: Dyson, *HMS Hermes.*

HESH, High-Explosive Squash Head
EXPLOSIVE DEVICE

High **explosive** squash head projectiles, also known as HEP, or high-explosive plastic, deform on hitting a hard target before exploding. The explosion causes parts of the rear surface to break away and fly about, so that a **tank** or fortification may be disabled even if the **armor** is not penetrated.

Hexamine Cooker. *See* Rations

Hien, Kawasaki Ki-61   AIRCRAFT

Looking remarkably like the **Me Bf109**, the Japanese Hien single-engine fighter **aircraft** was powered by a license-built liquid-cooled Daimler-Benz engine. It was code named "Tony" by the Allies. Despite its promising appearance, its record from its entry into service in 1942 was undistinguished. The Hien was armed with two **machine guns** and two cannon, and it had a top speed of 348 mph.

Higgins Boat

Developed by Andrew Higgins at New Orleans. The Higgins Boat was a small landing craft of shallow draught with a hinged bow ramp. Exceptionally useful in amphibious operations, the Higgins boat was once praised by President Eisenhower as critical to Allied Victory in World War II.

Additional Reading: Baker, *Allied Landing Craft*, 1985.

High Power, Model 1935. *See* Browning

Hipper. See Prinz Eugen

HMMWV. *See* Humvee

HMS, "Her Majesty's Ship"

HMS, "Her Majesty's Ship." *See by name of vessel*

Hobos   AMMUNITION

The HOBOS, or Homing Bomb System, was created under a U.S. Air Force program intended to convert "dumb" bombs dropped from **aircraft** into accurate guided weapons. It consisted of tail and nose assemblies fitted over the casings of two and three-thousand-pound bombs, producing a missile about 12 feet long. Originally working on a television guidance system, later models had **infrared** or **laser** seeking systems. Used in Vietnam, the idea underwent considerable subsequent development, producing the GBU-15 Planar Wing Weapon and other accurate glide bombs. HOBOS are generally acknowledged as the ancestors of more recent "**smart bombs**."

Holland. *See* **Submarine**

Hollow Charge   EXPLOSIVE

Also known as shaped charges, hollow charges of **explosive** are so formed as to focus their effect at a given point. They have particular value in antitank weapons and demolitions. Many weapons have employed the principle, including **shells, mines, bazooka** rounds, and **grenades**.

The hollow-charge phenomenon was observed as early as the 1880s by U.S. chemist Charles Munroe, who noted that explosive blocks with cavities caused the greatest effect adjacent to the cavity. In the 1920s the German researcher Neumann added metal liners to cavities in explosives and managed to multiply this "Munroe effect." It is now understood that a metal liner in a cone-shaped hollow is melted at the moment of detonation and shoots forward with extremely high energy and a very high temperature. Hollow charges work best when standing just clear of the target, approximately two to five cone diameters away, and when there is little rotation of the missile or round in which it is carried.

Additional Reading: Margiotta, *Brassey's Encyclopedia of Land Forces and Warfare*, 1996; Gander, *Anti Tank Weapons*; Weeks, *Men against Tanks*, 1975.

Honest John (MGR-1) Missile   MISSILE

The Honest John was a large, unguided U.S. artillery rocket, tests of which commenced in 1951. It was manufactured in large numbers by **Douglas** and Emerson Electric, and saw widespread deployment. Powered by a single-stage rocket motor, the missile was 24 feet 10 inches in length and could fly at Mach 1.5 to a range of 23 miles. Its nuclear or conventional warhead weighed 1,500 lb. The Honest John was replaced by the Lance.

Hood, **HMS**   WARSHIP

The British **battleship** (properly battle cruiser) Hood was laid down in 1916. Though originally intended to be one of a class of four, in the event she was the only vessel of the type completed, being launched in 1918 and commissioned in 1920. During her construction there were several changes to specification, most notably to her armor. As completed she displaced 41,200 tons, was powered by 24 Yarrow boilers, and was capable of 31 knots. Her complement was 1,477 officers and men. The main armament was eight 15-inch guns; her armored belt had a maximum thickness of 12 inches. Her protection included "crush tube" spaces, which gave good resistance to **torpedoes** and **shell** splinters. Yet at the time she was constructed, cover against long-range plunging fire was not considered particularly significant, a factor that would ultimately prove her Achilles' heel.

Hood served as flagship of the battle cruiser squadron in the Atlantic and in 1940 was at the successful action against the French fleet at Oran. On 24 May 1941 she was in combat with the *Bismarck* when plunging German fire caused a catastrophic explosion. Just three of her crew were rescued, by the **destroyer** HMS *Electra*.

Additional Reading: Kemp, *Bismarck and Hood*, 1991; Coles and Briggs, *Flagship Hood*, 1985; Roberts, *Battlecruiser Hood*, 2001; Bradford, *The Mighty Hood*, 1959; Bassett, *Battle Cruisers*, 1981.

Hornet, USS   WARSHIP

The *Essex*-class **aircraft carrier** USS *Hornet* (CV 12) was the eighth U.S. Navy warship to bear the name. Her famous forbears included the very first *Hornet*, built in 1775; the third *Hornet*, which fought in the War of 1812; and a **Yorktown** (CV 5)–class carrier. The eighth *Hornet* is 894 feet long and displaced approximately 30,000 tons; when she was launched in 1943 she had a complement of up to 90 **aircraft**. Fighting in the Pacific from March 1944, she took part in the liberation of the Philippines and raids on Japan, earning a total of nine battle stars and a Presidential Unit Citation. In 1969 she recovered the first moon landing astronauts of *Apollo 11* from the water. *Hornet* survives to this day as a museum ship at Alameda Point, California.

Additional Reading: Friedman, *US Aircraft Carriers*, 1983.

Hornet, F-18   AIRCRAFT

The US Navy's Northrop **McDonnell Douglas** Hornet first flew in 1978. Combining good fighter characteristics and self-defense, it exists in both single and two-seat versions. Its roles have been many and varied, including air defense, reconnaissance, and support, as well as strike missions. Since introduction there have been numerous improvements, of which night strike capability and engine enhancement are among the most important. An upgraded APG-73 **radar** was fitted in 1994. Published data for the F/A-18C model gives 16,000 lb thrust from F404-GE-400 turbofan engines, a wingspan of 37 feet, a maximum speed of 1,189 mph, range of 2027 miles, and armament that may include a 20 mm cannon and **Sidewinder** or **Sparrow** missiles.

The Hornet has been widely sold abroad, with Canada as the first and largest customer. The Canadian CF-18 has an unusual **camou-**flage scheme in which a dummy cockpit is painted on the underside, the intention being to confuse enemy pilots and gunners during combat.

Additional Reading: Crosby, *A Handbook of Fighter Aircraft*, 2002.

Horsa. *See* Gliders

Horten. *See* Stealth

Hotchkiss Machine Guns   FIREARM

The Paris-based Hotchkiss company (originally owned by American B. B. Hotchkiss) has been credited with the manufacture of the first really successful air-cooled heavy **machine gun**. This was remarkable at a time when the market was dominated by water-cooled guns like the **Maxim** and **Schwarzlose**. The first inspiration for an air-cooled design came from Austrian cavalry officer Baron von Odkalek in 1893. From this U.S.-born designer L. V. Benet and Frenchman Henri Mercie worked up a weapon in which reliable automatic fire was generated by means of a piston powered by gas from the barrel. **Cartridges** were fed from rigid strips. The initial gun was finalized in 1897.

These basic premises were applied to a number of subsequent arms. In the Model 1914 tripod-mounted gun the French army found a reliable 8 mm machine gun to carry it through World War I. A light-model Hotchkiss "automatic rifle" was used by British cavalry, in U.S. hands it was known as the Benet-Mercie. In Japan a number of similar machine guns were inspired, culminating in the **Type 92**.

Additional Reading: Bruce, *Machine Guns of World War I*, 1997.

Hovercraft (Landing Craft Air Cushion)
                                  WARSHIP

As early as 1877 John Thorneycroft put forward the idea that a vessel traveling on an air cushion would move across water with less friction and therefore more efficiently. He proved the theory by using a model and bellows; given the state of engine technology, however, there was as yet no practical application. Not until the 1950s did Englishman Christopher Cockerill (1910–1999) perfect an air-cushion machine, a small prototype of which was demonstrated in 1955. In this a vertical lift motor, or fan, blew downward around the edge of the craft, thus trapping air. Neither ship nor aircraft manufacturers wanted it, but the British Ministry of Defence took cautious interest, and eventually a working hovercraft appeared in 1959.

Remarkably a somewhat similar "aeromobile" machine was by now also being developed in the United States, but it was Cockerill's team that first solved two major problems. These were steering and the initial inability of the machine to cope with obstacles. The latter was successfully addressed by means of the now-familiar flexible skirt, which allowed the hovercraft to rise up and over small objects or travel up an incline.

By the early 1960s the hovercraft had been perfected and was tested by all three services in Britain in a program including crossings of the Libyan desert and Canadian Arctic. The United Kingdom now adopted the SRN6, a 10.7-ton, 45 mph machine capable of carrying 30 troops or a **howitzer**. Significant attributes included the ability to traverse any surface including ice and water; lack of ground pressure, and therefore relative safety from land or sea **mines**; lack of sonar signature; and speed for amphibious assault.

The United States took up an even faster modified Bell Aerosystems commercial craft, which became known as a PACV or Patrol Air Cushion Vehicle. From 1966 Navy PACVs proved particularly useful in Vietnam, carrying about a dozen men, **machine guns**, and a **grenade** launcher. On the downside, hovercraft proved difficult to service and even in 1967 cost about $1,000,000 each. The Soviet Navy was not slow to follow suit, operating 15-ton *Lebed*-class hovercraft from 1967 and later the larger *Gus* class, capable of taking 50 marines. In the 1970s the Soviets began to use the impressive 220 ton *Aist* class, which were 220 feet long and armed with two twin 30 mm cannon. These

gas turbine vessels could speed along at up to 70 knots.

Also in the 1970s, the U.S. Navy itself developed a new generation of what became known as the Landing Craft Air Cushion, or LCAC. These boast 16,000 horsepower twin lift fans and 18-foot carbon fiber propellers. They are capable of moving 75 tons of stores. Tactical usage of the "Swift Intruders" includes the ability to drive them aboard landing ships for long journeys, then released short of the target, to arrive at maximum speed. More than 90 LCACs have been ordered, and they have seen active service in the Persian Gulf and Somalia.

Howdah; Howdah Pistol; Elephant
FIREARM

The word "howdah," derived from the Arabic, means a pavilion or seat carried on the back of an elephant. In the ancient world they were used in warfare to carry archers and other troops into battle, use of elephants with howdahs being particularly widespread in the Indian subcontinent, Persia, and North Africa. Apart from their impact and value as a fighting platform, elephants were particularly frightening to horses. Some illustrations show howdahs in the form of small wooden "castles." The first documented use of military elephants was by King Pyrrhus in 280 B.C. Their most famous deployment was with the Carthaginian army of Hannibal during the crossing of the Alps in 218 B.C., though they fell out of favor thereafter.

Howdah pistols were large-bore handguns designed to be carried in the Howdah, primarily for emergency use during hunting. In the late nineteenth century they gained some popularity with army officers, by which time they were generally double barreled, giving one shot with each barrel.

Howitzer
ARTILLERY

The word "howitzer" derives from the Dutch *houwitser* and the German *haubitze*, and it means a species of **artillery** adapted to fire **shells** at higher angles and lower velocity than ordinary guns. The barrel is commonly short, and howitzers may therefore be regarded as bridging the gap between artillery and **mortars**. Probably known as early as the latter seventeenth century, howitzers were in general use by the Napoleonic period. Then they were often attached to field gun batteries and even began to be grouped as specialist units.

There have been many models of howitzer of widely differing sizes. Particularly noteworthy are the 30.5 cm Skoda howitzers developed at Pilsen in 1910. Capable of firing a 846 lb shell more than seven miles, they were used to batter enemy forts in 1914. A British 15-inch howitzer, initially crewed by the Royal Navy, was fielded a year later. This was nicknamed "Granny" by the troops, while a 9.2-inch model was called "Mother." A current type with the U.S. Army is the M284 155 mm howitzer.

Howitzer Motor Carriage. *See* **Self-Propelled Gun**

Huey, XH-40, Iroquois, etc. HELICOPTER

Derived from the XH-40 prototype of 1956, the Bell Huey and its derivatives are among the most, if not *the* most, widespread military **helicopters** of all time. The name "Huey" sprang from the original HU designation, later changed to UH. Important models have included the UH-1N, which entered service with the U.S. Marines in 1971; the German Dornier 352; the Italian Agusta AB 212 antisubmarine variant; and the H types, which saw widespread use in Vietnam.

The UH-1D Iroquois of 1963 was the first "stretch-bodied" version, capable of taking 12 soldiers or six stretcher casualties. Particularly remarkable was the UH-1D air cavalry night-operations machine, which used a cluster of landing lights to illuminate ground targets; other helicopters in the group would then pulverize the enemy with **Gatling**-type miniguns, rockets, and **machine-gun** fire. Hueys were also used with loudspeaker systems as part of the propaganda effort and as improvized bombers, dropping 81 mm mortar rounds. Specifications vary widely with precise model and engine fitted, but a top speed of about 130 mph and range of 250 miles loaded was typical.

Humvee (HMMWV) VEHICLE

The four-wheel-drive "High Mobility, Multipurpose, Wheeled Vehicle" (HMMWV) was developed by AM General with the U.S. government in the late 1970s and following testing and competitive bid processes was selected as the new light military vehicle. A contract for over 55,000 humvees was awarded in 1983, and within five years 70,000 were produced. At the end of the decade a further contract was issued, and by 1991 the decision had been taken to offer "Hummers" to the civilian market. At six feet high, over seven wide, and nearly 16 feet in length the humvee is big for a light vehicle, with a profile that puts a premium on stability. It is also well calculated for all-terrain use, being perfectly capable of scaling steep slopes and vertical two-foot brick walls. As one Australian journalist remarked, "The Hummer is the absolute antithesis of the **jeep**, the **Land Rover**, the European style of four wheel drive. Where the latter are small, minimal and nimble, the Hummer is large, substantial with all eventualities covered. . . . All in all it is a typical piece of 'money no object' military engineering."

Many variant HMMWVs have been produced for army, navy, and marines and for special purposes varying from ambulances to missile launching.

Additional Reading: Green, *Hummer: The Next Generation*, 1995.

Hunley. *See* **Submarine**

Hunter AIRCRAFT

The British **Hawker** Hunter swept-wing jet fighter aircraft flew in prototype in 1951, and it flew faster than the speed of sound in 1952. It entered Royal Air Force service in 1954 and has been in service around the world ever since, though frontline RAF use as an interceptor ended in 1963, after which its main use was ground attack. The Mark 6 Hunter was capable of 716 mph and had a range of 1840 miles.

Additional Reading: Jones, *Hawker Hunter*, 1998.

Hurricane   AIRCRAFT

The **Hawker** Hurricane was the most numerous **fighter** aircraft in the RAF inventory during the battle of Britain in 1940. Along with the better-known **Spitfire** it made a vital contribution to the Second World War. Initially dubbed the "Fury Monoplane," the single-seat Hurricane first flew in 1935 and entered service in 1937. Early models featured fabric-covered wings, but the aircraft was solid and able to absorb surprising amounts of punishment. Later models were produced for night fighting, naval operations, and ground attack. A total of over 14,000 were built in the United Kingdom and Canada.

The Hurricane Mark I was powered by a Rolls-Royce 12-cylinder engine, giving a maximum speed of 318 mph and a range of 460 miles. Its armament was eight **Browning machine guns**.

Additional Reading: Jackson, *The Hawker Hurricane*, 1987; Bishop, *Hurricane*, 1986.

Huskie H-43B   HELICOPTER

The first U.S. Kamen **helicopter** flew in 1947 and was much influenced by the German intermeshing-rotor **Kolibri**. The larger H-43B, which entered service in the late 1950s, was intended for crash rescue. It was distinctive for its unusual layout having a twin-boom tail and a long exhaust stack. The maximum speed was 120 mph. Unarmed Huskies saw extensive rescue use in Vietnam.

Hydrogen Bomb   NUCLEAR WARFARE

The United States tested the first thermonuclear, or hydrogen, device at Eniwetok in 1952, and the Soviet Union exploded its first full-size "H-bomb" in 1953, followed by the United States at Bikini Atoll in March 1954. The Bikini bomb was about 750 times the power of the atomic bomb used at Hiroshima. Hydrogen bombs represented a massive increase in power over atom bombs. This is because the H-bomb releases far more of the potential energy of the material employed, which is Uranium-235 or Plutonium and Uranium-238.

Hydrophone   DETECTION

The hydrophone is a listening device that takes advantage of the fact that sound travels great distances under water. Installed in submarines from World War I onward, hydrophones enabled estimates to be made of the enemy's direction by the sound of its propellers. Though primitive compared to later active **sonar** and **radar**, hydrophones had the advantage that they were usually passive devices, not themselves liable to detection. More advanced forms of hydrophone fitted in **U-boats** during World War II included the cluster *Gruppenhorchgerät*, which was aided by an electronic timing circuit, and the Balkon *Gerät* of 1943, which mounted 43 hydrophones capable of detecting a **destroyer** at 10 km. The last **U-boat** hydrophone was the SU-Apparat or Nibelung, which included both active and passive elements. Modern "passive systems" take advantage of the fact that they have no signal that can be detected.

Hyposcope; Hyposcope Rifle DETECTION

The hyposcope or periscope **rifle** combines mirrors and a "set down" mechanism to allow a weapon to be fired above the head of its user while still aiming at the enemy. This is of particular utility where the marksman can as a result remain under cover and thus be less vulnerable. It was quite widely used in the trenches of World War I, when a number of types were patented. A similar method has also been applied to **machine guns**.

I

Ilyushin Il-2. *See* **Shturmovik**

Image Intensifier   DETECTION

Mainly used for nighttime detection, image intensifiers receive light on a screen and amplify
the image electronically. In the U.S. arsenal,
one of the most widespread of the image-
intensifying devices has been the Starlight
scope, which entered service in 1965 and could
be handheld or fitted to infantry weapons, such
as the **M16**. In later models this battery-
powered model included an automatic gain control to allow a uniform level of illumination,
and flash protection to prevent damage from
bright light and allow the user to see rounds hit
the target. Though early types were limited to
about 300 m range, later types were useful at
greater distances. Vehicles can be fitted with
much more powerful devices.

In second and third-generation image intensifiers, a microchannel plate (MCP) is included
to multiply the electrons produced. The result
is a much better image for much less weight.
Indirect viewing is now often carried out using
LLTV, or low light television, coupled to image
intensifiers. Image intensifiers and laser illu-
minators have now largely superceded **infrared**
technology for small battlefield weapons.

Additional Reading: Richardson et al., *Surveillance
and Target Acquisition Systems*, 1997.

Independence Class   WARSHIP

Named after America's first **ship of the line**,
the *Independence* class of U.S. **aircraft carriers** was constructed from 1941 to 1943 in a
crash program. A total of nine 11,000-ton vessels were built using an adapted light **cruiser**
hull. The result was a slightly ungainly compromise, with a wooden flight deck, into which
aircraft were crammed; some that sailed to the
Pacific theater as ferries had over 100 aboard.
The normal complement of planes was 30. CVL
27 preserved the name of the original U.S. carrier, *Langley*. The *Independence* (CVL 22)
took part in the atomic tests at Bikini and was
scrapped in 1951.

Infrared Systems   DETECTION

Invisible to the naked eye, infrared radiation is
the portion of the electromagnetic spectrum that
extends from red, or long wavelength, to the
microwave range. Its existence was first discovered by Sir William Herschel in 1800, yet
technology to use infrared in sighting and surveillance systems was not developed until
World War II. IR detectors are of two main
types, thermal and photo. Since infrared radiation is not primarily dependent on color, it may
render camouflage ineffective, though carbon
added to camouflage materials in turn reduces
the effectiveness of infrared. Infrared systems
may be passive, as when used to detect enemy
infrared systems, or active, where, for example,
an infrared searchlight is used to illuminate a
target.

A wide range of military infrared devices
have been developed. These included **rifle** night
sights such as B8-V, in use with West German
forces in the 1970s; infrared field glasses, as
exemplified by the French NI-PE-38 Mark 4;
and airborne systems, such as the UK Linescan.

For thermal imaging, FLIR, or forward-looking infrared, systems may be used; they identify the temperature difference between hot engines, personnel, and cold objects. A recent development in this sphere is SPRITE, or Signal Processing in the Element, which reduces the amount of circuitry required in the detector. Many battlefield infrared devices have now been superceded by **image intensifiers**.

Ingram Submachine Gun, Models 6, 10, 11
FIREARM

Designed by Gordon B. Ingram following the Second World War, Ingram **submachine guns** are short (as little as 22 cm long), solidly built automatic weapons. Having lightweight bolts, they have extremely high rates of fire. Popular in the United States and South America from the 1950s, they have been produced in .45 inch, 9 mm, and .380 calibers. They have often been fitted with a form of **silencer** that allows the bullet to remain supersonic while reducing the emergent gas to subsonic. Latterly Ingram SMGs have been produced under the name Cobray.

Additional Reading: *Jane's Infantry Weapons.*

Intercontinental Ballistic Missile (ICBM)
MISSILE

The first Soviet SLBM, or submarine-launched ballistic missile, was tested in 1955; the USSR also launched a multistage missile known to the West as the SS-6 Sapwood as early as 1957. Spurred by this arms escalation, the United States completed its Thor and Jupiter IRBMs (intermediate-range ballistic missiles) and deployed them to the United Kingdom, Italy, and Turkey in 1958. Development of longer-range weapons was continued apace.

In the event, the SS-6 was not a great success; because its maximum range was 3,000 miles, it had to be stationed in the northern Soviet Union in order to reach the United States. Severe weather conditions made for difficult operation, and in 1960 a missile exploded, killing Mitrofan Ivanovich Nedelin, chief of the

Strategic Rocket Forces, and many others. It may have been these failings that prompted the Soviets to place SS-4 Sandal IRBMs in Cuba, thus triggering the Cuban missile crisis. Ultimately the U.S. response was more powerful ICBMs based on the American mainland. One of the first was the Atlas-D rocket, with 360,000 lb of thrust, a two-megaton warhead, radio inertial guidance, and a 7,500-mile range. Later variants increased the payload to four megatons and the thrust to 390,000 lb, and made silo deployment possible.

Early ICBMs were problematic, because, like the German **V2** of World War II, they used liquid fuel. In the Atlas and Titan types the hypercold fuels had to be pumped aboard before launch, taking about an hour. Reaction time was therefore lengthy, and, in a worst-case scenario, could mean that a first strike by the enemy might destroy the ability to reply. There was also a danger that one side or the other might become trigger happy, fearing that it would be unable to retaliate if attacked. In order to shorten the launch sequence, much work went into the development of high-speed fuel pumps.

In the Titan II, the Soviet SS-7 Saddler, and the SS-8 Sasin, deployed in 1963, systems were used that allowed fuel to be stored in rockets. This cut preparation time to about a minute. The Titan II was the largest ICBM developed by the United States, being in two stages and 100 feet in length. Its range was 9,000 miles. Chinese missile technology also made significant strides in the 1960s, with the advent of the Dong Feng, or East Wind, series of surface-to-surface missiles. The first successful firing of a Chinese ICBM was in 1970; the CSS-3, with a range of 3,500 miles, first flew in 1976.

As flying times contracted, speed of launch became ever more critical, and it was solid fuel that seemed to offer the swiftest and safest answer. The U.S. **Minuteman** I solid-fuel rocket, first developed as a rail-mobile system, was deployed in silos in 1962 and fully operational in 1963; it remained in service until 1973. Updated versions remain in use. The first Soviet solid-fuel ICBM was the SS-13 Savage, which became operational in 1969. This was capable of throwing a 750-kiloton warhead over 5,000 miles. France deployed the much shorter range IRBM S-3 in 1980. It was capable of 2,100 miles.

International Heavy Tank. *See* Liberty Tank

Interrupter Gear   MISCELLANEOUS

Interrupter gear allows guns to fire through the propeller of an **aircraft**. Lack of a suitable system was a serious handicap to early war planes. Efforts to solve the problem were made as early as 1913, with the German Franz Schnieder, the Russian Poplavko, and the English Edwards brothers competing in the field. Yet the first successful, if primitive, solution was that devised by a Frenchman, Raymond Saulnier. He had some success with mechanical means but fitted steel deflector plates to the propellor as a fail-safe extra. These deflector plates were used in combat, causing serious disquiet to the enemy. Very soon, however, **Fokker** introduced a linkage system of cams and push rods that effectively synchronized the firing of the guns with the rotation of the propeller, thus returning the advantage to the Germans. Nevertheless, the early systems had occasional spectacular failures, when pilots shot off their own propellers.

Intruder, A-6   AIRCRAFT

The **Grumman** A-6 Intruder first flew in 1960 and was accepted by the U.S. Navy in 1961. The twin-jet-engine **aircraft** was designed in answer to a requirement for an all-weather, close-support, night-attack fighter-bomber. With two crew members, seated side by side, the plane was a suitable platform for electronic systems and a variety of weapons, including bombs and rockets. It was heavily used in Vietnam.

Technologically the Intruder was remarkable for what was then advanced navigation and **radar** equipment. Devices fitted to various models included the DIANE, or Digital Integrated Attack Navigation Equipment; Sperry automatic flight control; Doppler **radar**; a ballistics computer; TRIM, with electro-optical sensors

that could detect targets invisible to radar or the naked eye; and ACLS, or Automatic Carrier Landing System.

Repeated upgrades to the Intruder produced the A-6E which first flew in 1970, and thereafter the A6-F, and A6-G. A four-seat variant that entered service in 1971 introduced a TJS, or tactical jamming system, and this led ultimately to the EA-6B Prowler, the U.S. Navy standard carrierborne electronic warfare aircraft of the 1990s. The latest Prowlers carried antiradar missiles and performed vital tasks but were not particularly fast aircraft, with a top speed of about 610 mph when carrying jammer pods.

Additional Reading: Treadwell, *The Ironworks: Grumman's Fighting Aeroplanes*, 1990; Francillon, *Grumman Aircraft since 1929*, 1989.

Invader, A-26   AIRCRAFT

The Douglas A-26 Invader **aircraft** was designed as a multirole twin-engine light bomber capable of low-level attack. Though test flights were made in 1942, it did not see operational service until November 1944. Speed and heavy armament were its main strengths; it was capable of 373 mph and of carrying 4,000 lb of bombs, as well as six **machine guns**. A version specifically intended for ground strafing mounted no fewer than 18 machine guns, mainly .5-inch **Brownings**. In a B-26 version the Invader was operational as late as the 1960s over Vietnam.

Additional Reading: Donald, *American Warplanes of World War II*, 1995.

***Invincible; Invincible* Class   WARSHIP**

Invincible has been the name of several British warships. The first was captured from the French in 1747 and lost accidentally in 1758. The fifth *Invincible* (1909–1916) is famous as the first of the large armored **cruisers** conceived by Admiral Sir John Fisher as a fast and hard-hitting commerce protector. Given that she displaced almost 20,000 tons, had 6-inch armor, and was armed with 12-inch guns it was fitting that she was redesignated as a battle cruiser in 1913. She was destroyed at the battle of Jutland in a catastrophic explosion when a shell hit her Q turret. All but six of her 1,027-man crew died.

Most recently the name *Invincible* has been applied to a class of 20,000-ton **aircraft carriers**. The *Invincible* herself was laid down in 1973 and commissioned in 1980; she was 677 feet long and had a top speed of 28 knots. During the Falklands War she operated **Harrier aircraft** with remarkable success. Her sister ships were *Illustrious* and *Ark Royal*.

Additional Reading: Lavery, *Royal Navy's First Invincible*, 1988; Tarrant, *Battlecrusier Invincible*, 1986; Bassett, *Battle Cruisers*, 1981; Beaver, *Invincible Class*, 1984.

Iowa Class   WARSHIP

Planned as fast **battleships** capable of engaging the latest Japanese ships, the six *Iowa*-class vessels were laid down between June 1940 and December 1942. By 1944, four—*Iowa*, *New Jersey*, *Missouri*, and *Wisconsin*—had been completed. With a displacement of 48,000 tons, a top speed of 32 knots, and a main armament of nine 16-inch guns, the *Iowas* were among the most powerful ships of the day. All four saw action in World War II and have since had the distinction of being the world's longest-serving and last true battleships.

The *Iowa* herself transported President Roosevelt to the Middle East in 1943 and later fought extensively in the Pacific campaigns, where strikes from smaller ships' 4.7 inch shells caused little damage. She was present at the surrender ceremonies in Tokyo Bay in 1945. She fought during the Korean War and, though decommissioned in 1958, was reactivated in 1984. An accidental explosion damaged her number-two turret in 1989, and she was decommissioned again in 1990. In later life she carried such modern equipment as nuclear **shells** and **Harpoon** and **Tomahawk** missiles. The last two vessels of the class, *Illinois* and *Kentucky*, were never completed, though *Kentucky* survived part finished as late as 1958.

Additional Reading: Sumrall, *Iowa Class Battleships*, 1988; Madsen, *Forgotten Fleet: The Mothball Navy*, 1999; Schwoebel, *Explosion aboard the Iowa*, 1999.

Ironclad. *See* **Battleship;** *Gloire; Monitor; Warrior*

Iroquois. *See* **Huey**

IS Heavy Tank. *See* **Joseph Stalin Tank**

Ivan Rogov   WARSHIP

The Soviet *Ivan Rogov* class of Landing Platform Docks, commenced in the mid-1970s, were 11,000-ton seagoing ships for carrying amphibious forces. At 522 feet they were powered by four diesel engines, and their maximum speed was 20 knots. Carrying capacity was a battalion of marines and 40 tanks, while the fixed armament comprised a twin SA-N-4 SAM missile launcher, a twin 76 mm gun, four 23 mm **Gatlings**, and a BM-21 rocket launcher.

J

Jagdtiger. *See* **Tiger**

Javelin. *See* **Blowpipe and Spear**

Jeep   VEHICLE

The jeep was described by Ernie Pyle of the *Washington Daily News* as "a divine instrument of wartime locomotion"; while this may be an exaggeration, the jeep has certainly became one of the most successful, and most famous, vehicles of all time. Designed in 1940 in answer to a requirement for a "general purpose" four-wheel drive capable of pulling a small antitank gun, it was the result of competition between the Bantam Company of Butler Pennsylvania and Willys-Overland of Toledo Ohio, the only two companies that submitted designs. In the event it was Bantam designer Karl Probst who came up with the best ideas, drawing up the initial plan in five days. Bantam delivered the first vehicles in December, just five months from the moment Probst had put pen to paper.

Nevertheless the Quartermaster Corps thought Bantam too small to fulfill all the orders and wished to examine further the work of other companies. Willys and Ford submitted improvements based on not only the Bantam but their "Quad" and "Pygmy" designs, with a result that a major contract for a quarter-ton "command reconnaissance" truck was now issued to Willys. About 660,000 jeeps had been made by 1945, the vast majority being either Willys MB or Ford GPW types. There is still argument as to how the name came about. Some have it that jeep comes from "GP," others that it was a name used in *Popeye* cartoons.

(Interestingly, the Dodge weapons carrier got the nickname "Beep.") Costing about $750, the Ford GPW had a 60 horsepower four-cylinder engine and could carry loads of 800 lb.

Used by many Allied countries, the jeep continued to be important after the war, with an M38 model produced from 1950, and a more powerful M38A1 from 1952. Thereafter a Mitsubishi jeep was made in Japan, and Ford produced the M151 in 1960. India also produced jeeps at this time. Willys became the Kaiser company in 1963, and in 1970 a subsidiary of AMC, as the Jeep Corporation. There have been myriad variant and experimental models. These include weapons carriers, ambulances, models fitted with snorkels for wading, the aluminum-bodied "Aero" jeep, and the "Mighty Mite," with Porsche engine and permanent all-wheel drive.

Additional Reading: Rifkind, *The Jeep: Its Development and Procurement*, 1988; Munro, *Jeep from Bantam to Wrangler*, 2000; Boniface and Jeudy, *US Army Vehicles of World War II*, 1991.

JLENS. *See* **Strategic Defense Initiative**

Joe-1. *See* **Nuclear Weapons**

John C. Butler Class   WARSHIP

This class of U.S. **destroyer** escorts commenced production with the laying down of the *John C. Butler* (DE 339) at the Consolidated yard in October 1943. Displacing 1,430 tons, they were significantly smaller than the *Fletcher, Gearing*, and *Allen M. Sumner* destroyers but well adapted to antisubmarine

John C. Stennis, *USS*

A jeep stuck on a jungle road Guadalcanal, Solomon Islands, 1942. This small rugged equipment carrier and runabout was a small but significant advance in military mobility. Most armies of the world now have their own modern equivalents. Courtesy of the Library of Congress.

work, having **hedgehog** and **depth charges**. In concert with the *Buckley, Rudderow,* and other destroyer escort types, it had significant successes against German **U-boats** and Japanese submarines. Some were later used as fast transports.

Additional Reading: Whitley, *Destroyers of World War II,* 1988.

John C. Stennis, USS   WARSHIP

The USS *John C. Stennis* (CV 74) is a *Nimitz*-class **aircraft carrier**. It was named by President Ronald Reagan in 1988, after the veteran Senator Stennis, who served in the Senate for 41 years. From 2000 the USS *Stennis* was a major unit of Carrier Air Wing 9. Though older, its specifications are similar to those of the **Harry S. Truman**.

Johnson, M1941   FIREARM

U.S. Marine Corps Reserve captain M. M. Johnson developed both an automatic **rifle** and a light **machine gun** in the 1930s. Though there was initially little demand, his .30 machine gun was later manufactured by Cranston Arms in Rhode Island as the model 1941 for marines and rangers. It weighed just over 14 lb. Its novel features included the fact that in single-shot mode it fired from a closed and locked bolt, while on full automatic it fired from an open bolt. Its 20-round magazine could be topped up from ordinary five-round clips.

Joint Strike Fighter (F-35)   AIRCRAFT

To be developed by a consortium including Lockheed Martin, **Northrop Grumman**, and **British Aerospace**, the F-35 fighter aircraft is estimated to cost $200 billion; it has been described as "the largest single military procurement programme in history." It has also been billed, perhaps prematurely, as the West's "last manned fighter." At the time of writing it is planned that Lockheed will make the front section, Northrop Grumman the midsection, and the British the rear. The partners will provide their sections "stuffed"—that is, with all wiring and components; the final assembly will take place at Fort Worth, Texas. Many small contractors will supply the main companies. Full production is scheduled for 2008, and it is hoped that a total of about 3,000 will be made, mainly for U.S. forces but also for Britain, the Netherlands, and other customers.

The F-35 is intended as a multirole craft, acting as a supersonic fighter but also having a short-takeoff capability for carrier and field operation. Significantly, computer-aided design (CAD) has been used from the outset. The whole plane is to be assembled in cyberspace before any metal is cut; it is believed that this will obviate compatibility problems well in advance.

"Jolly Green Giant." *See* Sikorsky, Igor

Joseph Stalin Tank   TANK

First produced at the end of 1943, the Joseph Stalin, or IS (for "Iosif Stalin"), was the first of a new generation of heavy **tanks** that took the Soviets a step beyond the **T-34**. With thicker and better-shaped armor than that of the old KV types, the IS boasted a new low, almost hemispherical, cast turret. The IS-2 and IS-3, of 1944 and 1945, respectively, mounted a powerful 122 mm gun, which put it in the same league as the **Tiger**. The Stalin name was dropped after the demise of the dictator, but the tank was influential on later designs, the T10 of 1956 being a late-model Stalin in all but name.

Additional Reading: Bean and Fowler, *Russian Tanks of World War II*, 2002.

Ju-52. *See* Junkers

Ju-87. *See* Stuka

Ju-88   AIRCRAFT

The twin-engine German **Junkers** Ju 88 was a fast bomber and **dive bomber** designed by Ernst Zindel and his team in the mid-1930s. It was test flown from 1936 and in action from September 1939. Thereafter it was one of Germany's better bombers and a mainstay of operations. When the Luftwaffe began to lose control of the skies, the Ju 88 was revisited for a variety of tasks, including **radar**-guided night fighting and antitank ground attack. Detailed specifications vary considerably from model to model, but the Ju 88 A-4 bomber had a wingspan of just over 65 feet, a maximum speed of 269 mph, and a bomb load up to 1,500 kg. Up to nine **machine guns** were carried.

Some of the more unusual modifications included the fitting of **skis** and **torpedo** bombing. Perhaps the weirdest conversion was known as "Beethoven," or "Mistrel," in which a redundant and uncrewed Ju 88 was filled with explosives and had a fighter attached to its back. The fighter pilot controlled the whole combination in a **kamikaze**-style attack, jettisoning his deadly load and escaping in the fighter at the last moment. Total production of all Ju 88 types was more than 14,000.

Additional Reading: Mackay, *Junkers Ju 88*, 2001.

Junkers, Dr. Hugo   INVENTOR

Professor Dr. Hugo Junkers (1859–1935) of Germany was both an inventor and a manufacturer of boilers long before his first collaboration on an **aircraft** project with the Aachen Technical High School in 1909. Nevertheless, his contribution to the field of military aviation would be significant; during World War I he was a prolific designer and tester. One important discovery was that thick-profile wings could be surprisingly efficient, a factor that would be particularly influential on his later work; another was that it was possible to make good aircraft of metal. So it was that he produced the J1, or "tin donkey," the world's first all-metal aircraft, in 1915. The J4, which followed, served as a reconnaissance machine. The J7 fighter of 1918 was an aircraft with the now-familiar corrugated duralumin skin that would characterize later Junkers production.

Though civil aircraft dominated Junkers efforts after 1918, several of his cargo-carrying planes, such as the W34 and giant G38, had clear military potential. Others served as trainers. Junkers also produced engines at his Dessau plant, these being popularly known as "Jumo" engines, a contraction of "Junkers Motorenbau." Perhaps his best-known craft was the Ju 52, which first flew as a single-engine passenger plane in 1930 but was redesigned as a trimotor in 1932. Following the renunciation of the Treaty of Versailles, the "Aunt Ju" would emerge as the main Luftwaffe transport; it saw action as a bomber in the Spanish Civil War. Production of the rugged and adaptable Ju 52 eventually reached almost 5,000, with the aircraft being used particularly for **parachute** drops and supply missions during World War II. Interestingly, the elderly Junkers refused to hand over his patent rights to the Nazis until colleagues were arrested and his family threatened.

Many of the best-known military aircraft postdated the death of Junkers himself. These included the Ju 86, the Ju 87 **Stuka dive bomber**, the **Ju 88** and **Ju 188** multirole aircraft, and the Ju 290 and 390 transports. The unusual Ju 287, with its four turbojet Jumo engines and forward-swept wings, flew in February 1945, but trials were incomplete at the end of the war.

Additional Reading: Walters, *Junkers*, 1997.

K

K98k. *See* **Mauser**

K Class SUBMARINE

The British K class of oceangoing **submarines** of 1915 to 1918 were some of the worst used by the Royal Navy, earning themselves the nickname "Kalamity Ks." The key problem was that in order to get maximum surface speed, steam power had been chosen. To dive, boilers had to be shut down—as with the old *Resurgam*—and this, plus the folding of the funnels, took about five minutes. Moreover, stability and watertight integrity were questionable; accidents claimed several K-class vessels. Some were later converted to M-class monitors.

Additional Reading: Everitt, *K Boats*, 1999.

K-36. *See* **Ejection Seat**

Kaga WARSHIP

The Japanese **aircraft carrier** *Kaga* was based on a **battleship** hull laid down in 1920. She was commissioned in 1928. For the time she was large, at 715 feet in length, and capable of carrying 60 aircraft. She was also heavily armed, with ten 8-inch guns. Later the guns were reduced, while the aircraft capacity was upped to 72. *Kaga* was originally built with a large, featureless flight deck; an island was added in the 1930s. *Kaga* was in the war against China, involved in Pearl Harbor, and the raid on Darwin, Australia, in 1942. She was sunk by aircraft from the *Enterprise* at Midway.

Kaiten "Human Torpedo" EXPLOSIVE DEVICE

Based on the big Long Lance, the Japanese Kaiten was a manned **torpedo** accepted into service in 1944. There were four major subtypes, though only the first of these would be used operationally. Though it had a nominal escape hatch, used in training, it is clear that the pilot was in effect a **kamikaze**, intended to perish in the attack. Indeed, one of the craft's inventors, Lieutenant Hiroshi Kuroki, died in a training accident before being committed to action.

Even so, the Kaiten was a formidable weapon, containing 3,418 lb of explosive, with a maximum range of about 85,000 yards. They were launched from submerged submarines or converted surface vessels. Though many missed their targets or were sunk, some successes were achieved against Allied ships.

Additional Reading: O'Neill, *Suicide Squads of World War II*, 1988.

Kalashnikov, AK-47, AKM, AIM, Tabuk, Type 56 FIREARM

The **assault rifle** designed by Mikhail T. Kalashnikov is deservedly one of the best-known weapons of all time. Manufactured in huge numbers, the original AK-47 and its many variants have been made in many countries and have equipped many armies. Sometimes referred to as the "peasant's gun," it has also been used by irregulars and terrorists; it is straightforward to use, can be stripped down without tools, and is powerful and murderously effective at short to medium ranges.

Kamikaze

The young Kalashnikov was a Soviet tank commander, wounded at the battle for Bryansk in 1941. According to legend he used his convalescence to begin his weapons-design career, although his early efforts were not accepted for production. It was not until 1946 that a prototype of what would later become the AK-47 was accepted for trials. It was soon taken as a supplement to the existing **SKS** carbine and was adopted by the army in 1949. In the 1950s it was recognized as a world-beater.

Though the Soviet version of events would have us believe in the uniqueness and genius of Kalashnikov, in fact the AK-47 built substantially on what had come before, albeit bettering existing designs. Thus it is that the AK-47 bears a general resemblance to the German MP 43 (or later "Sturmgewehr"), examples of which had been captured by the middle of the war. It used an intermediate **cartridge**, had a trigger similar to the **Garand**, and incorporated some features of existing Soviet arms. Moreover, Kalashnikov was assisted by a design collective, and Aleksandr Zaytsev also claimed a contribution.

Nevertheless, the AK-47 was a stunning weapon. The basic model was a 7.62 mm, with selective fire, using gas to operate the mechanism, which incorporated a rotating bolt. Weighing 4.3 kg and being feed from an easily detached 30-round box magazine, its simplicity and handiness were significant advances. Using a steel-cored bullet the AK-47 had good penetration and was accurate enough at 400 meters when using single shots. By 1959 an AKM model was in production; the improvement was mainly in the weight, which was reduced to 3.13 kg by means of pressed steel and riveted construction. This also saved on cost. An AKM-S was made featuring a folding stock, and the AKM was also made in East Germany, Hungary, Poland, and Romania. Chinese-produced weapons were known as Type 56.

From the late 1960s Soviet designers had the opportunity to study the **M16** and other Western weapons, coming to the conclusion that a better cartridge was required for their own arms. The result was the 5.45 mm ammunition that appeared in 1974, and redesign of the ex-

isting Kalashnikov to produce the AK-74. Apart from the improved characteristics of the round, the main innovation was a muzzle brake or compensator at the fore end of the barrel, which directed some of the gas forward on firing. This helped to keep the gun steady and acted to prevent the aim from climbing.

Since then there have been many variants and many weapons influenced by the Kalashnikov. In a modern Armenian version the configuration has been altered to create a **"bullpup,"** with the magazine to the rear of the trigger. In Bulgaria, the basic design is known as the AKK-74; in China, Norinco has produced a Type 81 assault rifle, similar to the AK-74, since 1982. The Polish KA-88 Tantal is effectively a folding AK-74 with a burst-fire facility. The Russian AK-74U takes compactness a stage farther, in what is essentially a short 2.7 kg **submachine gun** version. In the Gulf in 1991 and 2003 coalition forces faced an Iraqi Kalashnikov type known as the Tabuk.

Additional Reading: Long, *AK 47*, 1988; Walter, *Kalashnikov*, 1999; Jane's *Infantry Weapons*; Lamont (ed), *The AK-47 Assault Rifle*, 1969; Ezell, *AK 47 Story*; Ezell, *Small Arms*; Kalashnikov, *From a Stranger's Doorstep*, 1997.

Kamikaze   AIRCRAFT

Kamikaze, Japanese for "divine wind," has become generally associated with **aircraft** deliberately crashed into their targets. Yet this term was not particularly widespread in Japan in World War II, nor have suicide attacks been limited to traditional aircraft. The Japanese, for example, also used an **Ohka** piloted bomb and exploding motor boats.

Vice Admiral Takijiro Onishi, veteran of Chinese campaigns and **parachute** forces leader, is usually identified as father of the kamikaze. His first "special attack corps" was formed in the Pacific in late 1944; its sorties were conducted using Zeros carrying a 250 kg bomb mounted in place of the fuel drop tank. The first Allied ship to be hit was the HMAS *Australia* on 21 October, with 30 killed and 64 wounded, though this is believed to have been an impromptu act rather than the work of a spe-

142

cially designated aircraft. The U.S. tug *Sonoma* and the **Liberty Ship** *Augustus Thomas* were struck soon afterward. Kamikaze would be widely used at Leyte, where *Suwanee, St Lo*, and other vessels were sunk or damaged. Kamikaze attacks now became commonplace, with one calculation suggesting that more than half of all Allied vessels damaged or sunk from October 1944 to the end of January 1945 were due to suicide attack, with an increasing proportion thereafter.

Aircraft employed on kamikaze missions included not only the **Zero** and **Val** but adapted versions of the Kyushu Shiragiku (White Crysanthemum), the Kawasaki 99 Lily, the Nakajima Donryu Helen, and the Mitsubishi Flying Dragon Peggy. In the case of bomber types, turrets were sometimes removed and faired over and **explosives** mounted internally. Attacks were made diving, bow on, and horizontal to the target, with kamikaze pilots instructed to give priority to **aircraft carriers**, followed by **battleships** and other large vessels.

According to U.S. Navy instructions, the only certain way to avoid kamikaze strikes was to cause "total disintegration" before the aircraft impact. This was best achieved by heavy antiaircraft guns using **shells** with proximity **fuses**, and "wall of fire" tactics from 40 mm and 20 mm weapons. In one of the most extreme instances, on 16 April 1945, the **destroyer** USS *Laffey* was attacked by 22 kamikazes. In a period of 80 minutes she shot down 16 but suffered five aircraft and four bomb hits causing over 100 casualties.

Additional Reading: Hoyt, *The Kamikazes*, 1983; O'Neill, *Suicide Squads of World War II*, 1988.

Kashin Class   WARSHIP

The Kashin-class **destroyers** were commenced in the early 1960s and were a considerable advance in Soviet naval technology. They were the first major warships to rely solely on gas turbines for propulsion and they made extensive use of electronics. Good lines and four engines gave the 3,750-ton Kashins a top speed of 35 knots. They were armed with torpedoes, missiles, and antisubmarine launchers and carried

a **helicopter**. Updates during the 1970s saw added armament, including **Gatling**-type close-defense weapons and additional ASW launchers.

Katyusha   MISSILE

First used in action in mid-1941, the Katyusha was a truck-mounted rocket launching system developed by the Leningrad Gas Dynamics Laboratory. Initially deployed with 82 mm rockets, a later version used a 132 mm type. The latter is sometimes designated the BM-13-16. German troops nicknamed the weapon "Stalin's Organ." Post–World War II the Soviets would field a whole family of similar weapons, as for example the BM-21, BM-24, and BM-25.

KD6 Class   SUBMARINE

The KD6 class of **submarine**, built during the period 1934 to 1938, was one indicator of improving Japanese military technology in the interwar period. With a maximum surface speed of 23 knots, they were for a time the fastest submarines. Though a successful design, seven out of the eight in the class would be sunk during World War II, the I-70 being destroyed just three days after Pearl Harbor. KD6s were armed with four bow and two stern 21-inch **torpedo** tubes, plus deck guns.

Kent Class   WARSHIP

The British *Kent* class of 10,000-ton **cruisers** was laid down in 1924, with five vessels completed in 1927 and 1928. Their weight and eight 8-inch-gun armament was a result of building up to the parameters of the Washington Treaty of 1922. All saw copious active service in World War II, with *Cornwall* and *Cumberland* participating in the hunt for the *Graf Spee* and *Berwick* involved in action against the *Tirpitz*. *Cornwall* was sunk by the Japanese in 1942.

Kestrel. *See* Harrier

Kettenkrad VEHICLE

Kettenkrad is German for "tracked cycle." During World War II such a vehicle, with tracks at the rear and a motorcycle steering unit at the front, was produced for German forces for towing light artillery and supplies across rough terrain. Though ingenious, it was expensive for the results achieved.

Ki-45. *See* Toryu

Kiev Class WARSHIP

The 38,000-ton *Kiev*-class ships were the Soviet Union's most significant venture in the **aircraft carrier** field. The first in the series, the *Kiev* itself, was laid down at the Nikolayev yard in 1970 and commissioned in 1975. Nevertheless, it is arguable that these ships, built in the 1970s and 1980s, were effectively antisubmarine cruisers with a significant air capability. Thus it was that although they were through-deck carriers, they had large deck island and a heavy and varied armament. This included not only 33 **aircraft** and **helicopters** but a selection of up to 136 missiles, including the SS-N-12 Shaddock, **torpedoes**, and four 76.2 mm guns. With a crew of about 1,700, the *Kiev* class had a range of 13,000 miles and a top speed of about 32 knots. Bizarrely, one of the class, the *Minsk*, is now a floating theme park at Shenzen, China. The only major Russian carrier since the *Kiev* types has been the *Kuznetzov*.

Additional Reading: Jordan, *Soviet Warships 1945 to the Present*, 1991; Moore, *Warships of the Soviet Navy*, 1981.

Kilo Class SUBMARINE

The first 2,455-ton Kilo-class Soviet **submarine** was launched in 1980, and by 1998 there were 15 in Russian service. Kilos are also known as the *Vashavyanka* class. With a crew of 50 and six **torpedo** tubes, they are a relatively modern design powered by diesel and electric engines, making them quiet and giving a top speed submerged of just over 20 knots. Its main roles are antiship and antisubmarine warfare protecting naval installations and sea lanes. Sales have been conducted by state arms manufacturer Rosoboronexport; non-Russian users include India, Algeria, Poland, and Romania.

The latest model is the *Proiekt* 636, which appeared in 1997. It is reported as able to remain for up to 45 days at sea without refueling and having an anti-acoustic outer rubber coating. This created stories in the Western media during 2002 because purchases by China threatened the balance of power in the Taiwan Strait.

Additional Reading: Hutchinson, *Submarines, War beneath the Waves*, 2001.

Kingcobra. *See* Airacobra

King Kong. *See* Self-Propelled Gun

Kirov Class WARSHIP

The *Kirov* class of Soviet **cruisers** were the first large ships to be laid down after the Russian Revolution. A 9,000-ton three-turret type, it was loosely based on a contemporary Italian design. The main armament was nine 7.1-inch guns. Six ships were completed between 1938 and 1944, seeing extensive active service. Remarkably, all survived World War II, and the *Molotov* was last to be scrapped in 1978. A new *Kirov* Class of nuclear powered battle cruiser appeared in 1988, and four ships of this type were built.

"Knee" Mortar ARTILLERY

"Knee mortar" was a term erroneously applied by Allied troops during World War II to a small Japanese **grenade** launcher or **mortar**, the proper designation of which was the "tenth-year model." The mistake probably came about from the small curved base plate; if actually fired while rested on the leg it would cause serious injury.

Additional Reading: Markham, *Japanese Infantry Weapons of World War II*, 1976.

Knife. *See* Dagger; Knuckle Knife; Machete

Knobkerrie   CLUB WEAPON

The knobkerrie is the traditional club of the peoples of southern Africa, typically a single piece of wood with a straight shaft and spherical head. The name is a composition of Dutch and Hottentot, meaning literally "knot (or knob) stick." Though often thrown, it was made famous by the Zulus in hand-to-hand combat. During World War I the name was attached somewhat indiscriminately to various forms of **trench club**.

Additional Reading: Spring, *African Arms and Armour*, 1993; Stone, *A Glossary of the Construction, Decoration and Use of Arms and Armor*, 1934.

Knuckle Knife   BLADED WEAPON

The knuckle knife combines the attributes of the **dagger** and the knuckle duster, having both a blade and a knuckle guard with which to strike. Such weapons were available commercially from about 1900; during World War I the knuckle knife was adopted officially by the United States for trench fighting. Knuckle knives were quite widespread during World War II, with British, Australian, New Zealand and other models in use alongside the U.S. McNary. An unusual type was the British "Middle East" Commando model, which was of all-metal construction.

Additional Reading: Stephens, *Fighting Knives*, 1980.

Kolibri, Fl 282   AIRCRAFT

The German Kolibri, or "humming bird," first flown in 1941 and on active service from 1942, was the world's first mass-production military **helicopter**. Manufactured by the Flettner company, the Kolibri was a small machine, 21 feet 6 inches in length, with intermeshing rotors driven by a 160 horsepower BMW engine giving a maximum speed of 93 mph. The pilot's position was usually open to the elements, and there was often provision to carry an observer. A then novel feature was that in the event of engine failure the rotors continued to revolve, ideally bringing the machine to a controlled landing. The Kolibri was flown from ships and land.

Komintern   WARSHIP

The 6,338-ton Russian **cruiser** Komintern began life in 1905 as the *Pamiat Merkuriya* of the Czar's fleet. While others of her five-strong class were sunk or scrapped, the *Pamiat Merkuriya* led a charmed if complex existence. Surviving extensive war service, she raised the Ukrainian flag in November 1917, was turned over to the Bolsheviks in 1918, then was captured by the Germans. At the armistice she was turned over to White Russian service, then was briefly held by Allied troops until her capture by the Bolsheviks in 1919. She was renamed *Komintern* in 1922.

Repaired and upgraded to carry 16 5.1-inch guns, she was later refitted as a training ship. Despite her age and poor condition she performed sterling service in the early stages of World War II until being sunk for use as a breakwater in the channel of the Khopi River in October 1942. Recently she was still there.

Königsberg; Königsberg Class   WARSHIP

The Baltic city of Königsberg gave its name to several German warships of the early twentieth century, including a 5,300-ton cruiser constructed in the middle part of World War I. The 6,650 ton *Königsberg* commenced at Wilhelmshaven in 1926 lent its name to a class of three vessels and was unusual for a number of reasons. Triple-gun turrets were used for the first time, and six of the 15 cm guns faced aft, on the assumption that in a scouting role it was more likely to be chased than involved in head-on attack. The two rear-facing turrets were offset from the centerline. The *Königsberg* was powered by twin-shaft steam turbines but had "cruising" diesels installed on either side that could be engaged using a hydraulic coupling.

Despite such innovation, or because too much innovation was included in a new design all at once, the result was less than satisfactory. Stability problems became a significant issue. The *Königsberg* and the *Karlsruhe* were sunk in April 1940, while the *Köln* later served in the Baltic. The *Köln* was damaged in 1944, and during the course of a refit she was hit by a U.S. air raid. Nevertheless, she continued to resist, being used in a static role until 3 May 1945.

Krag-Jorgensen Rifle   FIREARM

The Norwegian Krag-Jorgensen **bolt-action rifle** of 1889 was unusual in that its five-round magazine was loaded through a hinged side gate. Surprisingly, the Krag was also adopted by the United States, but this relatively long and heavy rifle had a short service life, being replaced by the **Springfield**.

Krasnopol. *See* Copperhead

Kresta Class   WARSHIP

The Soviet Kresta class of guided missile **cruiser** was one of the most important in a line of such vessels that commenced with the Kynda class in 1960 and would be continued with the larger Kara class. Designed during the 1960s to oppose the U.S. **aircraft carrier** forces, the Krestas were very heavily armed 6,000-ton vessels, about 515 feet in length. They had good surface attack, antisubmarine, and antiaircraft capabilities and were capable of 34 knots.

Krivak Class   WARSHIP

The Soviet Krivak class of guided missile **frigate** entered service in 1970. These heavily armed multipurpose, 405-foot vessels were particularly well adapted for antisubmarine warfare, being equipped with SS-N-14 missiles as well as twin 76 mm guns and **torpedo** tubes. They were capable of 32 knots, though their range was inferior to that of similar Western vessels. The Krivak II, with its improved **sonar** and 100 mm guns, began to appear in 1976.

Additional Reading: *Jane's Fighting Ships*.

Krupp   MANUFACTURER

Few families or industrial concerns were as inextricably linked with armaments as Krupp of Essen, Germany. Founded by Arndt Krupp in the 1580s, the dynasty was thrust to prominence during the Thirty Years' War (1618–1648), when Anton Krupp supplied 1,000 gun barrels per year. Krupp **artillery** was important during the Franco-Prussian War of 1870–1871, but the Krupp who would ultimately become a worldwide household name was Bertha (1886–1957). The nickname "Big Bertha" was initially applied to 42 cm siege guns first deployed in 1914. Though members of the family were intimately associated with the Nazis, the firm survived World War II and postwar dismantling to reemerge under Alfried Krupp, once dubbed "the most powerful industrialist in the Common Market." In 1967 the company completed Germany's first nuclear plant, but financial collapse and the death of Alfried led ultimately to the dissolution of Krupp in 1968. The name is still preserved in the Thyssen-Krupp corporation.

Additional Reading: Manchester, *The Arms of Krupp*, 1969.

Kursk   SUBMARINE

The Russian nuclear **submarine** Kursk was named after a city near which occurred the greatest tank battle in history, in which the Red Army inflicted a serious reverse on German forces in 1943. The vessel was one of the most powerful in the Russian navy; an **Oscar** class vessel, it had an armament of 24 **nuclear** missiles and 28 **torpedoes**. On 10 August 2000 the *Kursk* was on a live-firing exercise in the Barents Sea when disaster struck. A torpedo exploded prematurely, and though the ballast tanks were blown the temperature in the torpedo room reached critical levels causing a second and much larger detonation. The hull was torn open, and *Kursk* sank in 350 feet of water.

Of the crew, 23 men survived the initial accident, gathered in the ninth compartment at the stern of the vessel. Only four days later did Russia acknowledge the problem; the British rescue submarine *LR 5* took a week to reach the *Kursk* but even then was not granted permission to act. The entire complement of the *Kursk* died, causing an international furor.

Additional Reading: Truscott, *Kursk, Russia's Lost Pride*, 2002; Moore, *A Time to Die: The Kursk Disaster*, 2002.

Kuznetsov   WARSHIP

Formerly known as the *Tbilisi* and *Leonid Brezhnev*, the 46,000-ton vessel now called the *Admiral Kuznetzov* is the largest Russian **aircraft carrier**. It had originally been intended that the *Orel* class, planned in the 1980s, would have several ships, but in the event only the *Kuznetsov* and one other vessel were built. The sister ship, *Varyaf*, was bought by a Chinese businessman, supposedly for "conversion into a static commercial attraction."

L

L Class   SUBMARINE

The L class was the U.S. Navy's first ocean-going **submarine** type, with a range of 4,500 miles. The first, *L-1* (SS-40), was laid down in 1914, and by 1917 a total of 11 vessels had been completed. The L type had a surface displacement of 450 tons and a surface speed of 14 knots. The crew was 28. After World War I the class was involved in trials of new **torpedoes** and **hydrophone** equipment, but all were scrapped by the 1930s.

LADAR. *See* Laser

La Galissonnière Class   WARSHIP

The six French cruisers of the *La Galissonnière* class were built between 1931 and 1937. Despite the weight of a substantial armored belt, the 7,600-ton ships performed well at sea, achieving a maximum speed of 35 knots. In addition to an armament of nine 6-inch guns, eight 3.5-inch guns, and 12 heavy **machine guns**, they also carried four **aircraft**. In the middle part of World War II, some vessels of the class served with the Vichy, others with the Allies. *La Galissonnière, Jean de Vienne*, and *Marseillaise* were scuttled at Toulon in 1942, but the *La Galissonnière* was refloated and given to Italy by the Germans as the *FR 12*. After Italy's surrender she was passed back to France but was sunk a second time by U.S. **B-25s** in 1944, being raised and finally scrapped in 1952.

Additional Reading: Whitley, *Cruisers of World War II*.

Lahti Pistol   FIREARM

Designed by Aimo Lahti (1896–1970), the 9 mm L35 **semiautomatic** pistol was adopted by the Finnish army in 1935. Well made and specifically intended to operate in subzero temperatures, the weapon bore an external resemblence to the **Luger**. It had an eight-round magazine and weighed 1.22 kg. Lahti was also known for his **submachine** gun designs.

Additional Reading: Ezell, *Small Arms of the World*, various editions.

Lancaster   AIRCRAFT

The Avro Lancaster **aircraft** was Britain's main heavy bomber during the latter part of World War II. Based on the existing Avro Manchester, it was developed by a team under chief designer Roy Chadwick. The Lancaster flew as a prototype in 1941 and began to reach the squadrons of Bomber Command in 1942. Lancasters took part in attacks on the *Tirpitz*, and along with **Wellingtons** and other craft were in Operation Millenium, the first thousand-bomber raid. Tough and practical, the Lancaster ranks with the **B-17** and **Liberator** among the most important Allied bombers. Moreover, the Lancaster had a surprising bomb capacity; on an "average" raid about 14,000 lb were carried, but it could also cope with both massive and unusual cargoes. From 1943 it was carrying single 8,000 lb bombs, soon switching to 12,000 lb deep-penetration "Tallboys." In March 1945 Lancasters were dropping the "Grand Slam" 22,000 lb bomb. It was also Lancasters that carried the **"bouncing bomb"** on the "dams raid."

With a crew of seven and four Merlin engines, the Lancaster B.I. had a range of 2,530 miles, a maximum speed of 275 mph, and a ceiling of 19,000 feet. Its defensive armament was eight or nine **machine guns**. Crew luxuries included automatic window de-icing, a first aid kit, and a dinghy and chemical toilet. Like other Allied bombers, Lancasters were often personalized by their crews. One of many was *Phantom of the Ruhr* (EE136), which flew in excess of 121 missions, those to Italy being painted on the nose as ice cream cones rather than bombs. A total of 7,366 Lancasters were made, of which almost half were lost. Ten Victoria Crosses were won by crewmen.

Technological oddities on Lancaster airframes would include experimental artificial icing and de-icing rigs; a Swedish Lancaster used for jet engine tests; the Mamba turbo jet tester; and Lancaster 10-P photo-reconnaisance aircraft, which remained in use until 1962. The Avro Lincoln and Lancastrian were also developed from the Lancaster. The Shackleton, which also owed much to the basic Lancaster design, served as an RAF reconnaisance aircraft from 1951.

Additional Reading: Robertson, *Lancaster*, 1965; Franks, *Claims to Fame: The Lancaster*, 1994; Wood, *The Design and Development of the Avro Lancaster*, 1991; Garbett and Goulding, *Lancaster*, 1992; Moyes, *Bomber Squadrons of the RAF and Their Aircraft*, 1964; Mason, *The Avro Lancaster*, 1989; Ashworth, *The Shackleton*, 1990; Hawks, *Bombers of the Present War*, 1944.

Lance. *See* **Spear**

Landing Craft Air Cushion, LCAC. *See* **Hovercraft**

Landing Craft Retriever   VEHICLE

The U.S. **landing craft** retriever produced in 1955 was a tall vehicle with a long gantry out to one side, to rescue vessels stranded in sand and mud. The most significant technological feature were the ten-foot-high tubeless tires and the electric motors that operated under air pressure to prevent the entry of water.

Landing Ship Tank (LST)   WARSHIP

The need for a special vessel to land large numbers of **tanks** was identified in the United States in 1941, and a preliminary plan was prepared in 1942. The final design, as drawn up by John Niedermair of the U.S. Bureau of Ships, was for a 328-foot vessel capable of carrying 2,100 tons of tanks and vehicles. The first keel was laid in June 1942, and by 1943 the ships were being produced in as little as four months. In combat from the time of the Solomons campaign LSTs gave vital service—though cynics were apt to describe them as "Large Slow Targets." A total of 1,051 were built during World War II, and smaller numbers of newer models thereafter. In the 1950s the *Terrebone Parish* and *De Soto County* classes were produced. Faster types, such as the *Newport* class, entered service in the late 1960s.

Additional Reading: Department of the Navy, *Dictionary of American Naval Fighting Ships*, 1959 onward; Baker, *Allied Landing Craft of World War II*, 1985.

Land Rover; Range Rover; "Pink Panther"   VEHICLE

Production of the British four-wheel-drive Land Rover began in 1948, and it was first ordered for military use the next year. Since then it has become the standard small utility vehicle of many forces. Over half a century there have been dozens of different military variants produced. These include long and short-wheel-base models, the armored Shorlands, ambulances, command post and reconnaisance vehicles, specific types for the Spanish and Portugese markets, and a floating model. The Centaur was an experimental **half-tracked** Land Rover, while the Cuthbertson had four tracked bogies and was intended for bomb disposal work. A "command car" Range Rover capable of 95 mph was first introduced at the London Motor Show in 1970, and civilian Range Rovers have also seen covert use. The company has changed hands several times, but the product has remained popular in many countries, the Land Rover Defender being a particularly widespread model in the 1990s. The XD was current by 2000.

The U.S. Navy's first aircraft carrier, the USS *Langley*, seen with eight biplanes on deck off the coast of Baltimore, 1924. From such modest beginnings would come the carrier group concept—capable of projecting air power all over the globe. © Hulton/Getty Images.

Arguably the best known Land Rover variant is the "Pink Panther." Though the SAS had used a modified Mark 3 Land Rover with **machine guns** and improved suspension for patrols as early as 1958, a new model for special forces was deemed necessary. A specification for a long-range patrol vehicle was duly worked up by the Fighting Vehicles Research and Development Establishment at Chertsey, and a contract, WV7218, was issued to the Marshall company of Cambridge in 1967. Following trials and modifications the new "Pink Panther" was in use by 1970. The nickname stemmed from the color of paint applied for use as **camouflage** on desert patrols.

Since then new models of "Pink Panther" have followed. "Pinkies"—which were later in

fact painted in more sandy and brown shades—saw distinguished service in the Gulf War of 1991. Here SAS columns used mixed groups of High-Capacity Land Rovers, mounting a variety of **Browning** machine guns, grenade throwers, and **Milan** launchers. Extras carried for work behind enemy lines included **mortars, grenades**, plastic **explosives, satellite navigation**, and night-vision equipment.

Langley, USS   WARSHIP

The USS *Langley*, commissioned in March 1922, was the first U.S. **aircraft carrier**. Converted from the collier *Jupiter*, the *Langley* was a 12,700-ton vessel, 519 feet in length. Capable of carrying 34 **aircraft**, its crew was 350. Its three Bureau boilers gave power for a 14-knot top speed. The conversion job was crude but practical, with a flight deck on stilts providing a flat landing surface over the main deck. The planes were stored much like cargo and were moved by cranes. Though out of date, she served as an aircraft transport in World War II, being badly damaged by Japanese bombers and then sunk in 1942. Its name was, however, re-used for an *Independence*-class carrier.

LAPES. *See* **Parachute**

Laser   DETECTION

Developed experimentally in 1960, the laser is a device that amplifies light in the visible, infrared, and ultraviolet parts of the electromagnetic spectrum. Laser is an acronym for "light amplification by stimulated emission of radiation." Basic types of laser include the solid-state, gas, and liquid.

   In the popular imagination, the military use of the laser is as a beam weapon. Though this has been worked on—as part of the **"Star Wars"** technology, for example—most military lasers currently in use are for such purposes as target illumination and acquisition. They are widely used in tracking and targeting systems, warning devices, and detectors, they may also be used in holograms in displays and instruments. They are therefore vital in **smart bomb** applications and in simulators. A LADAR (laser detection and ranging) system has been developed for the guidance of **cruise missiles**.

Additional Reading: Richardson et al., *Surveillance and Target Acquisition Systems*, 1997.

Launcher, Rocket, 2.36-inch. *See* **Bazooka**

LAW 66 mm Light Antitank Weapon. *See* **HEAT Rocket Launcher**

LAW 80   ANTITANK WEAPON

LAW 80 is a shoulder-fired, British, one-shot light antitank weapon introduced into general service in the 1980s. It consists of a telescoping filament-wound tube with the missile inside,

and it incorporates a five-round aiming device that allows the user to see where the missile will go when released. Claimed to be effective against main battle tanks at 500 meters its armor penetration is in excess of 600 mm.

Leander **Class (Cruiser and Frigate)**
                                                 WARSHIP

The British *Leander* class of five 7,000-ton **cruisers** was laid down in the early 1930s and completed by 1935. Armed with eight 6-inch guns they were distinguished by having one large streamlined funnel; maximum armor was three inches. The crew was 570. All five fought in World War II. *Leander* was loaned to New Zealand; *Ajax* fought the **Graf Spee** surviving seven hits from her guns. *Achilles* was also damaged at the River Plate, and later cooperated with U.S. forces in the Pacific; she became part of the Indian Navy in 1947, as INS *Delhi*. *Neptune* saw distinguished service in the South Atlantic and Mediterranean but was sunk by Italian mines in 1941; there was one survivor.

   The name *Leander* was revived in 1960 for a new class of British **frigates**, others of the type resurrecting the famous names *Dido* and *Ajax*. The new *Leander* herself left the Harland and Wolff yard in early 1963. She was 2,450 tons, 372 feet long, with semiautomatic-loading 4.5-inch guns, fire control **radar, sonar**, anti-**submarine mortar**, and antiaircraft guns. New vessels of this significant class were produced, and older ones updated over the years, with additions such as **Seacat**, target tracking radar, **Seawolf**, Ikara guided missiles, and new active sonar systems. *Leander* types were widely adopted; Australia, Chile, India, the Netherlands, and New Zealand all used the type.

Additional Reading: Osborne and Sowden, *Leander Class Frigates*, 1990.

Leather Gun   ARTILLERY

Used mainly by the Scots and Swedes, leather guns were small **artillery** pieces on wheeled carriages. Invented early in the seventeenth century, they were particularly light and mobile, coming to prominence around 1640. Contrary to their popular name, they were not mainly of leather but had a metal liner that was wound with wire or cord and covered in leather. Wire winding was later revisited, to more lasting effect, during the nineteenth century.

Leclerc Tank   TANK

At the time of writing the Leclerc is the latest French main battle **tank**, having entered production in 1990. With a welded steel shell, its armored resistance is improved by the addition of modular units of composite armor. These are intended to be replaceable. In the long, low turret is a 120 mm smoothbore gun, connected with a Creusot-Loire 22-round automatic loader. This is so designed that it can be filled with more than one type of **shell**, loading whatever is selected and enabling 12 or more shots per minute. The loader is fitted behind a bulkhead and is surrounded with blowout panels, the intention being to divert any accidental explosion away from the crew.

The three-man crew is assisted by a sophisticated computer management system, which may be programmed to give reports to headquarters automatically. The Leclerc has an eight-cylinder Uni-Diesel engine and an auxiliary gas turbine unit, giving a maximum speed of 44 mph.

Lee (or Grant) M3 Tank   TANK

By 1938 the United States had developed a lightly armored M2A1 medium tank, which it was imagined would fill most roles. Outbreak of war in Europe and the success of the German **panzers** therefore came as a considerable shock, leading to the quick production of a new model with a bigger gun and better armor. The M3 was an odd-looking stopgap but was produced with commendable speed; work at the Chrysler tank factory commenced in September 1940, and the first tank left the production line in April 1941. The M3 Lee had a 75 mm gun in a limited-traverse sponson and a 37mm in the turret, 60 mm armor, and a maximum speed of 21 mph. A Grant version built for the British lacked the additional machine gun cupola and

was marginally faster. About 6,000 M3s were made before the appearance of the **M4**.

Additional Reading: Forty, *United States Tanks of World War II*, 1983.

Leech. *See* Catapult and Maiale

Leopard Tank, 1 and 2   TANK

The Leopard is Germany's most important **tank** since 1945 and is claimed as Europe's most successful, being sold in large numbers to other armies. First orders for the Leopard 1 for the German army were placed with Krauss-Maffei of Munich in 1963, with deliveries commencing in 1965. The basic machine weighed 42,400 kg and had up to 70 mm of armor. It was driven by a ten-cylinder multifuel engine, giving a top road speed of 40 mph. The gun was a British-made 105 mm. The crew was four, the driver being in the front right hull, the remainder in the large, low, turret. Deep-wading equipment, night vision, and **NBC** protection were incorporated as standard. Later versions of the Leopard 1 included additional armor and new fire control. The Leopard L1A12 featured a low-light television system.

First prototypes of the Leopard 2 appeared in 1974; it was produced in large numbers in the 1980s and 1990s. Its crowning characteristic is said to be that it successfully balances the "armor triangle," having good speed, protection, and firepower—thus an excellent all-round tank. Useful features include a quick-change engine, passive night vision; and hydraulically assisted loading for the 120 mm smoothbore gun. Its fire control system is of an advanced **laser** and stereoscopic range-finder type. The armor is of a Chobham-type spaced multilayer construction, containing plates of steel and ceramics, giving good all-round protection against a wide range of projectiles.

Additional Reading: Crow (ed), *Modern Battle Tanks*, 1978; Hilmes, *Main Battle Tanks: Developments in Design since 1945*, 1987; Norman, *Chieftain and Leopard*, 1971.

Lepanto. *See* Battleship

Lewis Gun   FIREARM

Designed by the American Samuel Maclean, the Lewis light **machine gun** was originally conceived as a tripod-mounted weapon that would be a viable alternative to the **Maxim**. Only when it was further refined by Maclean's countryman Colonel Isaac Lewis and set on a bipod was the potential of the gun for easy battlefield movement recognized. A handful were used by the Belgians in 1914; thereafter the Lewis was enthusiastically adopted by the British. At first it was regarded merely as a useful extra automatic weapon, but it soon demonstrated that it could be used in a very different tactical way—giving covering fire for small bodies of troops in the front line and countering enemy machine guns. The Lewis therefore succeeded in the job for which the **Chauchat** turned out to be inadequate.

The mechanism of the Lewis was based on a turning-bolt system, somewhat like that of the Schmidt-Rubin **rifle**; a gas-driven piston and helical spring provided the motive force for automatic fire. Even before World War I the Lewis had been tried as an **aircraft** gun, and by 1916 it was also being used on **tanks**. The Lewis was also used to a more limited degree in World War II. In addition to British production they were also made in the United States.

Additional Reading: Easterly, *The Belgian Rattlesnake: The Lewis Automatic*, 1998; Bruce, *Machine Guns of World War I*, 1997; Truby, *Lewis Gun*, 1986; *The Complete Lewis Gunner*, 1941.

Lexington Class   WARSHIP

The USS *Lexington* (CV 2) and her sister ship *Saratoga* have been described as the "first effective carriers" of the U.S. Navy. Having flight decks grafted onto what had been intended to be fast battle cruiser hulls, they were completed in 1927. They were massive at 822 feet in length, well defended with 8 and 5-inch guns, and capable of 15 knots. The voluminous hangars of the *Lexington* could accommodate 80 aircraft. The odd arrangement of turrets to one side of the flight deck was a weakness, but the vessels were as heavily armed as international treaty would allow, and dozens of smaller antiaircraft and machine guns were added later. A count of *Saratoga*'s armament in 1945 saw her fitted with 16 20 mm and 96 40 mm guns. **Radars** and widened flight decks also featured in various refits.

The original *Lexington* sank following action against the Japanese in 1942, but *Saratoga* survived the war, being finally destroyed in the atomic bomb test at Bikini in 1946. A new *Lexington* (CV 16), of the *Essex* class, (originally laid down as the *Cabot*) was commissioned in 1943. That *Lexington* fought with distinction in the Pacific and survived the war despite being hit by **kamikaze** aircraft.

Additional Reading: Stern, *The Lexington Class Carriers*, 1993; Friedman, *US Aircraft Carriers*, 1983; Fry, *USS Saratoga CV-3*, 1996; Hone et al., *American and British Aircraft Carrier Development, 1919–1941*, 1999.

LGB. *See* Smart Bomb

Liberator, B-24   AIRCRAFT

The Consolidated B-24 Liberator U.S. four-engine bomber **aircraft** made its first flight in 1939. Heavily armed, with ten machine guns, its normal bomb load was 5,000 lb. Though often regarded as unremarkable compared to the **B-17** and **B-29**, over 18,000 were built and saw widespread service with many Allied air forces during World War II. The plane also had some interesting technical attributes, including a range of 2,100 miles and "roller shutter" bomb-bay doors designed to minimize drag. Its boxy shape proved suitable for conversion to many roles, including maritime and antisubmarine work; this would prove important in closing "the Atlantic gap" against **U-boats**. One even served as personal transport for Prime Minister Winston Churchill.

Additional Reading: Campbell, *Consolidated B-24 Liberator*, 1993; Donald, *American Warplanes of World War II*, 1995; Dorr, *US Bombers of World War Two*, 1989.

Liberator ("OSS") Pistol   FIREARM

First produced in 1942, the single-shot U.S. Liberator pistol, also known as the "Woolworth Gun," was crude and cheaply produced. It fired .45-caliber ammunition, but the empty **cartridge** was not ejected, having to be poked out with a stick before the next round was inserted. Manufactured at the behest of the Office of Strategic Services, the Liberator was designed to be dropped behind enemy lines and used by friendly populations against Axis forces. It came packed in cartons of 20 guns, with 200 rounds and pictorial printed instructions.

Additional Reading: Melton, *OSS Special Weapons and Equipment*, 1991; Ezell, *Handguns of the World*, 1981.

Liberty Ship   WARSHIP

With many merchantmen falling prey to **U-boats, mines**, and **aircraft** in the early part of World War II, President Franklin D. Roosevelt determined on a program of simple replacements, the "Liberty Ship." The first was launched on 27 September 1941, prior to America's entry into the war. Producing them ever faster became a matter of national pride. Newspaper reports stated that the building time of 260 days in early 1942 was reduced to just 40 by 1943. Over 2,700 were produced in 18 yards.

At the time of writing, two Liberty ships survive, the *Jeremiah O'Brien* and the *John W. Brown*. The latter is of the EC2-S-C1 type and was built at Bethlem-Fairfield, Baltimore, in 1942. It is 441 feet long with a beam of 57 feet and has an 8,500-ton capacity. The top speed is 11 knots. Its defensive armament comprised four guns of 3 and 5-inch caliber, and eight 20 mm.

Additional Reading: Sawyer and Mitchell, *Liberty Ships*, 1973; Elphick, *Liberty: The Ships That Won the War*, 2001.

Liberty Tank   TANK

Also known as the Mark VIII or "International Heavy Tank," the Liberty **tank** was an Anglo-American venture, planned to be built in France from 1918 onward. It was intended that monthly production would exceed 300 a month, providing the Allies with an unstoppable wall of armor that would bring the First World War to a rapid conclusion in the West. Designed by the Mechanical Warfare Supply Department of the Ministry of Munitions, it would have a U.S. engine and British armor and gun. In the event none had been finished at the armistice, and only small numbers were eventually completed for the U.S. Army, with which they would serve until 1932. In Canada they were later used as training vehicles.

Costing $85,000 each and weighing about 40 tons the lozenge-shaped Liberty tanks had a crew of from 10 to 12. The armament was a six-pounder gun on either side and up to seven **Browning machine guns**. The road speed was about 6.5 mph. Liberty engines were also used in **Christie** tanks.

Additional Reading: Crow, *AFVs of World War I*, 1998.

Light Strike Vehicle   VEHICLE

In use by the 1990s the Light Strike Vehicle (LSV) was developed for the British army by Longline Limited to operate over rough terrain. Effectively a modern form of **jeep**, it is a two-seater 4.16 meters long, capable of about 80 mph. It can carry **Milan** missiles, **machine guns**, a 30 mm cannon, or a Gecal **Gatling gun**.

Lightning, English Electric   AIRCRAFT

Development of the UK Lightning turbojet fighter **aircraft** began as early as 1947 with the issue of a research contract to the English Electric company. The machine that entered frontline service in 1960 was remarkable in several ways. Most impressive was its speed—a then staggering 1,320 mph. Its air-to-air missiles and nose **radar**, capable of searching above and below the horizon, were also significant. Sometimes regarded as the peak of British fighter development, it was the last solely British design. The last remained in RAF service until 1988.

Lightning, Lockheed P-38   AIRCRAFT

A remarkable U.S. twin-boom fighter, the P-38 Lightning was the first purely military **aircraft** to be produced by Lockheed. Designed by H. L. Hibbard and his team to answer Army requirements for a high-speed, high-altitude, long-range interceptor, it first flew as an XP-38 prototype in 1939. An instant record-breaker, it set a U.S. coast-to-coast time of seven hours and two minutes.

Deliveries to squadrons began in 1941, and before long the Lightning was showing its quality as a long-range fighter. Over the Mediterranean in late 1942 and 1943 it achieved significant successes against enemy transports, earning the German nickname *Gabelschwanz Teufel*, "fork-tailed devil." The Lightning was at its best at high altitude; below 15,000 feet German pilots discovered that their **Me Bf109s** were more manoeuvrable. Over northern Europe P-38s would later serve as **radar**-equipped pathfinders for bomber formations. In the Pacific, triumphs included the 40 kills of fighter ace Major Richard I. Bong. Lieutenant T. G. Lanphier used the range of the P-38 in the mission that resulted in the shooting down and death of Admiral Isoroku Yamamoto.

Major models of the P-38 included the D, F, G, J, and L types. The P-38J, of which almost 3,000 were produced, had such improvements as electrically activated dive flaps, power-boosted controls, and increased fuel capacity. It was powered by two 1,425 horsepower Allison engines, giving a top speed of 414 mph. The operational ceiling was a then-superb 44,000 feet. The powerful nose armament was a 20 mm cannon and four .5-inch **machine guns**.

Line of Battle (Ship)   WARSHIP

Though guns have been mounted on ships since about 1340, the great age of wooden sailing vessels fighting in "lines of battle"—broadside to broadside—spans the period from the early seventeenth century to about 1840. Such warships were marked by their heavy armament, firing through gun ports. The **artillery** itself was arranged on "gun decks." Ships of the line were generally of the largest classes; smaller types such as the **sloop, brig, schooner**, and **bomb vessel** had specific military tasks but were not part of the line of battle. So it was that early ships of the line were sometimes referred to as "great ships." The advent of the line of battle ship marked the move away from multipurpose ships to the specialized warship, manned by crews permanently retained by the state. This process is often thought of as commencing with the "ships royal" of Tudor and Stuart England, but it was given powerful expression in the Dutch, French, and Swedish navies, which dominated the seas during the seventeenth century.

Development over the 200-year reign of the ship of the line saw a gradual convergence of international thinking, an increase in size, and an increase in armament. Thus it is that the "three-decker" of the late seventeenth century was usually around 1,500 tons, a thousand less than the average three-decker of 1800. The smallest ships of the line of 1650 could carry as few as 30 guns; by 1800 anything less than 70 was regarded as inadequate.

Notable among the hundreds of ships of the line built were the Dutch *Brederode* and *Zevenwolden*, which helped gain Dutch mastery in the middle seventeenth century. Important British ships included ***Sovereign of the Seas*** and ***Victory***. For France the *Royal Louis*, built at Toulon in 1668, was the first 120-gun ship. The first American vessel accounted ship-of-the-line status was the *Independence*, a two-decker, built at Charleston in 1814. She was broken up a hundred years later.

Additional Reading: Gardiner, *Line of Battle*; Ireland, *Naval Warfare in the Age of Sail*, 2000; Lavery, *The Arming and Fitting of English Ships of War, 1600–1815*, 1987; Davies, *A Brief History of Fighting Ships*, 1996; Brown, *Before the Ironclad: Development of Ship Design, Propulsion and Armament in the Royal Navy 1815–1860*, 1990; Chapelle, *The History of the American Sailing Navy*, 1949.

Little David. *See* **Mortar**

Little Willie

Little Willie. *See* **Tank**

Livens Projector. *See* **Gas**

LL Sweep. *See* **Double "L" Sweep**

Locust, M22 Tank TANK

As early as February 1941, the U.S. Ordnance Department was considering the possibility of a **tank** that was airmobile. A T9 experimental model was made by Marmon-Herrington, and trials were under way by late 1942. The final M22 looked like a diminutive **Sherman**, had a crew of three, mounted a 37 mm gun, and weighed just eight tons. Total production was 830. Locusts were deployed with U.S. and British forces from 1944.

Additional Reading: Forty, *United States Tanks of World War II*, 1983.

London **Class** WARSHIP

The four British *London*-class, 10,000-ton **cruisers** were completed in 1929 and were an improvement on the existing *Kent* class. They were fitted to carry aircraft, were slightly faster than the *Kent* type, and had a complement of 784. Later modifications included **radar** and anti aircraft guns. All saw extensive war service; the *Sussex* was badly damaged in 1940 but survived; *Shropshire* served with the Australian navy, as *Canberra*, from 1942. All four were scrapped in the 1950s.

Longbow. *See* **Bow**

Longship WARSHIP

"Longship" is the general term covering vessels of the Norsemen. They were primarily sailing ships, though often capable of oared propulsion. First identified in the eighth century, they are commonly associated with Viking raiders, but similar types continued in use into the Middle Ages, as is shown by the Bayeux Tapestry. Frequently depicted with **shields** set along the sides, these wooden ships were built of oak, pine, and ash.

Additional Reading: Greenhill, *The Archaeology of Boats and Ships*, 1995.

Lorenz S40. *See* **Enigma**

Los Angeles **Class** SUBMARINE

The nuclear-powered *Los Angeles* class is the most numerous type of **submarine** on the U.S. Navy inventory, comprising 51 vessels at the time of writing. The majority are named after U.S. cities. The *Los Angeles* (SSN 688) was first to be commissioned, in November 1976; the most recent is *Cheyenne*, commissioned in September 1996. The class displaces 6,000 tons on the surface; the main armament is **Tomahawk** missiles and **torpedoes**. Interesting technological features include the ability of the class to operate under the Arctic ice, and the addition of acoustic-tile cladding to reduce noise. *Memphis* (SSN 691) was withdrawn from regular service to act as a research platform for submarine technology, while Augusta (SSN 710) has been used in trials of the BQQ-5D wide-aperture passive **sonar** system. The original role envisaged for the class was to act as escort for a carrier group. The cost was about $900 million per vessel.

Los Angeles submarines have been kept up to date with various technological innovations, including new navigational aids and mine and ice-avoidance systems. From 1996 the carrying of Predator and other unmanned aerial vehicles became possible, and in 1997 began the Acoustic Rapid COTS Insertion program. Under this program new BQQ-5 sonar was fitted, allowing annual updates to both software and hardware. Though some, including *Atlanta, Houston, New York City, Boston, and Baltimore*, have already been decommissioned, it is intended that *Los Angeles* submarines will still form two-thirds of the Navy nuclear attack force.

Additional Reading: Saunders (ed), *Jane's Fighting Ships 2001–2002*, 2001.

Lost. *See* **Mustard Gas**

LST. *See* **Landing Ship Tank**

Luger Pistol   FIREARM

Though the name of Austrian-born Georg Luger (1849–1923) will forever be associated with this famous German **semiautomatic**, the ideas of several designers over a number of decades made important contributions to its final appearance. The heart of the Luger was the "toggle lock" mechanism, known to engineers for some time and used by **Maxim** in his machine gun, and by **Borchardt** a pistol design dating back to 1893. The elegance of the Luger was that it married the mechanical efficiency of the toggle lock to a neat, ergonomic, back-swept grip containing the magazine.

Military trials commenced in 1898, with pistols in 7.65 mm caliber being tested by Switzerland, the Netherlands, the United States, Germany, and other countries over the next few years. About 1903 the weapon was first made to take a 9 mm Parabellum cartridge, the result being a weapon that not only shot easily and accurately and loaded quickly but had sufficient power for a military arm. Adopted by the German navy in 1904 and the German army in 1908, the gun soon acquired an enviable reputation. **Enfield** testers observed that it was well made, of good design, and handed comfortably; moreover "when the eight rounds have been fired . . . the magazine can be replaced by a full one and fire resumed in four or five seconds."

The army model 1908 Luger, or P 08, continued in service with the German army till 1945, and a variety of similar weapons in different calibers were used in other countries. A Lange, or long, model produced during World War 1 could be used with a shoulder stock and snail drum. Ultimately the Luger would be replaced, because it required far more machining than more modern, more robust pistols. Yet it never lost its appeal as a souvenir or symbol and has been reproduced in recent times.

Additional Reading: Walter, *The Luger Story*, 1995; Walter, *The Luger Book*, 1991.

M

M Class
SUBMARINE

The three completed British M-class monitor **submarines**, based on the **K class**, were constructed between 1916 and 1920. Their real peculiarity was the mounting of a 12-inch gun, which doubtless would have surprised an enemy but was of limited use as it could only be loaded on the surface. *M1* sank after a collision in 1925, and the other two were converted to carry an **aircraft** and lay **sea mines**, respectively.

M1 Abrams Tank. *See* Abrams

M1 Carbine
FIREARM

The M1 Carbine owes its existence to U.S. reactions to the events in Europe in 1939 and 1940, when German success demonstrated the need for high levels of combat mobility and for a weapon that could be used by rear-area troops in the event of an enemy breakthrough. The U.S. Ordnance therefore called for the introduction of a "light weight semi automatic rifle, as a possible replacement for the Cal .45 pistol and sub machine gun" and arranged for competitive tests in early 1941. A late entry and the outright winner was the **Winchester** gun, reputed to have been put together in a mere 34 days. It was adopted on 25 September 1941 as the "Carbine Cal .30 M1," and the government purchased the manufacturing rights for $886,000.

The M1 was just about as light and handy as any lethal shoulder arm of the period, weighing just 5 lb. Simple to use, it worked on a "short stroke" piston, or "gas tappet" principle, which had been developed by Winchester employee David M. Williams. It was useful up to about 300 yards. An M2 variant with a full-automatic capability was introduced in 1944. Over 3.5 million M1 carbines were produced by nine major manufacturers during the Second World War; many of the 60 component parts were subcontracted to smaller companies. Particularly popular with **parachutists**, the Marine Corps, and jungle fighters, the M1 achieved a considerable reputation. Later complaints that it lacked range and stopping power are perhaps unfair, because it was intended to be used only in instances where pistols or submachine guns could also be employed. Many of the U.S. military's M1 carbines were disposed of in 1963, but the weapon continued to be widely deployed overseas.

Additional Reading: Ruth, *War Baby: The US Caliber .30 Carbine*, 1992.

M1 Howitzer. *See* 8-Inch Howitzer

M1 Rocket Launcher. *See* Bazooka

M1 Thompson. *See* Thompson

M2 Carl Gustav. *See* Recoilless Guns

M2, M3 Tracked Armored Fighting Vehicles. *See* Bradley

M3 "Grease Gun"
FIREARM

Adopted by the United States in December 1942 the M3 .45-inch **submachine gun** was nicknamed the "grease gun," which it superficially resembled. General Motors and Buffalo Arms manufactured over 600,000 initially, with a further smaller contract during the Korean War. With a fairly slow rate of fire but costing just $25, the M3 was simple, lighter, and cheaper, than the **Thompson**. Weighing about 4 kg, it was fitted with a 30-round box magazine. Though not used by the U.S. infantry since the 1960s a modified M3A1 was kept as a tank crew weapon, and "grease guns" have been sold in other countries.

Additional Reading: Ezell, *Small Arms of the World*, various editions; Hogg, *Infantry Weapons of World War II*, 1977.

M3 Half Track. *See* **Half-Track**

M3 (M4, M5, Light). *See* **Stuart Tank**

M3 (Medium). *See* **Lee Tank**

M4. *See* **Sherman Tank**

M8. *See* **Greyhound**

M9, 92FS. *See* **Beretta**

M10. *See* **Tank Destroyer**

M11A1. *See* **Fragmentation Grenade**

M12. *See* **Self-Propelled Gun**

M14 Rifle   FIREARM

Having some similarity to the **Garand**, which it superseded, the 7.62 mm U.S. M14 semiautomatic, or self-loading, rifle was adopted by U.S. forces in the late 1950s. Approximately 1.3 million were made by **Springfield** Armoury, Harrington and Richardson, Thompson-Ramo-Wooldridge, and **Winchester**-Western before the end of production in 1964. The M14 weighed 5.1 kg and had a 20-round box magazine. Later models featured a fully automatic facility. The normal effective range was about 500 yards, increased to about 750 in models fitted with a bipod. Maximum range of the **cartridge** was a remarkable 4,000 yards.

Additional Reading: Stevens, *US Rifle M14*, 1991.

M16 "Meat Chopper." *See* **Half-Track**

M16 Rifle   FIREARM

Designed by Eugene **Stoner**, the M16 rifle was first ordered by the U.S. military in 1961. Since then this lightweight **assault rifle** has become not only an American standard but popular with armies around the world. Despite new research and trials it is likely to be a mainstay for years to come. Nevertheless, the M16 has a complex and sometimes controversial pedigree.

The M16 was rooted in the 1950s, when the U.S. Air Force was looking for a simple, lightweight weapon with which an airman could defend himself in a hostile environment. The Armalite division of Fairchild came up with the AR-5, a remarkably innovative **bolt-action** rifle that fired a high-velocity .22 Hornet **cartridge** and could be taken apart and stored in its own butt. As it made use of glass fiber and rubber components, it could float. Armalite's next major essay was the AR-10, which appeared in prototype in 1955. This was designed as a gas-operated automatic assault rifle from the outset; it was initially made by Euromataal in the Netherlands. It had a barrel jacket of fluted aluminum and a foam-filled plastic stock. Though cruder and squarer in appearance, it was recognizably similar to the later AR-15, which would ultimately become the service M16.

By the standards of the time the AR-10 and AR-15 were outlandish, with the appearance of futuristic toys rather than military rifles. What made them real candidates for the job was recent research, including Hall's *Ballistic Experience in Korea*, the Hitchman report, and S. L. A. Marshall's report on infantry weapons in Korea. Taken together these suggested that the vast majority of combat took place at close range and that a light, high-velocity cartridge would allow the soldier to carry more rounds and use them to greater effect. Though this was virtually proven by the **Sturmgewehr** and **AK47**, the U.S. Army would take some convincing to accept a rifle firing a round with anything less than the maximum range punch and accuracy given by the **Garand** and **M14**.

In the event, the Air Force pointed the way, and the Army sponsored the further development of the AR-15. **Colt** was engaged for full production. Experience of close-range combat in Vietnam rapidly demonstrated the wisdom of a weapon that was light to carry and could virtually cut an enemy in half with a full automatic burst. Though there were early problems, some because the M16 had been presented as virtually maintenance free, it was soon in demand due to its awesome lethality. Combat reports spoke of "explosive" wounds and limbs severed by the impact of the M16.

The M16A1 was a 5.56 mm selective-fire rifle loading from 20 or 30-round box magazines. It weighed 3.18 kg, was 99 cm long, and could be fitted with a **bayonet** or M203 **grenade** launcher. The muzzle velocity was 1,000 meters per second, to an effective range of about 400 meters, though the bullets would fly over a mile. Since the 1960s there have been many improvements.

In the M16A2, adopted as Standard A in 1983, the flash suppressor also became a muzzle brake, helping to keep the barrel down, and sights were improved. Perhaps most importantly, on the recommendation of the Marines, the full-automatic capability was replaced by a three-round "burst." This both saved on ammunition, and helped accuracy. There have also been many variations on the theme. The Colt Commando introduced a telescopic butt, while the Canadians produced their own C7 model. M16s have also been fitted with telescopes and **silencers**, shortened, and fitted with bipods and heavy barrels. They have found particular approval with special forces.

Additional Reading: Stevens and Ezell, *The Black Rifle: M16 Retrospective*, 1987; *Jane's Infantry Weapons*; Ezell, *Small Arms of the World*, various editions.

M18. *See* **Tank Destroyer**

M20. *See* **Greyhound**

M22. *See* **Locust Tank**

M24. *See* **Chaffee Tank**

M26. *See* **Pershing Tank**

M35. *See* **Browning**

M36. *See* **Tank Destroyer**

M41. *See* **Walker Bulldog Light Tank**

M47. *See* **Dragon (Missile)**

M47. *See* **Patton (Tank)**

M48 Medium Tank   TANK

The successor to the **Patton**, the U.S. M48 medium **tank** began development at the Detroit Arsenal in 1950. It first appeared as a Chrysler-built prototype in 1951, by which time contracts had also been placed with Ford and General Motors; it entered service in 1953. Of a cast-armor construction, the M48 weighed 49 tons and had a crew of four and a 90 mm gun. Its diesel Continental 750 horsepower engine gave a speed of 30 mph. Appearing in a multitude of variants, it was used by many other countries, including South Korea, Taiwan, and Turkey.

In the M48A5 a 105 mm gun was installed along with myriad other improvements. Some thousands of this model were still in service worldwide in 2000. The **M60** was developed from this vehicle.

Additional Reading: Tillotson, *M48*, 1981; Crow (ed), *Modern Battle Tanks*, 1978.

M60 Machine Gun   FIREARM

The M60 7.62 mm **machine gun** was a mainstay of U.S. forces in Vietnam and has been used in many situations from light squad support to pintle-mounted **helicopter** armament. Its prime inspiration was the German **MG42**. By the end of World War II what would later become the M60 had appeared as a T44 prototype, but it was only pushed along with the onset of the Korean War.

As an 1984 official *field manual* observed, the M60 is an air-cooled, belt-fed, gas-operated automatic. It is 110.5 cm in length and weighs 10.4 kg. Though the absolute maximum range is a remarkable 3,725 meters, its best results are achieved at up to 1,000 meters. Individual moving point targets can be engaged with short bursts and good chances of a hit at 200 meters. Sustained fire at 100 rounds per minute requires a barrel change about every ten minutes.

Additional Reading: Ezell, *Small Arms of the World*, various editions; Department of the Army, *Field Manual 23–67: Machine Gun 7.62mm, M60*, 1984; *Jane's Infantry Weapons*.

M60 Main Battle Tank   TANK

First produced as a prototype in 1958, the U.S. M60 main battle **tank** was essentially an M48 fitted with a British-type 105 mm gun. It entered service in 1960. Later the M60 would go through various modifications to produce the M60A1 with its all cast-steel construction, and the M60A3. Perhaps the most significant technological improvements would be applied to the fire control system, which would feature a **laser** range finder, computer, and thermal sight.

The M60A3 weighed 107,900 lb and had a Continental 12-cylinder diesel engine, giving a road speed of 30 mph and a range of 300 miles. It was fitted with both a coaxial **machine gun** and an antiaircraft machine gun. It was still in use in the Gulf War, where it was to be seen fitted with additional Explosive Reactive Armor (ERA) **armor** around the turret. Though replaced by the **Abrams** and taken out of front-line U.S. service in 1997, the M60A3 remains in use in countries as diverse as the Sudan, Israel, Brazil, and Austria.

Additional Reading: Crow (ed), *Modern Battle Tanks*, 1978; Hilmes, *Main Battle Tanks: Developments in Design since 1945*, 1987; Zalgoda and Loop, *Modern American Armor*, 1985.

M72. *See* HEAT Rocket Launcher

M79 Grenade Launcher   FIREARM

Commonly nicknamed the "Blooper" or the "Bloop Gun," the M79 **grenade** launcher was first delivered to the U.S. Army in 1961. Resembling a huge short **shotgun**, the M79 broke open to load a single 40 mm grenade. Maximum range was about 375 meters; accuracy was sufficient to put a grenade through a window at about 100 meters. With the ordinary high-explosive grenade, fragments were lethal up to five meters. A wide variety of other projectiles was developed, including CS **gas**, smoke, and even a **flechette** round.

M82A1. *See* Barrett "Light Fifty"

M102. *See* 105 mm Howitzer

M103 Heavy Tank   TANK

The U.S. M103 heavy **tank** had its beginnings in the T43 project, prototypes of which were produced in 1948. It was intended, like the British Conqueror, as an answer to the Soviet **Joseph Stalin** III and other heavies. The M103 entered service in the early 1950s but was found deficient in a number of areas and withdrawn until 1957, when an improved version was reintroduced. Nevertheless, the M103 had a relatively short service life and was replaced by the **M60**, the last examples of the M103 with the Marine Corps being phased out in 1973.

The M103 was fabricated of cast steel and had a crew of five; its Continental 810 horsepower diesel engine gave a road speed of 21 mph. Its main armament was an M58 gun, and its maximum armor thickness was 178 mm. It was expensive for its time, costing $300,000.

M109. *See* Paladin

M113, 113A APC   VEHICLE

The U.S. M113 fully tracked armored personnel carrier, developed in the 1950s, was one of the "real maids of all work" of the second half of the twentieth century. It is estimated that about 40,000 saw service in Vietnam and that it was used in 60 variants. In the M106 type, it was a

4.2 inch **mortar** carrier; in the M125, an 81 mm mortar carrier; in the M577A1, a field aid station; in the M132, a self-propelled **flame-thrower**. The basic M113 consisted of an aluminum body with up to 38 mm of armor. In addition to a commander and driver it could carry a maximum of 11 soldiers. Rubber seals, bilge pumps, and rubber blades on the tracks gave the "Bucket" or "Crackerbox," as it was nicknamed, an amphibious capability at speeds up to 3.5 mph. Early examples had a gasoline engine, but in Vietnam bad experiences with fire led to a general conversion to diesel.

Vietnam also exposed the vulnerability of the M113 to mines. Devices improvised to cure the problem included lining the floor of the vehicle with sand bags, and curious antenna-like "long controls" that wary drivers could operate while sitting in the top hatch. Later the problem was more effectively solved by titanium base shields. In the ACAV variant a small open-topped turret and additional machine guns were carried, allowing the crew to fight mainly from the vehicle. The M113 was used by many nations, including Australia, Belgium, Canada, Denmark, Germany, and Israel. Its basic design also influenced the layout of the British **FV 430**.

Additional Reading: Dunstan, *The M113 Series.*

M203. *See* **M16 Rifle**

M284. *See* **Howitzer**

M551. *See* **Sheridan**

M712. *See* **Copperhead**

M1911 Semiautomatic Pistol. *See* **Browning** and **Colt**

M1917 6-Ton Tank. *See* **Renault FT-17 Light Tank**

M1928, M1931 Tanks. *See* **Christie Tanks**

Mace   CLUB WEAPON

The mace is a handheld smashing weapon, often having a metal head and shaft. It has been distinguished from clubs or cudgels, which are usually made of single pieces of wood. The mace has been a popular weapon in many parts of the world. In medieval Europe it was accepted as a symbol of authority, and in some places it continues to be so to this day. The *morgenstern* (morning star) and flail are often categorized as forms of mace, the latter being distinguished by its chain between the shaft and the head or heads.

Additional Reading: Tarassuk and Blair, *The Complete Encyclopaedia of Arms and Weapons*, 1979.

Machete   BLADED WEAPON

Though first used as an agricultural tool, particularly by Spanish settlers in the Americas, the machete, with its broad blade, is well adapted to military use in jungle. In the 1890s machetes were purchased for the U.S. Army from the Collins company, and in 1904 a new model was introduced for use by the U.S. Hospital Corps. The machete was widespread during World War II. Interesting types included a folding-blade version by Camillus of New York, various models based on the Burmese *dah*, or **sword**, and the U.S. Air Force survival machete, which was carried in the seat-pack kit of the **parachute**. In 1966 a machete by Case Cutlery was even devised as a survival tool for astronauts.

Additional Reading: Stephens, *Fighting Knives*, 1980.

Machine Gun   FIREARM

The idea of firearms capable of rapid shooting or repeating fire is an old one. As early as the fourteenth century there were multibarrel ribaulds, or "organ" guns. There were also weapons charged with superimposed loads; once set off, they discharged in the manner of a Roman candle until empty. Many variations on the Roman candle theme were devised over the centuries, including that of Englishman Charles

Cardiffe, patented in 1682, and those of Americans Joseph Belton and Joseph Chambers, of 1777 and 1813, respectively.

Revolving cylinders also seemed a promising route to speed. In 1718 James Puckle patented "a portable gun or machine called a defence," which was effectively a giant **revolver** on a tripod. A similar concept, much improved and refined with a constant feed system, would reemerge in the multibarrel **Gatling** gun. The Dane N. J. Lobnitz produced an imaginative, if impractical, machine **air gun** in 1834.

Hand-cranked multibarrel volley guns, often mounted on wheeled carriages, were in particular vogue from about 1865 to 1890. In addition to the famous Mitrailleuse, the Nordenfeldt, the Hotchkiss "revolver cannon," and the Gardner offered promise. In the Swedish-invented but British-made Nordenfeldt, from two to twelve barrels of various calibers could be mounted. A back-and-forth working of the lever activated a series of springs, strikers, and extractors, while an assistant recharged the ammunition hopper with **cartridges**. About 100 rounds a minute could be fired. The French-manufactured Hotchkiss revolver of 1875, invented by American Benjamin B. Hotchkiss (1828–1885), used multiple barrels and an "endless screw" with a hand crank. Optimum rate of fire was about 60 rounds per minute; like the Nordenfeldt, Hotchkiss guns were often mounted on warships. The Gardner was invented by William Gardner of Toledo, Ohio. Patented in 1874, this often had a five-barrel assembly and a hand crank that fired two rounds from each barrel with each revolution of the handle. A remarkable 500 rounds per minute was possible under the best conditions.

Ingenious as these inventions were, they were not true machine guns, in the sense that external power was required to keep them firing. Moreover, they were often used as a species of short-range but deadly **artillery** rather than as a new class of tactical weapon. As early as 1663 it had been suggested in a paper to the Royal Society that the forces of recoil and escaping gas might be harnessed to reload a weapon. Such as gun could shoot fast automat-

ically "yet be stopped at pleasure." This fascinating idea remained only theory until the work of Hiram **Maxim** in the late nineteenth century.

Following the invention of the Maxim gun, the machine gun would achieve its deadly potential; by 1914 most European infantry battalions would have two machine guns. During World War I carnage was wrought by guns like the **MG 08 Vickers, Schwarzlose, Browning**, and **Hotchkiss Mle 1914** working from tripods. Yet this was but part of the story; the war would also see the deployment of automatic rifles and light machine guns, such as the **Lewis, Madsen**, BAR, and **Chauchat**. All of these were significant as weapons that were air cooled, thus requiring no cumbersome water supply, and fired from self-contained magazines, and thus having no trailing belts. These, together with **grenades**, would help bring about a revolution in infantry tactics. **Submachine guns** also made their appearance in World War I. Machine guns also formed an important part of the armament of **aircraft** and **tanks**.

During the interwar period the importance of the light machine gun would be confirmed with the production of weapons like the Czechoslovak ZB series, the **Bren** gun, the **Degtyarev** DP 1928, the Breda Model 1930, the **Johnson**, and the Japanese **Type 92**. Yet the most important of this series was the German **MG 34**, arguably the first truly "general purpose" machine gun. Its successor, the very rapid-firing **MG 42**, would continue to see use into the twenty-first century. Significant heavy machine guns of World War II included the Soviet **Goryunov**.

Though the division between automatic firing **assault rifles** and light machine guns has sometimes been blurred, machine guns have continued to be important. Particularly significant machine guns of the immediate postwar decades included the **M60, GPMG**, and the Soviet RPD. With the adoption of 5.56 mm and other smaller cartridges to machine gun use, a new generation of light machine guns would become possible; foremost in this category is the **Minimi**, or SAW.

Additional Reading: Chinn, *The Machine Gun*, 1951; Musgrave, *German Machineguns*, 1992; Ellis,

Madsen Machine Gun

The Social History of the Machine Gun, 1987; Longstaff and Atteridge, *Machine Gun*; Tarassuk and Blair, *The Complete Encyclopaedia of Arms and Weapons*, 1979; *Jane's Infantry Weapons*; Calef, *Machine Guns*.

Madsen Machine Gun — FIREARM

Produced by the Danish Dansk Industri Syndikat, the Madsen was an unusual and innovative **machine gun**. Its hinged block mechanism has been likened to an automatic version of the **Martini-Henry** or **Peabody** rifle. It was used in both world wars, and another model was produced in 1950. In its most common bipod-mounted configuration, with a detachable 30-round magazine, it was arguably one of the earliest automatic **rifles** or light machine guns. It was produced in many calibers, including .30, 7.92 mm, and 7.62 mm.

Additional Reading: Ezell, *Small Arms of the World*, various editions.

MAG. *See* General Purpose Machine Gun

Maginot Line — FORTIFICATION

Named after the minister of war, the Maginot Line was a complex of French defensive **fortifications** commenced in 1929. It was designed to cover the entire borders with Germany and Luxembourg. The southern sector was fronted by the Rhine, itself a formidable obstacle, so **pillboxes** and other light works sufficed. The northern and western parts from Haguenau to Longuyon received one of the most powerful defenses ever built; it included disappearing gun turrets, antitank ditches, underground barracks, and **railways**. Prior to the German invasion of 1940, 13 fortress divisions were committed to fixed defenses, but the strength of the Maginot Line was negated, since the enemy came through Belgium.

Maiale Manned Torpedo — EXPLOSIVE DEVICE

The Italian manned **torpedo** program commenced as early as the First World War, when the "Leech" was devised by Raffaele Rosetti and Raffaele Paolucci to attack Austrian warships. In this small craft, bow-mounted **explosive** metal canisters were carried; they could be covertly detached and attached, like leeches, to the enemy ship to be exploded by a clockwork mechanism after a time interval. A brave attack of the Leech on 31 October 1918 descended into farce when it was discovered that the "enemy" vessel being attacked had already been handed over to Yugoslavian control as a result of Austrian collapse.

Nevertheless, the Leech provided inspiration for interwar research into "special attack" weapons, and by 1940 the SLC, or "slow running torpedo," was ready to take on British ships. Whatever the official name, it was usually called the Maiale, or "pig," due to its poor handling characteristics. The electric-powered pig was 22 feet long and capable of full submergence to a depth of about 100 m; it was crewed by two men clad in rubber suits breathing bottled oxygen. In the first version of the craft, the crew were largely exposed; in the later SBB type they were partly enclosed in a form of cockpit. Like the Leech it carried a detachable warhead.

Interestingly, it was a captured Maiale that inspired the similar British Chariot, a manned torpedo with improved performance and a 700 lb warhead. This type was later used against the *Tirpitz*. It should be noted that neither Maiale nor Chariot, though extremely hazardous, were true suicide or **kamikaze** weapons, unlike the Japanese **Kaiten**; the Italian and British crews were seriously expected to make their escape. Modern versions of the Chariot are still used by certain navies.

Additional Reading: O'Neill, *Suicide Squads of World War II*, 1988; Southby-Tailyour, *Jane's Amphibious Warfare Capabilities*, 2000.

Mail. *See* Armor

Mainstay. *See* AWACS

Malyutka. *See* Sagger

Mangonel. *See* Catapult

Mannlicher Rifles   FIREARM

Originally designed by Karl F. von Mannlicher (1848–1904), Mannlicher **rifles** are noteworthy for their use of the box magazine. Austria's adoption of a Mannlicher in 1886 marked the first time that a rifle with a box magazine was issued. Nevertheless, Karl von Mannlicher was associated with other innovations, including various types of clip loading, straight-pull bolts, and rotating magazines. Mannlicher rifles remained standard issue in the Austro-Hungarian forces until the end of the empire in World War I.

Mark I. *See* Tank

Marsh Screw   VEHICLE

The U.S. amphibious Marsh Screw was a Chrysler-made military vehicle first developed in 1962 that traveled on two screwlike rotating pontoons. With its 2,330 lb weight well spread, the Marsh Screw was capable of moving across water, mud, or snow, at speeds up to 20 mph in any direction.

Martin Baker. *See* Ejection Seat

Martini Henry Rifle   FIREARM

The name "Martini Henry" is derived from the names of Hungarian-Swiss inventor Friedrich von Martini and the Scot Alexander Henry. Their single-shot **rifle** was patented in 1868 and soon was adopted by the British army, becoming famous as the main firearm of the Zulu War. Martini contributed the hinge-down breech mechanism operated by a lever, while the rifling was the work of Henry.

Additional Reading: Temple and Skennerton, *A Treatise on the British Military Martini*, 1983.

Martlet. *See* Wildcat

Mary Rose   WARSHIP

Named after a sister of King Henry VIII, the *Mary Rose* was one of the first purpose-built

Dutch musketeer, c. 1607, with matchlock musket, bandolier, musket rest and sword. Engraved by Goodnight, after an earlier work by Jacob de Gheyn. © Hulton/Getty Images.

English warships, completed at Portsmouth in 1510. She remained a significant vessel until her sinking in 1545; she is believed to have been a victim of an accident similar to the one that later claimed the *Wasa*. Like the Swedish ship, she has been the subject of intensive archaeological investigation; her remains were raised in 1982.

Additional Reading: McKee, *Mary Rose*, 1973; Rule, *The Mary Rose*, 1982; Bradford, *The Story of the Mary Rose*, 1982.

Maschinenpistole. *See* Submachine Gun

Match, Matchlock   IGNITION SYSTEM

A matchlock was a firearm that used a smouldering piece of match for ignition. The match itself was a cord of twisted flax or hemp, soaked in a solution of saltpeter. It could be kept glowing for long periods either by lighting both ends or by holding the lit portion in a ventilated metal container.

Though cords or pieces of red-hot iron had previously been applied manually to the touch holes of guns, the use of an actual mechanism, or lock, appeared in about 1400. A German illustration of 1411 shows a man using a gun with a polelike stock on which is mounted an elongated pivoted lever, or "serpentine," to hold the cord. The advent of the matchlock was a significant advance, since it allowed the shooter to hold the gun with both hands and keep his eyes on the target. By the third quarter of the fifteenth century the matchlock mechanism had evolved into a plate screwed to the side of the stock, and a shorter lever, or cock, which dipped mechanically into the priming pan. Springs were introduced to allow the cock to return to its original position, and triggers now allowed easy operation with one finger.

Improvements to lock, barrel, and **gunpowder** made the matchlock an ever more practical military weapon. The sixteenth century would see the publication of drill manuals for the use of lines or blocks of matchlock calivers or **muskets** on the battlefield. By about 1600 the matchlock firearm was the most important, and most numerous, of infantry weapons. Though early **flintlock** mechanisms now appeared, they were in a minority until after 1700. Matchlocks were cheaper and simpler than either the flintlock or the **wheel lock**, but they were more prone to accident and were apt to give away the user's position at night.

Additional Reading: Pegler, *Powder and Ball Small Arms*, 1998.

Matilda Tank   TANK

The British Matilda **tank**, officially designated "Tank, Infantry, Mark II," was a tough, small, 26.5-ton vehicle with up to 78 mm of armor. In the first year of World War II it was accounted one of the few machines capable of taking on the German **panzers**. Produced by the Vulcan foundry to meet the A12 infantry tank specification, it was ready for trials in 1938, with production commencing in 1939.

Eventually almost 3,000, of all variants, were manufactured. Also supplied to Russia, it would last see use by Australia in 1953. However its heyday was over by 1941, since its 2-pounder gun was soon outclassed, and the enemy was now using tank-busters like the **88 mm** on a regular basis.

Additional Reading: Perret, *The Matilda*, 1973.

Maus   TANK

In June 1942, Dr. Ferdinand Porsche, president of the **Panzer** Kommission, was interviewed in Berlin by Hitler and Albert Speer, the German armaments minister. Among other programs, he was asked to start work on a massive **tank** initially code-named *Mammut* (Mammoth). This was to feature armor up to 200 mm thick, a 128 mm gun, and a coaxial 75 mm gun. Later demands would up main armament to a 150 mm gun, add a **flamethrower**, and require submersibility to 26 feet, while the name was changed to *Maus* (mouse). Mockups were produced in 1943, and work continued to 1945, but changes of specification and the monstrous impracticality of a 185-ton tank ensured that this leviathan never reached the battlefield.

Additional Reading: Spielberger and Milsom, *Elefant and Maus*, 1973.

Mauser   FIREARM

The Mauser brothers, Peter Paul (1838–1914) and Wilhelm (1834–1883), of Oberndorf Germany are acclaimed as giants in the field of the **rifle**. The Mauser company still exists at the time of writing. Among the many children of a "parts filer" at the Royal Wurttemberg rifle factory, they themselves were employed there from an early age and by the 1860s were designing arms of their own.

Yet it was at Liege at the end of the decade that they produced their major breakthrough—an efficient **bolt-action** rifle mechanism with only three major components. When worked it not only opened the chamber but self-cocked the mechanism and extracted any empty **cartridge**. Combined with the rifling of the **Chassepot**, this created a highly effective military rifle. The original single-shot 1871 model Mauser was continually improved, being later superceded by a tube-magazine type in 1884, a clip-loading rifle in 1888, and finally by what is often regarded as the definitive 1898 model. According to one count no less than 35 countries quickly adopted Mauser-type rifles. Belgium, for example, rearmed with a model of 1889, while the Boers fought the South African War mainly with the model of 1896.

The Mauser Gewehr 98, or G98, was the main rifle used by Germany in World War I. It was 125 cm long, weighed 4.1 kg, and had a five-round magazine loaded from a charger. It initially fired round-nosed Patronen 88 **cartridges**, but an update during the period 1903 to 1905 converted the rifle to fire the superior pointed S-Patronen ammunition. A version was also adopted as a **sniper** weapon, and **carbine** models were also used. Mauser also produced the first **antitank rifle**. In 1935 a short, updated Karabiner 98k rifle became the standard rifle of the German army. About ten million were made, and though **semiautomatic** and **assault** rifles were introduced during World War II, the K98k remained the main weapon of the Wehrmacht.

Mauser rifles remained in use with many armies after World War II, some even being seen in Vietnamese hands. The Mauser action has similarly been prized in sniping and sporting circles. The Mauser company has also supplied many **pistols** for military service. Important among these are the C96, or "broomhandle," semiautomatic, in use from the 1890s, and the HSc.

Additional Reading: Götz, *German Military Rifles and Machine Pistols*, 1990; Walter, *The German Rifle*, 1979; Ezell, *Handguns of the World*, 1981; Law, *Backbone of the Wehrmacht: The German K98k*, 1998; Walter, *Dictionary of Guns and Gunmakers*, 2001.

Maxim   INVENTOR

Hiram S. Maxim (1840–1916) was of French and English descent, but American by birth, being born at Sangerville, Maine. With some justification he is regarded as the father of the

modern **machine gun**, for though **Gatling** and others produced practical rapid repeating weapons, these required an outside motive force, such as the cranking of a handle. The Maxim invention, by contrast, was a true machine gun that required only that the first shot be fired, reloading and firing continuing automatically thereafter until ammunition ran out or the operator ceased to press the trigger.

Maxim's first invention was said to be an elaborate mousetrap, and he also took out patents on things as varied as hair-curling irons, steam pumps, and electric lamps. He later claimed that even before the Civil War both he and his father had considered the idea of a repeating firearm. Yet in the event Maxim avoided the war by going to Canada, and it was June 1883 before he patented his first repeating weapon in London. This was based on an 1873 model **Winchester rifle**, modified by means of a spring system in the butt so that the recoil of firing would operate the reloading lever. A year later Maxim had produced a genuine machine gun, in which the barrel and breechblock recoiled together before unlocking, with a return spring that drove a bolt forward to chamber a fresh **cartridge**. The Maxim Gun Company was founded at Hatton Garden, London, on 5 November 1884.

By 1888 further refinements had created what the company was pleased to call the "World Standard Model"; for once this was no idle boast, since within a few years a majority of the advanced nations would be using Maxim-type guns. The new Maxim had a number of attributes that would be repeated time and again in future machine guns. Apart from the basics of the recoil mechanism, these included belt feed and a water jacket for cooling. Gun shields, tripods, and wheeled carriages would also feature in the Maxim repertoire.

Maxim dominance was achieved not merely by means of the weapons' obvious superiority over the competition but also by business and marketing acumen. The Maxim company merged with Nordenfelt and thus acquired both capital and factory premises at both Crayford and Erith, Kent, as well as the cooperation of Albert **Vickers**. Maxim himself made it his

Sir Hiram S. Maxim demonstrates the rifle caliber "Maxim gun." The weapon has a shield against return small arms fire, and can be fitted with wheels to improve mobility. Note the belt feed and spent cartridges. © Culver Pictures.

mission to demonstrate and promote the new machine gun, which he succeeded in showing to the Kaiser, the Prince of Wales, and Sir Henry Stanley the explorer, to name but a few. In celebrated trials for the Chinese ambassador, trees were cut down by bursts of machine-gun fire.

Italy bought a few World Standard guns straight away. Britain had some Maxim guns as early as 1889 and was soon using them in colonial campaigns. Germany made purchases soon after, subsequently adopting a Berlin-manufactured 1901 model. Russia made the 1905 and 1910 models at its Tula arsenal. Small orders were received from nations as diverse as Denmark; Australia, and the Congo. During World War I machine guns would make a major contribution to the carnage. Particularly significant Maxim-type models of the period included the German **MG 08** and the British Vickers. It is interesting to note that the breaking toggle-lock mechanism used on Maxim

guns was also utilized on a smaller scale on certain pistols, such as the **Borchardt** and **Luger.**

Additional Reading: Maxim, *My Life*, 1915; Ellis, *The Social History of the Machine Gun*, 1987; Goldsmith, *Devil's Paintbrush*, 1989; Musgrave, *German Machineguns*, 1992.

McDonnell Douglas   MANUFACTURER

U.S. defense contractor McDonnell Douglas was a massive conglomerate formed from McDonnell and Douglas in 1967, though at different times it also included other concerns—for example, Hughes Helicopters, which joined the group in 1984. McDonnell Douglas merged with **Boeing** in 1997.

Donald Wills Douglas (1892–1981), a U.S. citizen of Scottish ancestry, was born in New York. He started the Douglas company in 1920, and the first wholly Douglas-designed and built craft, the Cloudster, flew in 1921. U.S. Navy

Douglas Dauntless A-24 dive bombers pictured c. 1943. The A-24 was the army counterpart of the Navy SBD, intended for attacking ground troops and installations. Courtesy of the Library of Congress.

contracts for the DT-2 followed the next year. In 1924 the company made headlines when U.S. Army Douglas World Cruisers flew round the world. The Douglas C-1 transporter was then produced, based on the DWC design. The T2D-1 **torpedo** bomber was built in 1927. Thereafter Douglas was a key manufacturer of U.S. military aircraft. Among its many significant planes were the **Havoc; Dauntless;** Devastator; **Skyraider**, Skymaster, and **C-47 Skytrain**. Donald Douglas, Jr., became chairman of the company in 1957.

James Smith McDonnell (1899–1980) was born in Denver, Colorado, and like D. W. Douglas was of Scottish ancestry and a graduate of the Massachusetts Institute of Technology. The McDonnell company was started in 1939 at Lambert Field, Missouri, with just 15 employees. Having manufactured parts for other companies, it designed a fighter in 1940; the first order from the U.S. Army Air Corps came in October 1941. Other projects during World War II included **helicopters**. Experimen-

tal flights of the Phantom I jet fighter were also made.

The 1967 merger saw the redesignation of existing and new models as "MD," or McDonnell Douglas, and while James S. McDonnell became chairman of the board and chief executive officer Donald Douglas senior was honorary chairman. Particularly significant McDonnell Douglas military productions included the KC-10 Extender, the Globemaster, the **Phantom F-4**, the F-15 **Eagle**, the F-18 **Hornet**, the **Harrier**, the Goshawk, and the **Apache**.

Additional Reading: Francillon, *McDonnell Douglas*, 1988.

McNamara Line   FORTIFICATION

Named after Secretary for Defense Robert S. McNamara, the McNamara Line was proposed by John McNaughton and Professor Robert Fisher in 1966. The idea was that a physical and electronic barrier would be created between North and South Vietnam, thus preventing the enemy from moving men and supplies to attack the South. Project Dye Marker envisaged 160 miles of **barbed wire** and **mines**, interwoven with electronic sensors that would inform the defenders where crossings were being attempted. The sensors would be acoustic, **infrared**, seismic, and pressure activated. Ground troops, previously vulnerable, could be held farther back, ready to respond. Construction of the line commenced in 1967, but it was never completed. Nevertheless, the technology of electronic sensors and physical barriers was deployed quite widely, notably at Khe Sanh, and it remains important.

Me 109   AIRCRAFT

Arguably Germany's most famous fighter **aircraft** of World War II, the single-engine, single-seat Messerschmitt Bf109 first flew in 1935. It showed early promise seeing off competition from a Heinkel machine; the 109B model was delivered in 1937 to the Luftwaffe, with which it saw service in the Spanish Civil

War. In November 1937 it set a world speed record of 379 mph.

In 1938 the definitive 109E, or "Emil," was developed; it was produced not only by Messerschmitt at Regensburg but Fieseler at Kassel and Erla, Leipzig. About 1,500 had been produced by the end of 1939, making the Me 109 Germany's main fighter during the early part of the war. In action throughout the Blitzkrieg and battle of Britain it was proved superior to virtually everything except the **Spitfire**. One of the many minor variants was the Bf109E-7. This was powered by the Daimler Benz 1,200 horsepower engine, was 28 feet 8 inches long, and had a ceiling of 36,500 feet. Its armament was a 20 mm cannon firing through the nose, and four **machine guns**. Two significant advantages of the 109 were that its cannon gave a longer effective range than machine guns alone, and that its engine fuel-injection system was able to operate even during the most violent maneuver.

Though it was gradually outclassed and outnumbered by Allied planes, production of the 109 continued, and it served as a fighter-bomber until the end of the war. The G, or Gustav, model of 1942, with an improved DB 650 A engine, improved undercarriage, and a larger oil tank, would ultimately be the most numerous. The final wartime model was the K of 1944, subvariants of which included a three-cannon, two–machine gun Sturmjager model and a high-altitude machine. Production was continued by Czechoslovakia after World War II, and the 109 continued to be used, notably by Israel and Spain.

Additional Reading: Shacklady, *Messerschmitt Bf 109*, 2000; Ishoven, *Messerschmitt Bf 109 at War*, 1977.

Me 110   AIRCRAFT

The German twin-engine, two-seat Messerschmitt Bf110 was designed in the mid-1930s. It was intended as a long-range escort and "destroyer." At that time it was quite suitable for the task, as 340 mph was then considered fast, and its range of 565 miles was significant. Only in 1940, when the Bf 110 came up against mod-

ern fighters, did losses suddenly escalate to unacceptable levels. Thereafter it was generally redeployed to night-fighter duties, and from 1942 its effectiveness was improved by use of **radar**. In 1943 upward-firing cannon were fitted, allowing the 110 to attack enemy bombers while passing beneath. Perhaps surprisingly, total production of all types was over 6,000, and it continued to be made until early 1945.

Additional Reading: Taylor, *Combat Aircraft of the World*, 1969.

Me 163   AIRCRAFT

With design work commencing in 1941 and first powered flight in August 1943, the German Messerschmitt 163 was a stubby, liquid-fuel, rocket-powered **aircraft**. Constructed of duralumin with an armored nose, the craft was an advanced design but was able to remain in the air only for about 25 minutes. Production was 364 machines.

Additional Reading: Ransom and Cammann, *Me 163 Rocket Interceptor*, 2002; Dressel and Griehl, *The Luftwaffe Album*, 1999.

Me 262   AIRCRAFT

Nicknamed the Schwalbe, or "swallow," the German Messerschmitt 262 fighter, one of the first jet **aircraft**, first flew as a prototype under jet power in 1942. Early unreliability and Allied bombing delayed its general deployment until mid-1944. By the end of that year it was flying as interceptor, fighter-bomber, and reconnaissance machine. Its remarkable speed and huge offensive power made it almost the ideal anti-bomber weapon, but too few were available to turn the tide in the air over Europe.

Nevertheless, the Me 262 was one of the most advanced planes of its time, and only in maneuverability could piston-engine, propeller-driven craft like the **Mustang** hope to compete. The Me 262A-1a was powered by two **Junkers** Jumo turbojets, giving a top speed of 540 mph. Its armament was four cannon and up to 24 rockets. In the 2a Stormbird variant, racks were fitted for up to 500 kg of bombs.

Additional Reading: Baker, *Messerschmitt Me 262*, 1997; Morgan, *Me 262: Stormbird Rising*, 1994; Donald, *German Aircraft of World War II*, 1996; Kay, *German Jet Engine and Gas Turbine Development 1930–1945*, 2002.

Me 321 and 323 Gigant   AIRCRAFT

The Gigant was a giant Messerschmitt German troop and freight **aircraft** of World War II, with a 55 m wingspan. The 321 glider version was towed by three **Me 110s**, or a five-engine **Heinkel**. The 323D had six engines. Built in small numbers the Gigant failed, as it was an easy target for enemy planes.

Additional Reading: Dabrowski, *Messerschmitt Me 321/323*, 2002.

Meatball   MISCELLANEOUS

"Meatball" is the popular name for the landing-light cluster that guides pilots to **aircraft carriers**, such as those of the *Nimitz* class. Red and amber lights occupy the center and though they are always illuminated the lens lets only one type show at a time, depending on the pilot's angle of approach. This helps him to line up correctly. Flashing red lights on either side of a vertical amber bar indicate a "wave off"; the pilot must accelerate away to try again.

Mechanical Mule. *See* Mulo Meccanico

Memphis Belle. *See* Flying Fortress

Merkava, Main Battle Tank   TANK

The Merkava, meaning "**Chariot**," is Israel's main battle **tank**. Completed as a prototype in 1974, it first saw combat in the Lebanon in 1982. It has a well sloped small turret mounting a 105 mm gun, and it is powered by a Teledyne Continental diesel engine giving a maximum speed of 29 mph. The Mark 3, introduced in 1989, has a 120 mm gun, **laser** range finder, all electric controls, and new modular armor. What is unusual about the Merkava is its layout, for it has the engine at the front and a gap between the two layers of armor, part of it used for diesel fuel. The arrangement maximizes crew protection without losing any more space. Another oddity is the fitting of a 60 mm **mortar**, which can be fired from within the turret. When not fully stowed it is possible to carry additional personnel, who can enter via a rear door.

Additional Reading: Miller, *Tanks of the World*, 2001.

Merrimack. *See* Virginia

Meteor   AIRCRAFT

The twin-engine British Gloster Meteor was the only Allied jet fighter to see operational use in World War II. The first prototype flew in March 1943, and Meteors were in action during 1944, when it achieved successes in the interception of **V1** flying bombs. Late versions of the Meteor continued in RAF service long after World War II. The Mark 11 night-fighter variant had a 43-foot wingspan, a maximum speed of 579 mph, and an operational ceiling of 43,000 feet.

MG 08; MG 08/15   FIREARM

The 7.92 mm MG 08 was a German version of the **Maxim machine gun** that found lasting fame, or infamy, as a major killer of Allied troops during World War I. Developed from an earlier 1901 type, the MG 08 was heavy, belt fed, water cooled, and usually mounted on a "sledge," mount enabling it to be carried like a stretcher. In order to make the weapon more mobile, various "trench mounts" were also improvised, but it was not until a radical overhaul produced the MG 08/15 that a weapon managable by one man was produced. Even then the MG 08/15 was very heavy for a "light" machine gun.

Additional Reading: Musgrave, *German Machineguns*, 1992; Goldsmith, *The Devil's Paintbrush*, 1989; Bruce, *Machine Guns of World War I*, 1997.

MG 34   FIREARM

Produced with Swiss connivance in the interwar period, the German MG34 is arguably one of the most important **machine guns** of all time and the first true "general purpose" weapon.

MG 42

The basics were fairly straightforward, consisting of a recoil-operated mechanism with a revolving-bolt head and an air-cooled barrel within a perforated jacket. It could be fed with either 250 round belts or from small drums. Its cyclic rate was a very brisk 850 rounds per minute. The clever part was that the gun was just part of the system. On a bipod, it was a squad support; on a tripod, it became a heavy sustained-fire weapon; with special pintles and mounts, it became a **tank** or fortress weapon. This concept has been used with many, if not most, machine guns since.

Additional Reading: Myrvang, *MG34, MG42*, 2002; Bruce, *German Automatic Weapons of World War II*, 1996; Musgrave, *German Machineguns*, 1992.

MG 42   FIREARM

Renowned for its extremely rapid fire rate of 1,200 rounds per minute, the German MG 42 could burn its way through a 250 round belt of 7.92 mm cartridges in 13 seconds. It was one of the best **machine guns** of the World War II. Designed as a replacement for the **MG 34**, the MG 42 of 1942 was much easier to manufacture, making substantial use of steel stampings. Yet it was still a versatile general-purpose weapon and could be used as a squad weapon on a bipod, a tripod-mounted support weapon, or in vehicles. The mechanism was clever, having a nonrotating bolt that locked into the barrel extension by two rollers that cammed outward. The barrel, bolt, and barrel extension all recoiled together, while pawls fed the ammunition belt, the whole cycle taking but a fraction of a second and with very few malfunctions. After the war the MG 42 was reproduced in NATO caliber as the MG 1; it also inspired the **M60**.

Additional Reading: Myrvang, *MG34, MG42*, 2002; *MG-42 Machine Gun*, (undated); Bruce, *German Automatic Weapons of World War II*, 1996.

Microwave Bomb   EXPLOSIVE DEVICE

The theory of the microwave device is that the sudden production of powerful microwave energy will cause the failure of enemy electronics, communications, and the like, without large-scale casualties. Press reports of 2002 suggest that U.S. research is directed toward delivery of such a bomb by means of a UAV.

Midway Class   WARSHIP

The *Midway* class of U.S. **aircraft carriers** comprised three vessels—*Midway* (CVB 41), *Franklin D. Roosevelt* (CVB 42), and *Coral Sea* (CVB 43)—constructed between 1943 and 1947. At 48,000 tons they were bigger than the **Essex** class and very heavily armored. They were 900 feet long, carried 137 aircraft, and had a top speed of 33 knots. Their sides were lined with a total of 18 5-inch guns in single turrets. Remaining in service for many years, the *Midway* class underwent radical changes to keep up with new jet aircraft. Most obvious was the fitting of new angled flight decks and modifications to the bows, but new **radar**, catapult and armament changes, including missile batteries, made them virtually new ships. Interestingly, the *Midway* was used for the test-firing of captured **V-2** rockets in 1947. *Coral Sea* was the first carrier to test "PLAT," or "Pilot Landing Aid Television." She was finally decommissioned in 1990.

Additional Reading: Department of the Navy, *Dictionary of American Naval Fighting Ships* (many vols), 1959 onward; Polmar, *The Ships and Aircraft of the US Fleet*, 1981; Friedman, *US Aircraft Carriers*, 1983.

MiG-15, Fagot   AIRCRAFT

The Mikoyan-Gurevich 15 jet fighter **aircraft**, which first flew in 1947, was a mishmash of captured and copied technology, with a brutal snub-nosed appearance. Yet the MiG-15 was a highly advanced machine that shocked the West with its quality and performance. Even in December 1950, when it came up against the **Sabre** in Korea, it was still superior in terms of climb, turn, and armament.

The original engine of the MiG-15 was the RD-45, a copy of a Rolls-Royce type; later an improved VK-1 was fitted, giving a maximum speed of 668 mph. The MiG-15's range was 1,156 miles, and its armament three cannon.

Israeli troops pass the wreckage of a MiG-15 fighter at El Arish airport, during the Six Day War, June 1967. © Hulton/Getty Images.

When the two-seater MiG-15UTI is taken into account, well over 8,000 of the type were produced, with many used by Poland and Czechoslovakia. It was a frontline mainstay until the late 1960s and continued to be used in training long afterward.

Additional Reading: Gordon, *Mikoyan-Gurevich MiG-15*, 2001; Crosby, *A Handbook of Fighter Aircraft*, 2002; Butowski and Miller, *MiG: A History of the Design Bureau and Its Aircraft*, 1991; Belyakov and Marmain, *MiG: Fifty Years of Secret Aircraft Design*, 1994.

MiG-21, Fishbed   AIRCRAFT

The delta-wing Soviet MiG-21 has a reputation of being cost-effective, easy to handle, and hard hitting. It is one of the most widely used fighter **aircraft** of all time. It achieved particular prominence with the downing of Gary Powers's **U-2**. The initial model was in service from 1957. The MiG-21F, which soon followed, was 51 feet long and was powered by a Tumansky

R-25 turbojet, giving a maximum speed of 1,385 mph. In addition to a twin-barrel cannon, it was capable of carrying 3,000 lb of ordnance, including air to air missiles.

It was sold to many nations, including Arab states that used them against Israel, and there was also production in Czechoslovakia, China, and India. Later models included the 21PF, with a reshaped nose to accommodate the R1L **radar**, and a more powerful engine. The Mongol was a two-seat trainer adaption. The Rumanian MiG-21 Lancer was still for sale in 2000 and may be flying for some years to come.

Additional Reading: Crosby, *A Handbook of Fighter Aircraft*, 2002; Butowski and Miller, *MiG: A History of the Design Bureau and Its Aircraft*, 1991.

MiG-23, Flogger   AIRCRAFT

The delta-wing Soviet MiG-23 interceptor **aircraft**, developed for short takeoff and landing, first flew in 1967. Since then many different models have been produced; the 23M, with its pulse doppler **radar**; the lightweight 23ML, with various avionics improvements; the 23B attack variant; and the two-seat 23UB trainer; are just a few of them. The MiG-23ML, powered by an MNPK Soyuz turbojet with afterburner, has a top speed of 1,550 mph and can climb at 47,000 feet per minute to just over 60,000 feet maximum. Typical armament is a twin-barrell 23 mm cannon and a maximum ordnance load of 3,000 kg, including up to six missiles.

Additional Reading: Butowski and Miller, *MiG: A History of the Design Bureau and Its Aircraft*, 1991; Belayakov and Marmain, *MiG: Fifty Years of Secret Aircraft Design*, 1994.

Mighty Mouse. *See* **Sabre**

Milan Missile   MISSILE

The small French-designed Milan wire-guided missile was first produced in 1973. Also produced in Germany and the United Kingdom, it has since seen widespread NATO use. The missiles themselves are 1.26 meters long with shaped-charge warheads and come in sealed packages for use on a separate launcher unit. The Milan 2, introduced in 1984, had a claimed range of 2 km and armor penetration in excess of 1,000 mm.

Mills Bomb   EXPLOSIVE DEVICE

Inspired by a **grenade** designed in 1913 by Belgian Leon Roland, the Mills bomb, or "Number 5 grenade," was perfected by Briton William Mills, a marine engineer from Sunderland. It consisted of an cast-iron casing within which were central tubes to hold the fuse, detonator, and a spring-loaded striker. Once the pin was pulled the bomb remained safe until throwing, as the spring lever was held down by the hand. Once thrown the fuse was ignited, and the bomb exploded a few seconds later. It entered service in 1915. Described as "one of the most satisfactory types" produced by any nation during World War I, it was later produced in other

variants, including a Number 23 rodded **rifle** grenade, and a 36 type that could be fired from a cup discharger attached to the end of the rifle. Produced and used in huge numbers during both world wars, it was still in stocks as late as the 1970s.

Additional Reading: Skennerton, *An Introduction to British Grenades*, 1988.

Milstar. *See* **Satellites**

Mines; Land Mine   EXPLOSIVE DEVICE

The mine has existed as a method of warfare since classical times. Originally "mining" consisted of digging under a town wall or **fortification**, causing collapse. If this did not produce enemy surrender, the breach created could be stormed. An added subtlety was the use of wooden props, which, set on fire, would allow the miners more time to escape and potentially cause a more catastrophic collapse. At least one medieval manuscript describes how mines could be filled with flammable material, which was then ignited by means of driving a pitch-smeared flaming pig into the gallery.

With the invention of **gunpowder** came the possibility of exploding mines, tunnels with a powder chamber at the end, which, it has been suggested, were first used at Belgrade in 1439. Such mines were widely used in Europe and Asia to spectacular effect in many sieges, including that of the castle of Uovo in 1503, the siege of Kazan in 1552, and on numerous occasions in the Dutch, English Civil, and Thirty Years' Wars. Mines were sometimes "countermined," when the defenders dug "camouflets" in an attempt to intercept or blow up the attackers. Civilian miners were often engaged to dig military mines in war.

These methods continued to be used into the nineteenth century and were revived during the First World War, by which time the invention of more powerful **explosives** made them all the more deadly. Charges of 50,000 kg and more were by no means unknown, blasting craters more than 250 feet in diameter. Mine warfare was also made more complex with the use of listening devices, air pumping equipment, breathing equipment, and even electric lighting in the tunnels. On 1 July 1916, the battle of the Somme was opened by the detonation of several large mines; that at Hawthorn Redoubt was caught on film by a movie camera. At Messines Ridge, mine warfare reached its apogee when British and Empire troops dug 21 vast mines under the German lines. All but two were exploded on 7 June 1917 to devastating effect; one, not detonated during the battle, exploded in the 1950s.

The idea that a "land mine" could also be a smaller explosive device placed near the surface to injure personnel was probably current as early as the eighteenth century. In 1862, during the Confederate defense of Yorktown, **shells** were buried so as to detonate when stepped on or pulled. "Controlled mines" were also rigged to be exploded from a distance; Brigadier General Rains used 24 lb "ground **torpedoes**" with **fuses** that activated when crushed. It is noteworthy that the German word *Minen*, already applied to explosive projectiles or such munitions as **grenades** or **shells**, was now applied to the mine. Similar devices were used in World War I; antitank and antipersonnel mines made rapid strides in the interwar period and were well established by the Spanish Civil War.

During World War II mines were a staple of defense, being especially important in North Africa, specific Eastern Front engagements such as Kursk, and the **Atlantic Wall**. They were at their most useful where covered by other weapons, such as **machine guns** and **artillery**. Mines were laid both in marked fields and as scattered or individual nuisance mines. Techniques evolved for mixing antitank and antipersonnel mines. When simple "mine prods" for mine locating and clearance were supplemented with mine detectors, new mines with little or no metal were produced to make them difficult to locate.

Important mines of World War II included the small German S mine model 1935, which U.S. troops called the "Bouncing Betty." This was operated by direct pressure on the igniter or by trip wires rigged to fire on a pull system. When set off it would eject from the ground and explode, hurling 350 ball bearings up to 100 yards in all directions. In the German Glasmine model 1943, the body and top plate of the weapon were made of glass; this was hard to detect but produced particularly lethal fragments. *Schu* mines made of wood were similarly difficult to find. Teller, or plate-shaped, German antivehicle mines acted on pressure and were produced in a wide variety of different models. On the Allied side, the U.S. M-14 was a small device capable of blowing off a leg, while the M-16 jumped into the air to explode at waist height.

After 1945, mine technology advanced with plastic mines (already pioneered by Italy) and remotely delivered mines, or RDM. In the U.S. Picatinny Arsenal M56 system, mines were ejected in pairs from SUU-13 **helicopter**-mounted dispensers. The mines armed automatically on hitting the ground and could be set to self destruct after a given time. In the British Ranger system, mines were sewn from ground vehicles using a battery of launch tubes, each tube projecting 18 mines. Ranger was capable of laying a complete load of 1,296 mines in one minute.

Antitank mines have also employed some novel technology. The U.S. M-21 detonated underneath the belly of the tank, projecting a saucer-shaped charge upward to explode on contact. The Swedish FFV 028 used a **hollow charge** to produce a gas jet capable of penetrating 50 mm of armor. Others were developed to respond to heat or vibration. The innovative Astrolite was a "liquid mine," made by the Explosives Corporation of America. This was poured or sprayed onto the ground and could be detonated remotely or using pressure sensors. It became inert after a given period. Systems were also developed wherein a vehicle with a plough could lay antitank mines automatically, quickly creating a field.

The Claymore, or directional-type, antipersonnel fragmentation mine used an old idea to devastating effect. Set up facing the enemy or covering a defile, they were detonated remotely or by means of a booby trap to shower ball bearings or **shrapnel** on the enemy. Typical of this class was the U.S. M-18A1, used in Vietnam. Mounted on small steel legs, it was loaded with a charge of **C-4** explosive and 700 steel balls, and fired by electrically by a handheld device at the end of 50 feet of wire. It was lethal to over 30 meters, and could cause casualties at 250.

The proliferation of antipersonnel mines and the widespread mutilation of civilians, often long after conflicts had ceased, had become a cause of international concern by the 1980s. The banning of mines was a cause espoused by both individual celebrities, such as Diana, Princess of Wales, and human rights groups. Whether such a ban would ever be practical or enforceable was hotly debated. Even so, the Ottawa Treaty was signed in 1997, and by 2002 there were 118 nations committed to the concept, with a further 22 signatories that had not yet ratified the treaty. Despite this, there were antipersonnel mine incidents and myriad injuries reported in 27 countries during 2001 alone.

Additional Reading: Croll, *The History of Landmines*, 1998; Duffy, *Siege Warfare*, 1979; Gravett, *Medieval Siege Warfare*, 1990; Monin and Gallimore, *The Devil's Gardens: A History of Landmines*, 2002; *Jane's Infantry Weapons*; King, *Jane's Mines and Mine Clearance*, 1996; Barrie, *The War Underground: The Tunnellers of the Great War*, 1988; *Imperial War Museum, Review* (vol. 6); Sloan, *Mine Warfare*, 1986; Fitzsimons (ed), *The Illustrated Encyclopedia of Twentieth Century Weapons and Warfare,* 1967–1978; Department of the Army, *Technical Manual 31-200-1.*

Minesweepers. *See* **Sea Mines; Motor Minesweeper; Oropesa** and **Double "L" Sweeps;** *Admirable* and *Auk* **Classes**

Minié Ball; Minié Rifle   AMMUNITION

French captain Claude E. Minié (1814–1879) was the inventor of the "Minié ball," which was in fact **a rifle** bullet of cylindrical shape, in the base of which was a small iron cup. On firing the cup was driven up into the bullet, expanding the soft lead. This had the effect of making the bullet grip the rifling of the barrel, making the bullet seat firmly, delivering an accurate shot with the maximum power. Though there had

been attempts at similar devices earlier, Minié's bullet was the first to be widely accepted, seeing successful use in the Crimean War. Rifles firing this type of round were sometimes called "Minié rifles."

Additional Reading: Roads, *The British Soldier's Firearm*, 1964.

Minimi; Squad Automatic Weapon
FIREARM

The Belgian Fabrique Nationale 5.56 mm Minimi gas-operated light **machine gun** was first unveiled in 1974. Weighing only 6.9 kg, having an easily changed barrel and the ability to use belt or boxes, it was a versatile and promising weapon. Following competition against guns like the Maremont XM233, Philco-Ford XM234, and other submissions from **Colt, Stoner**, and Rodman, it was, finally selected as the U.S. Army's new SAW, or Squad Automatic Weapon M249. According to the U.S. Army manual, it may be used much like the **M16** rifles of the rest of the squad, but the SAW gunner is positioned near the squad leader in defense and is capable of engaging targets with heavier volumes of fire. The SAW has also been popular with special forces.

Additional Reading: Department of the Army, *Field Manual 23-14: Squad Automatic Weapon (SAW) M24*, 1985; *Jane's Infantry Weapons.*

Mini-Moke   VEHICLE

The tiny Mini-Moke was first developed as a lightweight air-transportable vehicle in 1960. Based on the civilian British Mini car designed by Alec Issigonis (1906–1988), it was used by the military in small numbers but achieved something of a cult status when made available to the public in 1964. It was tested by the U.S. Army, and an Austin Ant "Midi-Moke" was produced in 1966. Perhaps the most extraordinary of the family was the experimental "Twini-Moke," which had two engines driving the front and rear wheels separately. The basic 1962 model Mini-Moke had a BMC 948 cc engine, was front wheel drive, 9 feet 2 inches long, and weighed 1,180 lb.

An LGM-30G Minuteman III inside a silo near Grand Forks Air Force Base, 1989. Courtesy of the Department of Defense.

Minsk. *See Kiev* Class

Minuteman   MISSILE

The Minuteman is a three-stage solid-fuel **ICBM** with multiple nuclear warheads and a range of over 6,000 miles; it is operated by the U.S. Strategic Command. The programme commenced in 1958, with the first launch in 1961. Minuteman II, launched three years later, was capable of striking from six to eight targets simultaneously with greater accuracy. Minuteman III of 1968 increased not only accuracy but range. At the height of Minuteman production **Boeing** had 39,700 personnel on the project. By 1975 the United States had 1,000 Minuteman missiles of the types II and III, mainly deployed in silos. It is expected that the system will remain current until at least 2010.

The latest Minuteman, LGM-30G, is six feet in diameter, 59 feet in length, and weighs 76,000 lbs. Its top speed is in excess of 15,000 mph. The silo requires a hole 80 feet deep and 12 feet in diameter, with a launch pad total area of about two acres.

Additional Reading: Fitzsimons, *The Illustrated Encyclopedia of Twentieth Century Weapons and Warfare*, 1967–1978; *Jane's Weapon Systems*.

Miquelet. *See* Flintlock

Mirage I, III, IV, 2000, etc.   AIRCRAFT

The French Dassault Mirage family of fighter **aircraft** was founded as long ago as 1955, when the protoype Mirage I first flew. The original was powered by two turbojets, with a liquid-propellant rocket for extra thrust at takeoff. By 1956 the Mirage III was using a single Atar turbojet plus an SEPR rocket, which could be jettisoned. By 1958 the Mirage IIIA was able to achieve 1,450 mph and a ceiling of 82,000 feet. The delta-wing Mirage III was widely used, and its descendants—the simplified ground-attack Mirage 5, and the faster Mirage 50, which first flew in 1979—were recently still in use in some countries. The Mirage IV first flew in prototype in 1959. Its most obvious difference was that at 77 feet it was over 25 feet longer than the Mirage III, but it carried almost double the weight of ordnance which could include the ASMP standoff nuclear missile.

More recent Mirages include the F1, some versions of which could carry the **Exocet** missile, and the Mirage 2000. This last appeared in prototype at the end of the 1970s, and in its newest versions includes fly-by-wire technology and the ability to carry antiradar rockets, runway-denial cluster bombs, and 30 mm cannon.

Additional Reading: Taylor, *Combat Aircraft of the World*, 1969; *Jane's Aircraft*; Falck, *Jane's Advanced Tactical Fighters*, 1998.

Missouri, USS   WARSHIP

The U.S. *Iowa*-class **battleship** *Missouri* was completed in June 1944 and served in both the

An Army Tactical Missile System Missile (TACMS) is fired from a Multiple Launcher Rocket System (MLRS) launcher during testing at White Sands missile range, New Mexico. Courtesy of the Department of Defense.

Atlantic and Pacific during the latter stages of World War II, mainly engaged in screening **aircraft carriers** and in shore bombardments. She was struck and damaged by **a kamikaze** in April 1945 but fought on. After World War II she served in a training capacity. Despite an incident in which she ran aground in Hampton Roads in 1950 she was later sent to Korea, making several sorties to provide fire support. After time in reserve she was reactivated in 1984 and fitted with the latest missile armament; she was actively involved in bombardment during the Gulf War of 1991. Back in reserve again in 1995, she is one of the world's last battleships.

Additional Reading: Sumrall, *Iowa Class Battleships*, 1988; Garzke and Dulin, *Battleships: United States Battleships, 1935–1992*, 1995; Department of

the Navy, *Refloating of the USS Missouri*, 1950; Madsen, *Forgotten Fleet: The Mothball Navy*, 1999.

Mistral   MISSILE

The French Mistral shoulder-launched antiaircraft missile—also known as the SATCP—was in regular use by the 1980s. It homes on its target by means of **infrared** and is exploded by a proximity **fuse**. The launch is in two stages, with the missile leaving the firer at relatively slow speed before the main motor accelerates it to speeds in excess of Mach 2.6.

MLRS. *See* **Multiple Launch Rocket System**

MMS. *See* **Motor Minesweeper**

"Moaning Minnie." *See* **Nebelwerfer**

Mogami **Class**   WARSHIP

Design work for the Japanese *Mogami* class of 8,500-ton **cruisers** commenced in 1930, and four vessels were completed by October 1937. The *Mogamis* were 661 feet in length, with a main armament of 15 6.1-inch guns in five turrets, and armor up to 5.5 inches thick. Before the war with the United States, the *Mogami* class underwent considerable modification, including strengthening to deal with perceived hull weakness and lowering of the bridge because of instability. With the collapse of treaty limitations, the main guns were replaced with ten 8-inch.

Despite early successes, the entire *Mogami* class was sunk in World War II. *Mikuma* ran into *Mogami* at Midway; while the former was sunk by U.S. aircraft the *Mogami* escaped. It was later converted to an "aircraft cruiser"; crippled at Leyte Gulf, she was finally sunk with a torpedo. The *Suzuya* and *Kumano* were also destroyed in 1944.

Additional Reading: Lacroix and Wells, *Japanese Cruisers of the Pacific War*, 1997; Jentschura, *Warships of the Imperial Japanese Navy 1869–1945*, 1977.

Molotov Cocktail   EXPLOSIVE DEVICE

In use since at least the 1930s and named after Soviet foreign minister Vyacheslav Molotov, the Molotov cocktail is a petrol bomb, or improvised incendiary **grenade**. It usually consists of a bottle with a wick, which has to be lit before throwing. Refinements include additives to the fuel to make it stick.

Monitor, **USS**   WARSHIP

According to several contemporary naval architects, the *Monitor*, now one of the best known ships of all time, was an impossibility. Nevertheless, she was built and, incorporating ironclad protection with a turret and steam propulsion, has been recognized as a breakthrough in naval technology. The contract for her construction was granted by Abraham Lincoln to

Swedish designer John Ericsson on 4 October 1861, with the stipulation that if she was not built in a hundred days Ericsson would be paid nothing.

As completed the *Monitor* was 179 feet long, low and raftlike, with a drum-type turret mounted on a steam-powered spindle. The armament was two seven-ton smoothbore Dahlgren guns. The maximum armor, on the turret, was eight inches thick. Within her hull 41 crew were accommodated below the water line. Her moment came in May 1862, when she steamed into Hampton Roads under command of Lieutenant John L. Worden to do battle with the CSS *Virgina*, which was attacking other Union ships. Four hours of hard action resulted in 24 hits on *Monitor*'s turret and the wounding of Worden. *Virginia* was also hit, but her armor similarly prevented fatal damage. The *Virginia* withdrew. The *Monitor* was active for sometime afterward, but sank under tow in a storm off Cape Hatteras on 31 December 1862. With some justification it has been claimed that *Monitor* ended the age of the wooden fighting ship.

Additional Reading: Konstam, *Hampton Roads: First Clash of Ironclads*, 2002; Mokin, *Ironclad: The Monitor and the Merrimack*, 1991; Quarstein, *The Battle of the Ironclads*, 1999; Marvel (ed), *Monitor Chronicles*, 2000; Baxter, *The Introduction of the Ironclad Warship*, 1933; Tise, *Monitor: Meaning and Future*, 1978.

Morgenstern. See **Mace**

Morse Code

Born in Charlestown, Massachusetts Samuel Finley Breeze Morse (1791–1872) worked as a professional artist before turning to the invention and development of the electric **telegraph** in the 1830s. The dot and dash code system which bears his name was ideally suited to the technology since it was expressed as a series of breaks in a "continuous wave." An operator could therefore transmit messages merely by "tapping" a morse "key." Morse's original code, sometimes referred to as "American" Morse, was modified for international use by a

"Terrific" combat between the USS *Monitor* and the *Merrimac*. The steam powered *Monitor* with its metal construction, low lying form, and revolving turret has been justly credited with a quantum leap forward in warship technology. Forty years would elapse before all its advances were being regularly incorporated into general design. Courtesy of the Library of Congress.

Berlin Treaty of 1851 which changed a number of letters and made accented letters possible.

Mortar   ARTILLERY

The mortar is a type of **artillery** or projectile weapon, the usual characteristic of which is to throw large missiles at relatively low velocities and high angles. This makes it particularly useful for firing into fortifications or over obstacles. The relatively low speed of the projectile may lead to comparatively short range, but propellant charges can be small, so that the barrels of mortars can often be thinner and lighter than those of other types of artillery. The mortar and the **howitzer**, therefore, have some similarity, and in the German army the terms *Mörser*

(mortar), *Granatenwerfer* (grenade thrower), and *Haubitze* (**Howitzer**) have sometimes been interchangeable.

Though medieval **bombards** are their ancestors, mortars are usually regarded as having been invented in the late fifteenth century, appearing in written documentation by 1506. Mortars are depicted in sketches made by Albrecht Dürer in the Low Countries about 1520 and were used at Boulogne in 1544. Military treatises of the later sixteenth century describe how mortars could be used with solid, incendiary, or explosive projectiles, these last being known in English as "granadoes." By the seventeenth century the mortar was regarded as one of the prime tools of the military engineer and was a deciding factor in many sieges.

During the eighteenth and nineteenth centuries, mortars were used wherever warfare became static. The small portable mortar developed by the Dutch engineer Baron Menno van Coehorn (1641–1704) was important in the eighteenth century and was sometimes used in batteries from trenches. Mortars mounted in boats known as "bomb ketches," or **bomb vessels**, became popular in the eighteenth century. Extensive use was also made of mortars in the sieges of the American Civil War; at Petersburg in 1865 a 13-inch mortar was mounted on a railroad truck. The British developed the monstrous "Mallet mortar" in the late 1850s; it weighed about 7.5 tons and was capable of throwing a three-foot-diameter bomb containing 480 lb of explosive.

The mortar received a new lease of life from 1914, when myriad trench mortars were introduced to lob projectiles from trench to trench. The Germans were early leaders in the field, developing several models of *Minenwerfer* (literally, mine thrower), various of which were capable of firing **gas shells**, and missiles up to 100 kg (220 lb) in weight. An equivalent French heavy weapon was designed by the Société de Construction de Batignolles. Known to English-speaking troops as the "flying pig," this would later enter service with Allied armies as the 9.45-inch mortar. An innovative British model designed by Wilfred Stokes was trialed in early 1915. This consisted of a simple tube with a bipod support, first fabricated by Ransomes and Rapiers of Ipswich; it succeeded in combining portability with speed of firing and cost-effectiveness. After 1918 the majority of mortars would be made along similar lines.

By World War II most mortars were in one of three categories. The lightest, usually no more than 60 mm (2.5 inches) in caliber, were widely issued to the infantry and seldom had ranges in excess of 1,500 m. Important in this class were the Soviet 5 cm, first issued in 1938; the British 2 inch, which was simplified during the war and eventually produced as a lightened parachutists model; and the German Granatenwerfer 36, a 50 mm model that formed part of the equipment of every infantry platoon. The diminutive Japanese Type 89 mortar was some-

The British army shows off spoils of war in London: a German light "Lanz"-type trench mortar in front of a row of artillery. © Hulton/Getty Images.

times referred to as a **grenade** discharger, as it could also fire the standard Type 91 hand grenade. The U.S. 60 mm was based on a French design by the Edgar Brandt company, capable of firing explosive, illumination, and practice bombs to a range of just over a mile at a rate of up to 18 rounds per minute.

The second category of mortar was mainly used in battalion support companies, and most were about 80 mm in caliber. These included the simply made Soviet 82 mm, with its distinctive wheels; the U.S. 81 mm; the Italian 81 mm; and the 81 mm, German Granatenwerfer 34. The third and heaviest category of mortar was usually considered as part of the artillery; it encompassed such weapons as the 4.2-inch and the German 120 mm. One of the most extraordinary mortars of the period was the U.S. "Little David," a massive 915 mm weapon intended for smashing Japanese bunkers, though the war ended before it could be deployed.

The division of mortars into "infantry," "support," and "artillery" roles has continued, but in Vietnam the Americans discovered that the 81 mm was too heavy for use outside fire bases. The result was the development of an M224 lightweight company mortar. Lately, Finland and Israel have been prominent in mortar production, alongside the major powers. Recent developments include guided mortar projectiles like the Swedish Strix antiarmor round, the use of light alloys, and large mortars that can fire bombs containing smaller submunitions.

Additional Reading: *Jane's Infantry Weapons*; Hogg, *Mortars*, 2001.

Mosin-Nagant Rifle   FIREARM

Named after its designers, the Belgian Nagant brothers and the Russian colonel Mosin, the Mosin-Nagant family of **bolt-action rifles** was the mainstay of the Russian and Soviet infantry in two world wars. The first major model was that of 1891, which weighed 3.95 kg, fired a 7.62 mm round, had a five-round magazine, and was effective up to about 800 meters. Other important versions included the 1891/30 **sniper** model and the 1938 and 1944-type **carbines**.

Moskito Fw Ta 154   AIRCRAFT

The wooden **Focke-Wulf** "Moskito" Ta 154 of 1943 was doubtless inspired by, and nicknamed after, the British **Mosquito**. Perhaps surprisingly, given Focke-Wulf's success with other models like the Fw 190 and the Condor, this German twin-engine fast bomber was not a success. Despite a good top speed and the ability to carry **radar**, there were a number of crashes, and few were used.

Moskito Missile Launcher   MISSILE

The Swiss Moskito was a tiny, innovative, mobile antitank missile launcher based on the **Haflinger** four-wheel drive. Weighing just 680 kg, it incorporated a motor-driven conveyor system that allowed the firing of five missiles in succession. This was a very cheap, but possibly suicidal, way to deal with heavy armor. The main drawback seems to have been that a vehicle, however small, is more difficult to conceal than a missile team, which can hide very effectively in bushes and trenches.

Mosquito   AIRCRAFT

The British twin-engine **de Havilland** Mosquito multirole **aircraft** is interesting proof that the revisiting of old technology in new circumstances can sometimes be hugely successful. First designed in 1938, the Mosquito was initially intended to fly so fast that defensive armament would be superfluous. Yet most startling was the fact that this streamlined plane was made out of wood, which allowed the use of nonstrategic labor and materials. Faster than a **Spitfire**, the Mosquito could carry a similar bomb load to the much larger **Flying Fortress**, and it could fly two sorties to Berlin in a single night.

Ultimately, the Mosquito was used in a variety of roles, including fighter and **torpedo** bomber. Its armaments included up to four 20 mm cannon or **Browning** machine guns. Capable of 400 mph, the long-range models had an endurance of over 3,000 miles. By 1945, total production of all variants was 6,710, with manufacture in Canada and Australia as well as the United Kingdom.

Additional Reading: Birtles, *Mosquito*, 1998; Bowman, *De Havilland Mosquito*, 1998; Sharp and Bowyer, *Mosquito*, 1967.

Mother. *See* Tank

Motor Minesweeper   WARSHIP

Commonly referred to as the MMS, or "Mickey Mouse," the British motor minesweeper, introduced in 1941, was a wooden vessel 119 feet long displacing 165 tons. It was powered by a 500 horsepower diesel engine giving a maximum speed of about 11 knots. Its main task was the clearance of **sea mines**, a duty made slightly less dangerous by the fact that the MMS was nonmagnetic. Built at yards around the United Kingdom from Buckie in Scotland to Lowestoft in East Anglia, to Brixham and Looe in the southwest, the MMS was also produced in small numbers in Canada, India, Hong Kong, and elsewhere. Usually it was equipped with a **double-L sweep**, mounted on a giant drum when not in use, though many were retrofitted with **acoustic hammers**. Another version of the MMS was a 140 foot, 255-ton "Big Mickey," which had an extended range.

The MMS is usually distinguished from the BYMS, or British Yard Minesweeper, which was actually built in the United States. These were 130 to 135 feet in length, fitted with 3-inch and 20 mm antiaircraft guns, and capable of 14 knots. Among the many companies making them were Westergard of Biloxi, Associated of Seattle, Wheeler Shipbuilding, Campbell of San Diego, Stadium Yacht Basin of Cleveland, Greenport Basin of Long Island, and Weaver Shipyard. The fastest build recorded was three months and 18 days. In U.S. service such minesweepers were designated YMS. The BYMS and YMS were relatively luxurious, having such amenities for the 30-man crew as hot and cold running water, and they were capable of sweeping any type of mine then in service.

Additional Reading: Melvin, *Minesweeper*, 1992; Cocker, *Mine Warfare Vessels*, 1993; Elliott, *Allied Minesweeping*, 1979.

Mousetrap. *See* **Hedgehog**

MP 5 Submachine gun　　　FIREARM

Developed from the **G3 rifle**, the 9 mm **Heckler and Koch** MP 5 **submachine** gun appeared in the 1960s and has since become one of the most important and widely used weapons in this category. It weighs only about 2 kg in the lightest models, some of which have a collapsible butt, bringing down the overall length to just 61 cm. Usual magazines carry 15 or 30 rounds.

MP 38, MP 40　　　FIREARM

Designed by a team at the Ermawerk, the 9 mm MP 38 (Maschinenpistole 1938) **submachine gun** was one of the best-known weapons of World War II. Weighing 9 lb, it had a 32-round detachable box magazine and an innovative folding stock. Unusually for the time, there was no wooden furniture, the grip areas being of phenolic resin. The MP 40 update simplified the manufacturing process.

Additional Reading: Bruce, *German Automatic Weapons of World War II*, 1996; Götz, *German Military Rifles and Machine Pistols*, 1990.

MP 43, MP 44. *See* **Assault Rifle**

Mulberry Harbor　　　MISCELLANEOUS

Made of huge prefabricated units, the two Mulberry harbors were designed specifically to solve the logistical problems that would follow the 1944 Normandy landings. Towed across the channel, they provided instant docking facilities and so obviated the immediate necessity of seizing a major port. The remains of one of these structures is still to be seen on the French coast.

Mulo Meccanico　　　VEHICLE

Its name meaning literally "mechanical mule," the Italian Moto Guzzi Mulo Meccanico was a motor tricycle "power cart" for use in mountainous areas. Introduced in 1960, it had a 754 cc engine and weighed, 1000 kg; the payload was 500 kg in addition to the driver. It could be converted to a **half-track** configuration with small tracks and idlers at the rear. There was therefore some similarity to both the **Kettenkrad** and the **Tricar**. It is worth noting that the rather different U.S. M274 "mechanical mule" was a Willys-produced, four-wheel, four-wheel-drive platform utility vehicle.

Multiple Launch Rocket System, M270
MISSILE

The Multiple Launch Rocket System, or MLRS, consists of a fully tracked transporter that carries a missile container of 12 projectiles each 13 feet in length. Each unguided projectile has an M77 warhead that scatters submunitions over the target. A full salvo can devastate hundreds of square yards. The system was used to considerable effect by U.S. and British forces in the Gulf War of 1991. Similar weapons have been developed in other countries—for example, the Russian BM-27.

Musket; Musket Rest FIREARM

The term "musket" has been historically applied to various types of muzzle-loading **artillery** and smoothbore and **rifled** shoulder arms. As now used the word usually refers to smoothbore military shoulder arms of the type current between about 1580 and 1850. So important was this weapon in the eighteenth and early nineteenth centuries that the period is sometimes called the "horse and musket" period of military history.

The early musket was a **matchlock** of large caliber, heavy for a personal arm. For this reason it was often used from a "musket rest," a forked pole about four feet in length. Such rests had been generally discarded about 1640. By about 1700 the use of **bayonets** with muskets was making the **pike** redundant, and the increasing use of **flintlocks** began to make the musket more reliable. As the eighteenth century progressed muskets became more uniform in character; they were often put together in government workshops to established patterns.

It is often said that the musket was inaccurate and impractical. By modern standards this may be true, but at the time it was devastating, at least at short range. Part of the secret to the success of the musket was that it was used in large numbers and to standardized drills. Bodies of men shot at large targets, and the inefficiency or inaccuracy of any individual soldier became unimportant. The somewhat confusing term "rifled musket" came into use in the mid-nineteenth century with the spread of muzzle-loading **rifles**.

Additional Reading: Mowbray and Heroux (eds), *Civil War Arms Makers*, 1998; de Gheyn, *The Exercise of Armes*, 1986; Hughes, *Firepower*, 1974; Blair, *Pollard's History of Firearms*, 1983; Durdik, *Firearms*, 1981.

Mustang, P-51 AIRCRAFT

The single-engine, single-seat P-51 Mustang was not only one of the most successful fighter **aircraft** but an excellent example of U.S. and British military cooperation. Some regard the Mustang as the greatest fighter of World War II. Its origins date to April 1940, when the British Purchasing Commission approached North American Aviation to design and build an advanced fighter, with the stringent criterion that due to the critical situation the prototype should be completed in four months. Fortunately, designers Raymond Rice and Edgar Schmued already had ideas informed by air combat that had been taking place in Europe, and they did in fact complete the airframe on schedule, though the engine took longer to perfect.

By the end of 1941 the Mustang was in the air over Europe—a graceful aircraft with excellent speed and maneuverability, particularly at low levels, it was soon dubbed "the Cadillac of the skies." Range was also a strength, with the Mustang able to reach from the United Kingdom into Germany. Though the U.S. Army was already committed to the **P-38** and **P-47**, it soon recognized the quality of the Mustang and was flying its own variant by 1943. Total U.S. production of all types would be about 15,000, with a few additional examples built at the war's end in Australia.

Key to the ultimate success of the design was its engine; the original Mustang I had weaknesses in this department, but later versions were fitted with the Parkard-Merlin 1,590 horsepower motor, based on one of the best Rolls-Royce designs. From the first the Mustang also packed a heavy punch—the Mustang I had eight machine guns, four .303 and four .5-inch. Later models were even more heavily armed, with six .5-inch **machine guns** plus bombs or rockets on the P-51D. In the final lightweight P-51H, surface area and power were both increased, giving a maximum speed of 487 mph and making the P-51H the fastest Allied piston-engine aircraft.

Remarkably, the P-51 would eventually serve with 50 air forces and be used also in Korea. The Israelis flew Mustangs in the 1956 war, and as late as 1967 turboprop aircraft based on the Mustang were put back into production for counterinsurgency operations. A real Mustang oddity was the P-82 (later F-82) "Twin Mustang." First built in 1945, this was literally two Mustangs joined together during

Australian pilots stand by their Mustang fighters in Korea, c. 1950. Designed in World War II the Mustang was still viable in Korea. © Hulton/Getty Images.

production to create a twin-boom long-range fighter with two cockpits. This had the advantage that one pilot could rest or act as observer while the other flew; the range went up to the then-colossal 2,240 miles. The Twin Mustang flew in Korea and was sometimes also fitted with **radar**.

Additional Reading: Dorr, *US Fighters* of World War II, 1991; Coggan, *P-51 Mustang Restored*, 1995.

Mustard Gas   CHEMICAL WARFARE

Mustard **gas** (also known as "H," "H.S.," and even "Hun Stuff") is a blistering-agent chemical weapon first used by the Germans in July 1917. Called mustard gas because of its distinctive odor, it was particularly effective because, unlike **chlorine** or **phosgene**, it attacked all parts of the body. Settling as droplets, pure

mustard initially caused little pain but later resulted in severe burns and blisters that incapacitated and could prove fatal. Individuals not protected by **gas masks** suffered temporary or permanent blindness. Mustard gas was soon produced by several nations. In the United States, development and production were speeded by the aid of several eminent scientists, including J. B. Conant, Major Keyes of MIT, and Professor G. N. Lewis of the University of California.

Later variations on the mustard gas theme included the ammonia related "nitrogen mustards" (dichloro and trichloro-triethylamine), which were particularly toxic to eyes and skin; the garlic-smelling "distilled mustard"; Lewisite (dichloro 2-chlorovinyl arsine), which also acted as a systemic poison and caused such symptoms as diarrhea, heart and circulatory problems, and searing pain to the eyes; ethyldichloroarsine, ED; and phenyldichloroarsine, PD. In 1937 a compound known as "simulated mustard" was devised for training purposes. Though harmless unless swallowed, and based on molasses, simulated mustard behaved much like real mustard gas and could be dropped, sprayed, and projected, leaving a distinctive odor.

N

Nambu Pistol   FIREARM

Named after their designer Colonel (later General) Kirijo Nambu, the Nambu self-loading **pistols** were the main variety in service with Japanese forces prior to 1945. The first model was demonstrated in 1909, and a few were produced during World War I, but the best-known type, the 8 mm Taisho Type 14, was not designed until 1925. A 7 mm "baby" model was also produced. Despite their fame they were not in the same league as either the **Luger** or **Colt**.

Napalm; Napalm B   INCENDIARY
                                                 DEVICE

Though gasoline had been in use as an incendiary weapon for some time, it was realized that it was most effective when additives were included to make it stick to the target. In 1942 Harvard scientists mixed naphthelene and palmitate (hence *na-palm*) with gasoline, to make a brown sticky syrup that burned more slowly than raw gasoline. It was used in **flamethrowers** and bombs. More recently, the additives polystyrene and benzene have been used to create "super napalm" or "napalm B," the ignition of which is more easily controlled. Though napalm is most popularly associated with Vietnam, it has seen widespread use. It was back in the news recently when the U.S. Fallbrook Naval Station disposed of its accumulated stock over three million gallons.

Natter   UNCONVENTIONAL AIRCRAFT

The German Bachem Ba 349 Natter (Adder, or Viper) was a semi-expendable interceptor designed by Erich Bachem and Willy Fiedler in 1944 to counter Allied bombers. Powered by four solid-fuel rockets for vertical launch and a liquid-fuel motor for operations, the craft was 5.72 meters long. It was armed with 24 small Fohn rockets and two cannon in the nose. After high-speed interception the pilot and main part of the craft were intended to descend by separate parachutes. The first manned takeoff in February 1945 resulted in the death of the pilot, Lothar Sieber, and the Natter never entered service.

Additional Reading: Dressel and Griehl, *The Luftwaffe Album*, 1999; O'Neill, *Suicide Squads of World War II*, 1988.

***Nautilus,* USS**   SUBMARINE

Though there have been other military vessels called *Nautilus*, including a U.S. Navy **schooner** of 1799 and several **submarines**, the best known is the USS *Nautilus* (SSN 571) the world's first nuclear-powered submarine. Key to this breakthrough was the development of the pressurized water reactor, or PWR, by Hyman G. Rickover of the Naval Reactors Branch of the U.S. Atomic Energy Commission. The magnitude of this achievement is signaled by the fact that nuclear-powered submarines have almost unlimited range and may stay submerged for very long periods. Moreover, atomic power produces heat without the need for external sources of oxygen; also, the uranium fuel for the *Nautilus* weighed only about a pound. Though it required special storage facilities and screening, this still left much more space for weapons and crew.

The USS *Nautilus*, the first atomic powered submarine, entering New York harbor, 1956. Courtesy of the Library of Congress.

Laid down at General Dynamics yard at Groton, Connecticut, in 1952, the *Nautilus* was launched by Mamie Eisenhower and put to sea under Commander Eugene P. Wilkinson in January 1955. Her maiden voyage was a record breaker, setting the longest submerged distance to date. In 1957 she ventured under the polar ice, and in 1958, during a secret mission, she became the first vessel to reach the North Pole.

Capable of diving to 600 feet, the *Nautilus* was 324 feet long with a top speed of 25 knots. Armed with six **torpedo** tubes, she had a surface displacement of 3,533 tons and a complement of 105. During her service life she covered over 300,000 miles and took part in the blockade during the Cuban missile crisis. Decommissioned in 1980, she later became a museum ship at Groton.

Additional Reading: Anderson, *Nautilus*, 1959; Paine, *Ships of the World*, 1997; Polmar, *The American Submarine*, 1983; Hewlett and Duncan, *Nuclear Navy*, 1974; Blair, *The Atomic Submarine*, 1957.

NBC; NBC Suit   BIOLOGICAL WARFARE, CHEMICAL WARFARE, NUCLEAR WARFARE

Standing for "**nuclear, biological** and **chemical**," the acronym NBC is often used to denote systems that protect against these agents; thus an NBC suit is protective outerwear. The U.S. "Chemical Protective Outfit" is a two-piece suit of camouflaged or green charcoal-activated cloth with a nylon or twill outer layer, worn with **gas mask**, rubber boots, and gloves. NBC protection for **tanks** and ships may include airtight doors and hatches, pressurization, filtration systems, and lead shielding.

Additional Reading: Norris and Fowler, *NBC*, 1999; *Jane's NBC Systems*.

Nebelwerfer   MISSILE

Meaning literally "smoke" or "fog thrower," the German Nebelwerfer was one of the first really successful rocket equipments used on the modern battlefield. Developed prior to World War II, it was first operationally deployed against the Soviets in 1941. The commonest model consisted of six barrels on a carriage, the projectiles being electrically fired. The 150 mm rockets were launched one after the other, generally at two-second intervals, to a range of about 7 km. High-explosive, smoke, or chemical rounds could be fired, rapidly saturating a target—hence the unofficial motto of the Nebelwerfer troops, "Thump—don't tap." Allied troops nicknamed the Nebelwerfer "Moaning Minnie" or "Screaming Mimi" due to the noise it made.

Additional Reading: Gander, *Field Rocket Equipment of the German Army*, 1972.

Needle Gun. *See* **Dreyse**

"Nellie," NLE Trenching Machine
VEHICLE

The NLE owed its name to the fact that it was produced by the department of Naval Land Equipments; it was also known by the code words "Cultivator" and "White Rabbit No. 6." Manufacture of this British trench-digging machine was encouraged by Winston Churchill at the beginning of World War II. Nellie was a slow monster, weighing 130 tons and 80 feet long, advancing at half a mile per hour, excavating a trench 7 feet 6 inches wide. Since the war soon developed into campaigns of rapid movement, Nellie was not produced in quantity.

Additional Reading: Turner, *"Nellie": The History of Churchill's Lincoln Built Trenching Machine*, 1988; White, *British Tanks and Fighting Vehicles 1914–1945*, 1970.

Nelson Class
WARSHIP

The British *Nelson* class of **battleships** comprised the *Nelson* and *Rodney*, laid down in 1922 and completed in 1927. They were unusual in that their main armament of nine 16-inch guns was grouped forward in three triple turrets. This made them impossible to fire astern but allowed the overall reduction in vessel length required by the Washington Naval

Treaty. They displaced 33,300 tons, were 710 feet long, had a maximum armor of 14 inches, and a maximum speed of 23 knots.

The *Rodney* was involved in the final battle with *Bismarck* during which she fired 375 rounds from her big guns, inflicting 40 hits. She was not damaged by enemy fire, but damage caused by her own blast during this bombardment made repair work necessary. *Rodney* was scrapped in 1948. *Nelson* fought extensively in the Mediterranean and Far East, suffering damage from **sea mine** and **torpedo**. She survived to be used as a target ship in 1948 and was finally broken up in 1949.

Additional Reading: Raven and Roberts, *Battleships Rodney and Nelson*, 1979; Thompson, *HMS Rodney at War*, 1946.

New Jersey
WARSHIP

Completed in May 1943, the *New Jersey* was a U.S. **battleship** of the *Iowa* class and one of the most powerful ships afloat. She was soon engaged in the Pacific, at the Marshall Islands and Truk, demonstrating the immense range of her 16-inch guns by opening fire on the Japanese **destroyer** Nowake from the then-incredible range of 22 miles. Her later World War II actions included Okinawa and Iwo Jima. Involved in a collision with the U.S. destroyer *Franks*, she was soon back in action. During the Korean War the *New Jersey* made two tours of duty and was reactivated for Vietnam. After a period in reserve she was in action again off the Lebanon in 1983 and 1984. She was taken off the register in 1995.

Additional Reading: Stillwell, *Battleship New Jersey*, 1986; Turner, *USS New Jersey*, 1996; Sumrall, *Iowa Class Battleships*, 1988; Terzibaschitsch, *Battleships of the US Navy in World War II*, 1977.

New Orleans Class
WARSHIP

The *New Orleans* class of U.S. **cruisers** was laid down in the early 1930s and complete by 1937. The design was influenced by the realization that existing heavy cruisers were lacking in protection and that by shortening them the thickness of the armor belts could be increased.

Moreover they differed from each other in detail. As completed the seven ships of the class were 588 feet in length with a maximum armor of 5.25 inches. They mounted nine 8-inch guns, eight 5-inch, and eight .5-inch **machine guns**. Powered by Westinghouse turbines with eight boilers, they were capable of 32 knots. Modifications at the beginning of World War II included additional antiaircraft armament and the installation of **radar**.

New Orleans herself had a very eventful war. She was one of two heavy cruisers at Pearl Harbor during the Japanese attack but survived to fight in the Pacific. Following convoy duty she fought at the battles of the Coral Sea and Midway. At Tassafaronga she was hit in the magazine by a torpedo, which blew off her bow. Remarkably, she limped away for repair and was in the thick of the action again by late 1943. Her late war career included Saipan, Truk, and Leyte Gulf, where she participated in the sinking of the **aircraft carrier** *Chiyoda* and the **destroyer** *Hatsutsuki*. Put in reserve in 1947, she was sold for scrap in 1959.

Others in the class fought in the Pacific but had less charmed lives. *Astoria, Quincy*, and *Vincennes* were all sunk at Savo Island in August 1942. *Minneapolis*, also at Coral Sea and Midway, suffered damage similar to that of the *New Orleans* at Tassafaronga and was finally broken up for scrap in 1960. *Tuscaloosa* fought in the Atlantic and Mediterranean, covering the landings in North Africa and Normandy before joining the Pacific war, where she was at Iwo Jima. The *San Francisco* was under refit at Pearl Harbor on 7 December 1941 but suffered no additional damage. After actions at Wake, Huon Gulf, and the Eastern Solomons, she was badly damaged at Savo Island, returning to action again in early 1943. Thereafter she was constantly in the front line—at Wake, the Gilbert Islands, Saipan, Guam, the Bonin Islands, Iwo Jima, and elsewhere. After 1945 she served in China and Korea, being broken up in 1959.

Additional Reading: Friedman, *US Cruisers*, 1985; Terzibaschitsch, *Cruisers of the US Navy 1922–1962*, 1988.

Nibelung. *See* **Hydrophone**

Nick. *See* **Toryu**

Nieuport Scout Aircraft, XI, XVII, 28, etc.   AIRCRAFT

Designed by Gustave Delage, the Nieuport series of scout **aircraft** was a mainstay of the French air force in World War I, later serving with other Allied countries, notably the United Kingdom and Russia. The Nieuport XI biplane was derived from a civilian racing machine and was in use by the summer of 1915. Its maneuverability, **machine-gun** armament, and ability to carry rockets for attacking **balloons** was marred only by its propensity to break up in flight.

Nevertheless, the XI was an influential machine, inspiring both foreign imitators and the Nieuport XVII, which was first deployed in 1916. This model overcame many of the failings of its predecessor, being a relatively sturdy machine with a 110 horsepower engine giving a top speed of 106 mph. Its armament was two machine guns. The one mounted on the top wing was fitted on a Foster mount, which enabled the pilot to pull it back and down for reloading.

The Nieuport 28 was the first combat aircraft used by the United States during World War I. Among others, it was flown by ace Eddie Rickenbacker, who eventually achieved 26 victories. The 28 was powered by a 160 horsepower Gnome engine giving a top speed of 121 mph. It had a 26 foot 3 inch wingspan and two machine guns.

Additional Reading: Sanger, *Nieuport Aircraft of World War I*, 2002; Lowin, *Allied Aviation of World War I*, 2000.

Night Hawk. *See* **Stealth**

Nimitz, USS; *Nimitz* Class   WARSHIP

Chester W. Nimitz (1885–1966) was commander of the U.S. Pacific Ocean Area in World War II, eventually leading the biggest-ever U.S. naval force. He became Chief of Na-

The nuclear powered aircraft carrier USS *Nimitz*, founder of a new dynasty of super carriers which helped transform naval warfare. It is seen here crossing the Indian ocean in 1980. Courtesy of the Department of Defense.

val Operations, remaining until 1947. It is therefore fitting that the largest class of **aircraft carrier**, begun in 1968 with the *Nimitz* (CVN 68), should bear his name. The statistics associated with the nuclear-powered *Nimitz* class are astounding. The decks are approximately 1,030 feet in length, and the maximum number of aircraft carried is 89. It claimed that their range is a million nautical miles at 33 knots. Moreover, since the class has been 30 years in the building, there have been myriad changes and improvements over the years. Thus it is that the carriers of the class are not identical. The full list of *Nimitz*-type carriers in service in 2003 was: *Nimitz, Dwight D. Eisenhower, Carl Vinson, Theodore Roosevelt, Abraham Lincoln, George Washington,* **John C. Stennis, Harry S. Truman**, and *Ronald Reagan* (CVN 76).

Nipolit   EXPLOSIVE

Described in a secret document by Dr. von Holt in July 1944, Nipolit was a new German **explosive** developed at the Reinsdorfwerke of WASAG, the Westphalian and Anhalt explosives company. Potential use was seen for it as a projectile filling, engineer munitions, for bombs and rockets, and as a detonator.

It is said to have come about as an attempt to reuse old artillery propellant that was past its best. In the event, Nipolit was cheaper to produce and had the remarkable property of high mechanical strength. It was possible to cut and shape, and it was waterproof into the bargain. As a result it proved possible to manufacture Nipolit **grenades** that had no external casing, as well as preshaped fillings for **mines**, and other devices. It was used in the latter stages of the war but not fully exploited by May 1945.

NLE. *See* **Nellie**

Northampton **Class**   WARSHIP

The U.S. *Northampton* class of six **cruisers** was completed in the early 1930s. They displaced about 9,000 tons and were armed with nine 8-inch guns in triple turrets. Prior to World War II these ships were given much improved antiaircraft defense, and early in the war they received **radar**. War service included the *Northampton* itself fighting in the Pacific and supporting the Doolittle raid on Japan before being sunk in 1942. *Chicago* and *Houston* were also lost in action against the Japanese. *Louisville, Augusta, and Chester* survived the war.

Additional Reading: Friedman, *US Cruisers*, 1985.

General Leslie Groves and Dr. J. R. Oppenheimer examine the fragmentary remains of the tower on which an atomic test bomb was detonated in the New Mexico desert, 1945. Neither military technology, nor the world, would ever be the same again. Courtesy of the Library of Congress.

Nuclear, Thermonuclear, "Atomic" Weapons   NUCLEAR WARFARE

Fission, or the dividing of atoms to release energy, was discovered by German physicist Otto Hahn. By 1938 Hahn and Fritz Strassmann were able to demonstrate the principle using uranium-235. The fact that when the uranium was bombarded with neutrons it split, releasing more neutrons, suggested that a massive chain reaction was possible. The military potential was apparent. At about the same time that Nobel Prize–winning scientist Professor Werner Heisenberg returned to work in Germany in 1939, President Franklin D. Roosevelt established the American "Manhattan Project."

Fortunately, the German scientists were starved of "heavy water" and other necessary raw materials by bombing and guerrilla action, while the U.S. teams achieved success. A self-sustaining chain reaction was demonstrated in Chicago in 1942, and on 16 July 1945 scientists at Los Alamos New Mexico exploded the test bomb "Trinity." Within a month Hiroshima and Nagasaki were bombed, bringing the Second World War in the Far East to a conclusion. Thereafter there was a worldwide race to join the "nuclear club." In 1949 the Soviet Union tested its first bomb, the RDS-1, known as "Joe-1," to the Americans, after Joseph Stalin. The United Kingdom joined the nuclear club in 1952, with France, China, and India following by the 1970s. The discovery that fusion of atomic nuclei, as in a **hydrogen** bomb, could produce much greater power than fission produced a second-level nuclear race. The United States produced its first fusion bomb in 1952, a year before the Soviets.

Though difficult to achieve in practice without the right materials and manufacturing facilities, the basic theory of producing a nuclear detonation is not hugely complex. This was demonstrated in 1967 when a trio of new U.S. graduate physicists were set the task of designing a nuclear device using only published sources. In three years a plan was produced for a bomb that would have worked.

Initiation of the necessary chain reaction for a nuclear explosion relies on the production of a "critical mass" at the required moment. In gun-type devices, a small, or "subcritical," piece of fuel is fired into a larger amount; the two together exceed the critical mass. In implosion designs, conventional **explosives** are used to crush a hollow sphere of fissionable fuel to create a supercritical mass. Fusion requires extremely high temperatures, achieved using reflectors within the bomb to focus radiation pressure for perhaps a millionth of a second, crushing a cylinder of the fuel.

The destructive effects of a nuclear detonation are manifested in several ways: blast, thermal radiation, nuclear radiation, pulses of electrical and magnetic energy, and the creation of radioactive particles. Blast may reach 20 times normal pressure under a small air-bursting nuclear weapon, leveling reinforced concrete structures in a mile radius and creating winds of 500 miles per hour. Flying debris is likely to cause damage 12 miles away. The thermal radiation appears as heat and an enormous flash of light. The heat will kill those nearby, with first-degree burns up to seven miles from a one-megaton bomb. Burns will be worse on clear days, less serious when there is rain or smog. Flash blindness will often occur to observers farther away, up to 50 miles from a one-megaton burst, though these victims would probably recover their sight. Thermal radiation may well lead to combustion of objects and the starting of fires. In worst-case scenarios these may be of "firestorm" magnitude, with in rushing winds causing suffocation as well as burn and smoke casualties.

The electrical and magnetic pulse, or EMP, creates thousands of volts in a fraction of a second, damaging electrical equipment or causing power failures. (Later, similar theory has been directed toward the development of the "**microwave bomb**.") Direct nuclear radiation is intense but of limited range. Those close to a nuclear explosion, receiving a dose of 600 rem or more, are 90 percent likely to die within a few weeks. Doses of 50 rem or less are not usually fatal, but a small proportion of those effected may die prematurely of cancer in later years. Radioactive particles that rise as a result of the explosion return to earth as "fallout." Some is local and quick, some is borne by the wind, but some is likely to be stratospheric and may drop only years after the event. High doses will lead to sickness or death.

Official U.S. Congress studies postulating a one-megaton surface burst in Detroit suggest that about a quarter-million deaths and a half-million injuries would be caused as a result of one relatively small nuclear explosion. A 25 megaton air burst would cause over three million casualties, wiping almost all of Detroit from the map and filling every hospital bed in America, if the injured could be transported to them.

Though air-dropped bombs were the first nuclear weapons, the technology was quickly applied to other devices. Atomic cannon, **depth charges, torpedoes**, and missiles are just some of the possibilities. So it is that some smaller nuclear weapons have been regarded as "battlefield," naval, or tactical, intended to destroy armor, ships, or troops in the field. The "dirty bomb," suspected to be a potential terrorist weapon of the near future, is not a nuclear weapon in the strict sense. In dirty bombs, conventional explosives are used to spread radioactive material, thus contaminating cities and causing longer-term illness and disruption rather than a catastrophic explosion. Dirty bombs were investigated by Nazi scientists as early as World War II.

Additional Reading: Norris and Fowler, *NBC*, 1999; Office of Technology, *The Effects of Nuclear War*, 1980; Blackett, *Military and Political Consequences of Atomic Energy*, 1949; Cox, *Overkill*, 1977.

"Number 36." *See* **Mills Bomb**

O

O Class   SUBMARINE

Building on the experience gained from the **L class**, the U.S. Navy O-class **submarines** were oceangoing vessels; 16 were built in 1918. Built in two slightly differing subgroups, they were approximately 175 feet long and armed with four 18-inch **torpedo** tubes. The *0-12* saw post–World War I use with Wilkin's Arctic expedition, as *Nautilus*, while several were reused during World War II.

Oboe   MISCELLANEOUS

Developed by Alec Reeves at the British Telecommunications Research Establishment at Malvern in 1941, and in use from 1942, Oboe was a radar-based method of bomber **aircraft** navigation, particularly useful at night or in bad visibility. One **radar** post, known as the "Cat" station, ranged the known distance to the target, transmitting **Morse code** dots or dashes to inform the aircraft whether it was, quite literally, off the beam in either direction. A second, "Mouse," station, set at a distance from the Cat, signaled for bomb release when the intersection point of the Cat and Mouse transmissions was reached. The name Oboe arose from the fact that when the aircraft was flying along the center of the Cat beam it received a steady, reedy tone like the sound of that musical instrument.

Since Oboe required an attacking craft to follow a steady course, it was not particularly suitable for use with large bodies of heavy bombers, which might be intercepted or shot down by **flak**. It was therefore generally fitted to fast, high-flying aircraft like **Mosquitoes**, which would act as pathfinders by dropping flares. Large numbers of heavy bombers could then make their way to the target area by other routes and congregate where the target had been marked.

Oerlikon Gun   ARTILLERY

The Swiss Oerlikon company of Zurich is particularly associated with the production of **artillery**. A number of its best-known models have been quick-firing multibarrell antiaircraft weapons. During the latter part of the twentieth century these included the 25 mm Diana twin and the GBF-BOB twin dedicated trailer. The 20 mm GAI-BO1 was a single-barrel model that could be used against ground or air targets and had a claimed cyclic rate of 1,000 rounds a minute.

O'Higgins. *See* **General O'Higgins**

Ohio Class   SUBMARINE

The largest **submarines** in the U.S. Navy at the beginning of the twenty-first century are the *Ohio*-class strategic missile submarines, displacing approximately 17,000 tons. They are the primary U.S. strategic deterrent. *Ohio* (SSBN 726) was the first to be launched, in 1979, and there are now 18 such vessels in service. With the exception of the *Henry M. Jackson*, all bear the name of states. All have been built at General Dynamics, at Groton, Connecticut.

The main armament is 24 Lockheed **Trident** missiles with multiple thermonuclear warheads. It is claimed that the latest of these are accurate to within 90 meters. The *Ohio* class is also equipped with 4 21-inch Mk 68 **torpedoes**. The *Ohio*s are 560 feet long with a top speed of 24 knots and a complement of 155. Under the Strategic Arms Reduction Treaty it is expected that the force will be reduced to 14 vessels by 2007.

Additional Reading: Saunder's (ed), *Jane's Fighting Ships 2001–2002*, 2001.

Ohka Piloted Bomb EXPLOSIVE DEVICE

The Japanese Ohka, or "Cherry Blossom," piloted bomb of 1944 took the form of a small midwinged monoplane with alloy fuselage and wooden wings. Propelled by three rockets and equipped with simple controls, Ohka could be towed or carried to the target area prior to release. The craft exploded on impact. Other names applied to this weapon included Jinrai ("divine thunderbolt") and the Allied expression "Baka," or idiot bomb. A Kawanishi Baika, or "Plum Blossom," piloted bomb, based on a **V1** design was not completed.

Additional Reading: O'Neill, *Suicide Squads of World War II*, 1988.

Oliver Hazard Perry Class WARSHIP

The *Oliver Hazard Perry* class of **frigates** is the most numerous class of fighting vessel in the U.S. Navy. Some 35 were in service in 2002, having been commissioned in the decade 1979 to 1989. Displacing about 3,000 tons with a crew of 200, this type carries **Harpoon** missiles, a 3-inch gun, **torpedoes**, and two **helicopters**. Their range is about 4,500 miles, with a top speed of 29 knots. It is intended that these frigates will be eventually be replaced by the *Zumwalt* class.

Omaha Class WARSHIP

The U.S. *Omaha* class of ten **cruisers** were planned as early as 1917 but was completed in the mid-1920s. Relatively light at 7,050 tons, they had powerful machinery, with 12 boilers in four firerooms giving good speed. They had 12 6-inch guns and were distinctive in that four of the guns were grouped in forward case-

mates for maximum frontal fire. They were also well armed with **torpedoes**. The class saw extensive war service, with *Omaha* herself intercepting several blockade runners. *Milwaukee* was transferred to the Soviet Union as the *Murmansk*—remarkably, being handed back to the United States in 1949.

Oneida. See **Brigantine**

Ontos VEHICLE

Developed in the 1950s and used by the Marines from 1956, Ontos was a novel U.S. lightweight tracked vehicle designed to pack maximum punch in minimum space. The name was Greek for "the thing"—and the thing was air mobile. Essentially it was six 106 mm **recoilless** rifles, atop a nine-ton armored carrier, 12 feet 6 inches long, crewed by three men. The armament could be traversed up to 40 degrees on later models, but if reloading was required it had to be done from outside the vehicle. Two of the weapons could be dismounted to use separately. Ontos saw service in Vietnam until 1969. Though relatively few were made, some examples remain, including one each at Rock Island Arsenal and Aberdeen Proving Ground.

Additional Reading: Zaloga and Loop, *Modern American Armor*, 1985.

Oropesa Sweep MINE SYSTEM

Developed in 1919, the Oropesa sweep was a rope covered in serrated wire, with cutter devices at intervals, designed to be dragged through the sea. A "kite" kept the rope at the desired depth, while a wooden "otter" kept it away from the towing ship's stern. The intention was to cut the mooring cables of sea **mines**, allowing them to float free to the surface. Here they could be detonated by **rifle** fire or otherwise disposed. The method saw most use during World War II, being common to both the U.S. and Royal Navies.

Additional Reading: Elliott, *Allied Minesweeping*, 1979.

Oscar Class   SUBMARINE

The first huge Soviet Oscar-class nuclear-powered **submarines** were laid down in the late 1970s, and the first two, *Archangelsk* and *Murmansk*, were in service in the early 1980s. Intended to oppose **aircraft carrier** battle groups, these vast tublike submarines were equipped with a range of nuclear missiles and **torpedoes**. In 1985 the first boat of the Oscar II series appeared. These were even mightier, being 505 feet long and 60 feet in the beam, displacing 13,900 tons on the surface. Their armament would eventually comprise 24 SS-N-19 Shipwreck cruise missiles, Starfish antisubmarine weapons, and **depth charges** or torpedoes. In a minelaying role 32 sea **mines** would be carried instead of torpedoes. The main armament was held in 12 pairs of tubes, inclined to the side and outside the pressure hull. Eleven Oscar II submarines were completed, and a twelfth was commenced. The best known of these was the ill-fated *Kursk*. Most of the Oscars have now been decommissioned.

Additional Reading: *Jane's Warships*; Jordan, *Soviet Submarines*, 1989.

Osprey, V-22   AIRCRAFT

The U.S. vertical-lift Osprey V-22 is one of the most unusual military aircraft. Developed by Bell Helicopter Textron and **Boeing** Vertol in the 1980s, it is a "tilt-rotor" design. Turboshaft engines on each wingtip can be swiveled through about 98 degrees. When they point upward the Osprey can fly in **helicopter** mode; when swung down horizontally the propellers face to the front, and the craft operates as a twin-engine aircraft. With a top speed of 316 mph and a weight carrying capacity of 12,000 lb the Oprey is particularly useful for the transport of assault troops, special forces or stores.

Overland Train   VEHICLE

Claimed as the longest military vehicle, the USATRECOM experimental overland train was built by R. G. LeTourneau of Longview, Texas, in 1962. It was powered by gas turbines, driving generators, which in turn powered 54 electric wheels. The total length was 572 feet. Its segmented units comprised a control car, two power generator cars, and ten 15-ton cargo carriers.

P

P17. *See* Winchester

P-26 Peashooter   AIRCRAFT

This all-metal P-26 single-seat fighter **aircraft** was a **Boeing** design that first flew in March 1932. Ordered for the U.S. Army, it was acknowledged for its speed and maneuverability. With a 28-foot wingspan and a 600 horsepower Wasp engine, the P-26 was capable of 234 mph. The armament was two **machine guns** and a bomb load up to 200 lb. Though outclassed by World War II, it saw action and was supplied to the Chinese and other countries.

P-36. *See* Curtiss

P38 "Pistole." *See* Walther

P-38. *See* Lightning

P-39. *See* Airacobra

P-40. *See* Curtiss

P-47. *See* Thunderbolt

P-51. *See* Mustang

P-59. *See* Airacomet

P-61. *See* Black Widow

P-63. *See* Airacobra

P-82. *See* Mustang

PACV. *See* Hovercraft

PAK (PaK)   ARTILLERY

The German acronym PAK—*Panzer Abwehr Kanon*, literally "**tank** defense gun"—has been applied to many pieces of antitank **artillery** since the interwar period. Generally, though not exclusively, long barreled and having a high muzzle velocity, they have been well adapted to armor piercing. Significant examples have included the 3.7 cm Pak 35/36, also used by Finland and Turkey and manufactured under licence in the Soviet Union; the 5 cm Pak 38; the 7.5 cm PaK 40; and the **88 mm** PaK 43. The term remains in current usage for antitank guns.

Paladin, M109   ARTILLERY

Manufactured by United Ground Defense, the M109 Paladin is the current 155 mm self-propelled **howitzer** fielded by the U.S. Army. Mounted on a fully tracked hull, the Paladin is powered by a 440 horsepower diesel engine and is capable of 40 mph maximum. The M284 cannon is in a rotating turret and can fire up to eight rounds per minute. The crew is six men. It had been intended that the Paladin would be replaced by a new system called Crusader, but this program was terminated in 2002.

***Pampanito*, USS**   SUBMARINE

The USS *Pampanito* (SS 383) is a *Balao*-class **submarine** built during World War II. She undertook six Pacific patrols, during which she sank six Japanese ships. Recently restored, she is moored at Pier 45 on San Francisco's Fisherman's Wharf, where she is one of the most popular historic vessels in the United States.

Panhard   VEHICLE

The French Panhard company first received orders for **armored cars** as early as 1911. Yet it did not achieve any prominence in the field until the late 1920s, when it built the 175 model, used by French forces in Morocco. The 175 was conventional in that it used a passenger car chassis, but in 1935 the company produced the AMD 178, which was constructed entirely from scratch as a military vehicle. More than 360 of this neat turreted design were in use by May 1940, and many were later used by the Germans. A big-wheeled, nine-ton model 201 was only in prototype at this time but gave a significant lead to postwar development.

The work of Panhard recommenced in 1945, leading to the innovative Type 212, also known as the EBR 75 Modèle 1951, which was produced throughout the 1950s. Key features of this eight-wheeler included a hull only just over a meter high and a flat 12-cylinder engine mounted low in the center of the floor. On roads the middle wheels could be lifted clear of the ground when not needed. There were driving positions at both ends of the vehicle, obviating the need to turn round. The welded steel turret held a 75 mm gun, which was autoloaded on late models.

Many more models would follow. Prominent among them were the AML, produced in different variants (including missile and personnel carriers) as well as more conventional turreted types, and the VBL.

Panther Tank   TANK

The German Panther, or **Panzer** V, was one of the best tanks of the Second World War. Heavily influenced by the **T-34**, the MAN-designed Panther appeared as a trials model in September 1942. Being rushed into manufacture it had initial problems, and production levels were never enough to counter the Allied outpouring of armor, but the Panther was ultimately superior to the T-34 in all respects. Frontal protec-

tion was 120 mm of well sloped armor, and the Maybach V-12 engine gave a road speed of up to 30 mph. The long-barrel KwK 42 L/70 gun was capable of penetrating 120 mm armor at over 1,000 yards. The suspension, with its interleaved bogie wheels and sprung torsion bars, was excellent. Later models were improved and simplified to ease production. If the Panther had a weakness it was its complexity and cost; even so about 5,000 had been made by the end of the war. A **tank destroyer** variant was also built.

Additional Reading: Feist and Culver, *Panther*, 1998; Doyle, *Panther Variants 1942–1945*, 1997; Hughes and Mann, *The Panther Tank*, 2000.

Panzer; Panzer I, II, III, IV   TANK

Meaning "**armor**," the German word *panzer* was soon adopted to refer to **tanks**. *Panzerkampfwagen* (PzKpfw) is thus a literal translation of "armored fighting vehicle." Though an **A7V** tank had been produced during World War I, "panzers" are commonly thought of as the series of German tanks that commenced in the 1930s and continued to 1945.

Prototypes were ordered as early as 1926, in contravention of the Treaty of Versailles. The resulting tanks were tested in the Soviet Union under the cover designation of heavy and light "tractors." Experimental heavy tanks, then called *Neubaufahrzeug*, were also constructed as early as 1933. What was later built in quantity as the Panzer I was first tested at Kummersdorf the same year and approved by Hitler in 1934. This vehicle, apparently inspired by the small tracked carriers of the day, consisted of a **Krupp** chassis, with a Daimler-Benz superstructure and turret. Its armament was a pair of MG13 **machine guns**. With a crew of two, it was lightly armored and capable of about 23 mph on roads. In action in Spain in 1936, it was still in frontline service as late as 1941, and it also formed the base for a number of gun mountings.

The Panzer II was in production by 1935. Marginally better protected with up to 30 mm of armor, it was armed with a 2 cm gun as well as a machine gun and had a crew of three. Radios were usually fitted, and the maximum speed was 25 mph. The much superior Panzer III appeared in prototype in 1936 and was in service by 1939, forming the backbone of the German tank forces during the campaigns of 1940. At 18 feet in length it was five feet longer than the diminutive Panzer I and, having a larger turret ring, was capable of mounting a variety of armament during its service life. The original 3.7 cm gun was soon exchanged for a 5 cm gun, and later in the war, when the Panzer III chassis was used as a base for the turretless *Sturmgeschutz*, or **assault gun**, 75 mm and 105 mm guns were mounted. Nevertheless, the Panzer III was no match for up-to-date tanks like the **T-34**.

The Panzer IV was the only German tank to be in continuous production throughout World War II. Larger than the Panzer III, it was similar in general layout and had a crew of five; a V-12 diesel engine of 300 horse power gave a top speed of 25 mph. Unlike the Panzer III, it had an electric motor to traverse the turret. Originally mounting a low-velocity 7.5 cm gun for support duties, it was later fitted with long-barrel weapons for tank-to-tank battle. An even more powerful KwK 40 L/48 was fitted in 1943. Though a sound design, the Panzer IV was soon being challenged both by new Soviet vehicles and the **Sherman**. As a result new models were ever more heavily armored—extra plates, side skirts, and spaced plates around the turret being just some of the additions. By the end of the war production of the Panzer IV was well over 8,000, and there were also many assault-gun and **self-propelled-gun** variants. Remarkably, the Panzer IV was still in service with Syria as late as 1967.

The last of the Panzers were the V and VI, though these are better known by the names **Panther**, **Tiger**, and King Tiger. The panzers were all good fighting vehicles at the times of their introduction, yet it has to be said that their successes were as much due to tactics as technology. Until late 1941 it was the imaginative use of the panzer division, acting as a combined and concentrated unit of all arms, rather than any individual type of tank that made "blitz-krieg" warfare possible.

Additional Reading: Chamberlain and Doyle, *Encyclopaedia of German Tanks of World War II*, 1993; Schiebert, *Panzer*, 1990; Guderian, *Achtung-Panzer*, Aberdeen Proving Ground, *Tank Data*, (undated); Gudgin, *Armoured Firepower: The Development of Tank Armament 1939–1945*, 1997; War Department, *Handbook on German Military Forces*, 1945; School of Tank Technology, *Preliminary Report No.10. German Pz.Kw.I.*, 1943; Duncan, *Panzerkampfwagen I and II*.

Panzerfaust (Klein, 60, 150, 3, etc.)
ANTITANK WEAPON

The innovative German Panzerfaust ("tank fist") was a crudely simple but highly effective one-shot handheld antitank weapon. Development by HASAG commenced during 1942, and by November the short-bodied experimental *Faustpatrone* had been devised. A total of 350,000 of the first model of the Panzerfaust, the "Klein" (small), were made during 1943. Key to the weapon were two ideas: the **hollow-charge** warhead, which gave great penetrative power; and the very simple launch tube, which was relatively small in diameter.

Once the safety was removed and the weapon was pointed at the tank, a simple snap mechanism was operated. This set off a charge of black powder that launched the finned projectile from the tube. The hollow tube directed the great gout of exhaust gas and flame away behind the firer, making the Panzerfaust recoilless. The missile exploded on impact. Though the Panzerfaust was short range, only 30 to 200 meters depending on the model, its destructive impact was massive. The Panzerfaust Klein could break 140 mm of armor, while the final production type, the Panzerfaust 150, could cut through 200 mm. This was adequate to go through the turret of a **Sherman** and out the other side.

While Allied tanks had a healthy respect of the Panzerfaust, production of which reached a staggering 1,253,000 in the month of November 1944 alone, it required almost suicidal courage to use effectively. The Panzerfaust influenced the design of several postwar antitank weapons, including the West German Panzerfaust 3, developed in the 1980s. This was a somewhat more sophisticated weapon that employed the Davies countermass principle to allow firing in enclosed areas. Armor penetration now claimed was a remarkable 700 mm.

Additional Reading: Fleischer, *Panzerfaust*, 1994; Martin and Hitchins, *Development of the Panzerfaust*, 1945; *Jane's Infantry Weapons*; Weeks, *Men against Tanks*, 1975.

Panzerjäger. *See* **Tank Destroyer**

Panzerschreck   ANTITANK WEAPON

Meaning literally "tank terror," the German World War II Panzerschreck shoulder-fired antitank weapon was inspired by the **bazooka**. Though known more properly as the "8.8 cm Raketen Panzerbuchse," it was sometimes called the "Ofenrohr," due to its resemblance to a stove pipe. First issued in 1943, it fired a **hollow-charge** rocket projectile to an effective range of about 150 meters and could penetrate about 100 mm of armor.

Parachute   MISCELLANEOUS

The word "parachute" derives from the Italian, *parare*, to protect and the French, *chute*, to fall. Parachutes make possible safe descents through the air by means of their large surface area, which increases air resistance, slowing the fall of a person or object. The idea is of uncertain antiquity, being ascribed to various persons including, Leonardo da Vinci. The earliest parachutes were kept permanently open, or partially open, limiting problems with deployment. As early as 1691 Simon de la Loubère described parachutes, or "umbrellas," being used in "great leaps" to provide entertainment at the court of Siam. André Jaques Garnerin (1769–1823) made the first parachute jump from a **balloon** in Paris in 1797. The first recorded emergency escape using the device was by Pole Jordaki Kuparento in 1808, when his balloon caught fire. The traditional parachute canopy resembled a portion of a sphere, or cone, made in sections of light, strong natural material, such as silk. Nylon and rayon canopies appeared dur-

A parachutist steers his canopy towards a precision landing at the Andrews Air Force Base "Open House," 1981. Courtesy of the Department of Defense.

ing World War II, as did the increasing use of such alternative shapes as oblongs and triangles.

Military parachuting developed primarily as a method of exit from balloons, observers being issued with them during World War I to escape the threat of fighter **aircraft**. The main type of the period was the "Guardian Angel," which was stowed in a tube and attached to the user by a single rope and harness. As the parachutist fell, his weight pulled the canopy from the sleeve. Parachutes were later adapted for aircraft escape. Italian experiment with troops deliberately dropped from aircraft commenced in 1927, using the Salvatore parachute. This was packed on the jumper's back and opened by means of a static line attached to the aircraft. It was relatively quick and reliable, being possible to operate at relatively low altitudes. It suffered, however, from a lack of more than one suspension point and its tendency to leave the user dangling face downward.

Russia was in the forefront in the 1930s; there were 1,300 parachute clubs in the Soviet

Union by 1935, and battalion-sized units were dropped by 1936. Early Russian military experiments included square canopies and the use of rip cords operated by the jumper to deploy the parachute, but these required both greater height and greater skill on the part of the user. Another problem encountered was the lack of suitable aircraft for parachute jumping. In the slow-moving ANT-6 aircraft parachute troops were forced to climb out onto the wing, sliding off on the signal given by a jumpmaster, who stood up, facing rearward, in a forward pulpit. The Russians also pioneered a variety of drop containers, with and without parachutes.

At the same time, Germany began to use the static line–deployed RZ 1 parachute, but complaints of lack of stability led to the adoption of the RZ 16 and finally the RZ 20, which remained standard until 1945. The main German parachute aircraft was the **Junkers** 52, from which the jumper exited through a side door, adopting a spread-eagled position. The parachutes of the Western Allies, developed slightly later, were arguably better. In 1940, on the suggestion of Raymond Quilter, the British developed a parachute that combined an Irvin-type air-crew canopy with rigging lines that paid out before the main deployment. The system also employed a fine line to pull the canopy out to its full length before opening. The Statichute, or X type, proved to be an influential design.

Modern U.S. parachute troop development began in 1940 with a 48-man test troop under Major William Lee at Fort Benning, moving to New Jersey, where there were 250-foot jump towers available. The first parachute was the T-4, an Irvin design with a three-hook harness and a large square backpack. A feature unusual in other countries at this time, but later common, was the use of a reserve parachute worn on the front. The T-7 parachute came into use in 1941 and was remarkable in that it was effective in even very low altitude deployments.

There have been many new uses for parachutes since 1945. "Low level extraction" of stores from aircraft was extensively researched in the early 1960s as a way of delivering accurately without landing, so that nothing would fall into enemy hands. The first systems used fixed wires and hooks but were unreliable and potentially very dangerous. The U.S. Army Lolex system used a small extraction parachute, which was deployed during a low-level run, thus pulling the container from the plane. The U.S. Air Force version, LAPES, or Low Altitude Parachute Extraction System, was similar but used a larger parachute.

Military parachuting itself has been improved in numerous ways—new materials, new parachute shapes, and transport aircraft with large rear doors being most obvious. In HALO jumps, troops exit high and open their parachutes low.

Additional Reading: Lucas, *The Silken Canopy: A History of the Parachute*, 1997; Weeks, *Airborne Equipment: A History of its Development*, 1976; Richards, *World War II Troop Type Parachutes*, 2000.

Parasite. *See* **Goblin**

Paris Guns, Paris Kanonen, Wilhelmgeschutze ARTILLERY

The ultra-long-range, or Paris, gun was one of the outstanding technological achievements of the First World War. Even before German armies marched into France and Belgium, the **Krupp** company had given consideration to increasing the range of artillery projectiles by means of slender, pointed nose caps on shells to reduce drag. By 1916 von Eberhard was suggesting that heavy guns could be given extra-long rang by means of a sabbotted, spin-stabilized, subcaliber ammunition.

In the event, the final idea, worked out with Professor Dr. Fritz Rausenberger (1868–1926) and presented to Hindenburg and Ludendorff by Colonel Bauer (1869–1929) of the General Staff, was a simpler but equally radical alternative. The proposal was to take a 38 cm "Long Max" gun, line a much-extended barrel with a 21 cm insert, and blast the low-drag 106 kg projectile out with a charge of approximately 195 kg of C/12 propellant. The scheme for monster cannon was approved, and following range testing at Altenwalde in 1917, firing positions for three "Wilhelmgeschutze" were prepared at Crépy, west of Laon. The plan was to provide a support for, and diversion from, the 1918 spring offensive. On 22 March the Kaiser inspected the pieces, and firing on Paris commenced at a range of 120 km (70 miles). The shells were in flight for about two minutes before impact. Some 351 rounds were fired, the dropping of large shells on the French capital being at first interpreted by the inhabitants as the work of an aircraft.

Breech pressures in excess of 4,200 atmospheres caused catastrophic wear, repeated range calculations, and frequent barrel changes, but the Paris guns led directly to new areas of scientific and technological endeavour. Years later they would provide inspiration for Project Harp and the Iraqi "**supergun**."

Additional Reading: Bull and Murphy, *Paris Kanonen: The Paris Guns (Wilhelmgeschütze) and Project Harp*, 1988.

PATA   VEHICLE

One of the most bizarre experimental military vehicles of modern times was the U.S. "Pneumatic All Terrain Amphibian," or PATA, developed by Ling Temco Vought in 1965. Key to the concept were Firestone air-cell tracks; these were effectively a **tank**-type track consisting of a series of bloated cells on which the vehicle could ride across most surfaces. The ground pressure created was little more than a pound per square inch, and the PATA could manage up to 35 mph on good ground, 10 mph in water.

Patriot Missile   MISSILE

The U.S. Patriot missile system, produced by Lockheed Martin and Raytheon, is designed to deal with missiles and **aircraft**. It was used in the Gulf War of 1991 with only mixed results, though its deployment was one of the factors that helped prevent the war from spreading. The major components of the system are a **radar**; the "Engagement Control Station," or ECS, where the operators and computers are based; and the missile containers. The containers hold from six to eight missiles. Each five-meter-long

rocket-propelled missile has a range of over 100 km and is computer guided in flight.

Work to improve the Patriot is ongoing. The first of the Patriot Advanced Capability 2, with an enhanced guidance system, was delivered in 1995. The latest model under test is the smaller PAC-3, or Patriot Advanced Capability 3, launches of which were conducted in 2001 and 2002.

Patton Tank, M47   TANK

Named after General George Patton (1885–1945), the U.S. Patton M47 medium **tank** was developed in some haste at the beginning of the Korean War. It married together the turret of the experimental T42 with the hull of the existing **Pershing** to make a surprisingly successful vehicle. Though intended as an interim measure, a total of 8,676 were made by 1953, and a good number were sold to NATO countries. Iran also built an improved version, the **M47M**, in the early 1970s. The Patton weighed 48.6 tons, with a maximum armor of 112 mm and a 90 mm gun. The Continental 810 horsepower engine gave a maximum speed of 30 mph. It was succeeded by the **M48**.

Paveway Bomb. *See* **Smart Bomb**

Peabody Rifle   FIREARM

Invented by H. O. Peabody early in the American Civil War, the single-shot U.S. Peabody **rifle** was notable for its breechblock mechanism, which pivoted at the rear. A groove on top of the block guided the **cartridge** down into the correct position when loading. The Peabody had similarities with the Bavarian Werder and the **Martini Henry**.

Peashooter. *See* **P-26**

Pedersen Device. *See* **Assault Rifle**

Percussion Cap; Percussion Ignition
                              IGNITION SYSTEM

As long ago as the seventeenth century it was realized that certain chemical compounds would explode when struck. Initially this interesting property of metal fulminates proved difficult to harness for any practical purpose, due to accidental explosions. However, in 1807 the Reverend Alexander J. Forsyth (1768–1843) patented a gun lock in which a small container, shaped like a scent bottle, was rotated to deposit a few grains of fulminate. A hammer, worked by the trigger, then snapped down to set off this priming charge, which set off the main charge of the gun in the normal way. The system had the advantage of being quick; also, no flints and sparks were required.

Within twenty years many new methods had been devised to achieve the same result with the minimum of human intervention and the maximum reliability. Tube locks and pellet locks confined the fulminate in different ways, while tape primers contained measured amounts within a paper tape. Yet by far the most widely adopted military system would be the percussion cap. The metal cap, shaped like a minute top hat, contained a small charge of fulminate. Once the soldier had loaded his weapon with powder and ball, all he had to do was set a cap on the "nipple" of the gun lock. Pulling the trigger dropped the hammer on the cap, which detonated. Its explosion was communicated to the main charge down a hole through the center of the nipple.

By the middle of the nineteenth century, percussion **muskets** and **rifles** were the soldier's main arm. Particularly well known were the **Minié** rifle and Brunswick rifle. Many flintlocks such as U.S. **Springfield** muskets were also converted to the percussion system.

Additional Reading: Blair, *Pollard's History of Firearms*, 1983; Hoyem, *History and Development of Small Arms Ammunition*, 1981; Durdik, *Firearms*, 1981.

Periscope Rifle. *See* **Hyposcope**

Permit. See **Thresher**

Pershing Tank, M26   TANK

The M26 rose from the need for U.S. **tanks** with more powerful guns to take on German tanks like the **Tiger**. The M26 mounted a healthy 90 mm, had 110 mm armor, and was capable of 30 mph. Though 1,436 were produced by the end of World War II, few saw combat until the Korean War.

Additional Reading: Thiel, *The M26 Pershing and Variants*, 2002; Zalgoda and Loop, *Modern American Armor*, 1985.

Personnel Detector, Chemical   DETECTION

Popularly known as the "people sniffer," the U.S. Manpack Personnel Detector, Chemical was a device that saw limited use in the Vietnam war. It consisted of a backpack containing the processor unit and a tube with a probe, which could be fitted to the end of a **rifle**. It was supposed to detect a concealed enemy from the ammonia in his perspiration. In practice it detected many things, including dung, and was therefore unsatisfactory. However the idea was a useful one, and the personnel detector was a step on the way to more efficient devices, including some for finding **explosives** and drugs.

"Perspective" Glass. *See* **Telescope**

Petard   EXPLOSIVE DEVICE

A petard is an **explosive** device for demolition and blasting gates. In regular use in siege warfare by the seventeenth century, it usually took the form of a pot-shaped container of **gunpowder** mounted on a wooden board. Once it was attached to the target, the engineer lit the **fuse** and retired.

The term "petard" was later revived to describe the large projectiles shot from the short-barrel guns of engineer and assault tanks to destroy fortifications.

Additional Reading: Wagner, *European Weapons and Warfare, 1618–1648*, 1979.

Phalanx. *See* **Spear**

Phalanx, Close-In Weapon System

ARTILLERY

First produced in 1979, the U.S. ship-mounted General Dynamics Phalanx system consists of a 20 mm **Gatling**-type cannon with fire control **radar**. Its purpose is to home in on and shoot down any missiles coming near to the ship. Early models had a healthy 3,000 rounds-per-minute rate of fire, since increased to 4,500 by means of pneumatic gun drive. A similar 30 mm Goalkeeper system has been developed in conjunction with the Dutch Hollandse Signaalapparaten company.

Phantom, F-4

AIRCRAFT

The twin-engine U.S. F-4 Phantom, a two-seat jet fighter **aircraft** first flew in 1958. Originally designed to meet U.S. Navy requirements for a fleet defense interceptor for **aircraft carrier** operations, it was later used by the Marines in ground support and by the U.S. Air Force. It was also widely flown around the world, with the United Kingdom, Germany, Japan, and South Korea being just some of the users. By the end of production in 1979 over 5,000 had been made, the vast majority by **McDonnell Douglas** in St. Louis, a few by Mitsubishi.

Early in its career the Phantom was a record breaker, setting world records for altitude, speed, and low-altitude speed. Yet the aircraft was no prima donna; it won 280 air-to-air combats in Vietnam and the Gulf, and it was widely regarded as both versatile and reliable. Regular updates to **radar** and weaponry kept the type current for four decades, and a few are still expected to be flying in 2015. The Phantom FGR.2 (F4-M), which appeared in 1967, was powered by two Rolls-Royce Spey turbofans, giving a top speed of 1,386 mph, a climb of up to 32,000 feet in a minute, and a range of 1,750 miles. Its possible armament included Sky Flash, **Sparrow**, and **Sidewinder** missiles, as well as a 20 mm rotary cannon.

It is worth noting that the F-4 was not the first U.S. McDonnell jet fighter to bear the name "Phantom." In 1943 the U.S. Navy had requested a jet fighter capable of operation from carriers, and an FH-1 design had flown in 1945.

Though contracts were canceled a few were built in 1947 and 1948 and saw limited use, being later overtaken by more modern turbojets.

Additional Reading: Thornborough and Davies, *The Phantom Story*, 2000; Sgarlato, *Aircraft of the USAF*, 1978; Donald and Lake, *U.S. Navy and Marine Corps Air Power Directory*, 1992.

Phoenix. See **General Belgrano**

Phoenix Missile

MISSILE

The U.S. long-range Phoenix missile was ultimately used with the F-14 **Tomcat**. The concept was initiated as early as 1960, with Hughes selected as prime contractor in 1962. Test-firing commenced in 1965. With **radar** guidance, the Phoenix was an air-to-air weapon with a range of about 90 miles, though over the years performance has been continually improved. Its main purpose is to hit enemy bombers before they are close enough to strike.

Additional Reading: *Jane's Weapons Systems.*

Phosgene

CHEMICAL WARFARE

Phosgene, otherwise known as carbonyl chloride, or CG, was used as a **gas** and caused a majority of the chemical warfare casualties of World War I. It appears to have been identified as a potential weapon simultaneously by several powers during early 1915, but it was first employed by the Germans that December. Smelling like new-mown grass, phosgene was more effective than **chlorine** because it was both more lethal and less obvious, and since it did not cause immediate spasms of the glottis, it could be absorbed in large quantities. It attacked the lungs, but its full effects were delayed, so men might discover that they had been badly "gassed" only three or more hours after exposure. The main drawback of phosgene as a weapon was that it was a light gas, relatively easily dissipated. For this reason the British mixed it with the heavier chlorine to produce "White Star."

Though it has similar properties and virtually identical effects when ingested, diphosgene, or DP, is different chemically, being trichloromethyl chloroformate. It has the advantage of a higher boiling point; it is easier to handle and more suitable for shell filling. As it has a slight tear-gas effect, it is not so useful as a surprise weapon.

Additional Reading: Richter, *Chemical Soldiers*, 1992; Haber, *The Poisonous Cloud*, 1986.

PIAT   ANTITANK WEAPON

The British Projector Infantry Anti-Tank, or PIAT was inspired by Colonel Blacker, who was responsible for the Blacker **Bombard**. In 1941 a "baby" version of this was worked on by Major M. R. Jeffries and paired with a **hollow-charge** bomb. The rough-looking result, approved in August 1942, was a metal monstrosity with a huge spring that threw the bomb out of a small trough and set off its propellant, blasting it at the enemy. The PIAT was something of a work of desperation, but it did account for some enemy tanks, including on one occasion two **Tiger** tanks destroyed by one man. It also had some use as a "house breaker."

Additional Reading: War Office (UK), *Small Arms Training; Projector Infantry Anti-Tank*, 1943; Hogg, *Infantry Weapons of World War II*, 1977.

Pillbox   FORTIFICATION

"Pillbox" is a common term for a small **fortification**, and (as in the case of the military pillbox hat) arises due to supposed resemblances to medicine containers. In the twentieth century, pillboxes were commonly of concrete and had openings, or embrasures, for weapons. The direct ancestor of the modern pillbox is the blockhouse, a type of small fortification that was in vogue for many years but came to prominence during the war in South Africa, c. 1900, when the veldt was divided with defensive lines to protect against Boer commandos.

In Europe, the pillbox became important from 1915, when the Germans in particular started to use concrete works as part of the western front. German stand-alone concrete works were often referred to as "MEBUs," an acronym for *Mannschafts Eisenbeton Unterstande*, or literally, "reinforced concrete personnel dugouts." Commonly housing a garrison with one or more **machine-gun** teams, such structures helped produce a weblike frontline defense of individual posts, which by mid-1917 was becoming more important than continuous trench lines in many sectors. Where possible the Allies adopted similar ideas. By 1918 their lines included pillboxes like the cylindrical Moir type, with its block construction and steel lid, and the Australian Hobbs, with its small revolving steel cupola. Arguably the most influential pillbox design was the British GHQ line model, which was hexagonal, flat roofed, and had gun slits.

Pillboxes of various types would become a common feature of war. They would be famously incorporated into the **Maginot Line**, the German **Atlantic Wall**, and Japanese Pacific strongholds, where log bunkers and natural materials would be particularly important. Other small machine-gun pillboxes of World War II would include the British Tett turret and the German "Tobruk" machine-gun emplacement. Though often regarded as too slow to build and too inflexible for the modern battlefield, pillboxes have continued to have a role in fixed defenses particularly at airfields and other military installations.

Additional Reading: Wills, *Pillboxes*, 1985; Oldham, *Pill Boxes of the Western Front*, 1995.

Pilum. *See* **Spear**

Pink Panther. *See* **Land Rover**

Pistol   FIREARM

Pistols are commonly defined as small firearms capable of being held and fired by one hand. They are therefore relatively light to carry, easy to conceal, and a useful weapon of last resort. Conversely they are often inaccurate at all but very close range, and having short barrels, are prone to accident. These characteristics have tended to define the role of the military pistol as a back up to other arms, or a weapon of surprise, especially useful for confined spaces.

Early ignition systems required both hands, and the **matchlock** needed a burning match—both factors ill suited to the development of pistols. It was not therefore until the sixteenth century that **wheel lock** pistols became important military arms, primarily with the cavalry. Thereafter **flint** and **percussion** locks were similarly applied. In the latter nineteenth century the widespread use of **revolvers**, and the work of **Colt** and others with mass production techniques were significant advances. Yet by the close of the nineteenth century **semi automatics** were steadily gaining ground. By World War I **Luger** and **Browning** were household names. Other significant inventors and manufacturers of military pistols have included **Astra; Fabrique Nationale; Webley; Lahti; Walther; Beretta** and **Sig-Sauer**.

Additional Reading: Blair, *Pollard's History*, 1983; Myatt, *Illustrated Encyclopedia of Pistols and Revolvers*, 1980; Taylorson, *The Revolver*, 1970.

Platz, Reinhold. *See* **Fokker**

PLUTO   MISCELLANEOUS

Described by General Eisenhower as "second only in daring to the [**Mulberry**] artificial harbors," the PLUTO pipelines were laid from the United Kingdom to fuel the Normandy beachhead after D-Day in 1944. PLUTO was an acronym standing for either "Pipe Line under the Ocean" or "Pipe Line Underwater Transport of Oil," both versions appearing in official documents. There was not one pipe but several, the two main routes being "Bambi" from the Isle of Wight to Cherbourg, and "Dumbo" from Kent to Boulogne. The Pluto pipes were supplemented by "Tombola," shorter ship-to-shore pipes.

The high-pressure Pluto lines themselves were of two designs: HAIS, which was of lead with steel windings, and the steel HAMEL. A total of 710 miles of these three-inch-bore tubes were manufactured, 140 miles being provided by U.S. manufacturers. The piping was laid from a huge steel bobbin called a "Conun-drum"—so called because it was a "cone ended drum." A full drum, carrying 80 miles of cable, weighed 1,600 tons. The vast majority of PLUTO had been salvaged for recycling by 1949.

Polaris Missile   MISSILE

The **submarine**-launched US A-1 Polaris Fleet Ballistic Missile was developed in the late 1950s and was fired from the USS *George Washington* in July 1960. Its appearance marked a leap forward in submarine technology. In 1961 the improved A-2 was fired from the *Ethan Allen*. The A-3 was operational by 1964. The A-3 version was 9.44 meters long, with a range of 4,630 km, and weighed 13,600 kg. Its two-stage motor used solid-fuel propellant and glass-fiber construction. The nuclear payload was contained in three warheads, allowing a limited degree of distribution over the target. Over 20,000 contractors and U.S. government agencies were said to have been involved in the development and production of the FBM system.

With a service life spanning three decades, the Polaris system underwent many modifications. Fire control was revolutionized when the original punch-card systems were replaced with digital computers. With the Antelope penetration aid system, greater control and security against other nuclear weapons was achieved. The British Chevaline version, first test-fired at sea in 1980, deployed six smaller warheads. Polaris was steered during both its stages, in the first by means of four nozzles, in the second by the injection of a stream of liquid freon into the single nozzle, which caused a shock wave, deflecting the thrust.

Additional Reading: *Jane's Naval Weapons Systems; Jane's Weapons Systems.*

Poleaxe. *See* **Axe**

Pony   VEHICLE

The Dutch-made DAF Pony was developed in the early 1960s for U.S. Army use. Perhaps best described as a simple "platform carrier," it was a small four-wheel-drive vehicle powered by a 500 cc engine. Aside from magneto ignition, no electrical components were included in the design.

Poseidon Missile   MISSILE

The U.S. Poseidon **submarine**-launched ballistic missile was a two-stage weapon with many similarities to the **Polaris**; however, given that it carried up to 14 warheads and had a range of over 3,200 miles, it was claimed to be eight times more effective. Flight tests commenced in 1968. The first submarine to deploy the Poseidon was the USS *James Madison*.

Additional Reading: *Jane's Naval Weapons Systems.*

"Potato Masher." *See* **Steil Handgranate** and **Grenade**

Potez, Henri; Potez 630   INVENTOR

Together with Marcel Bloch and Louis Coroller, Henri Potez was a founder of the Société d'Etudes Aéronautiques in 1917. Despite limited early success in **aircraft** development, Potez would go on to become France's main designer of reconnaissance aircraft in the interwar period. His best-known productions would be the 630 series, construction of the first of which commenced in 1935. All twin-engine types, these would eventually include day and night fighters, light bombers and **dive bombers**.

Additional Reading: Taylor, *Combat Aircraft of the World*, 1969.

PP; PPK. *See* **Walther**

PPsh-1941G   FIREARM

Pronounced "pay pay shar," and standing for *pistolet pulyemet shapagin*, the Soviet PPsh was one of the outstanding **submachine guns** of World War II. Developed in 1940 to 1941, this 7.62 mm blowback weapon, manufactured by state arsenals, was notable for its distinctive

71-round drum magazine. It had a stamped steel body and a wooden stock, and it weighed 8 lb. Made in huge numbers, it sometimes equipped whole units. It was also captured in quantity by the Germans, who converted it to fire 9 mm **ammunition**.

Additional Reading: Barker and Walter, *Russian Infantry Weapons of World War II*, 1971.

Predator   UNMANNED AIRCRAFT

The Predator is a UAV (unmanned aerial vehicle) used by U.S. forces for surveillance; it can also be fitted with **Hellfire** laser-guided missiles. With a wingspan of 49 feet, a Rotax 85 horsepower engine, and "pusher" propeller, it is relatively slow, at 140 mph maximum speed. However it has a range of 450 miles and can remain airborne for long periods. It has recently been used over Afghanistan. The press reported two shot down over Iraq in late 2002.

Priest. *See* **Self-Propelled Gun**

Prince of Wales   WARSHIP

Launched in 1939 and still not quite complete when she sailed on the trail of the *Bismarck* in 1941, the **battleship** *Prince of Wales* was referred to by Winston Churchill as Britain's "newest, strongest, ship." In August 1941 she was scene of a historic meeting between Franklin D. Roosevelt and the British prime minister. With up to 15 inches of armor and ten 14-inch guns, she was 745 feet in length with a crew of 1,422.

Following the Japanese invasion of Malaya she cruised the coast in company with the *Repulse* to intercept enemy shipping. Unfortunately, the **aircraft carrier** sent to accompany them ran aground, and both warships were sunk by Japanese **torpedo** and bomber aircraft on 10 December 1941. Coming hard on the heels of the disaster at Pearl Harbor, there was now real reason to believe that the day of the battleship was at an end.

Additional Reading: Hamer, *Bombers versus Battleships*, 1999.

Prinz Eugen; Hipper Class — WARSHIP

The *Prinz Eugen* was a German heavy **cruiser** of the *Admiral Hipper* class, five vessels of which were commenced between 1935 and 1937. The idea for such a class had been put forward in the early 1930s, as vessels capable of taking on French ships like the *Algérie*. Orders were placed in 1934, yet actual work did not commence until Hitler renounced the Treaty of Versailles. The basic specification of the class was a displacement of 14,271 tons empty, a good top speed of 32.5 knots using high-pressure steam turbines, a main armament of eight 8-inch guns, a maximum armor of 80 mm, and a complement of 1,600. Nevertheless, there were variations within the type; the marginally superior *Prinz Eugen*, launched in 1938, was slightly longer than her earlier sisters *Admiral Hipper* and *Blucher*. **Radar** was added to the completed ships at a later date.

The final two vessels of the class, *Lutzow* and *Seydlitz*, never served as German warships. Lutzow was sold to Russia in 1940 under the Molotov pact, becoming the *Petropavlovsk*. Bizarrely, she saw action against German forces during the siege of Leningrad; from 1944 she served as the *Tallin* and was again renamed as the training ship *Dnepr* in 1953. Her final incarnation was as the barracks ship *PKZ-112*. The *Seydlitz* was incomplete when in 1943 it was decided that she should be converted to an **aircraft carrier**. This work was still not finished when the yard was overrun by the Soviet advance in 1945.

The *Blucher* was somewhat ignominiously dispatched by Norwegian shore batteries in 1940. *Admiral Hipper* served with distinction in the Scandinavian theater and Atlantic, part of the time acting in concert with the *Scharnhorst* and *Gneisenau*, but was badly damaged in a bungled convoy attack in December 1942. The *Prinz Eugen* fought off the coast of France alongside the *Bismarck* in her famous action with the *Hood*. Despite bomb damage she escaped through the Channel in 1942 but was later **torpedoed** on the way to Norway. She served in the Baltic until surrendered at Copenhagen in 1945. The United States later used her in the Bikini Atoll atomic bomb trial.

Additional Reading: Whitley, *German Cruisers of World War II*, London, 1985; Lenton, *German Warships of the Second World War*, 1975.

Prowler. *See* **Intruder**

Pulse Jet — MISSILE

The pulse jet is a simple jet-type engine devised by German professor Paul Schmidt c. 1928. It is essentially a tube with spring-loaded flaps, a gasoline injection system, and a sparking device. Movement through air opens the flaps and activates the fuel system, filling the void with air and fuel vapor. The spark ignites the mixture, forcing the forward flaps shut again; the blast exits to the rear, forcing the engine forward. As early as 1934 it was suggested that this idea might have use in an "aerial **torpedo**," but it was not until 1938, when the German Air Ministry began to examine jet engines, that the pulse jet came to prominence. It was later used in the **V1**.

Puma — HELICOPTER

Though the name "Puma" was used for a German **armored car** in World War II, it is now associated with the Puma transport **helicopter**. This Aérospatiale Westland collaboration first flew in 1965 and has since been used by many nations, particularly in Africa, the Middle East, and South America, in addition to France and the United Kingdom. The original SA 330 model seated up to 20 and was capable of lifting 7,000 lb in its cargo sling. Some buyers adapted the Puma for combat with gun and missile pods. Its twin engines were particularly useful, since it could fly on only one. The faster, longer-range, AS 332 Super Puma entered production in 1980.

Purple. *See* **Enigma**

PzKpfw. *See* **Panzer** and **Tank**

Q

QF, "Quick Firer," or "Quick Firing." *See*
Artillery

Queen Elizabeth **Class**   WARSHIP

Five British **battleships** of the *Queen Elizabeth*
class were completed during World War I:
Queen Elizabeth, Valiant, Barham, Warspite,
and *Malaya*. A sixth vessel was canceled. The
fastest battleships yet built, they were the first
to use oil for fuel and to have 15-inch guns.
Capable of a top speed of 24 knots, they had
crews of about 950 and maximum armor of 13
inches. Most of the class were at Jutland, and
all would be heavily engaged in World War II.
Barham was sunk by **torpedoes** from the *U-
331* in 1941; the massive explosion caused 862
fatalities.

All the others survived, being eventually
broken up between 1948 and 1950. The career
of *Warspite* was particularly remarkable, the
ship taking part in several bombardments before being damaged off Crete in 1941 and repaired in the United States. Following convoy
escort duties, she was again damaged by a
glider bomb near Salerno. She later fought during the Normandy invasion. In 1946, on the
way to be scrapped, she ran aground near
Land's End and so remained until salvaged and
beached near Marazion in 1950.

Additional Reading: Breyer, *Battleships*; Watton,
Warspite, 1986; Roskill, *HMS Warspite*, 1997;
Jones, *Battleship Barham*, 1979.

Quiver. *See* **Bow**

Q-ships   WARSHIP

Q-ships were World War I decoy vessels that
appeared to be merchantmen but were equipped
with hidden weapons to surprise **U-boats** or
other commerce raiders. The idea is often credited to Winston Churchill, who wrote to Admiral Meux on 26 November 1914 that "a small
or moderate size steamer should be taken up
and fitted very secretly with two twelve
pounder guns in such a way that they can be
concealed within deck cargo." The first success
for a Q-ship came in July 1915, when the
Prince Charles, commanded by Lieutenant
Mark-Wardlaw of the Royal Navy, sank *U-36*.

Additional Reading: Bridgland, *Sea Killers in Disguise: The Story of Q-Ships and Decoy Ships in the
First World War*, 1999.

R

R-35. *See* **Renault R-35 Light Tank**

Radar   DETECTION

An acronym standing for "radio detection and ranging," radar is a method of using electromagnetic waves to sense remotely the position, velocity, and characteristics of a target. The basic principle is that a radar device generates a radio frequency and then detects the "echo" of that emission, measuring the time delay. Commonly, microwave frequency bands of roughly 0.5 to 100 GHz are used. Different frequencies are suited to particular purposes. The highest frequencies, which may be directed as narrow beams, are best for short-range tracking, guidance, and imaging. The lowest frequencies are suited to long-range surveillance and are least effected by weather.

Radar as we know it today developed in the 1930s but was inspired by earlier work, notably Marconi's observation in 1922 that **aircraft** could create interference with radio communication. An important breakthrough was a paper presented by Robert Watson-Watt, superintendent at the Radio Department of the National Physical Laboratory, to the Committee for Scientific Survey of Air Defence in 1935. British defense analysts had been interested to know whether it might be possible to focus "radiated energy" to produce a "death ray" for use against aircraft. Watson-Watt stated that given the current state of technology it was not but that detection of aircraft might be.

A demonstration at the Post Office's Daventry wireless station using a Heyford bomber was sufficiently convincing for further funding.

This led eventually to a proposal to put RDF stations around the coast of Britain, proving a valuable addition to air defense in World War II. Active radar detection equipment, or *Funkmessortungsgerit*, was fitted to German surface ships from 1937. The first experimental use on a **U-boat** was made in 1939, though more general introduction did not occur until 1942. In the air, radar soon helped to revolutionize combat, especially when used to help night fighters home on targets. Radar was first used as a method to locate ground weapons in Italy in 1944, when they were used in to pinpoint **mortars**.

Modern radar may fulfill a variety of military purposes. The ASR, or air search radar, continually scans a volume of space to detect aircraft. SSR, or secondary surveillance radar, can be used with transponders to identify craft, thus producing what is referred to as IFF, or "identification friend or foe." In multifunction radars, such as that used by the U.S. Navy Aegis system, several tasks may be addressed simultaneously. With synthetic-aperture radar, or SAR, high-resolution images like photographs may be created. SAR is well adapted to airborne and space uses. In ground-based battlefield surveillance radar, relatively small, often man-portable units are used to locate ground-based targets, helicopters, and the like out to the local horizon.

Technically, radars may be of the pulse (or pulse doppler) continuous wave (CW), or moving target identification (MTI) types. In MTI, stationary clutter is ignored while the system focuses on a moving objects. "Bistatic" radar is a relatively new application for military purposes, in which the transmitting and receiving devices are physically separate, even a long way apart. This has the advantage that an otherwise vulnerable transmitter may be placed out of range, while the data is received elsewhere. **Stealth** technology is less effective against the latest bistatic techniques.

Additional Reading: Edde, *Radar*, 1993; Margiotta, *Brassey's Encyclopedia of Land Forces and Warfare*, 1996; Brinkman (ed), *Jane's Avionics*, various editions; *Jane's Radar*; Buderi, *The Invention That Changed the World*, 1996; Latham and Stobbs, *Radar*, 1996; Gough, *Watching the Skies: The History of Ground Radar in the Air Defence of the United Kingdom*, 1993; Richardson et al., *Surveillance and Target Aquistion Systems*, 1997.

Radio   COMMUNICATIONS

During the 1870s, British professor James Clerk Maxwell demonstrated that electrical waves can travel over distances. Subsequently the German Heinrich Heine, showed that these waves travel in straight lines but can be reflected. By 1896 Italian Gugliemo Marconi had built the equipment necessary to transmit and receive signals across the English Channel, and within five years signals had been sent across the Atlantic. Huge improvements were made in reception and amplification by 1914. Radio, or "wireless telegraphy," promised to free communications from the tyranny of fixed lines that had hitherto limited the usefulness of the **telegraph** and **telephone**.

In the early years of the twentieth century there was experimentation with the adaptation of radio to war on sea and land; radios were soon fitted to ships. Progress was slower for armies, since to be really useful, radios had to be easily transported. Nevertheless, radios were fitted to some tanks and aircraft in World War I. Man-portable radios were in general use in Western armies by World War II, a typical, though less than perfect example being the British No. 18 wireless set used for company and battalion communication. This weighed 14.4 kg and had a range of 8 km for voice communication, 16 km being possible for **Morse code** transmission. Radio soon helped make possible

subsequent advances in **radar** and microwave technology. As with civilian equipments, military radios have been successively revolutionized by the transistor and the silicon chip, which have made communications equipments ever smaller, lighter, and cheaper.

With diminishing size and increasing availability, military radio has been put to many additional tasks. Radio beacons aid search and rescue, and transmissions are commonly made from unmanned stations or such equipments as **sonobouys** and "bugs." Burst transmissions, in which much information is sent in short bursts, make it more difficult for the enemy to detect the location of the transmitter. Radio has similarly opened up new technological fields of electronic warfare, including jamming of enemy systems, and other countermeasures.

Railroads, Railways   MISCELLANEOUS

As the first system of rapid, mass land transport, railways have been of great strategic importance. Quicker to build and faster than canals, they have sometimes dominated campaigns. Though the first British line, Stockton to Darlington, was built in 1825, and the first U.S. line in 1828, it was arguably in the century 1850–1950 that they were most crucial. Moltke first demonstrated the potential when shifting army corps to face various real and potential opponents of Prussia. In the South African War, c. 1900, armored trains were used, while the Boer commandos showed the vulnerability of railroad tracks to guerrilla action.

During World War I, railways were so critical in determining mobilization and movement times that the campaigns of 1914 have sometimes been called war "by timetable." It was also in World War I that T. E. Lawrence ("Lawrence of Arabia") would seriously interfere with Turkish communications by attacking rail lines. Railroad guns, or railway **artillery**, made a contribution to the barrages of the western front, curved track being used for major alterations of aim, and tunnels to shelter guns from observation. Railway carriages served as mobile command posts; the armistice was signed in one of them.

In World War II, rail lines had a significant bearing on the Eastern Front campaign; the Russians and others would deploy trains with **tank** turrets for defensive firepower. Rail guns were also used for cross-Channel firing. With the growing importance of bomber and ground-attack **aircraft**, railways became more vulnerable. This factor was of particular importance in the latter stages of World War II, when special forces and Allied aircraft seriously hampered German deployments, particularly during the D-Day campaign.

Ramrod MISCELLANEOUS

The ramrod is a staff used to push shot or a charge into the barrel of a firearm. It probably began about the late thirteenth century with a rough wooden stick pushed down the muzzle of an early **artillery** piece, but hydraulic and automatic ramming devices are still used to push **cartridges** or **shells** into the breeches of guns. Ramrods were an integral fixture of military shoulder arms by the sixteenth century, commonly taking the form of a slender wooden shaft with a bell end stored in a recess under the barrel. In the early eighteenth century, wood gave way to metal, giving a more durable tool. Later rammers were sometimes permanently attached to their weapons by means of a swiveling system so they would not be lost in combat. By the late nineteenth century, ramrods on **rifles** had given way to cleaning rods, as on many **Mausers**.

RAP. *See* **Artillery**

Rapier. *See* **Sword**

Rapier Missile MISSILE

The British surface-to-air Rapier missile system was first developed in the 1960s and was operationally deployed in 1971. The basic components are the launch unit, generally mounting four missiles, and the **radar** tracker system. As a close-range system it is particularly well suited to local defense, in which role it was deployed after the Falklands landings in 1982. An improved Rapier 2000 was developed by

the 1990s, with a new "optronic" tracker and "intelligent" proximity **fuses** for the missiles.

Raptor, F-22 AIRCRAFT

The U.S. Lockheed F-22 Raptor "advanced tactical fighter" (ATF) is the successor to the F-15 **Eagle**. It was developed by Lockheed in conjunction with **Boeing** and General Dynamics. The F-22 brings together elements of **stealth** technology, with low wing loading and engine nozzles that can be turned, or vectored, for maximum maneuverability. The intention is that Raptor will be able to cruise to the target area at supersonic speed but then be able to fight with great agility. Statistics published in the late 1990s give the wingspan as 44 feet 6 inches, a Mach 1.7 top speed, and a ceiling of 50,000 feet. The weapons load may include a 20 mm cannon, **Sidewinder** missiles, and JDAM missiles. Extra fuel tanks or Standoff Attack Missiles may be carried under the wings.

RAT VEHICLE

The RAT was a tracked vehicle developed by the Canadian army in cooperation with Canadair of Montreal in 1955. Properly described as an articulated "utility carrier," it had wide tracks and was similar in general configuration to the **Snowcat**. The RAT was further developed to produce the Dynatrac in 1962, with the tracked snow scooter, or "Ski-do," appearing in 1966. Some of these vehicles have been supplied to the militaries of the United States and other nations.

Rations MISCELLANEOUS

From earliest times, food has been important in war. In the medieval era soldiers were usually kept under arms for campaigning "seasons," and war would be abandoned for the harvest. Sieges were frequently determined by the defenders' foresight in laying in provisions. By the seventeenth century most armies had commissaries to provide basic wants, while sutlers were able to sell extra provisions. Scotsman Sir James Turner stated in his *Pallas Armata* of 1683 that "the ordinary allowance for a soldier

An F-22 Raptor is prepared for a test flight at Edwards Air Force Base, March 1999. Photo by Staff Sergeant Andrew Dunnaway II USAF. Courtesy of the Department of Defense.

in the field, is daily two pound of bread, one pound of flesh, or in lieu of it one pound of cheese, one bottle of wine, or in lieu of it two bottles of beer." In practice, finance and nutrition lagged behind theory, and armies frequently survived on stale bread and cheese, with water or weak beer.

The use of "hard tack," or ship's biscuit, and the invention of canned food made major contributions to the durability of armies and range of navies. In the Royal Navy it became usual to serve food on square wooden platters, giving rise to the expression "square meal." The discovery by James Lind (1716–1794) that lime juice, a natural source of vitamin C, could be given to sailors to prevent scurvy gave the American nickname "limeys" to Englishmen.

By 1900 in most armies soldiers in the field were fed in groups, rations being prepared communally in field kitchens. Individual soldiers used metal mess tins or cans as food containers. Small rations of tobacco were now common. Many nations continued to issue alcoholic

drinks to their troops. What and when varied from nation to nation; the French, for example, received regular rations of wine, the British small "tots" of rum when on active service. When combat intervened, troops survived on "iron rations," small portions of high-energy canned food, together with water from canteens. At the beginning of World War I, German iron rations, or *Eiserner Bestand*, consisted of 250 grams of biscuit, 200 grams of meat, 150 grams of preserved vegetables, and 25 grams each of salt and coffee, per day. While the Germans grappled with food shortages through the introduction of many *Ersatz*, or substitute foods, the main problem for the United States would be sending vast quantities of foodstuffs to its expeditionary force and allies. Powdered eggs and soluble coffee were part of the transport solution, but it was the realization by J. C. Hormel that boning and compacting beef before transit that would make a 40 percent saving on refrigerated shipping space. Even so, the daily cost of feeding the United States Army alone would be $2,500,000.

During World War II the prepackaged ration became both the staple of combat and an item of barter, with U.S. "C" (Combat) and "K" rations having the best reputations. Though "trench cookers" had existed in World War I and "solidified alcohol" had been used for warming food, it was World War II that would see widespread distribution of individual cooking equipment. One of the earliest and most influential types was the German *Esbit Kocher*, a small metal folding stand using solid fuel tablets. NATO forces later generally adopted a nearly identical hexamine, or "hexy," burner. Freezing also became important, building on the interwar commercial work of Clarence Birdseye. Self-heating cans were similarly introduced.

After World War II, British forces in the field relied on a "24 Hour Ration GS" system, in which there were four basic packs, a different one being issued on each successive day. All packs included condensed milk and margarine in tubes, chewing gum, toilet paper, salt, matches, and miniature can opener. A type "A" pack (consumed by the author in 1974) also contained "breakfast" (oatmeal block, canned sausage and beans, hard biscuit, jam, tea and sugar); a "snack" (more biscuit, cheese, chocolate, boiled sweets, coffee and sugar); and a "main meal" (dehydrated onion soup, canned chicken curry, precooked rice, apple flakes, tea, sugar, and yet more biscuits). The U.S. "C" rations of the period were essentially similar, with one five-inch-square cardboard box containing about 3,000 calories, or enough to sustain one man for one day. The cans within the package were opened with the P-38 can opener supplied.

Bulk and weight made both GS and C rations unpopular to carry in quantity; in the 1960s freeze-drying helped make possible the "Lurp" ration, named after Long Range Reconnaissance Patrols. Food was rapidly frozen and the liquid extracted, the food being placed in a vacuum pack that was then returned to room temperature. The result was a light, malleable pouch that could be crammed comfortably into any small space. The Lurp could be cooked

properly, or when necessary just dampened and consumed from the bag.

Since then, military food technology has moved on. According to the National Research Council's Board on Army Science and Technology of 2001, many new developments are undergoing study. These include rations containing vaccines, confectionery bars with nutrients that raise body temperature in cold conditions, genetic modification of food to contain anti-infection agents, and even edible "biomarkers" that can identify friendly troops. In 2002 it was announced that the U.S. Army Soldier Systems Center at Natick, Massachusetts, had invented a sandwich, sealed in a laminated pouch, that would remain edible for up to three years. This was achieved with the use of chemical "humectants," which sealed the water content into the food, preventing the growth of bacteria or drying.

Raven, UH-12   AIRCRAFT

The U.S. Hiller Raven UH-12 **helicopter** was devised by Stanley Hiller, Jr., and entered service in 1950. It was a three-seater, designed for training and observation. It was initially powered by a 178 horsepower, later a 250 horsepower engine. Total production was in excess of 2,000, and Ravens were used by the armies of many nations; some were still in service as late as the 1980s.

Recoilless Gun; Recoilless Rifle
       ARTILLERY

Newton's law of "equal and opposite" forces has long been recognized as a limiting factor to projectile weapons. Large handguns can be difficult to aim because of their vicious backward and upward "kick." Early cannon, lacking any manner of recoil absorption, bounced dangerously backward as they fired, or had to be mounted on sloped platforms that would allow them to run forward again in a controlled manner. A potential solution was recognized in the creation of an opposite force at the time of discharge, which would have the effect of canceling out the rearward motion. In the Davis gun of World War I, two barrels were opposed, the projectile shooting forward while cotton wadding was blown out at the back.

During the interwar period and World War II, further work resulted in many more practical designs in which gas escape to the rear replaced the need for any backward-moving object. Often this gas escaped at very high speed through specially designed appertures, or "venturi." German experimentation led to the deployment of ultra-light **artillery** with the Luftwaffe as early as 1940. Particularly successful were the U.S. 57 mm and 75 mm "recoilless rifles," which saw service by 1945, and the 106 mm, which saw use afterward and has also been made elsewhere in the world.

Recoilless guns have also been produced in numbers by Russia, the United Kingdom, and Sweden. British research under Sir Dennis Burney during World War II led eventually to a series of light towed weapons, or BATS—the Battalion Anti Tank Guns. Improved models, in use until the late 1970s, would be known as the "Mobat" and "Wombat." Sweden's most successful venture in the recoilless field was undoubtedly the Carl Gustav shoulder-fired 84 mm M2. First produced in 1948, the M2 was particularly successful as an anti-armor weapon, being capable of firing a high-explosive antitank (HEAT) round to about 700 meters, with armor penetration of about 400 mm. A lightweight M3 model of the Carl Gustav was accepted by U.S. special forces as late as the 1990s.

Additional Reading: Weeks, *Men against Tanks*, 1975; *Jane's Infantry Weapons*.

Redeye Missile   MISSILE

Developed in the late 1950s, the U.S. Redeye was a shoulder launched antiaircraft missile manufactured by General Dynamics. The firer tracked the target through an optical sight and was informed by a buzzer when the missile was ready for launch. After firing an **infrared** sensor enabled the missile to seek the target.

A similar Russian weapon was the Grail (SA-7) shoulder-launched surface-to-air missile, first seen in the hands of the North Vietnamese in the latter stages of the Vietnam War. This has popularly been dubbed the SAM-7. Its range is about two miles, to a height of 15,000 feet. Widely used in many armies, it has also been fitted to boats.

Reisen. *See Zero*

Reising Submachine Gun   FIREARM

The U.S. Reising **submachine gun** was designed by Eugene Reising and patented in 1940. It fired from a closed bolt at all times and so had a relatively slow rate of fire. It was manufactured by Harrington and Richardson and was used by the Marine Corps. As it was not found particularly reliable, only about 100,000 were made.

Additional Reading: Iannamico, *Reising Submachine Gun Story*, 1999.

Renault FT-17 Light Tank   TANK

Louis Renault was first approached by General Estienne to provide a design for a light **tank** in July 1916. Though the first Renault efforts were little more than tracked lorries, by 1917 the company had produced what was for the time a highly practical little tank, with a then-novel 360-degree traversing turret. This was first fitted with a **machine gun**, later with a 37 mm gun.

The FT-17 first saw action in 1918, and by the end of the First World War about 3,000 had been made by several companies, including Renault. The FT-17 was also produced in the United States as the 6-Ton Tank, M1917, and widely used in other countries in a number of variants. Though mainly replaced by the **Renault R-35**, it was still in use in 1940, when a number were captured and subsequently used as the **PzKpfw** 18R 730 (f).

Additional Reading: Crow, *AFVs of World War I*, 1998.

Renault R-35 Light Tank   TANK

The unimpressive R-35, first ordered in May 1935, was the most numerous **tank** in French service at the outbreak of World War II. Made of cast sections bolted together, the R-35 was a two-man vehicle with a 37 mm main armament in the turret. There was also a coaxial **machine gun**. The tracks ran on rubber-tired wheels, and a "tail" was fitted to most R-35s to increase trench-crossing capability. Top speed was just under 13 mph. A **radio** was fitted to late production models. A self-sealing fuel tank and a fireproof bulkhead were intended to give added security to the crew, though armor was only 45 mm maximum. Large numbers were captured and used by the Germans as chassis for other vehicles after 1940.

Requin, USS   WARSHIP

Now moored at the Carnegie Science Center, Pittsburgh, the USS *Requin* (SS 481) is a 312-foot fleet **submarine** commissioned in April 1945. In use until 1971, the *Requin* was converted three times for different roles, ending its active life as a Naval Reserve trainer (IXSS 481). During her service she completed more than 5,000 dives.

Respirator. *See* Gas Mask

Resurgam. *See* Submarine

Revolver   FIREARM

A revolver is a firearm, usually a handgun but occasionally a **rifle** or larger weapon, in which a cylinder with chambers rotates to line up charges with a firing device. In some instances a complete unit of multiple barrels is rotated. The idea was in use by the sixteenth century but did not become common until much later. Important makers of revolvers have included **Colt, Smith and Wesson, Webley,** and many others. Revolving handguns have become progressively less common during the past century with the rise of automatic and **semiautomatic** systems.

Additional Reading: Blair, *Pollard's History of Firearms,* 1983; Taylorson, *The Revolver,* 1970.

Rhino G6. *See* Self-Propelled Gun

Rifle, Rifling   FIREARM

Rifling is the shaping, or spiral grooving, of a barrel to induce spin on the projectile. Such spin stabilizes the shot, after the manner of a gyroscope, so improving accuracy. There are many types of rifling, which differ in terms of profile, pitch of the groove, and number of grooves, which may be clockwise or counter clockwise. Rifling may be constant and consistent over the length of the barrel or "progressive," whereby the twist increases. Guns with rifling are known as "rifles," and though the term is now usually applied to shoulder arms the name has historically also been applied to certain **artillery**.

It is thought that the first rifled guns were made as early as 1500, but they were uncommon for another century as they were difficult and expensive to make and slow to load. Rifles were in limited military use by 1620, some **wheel lock** rifles being produced for the guard of King Christian IV of Denmark about that date. They played a minor role in the Thirty Years' War, and English Civil War, where it is known that civilian "screwed" (i.e., rifled) guns were also employed.

Though the combination of a rifled barrel and **flintlock** mechanism made the idea a more practical proposition, the majority of troops would remain armed with smoothbore **muskets** for another 200 years. Significant exceptions arose in heavily wooded or broken country where hunting with rifles had become established. Thus it is that German Jäger troops and American colonial militias were often rifle armed; also, there was limited Scandinavian use. Early American and German rifles were essentially similar, with barrels of about 30 inches in length and bores of about 0.6 inch.

By 1740 a distinctive American rifle had begun to emerge, with a longer barrel and smaller bore. Various states have claimed to be the prime mover in this process, with Virginia, North Carolina, and Pennsylvania all strong contenders. Only after 1800 would this type of rifle become generally known as the "Kentucky" rifle. As skirmishers, riflemen were crucial during the War of Independence, with a very small number being also deployed on the side loyal to Britain. Rifles would see limited but effective use in the Napoleonic period, particularly with the Prussians and British, who used the **Baker** rifle. An official-pattern U.S. rifle was adopted in 1803, to serve alongside the muskets then in use. A new type introduced in 1817 was known as the "common" rifle, to distinguish it from the latest **Hall breechloaders**.

By the middle of the nineteenth century, rifled muzzle loaders were in widespread use. The one in British service was the Brunswick, which was current from 1838 to 1851. **Percussion** ignition was now the norm. Significant breakthroughs came with the advent of the breechloading Prussian **Dreyse** "needle" gun and the **Minié** bullet, which reopened the question of breech loading with **bolt action** and produced a really effective round, respectively. The repeating **Spencer** rifle was similarly a major step forward, as was the lever action pioneered by **Winchester** arms. Yet it was arguably the development of the metal "fixed" **cartridge** by inventors such as Lefaucheux, Morse, Berdan, and Boxer that made swift, accurate, reliable, long-range breechloading rifles possible.

The period from 1860 to 1914 was arguably the apogee of the military rifle, during which infantry armed with rifles and **bayonets** became vastly more important than cavalry and even challenged the power of artillery on occasion. The era saw the rapid development of many different breechloading mechanisms and the introduction of magazine systems for general use. **Chassepot, Snider, Peabody, Martini, Lebel, Metford, Lee**, and **Mauser** were just the best known, and ultimately some of the most successful, innovators in the field. At the conclusion of this half-century of feverish development all of the major powers were armed with **bolt-action** repeating breechloaders. The armies of World War I were armed with slightly different systems, in the Mauser, **Mannlicher, Mosin-Nagant**, Lee-**Enfield**, and **Springfield**, but the effects were similar—large casualties, which, combined with the catastrophic impact of **artil-**lery and **machine gun**, helped bring about trench warfare.

Thereafter rifle development would be forced into different directions, as makers sought ways to make rifles swifter, lighter, handier, more destructive in confined spaces, and take bigger magazines. **Sniper** rifles became more important. The invention of the **submachine gun** and light machine gun challenged the dominancy of the rifle and introduced the concept of infantry armed with several different types of weapon acting together in platoons and squads. The Germans took one route, keeping their basic Mauser system and applying it to a light carbine, the K98k; the United States took a more radical line, with the adoption of the semi-automatic **Garand**. World War II would demonstrate that semi-automatic and automatic was the way ahead, as was shown by weapons like the **M1 carbine**, Tokarev SVT-40, and Gewehr 43.

Yet it was not until the middle of the war that the idea of combining the best of the submachine gun with the best of the rifle to produce an "**assault rifle**" really came into its own. In this respect the German **Sturmgewehr** was a ground-breaking design. After the war the Soviets would go one better with the **Kalashnikov AK-47**, and a new race was on to equip the armies of the world with either better semi-automatics or full-blown assault rifles. In this respect it may be argued that the Western powers were initially the more conservative, with arms like the U.S. **M14** and the **FN** Self-Loading Rifle, or SLR. Both of these strove to maintain the full power range of a traditional rifle and cartridge compatibility with machine guns while incorporating rapid fire.

Since Vietnam, however, virtually every industrialized nation has gone down the assault-rifle route, with weapons that use a smaller cartridge than the rifles of 1914, large-capacity magazines, short barrels, light overall weight, and automatic-fire capabilities. Important modern rifles include the **M16** family, the Kalashnikov derivatives including the AK-74, the Israeli **Galil**, the British **SA 80**, the Austrian Steyr **AUG**, the Heckler and Koch **G3**, and the French **FA MAS**. Experiments continue with things like new materials, caseless rounds, **grenade** launching systems, and other improvements.

Additional Reading: Blair, *Pollard's History of Firearms*, 1983; Ezell, *Small Arms of the World*, various editions; Patent Office, *Patents for Inventions: Class 119, Small Arms*, 1993; *Jane's Infantry Weapons*.

Rifle Grenade EXPLOSIVE DEVICE

Grenades and fireworks have been projected from shoulder arms since the seventeenth century, with cup-type launchers fitted to military **muskets** during the eighteenth century.

The father of the modern rifle grenade is arguably Frederick Marten Hale, of Faversham, Kent, United Kingdom, who developed the rodded "Hale grenade" in the decade prior to World War I. In the Hale system the grenade was fitted with a rod that was pushed into the barrel of the **rifle**, and the gun was loaded with a special blank **cartridge**. Firing the rifle shot out the grenade, which exploded on impact. Numerous grenades on this theme were used during World War I, the German model 1914 and the British "Number 3" being two examples. Cup discharger systems were also perfected during this period. In the French VB model, also used by the United States, an ordinary cartridge was used with a small cup. An ordinary round fired through the rifle and cup also passed through a channel in the bomb, both launching the grenade and lighting the fuse. The British later used the **Mills bomb** with a discharger.

Since then there have been myriad rifle grenades and grenade launcher systems. A wide range of such munitions were used by the Germans in World War II, including antitank rounds. Grenades were even developed to be shot from flare pistols. U.S. rifle grenades used after 1945 included the M31 high-explosive Antitank and the M19A1 phosphorus smoke types, though the dedicated **M79** launcher was issued in the 1960s. Other interesting examples have included the Belgian Mecar types, the Austrian Type 74, and the French STRIM models.

Additional Reading: *Jane's Infantry Weapons*; Skennerton, *An Introduction to British Grenades*, 1988; Hogg, *Infantry Weapons of World War II*, 1977.

Robat TANK

The U.S. Robotic Breaching Assault Tank, or Robat, is just one attempt of many to apply the science of robotics to the battlefield. It is essentially a remotely operated **M60 tank** fitted charges and rollers. Using radio control or fiber-optic links from a man-portable unit or another vehicle, it can clear minefields and obstacles.

Roborat MISCELLANEOUS

Funded by the Defense Advanced Research Projects Agency (DARPA), a U.S. military research arm, the Roborat project at the State University of New York aims to control rats by the use of electrodes. Though animals such as dolphins and dogs have been widely trained for military purposes, Roborat was hailed as a technological breakthrough in 2002. The key to its success is reported to be the fact that the rats are positively motivated by the stimulation of pleasure centers in their brains.

Rockeye. *See* **Cluster Bomb**

Rodney, **HMS.** *See* **Nelson Class**

Rome Plough VEHICLE

The Rome plough came into existence, along with some chemical **defoliants**, as an answer to the jungles of Vietnam. The "plough" itself was a 4,600 lb bulldozer blade with a spike attached, its name coming from the Rome Company of Georgia. The blade was mounted on a Caterpillar D7, or Allis-Chalmers fully tacked bulldozer. Tested in 1966, the Rome plough was later used in large numbers.

Rommel's Asparagus. *See* **Gliders**

Ross Rifle   FIREARM

Invented by Sir Charles Ross the Canadian Ross rifle of 1900 was a highly accurate **bolt-action** model. Later adopted by Canadian forces, it was found susceptible to dirt in the trenches of World War I. Even worse, there were occasional accidents in which the bolt flew out. Total loss of confidence followed, and the Ross was dropped as a general frontline weapon.

Royal Sovereign; Royal Sovereign Class
                                  WARSHIP

The name *Royal Sovereign* has been used on English, later British, warships for centuries, and there was a *Sovereign* afloat before 1495. The famous *Royal Sovereign* launched in 1787 was flagship of the Channel fleet and fought the on the "Glorious First of June" in 1794, as well as being caught up in the Spithead Mutiny. She later fought at Trafalgar and survived until 1849. In 1862 a three-deck wooden **battleship** of the same name was converted to an ironclad, having her upper decks cut away and four turrets mounted.

In 1892–1894 a whole *Royal Sovereign* class of seven battleships was constructed. These 14,150-ton ships mounted four 12-inch guns in barbettes: part of a huge naval expansion, they were made obsolete by *Dreadnought*. A much more modern, single-funnel *Royal Sovereign*, of the *Revenge* class, was begun in 1913. This 15-inch-gun ship, capable of 21 knots, saw action in World War I and following complete overhaul remained in service until 1949.

Additional Reading: Smith, *Battleship Royal Sovereign*, 1988; Whitley, *Battleships of World War II*, 1998; Breyer, *Battleships*.

RPG-7   ANTITANK WEAPON

Introduced in 1962, the Soviet rocket-propelled **grenade**, or RPG-7, was soon the standard man-portable, short-range antitank weapon of the Warsaw Pact. Consisting of a reusable launch tube with **hollow-charge** high-explosive antitank missiles, the system combined many of the useful features already found in the **bazooka** and **Panzerfaust**. Later versions featured a folding tube and other refinements. Published data for the RPG-7V gave a range of 500 meters against stationary targets, 300 against moving objects.

RPV. *See* **UAV**

Ryan X-13 Vertijet   UNCONVENTIONAL
                              AIRCRAFT

The X-13 was a small experimental aircraft built around a Rolls-Royce Avon 200 series engine, combining high thrust with low weight. During trials of 1956 and 1957 it became the first jet VTOL (vertical takeoff and landing) aircraft, ascending straight upward before transition to wing-borne horizontal flight, then returning to hover before landing. Though too small to carry armaments, it helped demonstrate the viability of "jump" jets, later perfected in the form of the **Harrier**.

Additional Reading: Rogers, *VTOL Military Research Aircraft*, 1989; Miller, *The X-Planes*, 1988.

S

S-61 helicopter. *See* Sikorsky, Igor

SA-2 (or SAM 2). *See* Guideline

SA-7 (or SAM-7). *See* Redeye

SA 80 Rifle   FIREARM

The SA 80 is the British army's current **rifle**—a short **bullpup** design, it is easy to handle and shoot but has been the subject of controversy. Also known as the IW, or "Individual Weapon," or **Enfield** L85A1, it was introduced in the 1980s. Weighing just under 4 kg empty and having a 30-round magazine, it was intended for mass production and ease of maintenance. It was also designed "en suite" with the Light Support Weapon, a heavy-barreled version with a bipod designed to support an infantry squad and replace the elderly **Bren gun** (LMG).

Additional Reading: *Jane's Infantry Weapons.*

Sabaton. *See* Armor

Sabot; APDS; FSADS   EXPLOSIVE
                                 DEVICE

The word "sabot" was originally French for a wooden shoe or clog. In the military sense it refers to a casing or guide that carries a projectile through the bore of an **artillery** piece. "Discarding" sabots separate from the **shell** as it leaves the barrel; this can be useful, as decrease in the diameter and weight of the projectile leads to an increase in velocity. Such an in-

crease leads to greater penetration against armored targets, such as **tanks**.

Sabot shells were developed by both sides during World War II. The Canadians, for example, pioneered the APDS, or armor-piercing discarding sabot, which was also worked on by Permutter and Coppock at the British Armaments Research Establishment. German experiment with discarding sabots, or *Treibspeigelgeschosse*, produced various shells with rings at the base and shoulder, "pot" sabots, with the hardened projectile sitting in an outer container; and "shoulder supports," in the shape of small fins that held the fore end of the shell true within the barrel.

Sabot rounds continue to be used. Many modern examples are fin stabilized for accuracy and stability, hence the acronyms FSADS (Fin Stabilized Armor Piercing Discarding Sabot) and APFSDS (Armor Piercing Fin Stabilized Discarding Sabot).

Sabre, F-86   AIRCRAFT

The F-86 Sabre jet fighter **aircraft** was the North American Company's first jet fighter. Groundwork had been laid in the latter stages of World War II, but the final machine, which first flew in 1947, also took advantage of captured German research. The Sabre was a single-seat swept-wing design with a top speed of 707 mph, a length of 40 feet 4 inches, and, in its **radar**-equipped F-86D variant, an armament of 24 Mighty Mouse high-explosive rockets.

The real test of the F-86 was Korea, where it came up against the **MiG-15**. Here the Sabre would achieve an almost legendary status, despite the fact that the F-86A originally in use was only **machine-gun** armed. Eventually Sabres achieved 757 combat victories for only 103 losses, creating 39 aces. Thereafter the Sabre served with friendly powers including the United Kingdom, Canada, and Australia, and it became the yardstick by which other fighters were judged.

Additional Reading: Pace, *X-Fighters: USAF Experimental and Prototype Fighters, XP-59 to YF-23,* 1991.

Saddle   MISCELLANEOUS

In use from the classical era, the horse rider's seat, or saddle, was of considerable importance to cavalry, particularly when edged weapons were used. Since the medieval period the European saddle has normally consisted of a wooden frame or "tree" with padding and a leather covering. It is secured by a girth, or surcingle, passing under the belly of the mount. **Stirrups** hang at either side.

The knightly, or war, saddle incorporated a high cantle, having the effect of holding the rider in his seat. More recently, military designs have been lower and may incorporate "buckets" for long arms, holsters for pistols, and holders for spare horse shoes as part of the furniture. Pack saddles have been used with horses, mules, and camels to carry many types of military equipment, up to and including **machine guns** and the component parts of mountain **artillery**.

Additional Reading: Tylden, *Horses and Saddlery,* 1965.

Saetta. *See* **Folgore, Macchi**

Sagger Missile   MISSILE

The Soviet AT-3 Sagger antitank missile, officially designated the 9K14 Malyutka, was first issued in 1963. It was more compact than the Snapper and Swatter types that it followed, and relatively cheap. Its success may be gauged by the fact that some Malyutka types were recently still in use. Released in salvos by Eygptian forces against the Israeli tanks, it was one of the successes of the 1973 war on the Arab side. With a range of about 3 km, it is a MCLOS (manual command to line of sight) type, with an armor penetration of 460 mm.

Saladin   VEHICLE

The British six-wheeled Saladin **armored car** appeared as a Crossley prototype in 1954 and was in use from 1958. Powered by a 160 horsepower engine, it weighed about 25,000 lb, offered a top speed of 45 mph, and had a crew of three. Its main armament was a 76 mm gun in the turret.

Salmon Class   SUBMARINE

The six vessels of the U.S. *Salmon* class of **submarines** were built between 1936 and 1938, the *Salmon* herself (SS 182) being commissioned on 15 March 1938. Armed with six torpedo tubes, these submarines were 308 feet long, with a complement of 55. The *Salmon* class sank 33 enemy ships during World War II, the *Seal* having the odd distinction of sinking a Japanese merchantman with its periscope during an attack on a convoy. Largely superseded by the more modern *Gatos*, the last of the *Salmon*s was sold for scrap in 1948. *Skipjack* (SS 184) took part in an atomic bomb test at Bikini Atoll.

Additional Reading: Polmar, *The American Submarine,* 1983.

SAM-7. *See* **Grail** under **Redeye**

Sampson Class   WARSHIP

The U.S. *Sampson*-class **destroyers** were built in World War I. Displacing 1,100 tons, they had a complement of 145 and carried 4-inch guns and **torpedo** tubes. Yarrow boilers and Curtis turbines gave a maximum speed of 29.5 knots. Just one of the type, the *Allen* (DD 66), survived to World War II, becoming a training ship at Pearl Harbor. She was finally scrapped in 1946.

Sänger HELICOPTER

During the latter part of World War II the German Eugen Sänger designed a rocket-powered orbital bomber capable of crossing the Atlantic to bomb American cities. Launching was to be from a monorail track, acceleration to over 1,000 mph being given by captive **V2** engines. Cruising at an altitude of 80 miles at several thousand knots, the Sänger was arguably more closely related to Space Shuttle technology than conventional bombers. It was never built, but after World War II Messerschmitt-Bälkow-Blohm developed an idea bearing the same name for a "piggyback" launch space vehicle. **Boeing** developed a similar concept into the X-20 Dyna-Soar project, which, like the Sänger, never flew.

Additional Reading: Myhra, *Sänger, Germany's Orbital Rocket Bomber*, Miller, *The X-Planes*, 1988; Dutton, *Military Space*, 1990.

Sappenpanzer ARMOR

Sappenpanzer is the general name for the most common type of body **armor** used by German troops in World War I. Made of silicon-nickel steel, it consisted of a breastplate that hung over the shoulders, with three other plates suspended below. It was first produced in 1916, and about 500,000 were made. A peculiarity was that it could be worn back to front, thus protecting a soldier lying down.

Additional Reading: Dean, *Helmets and Body Armour*; Dunstan, *Flak Jackets*, 1984.

Saracen, FV 603 VEHICLE

The Saracen Armored Personnel Carrier, made by Alvis entered British service in 1952. A ten-ton, six-wheeled design, capable of 30 mph on the road, it could carry 12 men. The basic model had a small turret with a machine gun, but there were also command carriers and other variants.

Saratoga. See Lexington and Forrestal

Sarin CHEMICAL WARFARE

Sarin, or GB, is the chemical nerve agent methylisopropoxyfluoro-phosphene oxide. First adopted in 1938, it is a colorless liquid, or vapor, highly toxic to the eyes and capable of penetrating the skin. It attacks the nervous system, causing symptoms such as breathing difficulty, vision problems, and convulsions. A sufficient exposure may cause death within a few minutes. It is often categorized with **Tabun, Soman**, and the **V-agents**.

Additional Reading: Burck and Flowerree, *International Handbook on Chemical Weapons Proliferation*, 1991.

Satellites COMMUNICATIONS; OBSERVATION; NAVIGATION; DETECTION

The launch of the Soviet Union's first artificial earth satellite, Sputnik 1, on 4 October 1957 opened a major new field of military technology. The 83 kg Sputnik I was able to transmit; Sputnik 2, launched just a month later, weighed 508 kg and carried cameras into orbit. The first satellite to be actually described as for military communications was the U.S. SCORE (Signal Communications by Orbital Relay Equipment). This was launched by an Atlas rocket in December 1958 and lasted just 13 days. Since then satellite capabilities have improved exponentially, becoming vital to communications, reconnaissance, and meteorology. ASAT, or antisatellite, weapon development began as early as 1959 with the SAINT "satellite interceptor" project. By 1964 the United States had two operational ASAT systems, Thor and Nike Zeus.

The use of geostationary orbits has made active tracking unnecessary, while the positioning of three or four satellites may achieve global coverage. Lower-altitude orbits opened the possibility of passing comparatively close to a target and then sending data to a specified area on the ground—a function now possible from other types of satellite using improved antenna. From 1965, using highly elliptical Molniya orbits, the Soviets created platforms that passed over both Russia and the West, had a wide field

Members of the 343rd Defense Artillery Squadron prepare their satellite communicatons system during a training exercise at Fort Bliss, June 1996. Courtesy of the Department of Defense.

of view, and were usable for about two-thirds of each 12-hour orbit.

From the 1960s, the Defense Satellite Communications System, DSCS (or "Discus") provided wideband communications for U.S. government agencies all over the world. The cube-shaped DSCS III–type satellites, current in the 1980s, weighed about 1,042 kg and mounted advanced multibeam lens antennas. By using solar arrays oriented toward the sun they were able to develop about 1,100 watts of power. Between 1978 and 1989 four Fleet Satellite Communications, or FLTSATCOM, satellites were also launched for the U.S. Navy and Air Force. This system was still operational 20 years later. Satellite deployment was revolutionized by the invention of the reusable Space Shuttle, though following the *Challenger* disaster there was new interest in "ELVs," or expendable launch vehicles.

President Ronald Reagan announced the new-generation Milstar, or Military Strategic

Tactical and Relay, satellite program in 1981. The first of the Milstars was launched in 1994. The second generation, Milstar II, commenced deployment in 1999, though the first launch malfunctioned, resulting in a $1.233 billion fiasco. A replacement in 2001 proved successful, placing a Milstar II in a geostationary orbit at 90 degrees west.

The relatively low-powered British Skynet 1 was the first of the geostationary defense communication satellites, launched in 1969. Skynet 4s, controlled from RAF Oakhanger in Hampshire, were in operation by the 1990s. Skynet 5 is expected in 2005. NATO satellites, facilitating communication across the Atlantic and based on the IDSCS, or Initial Defense Satellite Communications System, were first launched as early as 1970. During the late 1970s NATO satellites, fully compatible with U.S. systems were built by Ford Aerospace. By the 1990s NATO 4–type satellites were in use.

The navigational potential of satellite technology has developed rapidly from the use of "Transit" satellites to provide positional fixes in the early 1960s. The now general Navstar GPS, or Global Positioning System, was researched by the U.S. Navy and Air Force during the 1970s. Essentially GPS works by the generation of a highly accurate time signal using the satellite's atomic clock; measurements of the fractional delays between the transmission and reception from different satellites provide the position of a user. Eleven developmental satellites were launched by 1985, with the first operational GPS satellite on station in 1989. Since then GPS receiver systems have been mounted in all forms of craft and are now used as handheld navigation devices by individual soldiers. GPS also has many other uses, including the targeting of missiles and the calibration of early-warning systems.

The GPS system is controlled by the Master Control Station at the Falcon Air Force Base, Colorado Springs, Colorado. Two separate coded signals are used, a general "C/A" code at around 1 MHz being available to all and providing accuracy of about 35 to 100 meters, whilst the "P" code is used by the military to achieve a pinpoint fix. Measurements conducted by the U.S. Air Force Space Division in 1988 showed that the location given by the military system was then accurate to within ten meters. The improved Differential system, or DGPS, designed to reduce error and atmospheric distortion, is calculated to have an accuracy within four meters. The full "constellation" of 24 GPS satellites was agreed to by the U.S. Congress for the mid-1990s. Glonass, a similar Soviet system, saw the launch of 40 navigational satellites between 1982 and the end of the communist system.

Though there are various meteorological satellite systems, only some are specifically military. In the United States the Defense Meteorological Satellite Program operates its own satellites. These orbit at a comparatively low 500 km and transmit their information in coded form to U.S. forces. Command "readout" sites are provided at the U.S. Air Force Global Weather Center at Offut, Nebraska, and the U.S. Navy Fleet Numerical Oceanography Center at Monterey, California.

Satellite surveillance is of critical and growing importance; it has been calculated that well over a third of all satellites ever launched have been for surveillance purposes. Improvement of resolution in both the optical and electromagnetic spectra has been key. Data transmission is now instantaneous for all intents and purposes, though old-fashioned problems like atmospheric conditions and the timing of orbits remain.

In the United States the Keyhole Satellite Program commenced in the late 1950s with the Discoverer series, which has been reported as a cover for the Central Intelligence Agency's own secret Corona surveillance operation. From 1966 to 1984 KH-8 series satellites were used. The earliest relied on exposed film being delivered in canisters, or snatched from parachutes, with obvious drawbacks in terms of time and efficiency. The KH-9 Big Bird satellite, current from 1971 to 1986, incorporated a scanning and transmission facility, though this did not have the best definition. The 19-meter KH-11 type, first revealed (illegally) in 1984, relied entirely on electro-optics. Its data could be transmitted via other satellites, meaning a continuous flow of information whatever the orbit. Optical spy satellites are now capable of picking out individuals on the ground. SAR, or synthetic-aperture radar, satellites may sense at night or in bad weather. Hyperspectral satellites, which commenced operations in 2001, use different wavelengths across the light spectrum and are particularly useful for the differentiation of terrain types.

Military satellites are by no means inviolate. Press reports of 2002 suggested that computer hackers working for the Bosnian Serbs had managed to download data received from U.S. and allied satellites over the Balkans, thus giving them useful and otherwise secret data.

Additional Reading: Dutton, *Military Space*, 1990; Lee, *War in Space*, 1986; Hobbs, *Space Warfare*, 1986; Chetty, *Satellite Technology and Its Applications*, 1988; Tetley and Calcutt, *Electronic Navigation Systems*, 2001; Johnson, *Soviet Military*

Strategy in Space, 1987; Friedman, *Seapower and Space*, 2000.

SAW. *See* Minimi

SBR. *See* Strategic Defense Initiative

Scharnhorst WARSHIP

The name *Scharnhorst* has long been associated with German warships; a 11,600-ton **cruiser** *Scharnhorst* was built in 1907 and was sunk during the battle of the Falklands in World War I.

Its more famous **battleship** namesake was launched in 1936 and took part in the invasion of Norway in 1940, later sinking the British **aircraft carrier** *Glorious*. **Mined** in the English Channel in 1942, she was finally sunk by the *Duke of York* and other vessels in December 1943. The World War II *Scharnhorst* was 753 feet long, displaced 39,000 tons, and had a top speed of 32 knots. Her crew was 1,840 and her main armament nine 11-inch guns.

Additional Reading: Koop and Schmolke, *Battleships of the Scharnhorst Class*, 1999; Lenton, *German Warships of the Second World War*, 1975; Whitley, *German Capital Ships*, 1989.

Schmeisser, Hugo INVENTOR; FIREARM

The German Hugo Schmeisser is properly remembered as one of the fathers of the **submachine gun** and acknowledged as the designer of the Bergmann MP 18, as well as the improved model 1928. During World War II, working at Haenel, he also played a significant part in the development of the first successful **assault rifle**. Ironically, he had very little, if anything, to do with the **MP 38** and **MP 40** weapons, which were often popularly dubbed "Schmeissers."

Additional Reading: Ezell, *Small Arms of the World*, various editions; Bruce, *German Automatic Weapons of World War II*, 1996; Ellis and Chamberlain, *The Schmeisser*, 1999.

Schneider Assault Tank TANK

Cooperation between Holt Tractors and Schneider made possible the design and manufacture of the French Schneider **tank** during the latter part of World War I. It was first committed to action in April 1917 at the Chemin des Dames; about 400 had been built by August 1918. The Schneider was powered by a four-cylinder, 55 horsepower gasoline engine and was capable of 4.6 mph on the road. It had a crew of six and was armed with a 75 mm gun and two **machine guns**. Though useful, it was easily set alight.

Additional Reading: Crow, *AFVs of World War I*, 1998; Touzin and Gurtner, *Chars d'Assaut* (undated).

Schnorkel; *Schnorchel;* Snorkel MISCELLANEOUS

A schnorkel is a tube, or tubes, allowing men or machines to obtain air under water. It has been suggested that the word derives from the German *Schnorkel*, meaning "ornament" or "eccentricity," but *Schnorchel* may equally mean "snort." In its most primitive form, that of a hollow reed or tube, the schnorkel is of great antiquity. Attempts were also made to fit schnorkels to some of the earliest **submarines**. In 1894 U.S. pioneer Simon Lake applied the principle to his *Argonaut*, but Japanese experiment on similar lines led to disaster in April 1910 when a breathing tube flooded, leading to the loss of a vessel and its 16-man crew. Nevertheless, pioneering work by the Dutch navy in the 1930s improved on the basic concept by adding a sophisticated valve and an electric motor to raise the tube. From 1943 Schnorkels were fitted to German **U-boats**, allowing them to run the diesel engines underwater. Rather than delivering air straight to the engine however, the tube entered the main compartment, thus creating an air buffer. Schnorkels have since become a common feature of submarine design.

Schooner WARSHIP

The original sailing schooner, which originated about 1700, was a gaff-rigged vessel with two or more masts, the "gaff" being a spar to extend the head of a fore-and-aft sail. Though later widely used, this fast type was popularized in America, first printed mention of the name being credited to Boston in 1717. Use of schooners as small general-purpose warships and transports began during the French and Indian War of 1755–1763. Sailing schooners continued to be used well into the nineteenth century, and the name persisted thereafter.

Additional Reading: Chapelle, *The History of the American Sailing Navy*, 1949; Gardiner, *Line of Battle*.

Schu. *See* Mine

Schwarzlose   FIREARM

The Schwarzlose was the main **machine gun** of the Austro-Hungarian empire. Following less than satisfactory results with both a Salvator-Dormus weapon and an early-model **Maxim**, the Austrians went their own way and adopted the model 1907 weapon designed by Andreas Schwarzlose. This 8 mm, belt-fed, water-cooled gun had a relatively short barrel and weighed 40 kg when its tripod was included. It worked on a delayed blowback principle, and quite effectively. Later models were still in use in World War II.

Schwimmwagen   VEHICLE

The World War II German Schwimmwagen was a four-wheel amphibious car manufactured by Volkswagen. Made of welded sheet metal, its body resembled the hull of a small boat. Driven by a 1,131 cc engine, it was fitted with an extended crankshaft that could be engaged with a propellor shaft for use in water. A similar 1942 model quarter-ton truck was also built on a very limited basis by Trippelwerke Homburg.

After World War II the idea continued to appeal to both halves of the divided Germany. The German Democratic Republic forces operated a P2S amphibious field car. This was capable of 60 mph on roads, 6 mph in water, and had a payload of 450 kg. In the West, the Federal Republic experimented with BMW six-seater amphibians.

SCORE. *See* Satellites

Scud (SS-1) Missile   MISSILE

The Soviet Scud missile, a direct descendent of the **V2**, was first deployed in the mid-1960s. Unlike the **Frog** it was equipped with movable fins. Early versions (A, B, and C), were capable of less than 100 miles range and were seen on either tracked or wheeled launchers. Used in both the Yom Kippur War of 1973 and the Iran-Iraq War, they would later come to international prominence in the Gulf War of 1991.

Here Iraqi improved models, such as the Al Hussein and Al Abbas, would prove particularly problematic due to their increased range and ability to hit Israel and Saudi Arabia. With a range now estimated at up to 500 miles, the Scud is still thought to be a threat due to its ability to carry **nuclear, chemical** or **biological** warheads. Attempts were made to intercept Scuds using **Patriot** missiles, and since then **Arrow** has been produced for that purpose.

Additional Reading: *Jane's Weapons Systems*; Zaloga, *The Scud*, 2000.

SDI. *See* Strategic Defense Initiative

SdKfz 250, 251. *See* Half-Track

Sea Harrier. *See* Harrier

Sea Knight. *See* Chinook

Sea Mine   EXPLOSIVE DEVICE

The idea of floating **explosives** in water to damage enemy ships or works dates back to at least the sixteenth century. One method that proved promising was to use the flow of a river or estuary to carry a bomb to its target. Strictly speaking, however, such devices were delayed-action bombs rather than true sea mines. By 1776, during the American Revolution, David Bushnell had devised a charge, placed by a small **submarine**, that could be exploded underwater to destroy ships. He is thus popularly regarded as the father of sea mine warfare. This idea would later be updated in the **Maiale**.

About 1810 another American, Robert Fulton, put forward proposals for what was effectively the first contact mine. This consisted of a large copper container moored by means of a weight and anchor. Within the container was **gunpowder**, on top of which was a firing mechanism, set off when struck by a ship. "Controlled mining" appeared in 1843, when Samuel **Colt** succeeded in firing mines electrically from the shore. Mines of similar type were used in Schleswig-Holstein about 1850 and in defense of Russian ports during the Crimean War. The Russian mines used a glass tube **fuse** that broke on impact allowing acid and chemicals to mix, creating heat that initiated the main charge.

Sea mines were widely deployed in the American Civil War. Some types were deployed in pairs, linked by a line to detonate them when pulled. The more advanced Singer mine incorporated a safety-pin system. The Brooks shallow-water mine introduced the idea of the antisweeping device that exploded a larger mine underneath if the upper part of the system was interfered with.

A significant advance came in 1868, when Dr. Herz of the Prussian mine-defense committee invented the Herz "horn." These protuberances from the surface of a sea mine each contained a carbon plate, a zinc plate, and a glass tube containing a bichromate solution. When the horn was bent—as, for example, when struck against the hull of a ship—the liquid met the plates, creating the effect of a small battery. The electric discharge was enough to fire the detonator. Not long after came the countermine, a line of electrically fired mines that could be let out and exploded, for the express purpose of clearing enemy mines.

The Japanese and Russians both deployed mines in the war of 1904, in what has been noted as the first extensive use of independent, or open sea, mining. The Japanese used an electrically activated model set off when an inertia weight moved, completing a circuit; they

achieved success against the Russian flagship *Petropavlovsk*, which was sunk, and the battleship *Pobieda*, which was damaged. Later the Russians also scored notable victories, mining several cruisers and battleships. As a result many nations were forced to reappraise the importance of the sea mine.

By World War I the basic weapon was the moored contact mine. This consisted of a hollow steel **shell** containing a charge of perhaps 600 lb of TNT, or later Amatol, which was tethered to the seabed by means of an iron or concrete "sinker" and wire. Yet there were many variations; the Swedish designed Leon mine was cylindrical, rising and sinking by means of a small propellor and hydrostatic valve, while the Italian Scotti countermine sank after laying and exploded at a preset depth. The U.S.-produced antenna mine featured a projection above the body of the mine and an insulator some way below. A steel ship in contact set up a sea cell, and electrical discharge set off the mine. Though relatively delicate, antenna mines had the advantage of covering more vertical space. Another variation employed was the mined net, which formed a physical obstruction to **submarines**, which might also destroy them.

A common method of clearance during World War I was the A sweep, essentially a wire that ran between two **minesweeping** vessels, being secured at one end by a quick-release slip. The **Oropesa sweep** appeared at the end of the war. Sweep obstructors were designed to damage sweeps before they could deal with mines.

By 1939 sea mining had become a highly developed science, with new mines capable of rising and falling with the tides, preset depth adjustment, and delayed-action release of mines from the seabed. Minelayers also became more sophisticated, with the use of submarines and ship-mounted "chain conveyors" arming and dropping mines into the water without human intervention. Experiment with acoustic mines, designed to be set off by noise, had begun by 1937. A counter developed early in the war was the acoustic hammer, set in the bows of sweepers to create noise and vibration, thus exploding the mines. There was massive demand for mine clearance vessels; trawlers, drifters, and whalers were all adapted for sweeping. Allied navies alone had over 1,300 of these vessels. Purpose-built U.S. minesweeper types included the *Auk* and *Admirable* classes.

Development of magnetic mines had begun as early as 1917, but it was the Germans who deployed them to greatest effect early in World War II. These incorporated an electrical unit that picked up the magnetic fields of passing ships; a sufficiently strong interference closed contacts and detonated the mine. The G mine of 1941 was particularly dangerous, since it was less sensitive and would usually allow smaller ships, including minesweepers, to pass before exploding under larger targets. In addition to the ordinary **double L sweep**, mine destructor vessels were now employed that contained large electromagnets in their holds and over the bows. In theory, mines exploded at a distance, but the enemy introduced magnetic mines with delays, causing mine destructor ships to be hit.

Perhaps a better method of avoiding the magnetic mine was "degaussing," wrapping electric cable around vessels to reduce their magnetic signature. Wooden **motor minesweepers** were also part of the solution, but the enemy sought constantly to use new methods to frustrate mine clearance. German preventive measures in the latter part of World War II included static cutters, cone-shaped explosive charges on floats, and heavy mooring chains difficult for minesweepers to clear.

The sea mine remains a significant weapon, becoming ever more complex. Just some of the many of recent years are the French Thomson CSF series, the Italian MISAR, the Russian AMD, and a wide variety of U.S. types sown from the air. New antihandling measures, devices to attract submarines, and pressure-sensitive Oyster mines have proved especially problematic. In recent decades fast **hovercraft** and hydrofoils have been favored for countermeasures duties; having minimum draft, they are less likely to cause mines to detonate. In the German Troika system, three unmanned remote minesweepers were used. Yet in the absence of large fleets of minesweepers there has been em-phasis on disposal by divers, who place charges to cause controlled explosions.

Additional Reading: Cowie, *Mines, Minelayers and Minelaying*, 1949; Elliott, *Allied Minesweeping*, 1979; Lenton, *American Gunboats and Minesweepers*, 1974; Lord, *Civil War Collector's Encyclopedia; Jane's Weapons Systems;* Sueter, *The Evolution of the Submarine Boat, Mine and Torpedo*, 1907.

Sea Sparrow. *See* **Sparrow**

Seawolf Missile   MISSILE

The Seawolf missile is a close-range surface-to-air and surface-to-surface missile developed by **British Aerospace** Dynamics Group. Development under the code number PX430 commenced in 1967. The supersonic missile, 6 feet 7 inches long, carries a high-explosive warhead with proximity fuse and is guided by means of a Marconi **radar** system. Tests have shown it capable of intercepting both shells and other missiles in flight. On ships it is usually fired from a six-barrel launcher. The Seawolf served in the Falklands, and in 1985 a vertical launch version was tested for the first time.

***Seawolf* Class**   SUBMARINE

The U.S. *Seawolf* class of **submarines** comprises three vessels. The 8,000-ton vessels *Seawolf* (SSN 21) and *Connecticut* were commissioned in 1997 and 1998, respectively; the incomplete *Jimmy Carter* is delayed due to an intended increase in size. It is intended that the *Jimmy Carter* will be launched in 2004. Research and development alone cost more than a billion dollars.

The main armament of *Seawolf* submarines comprises **Tomahawk** missiles and **torpedoes**. The class was designed to be even quieter, and carry more weapons, than the *Los Angeles* class, while providing special forces support. It has even been claimed that the *Seawolf* is quieter under way than a *Los Angeles* when moored. Seawolf is 353 feet long and powered by a S6W pressurized water reactor, giving a top speed of 39 knots, though quietness is best at around 20 knots; it is capable of diving to almost 2,000 feet. The crew numbers 134. Roughly three-quarters of the earth's land mass can be reached by missiles fired from *Seawolf* submarines.

Additional Reading: Saunders (ed), *Jane's Fighting Ships*.

Self-Propelled Gun; Self-Propelled Artillery ARTILLERY

Self-propelled guns are artillery pieces with an integral method of propulsion. The widest definition therefore includes guns with small motors to allow localized maneuver, and fully tracked, heavily armored, and turreted armored fighting vehicles. Common subdivisions include *Sturmgeschütz* (StuG), or assault guns, intended for close support of infantry and **tank** attacks, and self-propelled artillery, which may be lightly armored, if at all, open topped, and designed to stand off at a distance while bombarding, in much the same way as conventional artillery.

The common ancestor of the modern self-propelled gun is the gun carrier developed by the British in 1917. This consisted of a tank-type hull with tracks; in it was mounted a 6-inch **howitzer**. During World War II a vast number of self-propelled guns were introduced. Famous among these were the U.S. Priest, which featured a 105 mm gun on a **Sherman**-type chassis, and the M12, with its 155 mm gun. A British 25 pounder self-propelled piece was known as the Sexton.

The German army fielded a particularly wide variety of self-propelled artillery, including the 105 mm Wespe, or "wasp," and the 150 mm Hummel. Many guns were also put on the chassis of captured foreign tanks. The German StuGs, commonly with 75 mm or 105 mm guns, were normally based on the **Panzer** III. These were fully armored and enclosed, and they were frequently used in support of infantry attacks. Perhaps the ultimate self-propelled gun of the period was the "King Kong," or U.S. 240 mm Howitzer Motor Carriage, only a handful of which had been completed by the end of hostilities.

Since 1945, self-propelled guns have continued to fill a significant niche, being particularly important in enabling artillery to keep up with and support tanks and armored infantry. Notable examples have included the French AMX-105 and 155, based on AMX tanks; the U.S. **Paladin** M109 and the M107, with its 175 mm gun; the small British FV 433 Abbot; and the **Bofors**-manufactured Swedish VK-155. The South African G6 Rhino 155 mm is particularly well regarded; it is based on a Canadian logging vehicle.

Additional Reading: Dunstan, *Self Propelled Howitzers*, 1988.

Semiautomatic FIREARM

Semiautomatic weapons, or "self-loading" arms, reload for the next shot after the previous one has been discharged. Typically all the firer has to do is squeeze the trigger again. The main methods by which such operation is achieved in **pistols** are "blowback" and "recoil." In either case the energy comes from the discharge of the cartridge. Blowback is generally used with the least powerful **cartridges**, operating from an unlocked breech mechanism. Recoil operation is generally applied with more powerful cartridges, where breechblock and barrel remain locked together for part of the cycle.

Semiautomatic long arms, such as **rifles**, are often described as gas operated and commonly work by trapping a portion of the gas caused by the discharge of the weapon to work pistons and cylinders. Nevertheless, some, such as the **Johnson** "automatic rifle," have used recoil operation. Particularly noteworthy military semiautomatic weapons have included the **Colt** model 1911, **Luger** and **Browning** pistols, the **Garand, M1 carbine**, and the **FN SLR**.

Additional Reading: Hogg and Weeks, *Military Small Arms of the Twentieth Century*, 1977, 1994.

Semtex EXPLOSIVE

Named by taking the first four letters of the Czech town Semtin, where it was first made, and the beginning of the word "**explosive**," Semtex is a highly malleable plastic explosive.

Sen Toku

Invented by Stanislav Brebera in 1966, it is most widely encountered in two forms. In Semtex A, the bulk is PETN (Pentaerythritol tetranitrate), while in Semtex H there are roughly equal proportions of RDX (Research Department Explosive) and PETN.

When Semtex became associated with terrorism, as at the infamous Lockerbie bombing, the manufacturers added a chemical to give it a distinctive odor, and metal traces to aid detection. Nevertheless, problems continued. The Explosia company was therefore taken into government control in 2002.

Sen Toku   SUBMARINE

The giant Japanese *Sen Toku* **aircraft**-carrying vessels were the largest **submarines** of World War II. At 400 feet long, they were equipped with three seaplanes, eight 21-inch **torpedo** tubes, and deck guns, the largest of which was 140 mm. Though 18 were planned, only three were completed, and the last of these, the *I-402*, was converted into a fuel carrier. The *Sen Toku*s were double hulled, with the hulls side by side, an arrangement later repeated in the Soviet **Typhoon.**

Additional Reading: Januszewski, *Japanese Submarine Aircraft*, 2002; Hutchinson, *Submarines: War beneath the Waves*, 2001; Treadwell, *Submarines with Wings*, 1985; Polmar and Carpenter, *Submarines of the Imperial Japanese Navy*, 1986.

Sentry. *See* **AWACS**

Sexton. *See* **Self-Propelled Gun**

Shackleton. *See* **Lancaster**

Shahine. *See* **Crotale**

Shaped Charge. *See* **Hollow Charge**

Sharps Carbine; Sharps Rifle   FIREARM

Invented by Christian Sharps in 1848 the Sharps is one of the best-known U.S. shoulder arms. Key to its success was a breechblock mechanism that moved vertically. Early **per**cussion models used automatic primers. At the end of the Civil War the weapon was adapted for use with metal **cartridges**.

Shell   SHELL

The word "shell" predates its military application by many centuries, appearing with the spelling "scell" or "scille," to denote the carapaces of shellfish and animals, as early as the eighth century. It was therefore natural that the name should be adopted for the hard outer case of an **explosive** device in the sixteenth century. In 1644 Nathaniel Nye referred explicitly to **grenades** as "small shels" filled with fine **gunpowder.** Falconer's *Marine Dictionary* of 1769 defined shell as "a great hollow ball filled with powder." The word was also soon applied to the outer covering of the **cartridge**, and it is interesting to note that in American English usage "shells" can be taken to mean small arms as well as **artillery** munitions. Most shells were spherical until the midnineteenth century, at which time the elongated shape we now regard as characteristic began to emerge.

The filling of artillery shells remained a purely manual operation for centuries; film footage as late as World War I shows women using jugs, wooden mallets, and tamping sticks. Yet the advances of metallurgy, chemistry, and engineering have all helped to make the shell more effective, and recently many of the processes have been automated. The production of more specialized types of shell has also become possible with the passage of time. Pyrotechnic, incendiary, and smoke shells were all known in the seventeenth century. Solid, hardened, or capped APC shells for **armor** piercing appeared in the later nineteenth century. Since then, message-carrying shells, **gas** shells, discarding **sabots**, submunitions, and chemical shells have all been introduced. **Fusing** has also become more reliable and more complex.

Sometimes a distinction is made between explosive shells and "carrier" shells, which release something on arrival. The antipersonnel and the antimaterial properties of the explosive shell rely on two main effects, blast and fragmentation. The fragments of the burst shell are

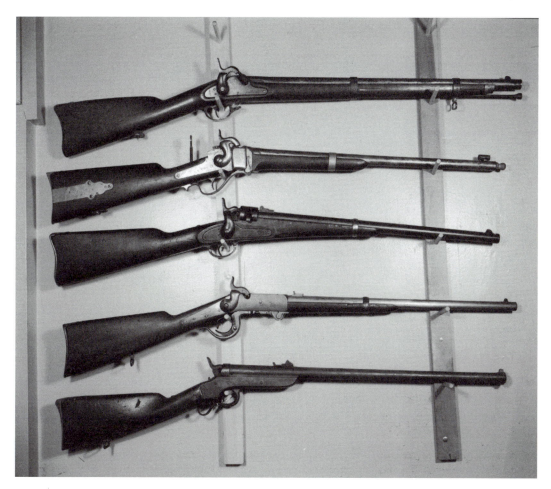

A selection of American Civil War period firearms. Top to bottom: a Confederate .58 caliber musket; a Sharps carbine; a Joslyn carbine; a Burnside carbine; and a Sharps and Hankins carbine. © Hulton/Getty Images.

often referred to as **"shrapnel."** In fixed-ammunition artillery shells, the metal **cartridge** and the shell itself are supplied as one unit. In such an instance the brass, or other metal, container for the propellant is refferd to as a "shell case."

Additional Reading: General Staff (UK), *Notes on German Shells*; Gudgin, *Armoured Firepower: The Development of Tank Armament 1939–1945*, 1997; Hogg, *British and American Artillery of World War II*, 1978; Hogg, *The Illustrated Encyclopedia of Ammunition*, 1985.

Sheridan Tank, M551   TANK

The U.S. Sheridan light **tank** was designed specifically for reconnaisance, having a light aluminum hull and steel turret. About 1,700 were produced by Allison between 1966 and 1970. The most novel feature was the 152 mm dual-purpose gun and launcher system, which could fire conventional **shells** or launch Shillelagh missiles. Though the retirement of the Sheridan was announced as early as 1978, some remained in service with the 82nd Airborne Division, seeing use in the Gulf War of 1991.

Sherman Tank, M4   TANK

The Sherman may not have been a technological wonder, but it was a miracle of industrial production. Eleven plants in the United States produced 49,000 of all variants. This figure exceeded the production of all tanks made by

The ubiquitous Sherman M4 tank, 1942. In a typical factory scene numerous Shermans are lined up to undergo checks before rolling off the assembly line. The Sherman may not have been the best tank in the world—but it was there, in numbers, just when it was needed. Courtesy of the Library of Congress.

Germany and Britain combined during World War II and led some to dub the Sherman "the tank that won the war." Though this statement might more accurately be applied to the **T-34**, the Sherman story is remarkable.

The Sherman began with the T6 Medium Tank project of 1941, which hoped to address the identified shortcomings of the M3 Grant. Objectives included improved gun performance and traverse, better silhouette, and better armor. To speed work it was decided to retain the basic engine, chassis, and suspension of the M3. The M4 Sherman had a 75 mm gun, a maximum of 80 mm armor, and a Continental R957C1 nine-cylinder radial engine giving a top speed of 24 mph. This made it a tolerable match for the **Panzer** IV and vastly superior to anything

fielded by the Japanese. Yet Germany was producing new tanks and antitank weapons, and the Sherman obtained a reputation as the "Ronson," or "Tommy Cooker"—because it lit at the first strike and had a habit of incinerating its crews.

There were therefore constant attempts to improve the Sherman. These included the diesel-engine M4A2, the slightly faster M4A2, the powerful British 17-pounder gun variant "Firefly," the M4(105) with close-support howitzer, and the heavily armored M4A3E2 "Jumbo." The tank had a long postwar existence with countries as diverse as Israel and Idi Amin's Uganda. **Tank destroyers**, troop carriers, and many other variants were produced.

Additional Reading: Forty, *M4 Sherman*, 1987; Forty, *United States Tanks of World War II*, 1983; Ford, *Sherman Tank*, 1999; Gudgin, *Armoured Firepower: The Development of Tank Armament 1939–1945*, 1997.

Shield   ARMOR

The word "shield" has been applied to a wide range of protective devices and structures; hence, **artillery** pieces may have shields to protect the crew, while lead can be used as a shield against radiation. Body shields may be part of **armor**. Nevertheless, "shield" is most commonly applied to a handheld object, often of metal, wood, or hide, used to parry or obstruct such weapons as **swords**. Archaeological evidence suggests that the idea is five or more thousand years old, and that shields were in regular use in ancient Egypt and Sumaria.

Various civilizations and historical periods have favored different types of shield. Classical Greek armies are best known for their large round shields, usually supported on the arm and gripped with a separate handle near the rim. Round and oval shields predominated in early Rome, while a distinctive coffin shape was often carried by the Celts. Legionaries of imperial Rome were distinguished by large oblong convex shields that could be linked to form a defensive *testudo*, or tortoise. The kite-shaped shield of the Normans was well adapted to cover a large proportion of the body, especially when mounted. The classic shorter, more triangular, definitive "shield" shape, was characteristic of the high Middle Ages.

Though carrying shields in European war became rare by the sixteenth century, at least in part due to the advent of effective firearms, they continued to have specialized functions and were still widely used in other parts of the world. Many cultures would retain local shield types until quite recently. So it was that the hippo leather shields of the Sudan and the large hide shields of the Zulu were encountered in combat until the end of the nineteenth century. In the Americas the availability of suitable materials appears to have been a particularly significant factor, with elk hide more common in the North, buffalo and deerskin in the Midwest, and wood and wicker in some other regions. Elaborate metal *dhal* were made in parts of India.

Specific types of shield used in the later European context included the round "targe" of the Scottish Highlander and the joust; small bucklers used to parry in sword fighting; and the "parvise," a large shield rested on the ground to shelter soldiers, such as **crossbow** men. Metal shields were revived on a limited scale during the trench warfare of World War I, and perspex shields still have some use in riot situations.

Additional Reading: Stone, *A Glossary of the Construction, Decoration and Use of Arms and Armor*, 1934; Tarassuk and Blair, *The Complete Encyclopaedia of Arms and Weapons*, 1979; Connolly, *Greece and Rome at War*, 1981.

Ship of the Line. *See* Line of Battle; Battleship

Shokaku Class   WARSHIP

The *Shokaku* class of Japanese **aircraft carriers** comprised two vessels, the *Shokaku*, commissioned in August 1941, and the *Zuikaku*, commissioned a month later. With 84 aircraft apiece, they were capacious, and reasonably fast, having a maximum speed of 18 knots. They were important vessels, and it has even been suggested that the timing of the Pearl harbor attack was influenced by their completion. Both were sunk in 1944.

Shotgun   FIREARM

Arguably the shotgun came into existence when, probably in the fifteenth century, handheld guns were first loaded with multiple shot. The idea soon gained currency for both sport and war, as shot spreads out when leaving the barrel of the gun, increasing the probability of a hit and causing devastating injury at close range. Though it is not invariably the case, shotguns tend to be smooth, relatively wide bored, and often short in the barrel. Bellmouthed blunderbusses saw limited military use from the sixteenth century and were subsequently fired from warships as a method of close-range deck clearance.

Ordinary muskets were also multishotted to similar effect, as was recorded in both the English Civil War and American Revolutionary War. From the eighteenth century, short double-barrel shotguns became the norm, and in the early nineteenth century an elevated central rib was added to the basic design, improving both sighting and rigidity. Such weapons saw quite widespread use in the American Civil War, when their ready availability and easy aiming made them suitable for poorly trained troops. With the advent of one-piece **cartridges**, shotguns attained a new level of efficiency, and automatic ejection of fired cases and hammerless **breechloaders** made their appearance. The 12 gauge or 12 bore shotgun became the commonest type, the 12 referring to the notional number of solid balls fitting the barrel required to make a pound weight. So it is that a 20 gauge shotgun has a small-diameter barrel, while a 10 gauge barrel is large.

Though lever-action repeating **Winchester** shotguns enjoyed some success from 1887, it was **Browning**'s work with pump and **semi-automatic** actions that made the shotgun a significant weapon of modern war. The 1897 Browning pump action, with a **bayonet** fitting, saw use as a "trench broom" or "trench sweeper" in World War I. In World War II and afterward, the shotgun was particularly used in jungle situations, where close-range firepower was at a premium.

Latterly, shotguns have been seen as useful for special forces and, contrary to their original rationale, have often been used to fire one large slug or ball. Such munitions may be specially adapted as miniature **grenades**; solid, to break engine blocks or doors; or lightweight, to limit the chance of causing indiscriminate casualties. Shotguns are extremely potent in the right situation, but the majority are not much use at more than fifty yards. Regarding the "pattern" when used with small shot, a modern rule of thumb is that the shot spread about one inch per yard of range. Thus, at five yards a shotgun

blast will commonly cause a huge, and usually fatal, wound perhaps five inches across, while at 60 yards the pellets are so dissipated as to be nearly ineffective.

Additional Reading: Swearengen, *The World's Fighting Shotguns*, 1978; Long, *Streetsweepers*, 1987; *Jane's Infantry Weapons*.

Shrapnel   AMMUNITION

In common usage the word "shrapnel" may be taken to denote any fragments of **shell** or bomb. It also has a more specific meaning in reference to Major General Henry Shrapnel (1761–1842), who produced a shell during the 1780s, to which was originally applied the name "spherical case shot." This consisted of a hollow iron ball filled with small shot, designed to burst over or within the target. This brought to the enemy, as the maker observed, the effects of **case shot** at long range. It was used at the siege of Surinam in 1804 and in the Napoleonic wars. Sadly, however, Shrapnel was not so much an inventor as a rediscoverer, as the same idea had been applied to **mortar shells** almost two centuries earlier.

Nevertheless, the name "shrapnel" stuck and has since been widely applied. By the beginning of the twentieth century, shrapnel shells were in common use by the field **artilleries** of many nations, a typical example being the British 18-pounder shrapnel round. This consisted of a brass case with a percussion cap in the base, into the open end of which was fixed the shell head. Striking the percussion cap set off the main charge of propellant, launching the shell down the barrel and leaving the case behind. The nose of the shell itself was fitted with a time fuse, which, if set to the correct range, would burst the projectile, showering the opposition with 364 fast-moving steel balls.

Britain alone produced 72 million 18-pounder shrapnel shells during the First World War. Yet a weakness of shrapnel rounds was a relative ineffectiveness against troops under cover, so after the onset of trench warfare it became less important.

Additional Reading: Bidwell and Graham, *Fire-power*, 1982; Hogg, *The Illustrated Encyclopedia of Ammunition*, 1985.

Shturmovik, Il-2 AIRCRAFT

Bronirovanni shturmovik is Russian for "armored attacker," a name commonly applied to the Soviet single-engine Ilyushin Il-2 ground-attack **aircraft**. Developed as a protoype in 1938 and first flown at the end of 1939, the two-seater Shturmovik was of mixed wood and duraluin construction, with heavy armor in vital areas. Though better than many Soviet aircraft of World War II, achieving some combat success against German planes, its prime attributes were twofold. Most importantly, it was made in huge numbers, total production being reported as 35,000. Secondly, it was able to carry 1,300 lb of bombs, or cannon up to 37 mm, making it a highly useful weapon in battles of encirclement, such as Stalingrad.

Additional Reading: Gordon and Khazanov, *Soviet Combat Aircraft of the Second World War*, 1998; Taylor, *Combat Aircraft of the World*, 1969.

Sidewinder Articulated Cargo VEHICLE

The Chevrolet Sidewinder was a U.S. experimental vehicle of 1964, developed in conjunction with GM Defense Research Laboratories. Powered by a 195 horsepower engine, it was intended for extreme terrain and was amphibious. The biggest novelty, however, was that it was constructed in three "modules," with the engine in the center compartment. The modules could rotate independently to allow for very rough surfaces. It could thus be seen as a further development of the **Gama Goat** idea. In 1966 a larger amphibious Chevrolet "Tactical Articulated Swimmable Carrier" was produced, based on the Sidewinder work.

Sidewinder Missile MISSILE

Probably the best-known air-to-air munition of all time, the U.S. Sidewinder family of missiles evolved from the AIM-9A, a prototype first fired successfully as early as 1953. In 1956 the first production model, the AIM-9B, went into service. The 9B was originally manufactured by Philco-Ford and in Germany, and a total of over 60,000 were made. It was 284 cm long, weighed 75 kg, and had a range of a little over a kilometer.

Since then there have been a multitude of updates and improvements, leading to an exponential improvement in performance over the years. The 9E, for example, features improved guidance and control, while the 9J improved on both maneuverability and speed, for use with the F-15. A Soviet counterpart to the Sidewinder was the Atoll (AA-2, or K-13A).

Additional Reading: Westrum, *Sidewinder*, 1999; *Jane's Weapons Systems*.

SIG-Sauer MANUFACTURER; FIREARM

The Schweizerische Industrie-Gesellschaft arms company was established in Switzerland in the nineteenth century. More recently SIG has come to prominence in conjunction with the German Sauer company as a supplier of **semi-automatic pistols**. Particularly acclaimed was the SIG-Sauer P6, or P225 **double-action** model, a 9 mm with an eight-round magazine. The P226, developed in the late 1980s, was intended as a candidate for use by U.S. forces, though ultimately it lost out to the **Beretta**.

Sikorsky, Igor HELICOPTER

Despite the parallel efforts of other inventors and early German successes, the Ukrainian Igor Sikorsky (1889–1972) is rightly regarded as the father of the modern **helicopter**. As early as 1909 he made a primitive prototype in his parents' summerhouse; it could glide across the floor, but as yet there was no engine with sufficient power-to-weight ratio to lift such a machine from the ground. Thereafter Sikorsky turned his attentions to more conventional fixed-wing designs, winning a prize in a military aircraft competition with his S-6B in 1912. The next year he produced the world's first successful four-engine plane, the RBVZ S-21 Great Baltic. During World War I improved Sikorsky-designed fighters and multi-engined planes, such as the Ilya Mouromatz bomber, ap-

Igor Sikorsky operates one of his experimental helicopters. © Culver Pictures.

peared. Armed with several **machine guns**, this was capable of dropping bombs up to 540 lb and was ultimately produced in several models. In the Mourometz G, a tail gunner's position was provided; the gunner occupied the main cabin on takeoff and pulled himself through the fuselage on a board on rails to reach the tiny open pulpit at the rear.

After the 1917 Russian Revolution, Sikorsky moved via London and Paris to the United States. In 1923 he formed Sikorsky Aero Engineering, in part funded by the composer Rachmaninoff, and recommenced aircraft construction. From impoverished beginnings he established a reputation for flying boats, and in 1929 the company became part of United Aircraft. Products of this period included the S-38 amphibian, used by U.S. forces. Despite this

success, Sikorsky never abandoned his dream of rotor-driven flight. Drawings of what we would understand to be a helicopter were made in 1930, and he patented an autogyro based on the S-38 in 1932. In 1939 his VS-300, with its main overhead rotor and small antitorque tail rotor, made its first brief hops from the ground.

Within three years similar machines were able to spend over an hour in the air, and military tests had commenced. In 1942 the 75 mph Sikorsky XR-4 was accepted by the U.S. Army and went into production as the R-4, thus establishing a claim as the first military helicopter outside Germany. On 6 May 1943 it achieved the first helicopter landing aboard a ship, when Colonel Frank Gregory landed on the USS *Bunker Hill*. It performed the first recorded helicopter mercy mission by bringing supplies for men injured on the **destroyer** *Turner* on 3 January 1944. Combat rescue missions started soon afterward, when in April 1944 crashed aircrew were retrieved from behind Japanese lines. Two more helicopter models were produced during the war, the more streamlined R-5 and the buglike R-6 observation and utility machine.

After the war Sikorsky continued to be a world leader, and in November 1945 a Sikorsky S-51 performed the first helicopter hoist rescue. The S-51 and S-55 served in Korea, and the advent of bigger machines helped make air assault possible. In the turbine-engine S-61 of 1959 was found a helicopter platform suited to submarine hunting, minesweeping, gunship duties, and spacecraft recovery. Described as "a quantum jump" in helicopter capability, the S-61 featured an amphibious hull, a maximum speed of 166 mph, and a range of 625 miles. Used all over the world, it has been produced in many different variants, from the U.S. Air Force armored combat "Jolly Green Giant" to the Japanese Mitsubishi-manufactured examples of the late 1970s and 1980s. Though Sikorsky himself died in 1972, his name would continue as a brand of United Technologies Corporation. Current products of the company include the UH-60L **Black Hawk**, and the RAH-66 **Comanche**.

Additional Reading: Hunt, *Helicopter*, 1998; Taylor, *Sikorsky*, 1998.

Silencer FIREARM

The silencer reduces the sound of a firearm, thus conferring tactical advantage. Most silencers consist of a tube containing a system of holes and baffles that slow and diffuse the gas from the weapon. They work best with subsonic munitions, since projectiles moving faster than the speed of sound produce a distinctive "crack." Despite the popular name, few if any guns are completely silenced, so silencers are often technically described as "sound moderators" or "suppressors." Patents for silencers are noted from the 1890s.

The military silencer became popular with special forces and saboteurs in World War II.

The U.S. Office of Strategic Services worked with the National Defense Research Committee and the Maryland Research Laboratory, producing several silenced weapons, including the modified **Colt** Woodsman and High Standard H-D MS **semiautomatics**. The latter was ordered in some quantity, with the OSS catalogue of 1944 claiming that the H-D MS achieved a "90 percent noise reduction" and a complete elimination of muzzle flash. British silenced weapons included the De Lisle **carbine** and **Welrod** pistol.

Since 1945 many military firearms have been fitted with silencers. Just a few of the better known are the Chinese Type 64, the British L34A1**Sterling**, the Swedish Kulspruta, and the **Ingram** Model 10 **submachine guns**.

Additional Reading: Paulson, *Silencer*, 1996; Pate, *US Handguns of World War II*, 1998; Melton, *OSS Special Weapons and Equipment*, 1991; Ladd and Melton, *Clandestine Warfare: Weapons and Equipment of the SOE and OSS*, 1988; Truby, *Silencers, Snipers and Assassins*, 2001.

Sioux, H-13; Bell 47 HELICOPTER

The Bell company's Sioux **helicopter** is a derivative of the original Bell 47. According to company history, the project had its roots in the 1930s, when inventor Arthur Young built a viable helicopter model. It so impressed entrepreneur Larry Bell of the Bell **Aircraft** Corporation that he established Young in a shop at Gardenville, New York. The result was the Bell 30, an open-cockpit machine that was fully developed only at the end of World War II. In 1946 the latest Bell model, the 47, was granted its first certification for general use. In Korea the Bell was used with a stretcher pod on either side for casualty evacuation.

With widespread acceptance and full-scale production, the Bell 47 and its derivatives would become more or less the universal small military helicopter, with users as diverse as the United States, Peru, Iran, and Malta. Apart from the United States there was also manufacture in Italy, Japan, and the United Kingdom. The name "Sioux" was common to both the U.S. and British armies, though there have been many different models. Depending on role, machines have been fitted with machine guns, rocket pods, and guided missiles.

Skis   MISCELLANEOUS

The ski, for travel over snow, has existed for several thousand years, and its use in war was recorded as early as 1200 at the battle of Isen, near Oslo. Ski training was introduced to the Swedish and Norwegian armies in 1718. Long, narrow skis were used for gliding, while short types with seal skin attached to the running surface could be used to climb. Generally only a long single ski stick was used, the Swedes using a version with a **bayonet** during the Napoleonic period. Russian troops set a ten-day 1,115-mile endurance record in 1891.

France, Germany, Italy, and Canada were among those who used, or experimented with, ski troops in World War I. The equipment used at this time was mainly of wood and other natural materials but was recognizably similar to modern types. Together with sledges, **Ski-do** and **Snowcats**, skis remain a regular feature of artic and winter warfare.

Ski-do. *See* RAT

Skipjack   SUBMARINE

The name *Skipjack* has been used by a number of military vessels, several of them U.S. submarines. In the 1950s the name was applied to a class of six nuclear-powered U.S. Navy **submarines**, the *Skipjack* (SSN 595) herself being laid down at General Dynamics, Groton, Connecticut, in May 1955. *Scamp, Scorpion, Sculpin, Shark*, and *Snook* followed, with all complete by late 1961. Costing about $40 million apiece, they were 252 feet long, displaced 3,075 surfaced, and were capable of 30 knots submerged. They had six 21-inch tubes and could use nuclear torpedoes. Their design benefited from experimental work done on the *Albacore*. *Scorpion* was lost with all 99 hands 400 miles from the Azores in 1968; the rest of the class were scrapped in the 1990s.

Skorpion Submachine Gun   FIREARM

Designed in the 1950s, the innovative 7.65 mm Czechoslovak Skorpion was one of the first really small **submachine guns**. Made by Omnipol, this blowback weapon with folding butt and 20-round magazine was just 27 cm long in the folded position. It was particularly useful for tank crews and in confined spaces.

SKOT   VEHICLE

The SKOT was a post–World War II armored vehicle made by Tatra and developed jointly by Czechoslovakia and Poland. The acronym stood for "medium wheeled amphibious transporter." Weighing 12,500 kg the vehicle was powered by a 192 horsepower engine and was provided with propellers for crossing water.

Skyhawk, A-4; Super Skyhawk
                              AIRCRAFT

The Douglas A-4 Skyhawk attack **aircraft** entered U.S. service in 1956 and was a mainstay of the U.S. Navy and Marine Corps for about 20 years. One of its nicknames was "Heinemann's Hot Rod." This was fitting, since designer Ed Heinemann had succeeded in packing a lot of performance into a small space, with minimum weight.

Though the Skyhawk went out of frontline U.S. Navy duty three decades ago, it is remarkable that it has remained in use in a number of countries for much longer. Argentina, Israel, and Kuwait have been some of the better-known international customers. As recently as the 1990s New Zealand's Skyhawks were updated with new avionics under Project Kahu. Specifications for the A-4S-1 Super Skyhawk give a wingspan of 27 feet six inches, 701 mph top speed, and empty weight of 10,250 lb.

Skyhook. *See* B-17 and **Harrier**

Skyraider   AIRCRAFT

Described by the U.S. Navy in Korea as the "most effective" close-support **aircraft** in the world, the single-seat Douglas AD Skyraider was developed in the closing stages of World War II. It was produced until 1957, by which time 3,160 had been made. Designed to be used from **aircraft carriers**, the Skyraider was a low-wing all-metal monoplane with a 2,400 horsepower Wright Cyclone engine. Its maximum speed was 366 mph, and it was usually armed with two 20 mm cannon and up to 6,000 lb of bombs or other weapons.

Additional Reading: Smith, *Douglas AD Skyraider*, 1999; Rausa, *Skyraider*, Charleston, 2001.

Skytrain. *See* **C-47**

SLC. *See* **Maiale**

Sloop   WARSHIP

The term "sloop," of Dutch derivation, was in use from the early seventeenth century to describe small single-masted sailing vessels. By the 1670s the name had been applied to small warships with gun armament mounted on top of the main deck only. In 1769 *Falconer's Marine Dictionary* defined the "sloop of war" as a vessel that had between eight and 18 cannon. Sloops were quite widely employed in American operations, the Royal Navy sloops *Cyane* and *Levant* being sunk by the **frigate *Constitution*** in 1815.

The name "sloop" has since been variously applied to more modern, mechanically powered vessels. In World War I, for example, specially designed sloops were employed in antisubmarine work.

Additional Reading: Gardiner, *Line of Battle*; Cocker, *Frigates, Sloops and Patrol Vessels of the Royal Navy*, 1985.

Smart Bomb   EXPLOSIVE DEVICE

"Smart bomb" is the common term for air-dropped munitions that are guided to the target. They are thus unlike "dumb," or "iron," bombs, which are simply jettisoned by the pilot or bomb aimer and fall. The first laser-guided bomb (LGB) was dropped in U.S. tests as early as 1965. The **Hobos** system was used in Vietnam, as was the Walleye TV camera–guided bomb, which proved its worth against point targets.

Nevertheless, the concept only began to fire popular imagination during the early 1990s. It was then that video footage of the Gulf War was made public showing how targets could potentially be hit with pinpoint accuracy, leading to their destruction and the avoidance of "collateral damage," or the killing of civilians. This was in part successful public relations, since targets cannot be hit unless correctly identified. Nevertheless, precision guided munitions have made possible operations hitherto unimagined and have enabled actions to take place that high casualties might otherwise have precluded. Smart bombs have also achieved with very little expenditure what would previously have required many aircraft and many tons of munitions.

Probably the best known of the smart bombs are the Paveway laser-guided bombs. Using guidance systems developed by Texas Instruments, the first "Pave Storm" **cluster bombs** were dropped experimentally in 1971, and second, third, and fourth generations—each more sophisticated than the last—soon followed. By the 1980s there were also LLLGBs, or low-level laser-guided bombs, which incorporated the latest microprocessors, high-lift folding wings, and improved seeking scanners.

Laser-guided bombs are frequently used in conjunction with a ground laser target marker, which "paints" the target so the bombs can home onto it. Such portable laser target marker equipments can be carried by battlefield observers or by special forces delivered behind the front line specifically for the purpose. Alternatively, aircraft may mark the target themselves with a laser from the air.

Additional Reading: *Jane's Weapons Systems*; Richardson et al., *Surveillance and Target Acquisition Systems*, London, 1997.

SMG. *See* **Submachine Gun**

Smith and Wesson   MANUFACTURER; FIREARM

The world-renowned partnership of Smith and Wesson was begun by gunsmiths Horace Smith (1808–1893) of Cheshire, Massachusetts, and

Daniel Baird Wesson (1825–1906) of Worcester, Massachusetts, in 1852. The Smith and Wesson company was formed in 1855. Though they had worked independently on various repeating **rifle** and **pistol** projects, S&W became best known for its combination of metal cartridges and bored-through turning cylinders. The basic idea of **revolvers** with cylinders loaded with one-piece metal cartridges remains current to this day.

Commercial success was the result not only of technological skill but of long-term business acumen. A particularly vital year for the company was 1856, when the Samuel **Colt** patent on mechanically rotated cylinders expired; Smith and Wesson then bought a license from patentee Rollin White to manufacture weapons in which the chambers of the revolving cylinder could be loaded from the rear. White gave up his rights in exchange for a royalty of 25 cents per gun and also agreed to defend the patent against infringement.

Some of the first revolvers produced by Smith and Wesson were the small "tip up" models, in which the barrel was rotated upward and the cylinder was removed for loading. Demand was stimulated by the Civil War, and by 1865 the partners were designing larger-caliber pistols. This work was facilitated by the purchase of further patents, including Rodier's idea for ratcheted cylinders and Dodge's patent for the simultaneous extraction of all cartridges from a cylinder, obtained in 1869. The next year a Russian contract helped to launch a .44 revolver, which was also ordered by Turkey and Japan. Cooperation with Colonel Schofield produced a modified revolver that was used by the U.S. cavalry on the frontier. In January 1880 the Smith and Wesson factory was featured on the front cover of *Scientific American*.

New models appeared thick and fast, including single-shot target pistols and double-action models that broke open at the top. In the "Safety Hammerless" of 1884 there was no external hammer to be knocked or to catch on clothing. From 1894 began the development of large frame revolvers with cylinders that swung out to the side for loading. Vast numbers in various calibers, frame types, and barrel lengths

were made for armies and police forces around the world, particularly during the two world wars. The company also made automatics, submachine guns, handcuffs, and some household items. Arguably the best-known Smith and Wesson product was the .44 Model 29 Magnum, popularized by Clint Eastwood in *Dirty Harry*. Toward the end of the twentieth century reduction in the popularity of revolvers, legal questions on gun safety, and corporate finances were factors in changes of company ownership. For some years Smith and Wesson was part of the British "guns to buns" industrial conglomerate Tomkins, but at the time of writing is again a U.S.-owned company.

Additional Reading: Jinks, *History of Smith and Wesson*, 1977; Pate, *U.S. Handguns of World War II*, 1998.

SMLE, Short Magazine Lee Enfield
FIREARM

As a result of the Boer War, it was decided in Britain that neither full-length **rifles** nor short **carbines** were fully effective on the modern battlefield. The former were too long, the latter not accurate enough at long range. The United Kingdom therefore introduced the .303-inch Short Magazine Lee Enfield in 1902. Handy enough for use in confined spaces, its **bolt action** was also relatively swift and easy to operate. Used in a number of variants, including the "Number 4" type introduced in 1941, the rifle continued in use until superceded by the FN self-loader. The SMLE had a ten-round magazine and was made in the United States and Canada as well as in the United Kingdom at factories such as Enfield and **BSA**.

Additional Reading: Skennerton, *Lee Enfield; Jane's Infantry Weapons*; Hogg, *Infantry Weapons of World War II*, 1977.

Smokeless Powder. *See* Gunpowder

Snaphance. *See* Flintlock

Snider Rifle
FIREARM

American Jacob Snider is best known for his system of converting muzzle-loading weapons to breechloading by the fitting of a hinged block and striker. Apart from improving efficiency, this had the advantage that many rifles could be reworked more cheaply than manufactured new. The idea was applied to Britain's existing **Enfield** rifles from 1865.

Sniper Rifles   FIREARM

Sniping with firearms is surprisingly old, sporting **rifles** having been used from cover in war for the purpose as early as the seventeenth century. By the eighteenth century the verb "to snipe" was in regular use, and by about 1800 telescopic sights were used experimentally. Specially equipped snipers saw use in India and in the American Civil War. A Dr. Common first fitted a telescope to the Lee-Enfield rifle in 1901.

Sniping saw large-scale use in World War I, when many hunting techniques were applied to stalking and scouting in trench warfare. Magnifying, or "Galilean," sights, which were in effect separate lenses near the muzzle and breech, were soon in use. Telescopic sights were rapidly applied to **Mausers** and later to **SMLEs** and **Springfields**. Important manufacturers of sniper scopes at this time included **Winchester** and Warner and Swasey in the United States, Zeiss in Germany, and the Periscopic Prism company in the United Kingdom. Technically advanced sniping veils, scrim, and painted robes to match the local scenery were all in use by 1916.

Sniper equipments have remained important ever since. During World War II the **Enfield** and **Mosin-Nagant** were just two of the many **bolt-action** weapons fitted with sniping sights. They were also used with the **semiautomatic Garand**, Tokarev, and G43 rifles. More recently, many sniper rifles have been semiautomatic, one of the best known being the Russian Dragunov SVD, which is based on the same system as the AK-47. Nevertheless, a number of countries (including the United States and United Kingdom) have continued to run bolt-action sniper weapons alongside their standard **assault** rifle on the grounds of greater long-range accuracy.

Sniper arms of current interest include the U.S. Marine Corps M40, with its synthetic stock and detachable bipod; the Russian VSS silent rifle; and the traditional but still widely used Steyr SSG. Thermal imagers and **infrared** countermeasures are combatted by screens or portable "umbrellas" that maintain the temperature of the surroundings rather than the sniper's body.

Additional Reading: Spicer, *Sniper*, 2001; Hogg, *The World's Sniping Rifles*, 2002; Department of the Army, *Field Manual 23-10: Sniper Training*, 1994.

Snot   EXPLOSIVE

The term "snot" has recently been used as semiofficial military slang to denote several different viscous or thick liquids, both sides of the Atlantic. Perhaps most importantly, it has been applied to **explosives** that can be poured. Snot can also mean polymer liquid fired at a bomb as a disrupter to neutralize it.

Snowcat   VEHICLE

Known to the English speaking world as the "Snowcat," the innovative Swedish Bandvagn is a snow-crossing, articulated, amphibious, military vehicle first introduced in 1963. Weighing 3,200 kg, the Snowcat is powered by a Volvo engine with power transmission to all four rubber tracks.

Soman   CHEMICAL WARFARE

Soman, or GD, is a colorless liquid chemical nerve agent discovered by the Germans in 1944, though it was still at the laboratory stage when World War II ended. Even more lethal than **Tabun** and **Sarin**, it is highly toxic to the eyes and rapidly penetrates the skin. Large doses may cause death within a minute or two, and the liquid may persist in dangerous state upon the ground for a day or more.

Somua S-35   TANK

The French Char Somua S-35 medium **tank** was built by the Société d'Outillage Mécanique et d'Usinage d'Artillerie at St. Ouen from 1935.

241

About 500 had been built by the time of war with Germany, and the Somua gave a good account of itself. The main armament was a 47 mm gun, the armor was 56 mm at maximum, and the top speed 23 mph. The crew was three. Its main weaknesses were the bolted construction of the armor and its small turret.

Additional Reading: Miller, *Tanks of the World*, 2001.

Sonar; Sonobuoy   DETECTION

Derived from the words "sound navigation and ranging," sonar is a system of determining direction and distance under water using sound. The idea was first proposed for avoiding icebergs, but by 1916 a primitive version consisting of **hydrophones** towed behind a vessel was being used as a method of **submarine** detection. A practical working sonar set, sometimes referred to as "asdic," was devised by U.S. and British scientists before the end of World War I.

Modern sonar may be active or passive. In passive sonar, a receiver system picks up noise generated by motors and propellers. A big advantage is that it does not make any noise of its own; on the down side, it is not good for range estimation. Commonly, hydrophones for passive sonars are towed in "arrays" behind vessels. Active sonars send an electrical pulse through a transducer, creating a sound signal. This passes through the water at about 1,500 meters per second, and any echoes received from an object are amplified. A simple calculation of the time, divided by two, allowing for the speed, gives an accurate measure of distance. Active sonars may be hull mounted or towed. When a towed system can be lowered it is known as VDS, or variable-depth sonar.

The sonobuoy is an important adjunct to antisubmarine warfare. Usually dropped into the water by aircraft, sonobuoys detect submarines and transmit the data to friendly forces. The simplest types are passive and nondirectional, such as the parachute-dropped U.S. Navy Sparton. More complex models have included the U.S. AN/SSQ-62B, which was active, direc-

tional, and command activated, and the British CAMBS.

Additional Reading: Kemp, *Convoy Protection*, 1993; *Jane's Weapons Systems*.

Sopwith   AIRCRAFT; MANUFACTURER

British-born Thomas O. M. Sopwith (1888–1989), pioneer aviator, aircraft designer, and entrepreneur, was **balloon** flying by the age of 18. He took to powered flight in 1910, winning the Baron de Forest Prize for the longest nonstop flight between Britain and mainland Europe. His first military **aircraft** was purchased by the naval wing of the Royal Flying Corps in 1912. Working with Harry **Hawker** and Harry Kauper, he established the Sopwith Company near Brooklands to produce seaplanes, including a 100 horsepower model that won the Schneider Trophy.

The advent of the First World War led to huge demand, with Sopwith producing both naval planes and the Sopwith Gunbus "pusher" plane. Yet the reputation of the company was established with the production of the Sopwith "One and a Half Strutter," or LCT in 1915. According to company tradition the outline of this two-seater aircraft was first sketched on the workshop floor at Kingston by Fred Sigrist. In its production form it featured a 110 horsepower Clerget engine giving a top speed of 96 mph, two Lewis guns, and a 300 lb bomb load capability. The LCT was followed successively by the Pup, Triplane, Camel, and Dolphin, each with improved performance or armament.

The 1916 Pup single-seat scout, credited largely to the efforts of Harry Hawker, was relatively easy to fly and superbly maneuverable. With an 80 horsepower engine, it had a maximum speed of 104 mph, as well as a **Vickers** machine gun with a Sopwith-Kauper **interrupter** gear, allowing firing through the propeller arc. The Triplane had a similar box girder structure to the Pup but was heavier, with a 110 horsepower engine. The larger Dolphin was also produced for the U.S. Air Service (USAS) and featured three, sometimes four, forward-firing machine guns.

The F1 Camel appeared as a prototype in December 1916 and first saw action on 4 June 1917. Though notoriously idiosyncratic to fly, it was one of the most effective planes of the war. Its twin Vickers machine guns claimed more enemy aircraft than any other "fighting scout" serving with the USAS and Belgian air force as well as the British. Modifications to different specifications and roles saw the Camel fitted with anything from a 100 horsepower Rhone engine to a 150 BR1 (Bentley Rotary 1), developed by the famous automotive engineer W. Bentley. This was innovative in that it used aluminum cylinders with steel linings, an arrangement that allowed both lightness and dissipation of heat. With a top speed of between 105 and 118 mph depending on power unit, and a service ceiling of 20,000 feet, the Camel was also capable of carrying four 20 lb bombs.

Sopwith was also at the forefront of experimental naval aviation. A dummy deck was laid out at Grain (United Kingdom), and landings were practiced with arrester hooks, "skid" undercarriages, and other devices. The very first landing on a moving **aircraft carrier** (the *Furious*) was achieved by a "Ship's Pup" on 2 August 1917, though the pilot, Squadron Commander E. H. Dunning, was killed in an attempt to repeat this feat five days later. On the suggestion of Lieutenant Commander C. H. B. Gowan, takeoff platforms for Sopwith Pups were mounted on the gun turrets of **battleships**, allowing the launch pad to be pointed in the direction of the prevailing wind. The first successful takeoff was from HMS *Repulse*, by Squadron Commander F. J. Rutland, on 1 October 1917.

A Sopwith Pup with folding wings was developed, and an experiment was made with Camels with narrower wingspans and split fuselages that could be demounted for stowage, the first "2F1" Camels appearing in October 1917. Trials with Sopwith B1 and B2 bombers led to the development of the Sopwith Cuckoo, built by Fairfield Engineering of Glasgow. This aircraft, with a wingspan of 46 feet and a 200 horsepower Sunbeam, Wolseley, or Rolls Royce engine, was the first ship-launched **torpedo** bomber. As the only such type available

for British carrier operation, it was retained after World War I. A few were purchased by Japan in 1921, and Sopwith designer Herbert Smith worked there from 1922 on the development of shipborne **torpedo** aircraft.

With peace, "Tommy" Sopwith's company diversified into civil aviation and automotive engineering but went into liquidation in 1920 over taxes. Later that year, however, he was back at work with H. G. Hawker Engineering, with many of his old colleagues, including not only Hawker but Sigrist, Eyre, and F. I. Bennett. Sopwith, chairman of the Hawker companies and later of the amalgamated Hawker-Siddeley, was awarded the CBE and knighted in 1953. He continued to be a significant force in the industry until his retirement in 1963.

Additional Reading: Davis, *Sopwith Aircraft*, 1999.

Sound Moderation. *See* **Silencer**

SPAD   AIRCRAFT

The French Société des Productions Armand Deperdussin was formed in 1910. During World War I it brought the word "aviation" into its name but retained what would become one of the most famous acronyms in military **aircraft**—"SPAD." Among the company's numerous productions was the Spad VII of 1916, which equipped many French, Italian, U.S., and Belgian squadrons. This single-seat fighter, with a 25-foot wingspan, had a top speed of 122 mph; more than 6,000 were made. The Spad XIII of 1917, built in even greater numbers, increased performance to 139 mph. A total of 893 of these were obtained for the U.S. Air Service. Spad was taken over by Blériot in 1921.

Spandau   FIREARM

Spandau was the home of both the German **rifle** testing commission and the Prussian state arsenal, which grew rapidly in the decades leading up to 1914. Machine guns produced here up to 1918 bore the name "Spandau" stamped on them, whatever their technical designation.

U.S. World War I air ace Eddie Rickenbacker with his SPAD XIII fighter. Note the famous "hat in the hoop" painted insignia of 94th Squadron U.S. Air Service. © Culver Pictures.

It was therefore natural that Allied troops should call German machine guns "Spandaus," a tradition kept up in World War II, when the **MG 34** and **MG 42** were encountered.

Sparrow Missile   MISSILE

The U.S. Sparrow is an air-to-air or surface-to-air, missile. Having medium range with active homing, it is produced by Raytheon and General Dynamics. A number of different models have been produced over the years. The AIM-7M, first manufactured in the 1980s, for example, was equipped with folding wings and clipped tail for the NATO Sea Sparrow launcher.

Spear   POLE WEAPON

Probably starting as a simple stick, the spear is one of mankind's oldest weapons. Its use was once universal, from the pre-Columbian Americas to the tribes of Celtic Europe and the ancient Chinese. The term may be used to cover most shafted thrusting weapons, like lances, and those that are thrown like javelins. Ethnographers and lexicographers have defined over 200 distinct varieties of spear. Just a few of the best known are the Zulu *assegai* (properly the *iklwa* and *isijula*), the Japanese *yari*, the Masai *engerebbe*, the Tibetan *dung*, and the Australian aboriginal *do-war*. The importance of the spear as a weapon of war is emphsized by the fact that some African tribes chose their leaders on the strength of their spear-fabricating prowess.

Fire-hardened points were first added to spears in the Paleolithic. Stone, flint, and bone heads followed. Spear throwers, commonly of wood, bone, or leather were also widely known, and operated as a form of lever to increase the effective range. Yet it was with metalworking and classical Greece and Rome, that the spear revolutionized warfare.

The long Greek *sarisa*, or hoplite spear, was most effective in dense formations, like the phalanx, and helped make infantry queen of the battlefield while also encouraging new forms of military and social organization. By the time of the Hellenistic period, about 400 B.C., Macedonian spears were anything up to 23 feet in length. Among the Romans there were several distinct sorts of *pilum*; in one model the metal neck below the point bent on throwing, making it difficult to cast back. The *pilum muralis* was of wood and is supposed to have been commonly used as an addition to fortifications.

With horses and the use of **stirrups**, spears gained a new lease of life in the form of the cavalry lance. Again the spear may be said to have made a change in society possible, for without the lance it is doubtful whether the knight could have come to such prominence in medieval Europe. By the fifteenth century and the beginning of the Rennaisance, the pike, a form of very long infantry spear, had made its appearance. Contemporary theoreticians made specific connection with the Greek and Roman methods of war, and it is therefore possible that the "military revolution" of the sixteenth and seventeenth centuries was itself a product of the "old learning." In any case, pikes, as an anticavalry weapon, were of vital importance from the late fifteenth to the seventeenth centuries and were only finally eclipsed after the appearance of the **bayonet**. Even then short spontoons and half-pikes lingered as a symbol into the nineteenth century, and some militias still had recourse to the pike. As late as 1941 pikes were held for the British Home Guard in expectation of German invasion.

Additional Reading: Stone, *A Glossary of the Construction, Decoration and Use of Arms and Armor*, 1934; Tarassuk and Blair, *The Complete Encyclopaedia of Arms and Weapons*, 1979; Connolly, *Greece and Rome at War*, 1981; Watson, *The Roman Soldier*, 1969; Ritchie and Ritchie, *Celtic Warriors*, 1985; Spring, *African Arms and Armour*, 1993; Gonen, *Weapons of the Ancient World*, 1975; Black-

more, *Arms & Armour of the English Civil Wars*, 1990; ffoulkes and Hopkinson, *Sword, Lance and Bayonet*, 1967.

Spencer Rifle   FIREARM

Designed by Christopher M. Spencer (1833–1922) and patented in 1860, the Spencer **rifle** was one of the first really successful repeating rifles. Used extensively by Federal forces in the American Civil War, it had a tube magazine in the butt, usually holding seven **cartridges**. A coil spring pushed the rounds forward, and closure of the breechblock loaded them individually. The hammer was cocked by hand. The Spencer company was sold in 1869, most of its assets being purchased by **Winchester**.

Spirit, B-2 Stealth Bomber   AIRCRAFT

The Northrop B-2 Spirit bomber **aircraft** built on the **stealth** technology of the F-117A fighter but if anything is an even more unusual-looking craft, being a "flying wing" design that looks like a blunt arrow in plan and a science-fiction invention head-on. It is very slow, with a maximum speed of about 500 mph, and large, with a wingspan of 172 feet, and has no conventional tail. Twin bays behind the two-man crew area carry the payload. The pilots sit side by side, provided with vertically operating **ejection seats**.

With its roots in the Cold War, the B-2 was the result of Project Senior, which called for an aircraft capable of attacking targets within the Soviet Union with stand-off nuclear weapons. It first flew on 17 July 1989, with the first operational example appearing in 1993. The maximum ordnance carried is a healthy 50,000 lb, making **sea mines, cluster bombs**, and missiles possible loads.

Additional Reading: Moeng, *Military Aircraft*, 1994; Richardson, *Stealth Warplanes*, 2001.

Spitfire   AIRCRAFT

Commonly accepted as one of the best fighter **aircraft**, the British single-seat Supermarine Spitfire found fame alongside the **Hurricane** in the battle of Britain in 1940. The Spitfire first

The Northrop built B-2 Stealth bomber is rolled out at Air Force Plant 42, Palmdale, California, November 1988. Courtesy of the Department of Defense.

entered service in 1938 and with various improvements remained in production until the end of World War II. Designed by R. J. Mitchell, the Spitfire was a descendent of the Supermarine S6B, which had won the Schneider Trophy in 1931. Key strengths of the Spitfire were its all-metal construction, heavy eight–**machine gun** armament, powerful Rolls-Royce Merlin engine, and superb all-round aerodynamics and structural strength.

The Spitfire I, which equipped 19 RAF squadrons at the beginning of the battle of Britain, had a top speed of 369 mph. It could climb to 20,000 feet in 7.5 minutes and had a range of 1135 miles. The wingspan was 36 feet 10 inches. Later models with improved engines would push the speed to over 400 mph, and the maximum service altitude was anything up to 45,000 feet, with the HF IX. Armaments would also be uprated with 20 mm cannon and a bomb-carrying capability. The potent Mark IX was more than a match for the **Focke-Wulf 190**

and actually succeeded in destroying **Me 262** jet fighters. Over 20,000 of all models were made, the Marks I, V, VIII, IX, and XVI, accounting for three-quarters of all production.

Additional Reading: Henshaw, *Sigh for a Merlin*, 1996; Oliver, *Supermarine Spitfire*, 1999.

Springfield; Springfield Rifle   FIREARM

The Springfield Armory, in Springfield, Massachusetts, founded in the late eighteenth century, is sometimes styled "the small-arms arsenal of America." One of the world's great centers of military production, its museum and grounds are a national historic site. Even before the Civil War, Springfield was notable for its use of machinery, such as the 1820s Blanchard lathe, in a business that had hitherto relied on individual craftsmen. This mechanization both reduced the numbers of skilled workers required and made possible more interchangeable

The legendary Spitfire on display at RAF Laken-heath, June 2000. This plane is part of the Battle of Britain Memorial Flight. Courtesy of the Department of Defense.

parts. Springfield also had a "proof house" for the testing of weapons.

After the abandonment of Harpers Ferry in April 1861, Springfield was the only government armory remaining to the North. The **Rifled Musket**, Model 1861, or "Springfield rifle"—also contracted out to other U.S. and foreign suppliers—was the principal infantry weapon of the Civil War. Including the **ramrod** and **bayonet**, the 1861 model was made of 53 pieces and cost $14.93 to manufacture. It was a single-shot, muzzle-loading, **percussion** weapon, firing a .58-caliber bullet. Slight improvements to the type produced the models of 1863 and 1864.

In 1865 the U.S. government adopted a **breechloading** mechanism by Erskine S. Allin of the Springfield Armory. This consisted of a forward-opening block, controlled by an external plunger. It was used to modernize existing muzzle-loading arms that would otherwise have been obsolete.

Arguably the most famous Springfield production was the model 1903 **bolt-action** rifle. This served with U.S. forces from 1905 and was still in active use in limited numbers as late as the Korean War. The U.S. Navy deactivated

examples as recently as the 1980s, and some chromium-plated pieces may yet be kept for parade-ground ceremonial. This highly accurate rifle, with its **Mauser**-type action and five-round magazine, was updated in several ways during its lifetime. Most importantly, it was modified to accomodate the .30, 1906 **cartridge** (or .30-06). The original rod-type bayonet was discontinued and replaced with a more conventional type, following objections from President Theodore Roosevelt. Other adaptations have included a **sniper** weapon, drill arm, heavy-barrel target rifle, and line thrower. It has also been widely used for **rifle-grenade** projection. It is claimed that the first shot from a flying **aircraft** was made by Lieutenant J. E. Rickel, using a 1903 type Springfield, in August 1910. During and after World War II surplus weapons were supplied to friendly nations including the United Kingdom, New Zealand, Thailand, and Taiwan.

Additional Reading: Poyer, *M1903 Springfield*, 2001; Canfield, *Collector's Guide to the 03 Springfield*, 1989; Mowbray and Heroux (eds), *Civil War Arms Makers*, 1998; Brophy, *The Springfield 1903 Rifles*, 1985.

SPRITE. *See* Infrared

Spruance Class   WARSHIP

The *Spruance* class of U.S. Navy **destroyers** are a mainstay of the fleets but, though commissioned as recently as the period 1975 to 1983, are now regarded as nearing the end of their useful frontline service. At the time of writing, 22 of these 6,000-ton ships are in service. They have a range of 6,000 miles, a top speed of 33 knots, and are armed with **Tomahawk** and **Sea Sparrow** missiles and two five inch guns. It is intended that the *Spruance* class will be replaced with the *Zumwalt* class.

Additional Reading: Polmar, *Ships and Aircraft of the US Fleet*, 1981; *Jane's Warships.*

Spurs   MISCELLANEOUS

Spurs, or prods, fastened to the feet of horsemen to urge on the animal, have been in existence since classical times. They were used almost universally by cavalry and still see some use, sometimes as part of ceremonial military dress. The simplest types were prick spurs, shaped like a wish bone, but later there were many types. Rowel spurs with a spiked wheel were popular from the Middle Ages.

Additional Reading: Stone, *A Glossary of the Construction, Decoration and Use of Arms and Armor*, 1934; Tarassuk and Blair, *The Complete Encyclopaedia of Arms and Weapons*, 1979.

Sputnik. *See* **Satellites**

Squid. *See* **Hedgehog**

SS-1. *See* **Scud**

"Stalin Organ." *See* **Katyusha**

Stalwart   VEHICLE

The British Alvis Stalwart was a military truck produced from 1962 in an amphibious PV2 model. A Mark 2 version was manufactured from 1966 until 1971. The five-ton Mark 2 had six wheels and was powered by a Rolls-Royce 6522 cc, 220 horsepower engine, giving a road speed of about 30 mph and a water speed of 6 mph.

Starfighter, F-104   AIRCRAFT

The U.S. Lockheed Starfighter F-104 jet fighter was a distinctive, stubby-winged **aircraft** that first flew in 1954. It has been described both as a "missile with a man in it" and as the "widow maker," due to its number of fatal crashes. Its extreme design arose from experience in the Korean War, where pilots engaging the **MiG-15** had called for a machine with the maximum of speed and agility. In this respect the Starfighter could be described as a success, becoming the first aircraft ever to hold the world records for speed and altitude simultaneously. A speed of 1,404 mph and an altitude of 91,243 feet were achieved on different flights in May

1958. The 100,000-foot altitude barrier was broken the following year.

Deliveries of the F-104G commenced to the German air force in 1960, and in the event about two-thirds of Starfighter production went overseas. A few were still in use in 2002.

Additional Reading: Pace, *X-Fighters: USAF Experimental and Prototype Fighters, XP-59 to YF-23*, 1991.

Starlight Scope. *See* **Image Intensifier**

"Star Wars." *See* **Strategic Defense Initiative**

Stealth; Stealth Fighter F-117A
                    DETECTION; AIRCRAFT

The basic idea of "stealth," camouflage from **radar**, or reduced radar signature, is much older than is commonly realized. As early as the 1930s pioneer Watson-Watt had noted that it might be useful for bombers to reduce their radar reflectivity. Engineers similarly observed that targets would be detected at greater or lesser ranges depending on the type of **aircraft** and its angle to the radar. While the Allies produced **chaff** to disguise formations, the German Horten brothers set about designing an aircraft that would be difficult for radar to detect at all. Their Horten HoIX had a steel-tube subframe but was mainly of plywood, within which was sandwiched glue, sawdust, and charcoal—the charcoal being intended to absorb radar waves. An attempt was also made to shield German **submarine snorkel** tubes from airborne radar using Tarnmatte synthetic rubber. Alberich experimental antiradar rubber-tile coating was applied to a **U-boat** hull as early as 1940. Unfortunately, much of it dropped off while the vessel was at sea.

After World War II the United States, United Kingdom, and Germany continued work on radar-absorbent material, or RAM, and in 1945 the Massachusetts Institute of Technology produced MX-410. This was a rubberized antiradar paint that contained disclike aluminum flakes. Nevertheless, it proved impossible to treat whole aircraft successfully. It was not until the late 1950s that C. L. Kelly Johnson and the Advanced Development Projects division of Lockheed, then working on the **U-2**, realized that shape had as important a role to play as materials. Thereafter antiradar experimentation on the Compass Arrow and **Blackbird** projects involved not only materials and paints, such as Eccosorb and Iron Ball, but basic design.

With the growing importance of radar-guided missiles the significance of such work was recognized by the U.S. Air Force, and in 1974 came the request for the development of an aircraft with a dramatically decreased radar cross section, or RCS. The Lockheed "Skunk Works" project was pushed forward, and the first significant breakthrough was achieved when it proved possible to apply to aircraft the century-old Maxwell equations on the predicted scattering of electromagnetic radiation. The solution applied was to design without curves and to use computers to work out how radar waves would be reflected. The result was the now-familiar facets, which have since also been applied to ships and the B-2 **Spirit** "stealth bomber."

In 1977 the stealth project was given the title "Have Blue," a contract, and much greater funding. Small demonstration models flew the same year. Detail turned out to be crucial, with the wrong types of screws or minute gaps between panels causing apparently disproportionate problems. Yet by 1980 an aircraft undetectable to most airborne radar and most ground radar at long range had been built. It was flown by test pilot Harold Farley from the Groom Lake facility on 18 June 1981. Though various names were applied officially and unofficially, such as Scorpion and Senior Trend, the official designation would be F-117, with the production models being F-117A from 1982.

From statistics published in the mid-1990s, the F-117A Night Hawk has a wingspan of 43 feet four inches and when operating at optimum altitude, fully laden, has a combat radius of 700 miles. It is powered by two General Electric turbofans and can carry up to 5,000 lb of ordnance, including Paveway bombs, gun pods, and missiles.

Additional Reading: Sweetman and Goodall, *Lockheed F-117A*, 1990; Richardson, *Stealth Warplanes*, 2001.

Steil *Handgranate*　　　EXPLOSIVE DEVICE

Meaning literally "stick hand **grenade**," the Steil *handgranate* was introduced in 1915. In various models it remained the main grenade of the German army until 1945. It consisted of a wooden handle, metal cylinder head containing detonator and **explosive**, and a pull cord attached to a friction igniter. A pull on the cord ignited the fuse; after a delay of five and a half seconds, the bomb exploded. In an improved model, a screw cap concealed the cord, and a porcelain button gave the soldier something to grip on the end of the cord. Further models were manufactured from 1924 and from 1939. These are distinguishable from the World War I type by their smaller heads and lack of belt hook. The German "potato masher" was by no means the only type of stick grenade; other types were made by Austria, China, the Soviet Union, and the United Kingdom.

Sten Gun　　　FIREARM

Named after its inventors R. V. Shepherd and H. J. Turpin, and **Enfield**, where it was first demonstrated in 1941, the Sten **submachine gun** looked very much like a piece of cheap plumbing equipment. Nevertheless, it filled a vital gap and was manufactured in huge numbers to meet the needs of Britain and several of its allies during World War II. It did not have the quality of the **Thompson**, but at less than £3, ten or more could be had for the price of a "Tommy gun." It was also light, at under 7lb, and could be stripped down, even by a relative novice, without the aid of tools. More than 250 British and Canadian companies were involved in its production, from makers of castors to toy manufacturers. The Sten had a side-mounted 32-round box magazine, and, using 9 mm **cartridges**, could take captured ammunition.

Additional Reading: Hogg, *Infantry Weapons of World War II*, 1977; Anon, *Sten Machine Carbine*, (undated); War Office (UK), *Small Arms Training: The Machine Carbine*, 1944.

Stennis. *See* **John C. Stennis**

Steyr AUG. *See* **AUG**

Sticky Bomb. *See* **Grenade**

Stinger Missile　　　　　　　MISSILE

Announced in 1983, the U.S. Stinger shoulder-launched missile had much in common with the old **Redeye** but featured many improvements. Perhaps most important was the incorporation of an electronic "friend or foe" identification system intended to preclude the shooting down of friendly aircraft. Stinger teams usually consist of two men with two launch units; they may assist each other or fire independently. The Stinger came to prominence in the hands of the Afghan mujahideen, who used it with success against Soviet **helicopter** gunships. It is worth noting that the name "Stinger" has also been applied to a spiked device stretched across roads to puncture tires.

Stingray Light Tank, I and II　　　TANK

The Cadillac Gage Stingray light **tank** came into existence in the mid-1980s specifically for use in situations where main battle tanks are not needed or are too bulky to operate with advantage. The first "Commando" model was sold to Thailand. The Mark II type, completed in 1996, has a British-type 105 mm gun and a Detroit Diesel engine giving a maximum speed of 44 mph. It weighs 22 tons.

Stirrup　　　　　　　　MISCELLANEOUS

Stirrups, suspended from a saddle and take a rider's feet, made a considerable early contribution to the effectiveness of cavalry. They made mounting simple and the use of weapons easier. Thought to have originated in Asia, they were brought to Europe by the horsemen of the steppes about 500 A.D. By the tenth century metal stirrups were in use in Europe, and since then there have been many and varied forms, some of which completely enclose the foot.

Stoner 63 System　　　　　　FIREARM

The designer of the **M16**, Eugene Stoner, is credited with a number of other small arms. Most important among these was the "63 System," in which one basic weapon could be fitted with different barrels, feed systems, etc., to create an arm, **rifle**, or **machine gun**, for whatever purpose was required. The concept had significant benefits in terms of flexibility, cost effectiveness, and training, though it should be noted that similar ideas had been employed with **swords** and **armor** as long ago as the medieval era. The innovative 63 System of 1963 was manufactured by Cadillac Gage and in the Netherlands. Though popular with special forces, it was never widely used.

Strategic Defense Initiative
　　　　　　　　　　　MISCELLANEOUS

Announced by President Ronald Reagan in March 1983, the Strategic Defense Initiative—popularly known as "Star Wars," after the George Lucas movies—was not one technology but several, some of which had been already under consideration prior to that time. These were linked under the Strategic Defense Initiative Office, known since 1993 as the Ballistic Missile Defense Organisation, with an annual budget of about $4 billion. Though in many ways desirable the initiative was diplomatically questionable, since it contravened the 1972 Anti-Ballistic Missile, or ABM, Treaty. In 1987, however, the Soviet Union revealed that it was undertaking similar investigation.

With the fall of communism the objectives of the SDI became less ambitious, but research continued and unsuccessful missile tests were held at Vandenburg Air Force Base in 2000. Under George W. Bush it is intended that "Son of Star Wars" will create a **radar** communications net capable of tracking incoming missiles, which will then be destroyed by sophisticated interception devices. The United States formally withdrew from the ABM Treaty on 13 June 2002. Among the many technologies developed for SDI are space, air, and ground-based radar systems; airborne and space based lasers; a variety of sensor systems; Theater High Altitude Area Defense; and Boost Phase Intercept.

Space-based radar, or "SBR," moves early warning out into space, using **satellites**, thus increasing its range and giving greater time for interception. The initial emphasis was on global cover, but now theater-support functions, aircraft identification, and the ability to track **cruise** missile–sized targets are primary objectives. JLENS, or the Joint Land Attack Cruise Missile Defense Elevated Netted Sensor, provides over-the-horizon surveillance for the engagement of cruise-type targets with such weapons as the existing **Patriot** missile. It achieves this using an aerostat platform, or tethered **balloon**, at an altitude of between 10,000 and 15,000 feet. Following tests this was designated as an Acquisition Category II program in 1999.

The airborne laser, or ABL, weapon system is essentially a high-powered laser mounted in a **Boeing** 747 aircraft, intended to destroy ballistic missiles. This futuristic concept was inspired by the development of COIL, the powerful chemical iodine oxygen laser. It was invented as early as 1977 and demonstrated in a lightweight form in 1996. A "lethality demonstration" test firing was carried out early in 2002.

Theater High-Altitude Area Defense, or THAAD, has been described as the "most mature" of the upper-tier systems. It is intended, by means of antimissile missiles, for the protection of both military installations and population centers. It therefore has elements in common with **Arrow**. Despite its advanced status, THAAD has suffered various setbacks blamed on short schedules, lack of quality assurance, and other problems. With Boost Phase Intercept, or BPI, the intention is to stop ballistic missiles. In this instance, the weapons would be destroyed over enemy territory before they could deploy any submunitions, using missiles launched from an **aircraft** or **UAV**.

Stratofortress. *See* **B-52**

Stratofreighter. *See* **C-97**

Stringbag. *See* **Swordfish**

Stuart, M3 (M4 and M5) Light Tanks
TANK

Approved in July 1940 the U.S. M3 light **tank** featured a 37 mm gun and a respectable top speed of 36 mph. Though it had a maximum armor thickness of 38 mm, which was rather greater than the M2A4 model, which had inspired it, this still proved grossly inadequate when facing the latest antitank weapons. The M3 first saw action with the British in North Africa, and 3,200 were shipped to Russia. It gained popularity for its ease of handling and mechanical reliability, but its armament was soon out of date.

As a result of many design changes, including the replacement of the Continental radial with Cadillac engines, the model designation was changed to M4, and later changed to M5 to avoid confusion with the M4 **Sherman**. Variants included a command tank and an M3 with Satan flame gun in the turret. The Stuarts were superseded by the **Chaffee**.

Additional Reading: Forty, *United States Tanks of World War II*, 1983.

STUG. *See* **Self-Propelled Gun**

Stuka, Ju 87
AIRCRAFT

"Stuka" is a contraction of *Sturzkampfflugzeug*, a German expression that loosely translates as "**dive bomber**." During World War II the name stuck to a specific model of **aircraft**, the **Junkers** Ju 87. The famous two-seat, gull-wing Ju 87 was developed from the interwar K 47 craft, which was tested under cover by the Germans in the USSR and Sweden from 1931 to 1934. Trials established that dives over 300 mph were perfectly feasible and that bombs could be delivered with significantly greater accuracy from a near-vertical attitude. Ultimately many K 47 characteristics would be carried over into the Stuka, including external bomb racks, underwing air brakes, and an automatic recovery system designed to allow the craft to level up in the event of pilot incapacitation.

With the death of Karl Plauth, Hermann Pohlmann, the Junkers chief designer, assumed key responsibility for the program. The first experimental Ju 87 flew in September 1935, and though there were other small dive bomber aircraft, such as the Fieseler Fi 98 and Henschel Hs 123 under development, it was the Stuka that found the greatest favor. The first production type was the 87A, or "Anton," manufactured in 1937 and 1938. An improved 87B, or "Bertha," was made from 1938, with the C or Ceasar folding-wing type produced experimentally in 1939. The 87R, "Richard," was a long-range variant of 1940–1941. The sleeker-looking, more powerful 87D, "Dora," was introduced in 1941. In 1943 a Ju 87G, or "Gustav," appeared mounting two under-wing 37mm Flak 18 cannon, designed for antitank work.

Early in the war the Stuka excelled in its intended army ground-support role, acting as the long-range **artillery** of the blitzkrieg in Poland and France. It also proved useful against ships. From late 1940, however, the Stuka began to show its age and vulnerability when faced with modern fighters. During 1944 many Stukas were converted to a night-bomber role.

The Ju 87B-2, produced from the end of 1939, weighed 6,064 lb empty and was 36 feet in length with a wingspan of 45 feet. The Junkers Jumo 211 Da engine gave a maximum speed of 236 mph, with a range of 373 miles and a ceiling of 26,000 feet. Its armament was three machine guns, two forward firing and one rear facing, operated by the wireless operator–observer. The bomb load allowed various configurations up to a total of 1,000 kg. It featured a strong fixed undercarriage and a "bomb crutch" device that ensured that large bombs mounted centrally under the aircraft would swing out clear of the propeller before release.

Additional Reading: Smith, *Junkers Ju 87 Stuka*, 1998.

Sturgeon Class   SUBMARINE

The U.S. *Sturgeon* class of nuclear-powered **submarine** was constructed between 1963 and 1975 and was in origin an improved version of the **Thresher** type. With a total of 37 commissioned, from *Sturgeon* (SSN 637) in March 1967, to *Richard B. Russell* (SSN 687) in August 1971, the type was rightly described as the workhorse of the U.S. fleet until the appearance of the **Los Angeles**. The basic Sturgeon was 292 feet long, displaced 3,640 tons on the surface, and has been armed with **Tomahawk** missiles, **torpedoes**, and Harpoon-type missiles. **Sea mines** and minelaying equipment could be substituted for the torpedoes. The crew was 107.

Some of the later vessels were built ten feet longer to increase internal space, and *Archerfish, Tunny, Cavalla*, and *L. Mendel Rivers* were equipped to support special forces. In these submarines a dry-dock shelter was mounted on the hull from which small vessels and Navy SEAL units could operate. Most of the class had been decommissioned at the time of writing, with all planned for decommissioning by the end of 2003.

Sturmgewehr, StG 44. *See* Assault Rifle

Su-27. *See* Sukhoi Su-27

Submachine Gun, SMG   FIREARM

The submachine gun is a firearm capable of automatic operation that can be fired by one man on the move. It is commonly distinguished by a short **rifled** barrel and relatively small pistol-type **cartridges**. Many are simple mechanically, relying on the "blowback" principle, in which the mass and inertia of the barrel and breechblock serve to prevent gas escape at the rear between rounds. Nonetheless they are particularly deadly in confined areas and have been favored by **parachutists** and commandos.

There has been argument as to the first true

submachine gun but general agreement that they appeared in the First World War. The Italian Villar Perosa designed by A. B. Revelli is sometimes regarded as the first SMG, but initially it had two barrels side by side and was used rather as a light **machine gun**. The German Maschinenpistole 18/I, or MP 18, may have a better claim, for though it was not issued until 1918 it was single barreled and used by one man as a trench-sweeping weapon. Its magazine was a small "snail" drum containing 32 cartridges of 9 mm parabellum **ammunition**, the same as that used in the **Luger** pistol. It was aptly nicknamed the "Kugelspritz," or "bullet squirter."

The **Thompson** submachine gun was essentially designed during World War I but not actually introduced until the interwar period. The **Schmeisser** MP 28, Bergmann MP 34, and others showed commitment to the idea, but it was the **MP 38** that became the quintessential German SMG at the outbreak of World War II. Arguably World War II would see the high point of the SMG, with many new models produced and huge issues to the infantry. In Russia whole units would be armed with the **PPsh**; the PPS-42, produced in Leningrad during the siege, would become part of the folklore of Soviet resistence. Britain would produce the Lanchester and later the very cheap **Sten** gun. The United States produced the **Reising** for the Marine Corps, but it was the **M3** "grease gun" that served the army. In Italy there were various models of **Beretta**, and even Australia had two models of SMG, the Owen and the Austen. Surprisingly, only the Japanese among the major combatants had very few submachine guns, producing very limited numbers of their Type 100.

The immediate postwar period would also see some interesting new SMGs. These included the **Ingram, Uzi, Dux**, Czech Models 24 and 25, Carl Gustav M45, Argentine PAM, **Skorpion** and **Sterling**; however, for mainsteam military use, the demand was beginning to wane. **Assault rifles**, such as the **AK-47**, could now do most battlefield duties, and the SMG would have to find new niches to fill. By

the 1970s it was finding such work, not only in police and security duties but with special forces and as an armored vehicle weapon of last resort—an area in which SMGs had in fact been used since World War II. Some would be specifically designed as "port firing" weapons for **tanks** and carriers. Very small submachine guns were now doing effectively what **pistols** and **revolvers** used to do. A good example that has stood the test of time is the Heckler and Koch **MP5**.

So it was that the last quarter of the twentieth century would also see a new wave of SMGs. These would include the Spectre, Mini-Uzi, Finnish Jati-Matic, and Soviet AKR, though this last used an intermediate cartridge.

Additional Reading: Nelson, *The World's Submachine Guns*, 1980, 1986; *Jane's Military Review* (1985); Ezell, *Small Arms of the World*, 12th ed., 1983; *Jane's Infantry Weapons*; Bruce, *Machine Guns of World War I*, 1997; Marchington, *Handguns and Sub-machine Guns*, 1997.

Submarine   SUBMARINE

The idea of the submersible, or vessel capable of underwater travel, goes back to at least the sixteenth century. As early as 1578, English gunner William Bourne (1535–1582) produced a design for "a ship or boat that may go under the water unto the bottom and so come up again at your pleasure." The nub of his idea was a practical application of hydrodynamic theories pioneered by Archimedes—most importantly, that increasing or decreasing the relative density of a body could cause it to sink or float. Bourne's craft, naturally buoyant, would submerge when compressed leather ballast tanks were allowed to flood with water. It incorporated oars and a hollow mast with air holes for breathing. Though it was not built, an oar-propelled wooden underwater vessel was tested on the Thames by Dutchman Cornelius Drebble (1572–1634) in the 1620s. Explicit statements were made about its application to the attack of ships at anchor.

Thereafter there were a number of submarine schemes of greater or lesser practicality, including those of Frenchmen Mersenne, De Son, and Fournier, the Italian Borelli, and John Wilkins's "underwater ark." One of the first recorded fatal accidents occurred when Devon ship's carpenter John Day sank in Plymouth Harbor in 1774. The first use in warfare was two years later, when American David Bushnell (1742–1824) used his wooden *Turtle* to attack the British warship *Eagle* in New York Harbor. The *Turtle*, described as looking like "two upper shells of a tortoise" joined together, was equipped with a charge, or mine, which the submariner was supposed to attach to the target. The attack failed.

During the Napoleonic wars another American, Robert Fulton (1765–1815), attempted to interest both the French and British in his *Nautilus*, which he used in successful tests. This relatively advanced machine was copper sheathed and armed with a charge mounted on a spar. It was 21 feet long and powered by hand-cranked screws. This method of propulsion would be repeated in the German *Brandtaucher* of 1850, from which its inventor, Wilhelm Bauer, made the first submarine escape when it sank in 1851.

The American Civil War saw increasing interest in submarines. The Confederates built a number of 40-foot steam-driven semisubmersible "David" boats, one of which attacked and damaged USS *Ironsides* in October 1863. McClintock and Watson's *Pioneer* saw use in Lake Ponchartrain, while their promising *American Diver* foundered in heavy seas in 1863. Another Confederate submarine, the *St. Patrick*, unsuccessfully attacked the USS *Octorara*. The Union produced the *Alligator*, which sank in 1863, and the *Intelligent Whale*. Nevertheless, it is the McClintock vessel *Hunley*, named after her first, ill-fated commander, that has most fired public imagination. Made from a second-hand steam boiler bolted together with rubber seals, and powered by eight crewmen working a long crank, she was armed with an explosive harpoon. During her brief career the *Hunley* sank three times, gaining the nickname "murderer," but she also sank the USS *Housatonic*. The casualties of this attack were the first

Submarine innovator John P. Holland seen climbing up into the hatch of his invention, the USS *Holland* submarine. Courtesy of the Library of Congress.

caused by a submarine. The *Hunley* was relocated in 1995 and has since been raised.

The British *Resurgam* claims the title of first fully powered submarine. Built at Birkenhead in 1879, the 45-foot vessel featured a steam engine but operated on stored latent heat when underwater. It was armed with externally mounted Whitehead **torpedoes**. She was lost in 1880, but her designer, the Reverend Garrett, went to work for Nordenfelt, which supplied submarines to other nations. Advances in battery technology and electric motors now led to new types of submarine: the French *Goubet* and *Gymnote*; the British *Nautilus*, trialed in 1886; and the Spanish *Peral* of 1888. Named after its inventor Lieutenant Isaac Peral, this vessel is preserved at Cartegena.

Yet it is the Holland types that may be claimed as the direct ancestors of the modern submarine. Irish-born American John Philip Holland (1841–1914) built his first submarine, an underpowered two-tonner, in 1877. In 1888 he entered a U.S. Navy competition for a "submarine torpedo boat" and formed the Holland Torpedo Boat company in 1893. In 1900, after lengthy trials, *Holland VI* was purchased for the United States for $165,000. Seven improved 64-ton A-type submarines were built for the U.S. Navy between 1900 and 1903, and Holland submarines were also made under license at Barrow in the United Kingdom. Japan purchased a further five. The historic *Holland 1*, the Royal Navy's first submarine, was relocated in 1981 and is now conserved at the submarine museum at Gosport.

By the run-up to World War I, advanced navies were using gasoline and electric-driven submarines capable of firing torpedoes from hull tubes. Particularly numerous were the British C-class coastal submarines, 38 of which were built from 1905 to 1910. Driven by 600 horsepower engines, they were capable of 13 knots on the surface or eight submerged. They were 143 feet in length with a crew of 16 and had two torpedo tubes with two reloads. From 1906 the first German **U-boats** avoided the problems of gasoline by using diesel engines. Diesel power was also adopted for the U.S. E and F coastal classes of 1911–1912. Submarine warfare was of crucial importance in World War I, coming to international prominence in 1915 with the sinking of the *Lusitania*. Unrestricted U-boat activity helped to bring the United States into the war. Significant submarines in use included the U.S. oceangoing **L** and **O** classes and British **H** and **K** classes. U-boats were developed for cargo carrying and minelaying as well as ship attack.

Between the wars, technology produced faster vessels like the Japanese **KD6** class; heavily armed British **M**-class monitors, and the U.S. *Salmon* type. Though Germany started the World War II with relatively few submarines, the U-boat "happy time" early in the war brought Britain close to strangulation. Eventually a combination of new technology like **asidic, radar, hedgehog**, and squid with new tactics and **aircraft** led to the destruction of three-quarters of all U-boats by Allied navies. In the Far East, eventual U.S. naval mastery led to significant successes for Allied submarines. Other submarine types of World War II included the US *Gato* class and the giant Japanese *Sen Toku*. Midget and "suicide" craft like the **Maiale, X-Craft**, and **Kaiten** also made remarkable contributions.

From a position of relative inferiority in 1945, submarines would make a remarkable resurgence. In 1955, following experiment with the US *Albacore*, the United States would produce *Nautilus*, the first nuclear-powered submarine. Thereafter the growing ability of submarines to launch conventional and nuclear missiles turned them into one of the most powerful instruments of deterrence. Significant classes of submarine since 1960 have included the U.S. *Skipjack, Thresher, Sturgeon, Los Angeles, George Washington*, and *Ohio*. Russian vessels have included the **Yankee, Kilo, Typhoon, Oscar**, and **Delta**, though the numerous **Foxtrot** class was arguably the most successful. European countries have produced vessels like the *Vanguard, Trafalgar*, and *Le Triomphant*. The British *Astute* class is expected.

Additional Reading: Hutchinson, *Submarines: War beneath the Waves*, 2001; Compton-Hall, *The Submarine Pioneers*, 1999; Watts, *Axis Submarines*, 1977; Burgess, *Ships beneath the Sea: A History of Submarines and Submersibles*, 1976; Jackson, *Submarines of the World*, 2000; Tall, *Submarines*, 2002; Roscoe, *United States Submarine Operations in World War II*, 1949; Murphy, *Father of the Submarine*, 1987; Bagnasco, *Submarines of World War II*, 2000; Padfield, *War beneath the Sea*, 1995; Polmar, *The American Submarine*, 1983; Bowers, *Garret Enigma*, 1999; Hewlett and Duncan, *Nuclear Navy*, 1974; Craven, *The Silent War: The Cold War beneath the Sea*, 2002.

Suffren **Class**   WARSHIP

The *Suffren* class of four French heavy **cruisers** was built at the Brest navy yard from 1926 to 1932. Based on the *Tourville* design but with added protection, they displaced 10,000 tons and had armor up to 60 mm thick. Their main armament was eight 8-inch guns. The *Colbert, Foch*, and *Dupleix* were all scuttled at Toulon in 1942, but the *Suffren* served with Admiral Godfroy, whose ships joined the Allies in 1943. The *Suffren* was finally broken up in 1974.

More recently the name was been applied to the French F-60 class of guided missile **destroyers**, D-602 bearing the name *Suffren*.

Additional Reading: Whitley, *Cruisers of World War II*, 1985.

Sukhoi Su-27 AIRCRAFT

Developed from the late 1960s by Pavel Sukhoi, the prototype of this long-range Soviet interceptor **aircraft** first flew in 1977. Though the Su-27 suffered many teething problems, not least with its advanced **radar**, its deployment in the mid-1980s came as a serious concern to the West, where it was known as the Flanker. Particular strengths would include its laser range finder, compatible with a helmet-mounted display, its combat radius of 930 miles, its fast climb, and its fly-by-wire control system. Understandably it has often been regarded as the zenith of Soviet fighter technology. Later models of the same family included the naval Su-27K, with folding wings; the Su-35, with a new radar with a 400 km range; and the Su-27IB, with a "side by side" cockpit.

Additional Reading: *Jane's All the World's Aircraft*.

Sunderland AIRCRAFT

Based on the C-class Empire flying boat, the four-engine Short-manufactured Sunderland bomber **aircraft** entered service with the Royal Air Force in 1938. Several different variants were used, often for coastal and **antisubmarine** duties. Armed with ten guns and carrying 2,000 lb of bombs, the Sunderland was nicknamed the "Stachelschwein," or porcupine, by its German adversaries. The final model, Sunderland V of 1945, continued in RAF use until 1958 and was still in service in New Zealand until 1966.

Additional Reading: Delve, *Short Sunderland*, 2000; Barnes, *Shorts Aircraft since 1900*, 1989.

Superfortress. *See* B-29

Supergun ARTILLERY

The work of maverick Canadian scientist Dr. Gerald Bull (1928–1990), the Iraqi Supergun, designed as part of Project Babylon, was a weapon evincing consummate technical skill and a major threat to world security. Its story is more fantastic than that of many novels. The basic concept was simple—build a gun big enough and one could fire from Iraq to Israel and all over the Middle East. **Nuclear**, biological, and conventional **shells** could then be delivered without any need for missile technology. Bull's inspirations were the **Paris Gun** and his own earlier work on project HARP, the High Altitude Research Program, which was the first to gun-launch **satellites**, using rocket-assisted Martlet projectiles.

Bull had previously operated from his Space Research Corporation, on the U.S.-Canadian border. This had offered the advantage that anything deemed illegal in the United States could be taken out of the north side of the complex; anything suspect in Canada could go south. For Project Babylon new companies and highly specialized manufacturing would be required. Though third parties Iraq purchased a controlling share in British company Matrix Churchill, and SRC bought Lear Fan, while Bull received a reported $25 million for the project from Baghdad. Interestingly, $1 billion was allotted in the United States for an official parallel project, SHARP.

In early 1990 the whole Babylon scheme abruptly unraveled. Employees of companies involved had kept British intelligence appraised of progress, and customs now impounded suspect sections of "high pressure" tube. Bull was murdered, allegedly by Israeli intelligence. Only small prototypes of the Supergun were ever fired. Parts of the monster Supergun barrel went to the Royal Armouries as museum exhibits. At the time of writing court cases relating to German gun technologies exported to Iraq are pending.

Additional Reading: Lowther, *Arms and the Man: Dr Gerald Bull, Iraq and the Super Gun*, 1991.

Sverdlov Class WARSHIP

Planned as part of a major postwar Soviet naval expansion, 17 *Sverdlov*-class, 16,000-ton **cruisers** were laid down. Though essentially an improvement of existing designs, they were heavily armed, with good range and antiaircraft capability. The *Sverdlov* herself was finished in 1952, and eventually 14 such ships would be completed before Khrushchev stopped the program. These 689-foot vessels are sometimes compared to the US *Cleveland* class.

Specifications of 1980 stated that the main armament of that time was twelve 6-inch guns in triple turrets, plus 100 mm and 37 mm guns, as well as missiles. Refits included the replacing of certain turrets with surface-to-air missile launchers and the fitting of helicopters, notably to the *Admiral Senyavin* and the *Zhdanov*.

Swingfire   MISSILE

The British Swingfire antitank missile system was first publicly announced in 1962 and went into service in 1969. Originally fully guided by command, it is latterly SACLOS (semiautomatic command to line of sight). For an old system it still has impressive statistics, including a range of 4 km and a 7 kg charge that can penetrate more than 800 mm of **armor**.

Sword   BLADED WEAPON

The sword has been popularly defined as a long bladed weapon, sharp on one or both edges and often the tip, for cutting or thrusting. Invented in the Bronze Age, it is one of the oldest pieces of military technology and is still carried, though usually by officers for ceremonial. Swords of distinctively different local patterns have existed at various times all over the world. Early bronze swords were commonly short, with leaf-shaped blades, and could be surprisingly well made, within the limits of the properties of the metal. One the first discoveries was that copper alone was less suitable for sword making than a mixture of copper and tin. Carried by warriors, swords soon achieved ritual and status connotations.

The next quantum leap was the use of iron, though bronze and iron swords coexisted while the techniques of forging, hammering, and tempering were gradually perfected. Swords of the Roman era included the short-bladed *gladius*,

the down-swept Spanish *falcata*, and the long-bladed cavalry *spatha*. By the Dark Ages, European swords were being "pattern welded," or fabricated from rods hammered and twisted together to produce a resilient blade and keen edge without brittleness. By A.D. 1000 the prototype of the knightly sword had been formed, long and straight bladed with a simple cross hilt. The expensive and well made sword became as symbolic of the knight and his place in society as his horse or his land. In the Far East these social and technological developments would be mirrored by the samurai and his very different, but very high-quality, swords.

From the fifteenth century, lighter and more complex military swords began to appear in Europe. Hilts evolved guards, scabbards more complex hangings. By the sixteenth the century the rapier had appeared, long, slender, and straight, well adapted for new styles of swordplay and deadly thrusts. Yet the rapier existed alongside curved "hangers"; heavy broadbladed falchions; double-handers, and other types in different areas. Shorter and relatively cheap swords now did duty with all classes of soldier, serving as backup to firearms and **pike**. Longer, and often "basket"-hilted, swords slowly became the norm for cavalry.

Distinctive styles were retained in many parts of the world. In Europe, just two of these were the *schiavona* of Venice and the claymore of Scotland and Ireland. The derivation of the claymore is disputed, research suggesting that this was originally a large two-handed "great sword." The term was only later applied to basket-hilted broadswords of the type used by Highland regiments.

In the eighteenth century Western military swords began to achieve a degree of uniformity and became distinct from the "small swords" carried by gentleman civilians. It was ironic that as the industrial revolution made high-quality edged weapons available in quantity, the advance of military technology would make them less relevant. Nevertheless, the sword continued to evolve into the nineteenth century, with curved cutting sabres for the light cavalry, influenced by eastern designs, and heavy straight blades for the heavy cavalry. Bandsmen, pioneers, drummers, and others all carried their own distinctive types of sword. Some national groups also continued to use their own traditional arm, such as the Cossack *shashqa*.

Practical fighting swords continued to be devised into the twentieth century, but the number of casualties caused by swords in battle declined rapidly in the face of improving **rifles, artillery** and **machine guns**. Though cavalry swords were carried to war in 1914 and family blades continued to be treasured by Scottish and Japanese officers alike, the technological advance of the sword was at an end.

Additional Reading: Connolly, *Greece and Rome at War*, 1981; Hakusuki, *Nippon-To: The Japanese Sword*, 1948; Stone, *A Glossary of the Construction, Decoration and Use of Arms and Armor*, 1934; Mollo, *Russian Military Swords, 1801–1917*, 1969; Wallace, *Scottish Swords and Dirks*, 1970; Albaugh, *Confederate Edged Weapons*, 1960; Robson, *Swords of the British Army*, 1975; Oakeshott, *The Sword in the Age of Chivalry*, 1994; Hayes-McCoy, *Sixteenth Century Irish Swords* (undated); Burton, *The Book of the Sword*, 1884; Harris and Ogasawara, *Swords of the Samurai*, 1990; Norman, *The Rapier and Small Sword 1460–1820*, 1980; Fuller and Gregory, *Military Swords of Japan 1868–1945*, 1987; Coe et al., *Swords and Hilt Weapons*, 1993; Bull, *European Swords*, 1994.

Swordfish   AIRCRAFT

The two-seater British Fairey Swordfish **torpedo** bomber **aircraft** entered service in 1936 and served throughout the Second World War. The "Stringbag" was remarkable in that it was an open-cockpit biplane with what has been described as a "painfully slow" laden top speed of 132 mph. Yet it still achieved successes, including the decimation of the Italian fleet at Taranto in 1940, and was responsible for inflicting damage on the *Bismarck*. Powered by a Bristol Pegusus engine, it had a range of 540 miles when carrying a 1,500 lb bomb load, and had two **machine guns**.

Additional Reading: Sturtivant, *The Swordfish Story*, 1993.

T

T3 Medium Tank. *See* **Christie**

T-34 Tank   TANK

The T-34 is one of the most important **tanks** in history, if not *the* most important. Conceived on the eve of war with Nazi Germany and ruthlessly mass produced in vast numbers to very basic standards, it helped to turn the tide of the "Great Patriotic War." The vehicle was the work of several designers, working under Mikhail Koshkin, head of the team at the Kharkov Locomotive Factory, to a specification laid out by General Dmitri Pavel of the Directorate of the Armed Forces. The **Christie**-type suspension and hull were the domain of Nikolai Kucherenko and P. Vasihev; the power train, of Alexsandr Morozov; M. Tarshinov was responsible for the armor.

Yet if compromises were made, the result was a superb balance of the "armor triangle": defense, offence, and mobility. The armor had a maximum thickness of 45 mm but was well sloped, improving its efficiency by another 50 percent, making it impregnable to all but the largest antitank guns of 1941. The 76 mm gun was more than adequate against German tanks of that date, and the 34 mph maximum speed remarkable. Wide tracks and independently mounted suspension for each wheel reduced ground pressure and improved cross-country performance. Perhaps best of all, simplicity and interchangeability of parts made high production figures possible. Almost 35,000 T-34s were made up until 1943, when the model was uprated to a T-34/85, featuring a larger gun to take account of the newer German tanks. An-

other 18,650 of the later model were made by the end of 1944, leaving the enemy vastly outnumbered. A T-44 began to appear at the end of the war.

Though the T-34 was ultimately outgunned by tanks like the **Tiger** and technically inferior to the **Panther**, it may reasonably be claimed that it made the greatest contribution of any weapon to the defeat of Germany. The hulls of T-34s were also used for **tank destroyers**, such as the SU-85 and SU-100, and for the SU 152 assault gun and other variants. After 1945 the T-34 and its derivatives would serve widely with Eastern European armies and in the Third World.

Additional Reading: Hughes and Mann, *The T-34 Tank*, 1999; Gudgin, *Armoured Firepower: The Development of Tank Armament 1939–1945*, 1997; Bean and Fowler, *Russian Tanks of World War II*, 2002.

T-54; T-55; T-62; T-64; T-72; T-80 Tanks   TANK

The T-54 through T-80 series of tanks represents the line of Soviet main battle tank development from the late 1940s to the fall of communism. Despite the range of significant developments, a familial similarity is apparent; all are powerfully armed, with low domed turrets and overall lengths around 30 feet. Most were made in massive numbers—world production of the T-54 and T-55 alone has been estimated at 65,000—making these the most widely used tanks of all time.

The T-72, introduced in 1972, was of particular concern to the West. It had a three-man

Soviet T-34 tanks loaded with "attached infantry" tank riders, during the final advances of 1945. Close support from infantry helped to keep enemy antitank weapons like the Panzerfaust away from the armor. © Hulton/ Getty Images.

crew, with the driver centrally positioned behind well-sloped armor, and the other two men in the turret. Modern features included the 125 mm smoothbore gun with automatic loader, and a lead-based synthetic liner to the tank body. This was intended as a protection against nuclear radiation and electromagnetic pulse. The road speed was a remarkable 50 mph. **Laser** range finders, missile-launching capabilities, and additional armor were fitted to later versions of the T-72.

The T-80 was the work of the Kartsev design bureau. Entering service in 1985, it had laminated armor and a new gas turbine engine. In 1984 a new version appeared with "explosive reactive armor" on its surface. ERA was intended to detonate when hit, causing enemy high-explosive antitank rounds to activate clear of the surface of the main armor.

Additional Reading: Hilmes, *Main Battle Tanks: Developments in Design since 1945*, 1987; Crow, *Modern Battle Tanks*, 1978; Miller, *Tanks of the World*, 2001.

T-90 Tank   TANK

Entering production in 1994, T-90 is the latest main battle tank to join frontline service with the army of the Russian Federation. Its 125 mm is the same main armament mounted by the **T-80** but can use a new fragmentation round that can be detonated as it passes over a target. It has composite armor with explosive reactive ERA, can travel at 37 mph on roads, and stands only 7 feet 4 inches high (more than two feet lower than the **Abrams**). Other interesting features include a multifuel engine, six 81 mm launchers on either side of the turret for **gre-**

nades, and a spray intended to confuse incoming missiles. Diesel fuel injected into the exhaust system may be used to create a smoke screen.

Tabun   CHEMICAL WARFARE

Discovered by Dr. Gerhard Schräder in 1936 during research into organo-phosphorus compounds, Tabun, or GA, is a rapid-acting "nerve agent" chemical weapon highly toxic to the eyes, with a vapor that easily penetrates the skin. Its victims suffer first from running eyes, tightness of the chest, and poor vision. If untreated immediately, vomiting, cramps, headache, and involuntary jerking are followed by the cessation of breathing and death. Large doses may result in fatality as quickly as a few minutes, while lower levels of contamination may take an hour or more to take effect.

Though it was not actually used during World War II, a significant quantity was produced by the German Anorganawerke near Dyhernfurth, in Silesia. The production facility was captured by the Soviets at the end of the war, and since then Tabun and the related agents **Sarin** and **Soman** have remained important chemical weapons. Production of such "weapons of mass destruction" persisted as a concern into the twenty-first century.

Additional Reading: Burck and Flowerree, *International Handbook on Chemical Weapons Proliferation*, 1991.

Tacoma Class   WARSHIP

The U.S. *Tacoma* class of World War II **frigate** was a 1,430-ton vessel of all-welded construction. Similar to the British River class, *Tacomas* were capable of about 20 knots and were 285 feet long, with a crew of up to 214. They were armed with 3-inch, and antiaircraft guns and **Hedgehog**. A total of 100 were built. They served with the U.S. Navy and the Royal Navy, as well as in the Soviet Union, South Korea, Japan, France, and others elsewhere.

Additional Reading: Lenton, *American Gunboats and Minesweepers*, 1974.

Taiho   WARSHIP

The 30,000-ton *Taiho*, commissioned in March 1944, has been described as "the largest and in many ways the most advanced Japanese purpose built **aircraft carrier**." *Taiho* capitalized on the work done on the ***Shokaku*** class but was the first Japanese carrier to have an armored flight deck. She was also fitted with **radar**. Despite her modernity she lasted a mere three months, being sunk in June 1944.

Takao Class   WARSHIP

The Japanese *Takao* class of four 10,000-ton **cruisers** was commenced in 1927 and complete by mid-1932. Their design was influenced both by intelligence regarding the British *Kent* class and by contemporary U.S. practice. A key feature was supposed to be that the main armament of ten 8-inch guns would be viable in an antiaircraft role as well as surface to surface. In the event, however, their antiair capability proved to be limited, and many smaller guns were added for this purpose.

Three of the class were sunk in World War II—*Atago, Maya*, and *Chokai*—in October 1944, following torpedo strikes from U.S. **submarines**. The damaged *Takao* barely escaped; despite attacks from **B-29s** and British **X-craft** midget submarines, it survived to be captured at Singapore.

Additional Reading: Skulski, *Takao*, 1994; Lacroix and Wells, *Japanese Cruisers of the Pacific War*, 1997.

Tank   TANK

Though armored vehicles were conceived in classical times and experiments with all of the vital elements necessary for tanks predated 1914, the combination of tracks, armor, firearms, and the internal combustion engine belongs to the Great War. By 1918 armor theorists would be thinking in terms of the armor, armament, and speed "triangle," even imagining a strategic role for tank armies.

The tank as we know it was a British answer to the very specific problems of cutting wire, crossing trenches, and attacking **machine guns**

British Mark V tank during the latter stages of World War I. Though similar in general appearance to the Mark I and Mark IV tanks the Mark V featured a number of improvements. Small numbers were also used by the U.S. 301st Tank Batallion. © Culver Pictures.

while remaining protected. As early as 1914 Major E. D. Swinton put forward an idea for a "machine gun destroyer," and soon Winston Churchill was urging the development of "armoured caterpillar tractors." Several experimental vehicles were produced for the Landships Committee, but the first really practical design was "Little Willie," put together by Walter Wilson and William Tritton at Foster's of Lincoln. In response to specific War Office specifications, improvements were made resulting in the familiar rhomboid that became known as "Mother" in January 1916. The name "tank" came about as a subterfuge, the new

weapons being described as "water tanks" to disguise their real purpose from the enemy.

After further refinements in Mark 1, there was produced both a "male" version, which included 6-pounder guns, and a "female," which had only machine guns. The debut of the tank on the Somme came in September 1916. Promising performance led to continual improvement through Marks II to VIII. In 1918, light Whippet tanks would also be committed. French armor in the form of **Schneider** and St. Chamond tanks went into action from the spring of 1917, with **Renault** light tanks seeing service in 1918, some of them with American units. Total production of the German **A7V** was about 20 vehicles. The final expression of allied armored power at this time was the **Liberty** tank.

In the interwar period tanks were an active area of research and development. With Russian assistance the Germans embarked upon the **panzers**, whilst in the United Kingdom new tanks were divided into heavy "infantry" types, like the new **Matilda**, and faster "cruisers." The United States would see **Christie**'s development of new suspension and wheel systems and the new M2 Medium. Among the new French tanks were the **Char B** and **Somua S-35**.

Following Germany's dramatic blitzkrieg campaigns, there would be an escalating race to produce better tanks—the best armored, best gunned, and most mobile. Armor not only increased massively in thickness but was sloped, while guns increased in velocity as well as caliber. The **Churchill, Lee, Stuart**, and above all huge numbers of M4 **Shermans** became mainstays of Western armored power. The remarkable **T-34** arguably saved the Soviet Union from collapse, and the **Joseph Stalin** pointed the way to the future. The German **Panther** and **Tiger** showed new levels of technical excellence but were never produced in sufficient quantity.

Tank destroyers and **self-propelled guns** complemented the work of both the armored divisions and the infantry. **Tank transporters** began to remove armor's dependence on **railroads**. The "**funnies**" showed that armor could carry out a multitude of tasks. Yet this was just part of the story. New types of antitank **artillery, mines, sabot shells**, tank-killing **aircraft**, the **Panzerfaust**, and the **bazooka** prevented the tank from achieving a complete battlefield dominance.

After World War II the NATO powers remained aware that armor, in the form of the T-34, **T-54**, and **T-55**, remained one of the Soviet Union's main strengths. Accordingly the United States and United Kingdom now developed some of the best tanks ever built, seeking to balance numbers with quality. From the **Pershing** and **Patton** the United States went on to develop the **M60** and finally the **Abrams**. The

British **Centurion** and **Chieftain** would be followed by **Challenger**. In Germany, the **Leopard** was an outstanding success.

Technological improvements over time have been legion. Gyroscopic stabilization of armament improved accuracy and ability to fire on the move. Bigger guns, fin-stablized rounds, automatic loading systems, and depleted-uranium projectiles all made tanks more deadly. **Infrared** and **image intensifiers** made night fighting ever more practical, until it has become standard practice. As missiles like the **Sagger, Dragon**, and **M72** have challenged armor, layered and reactive armors including "Explosive Reactive" armors have been developed to defeat them. Engine performance has improved, and multifuel engines allow the possibility of continued operation in the event of shortage of any one kind.

Computers and **GPS** have revolutionized navigation and communications; while "vetronics," the integration of computers and electronics, offers automatic fault diagnosis and interchangable modular electrical systems. **NBC** systems, such as cages, seals, filtration systems, and lead screening, have all improved survivability in the face of weapons of mass destruction. Along with traditional **camouflage**, sensors and signature-reduction technologies can now help tanks avoid being targets in the first place.

Some surprisingly advanced tanks are now being produced in various parts of the world, including the Israeli **Merkava**, Indian **Arjun**, and French **Leclerc**. The latest U.S. development is the **Future Combat System**.

Additional Reading: Wright, *Tank*, 2000; Margiotta, *Brassey's Encyclopedia of Land Forces and Warfare*, 1996; Gudgin, *Armoured Firepower: The Development of Tank Armament 1939–1945*, 1997; Dunstan, *Modern Tanks and AFVs*, 2002; Foss and Mckenzie, *The Vickers Tanks*, 1988; Brook, *Armoured Warfare*, London, 1980; Dunstan, *Nato Armoured Combat Vehicles*; School of Tank Technology, *Tank Terms*, 1944; Johnson, *Fast Tanks and Heavy Bombers: Innovation in the U.S. Army, 1917–1945*, 1999; Halberstadt, *Inside the Great Tanks*, 1998; Crow, *AFVs of World War I*, 1998.

Tank Destroyer TANK

The **tank** destroyer is an armored fighting vehicle intended specifically to destroy enemy tanks. Like a tank it usually has a fully tracked chassis, and some have a rotating turret; the division between tank destroyers and tanks themselves is therefore not hard and fast. Commonly, however, tank destroyers have featured a high power-to-weight ratio and heavy armament. They can thus intercept and knock out enemy tanks but are not suitable for protracted combat or the many general tasks that tanks may have to fulfill.

The German army of World War II was in the forefront of tank destroyer (or *Panzerjäger* and *Jagdpanzer*) development. Yet many of the early German "tank hunters" were extemporized or emergency measures based on captured tanks or obsolete German models. The Marder II and III types, for example, were based respectively on the **Panzer II** and the Czech 38 (t). The Ferdinand, named after Ferdinand Porsche but also known as the Elefant, was based on a **Tiger** chassis. It fared poorly against the Soviets at **Kursk**. Notably successful among the later **Jagdpanzer**, or "hunting tanks," were the Jagdpanzer IV, the diminutive Czech-manufactured Hetzer, and the Jagdpanther. This last carried an **88 mm** gun and was based on the successful **Panther**.

The U.S. Army was similarly an early enthusiast of the tank-destroyer concept, basing simple early models on trucks and **half-tracks**. The first really successful U.S. type was the M10, with a 3-inch gun; over 6,700 had been produced by 1943. This was followed by the M36, with its powerful 90 mm gun. This certainly had the firepower to take on enemy tanks but was limited by its relatively slight armor. Like the M10 it had an open-topped turret and a **Sherman**-type chassis. The M18 Hellcat model was different in that it was purpose built and had a **Christie**-type suspension. Very thinly armored, it had a remarkable 50 mph top speed.

Other Allied armies of World War II also featured tank destroyers. Late in the war the Soviets fielded models such as the SU-76, SU-100, and ISU-122. These were based on existing Soviet tanks, and some were retained by communist nations long after 1945. British examples included the surprisingly useful Archer with its 17-pounder gun, and the A30 Avenger. A number of new tank destroyers have been produced in the last half-century, major users having included West Germany, Switzerland, and Sweden. As late as the 1990s a new Russian model was produced. This is the 2S25, produced by the Volgograd plant. Looking very much like a conventional tank, it is, however, very lightly armored and packs a 125 mm gun. Its light weight makes it suitable for air deployment.

Tank Transporter VEHICLE

Early tanks were strictly limited by their durability and speed and thus required **railway** transport to move long distances. The appearance of road vehicles capable of moving tanks was therefore a significant breakthrough, reducing wear and tear, particularly to tracks and engines, and making speedy deployment to areas away from rail lines possible. Many transporters have been essentially commercial vehicles, often articulated tractor and flatbed units, with minor modifications. During World War II the U.S. Diamond T proved particularly useful to the Allies, while models by Thorneycroft and Scammell have since been important in the United Kingdom. A significant French example is the 20-ton Berliet TB015A, produced about 1970; this was capable of moving 50-ton tanks both on and off roads.

Additional Reading: Boniface and Jeudy, *US Army Vehicles of World War II*, 1991.

Tarnmatte. *See* Stealth

TASC. *See* Sidewinder Articulated Cargo

Telegraph COMMUNICATIONS

The "visual telegraph" system was invented by the French Chappe brothers at the time of Napoleon. Stations for the transition of signals were set up on hilltops and towers. Though sending messages was now often quicker, bad weather and movement of troops rendered the early telegraph little more useful than the beacon lighting system that had obtained in England as early as the 1580s.

The use of wires and electricity to convey simple messages was known soon after 1800, but the concept was made practical for widespread commercial and military use by U.S. inventor Samuel Morse. In 1835 he produced a model telegraph machine, and with it the code of dots and dashes—"**Morse Code**"—that remains in use to this day. The telegraph machine itself worked by creating breaks in current between the machines battery and the receiver. U.S. government funding made possible a telegraph link between Washington, D.C., and Baltimore, Maryland, completed in 1844. Thereafter the telegraph helped to revolutionize warfare, as messages that had previously been limited to the speed of a galloping horse could now be transmitted almost instantaneously.

Telescope; Binoculars   DETECTION

The idea of using convex and concave lenses of glass to alter the image seen through them was well known by the medieval era; eyeglasses were in use among the wealthier classes. In 1558 Giambattista della Porta observed specifically how distant objects could be made to appear larger by putting two lenses together. Portable "perspective glasses" to enlarge images were probably first carried in war around 1600, about which time their manufacture was becoming more common. Hans Lippershey of Holland (1570–1619) is sometimes credited with the actual "invention of the telescope," though it was Galileo who famously applied the device to astronomy and Keppler who explained the theory. During the eighteenth and early nineteenth centuries, telescopes were the main method of observation by land and sea.

The idea of "binoculars"–essentially pairs of small telescopes mounted in frames—was also known at an early date, but it did not become widespread until the nineteenth century. A practical version was invented by J. P. Lumière in 1825. Binoculars were much improved with

the use of prisms, prismatic binoculars stemming from Italian Ignatio Porro's patent of 1854. By the late nineteenth century, binoculars, or "field glasses," had overtaken telescopes in the military, though where ranges were long or the user was not required to move about, telescopes were retained. The German optics industry achieved an early lead, a factor that would be significant at the outbreak of World War I. Binoculars and telescopes remain important, the basic concepts being much enhanced by relatively new technologies such as **image intensification** and **infrared**.

Telescoped Ammunition. *See* Cartridge

Teracruzer   VEHICLES

U.S. Teracruzers (terrain cruisers) are among the most impressive military vehicles ever produced. First used in the mid-1950s, they consisted of large beds and power units with rectangular cabs, riding on huge Goodyear "Terra-tires," or "Rolligon" roller tires, invented by W. H. Albec. Important uses have included U.S. Air Force ground support and cargo transport. The Teracruzer I of 1955 weighed 28,160 lb.

TERCOM. *See* Cruise Missile

Terrier Missile   MISSILE

The supersonic U.S. ship-based surface-to-air Terrier missile was first developed in 1956 as the SAM-N-7; by 1963 it had developed into the "Advanced" Terrier (RIM-2F). The latter offered a beam-riding guidance system that increased effectiveness against low-flying and multiple targets, as well as adding a surface-to-surface capability. Manufactured by General Dynamics, the Advanced Terrier was 27 feet in length and was fired from a twin deck launcher, to a range of about 22 miles.

Thermobaric Bomb EXPLOSIVE DEVICE

Also described as a "vacuum bomb," the thermobaric bomb is designed to create heat so intense that it incinerates any contaminants released into the atmosphere at the time of its explosion. The explosion itself is of relatively low pressure, thus limiting dispersal. A development of **fuel-air** bomb technology, the thermobaric device is currently under development as an antidote to stockpiled chemical and biological weaponry. It is suggested that thermobaric devices may be used in conjunction with a "burrowing" warhead to penetrate bunkers.

Thetis, HMS   SUBMARINE

The *Thetis*, a British 1,330-ton T-class **submarine** built at Birkenhead in 1938, has the distinction of having been sunk twice. On the first occasion, in 1939, some 99 men died in an accident when both ends of a **torpedo** tube were opened simultaneously. Raised and renamed *Thunderbolt*, she performed well against the Italians in World War II. She was sunk again by the Italian **corvette** *Cicogna* in 1943.

The name *Thetis* was also used in the 1990s for a small class of Danish **frigates**, particularly adapted for fishery protection, ice breaking, and **helicopter** transport.

Additional Reading: Roberts, *HMS Thetis*, 1999.

Thompson Submachine Gun   FIREARM

Named after U.S. general John T. Thompson, design director of the Auto-Ordnance Corporation, the Thompson, or "Tommy gun," was a pioneering and influential model of **submachine gun**. Work started during World War I, but production did not commence until 1921, with a further model made from 1928. Reliable and powerful, firing a .45-inch **cartridge**, the Thompson was also heavy, at just over 10 lb, and expensive to make. Nevertheless, it was one of the few SMGs available at the outbreak of World War II and so was in immediate demand, seeing service in the United Kingdom before being standardized as the U.S. Army M1 SMG in 1942. The manufacturers were **Colt**, Savage, and Auto Ordnance, which made over 1,300,000 Thompsons during the war. Though usually fed from a 20 or 30-round detachable box magazine, it could also take a distinctive drum containing 50 or 100 rounds.

A U.S. tank crewman pictured with his .45 inch Thompson submachine gun at Fort Benning, 1942. The "Tommy gun" was not the first submachine gun, but it was sturdy and well made, with excellent close range firepower. Courtesy of the Library of Congress.

Additional Reading: Helmer, *The Gun That Made the Twenties Roar*, 1970; *Thompson Submachine Gun Mechanism* (undated); Hill, *Thompson: The American Legend*, 1996; Cormack, *Thompson Submachine Gun* (undated); Auto-Ordnance Corp., *Handbook of the Thompson*, 1940.

Thresher Class   SUBMARINE

The *Thresher* class of 14 U.S. nuclear-powered **submarines** was built between 1958 and 1968. The *Thresher* (SSN 593) was herself laid down at Portsmouth Navy Yard in May 1958 and was commissioned in August 1961. With a pressurized-water reactor, the *Threshers* had a crew of 112 and were capable of more than 30 knots submerged. Initial length was 278.5 feet, but the last built were slightly longer. The armament was **torpedo** tubes, plus missiles, including some of the SUBROC antisubmarine type. A bow-mounted **sonar** suite with active and passive AN/BQQ-2 sonar was fitted.

Though specifically designed for deep diving, the *Thresher* herself was lost with all hands on a test dive 220 miles east of Boston in April 1963, her final message being that she had exceeded the test depth. Her hull was crushed.

The wreck was later located in 8,400 feet of water, and her loss was attributed to a failure of the saltwater induction system, which had led to flooding. Modifications to design followed the loss of *Thresher*, and subsequently the class was often referred to as the *Permit* class, after the second vessel (SSN 594) in the series. The entire class was decommissioned by 1993 and scrapped at Puget Sound.

Additional Reading: Polmar, *Death of the Thresher*, 1964; Bentley, *The Thresher Disaster*, 1974; Deputy Commander Submarines, *United States Ship Thresher*.

Thunderbolt, P-47　　　　AIRCRAFT

The Republic P-47 Thunderbolt fighter was a large and heavy **aircraft** built around a powerful 2,800 horsepower radial piston engine. With a total production of 15,660 of all models, it was the most numerous, and one of the most successful, U.S. fighters of World War II. It first flew in May 1941. Though designed as an interceptor, its real forte was ground attack, **railway** train busting being a particular specialty. In the Far East in the latter part of the war, fighter-bomber P-47s were often used on a "cab rank" principle, with patrolling aircraft called in on rotation to deal with concentrations of enemy troops.

The P-47 was a single-seat all-metal design and boasted such technical innovations as air conditioning, gun bay heating, and electric fuel indicators. The most extensively built model was the P-47D, manufactured by **Curtiss-Wright**, as well as Republic. This had a Pratt and Whitney Double Wasp engine, a 40 foot wingspan, and a weight of 9,950 lb empty. It was capable of 433 mph. Its armament was eight .5-inch machine guns, and its bomb load was up to 2500 lb. An interesting version, though produced in small numbers, was the P-47M of December 1944. This was a special high-speed variant, capable of 470 mph, designed to counter **V-1** flying bombs and other jet craft.

Additional Reading: Shacklady, *P-47 Thunderbolt*, 2000; Glenn, *The P-47 Pilots*, 1998.

Thunderbolt II, A-10, A-10A　　AIRCRAFT

Also known as the "Warthog," the U.S. Fairchild-Republic A-10 Thunderbolt was conceived mainly as a **tank** destroying **aircraft**. The YA-10 prototype first flew in 1972. Though ugly and very slow, the Warthog can deliver a considerable punch, being built around the Avenger seven-barrel, revolving-barrel, 30 mm **Gatling**-type cannon, with its cyclic rate of up to 4,200 rounds per minute. The rounds have a depleted uranium core, giving exceptional penetration; guided missiles may also be carried. The A-10A, operational by the late 1970s, was powered by two General Electric turbofans, giving a maximum speed of 517 mph. Titanium armor "bathtubs" protect the ammunition and pilot. The A-10 weighs just over 20,000 lb empty; this figure doubles when the craft is fully fuelled and armed. The avionics of the A-10 were basic initially, but lately a LASTE modification added an autopilot.

Additional Reading: Moeng, *Military Aircraft*, 1994; Logan, *Republic's A-10 Thunderbolt II*, 1997.

Thunderchief, F-105　　　　AIRCRAFT

The U.S. Republic F-105 Thunderchief **aircraft**, which flew as a prototype in 1955, has been described as the "world's best" fighter of the early 1960s. It has also been claimed as the biggest single-engine, single-seat combat aircraft. The F-105D, in use c. 1960, featured sophisticated **radar** to enable blind air-to-air or ground attack. In the F-105F of 1963 a second crewman was incorporated for improved fighter-bomber capabilities. The Thunderchief earned a remarkable record in Vietnam, flying the majority of missions over enemy territory; nevertheless roughly half of the 833 manufactured were destroyed in that conflict.

The F-105 was intended for a variety of roles from the outset. Its bomb bay was designed to take a Mk-28, 57, or 61 nuclear bomb, and its nose a 20 mm Vulcan **Gatling**-type cannon. It had four under-wing pylons for additional armament or external fuel tanks and was equipped with the General Electric MA-8 electronic fire control system, **radar** ranging,

Tiara

and the E-30 toss-bomb computer. Statistics for the F-105D show a length of 64 feet 4 inches, a top speed of 1,390 mph, a ceiling of 41,200 feet, and 24,500 lb of thrust from the Pratt and Whitney J75-P-19W turbojet.

Additional Reading: Pace, *X-Fighters: USAF Experimental and Prototype Fighters, XP-59 to YF-23*, 1991; Sgarlato, *Aircraft of the USAF*, 1978.

Tiara   DETECTION

Tiara was an experimental U.S. developed light-emitting chemical first tested at Fort Benning and Elgin Air Force Base. It was intended to be smeared to mark equipment or fired in **artillery shells** to illuminate areas at night. Its perceived advantage was that unlike star shells or "illuminating" rounds, it was not based on combustion but remained naturally glowing for long periods. Field tests in Vietnam proved disappointing; its properties were compromised by the climate, and its smell was disgusting.

Ticonderoga Class   WARSHIP

The *Ticonderoga* class of guided missile **cruiser**, with the **Aegis** combat system, is one of the most important types of vessel in the U.S. Navy. In 2002 some 27 of these ships were serving, the oldest being *Ticonderoga* (CG 47), commissioned in 1983, and the most recent the *Port Royal* (CG 73), commissioned in 1994. Displacing 9,500 tons with a crew of 358, they have a top speed of about 30 knots and a range of 6,000 miles. A wide range of missiles is carried, including Tomahawk, Harpoon, and surface-to-air types. They also have two 5-inch guns, Vulcan **Phalanx**, and **torpedoes**.

Additional Reading: Firebaugh, *Naval Engineering and American Sea Power*, 2000; *Jane's Warships*; Silverstone, *US Warships since 1945*, 1986; Polmar, *The Ships and Aircraft of the U.S. Fleet*, 1981.

Tiger, F-5   AIRCRAFT

The first of the U.S. Northrop F-5 series of single-seat fighter aircraft flew in 1959. It was also known as the "Freedom Fighter"; the name "Tiger" came after its use in Southeast Asia,

where it had been dubbed the "Sokoshi," or little Tiger. Its main virtues were its relative lightness, cheapness, and versatility. Eventually over 2,700 F-5s of different types would be built, and many of them exported to countries friendly to the United States.

The F-5E International Fighter, or Tiger II, appeared in 1972. This was powered by two General Electric J85-GE-21 axial turbojets giving a maximum speed of 1,075 mph. It was 48 feet long with a wingspan of just 26 feet 8 inches, and it weighed 9,424 lb empty. Armed with two 20 mm cannon, it could carry up to 7,000 lb of ordnance including **Sidewinder** missiles. The latest version, the F-20 Tigershark, was developed in the 1980s and featured greatly improved engine power but was not adopted by the U.S. Air Force.

Additional Reading: Pace, *X-Fighters: USAF Experimental and Prototype Fighters, XP-59 to YF-23*, 1991; Sgarlato, *Aircraft of the USAF*, 1978.

Tiger Tank; Königstiger; Royal Tiger
TANK

The reputation of the Tiger tank was such that Allied soldiers in the latter part of the Second World War were apt to judge every German tank a Tiger. It set the pace in the armor race and had to be taken on, if at all, with respect and superior numbers. Yet the Tiger was itself a hasty reaction to the discovery that the Russians were developing tough and innovative tanks like the **T-34**. Work commenced in late 1941, capitalizing on existing experimental designs, the VK 3000, and VK 4500, produced by Henschel and Porsche. Prototypes were presented to Hitler on 20 April 1942, and orders were placed. In the event, the 90 completed Porsche bodies were used for the Elefant tank destroyer, while the Henschel design appeared as the PzKpfw VI, or Tiger I. Its first use was on the Eastern Front in September 1942.

Key to the Tiger was its **8.8** cm L/56 gun. This was capable of 5.45 inch (138 mm) armor penetration at 1,000 meters, enough to smash any tank in production and many then yet to be devised. Even so, some critics have suggested that a smaller-caliber higher-velocity weapon,

The much feared German PzKpfw VI Tiger I heavy tank. With 100 mm of frontal armor and an 88 mm gun the Tiger was immensely powerful, and probably the most effective tank when it was first produced in 1942. New models like the Joseph Stalin, Pershing, Panther, and Tiger II "King Tiger" made any superiority short lived. Courtesy of the Library of Congress.

such as that mounted in the **Panther**, might have been more suitable, since the **88 mm** was heavy, with large rounds, necessitating a bigger turret and bulkier tank. Though essentially a series of unimaginative near-vertical slabs, the armor was a maximum of 100 mm thick, making the hull and turret impervious to the **T-34** or **Sherman** at all but point-blank range. The total weight was 56 tons. Its weaker spots, later sought out by ground attack aircraft and artillery, were the rear and rear decking. With a Maybach HL230 P45 gasoline engine, the Tiger could manage 25 mph on roads. Cross-country performance was about half this, and for rail transport the width of the tank required the fitting of special narrower transport tracks. There were also early mechanical problems.

Used at Kharkov and **Kursk**, the Tiger I performed well, but total production was only 1,350, and losses meant that the maximum

number ever available was 671 (July 1944). That same month manufacture of the Tiger I ceased, and the first of the new Tiger II, or Königstiger, already seen in a training role, now reached front. The new Tiger was another powerful, heavy design but differed materially from its predecessor. It featured sloped armor up to 180 mm thick, a better 88 mm gun, and a radically different turret. Total weight was 69 tons. Though formidable, the Tiger II's basic power plant remained the same, so its mobility was limited. Only 492 were made. Variants of the Tiger included the monster Porsche Jägdtiger with a 12.8 cm PaK44 L/55 gun, and the Sturmtiger, which mounted an improbable short-barrel breechloading 38 cm rocket projector, originally conceived as an antisubmarine device, in a bunker-busting role. Only 18 Sturmtiger were made.

Additional Reading: Ford, *The Tiger Tank*, 1998; Fletcher, *Tiger!* 1986; Gudgin, *Armoured Firepower: The Development of Tank Armament 1939–1945*, 1997; Devey, *Jagdtiger*, 1999.

Tirpitz WARSHIP

Named after Grand Admiral Alfred von Tirpitz (1849–1930), renown as "father of the German High Seas Fleet," the *Tirpitz* was a ***Bismarck***-class **battleship** completed at Wilhelmshaven in 1941. She was feared as the largest surface unit of the German navy in World War II. Continually assaulted from sea and air, she was finally sunk during operation Catechism by **Lancaster** bombers at Tromso, Norway, in 1944.

Additional Reading: Whitley, *German Capital Ships of World War II*, 1989; Kennedy, *Menace: Life and Death of the Tirpitz*, 1979; Garzke and Dulin, *Battleships: Axis & Neutral Battleships in World War II*, 1985.

Tomahawk Cruise Missile. *See* Cruise Missile

Tomcat, F-14 AIRCRAFT

The U.S. Grumman F-14 Tomcat fighter **aircraft** had its genesis in the 1960s, when Grumman worked with General Dynamics on the abortive F-111B. Though this was canceled, Grumman continued to work on its own project, Design 303, eventually producing an excellent interceptor primarily for aircraft carrier use. The navy argument that carrier-based planes could now easily reach much of the populated areas of the world, and the fact that the Vietnam War was in progress, helped to make sure that the idea reached fruition.

Important aspects of the specification included the ability to carry **Phoenix, Sparrow,** or **Sidewinder** missiles, and a higher loading capacity than the F4J **Phantom**; suitability for use on *Hancock*-class carriers; two Pratt and Whitney TF30-P-412 engines; advanced weapons control systems; and a two-man crew seated in tandem. The two-man crew was intended specifically to maximize awareness, allowing one man to concentrate on sensors that required "head-down attention" while the other was "head up." The design work was assisted not only by computers and many thousands of hours of wind tunnel tests, as might be expected, but by EMMA, the Engineering Mockup Manufacturing Aid. This took the old concept of wood and plastic models to a new level, by creating a full-size aircraft from metal and sandcast aluminum to fit-check hydraulic lines, wiring, and control systems, and to practice the installation of real engines.

The F-14 first flew in late 1970, piloted by Robert Smythe, with William Miller in the "back seat." Testing made early use of the ATS, or Automated Telemetry System, in which data was captured from the aircraft in flight, processed, and viewed in real time. The F-14 was in service at sea within four years. At the peak of production Grumman would have 10,000 people at 14 facilities working on the Tomcat for a projected production of over 700 aircraft. Since then the aircraft has undergone many refinements and modifications to keep pace with changing technology. The F-14B with General Electric F-110 engines was introduced in 1987, and a much improved F-14D appeared in 1990.

The Tomcat has many interesting technological features. It was the first "variable geometry" carrier aircraft, being able to sweep its wings forward for maximum lift in slow flight or sweep them back to create the best silhouette for speed. An MSP, or Mach Sweep Program, can control the wing settings automatically, thus allowing the crew to concentrate on combat or other tasks; manual and emergency modes can also be selected. The F-14 makes extensive use of titanium and such composite materials as boron skinned aluminum honeycomb; also, chemical milling and electron beam welding are used in fabrication. Huge amounts of work were put into its air inlet systems, which rely on a series of ramps and doors to ensure the correct flows at widely differing speeds.

Performance data published in 2002 gives the F-14 a maximum speed of 1,545 mph, a range of 450 miles, and a ceiling of 60,000 feet, which can be reached in two minutes six seconds. The empty weight is 39,762 lb. Common weapons loads include a 20 mm cannon plus six Sparrow and four Sidewinder missiles, or six Phoenix missiles and two AIM-9s. The Tomcat has seen action both real and fictional. Two Tomcats from the *Nimitz* shot down two Libyan fighter bombers in 1981, and in 1989 Tomcats destroyed two Libyan MiG-23 **Floggers**. In 1995 they were used in **smart-bomb** attacks on Bosnia, in which role they were nicknamed "Bombcats." On the big screen the F-14 was the "star" of the Hollywood film *Top Gun*.

By the end of the twentieth century more than 30 U.S. Navy units had been equipped with the Tomcat. A number of these—including the VF-24 "Fighting Renegades," VF-33 "Starfighters," VF-74 "Bedevilers," VF-111 "Sundowners," VF-114 "Aardvarks," VF-124 "Gunfighters," VF-142 "Ghostriders," VF-154 "Black Knights," VF-191 "Satan's Kittens," VF-194 "Red Lightnings," VF-201 "Hunters," VF-202 "Superheats," VF-301 "Devil's Disciples," and VF-302 "Stallions"—have been disestablished, some during 1988, others to save costs after the Cold War. However it is expected that Tomcats will remain in service until at least 2015, when it is thought that they will be replaced by the **Joint Strike Fighter**.

Additional Reading: Baker, *Grumman F-14 Tomcat*, 1998; Rockwell, *F-14 Tomcat*, 1999; Polmar, *The Ships and Aircraft of the US Fleet*, 1981.

Tony. *See* **Hien**

Tornado, MRCA, ADV, GR, ECR
AIRCRAFT

The Panavia Tornado two-seater "Multi Role Combat **Aircraft**" was developed in the early 1970s by the United Kingdom, West Germany, and Italy; the prototype flew in 1974. It was intended as a successor to such craft as the **Lightning** and **Phantom**, and it has been described as a "technological, political and administrative triumph." In terms of general performance it compares well with the **Tomcat**, though it is less maneuverable than the **F-16**. Some versions are nuclear capable. The various British GR types were deployed specifically for reconnaisance, antiship duties, ground attack, and **radar** suppression. The German Tornado ECR is for electronic combat and reconnaisance.

The Tornado ADV, or "Air Defence Variant," was produced by the United Kingdom and flew in its F2 form in 1979. Delivery to the RAF commenced in 1984, though the full-specification GEC Marconi Foxhunter radar was not fitted until 1989. In 1990, Tornado F3s were among the first aircraft sent to the Gulf, and they have since served in Bosnia and elsewhere. The Tornado F3's wings may be swept from a full 45-foot 8-inch span down to 28 feet 3 inches at high speed. It is powered by two Turbo-Union turbofans giving a top speed of 1,480 mph. It carries a range of missiles and a 27 mm cannon. The intercept radius is 1,150 miles.

Additional Reading: Harkins, *Tornado*, 1995; Moeng, *Military Aircraft*, 1994.

Torpedo
EXPLOSIVE DEVICE

Named after the torpedo fish, which gives an electric shock to its prey, torpedoes were originally any **explosive** or incendiary device used in or on water against ships. Thus it was that many early antishipping devices were indis-

A Mk 46 exercise torpedo is launched from the U.S. Navy *Spruance* class destroyer USS *Moosebrugger*, during phase two of the Unitas exercises off Brazil, August 1996. Courtesy of the Department of Defense.

criminately called **sea mines** or torpedoes. The spar torpedo, used in the American Civil War, consisted of a charge on the end of a pole. Nevertheless, what we now understand as the torpedo is a self-propelled, cigar-shaped missile capable of traveling through water. They may be launched from **submarines**, ships, or shore stations, or dropped from the air. (The **Bangalore Torpedo** is an exception being a land-use weapon.)

Engineer Robert Whitehead (1823–1905) of Bolton, in the United Kingdom, is generally regarded as the father of the modern torpedo. While working in Austria in 1864 he was asked to formulate an idea for an explosive self-propelled boat that could be steered from its launch site into the enemy. Whitehead improved upon the suggestion almost beyond recognition, creating a weapon that needed no physical link to its launch platform and would strike its target where it was most vulnerable—below the water line. A workable compressed-air-powered torpedo with fins and a propellor, designed to be launched from a tube, was in existence by 1866. Keeping the missile running at a uniform depth was at first problematic, but within a couple of years an answer was found in the pendulum hydrostat.

Torpedo

Thereafter the torpedo was embraced as a potential wonder weapon, both by the major naval powers and by nations that were themselves weak in **battleships** and needed a method to even the score. Following successful trials Britain ordered Whitehead torpedoes in 1870. Italy first experimented with its own torpedoes before adopting the Whitehead model. Germany ordered Whitehead types before the German Schwarzkopf company started to make torpedoes, exporting them to Russia, Japan, and Spain.

In the United States a torpedo test station was set up at Newport, Rhode Island in 1870, and a number of alternatives were investigated. In the Lay torpedo the missile floated about surface level and was guided by means of wires. In other models, propelled by carbon dioxide, the torpedo ran under the water, depth being controlled by means of a float on the surface. Rocket-propelled torpedoes were proposed by Lieutenant F. M Barber. In the U.S. Hall torpedo of the 1880s, superheated steam fed from the boiler of the **torpedo boat** was used as the motive power. Yet the most successful of the American designs was the Howell. This used the simple but clever expedient of a large flywheel that was spun to 12,000 revolutions per minute before launch of the weapon through a tube. The spinning of the fly wheel also helped stabilize the torpedo, which could travel to just over 1,000 yards at a maximum speed of 30 knots, a performance not dissimilar to that of the early Whitehead. Other torpedoes of this early period included the Ericsson, which was electrically powered through a cable that ran out behind the torpedo as it went forward, and two types by Nordenfelt, one of which was battery powered. The innovative **Brennan torpedo**, which had shown early promise, fell by the wayside in the early twentieth century.

By 1892 the biggest weapon in the Whitehead arsenal was a 15-inch-diameter steel torpedo 18 feet 9.5 inches long. Each one cost £350. Later technological developments included the introduction of the gyroscope in 1896 and heater systems from 1904. In one version of the heater system, fuel was sprayed into the air vessel and ignited; in another, fuel and air were mixed to boil water. Though sometimes referred to as "steam torpedoes," these were still primarily powered by the hot air. Either way, heater systems improved the range and speed of the torpedo. One of the best heater systems was the RGF devised by Lieutenant Hardcastle.

Torpedoes tended to increase in size. A 21-inch diameter model appeared in 1908; bigger examples were made, but this eventually this became the common size. During the early part of the twentieth century antitorpedo netting was introduced in many anchorages in an attempt to protect shipping. Experimental torpedoes with blades and net-piercing caps were therefore devised. There were also constant efforts to improve torpedo speed. Propellers were improved, and the American Bliss-Leavitt company introduced the "air blast" gyroscope for improved stability over longer ranges. By 1914 the 21-inch Weymouth Mark II weighing 2794 lb was capable of 29 knots and a range of 10,000 yards. Many torpedoes were now "pattern runners." This meant that they could be set to run for a predetermined distance, then zigzag back and forth over a certain area.

Developments during World War II included magnetic pistols, which triggered the torpedo when under the hull of a vessel; electric drive; and the German "Fat" torpedo. This last was designed to run in circles after its initial straight run, maximizing its chance of a hit on a convoy. The German Falke torpedo, introduced in 1943, and the U.S. air-dropped "Fido," or "wandering Annie," were the first to home in on sound.

Ship and aircraft-launched lightweight torpedoes were introduced from the 1950s, providing another weapon in the antisubmarine warfare arsenal. First of these was the U.S. Mark 44, powered by a seawater battery and equipped with active **sonar**. Britain followed suit with Stringray, and many other countries including France, Italy, and Sweden all produced their own over the next couple of decades.

Modern torpedoes use many technologies for a variety of specialized tasks and have a much increased chance of first-shot hit. Acoustic active torpedoes generate sound and home in on echoes from the target. Passive acoustic types are attracted by noise generated by the target. Interestingly, torpedos launched from submarines have themselves become key anti-submarine weapons. Most modern torpedoes are powered by electric motors and have batteries. Just one of many current during the 1980s was the 21-inch-diameter U.S. Mark 48; this was 19 feet in length and weighed 3,474 lb. With wire guidance and passive and active homing, it had a reported speed of 55 knots and a range of over 23 miles. Captor systems are a hybrid of torpedo and sea mine, laid on the bottom until activated. When triggered by the sound of a submarine, they activate a torpedo, which rises to optimum depth and searches for its quarry.

Additional Reading: Sueter, *The Evolution of the Submarine Boat, Mine and Torpedo*, 1907; Miller, *U-Boats*, 2000; Hill, *Anti-Submarine Warfare*, 1984; Fitzsimons, *The Illustrated Encyclopedia of Twentieth Century Weapons and Warfare*, 1967–1978; Poland, *The Torpedomen*, 1993.

Toryu, Kawasaki Ki-45 AIRCRAFT

Its name meaning "dragon slayer" in English, the Toryu Kawasaki twin-engine **aircraft** was designed in the late 1930s to meet a Japanese army specification for a long-range fighter. However, it did not enter production until 1941 and did not score its first successes until sometime afterward. It eventually found its forte as a night fighter against U.S. bombers, where its maneuverability was made to count. The special Kai-C variant was fitted with upward-firing cannon, designed to devastate bombers as it passed underneath. The Ki-45 is also significant as the first Japanese aircraft to be used in **kamikaze** attacks against Allied shipping. Total Toryu production was about 1,700.

TOW Missile MISSILE

The U.S. BGM-71 TOW is one of the most successful and best known antitank missiles. In production since 1970, first by Hughes and later

Raytheon, it has seen worldwide service. Launched from a tube before the main motor cuts in, it is wire guided to the target. The latest models claim up to 900-mm armor penetration and a range of about 3.5 km. The TOW 2A features a smaller second charge near the end of the nose probe to explode and neutralize any reactive armor the target may carry. The 2B model has an even more cunning method of attack, being intended to detonate above the enemy vehicle, sending a high-temperature jet downward. The appropriately named TOW BLAAM is for demolition of masonry targets.

TOW has been fitted to many armored fighting vehicles, including **tanks** and **helicopters**. It is also carried on the turret of the U.S. Army's **Bradley** infantry fighting vehicle.

Additional Reading: *Jane's Weapons Systems*; Gander, *Anti Tank Weapons*, 2000.

Trebuchet. *See* **Catapult**

Trench Club CLUB WEAPON

Appearing during World War I, trench clubs were particularly useful for quiet close-range combat. Usually under 60 cm long they were of widely differing designs, some of which resembled the ancient **knobkerrie** or **mace**. A common design was shaped like a wooden baseball bat, with metal studs externally and a lead weight within. Some were locally improvized, one French model having lead wrapped around a stout stick, while some British Tommies took the hanging straps and handles from London subway trains on their way to the front.

Tribal Class WARSHIP

Built in the late 1930s, the 16 elegant-looking British Tribal-class **destroyers** were heavily armed with eight 4.7-inch guns. Displacing 1,854 tons, they were 377 feet long. Engaged in many diverse operations early in World War II, 12 were lost by the end of 1942. *Afridi* was sunk by **Stukas**, *Sikh* by shore batteries. *Bedouin* was claimed by Italian aircraft. Several others were victims of **U-boats**. Only *Ashanti*,

Eskimo, Nubian, and *Tartar* survived to be sold off in the late 1940s.

Tricar Parachutable   VEHICLE

The bizarre FN AS 24 "Tricar Parachutable" was the Belgian answer to ground mobility for airborne forces. Designed by Nicholas Straussler, it was first produced in prototype by German companies in 1958 and manufactured in quantity by **Fabrique Nationale** of Belgium from 1959. It was a motor tricycle with large low-pressure Lypsoid tyres and a 15 horsepower engine. It was capable of carrying four soldiers at up to about 30 mph. A telescopic frame helped make it compact for transport and storage.

Trident Missile   MISSILE

The U.S. Trident **submarine**-launched ballistic missile was the successor to **Poseidon**. The Trident I C-4 became operational in 1978. Its greatest operational advantage was increased range, achieved by high-energy fuel and reduced drag. The Trident II D-5 was test-fired from a submarine in 1989. With a range of over 6,000, miles the three-stage Trident II can carry up to 14 nuclear warheads. It weighs 130,000 lb.

Additional Reading: *Jane's Naval Weapons Systems.*

Trireme. *See* **Galley**

Trojan. *See* **FV 430, 432**

Tupolev T6-95. *See* **Bear**

Turtle. *See* **Submarine**

Type 14. *See* **Nambu**

Type 22 Frigate   WARSHIP

The contract for the first of the British Type 22 **frigates** was awarded in 1974. HMS **Broadsword** (F88), the first of the class, was launched in 1976. Eventually 14 were produced. Built in several batches, the Type 22s differed markedly

in displacement, the earliest examples being as little as 4,000 tons, while the last were over 5,000 tons. Batch One comprised *Broadsword, Battleaxe, Brilliant*, and *Brazen*; Batch Two, *Boxer, Beaver, Brave, London, Sheffield*, and *Coventry*, Batch Three, *Cornwall, Cumberland, Campbeltown*, and *Chatham*. Armament and other specifications have also altered with time, though during the 1990s weapons carried included **Exocet** and **Sea Wolf** missiles, multi-barrel cannon, guns, and **torpedoes**.

The general soundness of the design was confirmed by the performance of two ships in the Falklands in 1982. *Broadsword* acted as vital close-range escort to **Hermes** and claimed four Argentine aircraft. Despite being raked with cannon fire and bombed, she survived with relatively minor damage. Brilliant (F90) protected the *Invincible*, was at every major engagement, and was the first Royal Navy ship to spend more than 100 days at sea since World War II. She destroyed at least two aircraft. All Batch One Type 22s were sold to Brazil in the 1990s.

Additional Reading: Marriott, *Type 22*, 1986.

Type 23 Frigate   WARSHIP

Designed in the light of experience in the Falklands, the British Duke-class, Type 23, **frigates**, comprise 16 vessels launched between 1987 and 2000. They are named after British dukes, hence the first (F230) is HMS *Norfolk*; others include *Marlborough, Lancaster, Westminster*, and *Iron Duke*. While their main task is anti-submarine work using a towed **sonar** array and Merlin **helicopter**, they are good all-rounders. Taking advantage of **stealth** technology, they have reduced **radar** signatures. Weapons systems include **Seawolf**, Stingray torpedoes, 30 mm antiaircraft guns, and a 4.5-inch gun. Gas turbines give a top speed of almost 30 knots.

Type 56. *See* **Kalashnikov**

Type 92   FIREARM

The Japanese Type 92 heavy **machine gun** was an 8 mm weapon inspired by a **Hotchkiss** design, modified by General **Nambu** in the 1930s. Weighing 61 lb, it used ammunition fed from strips and had an oiler mechanism to lubricate the cartridges. Its relatively slow rate of fire led Allied troops to call it the "Woodpecker." An unusual feature was a set of slots in the tripod allowing poles to be inserted so that three men could carry the whole assembly between them.

Additional Reading: Markham, *Japanese Infantry Weapons of World War Two*, 1976.

Type 94 Pistol   FIREARM

The 8 mm Japanese Type 94 six-round **semi-automatic** is worthy of note as one of the worst military pistols. Introduced in 1934, it was crude, with a grip that was very small even by Japanese standards. Just over seven inches long, it weighed .79 kg. Though it has been argued that it was technically superior to the **Nambu**, poor wartime production obviated any advantage.

Additional Reading: Ezell, *Handguns of the World*, 1981.

Type 97 Tank. *See* **Chi-Ha**

Type 99. *See* **Val**

Typhoon (Eurofighter)   AIRCRAFT

The single-seat "Eurofighter" **aircraft**, known in the United Kingdom as the Typhoon, is a joint British, German, Italian, and Spanish project. France withdrew from the project at an early stage. First flown in 1994, it is intended primarily as a fighter, but it also has ground-attack capability. Powered by an EJ200 turbofan, it has a maximum speed of 1,255 mph and a range of 863 miles, climbing to 35,000 feet in two and a half minutes. Highly agile, the plane is "fly by wire"; the pilot has a wide-angle head-up display and a helmet-mounted weapon sight. Press reports suggest that each Eurofighter costs about $50 million. First production models appeared by 2002, but the crash of prototype DA6 in Spain caused delays.

Series Production Aircraft or "SPAs" were finally flown in early 2003.

Typhoon (Hawker)   AIRCRAFT

Originally intended as a successor to the **Hurricane**, the British Hawker Typhoon single-seat fighter first flew in 1941. Despite a healthy 400 mph top speed, it lacked a good rate of climb. Luckily it proved a useful ground-attack machine; armed with cannon and rockets it was very effective against communications and **tanks** in the latter part of World War II.

Additional Reading: Mason, *The Hawker Typhoon and Tempest*, 1998; Reed and Beaumont, *Typhoon & Tempest at War*, 1974.

Typhoon Class   SUBMARINE

The Russian Typhoon class are the largest **submarines** ever built. Intended to survive the opening stages of any exchange of **nuclear weapons** by waiting under the Arctic ice, these Type 941 strategic missile submarines could then surface and retaliate. The multi hulled design, with five inner hulls inside two parallel main hulls, and retractable hydroplanes, made breaking vertically through 12 feet of ice a fully practical proposition. The TK208 was the first of the class to be laid down at the Severodivinsk yard in 1977, and by 1989 a total of six vessels were completed. The Typhoons came as a particular surprise to the West, not only because of their complement of 20 SS-N-20 Sturgeon ballistic missiles, capable of hitting any land target from the ocean, but because of their quietness. Near silence was achieved by double laying the silencing system around the power train, active sound cancellation methods, and sound absorbent tiles. Difficulty in tracking the Typhoons inspired the Hollywood film *The Hunt for Red October*. Ironically most of the class have now been decommissioned, with U.S. aid under the "threat reduction program."

Additional Reading: *Jane's Warships*; Jordan, *Soviet Submarines*, 1989; Hutchinson *Submarines*, 2001.

U

U-2   AIRCRAFT

The U.S. Lockheed U-2 is probably the best known strategic reconnaissance **aircraft** of all time. Ordered by the CIA in 1954, it was operational over communist countries by 1958. With an 80-foot wingspan and a relatively slow top speed of 500 mph, it has been described as a "stratospheric glider" with auxiliary turbojet power. The U-2 was dramatically compromised in 1960 when missile-armed Soviet **MiG-21s** succeeded in downing one piloted by Francis Gary Powers over the USSR. He was tried and sentenced to ten years but later was released in an exchange.

An improved U-2R first flew in 1967 and was used in Vietnam, with further production from 1979 for the deployment of battlefield surveillance **radar**. Still serving recently, the U2-Rs have been reequipped with General Electric turbofans. They are credited with a maximum service ceiling of 80,000 feet and a 12-hour endurance, with a range of over 3,000 miles.

Additional Reading: Gunston, *Spy Planes*, 1983; Simsonsen, *US Spy Planes*, 1985; Fensch, *Top Secret: The CIA and the U2 Program*, 2001.

U-1; U-35; U-151, etc. *See* U-boat

UAV   UNMANNED AIRCRAFT

The UAV, or unmanned aerial vehicle, is an intelligent successor technology to drone and target aircraft, and to the pilotless **V1**. Able to carry more fuel relative to size and deployed without risk of human casualties, UAVs have proved particularly useful as spy planes. One of the first really successful examples was the Ryan QM-34 Firebee, a small swept-wing U.S. subsonic turbojet that saw extensive use in Vietnam (though this was referred to by the acronym RPV, remotely piloted vehicle).

A good current example of the UAV is the U.S. **Global Hawk**. Recent press reports suggest that the Pentagon is currently considering a range of UAVs, including silent versions with fuel cells, hypersonic types, "smart" planes with enhanced ability to identify individuals and objects, and high-endurance machines that can stay aloft for weeks at a time. Enthusiasts of the concept suggest that UAVs will soon outnumber manned craft.

U-boat   SUBMARINE

The English term "U-boat" is derived from the German *U-Boot* or *Unterseeboot*, literally "undersea boat," or **submarine**. Though there had been earlier German experiments and submarines ordered from Russia in 1904, the first, *U-1*, was launched from the Germaniawerft yard at Kiel in August 1906. Listed as a coastal type, it was 139 feet in length with a double hull, displacing 238 tons on the surface. She was powered by diesel and electric engines giving a top speed of 11 knots. The armament was one bow torpedo tube and a mine. Remarkably, she survived World War I, later becoming an exhibit in the Deutsches Museum Munich. Most of her type were not so lucky, for of the first eight experimental coastal U-boats, three were sunk by enemy action, two sunk by other German vessels, and the remainder surrendered or were broken up. A total of 178 U-boats were

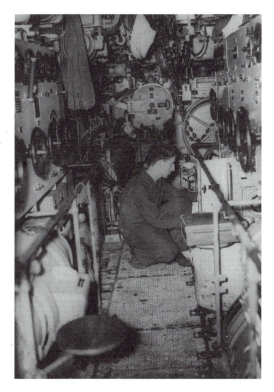

The cramped engine room of a captured German U-boat, pictured May 1945. As in all military submarines space was at a considerable premium, being filled with power plant, batteries, weapons, and supplies. Everything else was usually deemed wasted space. © Hulton/Getty Images.

lost to all causes in World War I, and the German submarine arm was disbanded in 1919—defeated by the convoy system, the **depth charge**, and British and U.S. shipbuilding.

Nevertheless, the U-boat had come of age between 1906 and the end of the war, graduating from a relatively small-scale novelty to a major strategic weapon. U-boats had sunk 5,282 vessels, severely damaging enemy trade in the Atlantic and causing a crisis for the allies; ironically, unrestricted submarine warfare had helped to bring the United States into the war. Significant technical improvements had also been made. As early as 1912 boats of the *U-19* class were being built for long-range patrols, armed with four torpedo tubes and an **88 mm** gun. It was *U-21* of this type that fired the

first torpedo of the war, in September 1914, and the *U-20* sank the *Lusitania* with a single torpedo in May 1915.

During the First World War, new types of U-boat included the *UB-II* coastal vessels, *UC-II* sea minelayers, the powerful *U-140* class, and the *U-151* class of ocean cruisers of 1917. These last were 213 feet long, and had a crew of 56. They were also capable of carrying cargo and a prize crew for taking over a captured vessel. The *Oldenburg, U-151* itself, carried out an epic 13-week patrol covering almost 10,000 miles, during which she was stationed off the East Coast of the United States, laid mines, and sank 23 ships. Top-scoring U-boat of the war was the *U-35*, launched in 1914, which destroyed a total of 224 ships during 25 patrols. One of its captains, Lothar von Arnauld de la Perière, holder of the Pour le Mérite, was arguably the most successful submarine commander of all time, with a score of 194 merchant and two warships.

Some German-designed submarines were built at foreign yards for other navies in the interwar period; the decision to revive the German U-boat arm came in 1932. The first new vessels were designated MVB, *Motorenversuchtboot*, or "experimental motor boats." The Type I U-boat mounted six 21-inch torpedo tubes, a 105 mm gun, and a net-cutting device on the bow. The Type IIA, based on an earlier design prepared for Finland, featured a light, strong, welded hull; the first of the series bore the famous *U-1* hull number. Types IIB, IIC, and IID followed. Remarkably, six U-boats of the IIB type were dismantled in 1942 and shipped overland to the Black Sea for action against Russia. The initial IIC was launched in May 1940; it was 144 long and had diesel-electric propulsion giving a maximum speed of 13 knots. Fifty Type II U-boats were built in all.

Most numerous of the U-boats of World War II were the Type VII, 709 of which were made from 1935 to 1945. The majority of these were of the Type VIIC subclass. Claimed as "one of the most important designs in the history of the submarine," the Type VIIs certainly made an impact, commonly by hunting as "wolf packs" under radio direction. The VIIBs alone sank a million and a half tons of Allied shipping by 1943. They included the *U-48*, the most successful submarine of World War II. Commissioned at Kiel in 1939, *U-48* carried out 12 patrols under five different captains, dispatching about a third of a million tons of shipping. Relegated to training in October 1943, she survived to be scuttled in May 1945.

The 88-boat VIIC/41 type, the first of which was launched in July 1943, was the epitome of the attack U-boat. Nonessentials were deleted, equipment lightened, and performance stretched to the maximum. With a surface displacement of 759 tons and a length of 220.5 feet, the VIIC/41 type was powered by two 2,200 horsepower diesels and two 750 horsepower electric motors, giving a maximum speed of 18.6 knots. A total of 16 torpedoes were carried; they could be fired through four bow and one stern tube. An 88 mm and a 20 mm gun plus up to 39 mines completed the armament. The sharklike bow was fitted with listening devices, underwater telephone transducers, and **hydrophones**. GEMA **radar** was installed on some vessels. Accommodation for the 45-man crew was typically cramped and basic, with just two toilets, only one of which was kept in use throughout the voyage. Most of the crew slept in the forward torpedo room, while only the captain qualified for a cabin, screened off by a curtain. The last of the type was the *U-1308*, built at Flensburg and commissioned in January 1945.

Partner to the VII Type boats was the larger Type IX, designed specifically for long-range patrols. The final models had ranges of up to 23,000 miles and a top speed of about 20 knots. The first Type IXA was the *U-37*, launched at Bremen in 1938, and the last the *U-883*, an IXD-42 type completed at the end of March 1945. Three Type IX boats were in Japanese ports at the end of the war, and a total of five actually served with the Japanese navy. Type IX vessels sent to the Far East were remarkable in that they carried diminutive Fa-330 **Focke**-Achgelis **helicopters**, perhaps better described as "rotary kites."

Other U-boats included the 294-foot XB type minelayer, the largest German submarine used in World War II; the bulbous XIV tanker, universally known as the *Milchkuh*, or "milk cow"; the Type XXIII coastal boat; and the XVIIG, with its revolutionary Walther geared turbines. Yet the Type XXI of 1944 was the most technologically significant, being designed to minimize hydrodynamic resistance and spend much of its time submerged. Sometimes known as the *elektroboot*, the Type XXI carried 239 tons of batteries. Capable of remaining underwater for three days at a time, the Type XXI could also "creep" quietly at three knots to avoid Allied attention. The class was also remarkable in its fabrication, being built on a diversified modular basis and brought together at the yard only during the final phase of construction. It was the inspiration of many postwar submarines. Fortunately for the Allies, few saw active service.

Additional Reading: Rössler, *The U-Boat*, 2001; Miller, *U-Boats*, 2000; Stern, *Type VII U-Boats*, 1998; Showell, *U-Boats under the Swastika*, 1987; White, *U-Boat Tankers*, 1998; Sharpe, *U-Boat Fact File*, 1998; Williamson, *U-Boats of the Kaiser's Navy*, 2002; Köhl and Rössler, *The Type XXI U-Boat*, 1991; Kemp, *U-Boats Destroyed*, 1997.

Uhu. *See* **He 219**

Unimog   VEHICLE

Unimog stands for *Universal Motor Gerät*, meaning "universal power plant." The four-wheel-drive vehicle that bears this name was first conceived in 1946 for multipurpose agricultural and industrial use. Production began at Boeringer in Göppingen in 1949 but was soon transferred to Daimler-Benz, later Mercedes-Benz. The vehicle has served German forces in many forms–as one-ton truck, radio van, snow plow, and cargo carrier to name but a few. Most recently it has gained fame as a support or mother vehicle for special forces, including the SAS.

United States, USS   WARSHIP

The USS *United States* (CVA 58) was begun in 1949 but was never completed. Nevertheless, it may be argued that in a sense this was the most important **aircraft carrier** of the period, as it marked a watershed in technology and design. Key to the plan was the perceived need to provide carrier transport for nuclear bombers that could strike deep into enemy territory. In order to accommodate the takeoff and landing of such planes, the *United States* was supposed to have had a totally flush deck 1,030 feet long. Instead of a superstructure, the vessel was to have had low sponsons either side of the deck.

Universal Carrier. *See* Bren Carrier

USS (United States Ship). *See by specific name of vessel*

Uzi   FIREARM

Designed by Lieutenant Colonel Uziel Gal (1923–2002) at the end of the 1940s, the Israeli 9 mm Uzi **submachine gun** entered production in 1955. Functional rather than elegant, it was just 44.5 cm long, space being saved by having the magazine in the grip and a bolt that wrapped around the rear of the barrel. It weighed 3.5 kg. Made to relatively wide tolerances, the Uzi was robust enough for use in desert conditions. Later versions were a Mini-Uzi, just 36 cm in length, and the Micro-Uzi, 25 cm long. Israeli Military Industries and **Fabrique Nationale** have made more than two million Uzis. They have now been withdrawn from Israeli front line service.

V

V1   MISSILE

The German Vergeltungswaffe 1 ("Vengeance Weapon 1"), or V1 project, code-named Kirschkern, or "cherry stone," began officially in 1942. By 1944 it had resulted in the small pilotless FZG 76 **aircraft**, known to the Allies as the "doodle-bug," or "buzz bomb." This consisted of a streamlined fuselage with short wings and a **pulse jet** engine to the rear. It contained 1,870 lb of high explosive, a fuel tank of 150 gallons, compressed-air tanks, a large battery, gyroscopes, and servos. Though parts production was dispersed, much of the construction work was done at Nordhausen in a massive underground complex using slave labor.

The craft was fueled and taken to a non-magnetic area to have its master compass set for the correct bearing from launch site to target. The V1 was now put on a trolley atop a 150-foot launch ramp, air was blown into the engine, and the sparking system was fired to start the jet. With the engine running at full power, superheated steam was released into the hollow tube within the launch ramp, driving a piston that propelled the trolley and the V1 up the ramp. Reaching 250 mph, the missile shot off the ramp, and the trolley fell away, leaving the V1 to climb to the operational height of 3,000 feet under control of a barometric (air pressure) sensor system. A good crew could fire a V1 every half-hour, with a rate of about 15 per night.

Gyroscopically steadied, the machine flew toward its target at speeds from 300 to 420 mph. The bomb armed about ten minutes into the flight. A small propeller turned by the air flow estimated distance, and when the required range was reached detonators acted, causing the control surfaces to lock, pushing the craft into a steep dive. The V1 exploded on impact.

From June to August 1944 about 9,000 V1s were launched against the London area. When the French ground ramp sites were overrun the Germans turned to air-launching from beneath **Heinkel** aircraft. A further thousand missiles were so delivered from September 1944 to January 1945; 275 shot from the Netherlands in a third wave of London attacks using an increased-fuel-capacity missile. Over 4,000 V1s were also used against Antwerp and Liege after Allied liberation. V1 attacks ceased on 30 March 1945. Though highly destructive, the V1 was by no means infallible; many were shot down by **antiaircraft guns** or aircraft, or missed. Of those directed at London more than a third were intercepted or otherwise lost before they reached the English coast, and less than a third reached London.

Additional Reading: Ramsey (ed), *The Blitz Then and Now*, 1990; Kay, *German Jet Engine and Gas Turbine Development 1930–1945*, 2002.

V2   MISSILE

Since heavy artillery had been denied to Germany by the Versailles Treaty, investigation of rockets was stimulated by the German military. Key figures were the chief of the Army Weapons Bureau, Karl Becker, and Walter Dornberger. As early as 1932 Werner von Braun was also part of the team involved in experiments with liquid-fuel rockets, which would ulti-

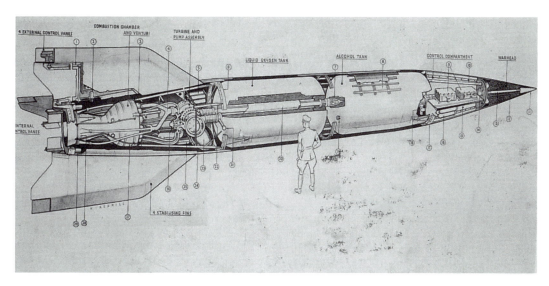

Sectional drawing of the German V2 rocket, showing the fuel tanks, venturi, and arrangement of the steering vanes. © Culver Pictures.

mately lead to advances in space travel as well as military technology. The A series rocket tests commenced. In 1934 A2 rockets were tested at Borkum, and by 1935 it was decided that trials had developed to a stage at which the traditional Kummersdorf testing range was no longer adequate or secure. A more isolated venue at Usedom Island near Peenemünde on the Baltic was selected.

Only with military reverses and the appointment of Albert Speer as armaments minister did rocket work assume urgency. Attention centered on the A4, later to be known as the V2. Though nominally in a series with the **V1**, and **V3**, the V2 was a totally different concept in both technology and scale. As completed, the V2 was a fin-stabilized rocket weighing 13.6 tons on firing, with a one-ton payload. It consisted, from top downward, of a pointed warhead with fuse; control gyroscopes; electrical equipment; four tanks containing, respectively, alcohol and liquid oxygen fuels, hydrogen peroxide, and calcium permanganate; burner and heat exchanger; combustion chamber; and venturi and jet steering carbon vanes.

The peroxide and permangante produced a reaction making superheated steam, which drove a turbine. The turbine drove high-speed pumps that delivered the alcohol and oxygen to

the combustion chamber, where it was lit initially by a pyrotechnic candle. The motor produced 25 tons of thrust. On 3 October 1943 an A4 was successfully launched; it flew 201 km along the Baltic to land within 4 km of its target. Ultimately, a maximum range of roughly double this would be achieved. There was now a race against bombing and the Allied invasion of Europe to get the V2 in production before its production facilities were destroyed and launch sites overrun.

In the event, active service commenced on 8 September 1944 with a launch on liberated Paris. Unlike the relatively slow-moving V1, it proved scarcely possible to detect, let alone to intercept the V2, which shot through the atmosphere almost vertically, reached an altitude of about 60 miles, and traveled at up to 3,600 mph. Moreover, the V2 had some strategic flexibility in that it could be used from a relatively simple launch pad, with the launch team and equipment moved in a convoy of vehicles. Well over 3,000 V2s were fired. This, however, was not the limit of the designers' ambitions; there were other experimental models and paper designs in progress as the war ended. The A9 was to have been lighter, with a range of 400 miles and radio guidance. The A10 project specified a two-stage rocket, with a range of 2,800 miles, capable of hitting the United States. Another idea, far-reaching but impractical in 1945, was to mount an A4 in a **U-boat** and sail the missile closer to the target before launching.

Additional Reading: Hogg, *German Secret Weapons of the Second World War*, 1999; Pocock, *German Guided Missiles*, 1967; Neufeld, *The Rocket and the Reich*, 1995; Ramsey (ed), *The Blitz Then and Now*, 1990.

V3   ARTILLERY

As early as about 1885, Americans Lyman and Haskell had proposed a large cannon in which there was not one gunpowder charge to shoot the projectile but several. Secondary chambers, set at an angle to the main bore and ignited by the gas from the first explosion, were to provide additional thrust as the projectile went up the barrel. The intended result was a very high-velocity shot with great range and improved accuracy. The theory was sound, but the reality proved unobtainable with nineteenth-century technology.

In 1943 a very similar concept was presented to Hitler by an engineer named Conders, who seized on the idea, proposing a large battery of 50 barrels using the booster technology. These would be emplaced in the Calais region of France and be used for the bombardment of London, 95 miles away. Work started on the French site, and, under the cover of the name "High Pressure Pump," tests were commenced at the Hillersleben proving ground. Work progressed slowly due to instability of the shells and premature ignition of charges. Moreover, as test firings on the Baltic demonstrated, obtaining the very high-velocity required for such a long-range target was problematic. The V3 program was overtaken both by the success of the **V2** and by Allied invasion. The V3 was also known to the Allies as "Busy Lizzie" or "Millipede."

Additional Reading: Hogg, *German Secret Weapons of the Second World War*, 1999. www.astronautix.com.

V-22. *See* **Osprey**

V-Agents   CHEMICAL WARFARE

The V-Agents, including VX, are chemical nerve agents that are generally colorless and odorless. They have the shared characteristic of low volatility, neither evaporating nor freezing easily, and may be spread in droplet or aerosol form. Their advantage over G agents, such as **Tabun** and **Sarin**, is that they settle more readily upon the skin, leading to better absorption and higher casualty rates.

Val Dive Bomber   AIRCRAFT

The first version of the Japanese Aichi D3A "Val" carrier-based **dive bomber** entered production in 1937, under the designation Type 99. A well designed two-seater machine influenced by Heinkel models, it carried a single 500 kg bomb. The standard Japanese type of 1941, it was in the forefront of the attack on Pearl Harbor. The later D3A2 model was outclassed and outgunned, suffering heavy losses.

Additional Reading: Francillon, *Japanese Aircraft of the Pacific War*, 1970.

***Vanguard* Class**   SUBMARINE

The *Vanguard* class, built at Barrow-in-Furness, represents Britain's latest ballistic missile **submarines**. At 491 feet long, they are shorter than the U.S. *Ohio* type, but of similar section to accommodate the **Trident** missile system. They are powered by Rolls-Royce PWR nuclear reactors, giving a top speed of 25 knots. *Vanguard*, the first of the class, was laid down in 1986 and was at sea by 1992. She was followed by *Victorious, Vigilant,* and *Vengeance*. The **Astute** class is now under construction.

Additional Reading: *Jane's Warships*; Hutchinson, *Submarines, War beneath the Waves*, 2001.

Variable Armor   ARMOR

The U.S. "Variable **Armor**, Small Arms—Fragmentation Protective," intended for ground troops, was first manufactured in 1968. Within a ballistic nylon shell were pockets in which were composite ceramic and glass-reinforced plastic plates. The vest gave good protection; it was "variable" in that it could be worn with or without the plates, depending on the level of risk and amount of weight the soldier was prepared to carry. Each vest cost $385.

Vashavyanka. *See* **Kilo Class**

Venturi. *See* **Recoilless Gun**

Vespa "ACMA" TAP   VEHICLE

Surely one of the oddest military vehicles, the Vespa "Scooter, Motor, 2-Wheel, Airborne" was in use by French paratroops from 1957. Weighing 90 kg and powered by a single-cylinder 146 cc two-stroke engine, it was fitted to carry a **recoilless** rifle.

Vickers Gun   FIREARM

The British .303-inch Vickers **machine gun** was an improved model of the **Maxim**, introduced in 1912. Lighter than its predecessor and with a reputation for reliability, it would serve the British army until the 1960s. Belt fed and water cooled, the Mark I model was tripod mounted and capable of cyclic rates of fire of about 500 rounds per minute. Sustained fire could be maintained for several hours at 10,000 rounds per hour, with a possible record of 120,000 being fired by a single gun one night in 1916. Depending on the type of **cartridge** used, its maximum range was between 2,900 and 3,500 yards. Various models, including the Vickers K, were adopted for use in vehicles and **aircraft**. Also used by other countries, the Vickers was adopted in the United States in 1915 and manufactured in small numbers by **Colt**.

Additional Reading: Goldsmith, *The Grand Old Lady of No Man's Land*, 1994; Bruce, *Machine Guns of World War I*, 1997; *Jane's Infantry Weapons* (1978); Hogg, *Infantry Weapons of World War II*, 1977.

Victory, HMS   WARSHIP

There have been five ships named *Victory* in the Royal Navy. The first, built in 1559 and originally called the *Great Christopher*, served as the flagship of Sir John Hawkins against the Spanish Armada in 1588. The next was designed by Phineas Pett and launched in 1620, while the third was built as *Royal James* in 1675 and later renamed. The fourth had a short career, being launched in 1737 and sunk in bad weather in 1744.

Undoubtedly the best known *Victory* was launched in 1769. She saw extensive service against France, the climax of which was as Lord Nelson's flagship at Trafalgar in 1805, when the admiral was mortally wounded on her deck. Her life as a frontline warship ended in 1812, but remarkably she remained afloat on various duties for another century before being permanently docked as a museum ship at Portsmouth, United Kingdom. She is 186 feet long and has been reasonably described as a "floating gun platform." At Trafalgar she carried 104 guns, the largest of which were 32-pounders. Her magazine contained 2,669 round shot.

Additional Reading: McKay, *Victory*, 2000; Fenwick, *HMS Victory*, 1959; Browne, *HMS Victory*, 1891.

VIFF, VIFFing. *See* **Harrier**

Viggen, JA 37   AIRCRAFT

The Swedish Saab Viggen (Thunderbolt) jet fighter **aircraft** first flew as a prototype in 1967. Armed with a 30 mm cannon and six missiles, it weighed 33,060 lb empty. The Volvo Flygmotor RM8B turbofan engine gave a top speed of 1,365 mph and a range of 620 miles with a ceiling of 60,000 feet. The Viggen was technologically remarkable for a number of reasons, making early use of a **head-up** display and a navigational computer. Most importantly, it could operate from short runways and had great maneuverability due to a large wing area. Manufacture ceased in 1990 after a total production of 329; since then the Viggen has been gradually replaced by the **Gripen**.

Additional Reading: *The Saab-Scania Story*, 1987.

Virginia

Virginia   WARSHIP

The Confederate ship **Virginia** started life as the U.S. **frigate** *Merrimack*, built at the Boston Navy Yard and commissioned in 1856. She served worldwide before returning to the United States, only to be burned by retreating Union forces in 1861. Thereafter she was raised by the Confederates and refitted as an ironclad ram, crewed by 320 men and armed with two 12-pounder **howitzers**.

She steamed out into Hampton Roads on 8 March 1862 and soon sank the *Cumberland*. Yet her most famous combat was the inconclusive duel with the ***Monitor*** the next day—the first fight between powered ironclads.

Additional Reading: Department of the Navy, *Dictionary of American Naval Fighting Ships*, 1959–; Baxter, *The Introduction of the Ironclad Warship*, 1933; Mokin, *Ironclad: The Monitor and the Merrimack*, 1991.

Vulcan Bomber   AIRCRAFT

Developed in the 1950s and deployed in squadrons from 1961, the Vulcan bomber was the main element of Britain's nuclear deterrent during the 1960s. An early delta-wing design owing much to the wartime work of Professor Alexander Lippisch, was first sketched by Roy Chadwick of Avro. Nevertheless, years of further work were required to perfect the long-range strategic Vulcan. As completed, the Vulcan B Mark 2 had a wingspan of 111 feet and was powered by four Rolls-Royce Olympus turbojets for a top speed of 645 mph. Its crew was five and the maximum bomb load 21,000 lb. Ultimately, Vulcans remained in service far longer than expected. Their long range and in-flight refueling capabilities were tested when they were used in Operation Black Buck in 1982. This entailed bombing the Argentinian-occupied Falklands from a distance of 3,900 miles.

Additional Reading: Laming, *The Vulcan Story*, 1993.

Vulcan Gun. *See* Gatling

Waco. *See* **Glider**

Walker Bulldog, M41 Light Tank   TANK

Authorized for production in 1949, the U.S. Little Bulldog light **tank** was subsequently renamed as the Walker Bulldog, after General W. W. Walker, who was accidentally killed in Korea in 1951. Produced by Cadillac, the M41 is often regarded as part of a family with the **M47** medium and **M103** heavy tanks, with which it shared common components.

The four-man M41 had a welded steel hull and a turret with both casting and welding. The six-cylinder gasoline engine developed 500 horsepower, giving a healthy on the road top speed of 45 mph. The main armament was a 76 mm gun. The M41 has been widely used by many nations, including Brazil, Denmark, Thailand, and Taiwan.

Walleye. *See* **Smart Bomb**

Walther; PP; PPK   FIREARM

Established by Carl Walther at Zella-Mehlis in the 1880s, the German Walther company has produced several significant military **pistols**. Originally intended for police use, the innovative PP model was introduced in 1929 and acquired for service use from 1935. This was a neat **semiautomatic**, the main advantage of which was that it was **double action**. The shorter PPK was introduced in 1931. In the mid-1930s the company began work on a new pistol for the German army. This eventually emerged as the 9 mm Walther P38, a pistol with an eight-round magazine and intended to replace the **Luger**.

Additional Reading: Ezell, *Handguns of the World,* 1981.

"Wandering Annie." *See* **Torpedo**

Warhawk. *See* **Curtiss**

Warrior Armored Personnel Carrier
                                        VEHICLE

The *Warrior* is Britain's current fully tracked armored troop carrier. Armed with a 30 mm Rarden cannon and a Hughes chain gun in the turret, it is powered by a Rolls Royce diesel engine giving a maximum road speed of 45 mph. A "Desert Warrior" version is used by Kuwaiti land forces.

***Warrior,* HMS**   WARSHIP

Designed by Isaac Watts, HMS *Warrior* was Britain's first ironclad **battleship**, laid down in 1859. At the time of her appearance the 9,137-ton vessel, armed with 110 and 68-pounder guns on her battery deck, was the most powerful warship in the world. Having a maximum speed of 17 knots with combined steam and sail, she was faster and better armed than the French *Gloire*. Her central armored belt had four and a half inches of iron backed with 18 inches of teak. For a time renamed *Vernon III*, she has now been restored and survives to this day as a visitor attraction at Portsmouth, England.

Additional Reading: Lambert, *Warrior,* 1987; Winton, *Warrior,* 1987; Wells, *The Immortal Warrior,* 1987.

Warspite

Warspite. See **Queen Elizabeth**

"Wart Hog." *See* **Thunderbolt, A-10**

Wasa   WARSHIP

With her 64 guns, the warship *Wasa*, named after the Royal house of Wasa, was pride of the Swedish navy. Unfortunately, she sank in Stockholm Harbour on her maiden voyage, on 10 April 1628. Though master builder de Groot was blamed for her sinking, overload of **artillery** and open gun ports were probably factors in the disaster. Her modern significance is as a milestone in nautical archaeology and salvage, which has taught us more about early modern warships than virtually any other vessel. She remains a major Stockholm tourist attraction.

Additional Reading: Ohrelius, *Vasa, The King's Ship*, 1962; Borgenstam and Sandström, *Why Wasa Capsized*, 1984; Saunder, *The Raising of the Vasa*, 1962.

Wasp, **Assault Ship**   WARSHIP

Seven of the U.S. *Wasp* class of amphibious assault ships (LHDs) were commissioned between 1989 and 2001, with a further vessel under construction at the time of writing. The primary purpose of these ships is the deployment of Marines and **aircraft**. Capable of carrying 1,870 troops plus 20 **Harriers** and various **helicopters**, they have a range of 9,500 miles and a top speed of 22 knots.

Wasp. *See* **Self-Propelled Gun**

Webley; Webley and Scott
              MANUFACTURER; FIREARM

Although it was rooted in older concerns, the Webley gun company was founded by Philip Webley (1813–1888) in Birmingham, United Kingdom, in 1838. The best known history claims Webley as "Britain's **Colt**," for though the company was responsible for many patents and also produced **shotguns** and **rifles**, it was best known for **revolvers**. The beginnings of the Webley service revolver may be dated to

1853, when James and Philip Webley were making single-action **percussion** models. By the latter part of the nineteenth century the company was Britain's premier revolver manufacturer. In 1900 the Webley-Fosbery hybrid "automatic revolver," designed by Colonel G. V. Fosbery (1832–1907), was produced. The manufacture of true **semiautomatics** commenced in 1903.

During World War I the company supplied large numbers of revolvers and Very pistols. The largest orders were for the Mark VI—a heavy six-shot revolver with a six-inch barrel. This weapon was already old fashioned, but it had the significant advantages of ruggedness, simplicity, reliability, and the ability to fire the powerful .455-inch standard **cartridge**. In World War II the company's main product was the .38-inch revolver, often marked "War Service" to explain why its finish was not up to the usual peacetime standard. Postwar decline in demand led eventually to the cessation of firearms manufacture in 1979. In 2002 the Webley name still appears on **air guns**, a market that the company had entered in 1924.

Additional Reading: Dowell, *The Webley Story*, 1962; Bailey and Nie, *English Gunmakers*, 1978.

Wellington Bomber   AIRCRAFT

The British Wellington twin-engine bomber **aircraft** was developed in the mid-1930s in response to Air Ministry specification B.9/32. Though it had originally been intended to call it "Crécy," the name "Wellington" was applied as early as 1936; crews often called it the "Wimpey," after the J. Wellington Wimpey character in Popeye cartoons. It entered service in 1938 and was the mainstay of RAF Bomber Command until 1942, when 599 of the aircraft involved in the first "thousand-bomber raid" were Wellingtons. Thereafter it was steadily eclipsed by four-engine designs, such as the **Lancaster**. Total production was 11,460.

Capable of carrying 4,500 lb of small bombs or two **torpedoes**, or one 4,000 lb "cookie" or "blockbuster" bomb, the Wellington originally carried four **machine guns** in **Vickers** turrets.

Later up to seven machine guns were fitted, and Frazer-Nash turrets were used. The original Hercules engines were also replaced, and larger tanks allowed ranges up to 2,000 miles. Though technically advanced when introduced, the Wellington later suffered heavy losses and so was removed to coastal and night operations. It was also used with the Directional Wireless Installation for magnetic mine hunting. Wellingtons remained in limited use until 1953.

The aircraft was technologically significant for several reasons. The airframe was of geodetic construction, meaning that it was a basketlike framework of light metal bars—what its designer Barnes Wallis called "a self supporting structure without any nonsense inside at all." The placing of individual bars was planned according to principles similar to those employed by navigators to find the shortest distance between two points on a globe. Tests showed that this method was twice as strong as that used on conventional craft but with only two-thirds the weight; however, the structure was fabric covered and thus vulnerable to burning. In addition to the usual dinghy, the Wellington was equipped with 14 inflatable floatation bags, controlled by an immersion switch that filled the bags with carbon dioxide automatically on contact with saltwater. Ideally, however, the crew would dump all ordnance, shut the bomb doors, and activate the bags before hitting the water at a shallow angle. This gave anything up to ten minutes' floatation, allowing escape.

The Wellington was built at Weybridge, Squires Gate Blackpool, and Chester. The new Broughton works near Chester was interesting, its vast assembly shop having, at that time, the largest unsupported roof span in Europe. Moreover, aircraft were made using components from 500 subcontractors—yet there was no parts storage in the initial factory design. Components were to be delivered "just in time" and fed direct to the production line.

Additional Reading: Lumsden, *Wellington*, 1974; Delve, *Vickers-Armstrong's Wellington*, 1998; Mason, *The British Bomber since 1914*, 1994; Rapier and Bower, *Halifax and Wellington*, 1994.

Welman. *See* **X-Craft**

Welrod Pistol   FIREARM

The British Welrod **silenced** pistol was a World War II firearm intended for use by agents behind enemy lines. The name came from the Welwyn Experimental Laboratory at Welwyn Garden City. Though originally designed in 7.65 mm, the more common Mk I was capable of firing any type of 9 mm parabellum **cartridge**. Accurate up to 30 meters, the Welrod weighed 3.5 lb.

Additional Reading: Ladd and Melton, *Clandestine Warfare: Weapons and Equipment of the SOE and OSS*, 1988.

West Spring Gun. *See* **Catapult**

West Virginia, **USS**   WARSHIP

Laid down in 1920, the *West Virginia* was a 32,600-ton U.S. **battleship** of the *Colorado* class. It had a main armament of eight 16-inch guns, was 624 feet long, and carried a complement of 1,080. Caught at Pearl Harbor in 1941, she sustained no less than seven **torpedo**, and two bomb, strikes, resulting in the death of her captain and over 100 men. Remarkably, she was refloated in 1942 and following substantial rebuilding rejoined the Pacific War in 1944. She was finally broken up at Seattle in the 1960s.

Additional Reading: Whitley, *Battleships of World War II*, 1998; Terzibaschitsch, *Battleships of the US Navy in World War II*, 1977; Martin, *USS West Virginia*, 1997.

Wheelbarrow   VEHICLE

The modern Wheelbarrow is a small unmanned tracked robot vehicle, normally used by ordnance technicians to examine or disarm suspected **explosive** devices. By such "remote handling," the lives of the operatives are not put at risk. The first Wheelbarrow, which entered service with the British army in Northern Ireland in 1971, was so named because it had three wheels. Since then the device has been continuously upgraded in the light of new technology.

By the end of that decade the Mark 7 Wheelbarrow was in service and was being sold widely around the world. This tracked machine, 122 cm long and weighing 195 kg, had the ability to view with a television camera, lay explosive charges, fire a **shotgun**, and attach towing cables as well as manipulate objects. It could also climb stairs, and it was equipped with a nail gun that could be used to keep doors open or closed. Other variants manufactured have included the Marauder and Hunter. In France during the 1980s an Andros Robot was developed, which, though similar to a wheelbarrow, featured tracks that could be folded upward, allowing turns in very confined spaces.

Wheelbarrows and their equivalents are still important in the war on terrorism. Types of bomb-disposal robot in recent use in the United States have included the TR-2000 "Max" and the Andros Mark V A. As recently as 2002 a Wheelbarrow was seen in use by Israeli forces, pulling away a wounded Palestinian bomber.

Additional Reading: *Jane's Infantry Weapons* (1978); Tomajczyk, *Bomb Squads*, 1999.

Wheel Lock IGNITION SYSTEM

The wheel-lock ignition system for firearms dates to about 1500 and has been claimed as an invention of Leonardo da Vinci. Whether or not this is the case, there is evidence from Nuremberg for the existence of a wheel-lock device made by, or for, Martin Löffelholz c. 1505, and wheel-lock guns were certainly in use in central Europe soon after. Wheel locks were fairly common by the middle of the sixteenth century, and while they were more complex and expensive than **matchlocks**, they offered certain distinct advantages. The wheel lock required no smoldering **match**; once loaded they could be left for some time before firing; and a wheel-lock **pistol** could be discharged with one hand. This was particularly significant for cavalry.

The basic wheel lock itself consisted of a small wheel with a rough outer edge, a spindle and chain, and an arm, or cock, in the jaws of which was a piece of iron pyrite. The end of the spindle was fitted for a separate key or spanner, with which the lock could be wound up, or "spanned." This rotated the chain around

the spindle and compressed a mainspring. Pressure on a trigger released a sear, and the wheel revolved in contact with the pyrite, creating sparks that ignited the **gunpowder**.

Wheel locks were to be seen all over Europe in slightly varying forms. In France, for example, a type predominated in which the wheel was contained within a recess of the stock of the weapon. They continued to be used well into the seventeenth century but were gradually eclipsed by various forms of **flintlock**.

Additional Reading: Blair (ed), *Pollard's History of Firearms*, 1983; Durdik et al., *Firearms*, 1981.

White Star. *See* Phosgene

Wickes Class WARSHIP

The 111 U.S. *Wickes*-class **destroyers** were constructed in the latter part of, and just after, World War I. Displacing 1,100 tons, they were capable of the then very fast top speed of 35 knots, making them possible partners for the swift *Omaha* scout **cruisers**. Some 33 of the type survived to see service in World War II, undergoing conversions to various specialized duties, including anti submarine, minesweeping, and minelaying. The last of the *Wickes* were scrapped in 1947.

Wildcat, F4F, FM-2 AIRCRAFT

The **Grumman** Wildcat, which first flew as a prototype in 1937, was the U.S. Navy's first monoplane fighter **aircraft** to see general service. Though not immediately ordered, it underwent some redesign and was beginning to equip Navy squadrons by 1940. The same year, Wildcats were supplied to Britain, where they saw action against the Germans under the designation Martlet I. Wildcats later saw distinguished service in Pacific **aircraft carrier** operations. Flying a Wildcat from Guadalcanal, U.S. Marine Corps pilot Captain Joe Foss shot down 26 Japanese aircraft, five of them in a day, winning the Congressional Medal of Honor.

One of the later versions of the Wildcat was the General Motors–built FM-2. This first flew in March 1943 and mounted six **machine guns**.

It was capable of up to 332 mph, with a ceiling of 34,700 feet and a range of 900 miles. It featured self-sealing fuel tanks, folding wings, and pilot armor. Though a respected aircraft, the Wildcat is perhaps best remembered as the precursor of the **Hellcat**.

Additional Reading: Dorr, *US Fighters of World War II*, 1991.

Wilhelmgeschätze. *See* **Paris Gun**

Wimpey. *See* **Wellington**

Winchester Repeating Arms
MANUFACTURER

Founded by Oliver F. Winchester (1810–1880), the Winchester Repeating Arms Company of New Haven, Connecticut, is best known for its lever-action **rifles**, including, for example, models of 1866, 1873, and 1895. Though Winchester is recognized as the company that developed and manufactured the gun "that won the West," the lever action predated it. Importantly it was used by the Volcanic Company, which Winchester bought out in 1857. It is also noteworthy that the Winchester lever action, as improved by B. T. Henry, was used as a military arm outside the United States. Its most notable success was in the hands of the Turks at Plevna in 1877, a victory over the Russians that signaled the importance of repeating rifles.

Winchester's later contributions are less well known but significant. The 1895 model rifle, designed by J. P. Lee, saw use in the hands of U.S. Marines and the Russians, and in World War I the company produced large amounts of munitions. These included the P17 **Enfield** ri-

fle, originally British designed, with a **Mauser** type **bolt action**; **Browning** automatic rifles; **sniper** telescopes; and **shotguns**. Almost a billion **cartridges** were made. A semiautomatic rifle was developed but saw little use. In World War II **Garand** rifles and **M1 carbines** were produced, along with an estimated 13,000,000,000 rounds of ammunition.

Additional Reading: Houze, *The Winchester Repeating Arms Company*, 1994; Canfield, *Winchester in the Service*.

Window. *See* **Chaff**

Windsor Carrier. *See* **Bren Carrier**

***Wisconsin*, USS** WARSHIP

The US *Iowa* class **battleship** *Wisconsin* was completed in April 1944. Following service in World War II, she was reactivated for Korea, where though hit by enemy shore batteries in March 1952 she sustained relatively little damage. Following a collision in 1956, her bows were replaced using parts of the unfinished sister ship *Kentucky*. Following another rest she returned from retirement in 1988 and along with the *Missouri* was again firing her guns in the Gulf War during February 1991. She was back in reserve again at the end of that year.

Additional Reading: Garzke and Dulin, *Battleships: United States Battleships, 1935–1992*, 1995; Pater, *United States Battleships*, 1968; Madsen, *Forgotten Fleet: The Mothball Navy*, 1999.

Wombat. *See* **Recoilless Gun**

"Woolworth Gun." *See* **Liberator Pistol**

X

X-1   AIRCRAFT

The Bell U.S. X-1 experimental rocket **aircraft** program, sponsored by the USAAF, was initiated in the latter stages of World War II to investigate the possibilities of supersonic flight. The craft first flew in January 1946, though only in a test-glide mode, released from 27,000 feet. Powered flights commenced at the end of the year, and in 1947 Charles E. "Chuck" Yeager flew the plane to 700 mph, thus breaking the sound barrier and setting new records for manned flight. In March 1948 a speed of 957 mph was achieved, while an altitude record of 71,902 was set in 1949. The program was continued into the 1950s with the X-1A to X1-E, during which speeds of up to 1,650 mph were achieved.

X-5. *See* X-Craft

X-22A   AIRCRAFT

The U.S. experimental Bell Aerospace Textron X-22A was built in order to test the idea of a ducted-fan vertical takeoff craft. Resembling an aircraft fuselage with a tail, it was fitted with four huge rings housing propellers, which could be angled horizontally and vertically to provide horizontal and vertical flight or to hover. The project commenced in the late 1950s, with test flights from 1966 onward.

Additional Reading: Rogers, *VTOL Military Research*, 1989; Miller, *The X-Planes*, 1988.

X-25. *See* Bensen

X-craft, X-3; X-5; XE; Welman, etc.   SUBMARINE

Based on an idea put forward by Commander C. H. Varley, British X-craft midget **submarines** were first built in secret during 1942. Their main purpose was the covert attack of ships at anchor. The X-3 and X-4 prototypes were followed by 12 boats of the X-5 class. The X-5 type was a 30-ton diesel-electric vessel, just over 51 feet in length, capable of six knots and having a crew of four. When near a target the X-craft could release a diver to clear obstacles or fix demolition charges, but the main armament was two side charges, each 4,400 lb of torpex **explosive**. These were dropped under the enemy vessel to explode up to 36 hours later. The best known X-craft action was the attack on the *Tirpitz*. X-craft were also used to survey the Normandy landing beaches in 1944.

The XE-type midgets were developed from the X-craft and saw action in the Pacific in 1945, badly damaging the Japanese cruiser *Takao*. Four Victoria Crosses were awarded for the *Tirpitz* and *Takao* actions. The Welman one-man British submarine was made mainly by Morris Cars at Oxford but was technically not an X-craft. Superficially it was a similar concept to the Japanese **Kaiten**, though its 560 lb detachable warhead had magnetic clamps and a delayed action, giving its pilot a chance to escape. It was used by Norwegian volunteers in 1943 but failed to penetrate the port of Bergen, though the operators survived.

Additional Reading: O'Neill, *Suicide Squads of World War II*, 1988.

Y

Yahoody the Impossible. *See* **Camouflage**

Yak-38. *See* **Forger**

Yamato **Class**   WARSHIP

The Japanese *Yamato*-class **battleships** were the largest and most heavily armed of all time. Though five were planned, only two, the *Yamato* and *Musashi*, were completed as battleships, with a third finished as an **aircraft carrier**. Construction commenced in 1937, with the *Yamato* finished in 1940 and the *Musashi* completed in 1941. They displaced 62,315 tons and were 863 feet long and 121 wide. Their main armament was nine 18-inch guns, and the maximum armor was 16 inches thick. The complement was 2,500. Both vessels were sunk by U.S. aircraft, the *Musashi* in October 1944, the *Yamato* in April 1945. With the *Yamato* went 2,498 men. Her loss was said to have ended "five centuries of naval warfare." It certainly ended the battleship era.

Additional Reading: Matsumoto, *Design and Construction of the Battleships Yamato and Musashi*, 1961; Watts and Gordon, *The Imperial Japanese Navy*, 1971; Jentschura, *Warships of the Imperial Japanese Navy 1869–1945*, 1977.

Yankee Class   SUBMARINE

The Yankee class of nuclear-powered ballistic missile **submarine** was the first such purpose-designed type in the Soviet navy. Displacing 7,800 tons on the surface, the Yankees had 16 missile and six **torpedo** tubes, and a maximum submerged speed of 30 knots. The first vessel was launched in 1967; soon there would be three or four on patrol off the U.S. eastern seaboard at any given time. Their mission would be to destroy bomber bases and aircraft carriers in the event of war. The new **Delta** class was based on the Yankees.

Additional Reading: Jordan, *Soviet Submarines*, 1989.

YMS. *See* **Motor Minesweeper**

Yorktown **Class**   WARSHIP

The first of the *Yorktown* class of U.S. **aircraft carriers** was laid down in 1934. The 20,000-ton vessels were capable of carrying up to 96 aircraft and had crews of 1,890. It was originally intended that the vessels should have fold-down funnels, but in the end a conventional "island" arrangement was settled upon. The hangars were built upon rather than part of the hull and had large roller shutters on the sides for easy loading and ventilation during running of engines. *Yorktown* (CV 5) and *Enterprise* (CV 6), commissioned in 1937 and 1938, were much the same, but the *Hornet* (CV 8) featured various improvements.

Yorktown (CV 5) was sunk at Midway but was replaced by a new *Essex*-class vessel of the same name (CV 10) in 1943. This vessel was decommissioned in 1947 but was refitted to appear during the Korean War and Vietnam. Finally taken out of service in 1970, *Yorktown* (CV 10) became a museum at Charleston, South Carolina.

Z

Zeke. *See* **Zero**

ZELL UNCONVENTIONAL AIRCRAFT

"Zero Length Launch" was an experimental method of launching fighters for quick interception pioneered in Europe after World War II to counter the supposed Soviet bomber threat. It consisted of blasting the fighter up a ramp by means of booster rockets.

Zeppelin AIRSHIP

Count Ferdinand von Zeppelin's (1838–1917) distinctive cigar-shaped **airship** *Luftschiff Zeppelin 1* made its first short flight over Lake Constance in 1900. A more durable *LZ 2* with twin engines followed, and with *LZ 3* the German government was interested enough to make serious investment in the program. Despite several accidents the count persisted until viable long-range machines had evolved. Later German army airships retained the "LZ" designation, while the Navy used an "L" prefix. By now the basic form of the craft was fixed— a lightweight metal frame within which gas bags of hydrogen provided the lift. Below the huge envelope hung gondolas in which were situated the engines and command, control, and bombing equipment.

The zeppelins first bombed Britain in 1915, the most destructive raid coming on 8 September 1915. Yet by 1916 more effective anti-zeppelin tactics were being evolved, including fighter **aircraft**, better antiaircraft guns, and incendiary bullets. The next generation of zeppelins was therefore adapted to high-altitude flight, with oxygen breathing. They were now capable of flying at 24,000 feet. Typical of the late war machines was the *LZ 113* of July 1918. This had a length of 743 feet and a diameter of 78 feet. Her gas volume was 2,418,700 cubic feet.

After the war zeppelin technology did not die but continued to progress under the leadership of Hugo Eckener. Nevertheless no real use was found for them in World War II, and the last of the extant examples was dismantled during the war. Civil zeppelin construction at Friedrichschafen recommenced in 1997, with passenger flights from 2001.

Additional Reading: de Syon, *Zeppelin!* 2002, Eckner, *My Zeppelins*, 1958; Hartcup, *The Achievement of the Airship*, 1974.

Zero Fighter AIRCRAFT

The famous World War II Japanese Zero fighter **aircraft**, designed by Mitsubishi engineer Jiro Horikoshi, was first approved by the Naval Aeronautical Establishment at Yokosuka in 1938. It flew in 1939. Though officially called the Reisen, the name "Zero-Sen" came about because the year 1940 was 2600 in the Japanese calendar. Also known by the Allied code name "Zeke," it would become the most numerous Japanese fighter of the war. Total production was almost 11,000, with many flying from **aircraft carriers**. Key to the Zero's legendary maneuverability was lightness of construction, which made liberal use of ESD, or extra-super duralumin metal. Safety features such as pilot armor and self-sealing fuel tanks were omitted

The German Zeppelin SL-20 on the air field, October 1917. Though its bomb capacity was relatively low for the size of the craft, the Zeppelin first made long range, high altitude, bombing raids a reality during World War I. Courtesy of the Library of Congress.

in favor of the maximum armament of two 20 mm cannon and two **machine guns**.

One of the most common types was the A6M2 Model 21, first built in April 1941. This was manufactured by both Mitsubishi and Nakajima; it had a NK1c Sakae 12, 940 horsepower engine, giving a maximum speed of 325 mph. It was capable of carrying two 60 kg bombs. At first hugely successful, the Zero later proved extremely vulnerable when hit. Though improved types such as the A6M8 were introduced, the Zero was both outnumbered and outclassed in the later stages of the war. It was finally used as a **kamikaze** weapon.

Additional Reading: Yoshimura, *Zero Fighter*, 1996; Bueschel, *Mitsubishi A6M1/2/-2N Zero-Sen*, 1995.

Zumwalt Class   WARSHIP

Zumwalt is the title of the DD-21 class of vessels proposed as replacements for the *Spruance* class destroyers and *Oliver Hazard Perry* class of **frigates** currently in service with the U.S. Navy. It is expected that the *Zumwalt* destroyers will have a displacement of 12 to 14,000 tons and be primarily designed for land attack.

Zündnadelgewehr. *See* **Dryse**.

Appendix

Chronology of Crucial Advances in Military Technology

Note: All dates are approximate since first concept, first test, and first successful use in war are frequently separated by a considerable period.

Spear, pike, javelin	Prehistory	Maxim machine gun	c. 1885
Bow	Prehistory	Smokeless powder	c. 1885
Shield	Prehistory	Radio	c. 1900
Armor	Prehistory	Dreadnought	c. 1905
Sword	Prehistory	Modern flamethrower	c. 1910
Biological weapons	Prehistory	Observation aircraft	c. 1910
Catapult	Classical era	Aircraft carrier	c. 1914
Stirrup	Classical era	Bombing aircraft	c. 1914
Greek fire	Classical era	Fighter aircraft	c. 1914
European longbow	c. 1200	Poison gas	c. 1915
Gunpowder	c. 1240	Tank	c. 1916
Gun	c. 1300	Sonar	c. 1917
Explosive shell	c. 1450	Strategic-range artillery	c. 1918
Breechloading	c. 1450	Radar	c. 1935
Musket	c. 1500	Helicopter	c. 1935
Rifle	c. 1500	Nerve gas	c. 1940
Flintlock mechanism	c. 1560	Unmanned aircraft	c. 1942
Bayonet	c. 1650	Guided missiles	c. 1942
Submarine	c. 1750	Computer	c. 1943
Sea mine	c. 1770	V-2 missile	c. 1944
Observation balloon	c. 1790	Atom bomb	c. 1945
Shrapnel	c. 1790	Hydrogen bomb	c. 1952
Percussion cap	c. 1820	Nuclear powered submarine	c. 1955
Railway	c. 1825	Satellite	c. 1957
Telegraph	c. 1835	Intercontinental ballistic missile	c. 1960
Bolt action	c. 1840	Laser	c. 1960
Armored warship	c. 1850	Mechanically scattered mines	c. 1960
Land mine	c. 1860	Smart bomb	c. 1965
Gatling gun	c. 1860	Cruise missile	c. 1975
Naval gun turret	c. 1860	Global Positioning System	c. 1980
Barbed Wire	c. 1870	Antiballistic missile	c. 1990
Torpedo	c. 1870	Airborne Laser	c. 1995

Bibliography

Aberdeen Proving Ground *Tank Data*. WE Inc., Old Greenwich, Conn., undated.

Albaugh, W. A. *Confederate Edged Weapons*. Harper, New York, 1960.

Allsop, D. F. and M. A. Toomey. *Small Arms*. Brassey, London, 1999.

Alm, J., et al. *European Crossbows*. Royal Armouries, London, 1994.

Anderson, W. R. *Nautilus*. Hodder and Stoughton, London, 1959.

Angelucci, E. *The World Encyclopedia of Military Aircraft*. Guild, London, 1985.

Apps, M. *The Four Ark Royals*. William Kimber, London, 1976.

Ashworth, C. *The Shackleton*. Aston, Bourne End, 1990.

Auto Ordnance Corporation. *Handbook of the Thompson Submachine Gun*. Auto Ordnance, Bridgeport, 1940.

Baer, L. *The German Steel Helmet*. Bender, San Jose, 1985.

Bagnasco, E. *Submarines of World War II*. Cassell, London, 2000.

Bailey, D. W. *British Military Longarms*. Arms and Armour, London, 1986.

Bailey, D. W., and D. A. Nie. *English Gunmakers*. Arms & Armour Press, London, 1978.

Bain, G. *DeHavilland*. Airlife, Shrewsbury, 1992.

Baker, A. D. (ed). *Allied Landing Craft of World War II*. Arms and Armour, London, 1985.

———. (ed). *Japanese Naval Vessels of World War II*. Arms and Armour, London, 1987.

Baker, D. *Messerschmitt Me 262*. Crowood, Marlborough, 1997.

———. *Grumman F-14 Tomcat*. Crowood, Marlborough, 1998.

Ballard, R. D. *The Discovery of the Bismarck*. Warner, New York, 1990.

Barger, C. J. *Communications Equipment of the German Army*. Paladin, Boulder, 1989.

Barker, A. J., and J. Walter. *Russian Infantry Weapons of World War II*. Arms and Armour, London, 1971.

Barnaby, W. *The Plague Makers*. Vision, London, 1999.

Barnes, C. H. *Handley Page Aircraft Since 1907*. Putnam, London, 1976.

———. *Shorts Aircraft Since 1900*. Putnam, London, 1989.

Barnes, F. C., and K. Warner. *Cartridges of the World*. DBI, Northbrook, many editions.

Barrie, A. *War Underground: The Tunnellers of the Great War*. Tom Donovan, London, 1988.

Basset, R. *Battle Cruisers*. Macmillan, London, 1981.

Baxter, J. P. *The Introduction of the Ironclad Warship*. Cambridge, Mass., Harvard University Press, 1933.

Bean, T., and W. Fowler. *Russian Tanks of World War II*. Amber Books, London, 2002.

Beaver, P. *Ark Royal*. Patrick Stephens, Cambridge University Press, 1979.

———. *The British Aircraft Carrier*. Patrick Stephens, Wellingborough, 1984.

———. *Invincible Class*. Ian Allan, London, 1984.

———. *German Capital Ships*. Patrick Stephens, Cambridge University Press, 1980.

Beaver, P., and T. Gander. *Modern British Military Missiles*. Patrick Stephens, Wellingborough, 1986.

Belyakov, R. A., and J. Marmain. *MiG: Fifty Years of Secret Aircraft Design*. Naval Institute Press, Annapolis, Md., 1994.

Bennett, T. *617 Squadron*. Patrick Stephens, Wellingborough, 1986.

Bentley, J. *The Thresher Disaster*. Doubleday, New York, 1974.

Bercuson, D. J., and H. H. Herwig. *Bismarck*. Hutchinson, London, 2002.

Bibliography

Berry, F. C. *Gadget Warfare*. Bantam, New York, 1988.

Bidwell, P. *Roman Forts in Britain*. Batsford, London, 1997.

Bidwell, S., and D. Graham. *Fire-Power*. Allan and Unwin, Winchester, Mass., 1982.

Bickers, R. T. *Airlift*. Osprey, London, 1998.

Birtles, P. *Mosquito*. Jane's, London, 1980.

———. *Mosquito*. Sutton, Stroud, 1998.

Bishop, E. *Hurricane*. Airlife, Shrewsbury, 1986.

Blackett, P. M. S. *Military and Political Consequences of Atomic Energy*. Turnstile Press, London, 1949.

Blackmore, D. *Arms & Armour of the English Civil Wars*. Royal Armouries, London, 1990.

Blackmore, H. L. *British Military Firearms*. Herbert Jenkins, London, 1961.

———. *The Armouries of the Tower of London Ordnance* (vol. 1). HMSO, London, 1976.

Blair, C. *The Atomic Submarine*. Odhams, London, 1957.

———. *European Armour*. Batsford, London, 1958.

———. (ed). *Pollard's History of Firearms*. Macmillan, New York, 1983.

Blazey, S. (ed). *The Official Soviet Army Handgrenade Manual*. Paladin, Boulder, 1998.

Boatman, R. *Living with Glocks*. Paladin, Boulder, 2002.

Boniface, J. M., and J. G. Jeudy. *US Army Vehicles of World War II*. Haynes, Newbury Park, 1991.

Borgenstam, C., and A. Sandström. *Why Wasa Capsized*. National Maritime Museum, Stockholm, 1984.

Bowcock, A. *CSS Alabama*. Chatham, Rochester, 2002.

Bowers, P. *The Garret Enigma*. Airlife, Shrewsbury, 1999.

Bowman, M. W. *Boeing B-17 Flying Fortress*. Crowood Press, Marlborough, 1998.

———. *De Havilland Mosquito*. Crowood, Marlborough, 1998.

———. *Lockheed Hercules C-130*. Crowood, Marlborough, 1999.

Boyne, W. J. *Boeing B-52*. Schiffer, Atglen, 1994.

Bradbury, J. *The Medieval Siege*. Boydell, Woodbridge, 1992.

Bradford, E. *The Mighty Hood*. Hodder and Stoughton, London, 1959.

———. *The Story of the Mary Rose*. Hamish Hamilton, London, 1982.

Brassey's. *Warship*. Brassey's, London, various editions.

Brettingham, L. *Royal Air Force Beam Benders*. Midland, Leicester, 1997.

Brew, A. *The Turret Fighters*. Crowood, Marlborough, 2002.

Bridgland, T. *Sea Killers in Disguise: The Story of Q-Ships and Decoy Ships in the First World War*. Leo Cooper, London, 1999.

Brinkman, D. (ed). *Jane's Avionics*. Jane's, Alexandria, Va., various editions.

Brook, P. *Warships for Export 1867–1927*. World Ship Society, Gravesend, 1999.

Brook, S. *Armoured Warfare*. Imperial War Museum, London, 1980.

Brophy, W. S. *The Springfield 1903 Rifles*. Stackpole, Harrisburg, 1985.

Brown, D. *Carrier Fighters 1939–1945*. MacDonald and Jane, London, 1975.

Brown, D. K. *Before the Ironclad: Development of Ship Design, Propulsion and Armament in the Royal Navy 1815–1860*. Conway, London, 1990.

Brown, G. I. *The Big Bang*. Sutton, Stroud, 1998.

Browne, C. O. *HMS Victory*. Engineer, London, 1891.

The Browning Heavy Machine Gun Mechanism Made Easy. Gale and Polden, Aldershot, undated.

Browning, J., and C. Gentry. *John M. Browning: American Gunmaker*. Doubleday, New York, 1964.

Bruce, R. *Machine Guns of World War I*. Windrow and Greene, London, 1997.

———. *German Automatic Weapons of World War II*. Crowood, Marlborough, 1996.

Buderi, R. *The Invention That Changed the World*. Little, Brown, New York, 1996.

Buerlein, R. A. *Allied Military Fighting Knives*. Paladin, Boulder, 2001.

Bueschel, R. M. *Mitsubishi A6M1/2/-2N Zero-Sen*. Schiffer, Atglen, 1995.

Bull, G. V., and C. H. Murphy. *Paris Kanonen: The Paris Guns (Wilhelmgeschütze) and Project Harp*. Mittler, Herford, 1988.

Bull, S. B. *An Historical Guide to Arms and Armor*. Facts On File, New York, 1991.

———. *European Swords*. Shire, Princes Risborough, 1994.

Burck, G. M., and C. C. Flowerree. *International Handbook on Chemical Weapons Proliferation*. Greenwood, Westport, 1991.

Burgess, R. F. *Ships beneath the Sea: A History of Submarines and Submersibles*. Robert Hale, London, 1976.

Burrard, G. *The Identification of Firearms and Forensic Ballistics*. Herbert Jenkins, London, 1934.

Burton, R. F. *The Book of the Sword*. Chatto and Windus, London, 1884.

Butowski, P., and J. Miller. *MiG: A History of the Design Bureau and Its Aircraft*. Aerofax, Stillwater, 1991.

Byron, D. *The Official Guides to Gun Marks*. Border Press, Brecon, 1990.

Calef, J. H. *Description and Service of Machine Guns*. U.S. Artillery School, Fort Munroe, Va., 1886.

Campbell, D. *War Plan UK*. Burnett Books, London, 1982.

Campbell, J. M. *Consolidated B-24 Liberator*. Schiffer, Atglen, 1993.

Canfield, B. N. *Collector's Guide to the 03 Springfield*. Andrew Mowbray, Lincoln, 1989.

Careless, R. *Battleship Nelson*. Arms and Armour, London, 1985.

Carter, A., and J. Walter. *The Bayonet*. Arms and Armour, London, 1974.

Caruana, A. B. *History of English Sea Ordnance*. Jean Boudriot, Rotherfield, 1994.

Chamberlain, P., and H. Doyle. *Encyclopaedia of German Tanks of World War II*. Arms and Armour, London, 1993.

Chamberlain, P., and C. Ellis. *Making Tracks: The British Carrier Story 1914–1972*. Profile, Windsor, 1973.

Chant, C. (ed). *Early Fighters*. Grange Books, London, 2002.

Chapelle, H. I. *The History of the American Sailing Navy*. Bonanza, New York, 1949.

Chesneau, R. *Aircraft Carriers*. Arms and Armour, London, 1992.

Chetty, P. R. K. *Satellite Technolgy and Its Applications*. TAB, Blue Ridge Summit, 1988.

Chin, G. M. *The Machine Gun*. U.S. Department of the Navy, 1951.

Churchill Tank: Vehicle History and Specification. HMSO, London, 1983.

Clarke, G. S. *Fortification*. London, 1907, reprinted Beaufort, undated.

Clarke, R. W. *British Aircraft Armament* (2 vols). Patrick Stephens, Sparkford, 1993, 1994.

Cocker, M. P. *Destroyers of the Royal Navy 1893–1981*. Ian Allan, London, 1981.

———. *Frigates, Sloops and Patrol Vessels of the Royal Navy*. Westmoreland Gazette, Kendal, 1985.

———. *Mine Warfare Vessels*. Airlife, Shrewsbury, 1993.

Cockle, M. J. D. *A Bibliography of Military Books up to 1642*. Holland Press, London, 1978.

Cocroft, W. D. *Dangerous Energy: The Archaeology of Gunpowder and Military Explosives Manufacture*. English Heritage, Swindon, 2000.

Coe, M. D., et al. *Swords and Hilt Weapons*. MMB, London, 1993.

Coggan, P. *P-51 Mustang Restored*. Motorbooks, Osceola, 1995.

Coles, A., and E. Briggs. *Flagship Hood*. Robert Hale, London, 1985.

Collier, B. *The Airship*. Granada, London, 1974.

Collingwood, D. *The Captain Class Frigates*. Leo Cooper, Barnsley, 1998.

Collinson, R. P. G. *Introduction to Avionics*. Chapman and Hall, London, 1986.

The Complete Lewis Gunner. Gale and Polden, Aldershot, 1941.

Compton-Hall, R. *The Submarine Pioneers*. Sutton, Stroud, 1999.

Connolly, P. *Greece and Rome at War*. Macdonald, London, 1981.

Conti, M. E. *Beyond Pepper Spray*. Paladin, Boulder, 2002.

Cooper, A. *The Dambusters Squadron*. Sterling, New York, 1993.

Cormack, A. J. R. *The Luger*. Profile, Windsor, 1971.

———. *Thompson Submachine Gun*. Weapons Review, undated.

Couhat, J. L. *French Warships of World War I*. Ian Allan, London, 1971.

Cowie, J. S. *Mines, Minelayers and Minelaying*. Oxford University Press, Oxford, 1949.

Cox, J. *Overkill*. Penguin, New York, 1977.

Craven, J. P. *The Silent War: The Cold War beneath the Sea*. Touchstone, New York, 2002.

Creed, R. *PBY: The Catalina Flying Boat*. Airlife, Shrewsbury, 1986.

Croddy, E. *Chemical and Biological Warfare*. Copernicus, New York, 2002.

Croll, M. *The History of Landmines*. Leo Cooper, Barnsley, 1998.

Cromwell Tank. HMSO, London, 1983.

Crosby, F. *A Handbook of Fighter Aircraft*. Hermes House, New York, 2002.

Bibliography

Crow, D. (ed). *Modern Battle Tanks*. Barrie and Jenkins, London, 1978.

Crow, D., et al. *AFVs of World War I*. Cannon Books, Retford, 1998.

Cruickshank, C. G. *Elizabeth's Army*. Oxford University Press, Oxford, 1966.

Culver, B. *The SdKfz 251 Half Track*. Osprey, London, 1983.

Curry, A., and M. Hughes. *Arms, Armies and Fortifications in the Hundred Years War*. Boydell Press, Woodbridge, 1994.

Dabrowski, H. *Messerschmitt Me 321/323*. Schiffer, Atglen, 2002.

Dastrup, B. L. *The Field Artillery: History and Sourcebook*. Greenwood, Westport, 1994.

Davies, D. *A Brief History of Fighting Ships*. Constable, London, 1996.

Davies, P. E., and A. M. Thornborough. *F-111 Aardvark*. Crowood, Marlborough, 1997.

Davis, M. *Sopwith Aircraft*. Crowood, Marlborough, 1999.

de Gheyn, J. *The Exercise of Armes*. Greenhill Books, London, 1986.

de Syon, G. *Zeppelin!* John Hopkins University Press, Baltimore, 2002.

Delve, K. *Vickers-Armstrong's Wellington*. Crowood, Marlborough, 1998.

———. *Short Sunderland*. Crowood, Marlborough, 2000.

Department of the Army. *Field Manual 23-30: Grenades and Pyrotechnics*. Washington, D.C., 1959.

———. *Field Manual 5-31: Boobytraps*. Washington, D.C., 1965.

———. *Technical Manual 31-200-1: Unconventional Warfare*. Washington, D.C., 1966.

———. *Field Manual 23-67: Machine Gun 7.62mm, M60*. Washington, D.C., 1984.

———. *Field Manual 23-14: Squad Automatic Weapon (SAW) M24*. Washington, D.C., 1985.

———. *Field Manual 23-10: Sniper Training*. Washington, D.C., 1994.

Department of the Navy. *Refloating the USS Missouri*. Washington, D.C., 1950.

———. *Dictionary of American Naval Fighting Ships*. Washington, D.C., 1959 onward.

———. *United States Ship Thresher*. Washington, D.C., 1964.

———. *SW 370.AA.OPI.010: Operator's Manual, Pistol Semiautomatic, 9mm, M9*. Washington, D.C., 1985.

Devey, A. *Jagdtiger* (2 vols). Schiffer, Atglen, 1999.

Dibbs, J. *Harrier*. Osprey, London, 1992.

Dierikx, M. L. J. *Fokker: A Transatlantic Biography*. Smithsonian, Washington, D.C., 1997.

Donald, D. *American Warplanes of World War II*. Airtime, Westport, 1995.

———. *German Aircraft of World War II*. Orbis, London, 1996.

Donald, D., and J. Lake (eds). *US Navy and Marine Corps Air Power Directory*. Airtime, Westport, 1992.

Dorr, R. F. *US Bombers of World War Two*. Arms and Armour, London, 1989.

———. *US Fighters of World War II*. Arms and Armour, London, 1991.

Dorr, R. F., and J. C. Scutts. *Bell P-39 Airacobra*. Crowood, Marlborough, 2000.

Dowell, W. C. *The Webley Story*. Skyrac, Leeds, 1962.

Doyle, H., et al. *Panther Variants 1942–1945*. Osprey, London, 1997.

Dressel, J., and M. Griehl. *The Luftwaffe Album*. Arms and Armour, London, 1999.

Duffy, C. *Siege Warfare*. Routledge, London, 1979.

Dufty, A. R. *European Swords and Daggers in the Tower of London*. HMSO, London, 1974.

Dugelby, T. B. *The Bren Gun Saga*. Collector Grade, Toronto, 1986.

Dunstan, S. *Flak Jackets*. Osprey, London, 1984.

———. *Self Propelled Howitzers*. Arms and Armour, London, 1988.

———. *The Chieftan Tank*. Arms and Armour, London, 1989.

———. *Modern Tanks and AFVs*. Airlife, Shrewsbury, 2002.

Durdik, J., et al. *Firearms*. Hamlyn, London, 1981.

Dutton, L., et al. *Military Space* (vol. 10, Air Power Series). Brassey's, London, 1990.

Easterly, W. M. *The Belgian Rattlesnake: The Lewis Automatic*. Collector Grade, Ontario, 1998.

Eckner, H. *My Zeppelins*. Putnam, London, 1958.

Edde, B. *Radar*. Prentice Hall, Upper Saddle River, New Jersey, 1993.

Elliott, P. *Allied Minesweeping*. Patrick Stephens, Cambridge, 1979.

Ellis, C., and P. Chamberlain. *The 88*. PRC, London, 1998.

———. *The Schmeisser*. PRC, London, 1999.

Ellis, J. *The Social History of the Machine Gun*. Cresset, London, 1987.

Elphick, P. *Liberty: The Ships That Won the War*. Chatham, Rochester, 2001.

Endres, G. *British Aircraft Manufacturers since 1908*. Ian Allan, Shepperton, 1995.

English, J. *The Hunts*. World Ship Society, Cumbria, 1987.

Esvelin, P. *D-Day Gliders*. Heimdal, Bayeux, 2001.

Evans, A. *BAe/McDonnell Douglas Harrier*. Crowood, Marlborough, 1998.

Evans, C. M. *War of the Aeronauts*. Stackpole, Mechanicsburg, Pa., 2002.

Everitt, D. *K Boats*. Airlife, Shrewsbury, 1999.

Ezell, E. C. *Handguns of the World*. Barnes and Noble, New York, 1981.

———. *Small Arms of the World*. Stackpole, Harrisburg, Pa., various editions.

Falck, J. *Jane's Advanced Tactical Fighters*. HarperCollins, New York, 1998.

Fay, J. *The Helicopter*. Hippocrene, New York, 1987.

Feist, U., and B. Culver. *Panther*. Ryton, Bellingham, 1998.

Fensch, T. *Top Secret: The CIA and the U2 Program*. New Century, Woodlands, 2001.

Fenwick, K. *HMS Victory*. Cassell, London, 1959.

Feugère, M. *Weapons of the Romans*. Tempus, Stroud, 2002.

ffoulkes, C. *The Gun Founders of England*. Arms and Armour, London, 1969.

ffoulkes, C., and E. C. Hopkinson. *Sword, Lance and Bayonet*. Arms and Armour, London, 1967.

Firebaugh, M. S. *Naval Engineering and American Sea Power*. Kendall Hunt, Dubuque, Iowa, 2000.

Fisch, R. *Field Equipment of the Infantry 1914–1945*. Greenberg, Sykesville, 1989.

Fitzsimons, B. (ed). *The Illustrated Encyclopedia of Twentieth Century Weapons and Warfare* (24 vols). Columbia House, New York, 1967–1978.

Fleischer, W. *Panzerfaust*. Schiffer, Atglen, 1994.

Fletcher, D. *British Tanks 1915–1919*. Crowood, Marlborough, 2002.

Fletcher, D. (ed). *Tiger!* HMSO, London, 1986.

Ford, R. *The Tiger Tank*. Spellmount, Staplehurst, 1998.

———. *Sherman Tank*. Spellmount, Staplehurst, 1999.

Fortress Study Group. *Fort: Journal of the Fortress Study Group*. Liverpool, continuing.

Forty, G. *United States Tanks of World War II*. Blandford, New York, 1983.

———. *M4 Sherman*. Blandford, Poole, 1987.

Foss, C. F. *Artillery of the World*. Ian Allan, Shepperton, 1976.

———. *Jane's Main Battle Tanks*. Jane's, London, 1983.

———. *Jane's Light Tanks and Armoured Cars*. Jane's, London, 1984.

———. *Jane's Tank and Combat Vehicle Recognition Guide*. HarperCollins, New York, 2000.

———. *The Encyclopedia of Tanks and Armoured Fighting Vehicles*. Amber, London, 2003.

Foss, C. F., and P. McKenzie. *The Vickers Tanks*. Patrick Stephens, Wellingborough, 1988.

Francillon, R. J. *Japanese Aircraft of the Pacific War*. Pitnam, London, 1970.

———. *Lockheed Aircraft since 1913*. Putnam, London, 1982.

———. *McDonnell Douglas Aircraft since 1920*. Putnam, London, 1988.

———. *Grumman Aircraft since 1929*. Putnam, London, 1989.

———. *McDonnell Douglas* (2 vols). Putnam, London, 1988.

———. (ed). *World Military Aviation*. Naval Institute Press, Annapolis, Md., 1997.

Franks, N. *Claims to Fame: The Lancaster*. Arms and Armour, London, 1994.

Freeman, R. A. *The B-17 Flying Fortress Story*. Sterling, 1998.

Freeman, R. A., and D. A. Anderton. *B-17 Fortress and B-29 Superfortress at War*. PRC, London, 1996.

Friedman, N. *US Aircraft Carriers*. Arms and Armour, London, 1983.

———. *US Cruisers*. Arms and Armour, London, 1985.

———. *World Naval Weapons Systems*. Naval Institute Press, Annapolis, Md., 1991.

———. *Seapower and Space*. Chatham, London, 2000.

Fry, J. *USS Saratoga CV-3*. Schiffer, Atglen, 1996.

Fuller, R., and R. Gregory. *Military Swords of Japan 1868–1945*. Arms and Armour, London, 1987.

Gander, T. J. *Field Rocket Equipment of the German Army*. Almark, London, 1972.

———. *German Anti-Tank Guns 1939–1945*. Almark, London, 1973.

———. *Anti-Tank Weapons*. Crowood, Marlborough, 2000.

———. (ed). *Jane's NBC Protection Equipment*. Jane's Information Group, Alexandria, Va., 1988.

Garbett, M., and B. Goulding. *Lancaster*. Promotional Reprint, Leicester, 1992.

Gardiner, R. (ed). *The Eclipse of the Big Gun Warship 1906–1945*. Conway, London, 1992.

———. *Line of Battle*. Conway, London, 1994.

Bibliography

———. *Cogs, Caravels and Galleons*. Conway, London, 1994.

———. *Frigates of the Napoleonic Wars*. Md., Chathan London, 2000.

Garzke, W. H., and R. O. Dulin. *Battleships: Axis and Neutral Battleships in World War II*. Naval Institute Press, Annapolis, Md., 1985.

———. *Battleships: United States Battleships, 1935–1992*. Naval Institute Press, Annapolis, 1995.

Gelbart, M. *Tanks*. Brassey's, London, 1996.

Giehl, F. *The F-4 Phantom II and the Sixth U.S. Fleet*. Vantage, New York, 1976.

Glenn, T. *The P-47 Pilots*. MBI, Osceola, 1998.

Goldsmith, D. L. *The Devil's Paintbrush*. Collector Grade, Toronto, 1989.

———. *The Grand Old Lady of No Man's Land*. Collector Grade, Ontario, 1994.

Goldstine, H. H. *The Computer from Pascal to von Neumann*. Princeton University Press, Princeton, N.J., 1972.

Gonen, R. *Weapons of the Anicient World*. Cassell, London, 1975.

Goodwin, P. *The Bomb Vessel Granado*. Conway, London, 1989.

———. *The Construction and Fitting of the Sailing Man of War, 1650–1850*. Conway, London, 1987.

Gordon, Y. *Mikoyan-Gurevich MiG-15*. Aerofax, Midland, Hinckley, 2001.

Gordon, Y., and D. Khazanov. *Soviet Combat Aircraft of the Second World War*. Midland, Leicester, 1998.

Götz, H. D. *German Military Rifles and Machine Pistols*. Schiffer, West Chester, 1990.

Gough, J. *Watching the Skies: The History of Ground Radar in the Air Defence of the United Kingdom*. HMSO, London, 1993.

Grancsay, S. V. *Arms and Armour*. Hamlyn, London, 1964.

———. (ed). *The Art of Archerie*. Arms and Armour, London, 1968.

Gravett, C. *Medieval Siege Warfare*. Osprey, Oxford, 1990.

Green, M. *M1 Abrams*. Motorbooks, Osceola, 1992.

———. *Hummer: The Next Generation*. MBI, Osceola, 1995.

Green, W., and G. Swanborough. *US Navy and Marine Corps Fighters*. MacDonald and Jane's, London, 1976.

Greenhill, B. (ed). *The Ship* (10 vols.). HMSO, London, 1980.

Greenhill, B., and J. Morrison. *The Archaeology of Boats and Ships*. Conway, London, 1995.

Gregg, W. A. (ed). *Canada's Fighting Vehicles*. Hayward Designs, Rockwood, Ont., 1980.

Griffin, R. *Chieftan*. Crowood, Marlborough, 2001.

Gröner, E. *German Warships 1815–1945*. Conway, London, 1991.

Gudgin, P. *Armoured Firepower: The Development of Tank Armament 1939–1945*. Sutton, Stroud, 1997.

Gunston, W. *AH-64 Apache*. Osprey, London, 1986.

———. *Spy Planes*. Salamander, London, 1983.

———. (ed). *Jane's Fighting Aircraft of World War II*. Random House, London, 2001.

Haber, L. F. *The Poisonous Cloud*. Clarendon, Oxford, 1986.

Hakusui, I. *Nippon-To: The Japanese Sword*. Japan Sword, Tokyo, 1948.

Halberstadt, H. *Inside the Great Tanks*. Crowood, Marlborough, 1998.

Hall, B. S. *Weapons and Warfare in Rennaissance Europe*. John Hopkins University, Baltimore, 1997.

Hamer, D. *Bombers versus Battleships*. Conway, London, 1999.

Hara, T. *Japanese Medium Tanks*. Profile, Windsor, 1972.

Harding, D. (ed). *Weapons: An International Encyclopedia*. Macmillan, London, 1990.

Hardy, R. *The Longbow*. Mary Rose Trust, Portsmouth, 1986.

Harkins, H. *Tornado*. Pentland, Bishop Auckland, 1995.

Harris, V., and N. Ogasawara. *Swords of the Samurai*. British Museum, London, 1990.

Hartcup, G. *The Achievement of the Airship*. David & Charles, Newton Abbot, 1974.

———. *Camouflage*. David and Charles, Newton Abbot, 1979.

———. *The War of Invention: Scientific Developments, 1914–1918*. Pergamon-Brassey's, New York, 1988.

Haselgrove, M. J., and B. Radovic. *Helmets of the First World War*. Schiffer, Atglen, 2000.

Hatcher, J. S. *The Textbook of Pistols and Revolvers*. Small Arms Technical, North Carolina, 1934.

Hawkins, G. W. *Treatise on Ammunition*. HMSO, London, 1887.

Hawks, E. *Bombers of the Present War*. Real Photographs, Southport, 1944.

Hayes-McCoy, G. A. *Sixteenth Century Irish*

Swords. National Museum of Ireland, Dublin (undated).

Hegener, H., and B. Robertson. *Fokker: The Man and the Aircraft.* Harleyford, Letchworth, 1961.

Helmer, W. J. *The Gun That Made the Twenties Roar.* Macmillan, New York, 1970.

Henderson, J. *The Frigates.* Coles, London, 1970.

Henshaw, A. *Sigh for a Merlin.* Air Data, Wilmslow, 1996.

Hersh, S. M. *Chemical and Biological Warfare.* Panther, London, 1970.

Herzog, S. *Defense Reform and Technology.* Praeger, Westport, 1994.

Hewlett, R. G., and F. Duncan. *Nuclear Navy.* University of Chicago Press, Chicago, 1974.

Hill, J. R. *Anti-Submarine Warfare.* Ian Allan, London, 1984.

Hill, Norton P. J. *Seapower.* Faber and Faber, London, 1982.

Hill, T. L. *Thompson: The American Legend.* Collector Grade, Ontario, 1996.

Hilmes, R. *Main Battle Tanks: Developments in Design since 1945.* Brassey's, London, 1987.

Hinsley, F. H., and A. Stripp. *Code Breakers.* Oxford University Press, Oxford, 1994.

Hobbs, D. *Space Warfare.* Prentice Hall, New York, 1986.

Hodges, P. *Royal Navy Warship Camouflage.* Almark, London, 1973.

———. *The Big Gun: Battleship Main Armament 1860–1945.* Conway, Greenwich, 1981.

Hogg, I. V. *Infantry Weapons of World War II.* Bison, London, 1977.

———. *British and American Artillery of World War II.* Hippocrene, New York, 1978.

———. *The Illustrated Encyclopedia of Ammunition.* Apple, London, 1985.

———. *The Illustrated History of Ammunition.* New Burlington, London, 1985.

———. *German Artillery of World War II.* Stackpole, Mechanicsburg, Pa., 1997.

———. *German Secret Weapons of the Second World War.* Stackpole, Mechanicsburg, Pa., 1999.

———. *Mortars.* Crowood, Marlborough, 2001.

———. *Anti-Aircraft Artillery.* Crowood, Marlborough, 2002.

———. *The World's Sniping Rifles.* Greenhill, London, 2002.

———. *The American Arsenal.* Greenhill, London, 1996.

Hogg, I. V., and J. Weeks. *Military Small Arms of the Twentieth Century.* Hippocrene, New York, 1977, 1994.

Hollet, D. *The Alabama Affair.* Sigma, Wilmslow, 1993.

Holmes, M. R. *Arms and Armour in Tudor and Stuart London.* London Museum, HMSO, 1957.

Hone, C., et al. *American and British Aircraft Carrier Development, 1919–1941.* Naval Institute Press, Annapolis, Md., 1999.

Hough, R. *Dreadnought.* Michael Joseph, London, 1964.

Houze, H. G. *The Winchester Repeating Arms Company.* Krause, Lola, 1994.

Hoyem, G. A. *The History and Development of Small Arms Ammunition.* Armory, Tacoma, Wash., 1981.

Hoyt, E. P. *The Kamikazes.* Burford Books, Short Hills, 1983.

Huenecke, K. *Modern Combat Aircraft Design.* Airlife, Shrewsbury, 1987.

Hughes, B. P. *Firepower.* Arms and Armour, London, 1974.

Hughes, M., and C. Mann. *The T-34 Tank.* Spellmount, Staplehurst, 1999.

———. *The Panther Tank.* Spellmount, Staplehurst, 2000.

Hundleby, M., and R. Strasheim. *The German A7V Tank.* Foulis, Newbury Park, Calif., 1990.

Hunnicutt, R. P. *Half-Track.* Presidio, Novato, Calif., 2001.

———. *Armored Car: A History of American Wheeled Combat Vehicles.* Presidio, Novato, Calif., 2002.

Hunt, W. E. *Helicopter.* Airlife, Shrewsbury, 1998.

Hutchinson, G. *Medieval Ships and Shipping.* Leicester University Press, Leicester, 1994.

Hutchinson, R. *Submarines, War beneath the Waves.* HarperCollins, New York, 2001.

Iannamico, F. *Reising Submachine Gun Story.* Moose Lake, Harmony, 1999.

Imperial War Museum Review (12 vols.). IWM, London, 1986–1999.

Ireland, B. *Warship Construction.* Ian Allan, London, 1987.

———. *Naval Warfare in the Age of Sail.* HarperCollins, London, 2000.

Ishoven, A. *Messerschmitt Bf 109 at War.* Ian Allan, Shepperton, 1977.

Jackson, D. *Swiss Army Knives.* Apple Press, London, 1999.

Bibliography

Jackson, J. *The Hawker Hurricane*. Blandford, London, 1987.

Jackson, R. *Submarines of the World*. Grange Books, Rochester, 2000.

James, B. *The Hawker Hunter*. Crowood, Marlborough, 1998.

James, D. N. *Gloster Aircraft*. Putnam, London, 1987.

Jameson, W. *Ark Royal 1939–1941*. Rupert Hart-Davis, London, 1957.

Jane, F. T. *The British Battle Fleet*. Partridge, London, 1912.

Jane's Military Review. London and New York, various editions.

Jane's Infantry Weapons. London and New York, various editions.

Jane's Radar and EW Systems. London and New York, various editions.

Jane's Naval Review. London and New York, various editions.

Jane's Aviation Review. London and New York, various editions.

Janitch, M. *A Source Book of Twentieth Century Warships*. Ward Lock, London, 1977.

Januszewski, T. *Japanese Submarine Aircraft*. Stratus, Sandomierz, 2002.

Japanese Aircraft Carriers and Destroyers. MacDonald, London, 1964.

Japanese Tanks and Tank Tactics. ISO, London, undated.

Jarrett, P. *Aircraft of the Second World War*. Putnam, London, 1997.

Jenkins, D. R., and A. Landis. *North American XB-70A*. Speciality, North Branch, 2002.

Jentschura, H., et al. *Warships of the Imperial Japanese Navy 1869–1945*. Arms and Armour, London, 1977.

Jinks, R. G. *History of Smith and Wesson*. Beinfeld, North Hollywood, 1977.

Johnsen, F. A. *P-40*. MBI, Osceola, 1998.

Johnson, D. E. *Fast Tanks and Heavy Bombers: Innovation in the US Army, 1917–1945*. Cornell University Press, Ithaca, N.Y., 1999.

Johnson, N. C. *Soviet Military Strategy in Space*. Jane's, London, 1987.

Johnston, I., and R. McAuley. *Battleships*. Channel 4, London, 2000.

Johnstone-Bryden, R. *HMS Ark Royal IV*. Sutton, Stroud, 1999.

Jones, B. *Hawker Hunter*. Crowood, Marlborough, 1998.

Jones, D. N. *Westland Aircraft since 1915*. Putnam, London, 1991.

Jones, G. *Battleship Barham*. William Kimber, London, 1979.

Jordan, J. *An Illustrated Guide to Modern Destroyers*. Salamander, New York, 1986.

———. *Soviet Submarines*. Arms and Armour, London, 1989.

———. *Soviet Warships 1945 to the Present*. Arms and Armour London, 1991, 1992.

Journal of the Ordnance Society. Leeds, Continuing.

Kalashnikov, M. T. *From a Stranger's Doorstep*. Publishing House, Moscow, 1997.

Kay, A. L. *German Jet Engine and Gas Turbine Development 1930–1945*. Airlife, Shrewsbury, 2002.

Kay, A. L., and J. R. Smith. *German Aircraft of the Second World War*. Putnam, London, 2002.

Keen, M. (ed). *Medieval Warfare*. Oxford University Press, Oxford, 1999.

Kelly, O. *Hornet*. Airlife, Shrewsbury, 1990.

Kemp, P. *Bismarck and Hood*. Arms and Armour, London, 1991.

———. *Convoy Protection*. Arms and Armour, London, 1993.

Kennard, A. N. *Gunfounding and Gunfounders*. Arms and Armour, London, 1986.

Kennedy, L. *Menace: Life and Death of the Tirpitz*. Sidgewick and Jackson, London, 1979.

Kern, P. B. *Ancient Siege Warfare*. Souvenir, London, 1999.

King, C. (ed). *Jane's Mines and Mine Clearance*. Jane's Information Group, Surrey, 1996.

Köhl, F., and E. Rössler. *The Type XXI U-Boat*. Conway, London, 1991.

Konstam, A. *Hampton Roads 1862: First Clash of Ironclads*. Osprey, Oxford, 2002.

Koop, G., and K. P. Schmolke. *Battleships of the Bismark Class*. Greenhill, London, 1998.

———. *Battleships of the Scharnhorst Class*. Greenhill, London, 1999.

Kroschwitz, J. I. (ed). *The Encyclopedia of Chemical Technology* (vol. 10). Wiley-Interscience, New York, 1993.

Labett, P. *Military Small Arms Ammunition of the World, 1945–1980*. Arms and Armour, London, 1980.

Lacroix, E., and J. Wells. *Japanese Cruisers of the Pacific War*. Chatham, London, 1997.

Ladd, J., and K. Melton. *Clandestine Warfare: Weapons and Equipment of the SOE and OSS*. Blandford, London, 1988.

Laidler, P., and D. Howroyd. *The Guns of Dagenham*. Collector Grade, Ontario, 1995.

Lambert, A. *Warrior*. Conway, London, 1987.

Laming, T. *The Vulcan Story*. Arms and Armour, London, 1993.

LaMont, W. (ed). *The AK-47 Assault Rifle*. Normount, Wickenburg, 1969.

Latham, C., and A. Stobbs. *Radar*. Sutton, Stroud, 1996.

Lavery, B. *The Ship of the Line* (vol. 1). Conway, London, 1983.

———. *The Arming and Fitting of English Ships of War, 1600–1815*. Conway, London, 1987.

———. *The Royal Navy's First Invincible*. Invincible Conservations, Portsmouth, 1988.

———. *Nelson's Navy*. Conway, London, 1999.

Law, R. D. *Backbone of the Wehrmacht: The German K98k*. Collector Grade, Ontario, 1998.

Leaman, P. *Fokker Aircraft of World War I*. Crowood, Marlborough, 2001.

Lee, C. *War in Space*. Hamish Hamilton, London, 1986.

Lee, R. G. *Introduction to Battlefield Weapons Systems and Technology*. Brassey's, Washington, D.C., 1985.

Lehmann, E. A., and H. Mingos. *The Zeppelins*. Putnam, London, 1927.

Lens, B. *The Grenadier's Exercise*. National Army Museum, London, 1967.

Lenton, H. T. *American Battleships, Carriers and Cruisers*. MacDonald, London, 1968.

———. *American Gunboats and Minesweepers*. MacDonald, London, 1974.

———. *German Warships of the Second World War*. MacDonald and Janes, London, 1975.

Lewis, J. *Handguns*. DBI Books, Northbrook, Ill., various editions.

Logan, D. *Republic's A-10 Thunderbolt II*. Schiffer, Atglen, 1997.

Long, D. *Modern Ballistic Armor*. Paladin, Boulder, 1986.

———. *Streetsweepers; The Complete Book of Combat Shotguns*. Paladin, Boulder, Colo., 1987.

———. *AK 47*. Paladin, Boulder, 1988.

Longridge, C. N. *The Anatomy of Nelson's Ships*. Percival Marshall, London, 1955.

Lowin, H. W. *Allied Aviation of World War I*. Osprey, Oxford, 2000.

Lowther, W. *Arms and the Man: Dr Gerald Bull, Iraq and the Super Gun*. Macmillan, London, 1991.

Lucas, J. *The Silken Canopy: A History of the Parachute*. Airlife, Shrewsbury, 1997.

Lumsden, A. *Wellington*. Ian Allan, London, 1974.

Lyon, D. *The First Destroyers*. Caxton Editions, London, 2001.

Mackay, R. *Junkers Ju 88*. Crowood, Marlborough, 2001.

Madsen, D. *Forgotten Fleet: The Mothball Navy*. Naval Institute Press, Annapolis, Md., 1999.

Manchester, W. *The Arms of Krupp*. Michael Joseph, London, 1969.

Mangold, T., and J. Goldberg. *Plague Wars*. MacMillan, London, 1999.

Marchington, J. *Handguns and Sub-machine Guns*. Brassey's, London, 1997.

Margiotta, F. D. (ed). *Brassey's Encyclopedia of Land Forces and Warfare*. Brassey's, Washington, D.C., 1996.

Markham, G. *Japanese Infantry Weapons of World War Two*. Hippocrene, New York, 1976.

Marriott, J. *Brassey's Fast Attack Craft*. Crane Russak, New York, 1978.

Marriott, L. *Type 22*. Ian Allan, Shepperton, 1986.

Marshall, S. L. A. *Infantry Operations and Weapons Usage in Korea*. Presidio, Novato, Calif., 1988.

Marshall, T. C. *British Grenades*. Published by the author, Novato, Calif., 1982.

Martin, A. R. F., and S.A.B. Hitchens. *Development of the Panzerfaust*. British Intelligence Objectives Sub Committee, 1945.

Martin, J. *USS West Virginia*. Turner, Puducah, Ky., 1997.

Marvel, W. (ed). *The Monitor Chronicles*. Simon and Schuster, New York, 2000.

Mason, F. K. *Gloster Gladiator*. MacDonald, London, 1964.

———. *The Avro Lancaster*. Aston, Bourne End, 1989.

———. *The British Bomber since 1914*. Putnam, London, 1994.

———. *The Hawker Typhoon and Tempest*. Aston, Bourne End, 1998.

———. *The Hawker Hurricane*. Crecy, Manchester, 2001.

Massie, R. K. *Dreadnought: Britain Germany and the Coming of the Great War*. Jonathan Cape, London, 1992.

Matsumoto, K. *Design and Construction of the Battleships Yamato and Musashi*. Haga, Tokyo, 1961.

Maxim, H. S. *My Life*. Methuen, London, 1915.

McCart, N. *Three Ark Royals*. Fan, Cheltenham, 1999.

McKay, J. *Victory*. Conway, London, 2000.

McKee, A. *Mary Rose*. Souvenir, London, 1973.

Bibliography

Mead, P. *The Eye in the Air*. HMSO, London, 1983.

Mearns, D., and R. White. *Hood and Bismarck*. Macmillan, London, 2001.

Meister, J. *Soviet Warships of the Second World War*. McDonald Janes, London, 1977.

Melton, H. K. *OSS Special Weapons and Equipment*. Sterling, New York, 1991.

Melvin, M. J. *Minesweeper*. Square One, Worcester, 1992.

Mercer, N. *The Sharp End: Sea Harrier Front Line*. Airlife, Shrewsbury, 1995.

The MG-42 Machine Gun. Moose Lake, Harmony, undated.

Miller, D. *Tanks of the World*. Greenwich Editions, London, 2001.

Miller, D. *U-Boats*. Pegasus, Limpsfield, 2000.

———. *Warships*. Salamander, 2001.

Miller, J. *The X-Planes*. Aerofax, Arlington, 1988.

Milsom, J. *Panzerkampfwagen 38 (t) and 35 (t)*. Profile, Windsor, 1979.

Milsom, J., and P. Chamberlain. *German Armoured Cars of World War II*. Arms and Armour, London, 1974.

Ministry of Defence. *General Purpose Machine Gun*. HMSO, 1966.

Ministry of Munitions. *History of the Ministry of Munitions*. (12 vols.). War Office, London, 1920–1921.

Moeng, S. (ed). *Military Aircraft*. Airlife, Shrewsbury, 1994.

Mokin, A. *Ironclad: The Monitor and the Merrimack*. Presidio, Novato, Calif., 1991.

Mollo, E. *Russian Military Swords, 1801–1917*. Historical Research Unit, London, 1969.

Mondey, D. *American Aircraft of World War II*. Chancellor, London, 1996.

Monin, L., and A. Gallimore. *The Devil's Gardens: A History of Landmines*. Pimlico, London, 2002.

Moore, C. K. *Colt Single Action Army Revolvers*. Andrew Mowbray, Lincoln, 1999.

Moore, J. *Warships of the Soviet Navy*. Jane's, London, 1981.

———. (ed). *Jane's Fighting Warships of World War I*. Random House, London, 2001.

Moore, R. *A Time to Die: The Kursk Disaster*. Doubleday, New York, 2002.

Morgan, H. *Me 262: Stormbird Rising*. Osprey, London, 1994.

Mowbray, S. C., and J. Heroux. (eds). *Civil War Arms Makers*. Andrew Mowbray, Lincoln, 1998.

Mowthorpe, C. *Battlebags: British Airships of the First World War*. Wrens Park, Stroud, 1998.

Moyes, P. *Bomber Squadrons of the RAF and Their Aircraft*. MacDonald and Janes, London, 1964.

Müllenheim-Rechberg, B. *Battleship Bismarck*. Naval Institute Press, Annapolis, Md., 1990.

Munro, W. *Jeep From Bantam to Wrangler*. Crowood, Marlborough, 2000.

Munson, K. *Fighters and Bombers of World War II*. Peerage, London, 1969.

Murphy, W. S. *Father of the Submarine*. William Kimber, London, 1987.

Musgrave, D. D. *German Machineguns*. Ironside, Alexandria, 1992.

Musgrave, D. D., and T. B. Nelson. *The World's Assault Rifles*. TBN, Alexandria, (undated).

Myatt, F. *The Illustrated Encyclopedia of Pistols and Revolvers*. Salamander Books, London, 1980.

Myrvang, F. *MG 34, MG 42*. Collector Grade, Ontario, 2002.

Natola, M. (ed). *Boeing B-47 Stratojet*. Schiffer, Atglen, 2002.

Nelson, T. B., and H. B. Lockhoven. *The World's Submachine Guns* (2 vols.). TBN, Alexandria, 1980, 1986.

Neufeld, M. *The Rocket and the Reich*. Harvard University Press, Cambridge, Mass., 1995.

Nicolle, D. *Medieval Siege Weapons*. Osprey, Oxford, 2002.

Noble, A. *Artillery and Explosives*. John Murray, London, 1906.

Nonte, G. C. *Firearms Encyclopedia*. Harper and Row, New York, 1973.

Norman, A. *HMS Hood*. Spellmount, Staplehurst, 2002.

Norman, A.V.B. *The Rapier and Small Sword 1460–1820*. Arno, New York, 1980.

Norman, M. *Chieftain and Leopard*. Profile, Windsor, 1971.

Norris, J., and W. Fowler. *NBC*. Brassey's, London, 1999.

Nowarra, H. *Heinkel He 111*. James, London, 1980.

Oakeshott, E. *The Sword in the Age of Chivalry*. Boydell, Woodbridge, 1994.

Office of Technology. *The Effects of Nuclear War*. Allanheld Osmun, Montclair, 1980.

Ogorkiewicz, R. M. *Panhard Armoured Cars*. Profile, Windsor, 1972.

Ohrelius, B. *Vasa, The King's Ship*. Cassell, London, 1962.

Oldham, P. *Pill Boxes of the Western Front*. Leo Cooper, London, 1995.

Oliver, D. *Supermarine Spitfire*. HarperCollins, New York, 1999.

O'Neill, R. *Suicide Squads of World War II*. Military Heritage, New York, 1988.

Osborne, R., and D. Sowdon. *Leander Class Frigates*. World Ship Society, Kendal, 1990.

Owen, D. *Lighter than Air*. Apple, London, 1999.

Owen, J. I. H. (ed). *NATO Infantry Weapons*. Brassey's, London, 1976.

Owers, C. *De Havilland Aircraft of World War I* (2 vols.). Flying Machines, Boulder, Colo., 2001.

Pace, S. *X-Fighters: USAF Experimental and Prototype Fighters, XP-59 to YF-23*. Motorbooks International, Osceola, 1991.

Padfield, P. *War beneath the Sea*. John Murray, London, 1995.

———. *Battleship*. Birlinn, Edinburgh, 2000.

Paine, L. P. *Ships of the World*. Houghton Mifflin, New York, 1997.

Palazzo, A. *Seeking Victory on the Western Front*. University of Nebraska Press, Lincoln, 2000.

Parker, J. *The Killing Factory: The Top Secret World of Germ and Chemical Warfare*. Smith Gryphon, London, 1996.

Parker, S. P. (ed). *Encyclopedia of Science and Technology*. McGraw-Hill, New York, 1997.

Parkinson, R. *Encyclopedia of Modern War*. Paladin, New York, 1979.

Partridge, C. *Hitler's Atlantic Wall*. D. I., Guernsey, 1976.

Pasco, D. *Tested: Marshall Test Pilots*. Grub Street, London, 1999.

Pate, C. W. *U.S. Handguns of World War II*. Andrew Mobray, Lincoln, 1998.

Patent Office. *Patents for Inventions: Class 119, Small Arms*. Armory Publications, Oceanside, 1993.

Pater, A. F. *United States Battleships*. Monitor, Beverly Hills, Calif., 1968.

Paulson, A. C. *Silencer*. Paladin, Boulder, Colo., 1996.

Payne-Gallwey, R. *The Crossbow*. Holland, London, 1990.

Pearcy, A. *Lend-Lease Aircraft in World War II*. Airlife, Shrewsbury, 1996.

Peck, T. *Round-Shot to Rockets: A History of Washington Navy Yard*. Naval Institute Press, Annapolis, Md., 1949.

Peebles, C. *Dark Eagles*. Presidio, Novato, Calif., 1995.

Pegler, M. *Powder and Ball Small Arms*. Crowood, Marlborough, 1998.

Perrett, B. *The Matilda*. Ian Allan, London, 1973.

———. *Iron Fist. Classic Armoured Warfare Case Studies*. Arms and Armour, London, 1995.

Pfaffenbichler, M. *Armourers*. British Museum, London, 1992.

Pocock, R. F. *German Guided Missiles*. Ian Allan, London, 1967.

Poland, E. N. *The Torpedo Men*. M. Books, Wilton, 1993.

Polmar, N. *Death of the Thresher*. Chilton, Philadelphia, 1964.

———. *The Ships and Aircraft of the U.S. Fleet*. Naval Institute Press, Annapolis, Md., 1981.

———. *The American Submarine*. Nautical and Aviation, Annapolis, Md., 1983.

Polmar, N., and D. B. Carpenter. *Submarines of the Imperial Japanese Navy*. Conway, London, 1986.

Poolman, K. *Ark Royal*. William Kimber, London, 1956.

Poyer, J. *The M1903 Springfield Rifle*. North Cape, Tustin, 2001.

Preston, A. *V and W Class Destroyers, 1917–1945*. MacDonald, London, 1971.

Pretty, R. T. and D. H. R. Archer. (eds). *Jane's Weapons Systems*. Jane's Yearbooks, London, various editions.

Putnam, T., and D. Weinbren. *A Short History of the Royal Small Arms Factory Enfield*. Middlesex University, Middlesex, 1995.

Pyle, W. *The Gas Trap Garand*. Collector Grade, Ontario, 1999.

Quarstein, J. V. *The Battle of the Ironclads*. Arcadia, Charleston, S.C., 1999.

Ramsey, W. G. (ed). *The Blitz Then and Now* (3 vols.). Battle of Britain Prints, London, 1990.

Ransom, S., and H. Cammann. *Me 163 Rocket Interceptor*. Classic, Crowborough, 2002.

Ransom, S., and R. Fairclough. *English Electric Aircraft*. Putnam, London, 1987.

Rapier, B. J., and C. Bower. *Halifax and Wellington*. PRC, London, 1994.

Rausa, R. *Skyraider*. Nautical and Aviation, Charleston, S.C., 2001.

Raven, A., and J. Roberts. *Battleships Rodney and Nelson*. RSV, New York, 1979.

Raven, A., and J. Roberts. *British Cruisers of World War II*. Arms and Armour, London, 1980.

Bibliography

Reed, A. *Jaguar*. Ian Allan, London, 1982.

Reed, A., and R. Beaumont. *Typhoon and Tempest at War*. Ian Allan, London, 1974.

Reynosa, M. A. *The M-1 Helmet*. Schiffer, Atglen, 1996.

Riccio, R. *Italian Tanks and Fighting Vehicles of World War II*. Pique, London, 1975.

Rice, D., and A. Gavshon. *The Sinking of the Belgrano*. Secker and Warburg, London, 1984.

Richards, G. *World War II Troop Type Parachutes*. Schiffer, Atglen, 2000.

Richardson, D. *Stealth Warplanes*. Salamander, London, 2001.

Richardson, M., et al. *Surveillance and Target Acquisition Systems*. Brassey's, London, 1997.

Richter, D. *Chemical Soldiers*. University of Kansas Press, Lawrence, 1992.

Rifkind, H. *The Jeep, Its Development and Procurement*. ISO Galago, London, 1988.

Rimington, C. *Fighting Fleets*. Dodd Mead, New York, 1944.

Ritchie, W. F., and J. N. G. Ritchie. *Celtic Warriors*. Shire, Aylesbury, 1985.

Roads, C. H. *The British Soldier's Firearm*. Herbert Jenkins, London, 1964.

———. *The Gun*. BBC, London, 1978.

Roberts, D. *HMS Thetis*. Avid, Bebington, 1999.

Roberts, J. *Battlecruiser Hood*. Conway, London, 2001.

Robertson, B. *Lancaster*. Aero, Fallbrook, 1965.

Robinson, H. R. *The Armour of Imperial Rome*. Arms and Armour, London, 1975.

Robson, B. *Swords of the British Army*. Arms and Armour, London, 1975.

Rockwell, D. *F-14 Tomcat*. HarperCollins, New York, 1999.

Rogers, H. C. B. *A History of Artillery*. Citadel, New Jersey, 1975.

Rogers, M. *VTOL Military Research Aircraft*. Foulis, Sparkford, 1989.

Rolf, R. *Atlantikwall*. AMA, Hague, Netherlands, 1983.

———. *Fortress Europe*. Airlife, Shrewsbury, 1986.

Rosa, J. G. *Colt Revolvers*. Royal Armouries, London, 1988.

Roscoe, T. *United States Submarine Operations in World War II*. Naval Institute Press, Annapolis, Md., 1949.

Rosendahl, C. E. *What about the Airship?* Charles Scribner, New York, 1938.

Roskill, S. W. *HMS Warspite*. Naval Institute Press, Annapolis, Md., 1997.

Rössler, E. *The U-Boat*. Cassell, London, 2001.

Royal Armouries. *Yearbook*. Leeds, 1996 (continuing).

Rule, M. *The Mary Rose*. Conway, London, 1982.

Ruth, L. L. *War Baby: The US Caliber .30 Carbine*. Collector Grade, Toronto, 1992.

The Saab-Scania Story. Streiffert, Stockholm, 1987.

Sanger, R. *Nieuport Aircraft of World War I*. Crowood, Marlborough, 2002.

Saunder, R. *The Raising of the Vasa*. Oldbourne, London, 1962.

Saunders, A. *Hitler's Atlantic Wall*. Sutton, Stroud, 2001.

———. *Weapons of the Trench War*. Sutton, Stroud, 1999.

Saunders, S. (ed). *Jane's Fighting Ships 2001–2002*. Jane's Information Group, Alexandria, 2001.

Sawyer, L. A., and W. H. Mitchell. *The Liberty Ships*. David and Charles, Newton Abbot, 1973.

Schmeelke, K. H., and M. Schmeelke. *Fortress Europe: The Atlantic Wall Guns*. Schiffer, Atglen, 1993.

———. *German Defensive Batteries*. Schiffer, Atglen, 1995.

Schiebert, H. *Panzer*. Schiffer, Atglen, 1990.

Schmidt, P. A. *Hall's Military Breechloaders*. Andrew Mowbray, Lincoln, 1996.

School of Tank Technology. *Preliminary Report No. 10. German Pz.Kw.I*. Egham, April 1943.

School of Tank Technology. *Tank Terms*. School of Tank Technology, Chertsey, 1944.

Schultz, R. H., et al. *The Role of Naval Forces in 21st Century Operations*. Brassey's, Washington, D.C., 2000.

Schwoebel, R. L. *Explosion aboard the Iowa*. Naval Institute Press, Annapolis, Md., 1999.

Sebag-Montefiore, H. *Enigma*. Weidenfeld and Nicholson, London, 2000.

Sellier, K. G., and B. P. Kneubuehl. *Wound Ballistics*. Elsevier, Amsterdam, 1994.

Senior, T. *F-16 Fighting Falcon*. Key Books, Stamford, 2002.

Sgarlato, N. *Aircraft of the USAF*. Arms and Armour, London, 1978.

Shacklady, E. *P-47 Thunderbolt*. Arcadia, Charleston, S.C., 2000.

———. *Messerschmitt Bf 109*. Tempus, Stroud, 2000.

Shacklady, E., and T. C. Treadwell. *Classic World War I Aircraft Profiles*. Cerberus, Bristol, 2002.

Sharp, C. M., and M. J. F. Bowyer. *Mosquito*. Faber and Faber, London, 1967.

Sharpe, P. *U-Boat Fact File*. Midland, Leicester, 1998.

Showell, J.P.M. *U-Boats under the Swastika*. Ian Allan, London, 1987.

Silverstone, P. H. *Directory of the World's Capital Ships*. Ian Allan, Shepperton, 1984.

———. *US Warships since 1945*. Ian Allan, London, 1986.

Simkins, P. *Battleship*. Imperial War Museum, London, 1979.

Simonsen, E. *US Spy Planes*. Arms and Armour, London, 1985.

Singh, S. *The Code Book*. Fourth Estate, London, 1999.

Skennerton, I. D. *British Small Arms of World War II*. Margate, Australia, 1988.

———. *An Introduction to British Grenades*. Margate, Australia, 1988.

Skulski, J. *Takao*. Conway, London, 1994.

———. *The Battleship Yamato*. Conway, London, 1988.

Sloan, C. E. E. *Mine Warfare on Land*. Brassey's, London, 1986.

Smith, J. R. *Focke-Wulf*. Ian Allan, London, 1973.

Smith, M. *The Emperor's Codes*. Bantam, London, 2000.

———. *Station X: The Codebreakers of Bletchley Park*. Macmillan, London, 1998.

Smith, P. C. *Battleship Royal Sovereign*. William Kimber, Wellingborough, 1988.

———. *Junkers Ju 87 Stuka*. Crowood Press, Marlborough, 1998.

———. *Dive Bomber*. Naval Institute Press, Annapolis, Md., 1982.

———. *Douglas SBD Dauntless*. Crowood, Marlborough, 1997.

———. *Douglas AD Skyraider*. Crowood, Marlborough, 1999.

Smith, R. D., and R. R. Brown. (eds). *Guns from the Sea: Ships' Armaments in the Age of Discovery*. Academic, London, 1988.

Smith, R. D. *British Naval Armaments*. Royal Armouries, London, 1989.

Smith, R. D., and R. R. Brown. *Bombards: Mons Meg and Her Sisters*. Royal Armouries, London, 1989.

Smith, W. H. B. *Smith's Standard Encyclopedia of Gas, Air and Spring Guns*. Castle Books, New York, 1957.

Southby-Tailyour, E. *Jane's Amphibious Warfare Capabilities*. Jane's, Alexandria, 2000.

Sowinski, L., and T. Walkowiak. *United States Navy Camouflage of the World War II Era*. Floating Drydock, Philadelphia, 1976.

Spicer, M. *Sniper*. Salamander, London, 2001.

Spick, M. *BAe and McDD Harrier*. Salamander, London, 1991.

Spielberger, W. J., and J. Milsom. *Elefant and Maus*. Profile, Windsor, 1973.

Spielberger, W. J., et al. *Schützenpanzerwagen SdKfz 251, 251*. Profile, Windsor, 1979.

Spring, C. *African Arms and Armour*. British Museum Press, London, 1993.

Stanley, R. M. *To Fool a Glass Eye: Camouflage versus Photoreconnaissance in World War II*. Airlife, Shrewsbury, 1998.

The Sten Machine Carbine. Gale and Polden, Aldershot, undated.

Stephens, F. J. *Edged Weapons of the Third Reich*. Almark, London, 1972.

———. *Fighting Knives*. Fortress, Ontario, 1980.

Stern, R. C. *The Lexington Class Carriers*. Arms and Armour, London, 1993.

———. *Type VII U-Boats*. Brockhampton, London, 1998.

Stevens, R. B. *US Rifle M14*. Collector Grade, Ontario, 1991.

Stevens, R. B., and Ezell, E. C. *The Black Rifle: M16 Retrospective*. Collector Grade, Toronto, 1987.

Stevens, R. B., et al. *The FAL Rifle*. Collector Grade, Ontario, 1993.

Stillwell, P. *Battleship New Jersey*. Arms and Armour, London, 1986.

———. *Battleship Arizona*. Naval Institute Press, Annapolis, Md., 1991.

Stone, G. C. *A Glossary of the Construction, Decoration and Use of Arms and Armor*. Southworth, New York, 1934.

Sturtivant, R. *The Swordfish Story*. Sterling, New York, 1993.

Sueter, M. F. *The Evolution of the Submarine Boat, Mine and Torpedo*. Griffin, Portsmouth, 1907.

Sumrall, R. F. *Iowa Class Battleships*. Conway, London, 1988.

Swanborough, G., and P. M. Bowers. *United States Navy Aircraft since 1911*. Putnam, London, 1968.

Swearengen, T. F. *The World's Fighting Shotguns*. Chesa, Alexandria, 1978.

Sweetman, W. *Advanced Fighter Technology*. Air-life, Shrewsbury, 1997.

———. *F-22 Raptor*. MBI, Osceola, 1998.

Sweetman, W., and J. Goodall. *Lockheed F-117A*. Motorbooks, Osceola, 1990.

Tall, J. *Submarines*. Silverdale Books, Leicester, 2002.

Tarassuk, L., and C. Blair. *The Complete Encyclopaedia of Arms and Weapons*. Batsford, London, 1979.

Tarrant, V. E. *Battlecruiser Invincible*. Arms and Armour, London, 1986.

———. *Battleship Warspite*. Arms and Armour, London, 1990.

Taylor, J. C. *German Warships of World War I*. Ian Allan, London, 1969.

Taylor, J. W. R. *Combat Aircraft of the World*. Ebury, London, 1969.

———. *Sikorsky*. Tempus, Stroud, 1998.

Taylor, M. J. H. *Missiles of the World*. Ian Allan, London, 1980.

———. *Boeing*. Jane's, London, 1982.

———. *The Aerospace Chronology*. Tri-Service, London, 1982.

Taylorson, A. *The Revolver* (3 vols.). Arms and Armor, London, 1966–1970.

Teesdale, E. B. *Gunfounding in the Weald in the Sixteenth Century*. Royal Armouries, London, 1991.

Temple, B. A., and I. D. Skennerton. *A Treatise on the British Military Martini*. Arms and Armour, London, 1983.

Temple, B. A. *World War I Armaments and the .303 British Cartridge*. Published by the author, Kilcoy, 1995.

Terry, T. W., et al. *Fighting Vehicles*. Brassey's, London, 1991.

Terzibaschitsch, S. *Battleships of the US Navy in World War II*. Brassey's, London, 1977.

———. *Cruisers of the US Navy 1922–1962*. Arms and Armour, London, 1988.

Tetley, L., and D. Calcutt. *Electronic Navigation Systems*. Butterworth-Heineman, Oxford, 2001.

Thiel, T. D. *The M26 Pershing and Variants*. Schiffer, Atglen, 2002.

Thompson, K. *HMS Rodney at War*. Hollis and Carter, London, 1946.

The Thompson Submachine Gun Mechanism Made Easy. Gale and Polden, Aldershot, undated.

Thornborough, A. M., and P. E. Davies. *The Phantom Story*. Sterling, New York, 2000.

Tillman, B. *The Dauntless Dive Bomber of World War II*. Naval Institute Press, Annapolis, Md., 1976.

———. *Hellcat: The F6F in World War II*. Naval Institute Press, Annapolis, Md., 1979.

———. *Corsair*. Naval Institute Press, Annapolis, Md., 1979.

Tillman, B., and R. L. Lawson. *U.S. Navy Dive and Torpedo Bombers of World War II*. MBI, St. Paul, 2001.

Tillotson, G. *M48*. Ian Allan, Shepperton, 1981.

Tise, L. E., et al. *The Monitor: Its Meaning and Future*. Preservation, Washington, D.C., 1978.

Tomajczyk, S. F. *Bomb Squads*. MBI, Osceola, 1999.

Touzin, P., and C. Gurtner. *Chars d'Assaut*. Bellona, Hemel Hempstead (undated).

Trawin, L. *Early British Quick Firing Artillery*. Nexus, Hemel Hempstead, 1997.

Treadwell, T. C. *Submarines with Wings*. Conway, London, 1985.

———. *The Ironworks: Grumman's Fighting Aeroplanes*. Airlife, Shrewsbury, 1990.

Treadwell, T. C., and A. C. Wood. *Airships of the First World War*. Tempus, Stroud, 1999.

Truby, J. D. *The Lewis Gun*. Paladin, Boulder, 1986.

———. *Silencers, Snipers and Assassins*. Paladin, Boulder, Colo., 2001.

Truscott, P. *Kursk: Russia's Lost Pride*. Simon and Schuster, London, 2002.

Tubbs, F. R., and R. W. Clawson. *Stahlhelm*. Kent State University Press, Kent, 2000.

Tucker, S. *Arming the Fleet: U.S. Navy Ordnance in the Muzzle Loading Era*. Naval Institute Press, Annapolis, Md., 1989.

Tunstall, B. *Naval Warfare in the Age of Sail*. Conway, London, 1990.

Turner, D. *USS New Jersey*. Turner, Publishing, Pudcah, Ky., 1996.

Turner, J. T. *"Nellie": The History of Churchill's Lincoln Built Trenching Machine* (vol. 7). Society for Lincolnshire History and Archaeology, Gainsborough, 1988.

Tylden, G. *Horses and Saddlery*. J. A. Allen, London, 1965.

Ulrich, A. L. *A Century of Achievement 1836–1936*. Colt Firearms, Hartford, 1936.

Vader, J. *Pacific Hawk*. MacDonald, London, 1970.

Vanderveen, B. H. *The Observer's Military Vehicles Directory*. Warne, New York, 1972.

———. (ed). *Military Wheeled Vehicles*. Ward Lock, London, 1972.

Wagner, E. *European Weapons and Warfare 1618–1648*. Octopus, London, 1979.

Wahl, P., and D. Toppel. *The Gatling Gun*. Jenkins, London, 1966.

Walker, F., and P. Mellor. *The Mystery of X-5*. William Kimber, London, 1988.

Walker, P. B. *Early Aviation at Farnborough*. MacDonald, London, 1971.

Wallace, J. *Scottish Swords and Dirks*. Arms and Armour London, 1970.

Walter, J. *The German Rifle*. Fortress, Ontario, 1979.

———. *The Luger Book*. Sterling, New York, 1991.

———. *The Luger Story*. Stackpole, Mechanicsburg, 1995.

———. *Kalashnikov*. Greenhill Books, London, 1999.

———. *Dictionary of Guns and Gunmakers*. Stackpole, Mechanicsburg, 2001.

Walters, B. *Junkers*. Chalford, Stroud, 1997.

War Department (US). *Handbook on German Military Forces*. Washington, D.C., 1945.

———. *Browning Machine Gun Caliber .30*, Washington, D.C., 1940.

War Office (UK). *Dannert Concertina Wire Obstacles*. 1939.

———. *Enemy Weapons*. HMSO, London, 1942.

———. *Small Arms Training; Projector Infantry Anti-Tank*. HMSO, London, 1943.

———. *Small Arms Ammunition*. HMSO, London, 1944.

———. *Small Arms Training: The Machine Carbine*. HMSO, London, 1944.

Ward, D. M. *The Other Battle, Being a History of the Birmingham Small Arms Company Limited*. Ben Johnson, York, 1946.

Watson, G. R. *The Roman Soldier*. Thames and Hudson, London, 1969.

Watton, R. *The Cruiser Belfast*. Naval Institute Press, Annapolis, Md., 1985.

———. *The Battleship Warspite*. Conway, London, 1986.

Watts, A. J. (ed). *Warships and Navies Review*. Ian Allan, London, 1974.

Watts, A. J., and B. G. Gordon. *The Imperial Japanese Navy*. MacDonald, London, 1971.

Watts, J., and P. White. *The Bayonet Book*. Published by authors, Birmingham, 1975.

Watts, R. J. *Axis Submarines*. MacDonald and James, London, 1977.

Webb, A. *Archaeology of Archery*. Glade, Tolworth, 1991.

Webber, P., et al. *Crisis over Cruise*. Penguin, New York, 1983.

Weeks, J. *Men against Tanks*. David and Charles, Newton Abbot, 1975.

———. *Airborne Equipment: A History of Its Development*. David and Charles, Newton Abbot, 1976.

Weland, G. *A Collectors Guide to Swords Daggers and Cutlasses*. Quintet, London, 1991.

Wells, J. *The Immortal Warrior*. Kenneth Mason, Emsworth, 1987.

Westrum, R. *Sidewinder*. Naval Institute Press, Annapolis, Md., 1999.

White, B. T. *British Tanks and Fighting Vehicles 1914–1945*. Ian Allan, London, 1970.

White, J. F. *U-Boat Tankers*. Airlife, Shrewsbury, 1998.

Whitelaw, C. E. *Scottish Arms Makers*. Arms and Armour Press, London, 1977.

Whitford, R. *Design for Air Combat*. Jane's, London, 1987.

Whitley, M. J. *Cruisers of World War II*. Arms and Armour, London, 1985.

———. *Destroyers of World War II*. Arms and Armour, London, 1988.

———. *German Capital Ships of World War II*. Arms and Armour, London, 1989.

———. *German Destroyers of World War II*. Arms and Armour, London, 1991.

———. *Battleships of World War II*. Cassell, London, 1998.

Williamson, G. *U-Boats of the Kaiser's Navy*. Osprey, Oxford, 2002.

Williamson, H. *A Dictionary of Great War Abbreviations*. A. Williamson, Harwich, 1996.

Williamson, H. F. *Winchester*. Combat Forces, Washington, D.C., 1952.

Willmot, H. P. *Pearl Harbor*. Sterling, New York, 2001.

Wills, H. *Pillboxes*. Leo Cooper, London, 1985.

Wilson, H. W. *Battleships in Action* (2 vols.). Conway, London, 1995.

Wilson, G. M. *Crossbows*. HMSO, London, 1976.

Winton, J. *Warrior*. Maritime Books, Liskeard, 1987.

———. ed. *Warships in Profile* (3 vols.). Profile, Windsor, 1970.

Wood, D. C., et al. *The Design and Development of the Avro Lancaster*. Royal Aeronautical Society, Manchester, 1991.

Woolliscroft, D. J. *Roman Military Signalling*. Tempus, Stroud, 2001.

Bibliography

Wright, P. *Tank*. Faber and Faber, London, 2000.

Yoshimura, A. *Zero Fighter*. Praeger, Westport, Conn., 1996.

Zaloga, S. J. *The M1 Abrams Battle Tank*. Osprey, London, 1985.

———. *The Scud*. Concord, Tsuen Wan, 2000.

Zaloga, S. J., and M. Green. *Tank Attack*. Motorbooks, Osceola, 1991.

Zaloga, S. J., and J. W. Loop. *Modern American Armor*. Arms and Armour, London, 1985.

Zaloga, S. J., and J. Magnuski. *Soviet Mechanised Firepower, 1941–1945*. Sterling, New York, 1989.

Useful Web Sites

www.colt.com	Colt firearms (U.S.)
www.heckler-koch.de	Heckler & Koch firearms (Germany)
www.raytheon.com	Raytheon Defense and Aerospace (U.S.)
www.firepower.org.uk	Firepower Museum of Artillery (UK)
www.msichicago.org/exhibit/U505	U505 and submarine site of Chicago Museum of Science and Industry (U.S.)
www.maritime.org/hnsa-guide.htm	Historic and Naval Ships Association Visitors Guide (U.S.)
www.ussnautilus.org	USS *Nautilus* and Submarine Museum (U.S.)
www.msubmus.co.uk	Royal Navy Submarine Museum, Gosport (UK)
www.cwartillery.org	Civil War Artillery Page (U.S.)
http:airdefense.bliss.army.mil/	United States Army Air Defense School, Fort Bliss (U.S.)
www.army-technology.com	Defense Industries—Army (U.S.)
www.Boeing.com	Boeing (U.S.)
www.nmm.ac.uk	National Maritime Museum (UK)
www.nns.com	Northrop Grumman (U.S.)
www.navy.mil	U.S. Navy Official Web site (U.S.)
www.si.edu	Smithsonian Institution and firearms bibliography (U.S.)
www.apg.army.mil	Aberdeen Proving Ground (U.S.)
www.tankmuseum.org.uk	Tank, and Royal Armoured Corps Museum (UK)
www.wpafb.af.mil/museum	USAF Museum, Wright-Patterson Air Force Base (U.S.)
www.af.mil	U.S. Air Force Official Web site (U.S.)
www.afrl.af.mil	Air Force Research Laboratory (U.S.)
www.history.navy.mil	Naval Historical Center (U.S.)
www.royal-navy.mod.uk	Royal Navy Official Web site (UK)
www.army.mod.uk	British Army Official Web site (UK)
www.armouries.org.uk	Royal Armouries Official Web site (UK)
www.iwm.org.uk	Imperial War Museum (UK)
www.fleetairarmarchive.net	Alphabetical listing of world aircraft and aviation museums (UK)
www.edwards.af.mil	Edwards Air Force Base and Test Center (U.S.)
www.cdi.org	Center for Defense Information (U.S.)
www.quarry.nildram.co.uk	Cannon, Machine Guns and Ammunition (UK)
www.fas.org/man	Federation of American Scientists (U.S.)
www.ednet.co.uk/~chris/nuke	Frequently Asked Questions, Nuclear (UK)

Index

Locators in **bold** indicate the main discussion of the topic. Locators in *italic* indicate pictures.

Index

Index

Index

Index

About the Author

STEPHEN BULL is the author of a dozen military history books, including *Trench Warfare: Battle Tactics, 20th Century Arms and Armament*, and *An Historical Guide to Arms and Armor*. He is currently Curator of Military History and Archaelogy at the Museum of Lancashire, England, and previously worked at the National Army Museum (London).